International Business

Mike W. Peng and Klaus E. Meyer

CENGAGE
Learning

Australia • Brazil • Japan • Korea • Mexico • Singapore • Spain • United Kingdom • United States

International Business
Mike Peng and Klaus Meyer

Publishing Director: Linden Harris

Publisher: Brendan George

Editorial Assistant: Charlotte Green

Content Project Editor: Adam Paddon

Production Controller: Tom Relf

Marketing Manager: Amanda Cheung

Typesetter: S4Carlisle Publishing Services

Cover design: Adam Renvoize

For product information and technology assistance, contact **emea.info@cengage.com.**
For permission to use material from this text or product, and for permission queries,
email **clsuk.permissions@cengage.com**

This work is adapted from Global Business by Mike W. Peng published by South-Western Higher Education, a division of Cengage Learning, Inc. © 2009.

British Library Cataloguing-in-Publication Data
A catalogue record for this book is available from the British Library.

ISBN: 978-1-4080-1956-6

Cengage Learning EMEA
High Holborn House, 50-51 Bedford Row
London WC1R 4LR

Cengage Learning products are represented in Canada by Nelson Education Ltd.

For your lifelong learning solutions, visit
www.cengage.co.uk
Purchase your next print book, e-book or e-chapter at
www.cengagebrain.co.uk

Printed by Seng Lee, Singapore
1 2 3 4 5 6 7 8 9 10 – 13 12 11

To our students:
past, present and future.

BRIEF CONTENTS

CONTENTS

PART ONE

FOUNDATIONS 1

PART TWO

BUSINESS ACROSS BORDERS 127

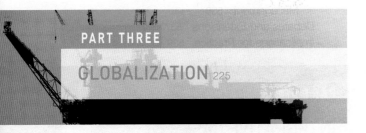

PART FIVE

OPERATIONS IN THE GLOBAL MNE 453

PART SIX

INTEGRATIVE CASES 545

LIST OF IN-TEXT CASES

LIST OF INTERGRATIVE CASES

PREFACE

A EUROPEAN VIEW ON INTERNATIONAL BUSINESS

This book offers a European perspective on international business. In the age of globalization, isn't that a contradiction? Why did we set out to write a textbook specifically for you as students in Europe? There are five considerations why we have been writing this book:

- Students learn best from cases and examples that they can relate to. Thus, we have developed a number of cases and examples specifically for this book that tell the experiences of European businesses. At the same time, we wish to broaden your horizon and equip you with an understanding of businesses in different parts of the world. As an international manager you will need to understand both, the regional and the global dimensions of business. Thus, we also include a large number of cases and examples from all over the world.

- In Europe, international business (IB) is relevant for (almost) every business. Most textbooks in this field have been written primarily for American students, and thus treat global business primarily as a phenomenon that big companies have to deal with, with internationally operating entrepreneurs being an exception. That is understandable given the vast size of the domestic market of the USA. However, in Europe, where national markets are much smaller, even small- and medium-sized firms soon hit the limits of their domestic markets, and IB becomes a natural part of everything they do. Thus, we relate much more to the needs and challenges faced by smaller firms, especially in a European context.

- Textbooks written by American authors typically draw primarily on scholarly work by US-based authors. However, there is important work by European scholars that is, in our view, not sufficiently appreciated in these textbooks. Thus, we pay special attention to work by European scholars, for example the work by Hall and Soskice on varieties of capitalism, and by Zweigert and Kötz on legal systems (Chapter 2), by Hofstede and other Dutch authors on culture and by Marschan-Piekkari on languages (Chapter 3), by Dunning, Buckley and Casson on foreign direct investment (Chapter 6), by Matten, Moon and others on corporate social responsibility (Chapter 10), by Nordic scholars in the tradition of Johansen and Vahlne on internationalization processes (Chapter 11), and by scholars across Europe on knowledge management and governance (Chapter 15) and on expatriate management (Chapter 16).

- European businesses deal with a variety of subtle differences when engaging in neighbouring countries as well as with big differences when going to, for example, China. This contrasts with US businesses for whom IB is a big strategic change from domestic operations (unless they go to Canada), and thus involves substantial differences. Thus, we treat IB as a natural and integrated part of business activity, but subject to a range of subtle differences when dealing with nearby yet still foreign institutions and businesses.

- European businesses do most of their IB elsewhere in the Europe, where they operate within the institutional framework of the European Union (EU).

Understanding this framework is thus essential. Therefore, we devote one entire chapter specifically to the institutional framework of the EU (Chapter 8), and we relate to the EU regulatory framework in later chapters of the book, for example EU competition policy in Chapters 13 and 14.

Of course, as an alternative to using an English-language 'European' textbook such as ours, instructors may consider adapting a textbook in local languages, for example in German or French. This approach has advantages – students may be more at ease with their own language, and examples are even more local. However, we would encourage instructors to adopt our textbook as a core or recommended reading because:

- Engaging in global business in most parts of the world requires competences in English, and the classroom is an ideal place to acquire and polish English language skills.

- An important aspect of building competences for IB is to put oneself in the position of a business partner or competitor in order to understand how they would handle a certain situation. Successful international managers are also able to critically reflect on the merits and demerits of their own country, its institutions and its businesses. The development of these capabilities requires looking 'beyond the horizon' of your national economy, and engaging with individuals and businesses in other countries. Our European view encourages students to broaden their horizon beyond national boundaries.

- Both authors being non-native speakers of English, we remember how hard it is to start using English in a classroom setting. Thus, we have written the text avoiding unnecessarily complex or colloquial expressions that may be inaccessible to students whose first language is not English.

OUR PERSPECTIVE AS AUTHORS

We, your authors, have studied, worked and taught global business throughout our careers. This personal experience and expertise gives us our foundation for writing this book, and enables us to offer you diverse yet complementary perspectives on international business:

- We have conducted research ourselves on many of the issues discussed in this text. Mike Peng has investigated, for example, the institutions-based view of business (Chapters 2 and 3), the resource-based view (Chapter 4) and strategies of global firms (Chapters 13 and 14). Klaus Meyer has also contributed to the institution-based view (Chapter 2), and investigated in particular foreign direct investment (Chapter 6) and foreign entry strategies (Chapters 11 and 12). This work has been published in leading scholarly journals in the field, such as the *Journal of International Business Studies, Strategic Management Journal* and *Journal of Management Studies*.

- In our research, we have investigated a wide range of different contexts, including in particular emerging economies. Mike Peng's research has focused on contemporary management research in China and other transition economies, while Klaus Meyer has studied businesses in the countries of Central and Eastern Europe as well as Asian economies such as Vietnam and Taiwan, and multinational firms from Germany, Denmark and the UK.

- We have taught at universities quite literally around the globe, and thus learned from discussions with students offering a wide variety of perspectives and experiences. Mike Peng has taught at the University of Hawaii at Manoa, Ohio State University and University of Texas at Dallas (all USA) as well as at Chinese University of Hong Kong and a number of universities in mainland China. Klaus Meyer has taught at Copenhagen Business School (Denmark), Hong Kong University of Science and Technology (Hong Kong), National Cheng-Chi University (Taiwan) as well as the University of Reading and the University of Bath (both UK). In addition, both of us have given numerous guest lectures at other universities throughout Europe, Asia and North America.

- Last but not least, we have lived in different countries, and thus complement each others' personal experiences. Mike Peng grew up in China and has spent most of his professional life in the USA, while Klaus Meyer grew up in Germany and has spent most of his professional life in Denmark and the UK. These personal experiences help us in linking theory to practice, notably on cross-cultural matters.

PEDAGOGICAL FEATURES OF THIS BOOK

In designing this book, we have been guided by three main pedagogical ideas:

1 We want to provide a comprehensive yet solidly research-grounded overview of the field.

2 We want to facilitate learning of the essential concepts and analytical framework.

3 We want to stimulate students' own critical reflection and discussions that go beyond rote learning of the material presented in the text.

COMPREHENSIVE, RESEARCH-GROUNDED

International business is a very broad topic that integrates many scholarly disciplines. In selecting and presenting the material, we have been guided by two objectives: to integrate complex materials in an accessible style and to build on contemporary research. First, to provide a consistent structure that helps to analyze this complex subject, we organize the book around a unified framework that integrates all chapters. Given the wide range of topics in IB, many textbooks present the discipline item by item: 'This is how MNEs manage X'. Rarely do authors address: '*Why* do MNEs manage X in this way?' More importantly, What are the big questions that the field is trying to address? Our framework suggests that the discipline can be united by one big question and two core perspectives. The big question is: What determines the success and failure of firms around the globe? To address this question, we introduce two core perspectives: (1) an institution-based view and (2) a resource-based view. The unified framework presents an extension of our own research that investigates international business topics using these two perspectives. This focus on one big question and two core perspectives enables this book to analyze a variety of IB topics in a coherent fashion.

Second, this book engages leaders through an evidence-based approach. We have endeavoured to draw on the latest research, as opposed to the latest fads. The comprehensive yet research-grounded coverage is made possible by drawing on the most comprehensive range of the literature. Specifically, we have read and considered every article over the past ten years in the *Journal of International Business Studies* and other leading IB and general management journals. In addition, we have consulted numerous specialty journals for specific chapters. As research for the book progressed, our respect and admiration for the diversity of insights of our field and the relevance of neighbouring disciplines grew substantially. The result is a comprehensive set of evidence-based insights on IB. While citing every article is not possible, we cover work from a wide range of relevant scholars. Feel free to check the authors found in the Name Index to verify this claim.

Furthermore, we provide evidence through contemporary examples that illustrate theoretical concepts in practice. These up-to-date examples are found all over the world, with an emphasis on European business. They not only encourage students to build bridges between theoretical frameworks and the contemporary world of business, but also encourage them to find further examples in newspapers and magazines, such as *Financial Times* and *The Economist*. Many of the cases have been contributed by scholars from around the world who have first hand knowledge of the companies and contexts concerned, including Finland, Italy, France, Germany, the UK and the USA.

SUPPORTING LEARNING

The comprehensive nature of IB means that students of the subject have to engage with a wide range of concepts and frameworks based on current research. To facilitate the accessibility of this material, we use a clear, engaging, conversational style to tell the 'story'. Relative to other books, our chapters are generally more lively. Moreover, we have introduced a number of features aimed to facilitate the learning of key concepts, facts and frameworks:

- We explicitly state **learning objectives** at the outset and in the margin throughout each chapter. These learning objectives are the basis for a brief **chapter summary** at the end of each chapter.
- An **opening case** about a firm or country provides a taster of the issues from a real world perspective, and a basis to reflect over issues introduced in the Chapter.
- Engaging in international business requires knowledge of many concepts. We therefore state the definitions of key concepts as **margin notes** when they are first introduced, and we include a **Glossary** at the end of the book containing all key concepts in alphabetical order.
- 'In Focus' boxes illustrate key concepts on the basis of shorter, real world examples.
- So what? We conclude every chapter with 'Implications for practice' that clearly summarizes the key learning points from a *practical* standpoint in one or more tables.

CRITICAL REFLECTION AND DISCUSSION

The field of IB is subject to many debates, and many broader debates on globalization affect internationally operating MNEs. While it is important to 'learn' concepts and frameworks, we strongly believe that, it is also important to critically engage with the 'how' and 'why' questions surrounding the field. It is debates that drive the field of practice and research forward. We therefore aim to encourage students to critically reflect over the material presented (We expect most students to find at least one argument where they disagree with us) and to engage in cutting-edge debates. Several features aim to provoke discussion and critical reflections in each chapter:

- 'Debates and Extensions' section for *every* chapter (except Chapter 1, which is a big debate in itself).

- **Photo questions** challenge you to think about the consequences of the material presented. We use photos not only to illustrate the text, but as a stimulus for developing your own ideas and arguments.

- **Recommended readings** provide a basis for further study, for example when you want to prepare a class assignment of a dissertation on a topic

- **Critical discussion questions** at the end of each chapter provide a basis for group discussions or individual work on the issues in the chapter, and their broader implications for society. Many of these questions concern ethical issues that have increasingly come to the forefront of public debates on international business.

- **Closing cases** to each chapter provide the story of a specific company engaged in international business. Analysis of this case along the questions provided will help gain deeper insights on the topic of the chapter, and help relating concepts to the real world of business.

- A set of **Integrative Cases** provide further opportunities to deepen the study material, and to discuss how firms may handle specific challenges they encounter in international business.

Our ambitions in writing this book have been quite high, aiming to provide a teaching and learning foundation for students in Europe and beyond that is comprehensive and specific, theoretically grounded and hands-on, and explaining concepts while stimulating critical thought. The writing process has been challenging, but with the support of numerous colleagues we believe we have produced a solid and innovative book. We hope you enjoy studying and working with this book and, in the process, become as enthusiastic about international business as we are. Happy reading!

Mike W. Peng and Klaus E. Meyer
Dallas, Texas and Bath, Somerset
June 2010

ACKNOWLEDGEMENTS

Undertaking a project of this magnitude makes us owe a great deal of debt – intellectual, professional, and personal – to many people, whose contributions we would like to acknowledge. Intellectually, we are indebted to our teachers as well as our colleagues at the institutions where we have studied and worked over the past two decades. Numerous people, too many to mention individually, have contributed in small and large ways to our understanding of international business, and the theoretical perspectives and empirical techniques to analyze international business phenomena.

In the preparation of this book, the following colleagues and friends for have provided helpful comments on drafts of specific chapters, for which we wish to express special thanks:

- David Ahlstrom (Chinese University of Hong Kong, China)
- Gabriel Benito (BI Oslo, Norway)
- Alan Butt-Philip (University of Bath, England)
- Alvaro Cuervo-Cazurra (University of South Carolina, USA)
- Felicia Fai (University of Bath, England)
- Irina Jormanainen (Aalto University, Finland)
- Amit Karna (European Business School, Germany)
- Andreas Klossek (Technical University of Freiberg, Germany)
- Jette Steen Knudsen (Copenhagen Business School, Denmark)
- Johan Lindeque (Queens University Belfast, Northern Ireland)
- Steven McGuire (University of Aberystwyth, Wales)
- Horst Meyer (corporate lawyer Germany)
- Eleanor Morgan (University of Bath, England)
- D. Mario Nuti (University La Sapienza, Italy)
- Niels Mygind (Copenhagen Business School, Denmark)
- Can-Seng Ooi (Copenhagen Business School, Denmark)
- Magdolna Sass (Corvinus University, Hungary)
- Evis Sinani (Copenhagen Business School, Denmark)
- Gabriele Suder (SKEMA Business School, France)
- Phil Tomlinson (University of Bath, England)
- Leon Zucchini (University of Munich, Germany)

In addition, we thank numerous colleagues that have supported Mike Peng's work on his earlier textbooks, and whose comments indirectly have benefited this book.

The following colleagues have contributed original case material to this book, thus greatly enhancing its practical relevance and its Europe-wide reach:

- Christoph Barmeyer (University of Passau, Germany) and Ulrike Mayerhofer (University of Lyon, France) – Opening Case to Chapter 16
- Mehdi Bousseebaa (University of Bath, England) – Opening Case to Chapter 15
- Jens Gammelgaard (Copenhagen Business School, Denmark) – Closing Case to Chapter 15

- Anna Gryaznova (Moscow State University, Russia) and Olga Annushkina (Bocconi School of Management, Italy) – Opening Case to Chapter 11
- Amber Guan (MBA Graduate, University of Bath, England) – Closing Case to Chapter 11
- Irina Jormanainen (Aalto University, Finland) – In Focus 12.2
- Lianlian Lin (California State Polytechnic University, USA) – In Focus 5.3
- Bernd Michael Linke (University of Jena, Germany) and Andreas Klossek (University of Freiberg, Germany) – Integrative Case 9
- Ajit Nayak (University of Exeter, UK) – Closing Case to Chapter 5
- Sunny Li Sun and Hao Chen (both University of Texas Dallas, USA) – Closing Case to Chapter 12
- Bernd Venohr (Berlin School of Economics, Germany) – Closing Case to Chapter 14

Cengage Learning would like to thank the following academics for their valuable suggestions:

- Ursula Ott – (Loughborough University, England)
- Robert Read – (Lancaster University, England)
- Sangeeta Khorana – (University of Wales, Aberystwyth, Wales)
- Saleema Kauser – (Manchester Metropolitan University, England)
- Gabriel R.G. Benito – (BI Norwegian School of Management, Norway)
- Erik de Bruijn – (University of Twente, the Netherland)
- Camilla Jensen – (Kadir Has University, Turkey)

In addition, special thanks go to Tom Rennie, Charlotte Green, Anna Carter and their team at Cengage Learning for initiating and supporting the writing of the book, and for managing the production process.

SCHOLARLY JOURNALS

Throughout this book, we make extensive references to publications in scholarly journals. To report these references in an efficient way, we use abbreviations such as *JIBS*, *AMJ*, *JMS* or *IBR*, as reported below. You will normally find these sources through your university library's databases, though a search through Google Scholar may also get you to the right place. When citing newspapers and magazine, we report the full name (*Business Week, The Economist*). To trace such an article, it is often easiest to go to these publications' own homepage and type the full title of the article in the search engine.

JOURNAL ACRONYMS

The most frequently cited journals are set in **bold**.

AE – *Applied Economics*; AER – *American Economic Review*; AIM – *Advances in International Marketing*; AJS – *American Journal of Sociology*; AME – *Academy of Management Executive*; AMJ – ***Academy of Management Journal***; AMLE – *Academy of Management Learning & Education*; AMR – ***Academy of Management Review***; APJM – ***Asia Pacific Journal of Management***; ASR – *American Sociological Review*; ASQ – *Administrative Science Quarterly*; ARS – *Annual Review of Sociology*; BEQ – *Business Ethics Quarterly*; BH – *Business History*; BSR – *Business Strategy Review*; CBR – *China Business Review*; CEP – *Comparative European Politics*; CES – *Comparative Economic Studies*; CH – *Current History*; CIEF – *Current Issues in Economics and Finance (Federal Reserve Bank of New York)*; CJAS – *Canadian Journal of Administrative Studies*; CJE – *Canadian Journal of Economics*; CJWB – *Columbia Journal of World Business*; CMR – *California Management Review*; EAIQ – *East Asia: An International Quarterly*; ECLR – *European Competition Law Review*; EE – *Ecological Economics*; EER – *European Economic Review*; EJ – *Economic Journal*; EJE – *European Journal of Education*; EJM – *European Journal of Marketing*; EJPE – *European Journal of Political Economy*; ELJ – *European Law Journal*; EMJ – *European Management Journal*; EMR – *European Management Review*; EoT – *Economics of Transition*; ETP – *Entrepreneurship Theory and Practice*; FA – Foreign Affairs; GP – *German Politics*; HJE – *Hitotsubashi Journal of Economics*; HBR – ***Harvard Business Review***; HR – *Human Relations*; HRM – *Human Resource Management*; HRMR – *Human Resource Management Review*; IA – International Affairs; IBR – ***International Business Review***; ICC – *Industrial and Corporate Change*; IE – *International Economy*; IJCCR – *International Journal of Cross-Cultural Management*; IJHRM – ***International Journal of Human Resource Management***; IJKM – *International Journal of Knowledge Management*; IJMR – *International Journal of Management Reviews*; IJPE – *International Journal of Production Economics*; ILR – *International Labour Review*; IMR – *International Marketing Review*; IPSR – *International Political Science Review*; JAMS – *Journal of the Academy of Marketing Science*; JAP – *Journal of Applied Psychology*; JB – *Journal of Business*; JBE – ***Journal of Business Ethics***; JBF – *Journal of Banking and Finance*; JBR – *Journal of Business Research*; JBV – *Journal of Business Venturing*; JCMS – *Journal of Common Market Studies*; JCR – *Journal of Consumer Research*; JEBO – *Journal of Economic Behavior and Organization*; JEI – *Journal of Economic Issues*;

JEL – *Journal of Economic Literature*; JEP – *Journal of Economic Perspectives*; JEPP – *Journal of European Public Policy*; JES – *Journal of Economic Surveys*; JFE – *Journal of Financial Economics*; JHE – *Journal of Health Economics*; JIA – *Journal of International Affairs*; JIBS – *Journal of International Business Studies*; JID – *Journal of International Development*; JIE – Journal of International Economics; JIM – *Journal of International Management*; JIMktg – *Journal of International Marketing*; JKM – *Journal of Knowledge Management*; JLAS – *Journal of Latin American Studies*; JM – *Journal of Management*; JMM – *Journal of Marketing Management*; JMS – *Journal of Management Studies*; JMR – Journal of Marketing Research; JOB – *Journal of Organizational Behavior*; JOM – *Journal of Operations Management*; JPA – *Journal of Public Affairs*; JPE – *Journal of Political Economy*; JSM – *Journal of Strategic Management*; JWB – *Journal of World Business*; JWT – *Journal of World Trade*; LODJ – *Leadership and Organizational Development Journal*; LRP – *Long Range Planning*; MI/IM/GI – *Management International / International Management / Gestiòn Internacional*; MIR – *Management International Review*; MQ – *McKinsey Quarterly*; MS – *Management Science*; OBES – *Oxford Bulletin of Economics and Statistics*; OD – *Organizational Dynamics*; ODS – *Oxford Development Studies*; OEP – *Oxford Economic Papers*; OSc – *Organization Science*; OSt – *Organization Studies*; PB – *Psychological Bulletin*; POM – *Production and Operations Management*; PoP – *Perspectives on Politics*; PSJ – *Policy Studies Journal*; QJE – *Quarterly Journal of Economics*; RDM – *R&D Management*; RegP – *Regional Policy*; RES – *Review of Economics and Statistics*; RIE – *Review of International Economics*; RIO – *Review of Industrial Organization*; RP – *Research Policy*; SC – *Strategic Change*; SJM – *Scandinavian Journal of Management*; SMJ – *Strategic Management Journal*; SMR – *MIT Sloan Management Review*; S&P – *Society and Politics*; TFSC – *Technological Forecasting and Social Change*; TIBR – *Thunderbird International Business Review*; TNC – *Transnational Corporations (United Nations)*; WD – *World Development*; WE – *World Economy*; YLJ – *Yale Law Journal*; ZfS – *Zeitschrift für Soziologie*.

ABOUT THE AUTHORS

MIKE W. PENG

Mike W. Peng is the Provost's Distinguished Professor of Global Business Strategy at the University of Texas at Dallas. He holds a bachelor's degree from Winona State University, Minnesota and a PhD degree from the University of Washington, Seattle, where he was advised by Professor Charles Hill. Prior to joining UTD, Professor Peng had been on the faculty at the Ohio State University, Chinese University of Hong Kong, and University of Hawaii. In addition, he has served as a visiting scholar in Australia (University of Sydney and Queensland University of Technology), Britain (University of Nottingham), China (Xi'an Jiaotong University, Sun Yat-sen University, and Cheung Kong Graduate School of Business), Denmark (Copenhagen Business School), Hong Kong (Chinese University of Hong Kong and Hong Kong Polytechnic University), Vietnam (Foreign Trade University), and the United States (University of Memphis, University of Michigan and Seattle Pacific University).

Professor Peng's research focuses on firm strategies in countries such as China, Hong Kong, Japan, Russia, South Korea, Thailand and the United States. He has published over 80 articles in leading academic journals such as the *Academy of Management Review, Strategic Management Journal* and *Journal of International Business Studies*. He published two textbooks with Cengage Learning, *Global Strategic Management* (2nd edition 2009) and *Global Business* (2nd edition 2010), which have become best sellers around the world, and have been translated into other languages such as Chinese, Portuguese, and Spanish.

Professor Peng is active in leadership positions in his scholarly associations such as the Academy of International Business (Co-Program Chair for the Research Frontiers Conference, San Diego, 2006 and Track Chair for the 2011 conference in Nagoya) and the Strategic Management Society (Program Chair of the Global Strategy Interest Group, 2005–07). He co-edited a special issue of the *Journal of International Business Studies* published in 2010, and from 2007 to 2009, he served as the Editor-in-Chief of the *Asia Pacific Journal of Management*. Professor Peng's personal website is available at: www.utdallas.edu/~mikepeng/.

KLAUS E. MEYER

Klaus E. Meyer is Professor of Strategy and International Business at the University of Bath, where he also serves in the role of Director of Research in the School of Management. He is also an Adjunct professor in the Department of International Economics and Management at the Copenhagen Business School. He holds a Diplom-Volkswirt degree (MSc Economics) from the University of Göttingen, Germany and has been an exchange student at the University of California, Santa Barbara, USA. He obtained his PhD at the London Business School with a study on foreign direct investment in Central and Eastern Europe. Prior to his appointment at the University of Bath, he has been a Professor at the University of Reading and at the Copenhagen Business School. Moreover, he spent a semester each teaching at the Hong Kong University of Science and Technology and at the National

Cheng-Chi University in Taipei. He is teaching at CEIBS in Shanghai China from September 2010.

Professor Meyer's research focuses on strategies of multinational enterprises in emerging economies. He is particularly interested in how firms adapt their business strategies to the specific conditions prevailing in each emerging economy. His work also extends to the impact of foreign investors on the economic transition and development of the host economies. Another stream of research focuses on the global strategies that may bring multinational enterprises into emerging economies in the first place, considering in particular firms originating from emerging economies. This work has led to four books and about 50 articles in leading scholarly journals such as the *Journal of International Business Studies, Journal of Management Studies,* and *Strategic Management Journal.*

Related to research, Professor Meyer holds responsibilities in scholarly journals, including the role of Senior Editor of the *Asia Pacific Journal of Management*, and Consulting Editor of the *Journal of International Business Studies.* He also served in numerous roles in the Academy of International Business, most notably as Track Chair for its conferences in Beijing (2006), Rio de Janeiro (2010) and Nagoya (2011). Professor Meyer maintains a personal website at www.klausmeyer.co.uk that includes a blog on contemporary matters related to International Business (www.klausmeyer.co.uk/blog).

GUIDED TOUR

Learning Objectives Each chapter starts with a list of objectives to help you identify the main topics and monitor your understanding as you progress through the book. They are repeated at the heading of the relevant section within the Chapter

Chapter Summary Provides a recap of the key information covered in each chapter and a summary of the chapter content for each learning objective.

Opening Case Appears at the start of each chapter to provide a taster of the topics discussed later in the chapter from a real world perspective.

Margin Notes Highlight key concepts throughout the text and state the definitions in the margin when they are first introduced.

Glossary Provides all key concepts and their definitions in alphabetical order.

In Focus Illustrates key concepts on the basis of shorter real world examples throughout the text.

Implications for practice Concludes every chapter by summarizing the key learning points from a practical standpoint.

Key Terms Listed at the end of each chapter along with their page reference for easy review.

Critical Discussion Questions Provided at the end of each chapter to help reinforce and test your knowledge and understanding, and provide a basis for group discussions and activities.

Closing Case Offers opportunities for analyses and discussion of the chapter's main issues applied in real life business situations. Each case is accompanied by questions to help test the reader and extend their understanding of the key issues.

Recommended Reading with brief annotations provide students with starting points for further study, for example when preparing a course assignment.

Integrative Case Offer further opportunity for analyses and discussion of the main issues and concepts covered in the book, applied to a variety of real life international business situations.

About the website

All of our Higher Education textbooks are accompanied by a range of digital support resources. Each title's resources are carefully tailored to the specific needs of the particular book's readers. Examples of the kind of resources provided include:

- A password protected area for instructors with, for example, a Testbank, PowerPoint Slides and an Instructor's Manual.
- An area for students including, for example, Multiple Choice Questions and Web-links.

To discover the dedicated digital support resources accompanying this textbook please go to:
www.cengage.co.uk/pengmeyer

For lecturers

- Instructor's Manual
- EvamView Test Bank
- PowerPoint Slides
- Updates on Cases

For students

- PowerPoint Slides
- Revision Questions
- Revision Quizzes
- Name Index
- Company Index

CENGAGENOW™

Designed by lecturers for lecturers, CengageNOW™ for Peng & Meyer's *International Business* mirrors the natural teaching workflow with an easy-to-use online suite of services and resources, all in one program. With this system, lecturers can easily plan their courses, manage student assignments, automatically grade, teach with dynamic technology, and assess student progress. CengageNOW™ operates seamlessly with Blackboard/WebCT, Moodle and other virtual learning environments. Ask your Cengage Learning sales representative for a demonstration of what CengageNOW™ for Peng & Meyer's *International Business* can bring to your courses (http:/edu.cengage.co.uk/contact_us.aspx).

Global Economic Watch

Cengage Learning's Global Economic Watch is a powerful, continuously updated online resource which stimulates discussion and understanding of the global downturn through articles from leading publications, a real-time database of videos, podcasts and much more. For more information about these digital resources, please contact your local Cengage Learning representative.

PART ONE

FOUNDATIONS

CHAPTER ONE

GLOBALIZING BUSINESS

© Hanquan Chen/iStock

LEARNING OBJECTIVES

After studying this chapter you should be able to:

1 Explain the concepts of international business (IB) and global business.

2 Articulate what you hope to learn by reading this book and taking this course.

3 Identify one fundamental question and two core perspectives that provide a framework for this field.

4 Participate in the debate on globalization with a reasonably balanced and realistic view.

5 Have a basic understanding of the global economy and its broad trends.

6 Draw implications for action around the world and recognize your own likely biases.

OPENING CASE

Thomas Friedman's notebook

My computer was conceived when I phoned Dell ... on April 2, 2004, and was connected to sales representative Mujteba Naqvi, who immediately entered my order into Dell's order management system. He typed in both the type of notebook I ordered as well as the special features I wanted, along with my personal information, shipping address, billing address and credit card information. My credit card was verified by Dell through its work flow connection with Visa, and my order was then released to Dell's production system. Dell has six factories around the world – in Limerick, Ireland; Xiamen, China; Eldorado do Sul, Brazil; Nashville, Tennessee; Austin, Texas [both USA]; and Penang, Malaysia, where the parts for the computer were immediately ordered from the supplier logistics centres (SLCs) next to the Penang factory. Surrounding every Dell factory in the world are these SLCs, owned by the different suppliers of Dell parts. These SLCs are like staging areas. If you are a Dell supplier anywhere in the world, your job is to keep your SLC full of your specific parts so they can constantly be trucked over to the Dell factory for just-in-time manufacturing. 'In an average day, we sell 140 000 to 150 000 computers', explained Dick Hunter, one of Dell's three global production managers ...

So, where did the parts for my notebook come from? I asked Hunter. To begin with, he said, the notebook was codesigned in Austin, Texas, and in Taiwan by a team of Dell engineers and a team of Taiwanese notebook designers. 'The customer's needs, required technologies and Dell's design innovations were all determined by Dell through our direct relationship with customers', he explained. 'The basic design of the motherboard and case – the basic functionality of your machine – was designed to those specifications by an ODM (original design manufacturer) in Taiwan. We put our engineers in their facilities and they come to Austin and we actually codesign these systems. This global teamwork brings an added benefit – a globally distributed virtually 24-hour-per-day development cycle. Our partners do the basic electronics and we help them design customer and reliability features that we know our customers want. We know the customer better than our suppliers and

our competition, because we are dealing directly with them every day.' Dell notebooks are completely redesigned roughly every 12 months, but new features are constantly added during the year – through the supply chain – as the hardware and software components advance.

It happened that when my notebook order hit the Dell factory in Penang, one part was not available – the wireless card – due to a quality control issue, so the assembly of the notebook was delayed for a few days. Then the truck full of good wireless cards arrived. On April 13, at 10:15 a.m., a Dell Malaysia employee then took out a 'traveller' – a special carrying tote designed to hold and protect parts – and started plucking all the parts that went into my notebook.

Where did those parts come from? Dell uses multiple suppliers for most of the 30 key components that go into its notebooks. That way if one supplier breaks down or cannot meet a surge in demand, Dell is not left in the lurch. So here are the key suppliers for my Inspiron 600m notebook: The Intel microprocessor came from an Intel factory either in the Philippines, Costa Rica, Malaysia or China. The memory came from either a Korean-owned factory in Korea (Samsung), a Taiwanese-owned factory in Taiwan (Nanya), a German-owned factory in Germany (Infineon) or a Japanese-owned factory in Japan (Elpida). My graphics card was shipped from either a Taiwanese-owned factory in China (MSI) or a Chinese-run factory in China (Foxconn). The cooling fan came from a Taiwanese-owned factory in Shanghai (Quanta), or a Taiwanese-owned factory in Taiwan (Compal or Wistron). The keyboard came from either a Japanese-owned company in Tianjin, China (Alps), a Taiwanese-owned factory in Shenzhen, China (Sunrex) or a Taiwanese-owned factory in Suzhou, China (Darfon). The LCD was made in either South Korea (Samsung or LG Philips LCD), Japan (Toshiba or Sharp) or Taiwan (Chi Meu Optoelectronics, Hannstar Display or AU Optronics). The wireless card came from either an American-owned factory in China (Agere) or Malaysia (Arrow), or a Taiwanese-owned factory in Taiwan (Askey or Gemtek) or China (USI). The modem was made by either a Taiwanese-owned company in China (Austek or Liteon) or a Chinese-run company in China (Foxconn). The battery came from

How does Dell manage to deliver its computers fast and at low costs?

© Ed Kashi/Corbis

an American-owned factory in Malaysia (Motorola), a Japanese-owned factory in Mexico or China (Sanyo) or a South Korean or Taiwanese factory in either of those countries (SDO or Simplo). The hard disk drive was made by either an American-owned factory in Singapore (Seagate), a Japanese-owned company in Thailand (Hitachi or Fujitsu) or a Japanese-owned factory in the Philippines (Toshiba). The CD/DVD drive came from either a South Korean-owned factory in China or Malaysia (NEC); a Japanese-owned factory in Indonesia, China, or Malaysia (NEC); a Japanese-owned factory in Indonesia, China or Malaysia (Teac); or a Japanese-owned factory in China (Sony). The notebook carrybag was made by either an Irish-owned company in China (Tenba) or an American-owned factory in China (Targus, Samsonite, or Pacific Design). The power adaptor was made by

either a Thai-owned factory in Thailand (Delta), or a Korean-, Taiwanese- or an American-owned factory in China (Liteon, Samsung or Mobility). The power cord was made by a British-owned company with factories in China, Malaysia and India (Volex). The removable memory stick was made by either an Israeli-owned company in Israel (M-System) or an American-owned company with a factory in Malaysia (Smart Modular). ...

'We have to do a lot of collaborating', said Hunter. 'Michael [Dell] personally knows the CEOs of these companies, and we are constantly working with them on process improvements and real-time demand/supply balancing.'

Source: T. L. Friedman, 2007, The World is Flat, 3rd ed., New York: Picador (pp. 580–583).

Were you surprised to learn how international your computer has been, even before it reached you? Did you expect so many companies to be involved in the creation of your work companion? International business has become an integral part of many businesses – and products. Yet, managing international business activities – for example coordinating multiple suppliers of 30 major components – is challenging even for experienced managers. This book is about these sorts of challenges faced by managers of firms operating around the globe. In particular, we will be exploring, what determines the success and failure of firms engaged in international business.

EUROPEAN AND GLOBAL BUSINESS

International business (IB)
(1) A business (firm) that engages in international (cross-border) economic activities and/or (2) the action of doing business abroad.

Multinational enterprise (MNE)
A firm that engages in foreign direct investments and operates in multiple countries.

Foreign direct investment (FDI)
Investments in, controlling and managing value-added activities in other countries.

International business (IB) is about (1) businesses (firms) engaging in international (cross-border) economic activities and/or (2) the activity of doing business abroad. The IB course thus adds an explicitly international dimension to the curriculum of your business education. Traditionally, IB textbooks have focused on the foreign entrant's perspective, often focusing on issues such as how to enter foreign markets and how to select alliance partners. The most frequently discussed foreign entrant is the multinational enterprise (MNE), defined as a firm that engages in foreign direct investment (FDI) by directly investing in, controlling and managing value-added activities in other countries.[1] For example, Dell, an MNE, has under taken many FDI projects, such as a plant in Ireland, where most of its computers sold in Europe are assembled. In addition it has a variety of relationships with other businesses, from the suppliers outlined in the Opening Case to distributors, marketers and customers. These other firms may not be MNEs themselves, but they engage in international business too. Facing foreign entrants, domestic firms actively compete and/or collaborate with them. They are the other side of the coin of international competition.[2]

There are two key words in IB: *international* (I) and *business* (B). The IB course is probably the only business school course with the word *business* in its title. All other courses are labelled as management, marketing, finance and so on, representing one function but not the overall picture of business. Does it matter? Of course! It means that your IB course is an *integrative* course that has the potential to provide you with an overall business perspective (as opposed to a functional view) grounded in a global environment. Consequently, this textbook aims to give you both the I and B parts.

The realities of international and domestic business are increasingly blurred because many previously national (domestic) markets have opened to international competition. For example, suppliers of computer parts need to be able and willing to cooperate with Dell at multiple sites around the world if they want to sell to Dell. Moreover, with creation of the single market in the European Union (EU), the definition of a home market is increasingly ambiguous. Especially in business-to-business markets, such as computer parts, customers are often operating internationally as well, such that competition in a single country would hardly be sustainable. Thus, it becomes difficult to tell what is international and what is domestic.

This book goes beyond traditional IB textbooks in two important ways. First, we discuss issues worldwide as they are relevant to European businesses and managers. In Europe, domestic markets are smaller than for example in the USA and China. Hence, international business is an important element of business for almost all firms – large and small. This international business activity by European firms is primarily conducted within Europe. Even UK exporters earn 57 per cent of their overseas sales within the EU, while their Czech counterparts sell 85 per cent within the EU (see Figure 1.1). That is like working Monday to Saturday on EU markets and Sunday on the rest of the world. Even the biggest MNEs do most of their business in their home region,[3] and even those that do business in all parts of the world often have a organizational structure divided by regions.[4] Within their own region, however, businesses face different kinds of challenges than when expanding beyond

Figure 1.1 International trade in Europe

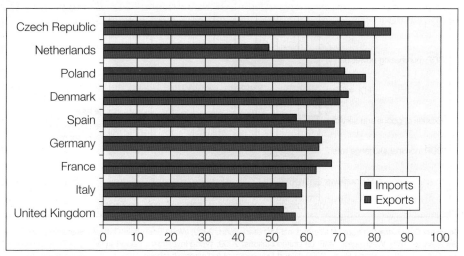

Note: Share of intra-EU exports and imports in the countries' total exports and imports, in percent.

Source: 'International Trade in Europe' from the Eurostat database, epp.eurostat.ec.europa.eu accessed August 18, 2009. Copyright © European Communities 2009–2010. Reproduced with permission.

their home region. Notably, they operate under the auspices of the EU and the rules that the EU has established for business (see Chapter 8). Moreover, a lot of business is conducted in neighbouring countries where differences are relatively small, yet nonetheless important. On the other hand, the rest of the world presents some of the most attractive (profitable) business opportunities. Hence, as an IB executive you need competences for *both*, Europe and beyond.

This books aims to give you both, which distinguishes it from most English-language textbooks, which have been written by leading scholars based in the USA, and thus focus on the issues of interest to Americans going international: Typically, these are large companies dealing with distant markets because the home market in the USA is so big. Thus, our European focus implies that we are paying more attention than other textbooks to (1) business in nearby countries, (2) institutions of the EU, (3) small and medium-sized enterprises (SMEs) and (4) research by European scholars on these issues.

Second, this book is going beyond developed economies by devoting extensive space to emerging economies (also known as emerging markets). These are economies that only recently established institutional frameworks that facilitate international trade and investment, typically with low or middle level income and above average economic growth, for example Brazil, Russia, India and China (BRIC) (see Closing Case). How important are emerging economies? Shown in Figure 1.2, collectively, they contribute about 26 per cent of the global gross domestic product (GDP) at market prices.[5] This share increases to 45 per cent when adjusted to purchasing power parity (PPP), an adjustment that reflects the differences in cost of living (see In Focus 1.1). Why is there such a huge difference between the two measures? This is because cost of living in emerging economies, especially services such as housing and haircuts, tends to be lower than that in developed economies. For example, €1 spent in Łodz, Poland can buy a lot more than €1 spent in Munich, Germany. The rapid growth of some emerging economies is evident.[6] Today's students – and tomorrow's business leaders – will find rich opportunities in emerging economies. This book will help you to recognize them.

Emerging economies (emerging markets)
Economies that only recently established institutional frameworks that facilitate international trade and investment, typically with low or middle level income and above average economic growth.

Gross domestic product (GDP)
The sum of value added by resident firms, households and governments operating in an economy.

Purchasing power parity (PPP)
A conversion that determines the equivalent amount of goods and services different currencies can purchase. This conversion is usually used to capture the differences in

Figure 1.2 The contributions of emerging economies

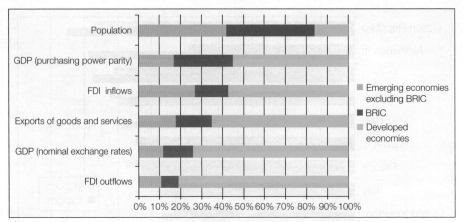

Sources: Data extracted from (1) International Monetary Fund, 2009, World Economic Outlook: Sustaining the Recovery (p. 162), Washington: IMF; (2) United Nations, 2009, World Investment Report 2009 (p. 247), New York and Geneva: UN; (3) World Bank, 2009, World Development Indicators database, Washington: World Bank. All data refer to 2008.

WHY STUDY INTERNATIONAL BUSINESS?

LEARNING OBJECTIVE

2 Articulate what you hope to learn by reading this book and taking this course

International business is one of the most exciting, challenging, and relevant subjects offered by business schools. In addition to the requirements at your university or business school that usually classify this course as a core or recommended course, there are at least two compelling reasons you should study it.

First, for many ambitious students who aspire to lead a business unit or an entire firm, expertise in global business is normally a prerequisite. It is increasingly difficult, if not impossible, to find top managers without significant international competences, even in medium-sized firms. Of course, eventually, hands-on global experience, not merely knowledge acquired from this course, will be required.[7] However, mastery of the knowledge of, and demonstration of interest in, international business during your education will set you apart as a more ideal candidate for fast-track career development that involves expatriate assignments – job assignments located abroad – where you can gain such experience (see Chapter 16).

Expatriate assignments
A temporary job abroad with a multinational company.

Thanks to globalization, low-skill jobs not only command lower salaries but are also more vulnerable to international competition. However, top management capabilities, especially those that create connections across the world, are both paid more handsomely and are in demand even during a recession. To put it bluntly, if a factory in Europe is shut down and the MNE sets up a similar factory in China, only a few dozen people may keep their jobs. Yes, you guessed it: These jobs are top-level positions such as the chief executive, chief financial officer, factory director and chief engineer. They may be sent by the MNE as expats to China to start up operations there. To motivate their best people to take such challenging assignments, MNEs typically offer them a higher salary and extra perks during the stay in China. Moreover, when these expats return after a tour of duty, if their current employer does not provide attractive career opportunities, they are often hired by competing firms. This is because competing firms are also interested in globalizing their business by tapping into the expertise and experience of these former expats. And yes, to hire away these internationally experienced managers, competing firms will have to pay them an even larger premium. This indeed is a virtuous cycle for those with sought-after skills and capabilities.

IN FOCUS 1.1

Setting the terms straight

GDP, GNP, GNI, PPP – there is a bewildering variety of acronyms that are used to measure economic development. It is useful to set these terms straight before proceeding. Gross domestic product (GDP) is measured as the sum of value added by *resident* firms, households and government operating in an economy. For example, the value added by foreign-owned firms operating in Mexico would be counted as part of Mexico's GDP. However, the earnings of *non-resident* sources that are sent back to Mexico (such as earnings of Mexicans who do not live and work in Mexico and dividends received by Mexicans who own non-Mexican stocks) are not included in Mexico's GDP. One measure that captures this is gross national product (GNP). More recently, the World Bank and other international organizations have used a new term, gross national income (GNI), to supersede GNP. Conceptually, there is no difference between GNI and GNP. What exactly is GNI/GNP? It comprises GDP plus income from non-resident sources abroad.

While GDP, GNP, and now GNI are often used as yardsticks of economic development, differences in cost of living make such a direct comparison less meaningful. A dollar of spending in, say, Thailand can buy a lot more than in Japan. Therefore, conversion based on purchasing power parity (PPP) is often necessary. The PPP between two countries is the rate at which the currency of one country needs to be converted into that of a second country to ensure that a given amount of the first country's currency will purchase the same volume of goods and services in the second country (Chapter 7 has more details). The Swiss per capita GNI is US$64 011 based on official (nominal) exchange rates – *higher* than the US per capita GNI of US$46 716. However, everything is more expensive in Switzerland. A Big Mac costs US$5.98 in Switzerland versus US$3.57 in the USA. Thus, Switzerland's per capita GNI based on PPP becomes US$42 534 – *lower* than the US per capita GNI based on PPP, US$46 716 (the World Bank uses the USA as benchmark in PPP calculation). On a worldwide basis, measured at official exchange rates, emerging economies' share of global GDP is approximately 26 per cent. However, measured at PPP, it is about 43 per cent of the global GDP. Overall, when we read statistics about GDP, GNP and GNI, always pay attention to whether these numbers are based on official exchange rates or PPP, which can make a huge difference.

Sources: Based on (1) *The Economist*, 2009, The Big Mac index: Cheesed off, July 18; (2) *The Economist*, 2006, Measuring economies: Grossly distorted picture, February 11; (3) World Bank, 2009, *World Development Indicators* Database, www.worldbank.org, accessed October 2009.

This hypothetical example serves two purposes in motivating you: (1) Study hard, and someday you can become one of these sought-after, globetrotting managers. (2) If you do not care about an expatriate job, do you really want to join the ranks of the unemployed due to such layoffs?

Second, even if you become self-employed, or do not have the aspiration to compete for the top job, you may find yourself dealing with foreign-owned suppliers and buyers, competing with foreign-invested firms in your home market, and perhaps even managing investments abroad. Very few companies in Europe are able to pursue their business without regular interaction across international borders. Moreover, you may also find yourself working for a foreign-owned firm, as your domestic employer is acquired by a foreign player. This is a very likely scenario because approximately 80 million people worldwide, including 18 million Chinese, six million Americans and one million British, are employed in subsidiaries of foreign-owned MNEs. Understanding how global business decisions are made may facilitate your own career in such MNEs.[8] If there is a strategic rationale to

Gross national product (GNP)
Gross domestic product plus income from non-resident sources abroad.

Gross national income (GNI)
GDP plus income from non-resident sources abroad. GNI is the term used by the World Bank and other international organizations to supersede the term GNP.

downsize your unit, you would want to be able to figure this out and be the first one to post your c.v. on a job search website such as Monster.com. In other words, it is your career that is at stake. Don't be the last in the know! In short, in this age of global competition, how do you prevent your job from being outsourced to India or China? A good place to start is to study hard and do well in your IB course.

A UNIFIED FRAMEWORK

LEARNING OBJECTIVE

3 Identify one fundamental question and two core perspectives that provide a framework for this field

International business is a vast subject area. It is one of the few courses that will make you appreciate why your university requires you to take a number of (seemingly unrelated) general education courses. Here, we draw on major social sciences, such as economics, geography, history, political science, psychology and sociology, as well as a number of business disciplines such as finance and marketing. It is very easy to lose sight of the 'forest' while scrutinizing various 'trees' or even 'branches'. The subject is not difficult, and most students find it to be fun. The number one student complaint (based on previous student feedback) is an overwhelming amount of information, which is also our number one complaint as your authors.

To address your possible complaint and make your learning more manageable (and ideally, more fun), we develop a unified framework as a consistent theme throughout this book (Figure 1.3). This will provide continuity to facilitate your learning. Specifically, we will focus on one fundamental question. This question acts to define a field and to orient the attention of students, practitioners and scholars in a certain direction. Our 'big question' is: *What determines the success and failure of firms around the globe?*[9] To answer this question, we focus on two core perspectives throughout this book: (1) an institution-based view and (2) a resource-based view. The remainder of this section outlines why this is the case.

One fundamental question

What is it that we do in IB? Why is it so important that practically every student in a business school around the world is either required or recommended to take such a course? Although there are certainly a lot of questions, 'what determines the success and failure of firms around the globe?' serves to focus our studies. IB,

Figure 1.3 A unified framework for global business

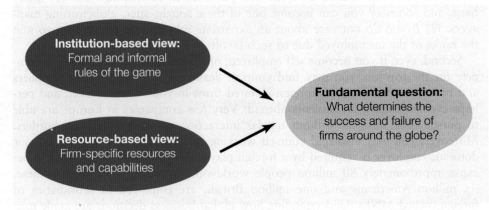

fundamentally, is about not limiting yourself to your home country and about treating the entire global economy as your potential playground (or battlefield). Some firms may be successful domestically. However, when they venture abroad, they fail miserably. Other firms successfully translate their strengths from their home market to other countries. If you were to lead your firm's efforts to enter a particular foreign market, wouldn't you want to find out what is behind the success and failure of other firms in that market?

Overall, firm performance in all their operations around the globe is, more than anything else, of concern to managers in internationally operating firms. Numerous other questions all relate in one way or another to this most fundamental question. For example, how do firms affect those they cooperate or compete with, their employees and suppliers and society as a whole? This broader perspective is part of what constitutes the 'success' of firms looking beyond profits. In this spirit, the primary focus of the field of IB – and of this book – is: *what determines the success and failure of firms around the globe?*

First core perspective: an institution-based view

In layperson's terms, institutions are the 'rules of the game'. Doing business around the globe requires intimate knowledge about the formal and informal rules of doing business in various countries. It is difficult to imagine that firms not doing their 'homework' to study the rules of the game in a certain country will emerge as winners. In a nutshell, an institution-based view suggests that success and failure of firms are enabled and constrained by the different rules of the game.[10]

Some *formal* rules of the game, such as the requirements to treat domestic and foreign firms as equals, would enhance the potential odds for foreign firms' success. Hong Kong is well known to treat all comers, ranging from neighbouring mainland China (whose firms are still technically regarded as 'non-domestic') to far-away Chile, the same as it treats indigenous Hong Kong firms. It is thus not surprising that Hong Kong attracts a lot of outside firms. Other rules of the game, which may discriminate against foreign firms, would undermine the chances for foreign entrants. For example, the recent attraction of Central and Eastern Europe as a site for foreign investment emerged only after it had shed the legacies of socialism, removed barriers to foreign investment, and introduced new regulations that correspond to those already in place in the EU.

In addition to formal rules, *informal* rules such as culture, norms and values play an important part in shaping the success and failure of firms around the globe. For example, because founding new firms tends to deviate from the social norm of working for other bosses, individualistic societies, such as Australia, Britain and the USA, tend to have a relatively higher level of entrepreneurship as reflected in the number of business start-ups. Conversely, collectivistic societies such as Japan often have a hard time fostering entrepreneurship; most people feel discouraged from sticking their neck out to found new businesses, which is against the norm.[11] Yet, such collectivist societies may find it easier to mobilize teams to work towards common goals over long periods of time.

Overall, an institution-based view suggests that the formal and informal rules of the game, known as institutions, shed a great deal of light on what is behind firms' performance around the globe.

Second core perspective: a resource-based view

The institution-based view suggests that firms' success and failure around the globe are influenced by their environments. However, insightful as this perspective is,

© Getty Images

Why is EU membership important for doing business with Poland?

there is a major drawback. If we push this view to its logical extreme, then firms' performance around the globe would be entirely determined by their environments. The validity of this extreme version is certainly questionable.

This is where the resource-based view comes in.[12] While the institution-based view primarily deals with the *external* environment; the resource-based view focuses on a firm's *internal* resources and capabilities. It starts with a simple observation: In harsh, unattractive environments, most firms either suffer or exit. However, against all odds, a few superstars thrive in these environments. For instance, the worldwide automotive industry has been under pressure of overcapacity. Yet, some Japanese and European manufacturers have been increasing their market share, while US manufacturers GM and Ford needed a government bail-out in 2009. On the other hand, Toyota suffered a major drop in sales due to quality control problems. Likewise, in the global airline industry, where most of the major airlines around the world have been losing money in recent years, a small number of players, such as Southwest in the USA and Ryanair in Ireland, have been raking in profits year after year. Also in countries with a business environment generally hostile to business, some firms succeed. For example, PepsiCo has been building market share in Russia even before the reforms of the 1990s. How can these firms succeed in highly unattractive and often hostile environments? A short answer is that Southwest, Ryanair and PepsiCo must have certain valuable and unique *firm-specific* resources and capabilities that are not shared by competitors in the same environments.

Liability of outsidership
The inherent disadvantage that outsiders experience in a new environment because of their lack of familiarity.

Doing business outside one's home country is challenging. Foreign firms have to overcome a liability of outsidership, which is the inherent disadvantage that outsiders experience in a new environment because of their lack of familiarity (see Figure 1.4).[13] Just think about all the differences in regulations, languages, cultures and

What are some factors that have contributed to PepsiCo's success in Russia, despite a challenging business environment?

norms. Your ability to operate depends on your familiarity with the local context. Thus, the liability of outsidership increases the more a firm's origins differ from the host environment,[14] the less the firm has experience in the host country[15] and the further away its nearest prior affiliate.[16] Against such significant odds, the primary weapon of foreign firms is overwhelming resources and capabilities that after offsetting the liability of outsidership, still result in some significant competitive advantage. Today, many of us take it for granted that year in and year out, Coca-Cola is the best-selling soft drink in many countries, and Microsoft Word is the market-leading word processing software virtually everywhere around the world. We really shouldn't take it for granted because it is *not* natural for these foreign firms to dominate non-native markets. Behind such remarkable success stories, these firms must possess some powerful firm-specific resources that enabled them to attain these leadership positions around the globe.

UNDERSTANDING GLOBALIZATION

The rather abstract word 'globalization' is now frequently heard and debated across the world. Those who approve of globalization praise its contributions to economic growth and standards of living, sharing of technologies and more extensive cultural exchange. Critics argue that globalization undermines wages in rich countries, exploits workers in poor countries and gives MNEs too much power. So, what exactly is globalization? This section (1) provides a first glance of what globalization is all about, (2) sets it in a historical perspective and (3) outlines the current wave of globalization.

LEARNING OBJECTIVE

4 Participate in the debate on globalization with a reasonable balanced and realistic view

Figure 1.4 Liability of outsidership

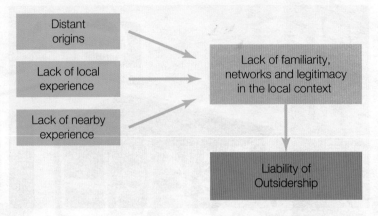

Views on globalization

Many people talk about globalization, yet they do not necessarily mean the same thing (see Table 1.1). For young people, globalization is often first and foremost the internet and all the information and communication technology that comes with it. It is now so easy to chat with your friends at the other end of the world, as if sitting in the same room. Imagine the days when letters took days or even weeks to be delivered. You may be studying anywhere in the world, but you can easily update yourself about activities of the authors of your textbook over the internet – what a difference to your fellow students only a decade ago. Facebook and Twitter, You-Tube and Flickr are certainly expressions of globalization affecting your daily life. The accelerated pace at which technologies spread around the globe is an important aspect of globalization.

A second view associates globalization primarily with the rising power of MNEs and the growing inequality in the world.[17] Many people feel that they are losing control over their lives as a result of forces unleashed by globalization, and beyond the control of even their elected representatives. MNEs have grown big (see next section), and have attained considerable bargaining power when negotiating with national governments. Nations appear to have less control over what happens within their borders, and politicians have lost some of their power to shape events.[18] For example, in 2009 the EU banned the import of seal-based products, notably sealskin, following a long period of lobbying by environmental groups and a vote by the European Parliament. Yet, it is doubtful whether the strong popular desire to protect seals will translate into action: Canada immediately announced that it would challenge the EU's import ban in the World Trade Organization (see Chapter 5) because it is 'a trade decision ... which is not based on science',[19] So, despite popular support, it remains unclear to what extent the ban on seal-based products will be implemented. No wonder citizens sometimes feel dis-empowered! The legitimacy of globalization is an ongoing concern for businesses, and thus for this book.

Third, unskilled workers appear to have lost out, at least in relative terms. In developed countries, international competition creates pressures on the welfare state,[20] while low skill workers fear that their job is offshored to India, China, Poland or Romania. At the same time, the poorest nations seem to fall further behind. The share in world GDP of the poorest fifth of the world has dropped from 2.3 per cent to 1.4 per cent between 1989 and 1998.[21] Many economists acknowledge

Table 1.1 What is globalization?

- Accelerated spread of communication and transportation technology?
- Rising power of MNEs and increased inequality in the world?
- Increased competition for jobs, especially for low skilled workers?
- A force eliminating differences among distinctive national cultures and identities?

such concerns, but point to the fundamentally positive effects. In particular, increased global trade allows greater specialization and greater synergies of pooling resources, which increases productivity and thus creating potentially more wealth that should eventually benefit all (Chapter 5). Advocates of this view thus argue that fine-tuning of regulations – rather than wholesale rejection of globalization – would be the appropriate way to ensure benefits of globalizations are shared more broadly.[22]

Fourth, some interpret globalization as a force that makes us all more similar, and that eliminates the distinctiveness of our national cultures and identities. Some scholars, especially in marketing, argue that the world is on a path of convergence where consumers become more alike, and companies thus sell the same products everywhere on the globe.[23] This expectation has created substantial anxieties, especially in more traditional communities.[24] For some consumer electronics, it may hold true as demonstrated by the success by Japanese consumer electronics made by Sony or Panasonics. Yet such strategies have their limits, and in fact almost all products (even the infamous Coca-Cola Classic) are in one way or another adapted to local contexts. People around the world may be watching Hollywood movies, yet they live their daily lives in distinctly different ways. Thus, we may see some convergence – especially among the middle class – but there is little evidence to suggest that globalization would create a homogenous 'global culture' any time soon.

The following definition by sociologist Mauro Guillén nicely sums up this discussion: globalization is '*a process leading to greater interdependence and mutual awareness (reflexivity) among economic, political and social units in the world, and among actors in general*'.[25] In other words, globalization has created unprecedented contacts between cultures, but it has only marginally reduced clashes between them. Hence, in business you have to work more frequently with others who operate under quite different conditions than yourself. This book aims to help you deal with the challenges and opportunities that this creates.

Globalization
A process leading to greater interdependence and mutual awareness among economic, political and social units in the world, and among actors in general.

Trends of globalization

Globalization is not new; it has always been part and parcel of human history. People have been trading over long distances for more than five millennia, with early traces of internationally operating businesses going as far back as the Assyrian and Phoenician Empires.[26] From 50 B.C. to 500 A.D., the Roman Empire ruled the Mediterranean region and created road and shipping infrastructure as well as political and legal structure, notably a common currency, that facilitated trade, while the Silk Road connected Europe to Asia. In the Middle Ages, the Hanseatic League created a trading network of cities in Northern Europe that stretched from Novgorod in Russia to London in England. The League established common rules (or institutions) that applied to merchants in member cities, and thus overcame the fragmented political structures at the time. Technological progress, notably in shipping and navigation techniques, has been advancing the speed and scope of international trade throughout the Middle Ages and into modern times.

Globalization accelerated in the 19th century following major innovations in manufacturing, communication and transport, as well as legal changes.[27] Industrialization took off with the invention of the steam engine, which powered the new railway networks and steam ships as well as mechanized mass production. Communication accelerated first by faster transport, and then by the invention of the telegraph in 1838. However, these technological changes alone would probably not have brought about the rapid economic growth of the 19th century; they were accompanied by major liberalization, the removal of regulatory restrictions on business, such as the abolishment of guild system for trades and crafts. The introduction of the limited liability company permitted new forms of ownership and thus larger companies, while new patent laws encouraged entrepreneurs to innovate – and reap the benefits of their innovations. Many countries adopted the gold standard, which provided stable exchange rates, and allowed unrestricted transfers of capital. Migration was uninhibited by passport controls, visas or work permits. MNEs played a major role in this global economy (see In Focus 1.2), the level of world FDI relative to GDP reached an estimated 9 per cent in 1913, a level that was reached again only in the 1990s (see Figure 1.5).

The wave of globalization of the 19th century peaked with the outbreak of World War I. While technological advances continued, politics basically messed up a lot of the benefits that our grandparents might have enjoyed. Tariffs started to be introduced from the 1850s; by 1914 only Britain, the Netherlands and Denmark were committed to free trade. During the 1920s, many countries raised tariffs to record levels, and new quotas and trade barriers were created as countries aimed to protect their domestic industries. During World War I, many MNE subsidiaries were expropriated, and all foreign investors lost their assets in Russia after the revolution of 1917. Many developing countries nationalized natural resource investments between the 1930s and 1960s. New FDI was made less attractive by

Liberalization
The removal of regulatory restrictions on business.

Figure 1.5 Waves of globalization

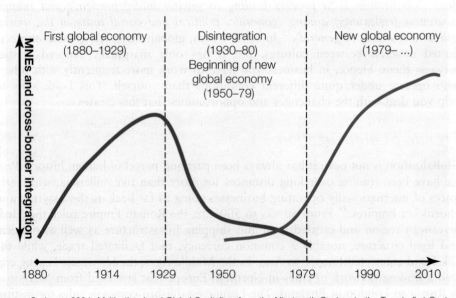

Source: G, Jones, 2004, *Multinational and Global Capitalism from the Nineteenth Century to the Twenty first Century*, Oxford: Oxford University Press (p. 20). Reproduced by permission of Oxford University Press, www.oup.com.

restrictions on foreign ownership and by exchange controls that inhibited the repatriation of profits. Migration has become more restricted since World War I. The USA started requiring passports and visas, and soon added work restrictions: its annual immigration rate fell from 1.16 per cent of the population in 1913 to 0.04 per cent after the war. The stable exchange rate system broke down when Britain abandoned the gold standard in 1931, and others followed with competitive devaluations, thus raising the costs and uncertainty of trading across currency areas. In consequence, international trade declined during World War I, recovered moderately during the 1920s, and then collapsed in the depression of the 1930s. In a nutshell, globalization is nothing new and it is marching on, but there have been quite substantial and costly setbacks. Following business historian Geoff Jones, we suggest that waves of globalization may appropriately describe the world economy (see Figure 1.5).

Waves of globalization
The pattern of globalization arising from a combination of long-terms trends and pendulum swings.

What is Globalization?

The current wave of globalization gradually evolved since World War II. A new fixed exchange rate system was created and provided stability until the late 1960s (see Chapter 7). However, in the 1950s and 1960s barriers to trade and capital movements were pervasive, even among the countries that had embraced the principles of a market economy. Many developing countries, such as Argentina, Brazil, India and Mexico, focused on fostering and protecting domestic industries, while socialist countries, such as China and the (former) Soviet Union, sought to develop self-sufficiently. Even in Western Europe, trade barriers were substantial – not only shielding European businesses from outside competition, but also inhibiting companies operating across borders within Europe.[28] However, barriers to global trade and investment ended up breeding uncompetitive industries that focused on domestic markets.

Gradually, international integration gathered pace. At a regional level, initiatives such as the European Communities, predecessor of the EU, created an institutional framework for intra-regional trade (see Chapter 8), while global agreements such as the GATT aimed to liberalize trade globally (see Chapter 9). However, in the 1970s and 1980s, globalization remained largely a matter for the developed economies in the Triad, three regions that consist of North America, Western Europe and Japan. In addition, four developing economies in Asia – namely, Hong Kong, Singapore, South Korea and Taiwan – earned their stripes as the 'Four Tigers' by embracing the global economy. They have become the *only* economies once recognized as less developed (low-income) by the World Bank to have subsequently achieved developed (high-income) status.

Triad
Three regions of developed economies (North America, Western Europe and Japan).

Globalization accelerated dramatically in the 1990s. While world output grew by 23 per cent over the decade, global trade expanded by 80 per cent and the total flow of FDI increased fivefold.[29] A major contributor to the acceleration were emerging economies that joined the global stage, bringing billions of people with much lower incomes into the fold. Inspired by the Four Tigers, more and more countries, such as China and Latin America in the 1980s, and Central and Eastern Europe and India in the 1990s, realized that joining the world economy was a must. As these countries started to emerge as new players in the world economy, they become collectively known as 'emerging markets'[30] or 'emerging economies'. The largest emerging economies, Brazil, Russia, India and China (collectively known as BRIC) have emerged and not only achieved economic development, but have become major political players as well.[31]

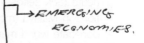
EMERGING ECONOMIES.

The active participation of emerging economies in international business has created new awareness of the pyramid structure of the global economy (Figure 1.6).

IN FOCUS 1.2

Globalization in the year 1900

The world economy was highly globalized at the start of the 20th century. By some measures, the same levels of global integration were only reached again in the 1990s. For instance the ratio of FDI-stock to GDP reached 9 per cent in 1913, dropped to 4.4 per cent by the 1960s before rising to 8.8 per cent in 1990 and 28.4 per cent in 2007 (before falling back to 24.5 per cent in 2008). However, the nature of global business was quite different. European powers ruled large colonial empires, and a lot of international trade was bringing raw materials to Europe, and manufactured goods from Europe were sold worldwide.

The mining industry led international investment. Many natural resources required by the rapidly industrializing nations of Europe and North America were found in colonies: petroleum, copper, tin and other metals. MNEs led the exploitation of these resources employing imported technologies and capital. Concessions, once obtained, were relatively generous giving these early MNEs a free hand to manage their affairs, and few taxes or charges were levied by the host countries. The notion that natural resources underground belong to the nation was only developed early in the 20th century. A leading player in the global exploitation of natural resources was Standard Oil, one of the largest companies of the world until it was broken up by US anti-trust legislation in 1911.

Many renewable resources in demand by the early industrial societies were also found in the colonies. In some industries, MNEs controlled the entire value chain from the plantation to the retailer. For instance, United Fruit controlled the banana trade between Central America and North America, while British trading houses not only imported tea but invested in tea plantations in South Asia. Elsewhere, British entrepreneurs took seeds from Brazil to build rubber plantations in Malaya (modern day Malaysia) that came to dominate world markets. In other industries, such as cotton, tobacco and coffee, multinational trading houses sourced from local farmers and sold on the big exchanges in Europe and North America.

Resource exploiting companies were often organized as free-standing MNEs. They would be headquartered in the leading financial markets of London or New York, but operate solely in distant locations or colonies. Often, these firms started out designing and implementing major projects such as railways and mines. Entrepreneurs would bring together engineering skills and capital from the home country with knowledge of local geology, geography, economics and politics. This business model enabled entrepreneurs to raise risk capital from European or American investors, and used it where high returns could be earned. After the initial construction phase, the operation of the railway or mine was often transferred to a local management company – similar to modern build-own-operate contracts.

The earliest manufacturing MNEs were established in the 1850s, including Singer Sewing Machines (USA) and Siemens (Germany). Yet, integrated global operations as we know them in the 21st century were rare in the year 1900 because distance – in particular the time it took to communicate over long geographic distances – inhibited the establishment of effective control mechanisms. Many businesses thus entrusted subsidiaries to a family member or clan member, and gave him (rarely her) a free hand to manage it locally. Hierarchical organizational forms to manage MNEs only evolved later with advances of technology and marketing practices.

In many industries, businesses organized international cartels to reduce the uncertainty created by free competition, and to protect their profits. Especially in small countries, many industries thus were highly concentrated, with tacit or even formal agreements between international competitors not to enter each others' home markets. Liberal policies at the time also meant absence of effective merger control or constraints on private monopolies. Moreover, protection of industrial workers was still in its infancy. Unprecedented wealth was created in the late 19th century, but it took several decades longer for this wealth to spread to all strata of society.

Sources: J.F. Hennart, 1994, International financial capital transfers, *BH*, 36, 51–70; M.C. Casson, 1994, Institutional diversity in overseas enterprise, *BH*, 36, 95–108; G. Jones, 2005, *Multinationals and Global Capitalism*, Oxford: Oxford University Press; S. Fellman, M.J. Iversen, H. Sjögren & L. Thue, eds., 2008, *Creating Nordic Capitalism*, Basingstoke: Palgrave-Macmillan; M. Bucheli, 2008, Multinational corporations, totalitarian regimes and economic nationalism: United Fruit Company in Central America 1899–1975, *BH*, 50, 433–454.

Figure 1.6 The global economic pyramid

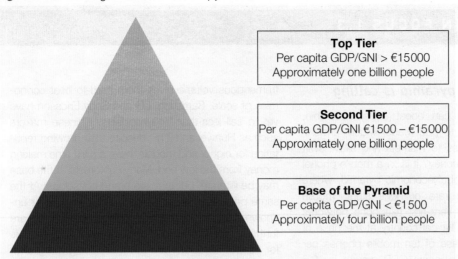

Top Tier
Per capita GDP/GNI > €15000
Approximately one billion people

Second Tier
Per capita GDP/GNI €1500 – €15000
Approximately one billion people

Base of the Pyramid
Per capita GDP/GNI < €1500
Approximately four billion people

Sources: Adapted from (1) C. K. Prahalad & S. Hart, 2002, *The fortune at the bottom of the pyramid, Strategy + Business*, 26: 54–67, and (2) S. Hart, 2005, *Capitalism at the Crossroads* (p. 111), Philadelphia: Wharton School Publishing.

The top consists of about one billion people with per capita annual income of €15 000 or higher. However, the vast majority of humanity, about four billion people, lives at the base of this pyramid making less than €1500 a year. These people at the base of the pyramid provide new resources, and new demand (see In Focus 1.3).[32]

Yet, are we really living in a globalized world? Is selling and investing abroad just as easy as at home? Obviously not. Most measures of market integration (such as trade and FDI) have recently reached new heights but they still fall far short of complete globalization. In other words, we live somewhere between total isolation and total globalization. Barriers to market integration at borders are high but not high enough to completely insulate countries from each other. Businesses still need more than one way of doing business around the globe. Total isolation on a nation-state basis would suggest localization (treating each country as a unique market) and total globalization would lead to standardization (treating the entire world as one market). However, the world is more complex, and there is no single correct strategy.[33]

Globalization has been accelerating since the 1990s. Yet, like a pendulum, globalization is unable to keep going in one direction. The late 1990s saw some significant backlash. First, it created fear among many people in developed economies because emerging economies not only seem to compete away many low-end manufacturing jobs but also increasingly appear to threaten some high-end jobs. Second, some factions in emerging economies complained against the onslaught of MNEs, which allegedly not only destroy local companies but also local cultures and values as well as the environment. During the 2008/09 crisis, many citizens in countries in Eastern and Southern Europe, such as Greece, Hungary, Latvia and Romania, were bitter.[34] Prior to 2008, these countries were enthusiastic about their integration with the EU, and many consumers felt they could afford to enjoy rich Europe's living standards by borrowing from the banks. However, when the financial crisis upset exchange rates and triggered a recession, the region was hard hit, the International Monetary Fund (IMF) came to the rescue, but not without harsh medicines of belt tightening, credit squeezing and spending cuts. Not surprisingly, many citizens in emerging Europe resented the IMF's 'rescue' policies (see Chapter 9).

Base of the pyramid
The vast majority of humanity, about four billion people, who make less than €1500 a year.

IN FOCUS 1.3

The base of the pyramid is calling

What magical device can boost entrepreneurship, provide an alternative to bad roads, widen farmers' and fishermen's access to markets and allow swift and safe transfers of money? It is … a mobile phone! At the base of the global economic pyramid, where fixed-line phones are rare or nonexistent, mobile phones are often the very first telephone networks widely deployed. In a typical country at the base of the pyramid, an increase of ten mobile phones per 100 people reportedly boosts GDP growth by 0.6 per cent. The growth is spectacular: In 2000, about a quarter of the world, 700 million mobile phone subscriptions, were in emerging economies.

The world's largest market, China now has 700 million users. In 2009, an additional 89 million signed up in China, 128 million in India, and 96 million across Africa. As demand takes off at the base of the pyramid, mobile phone makers and service providers cannot be happier. The reason is simple: At the top of the pyramid, market penetration is reaching saturation. The 'race to the bottom' is challenging, since many customers demand rock bottom prices of €40 or less per handset. For now, the only serious contenders for this segment are Nokia and Motorola, the world's No. 1 and No. 2 makers, respectively. Their tremendous volume gives them hard-to-beat economies of scale. Samsung, LG and Sony Ericsson have yet to sell less-than-€40 handsets. Chinese makers such as Huawei and ZTE, despite their growing reputation for higher end models, have a hard time making money from the low end. Many customers at the base may be illiterate, but they are brand conscious. At the same price, they prefer Nokia and Motorola over unknown brands. Already, both Nokia and Motorola are further consolidating their position by making models for as little as €20, while still maintaining margins at approximately 30 per cent, which is comparable to their margin around the world. Overall, this is a win-win solution for numerous emerging economies eager to develop and for the few farsighted and capable mobile phone makers to do what C. K. Prahalad, a guru on the base of the pyramid, preaches: serving the world's poor, *profitably*.

Sources: Based on: (1) C. K. Prahalad & A. Hammond, 2002, Serving the world's poor, profitably, *HBR*, September: 48–57; (2) C. K. Prahalad & S. Hart, 2002, The fortune at the bottom of the pyramid, *Strategy + Business*, 26, (3): 2–14; *Business Week*, 2005, Cell phones for the people, November 14; (4) *The Economist*, 2005, Economic Focus: Calling across the divide, March 12; (5) *The Economist*, 2009, Mobile marvels, special report (16 pages), September 26.

At the beginning of the 21st century, worldwide economic growth was again humming on all cylinders. World GDP, cross-border trade and per capita GDP have all soared to historically high levels. More than half of the world GDP growth now came from emerging economies, whose per capita GDP grew 4.6 per cent annually in the decade ending 2007. Developed economies have also been doing well, averaging 2 per cent per capita GDP growth during the same period. *Fortune* in 2007 declared that 'for your average globetrotting *Fortune* 500 CEO, right now is about as good as it gets'.[35] Yet, the same article almost prophetically cautioned, 'Assuming history at some point proves yet again unkind … it pays to be vigilant'. Indeed, the party suddenly stopped in 2008. The 2008/09 global economic crisis was unlike anything the world has seen since the Great Depression (1929–1933). In 2008, essentially everyone became aware how interconnected the global economy has become. Deteriorating housing markets in the USA, fuelled by unsustainable subprime lending practices, led to massive government bailouts of financial services firms starting in September 2008. The crisis quickly spread around the world, forcing numerous governments to bail out their own troubled banks. Global output, trade and investment plummeted, while unemployment started rising.[36]

After unprecedented intervention throughout developed economies, from mid 2009 there was growing confidence that the global economy had turned the corner. However, economic recovery was slow in developed economies, whereas some emerging economies rebounded faster. The recession reminded all firms and managers of the importance of risk management – the identification and assessment of risks and the preparation to minimize the impact of high-risk, unfortunate events.[37] As far as the direction of economic globalization is concerned, the recovery may see more protectionist measures, since various governments, in their stimulus packages and job creation schemes, emphasize 'buy national' (such as 'buy American') and 'hire locals.'

Overall, globalization is seen by everyone and rarely comprehended. Some aspects of globalization are continuously advancing – notably transport and communication technology.[38] Other aspects – notably politics – are more like a pendulum swinging back and forth. Thus, the world economy may best be described as a combination of continuous technological advance and pendulum swings in government policies, resulting in waves of globalization (see Figure 1.5). This view suggests that the downturn that commenced in 2008 might lead to a temporary reversal of some aspects of globalization, though communication technologies and thus the intensity of cross-border interfaces is unlikely to roll back.

Risk management
The identification, assessment and management of risks.

A GLANCE AT THE GLOBAL ECONOMY

LEARNING OBJECTIVE

5 Have a basic understanding of the global economy and its broad trends

The global economy is driven by the competitive interplay between nations and firms. To add some substance to the trends explored in the previous section, we now offer some specific data. Who are the biggest players in the global economy?

Let's have a look at countries first (Table 1.2). The USA accounts for €10 trillion or about 25 per cent of world GDP, followed by Japan with €3.4 trillion. China has risen to the 3rd largest economy achieving a GDP of €3.0 trillion, and with regularly higher growth rates its weight in the global economy is continuously growing. The EU as a whole is however bigger than any of these countries; its combined GDP adds to about €12 trillion. Looking at other indicators of economic power, however, quite different rankings emerge. Four of the five most populous countries are emerging economies: China (1.34 billion people), India (1.18 billion), Indonesia (226 million) and Brazil (192 million). The biggest exporters in 2008 were Germany (€1.0 trillion) and China (€980 million). The countries of the EU together export about €6.0 trillion, most of which is traded within the EU. Yet, exports to the rest of the world still account for €1.5 trillion, more than any country of the world. The country with the largest number of MNEs is again the USA with €2.3 trillion of assets overseas, followed by the UK, France and Germany.[39] However, look further in the table and you will note that some smaller countries also are major homes to MNEs, notably the Netherlands and Switzerland.

Do study the numbers in Table 1.2 in more detail, or better even download and analyze the latest data from databases on the internet or held in your university library. You will note that these numbers are highly volatile because growth trends and exchange rates fluctuate. The GDP data refer to 2008, and thus the recession of 2008/09 is only party captured by these data. Exchange rate realignments affect the relative position of countries, for instance, the British pound lost over 25 per cent of its value in 2008/09 (see Chapter 7).

A frequent observation in the globalization debate is the enormous size of MNEs. The size of these leading MNEs is indeed striking: The two largest MNEs, oil and gas majors Exxon Mobile and Shell, are generating more turnover (Table 1.3) than the

Table 1.2 Top 30 economies

	Country	GDP (€ billion)	Population (million)	Exports (€ billion)	Stock of Outward FDI (€ billion)
1	USA	9737	302	884	2272
2	Japan	3351	128	510	489
3	China	2954	1337	979	106
4	Germany	2488	82	1023	1042
5	France	1948	62	411	1004
6	UK	1825	61	323	1085
7	Italy	1570	59	373	372
8	Spain	1095	44	195	432
9	Russia	1153	142	322	146
10	Brazil	1076	192	135	117
11	Canada	1025	33	316	374
12	India	851	1181	120	44
13	Mexico	687	105	199	33
14	Australia	690	21	130	140
15	South Korea	634	49	296	69
16	Netherlands	595	17	365	606
17	Turkey	442	74	96	10
18	Poland	359	38	121	16
19	Indonesia	349	226	95	20
20	Belgium	344	11	255	423
21	Switzerland	335	8	165	521
22	Sweden	327	9	127	229
23	Saudi Arabia	320	24	160	17
24	Norway	308	5	115	123
25	Austria	282	8	118	110
26	Greece	243	11	20	23
27	Denmark	232	5	78	138
28	Argentina	225	40	48	21
29	Venezuela	219	28	64	12
30	Iran	192	71	57	1

Notes: Data refer to 2008.

Sources: (1) IMF (2009): International Financial Statistics, Washington: IMF; (2) UNCTAD (2009): World Investment Report, Geneva: United Nations.

Table 1.3 Top 30 companies by revenues in the global economy

	Company	Country	Industry	Sales € bn	Assets € bn	Employment	TNI*
1	Exxon Mobile	USA	Petroleum	313.8	163.9	79 900	67.9%
2	Royal Dutch/ Shell	Netherlands/UK	Petroleum	312.9	202.9	102 000	73.0%
3	Wal-Mart	USA	Retail	273.9	117.4	2 100 000	31.2%
4	BP	UK	Petroleum	249.7	164.0	92 000	80.8%
5	Chevron	USA	Petroleum	186.4	115.8	67 000	58.1%
6	Total	France	Petroleum	171.0	118.3	96 959	74.5%
7	Mitsubishi	Japan	Cars	168.4	86.4	33 390	35.4%
8	Conoco Philips	USA	Petroleum	164.4	102.7	33 800	43.4%
9	Toyota Motor	Japan	Cars	154.4	230.1	320 808	53.1%
10	General Electric	USA	Electrical/elec-tronic equipment	124.6	573.2	323 000	52.2%
11	Volkswagen	Germany	Cars	108.1	167.9	357 207	59.6%
12	ENI	Italy	Petroleum	102.7	116.6	78 880	56.4%
13	General Motors	USA	Cars	101.7	65.4	243 000	51.2%
14	Daimler	Germany	Cars	91.1	132.2	273 216	54.5%
15	Ford Motor	USA	Cars	88.2	160.2	213 000	55.9%
16	Arcelor Mittal	Luxembourg (India)	Steel	85.3	95.6	315 867	91.4%
17	China National Petroleum	China	Petroleum	83.5	137.4	1 167 129	2.7%
18	Carrefour	France	Retail	82.6	52.1	495 287	54.8%
19	EON	Germany	Utilities	82.4	157.1	96 573	55.2%
20	Samsung	Korea	Electrical/elec-tronic equipment	80.8	81.4	321 000	58.9%
21	Hewlett Packard	USA	Computers and software	80.8	81.4	321 000	58.9%
22	Honda	Japan	Cars	75.3	93.5	186 421	81.4%
23	Siemens	Germany	Electrical/elec-tronic equipment	73.5	94.5	427 000	78.8%
24	IBM	USA	Computers and software	70.7	78.7	398 455	61.1%
25	Nestlé	Switzerland	Food products	70.5	71.8	283 000	75.8%
26	Hitachi	Japan	Electrical/elec-tronic equipment	67.2	66.4	347 810	32.0%

	Company	Country	Industry	Sales € bn	Assets € bn	Employment	TNI*
27	Petroléos de Venezuela	Venezuela	Petroleum	65.7	77.4	61 909	16.9%
28	Metro	Germany	Retail	64.6	33.8	265 974	58.2%
29	GDF Suez	France	Utilities	64.5	167.2	234 653	58.6%
30	Statoil	Norway	Petroleum	64.0	59.3	29 496	36.4%

Notes: Data refer to 2008; * TNI (transnationality index) = average of three ratios: foreign/total assets, foreign/total employment and foreign/total sales.

Source: UNCTAD, 2009, World Investment Report 2009, Geneva: United Nations.

GDP of the country ranked 24th, Norway (Table 1.2), while Wal-Mart sells more products (Table 1.3) than the entire output of Denmark or Greece, ranked 26 and 27 (Table 1.2). Of course, you can't quite compare sales revenues and GDP figures, but this comparison indicates the economic power that some of these MNEs may attain, especially when operating in smaller countries. Many of these big companies do most of their business overseas, as indicated by the transnationality index (TNI), which measures the share of activities outside the home country. Most of the largest firms do more than half of their business abroad, especially those originating from a small country. An unusual case is Arcelor Mittal (TNI = 91.4 per cent), which is registered in Luxemburg, though it is controlled by the Indian Mittal family and has operations spread across Europe and Asia.

A group of particular powerful players in the global economy are banks, insurances and other financial intermediaries. They do not appear in rankings by sales turnover, but they manage very large amounts of assets. In 2008, the largest was Royal Bank of Scotland with €2.5 trillion, part owned by the British state as a result of the financial crisis. It was followed by Deutsche Bank (Germany, €2.3 trillion), Barclays (UK, €2.2 trillion), BNP Paribas (France, €2.1 trillion) and HSBC (UK, €1.8 trillion).

In 2008, over 80 000 MNEs controlled at least 790 000 subsidiaries overseas.[40] Total annual sales of the largest 500 MNEs exceed $20 trillion (about 40 per cent of global output). Table 1.4 documents the change in the makeup of the 500 largest MNEs. In general, over 80 per cent of the 500 largest MNEs come from the Triad. Since 1990, the USA have contributed about one-third of these firms, the EU has maintained a reasonably steady increase, and Japan has experienced the most dramatic variation (roughly corresponding to its economic boom and bust with several years of delay).

Among MNEs from emerging economies, those from South Korea and Brazil have largely maintained their presence in the *Fortune* Global 500. MNEs from China have come on strong – from zero in 1990 to 37 in 2008. Beijing is now headquarters of 26 *Fortune* Global 500 firms, eight more than New York. Clearly, Western rivals cannot afford to ignore them, and students of business need to pay attention to them.

LEARNING OBJECTIVE

6 Draw implications for action and recognize your own likely biases.

IMPLICATIONS FOR PRACTICE

At the onset of the 21st century, globalization has started to show its volatile nature, which has direct ramifications for you as a future business leader, a consumer

Table 1.4 Changes in the *Fortune* global 500, 1990–2008

Country/bloc	1990	1993	1996	1999	2002	2005	2008
USA	164	159	162	179	192	170	140
European Union	129	126	155	148	150	165	163
Japan	111	135	126	107	88	70	68
Canada	12	7	6	12	14	14	14
South Korea	11	12	13	12	13	12	14
Switzerland	11	9	14	11	11	12	15
China	0	0	3	10	11	20	37
Australia	9	10	5	7	6	8	9
Brazil	3	1	5	3	4	4	6
Others	50	46	11	11	11	25	34
Total	**500**	**500**	**500**	**500**	**500**	**500**	**500**

Sources: Based on data from various issues of *Fortune* Global 500. Finland and Sweden are included as 'others' prior to 1996 and as European Union after 1996.

and a citizen. At least three sets of high-profile events have highlighted the need for firms to respond flexibly to the unexpected: (1) anti-globalization protests, (2) risks of disruptions to global business and (3) the global recession.

First, large-scale anti-globalization protests have become a regular feature at meetings of world leaders. They were protesting against a wide range of issues, including job losses resulting from foreign competition, downward pressure on unskilled wages and environmental destruction. It is obvious that numerous individuals in many countries believe that globalization has detrimental effects on living standards and the environment. These issues are – rightly or wrongly – associated with globalization, and with globally operating MNEs in particular. They are often represented by non-governmental organizations (NGOs), such as environmentalists, human rights activists and consumer groups.[41] If you are working for an MNE, you need to engage with these concerns, and you may find yourself arguing with some NGOs, while working with other NGOs to jointly address an issue of mutual concern.

Second, global linkages also imply exposure to global risks. MNEs that are operating supply chains across countries and continents may face disruptions to this supply chain through events that are outside their control, and that may occur in a specific part of the world but impact their operations at the other end of the world. Many such disruptions arise from natural disasters such as epidemics (like SARS or Avian flu), earthquakes, typhoons, tsunamis or volcanic eruptions. For example, when volcano Eyjafjallajökull erupted unexpectedly in 2010, aircraft across Europe were grounded and many firms had to stop production because components could not be delivered on time. Other sources of disruptions are man-made, in particular wars and acts of terrorism.[42] Businesses operating around the globe thus have to be prepared for the unexpected – in other words, they need to be able to

Non-governmental organizations (NGOs)
Organizations, such as environmentalists, human rights activists and consumer groups that are not affiliated with governments.

react to crises in ways that minimize the impact on their business – and their customers. As a manager, you have to learn to manage such risks.

Third, the financial crisis that commenced in 2008 has highlighted global interdependencies. The credit crunch spread rapidly from the USA through the financial sector to banks in numerous countries, and caused an unprecedented credit squeeze as inter-bank lending came to a virtual holt. This in turn hit the real economy as businesses faced liquidity squeezes and consumers cut back their expenses.[43] The crisis caused subtle shifts in politics as protectionism was politically advocated by more and more pressure groups. As a manager, you have to react to such economic changes and their possible political and social consequences.

The examples illustrate how globalization debates directly affect *your* future. The debate tends to pit cosmopolitan tolerance versus traditionalist, nationalists or fundamentalists.[44] Cosmopolitans embrace the cultural diversity and the personal and professional opportunities that globalization brings. Most elites in both developed and emerging economies – executives, policy makers and scholars – tend to adopt cosmopolitan views.[45] Although it has long been known that globalization carries both benefits and costs, many elites have failed to take into sufficient account the social, political, and environmental costs associated with globalization. However, that these elites share certain perspectives on globalization does *not* mean that most other members of the society share the same views.

Cosmopolitans
The people embracing cultural diversity and the opportunities of globalization.

Many business school students already share the beliefs and biases in favour of globalization similar to those held by executives, policymakers and scholars. Shown in Table 1.5, relative to the American general public, US business students have significantly more positive (almost one-sided) views toward globalization. While these data are based on US business students, our teaching and lectures around the world suggest that business students worldwide – regardless of their nationality – seem to share such positive views on globalization. This is not surprising. Both self-selection to study business and socialization within the curriculum, in which free trade is widely regarded as positive, may encourage attitudes in favour of globalization. Consequently, business students may focus more on the economic gains of globalization and be less concerned with its darker sides.

Current and would-be business leaders need to be aware of their own biases. Possibly, business schools not only train functional skills but also promote the dominant values that managers hold. However, to the extent that there are strategic

Table 1.5 Views on globalization: American general public versus business students

Percentage answering 'good' for the question:		
Overall, do you think globalization is *good* or *bad* for	General public[1] (N = 1024)	Business students[2] (N = 494)
• US consumers like you	68%	96%
• US companies	63%	77%
• The US economy	64%	88%
• Strengthening poor countries' economies	75%	82%

Sources: Based on (1) A. Bernstein, 2000, Backlash against globalization, *Business Week*, April 24: 43; (2) M.W. Peng & H. Shin, 2008, How do future business leaders view globalization? (p. 179), *TIBR*, 50 (3): 175–182. All differences are statistically significant.

blind spots in the views of the current managers (and professors), these findings suggest that business students may already share these blind spots. Knowing such potential biases, business professors and students need to work especially hard to attain, and retain, a broader horizon.[46]

To combat the widespread tendency to have one-sided, rosy views of globalization, a significant portion of this book is devoted to debates. These are introduced in *every* chapter to provoke critical thinking and discussion. The field of IB is subject to many debates, and businesses operating internationally are confronted with many of the big questions of our times. No doubt, it is debates that drive practice and research forward. Therefore, it is imperative that you be exposed to cutting-edge debates and form your own views by engaging in these debates and learn to critically evaluate both business practice and conceptual frameworks. In particular, Chapter 9 discusses global integration and the role of multilateral organizations, while Chapter 10 on corporate social responsibility discusses the role and contribution of MNEs in this globalizing society.

In closing, most of you were probably surprised how much globalization influences almost every aspect of business, even in small- and medium-sized enterprises. Globalization is fascinating, isn't it? This book will reduce the element of surprise by providing a road map as you embark on this journey. Welcome aboard!

CHAPTER SUMMARY

1 Explain the concepts of international business (IB) and global business

- IB is defined as (1) a business (firm) that engages in international (cross-border) economic activities and (2) the action of doing business abroad.

- This book places special emphasis on the challenges faced by European businesses, and the challenges of emerging economies.

2 Articulate what you hope to learn by reading this book and taking this course

- To better compete in the corporate world that will require global expertise.

- To enhance your understanding of what is going on in the global economy.

3 Identify one fundamental question and two core perspectives that provide a framework for studying this field

- Our most fundamental question is: What determines the success and failure of firms around the globe?

- The two core perspectives are (1) the institution-based view and (2) the resource-based view.

- We develop a unified framework by organizing materials in *every* chapter according to the two perspectives guided by the fundamental question.

4 Participate in the debate on globalization with a reasonably balanced and realistic view

- Globalization has created unprecedented contacts between nations and cultures, with both positive and negative consequences for individuals.

- Globalization has been evolving in waves, with a major peak in the late 19th/early 20th century.

- The recent wave of globalization has accelerated with the rising powers of emerging economies, yet it remains highly volatile.

5 Have a basic understanding of the global economy and its broad trends

- MNEs, especially large ones from developed economies, are sizable economic entities.

6 Draw implications for action around the world and recognize your own likely biases.

- Globalization requires business leaders to stay up-to-date with economic, social and political developments around the world.

- Current and would-be business leaders need to be aware of their own hidden pro-globalization biases.

KEY TERMS

Base of the pyramid
Cosmopolitans
Emerging economies (emerging markets)
Expatriate assignments
Foreign direct investment (FDI)
Globalization

Gross domestic product (GDP)
Gross national income (GNI)
Gross national product (GNP)
International business (IB)
Liability of outsidership
Liberalization
Multinational enterprise (MNE)

Non-governmental organizations (NGOs)
Purchasing power parity (PPP)
Risk management
Triad
Waves of globalization

CRITICAL DISCUSSION QUESTIONS

1 A classmate says: 'Global business is relevant for top executives such as CEOs in large companies. I am just a lowly student who will struggle to gain an entry-level job, probably in a small domestic company. Why should I care about it?' How do you convince her that she should care about it?

2 A classmate says: 'The world economy has changed so much; all those textbooks and historical cases don't really help me in the 21st century'. How do you convince him that he should care about lessons from the past?

3 What are some of the darker sides (in other words, costs) associated with globalization? How can

business leaders make sure that the benefits of their various actions outweigh their drawbacks (such as job losses in developed economies)?

4 Some argue that aggressively investing in emerging economies is not only economically beneficial but also highly ethical because it may potentially lift many people out of poverty (see Closing Case). However, others caution that in the absence of reasonable hopes of decent profits, rushing to emerging economies is reckless. How would you participate in this debate?

CLOSING CASE

GE innovates from the base of the pyramid

Although the 130-year-old General Electric (GE) is usually regarded as a model of management excel-

lence, the recent recession has been brutal. An *Economist* article in March 2009 on GE used the following unflattering title: 'Losing Its Magic Touch' – for a good reason. Since 2008, GE has slashed its dividends by two-thirds, lost a prized AAA credit rating and seen

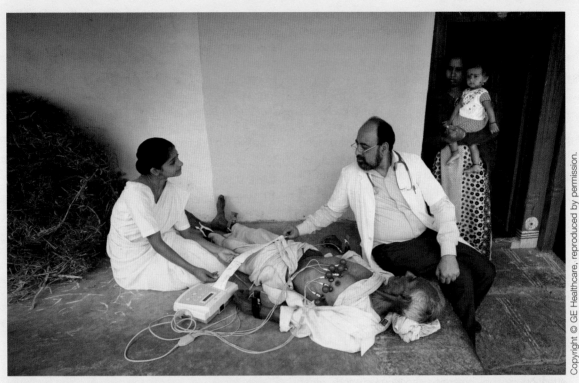

Does it signal news ways of managing innovation, knowledge transfer and corporate growth in global companies? The Mac 400 portable ultrasound by GE Healthcare is helping doctors in rural areas, www.gereports.com

$269 billion wiped off its stock market value due to concerns about the quality of some loans made by its financial services unit, GE Capital.

One glimmer of hope out of GE's recent crisis is a new initiative called 'reverse innovation', which has attracted GE chairman and CEO Jeff Immelt's personal attention. MNEs such as GE historically innovate new products in developed economies, and then localize these products by tweaking them for customers in emerging economies. Unfortunately, a lot of these expensive products, with well-off customers in developed economies in mind, flop in emerging economies not only because of their price tag, but also because of their lack of consideration for the specific needs and wants of local customers. Being the exact opposite, reverse innovation turns innovative products created for emerging economies into low-cost offerings for developed economies.

Take a look at GE's conventional ultrasound machines, originally developed in the USA and Japan and sold for $100 000 and up (up to $350 000). In China, these expensive, bulky devices sold poorly because not every sophisticated hospital imaging centre could afford to have them. GE's team in

China realized that more than 80 per cent of China's population relies on rural hospitals or clinics that are poorly funded. Conventional ultrasound machines are simply out of reach for these facilities. Patients thus have to travel to urban hospitals to access ultrasound. However, transportation to urban hospitals, especially for the sick, is challenging. Since most Chinese patients could not come to the ultrasound machines, the machines, thus, have to go to the patients. Scaling down its existing bulky, expensive, and complex ultrasound machines was not going to serve that demand. GM realized that it needed a revolutionary product – a compact, portable ultrasound machine. In 2002, GE in China launched its first compact ultrasound, which combined a regular laptop computer with sophisticated software. The machine sold for only $30 000. In 2008, GE introduced a new model that sold for $15 000, less than 15 per cent of the price tag of its high-end conventional ultrasound models. While portable ultrasounds have naturally become a hit in China, especially in rural clinics, they have also generated dramatic growth throughout the world, including developed economies. These machines combine a new dimension previously unavailable to ultrasound machines – portability – with an unbeatable price, in developed economies where containing health care cost is increasingly paramount. Before the global recession hit, portable ultrasounds by 2008 were a $278 million global product line for GE, growing at 50 per cent to 60 per cent annually. Even in the midst of a severe global recession, this product line is expected to grow 25 per cent annually in China.

GE's experience in developing portable ultrasound machines in China is not alone. For rural India, it has pioneered a $1000 handheld electrocardiogram (ECG) device that brings down the cost by a margin of 60 per cent to 80 per cent. In the Czech Republic, GE developed an aircraft engine for small planes that slashes its cost by half. This allows GE to challenge Pratt & Whitney's dominance of the small turboprop market in developed economies.

Such outstanding performance in and out of emerging economies, in combination with GE's poor performance in developed economies, has rapidly transformed GE's mental map of the world. Ten years ago, it focused on the Triad and paid relatively minor attention to the 'rest of the world'. Now strategic attention is on emerging economies and other resource-rich regions, and the Triad becomes the 'rest of the world'. The company is also embracing reverse innovation for defensive reasons. Thus, CEO Jeffrey Immelt noted in an Harvard Business Review: '*If GE doesn't come up with innovations in poor coun-*

tries and take them global, new competitors from the developing world – like Mindray, Suzlon, Goldwind and Haier – will ... GE has tremendous respect for traditional rivals like Siemens, Philips and Rolls-Royce. But it knows how to compete with them; they will never destroy GE. By introducing products that create a new price-performance paradigm, however, the emerging giants very well could. Reverse innovation isn't optional; it is oxygen.'

CASE DISCUSSION QUESTIONS:

1 What are the similarities and differences between GE's traditional innovation and reverse innovation?

2 Why is GE so interested in reverse innovation?

3 What are the main concerns that prevent Western MNEs from aggressively investing in emerging economies? What are the costs if they choose not to engage in emerging economies?

4 Why is a leading US MNE such as GE afraid of emerging multinationals from emerging economies?

Sources: Based on (1) *Business Week*, 2009, The joys and perils of 'reverse innovation', October 5; (2) *The Economist*, 2009, GE: Losing its magic touch, March 21; (3) GE Report, 2009, www.gereports.com; (4) J. Immelt, V. Govindarajan & C. Trimble, 2009, How GE is disrupting itself, *HBR*, October: 56–65.

RECOMMENDED READINGS

J.N. Bhagwati, 2004, *In Defence of Globalization*, Oxford: Oxford University Press – an esteemed economist outlines the benefits of globalization, and how they can be made even better.

P. Dicken, 2007, *Global Shift: Mapping the Changing Contours of the World Economy*, 5th ed., London: Sage – a thorough analysis of the economic trends of globalization in a variety of industries.

G. Jones, 2004, *Multinationals and Global Capitalism from the Nineteenth Century to the Twenty-first Century*, Oxford: Oxford University Press – a historical account of globalization and multinational enterprises.

K.E. Meyer, 2004, *Perspectives on multinational enterprises in emerging economies*, JIBS, 34: 259–277 – outlines an agenda for IB scholars looking beyond the firm to its wider impact on society.

M.W. Peng, 2004, *Identifying the big question in international business research*, JIBS, 35: 99–108 – outlines an agenda for IB scholars focused on the performance of firms in the global economy.

NOTES:

"FOR JOURNAL ABBREVIATION, PLEASE SEE PAGE XXVI-XXVII."

1 This definition of the MNE can be found in R.E. Caves, 1996, *Multinational Enterprise and Economic Analysis*, 2nd ed. (p. 1), Cambridge: Cambridge University Press; J.H. Dunning & S. Lundan, 2008, *Multinational Enterprises and the Global Economy*, Cheltenham: Elgar. Other terms are multinational corporation (MNC) and transnational corporation (TNC), which are often used interchangeably with MNE. To avoid confusion, in this book, we use MNE.

2 O. Shenkar, 2004, One more time: International business in a global economy (p. 165), *JIBS*, 35: 161–171. See also J. Boddewyn, B. Toyne & Z. Martinez, 2004, The meanings of 'international management', *MIR*, 44: 195–215.

3 A.M. Rugman & A. Verbeke, 2004, A perspective on the regional and global strategies of multinational enterprise, *JIBS*, 35: 3–18; A.M. Rugman, 2005, *The Regional Multinational*, Cambridge: Cambridge University Press.

4 A.J. Morrison, D.A. Ricks & K. Roth, 1991, Globalization versus Regionalization: Which way for the multinational, *OD*, 19 (3): 17–29; M. Lehrer & K. Asakawa, 1999, Unbundling European operations: Regional management and corporate flexibility in American and Japanese MNCs, *JWB* 34: 267–286; P. Ghemawat, 2007, *Redefining Global Strategy*, Cambridge, MA: Harvard Business School Press.

5 *The Economist*, 2006, Emerging economies: Climbing back, January 21.

6 R.E. Hoskisson, L. Eden, C.M. Lau & M. Wright, 2000, Strategy in emerging economies, *AMJ*, 43: 249–267; K.E. Meyer, 2004, Perspectives on multinational enterprises in emerging economies, *JIBS*, 35: 259–276; R. Ramamurti, 2004, Developing countries and MNEs, *JIBS*, 35: 277–283; K.E. Meyer & M.W. Peng, 2005, Probing theoretically into Central and Eastern Europe, *JIBS*, 36: 600–621; M. Wright, I. Filatotchev, R.E. Hoskisson & M.W. Peng, 2005, Strategy research in emerging economies, *JMS*, 42: 1–33.

7 A. Yan, G. Zhu & D. Hall, 2002, International assignments for career building, *AMR*, 27: 373–391; M. Dickman & H. Harris, 2005, Developing career capital for global careers: The role of international assignments, *JWB,* 40: 399–408; N.J. Adler & A. Gundersen, 2008, *International Dimensions of Organizational Behaviour*, 5th ed., Cincinnati, OH: South-Western.

8 W. Newburry, 2001, MNC interdependence and local embeddedness influences on perceptions of career benefits from global integration, *JIBS*, 32: 497–508.

9 M.W. Peng, 2004, Identifying the big question in international business research, *JIBS*, 35: 99–108.

10 C. Oliver, 1997, Sustainable competitive advantage: combining institutional and resource based views. *SMJ* 18: 697–713; M.W. Peng 2003. Institutional transitions and strategic choices, *AMR*, 28: 275–296. W. Henisz & B. Zelner, 2005, Legitimacy, interest group pressures, and change in emergent institutions, *AMR*, 30: 361–382; I.P. Mahmood & C. Rufin, 2005, Government's dilemma, *AMR*, 30: 338–360; P. Ring, G. Bigley, T. D'Aunno & T. Khanna, 2005, Perspectives on how governments matter, *AMR*, 30: 308–320; M. Gelbuda, K.E. Meyer & A. Delios, 2007, International business and institutional development in Central and Eastern Europe, *JIM,* 14: 1–11; M.W. Peng, D. Wang & Y. Jiang, 2008, An institution-based view of international business strategy, *JIBS,* 39: 920–936;

11 S. Lee, M.W. Peng & J.B. Barney, 2007, Bankruptcy laws and entrepreneurship development, *AMR*, 32: 257–272; N. Bosma, Z.J. Acs, E. Autio, A. Coduras & J. Levie, 2008, *Global Entrepreneurship Monitor, Executive Report 2008*, mimeo, Global Entrepreneurship Research Consortium.

12 J.B. Barney, 1991, Firm resources and sustained competitive advantage, *JM,* 17: 99–120, R.M. Grant, 1996, Towards a knowledge-based theory of the firm, *SMJ*, 17 (winter special issue): 109–122; M.W. Peng, 2001, The resource-based view and international business, *JM*, 27: 803–829; M.A. Peteraf, 2003, The foundations of competitive advantage: a resource-based view, *SMJ*, 14: 179–191.

13 J. Johansen & J.E. Vahlne, 2009, The Uppsala internationalization process model revised: From liability of foreignness to liability of outsidership, *JIBS,* 40, 1411–1432. Originally this concept was known as liability of foreignness, see J. Johanson & J.E. Vahlne, 1977, The internationalization process of the firm, *JIBS*, 8: 23–32; S. Zaheer, 1995, Overcoming the liability of foreignness, *AMJ*, 38: 341–363; J. Mezias, 2002, Identifying liabilities of foreignness and strategies to minimize their effects, *SMJ*, 23: 229–244; D. Sethi & W. Judge, 2009, Reappraising liabilities of foreignness within an integrated

perspective of the costs and benefits of doing business abroad, *IBR,* 18: 404–416.

14 B. Kogut & H. Singh, 1988, The effect of national culture on the choice of entry mode, *JIBS,* 19: 411–432; D. Xu & O. Shenkar, 2002, Institutional distance and the multinational enterprise, *AMR,* 27: 608–618; S. Estrin, D. Baghdasaryan & K.E. Meyer, 2009, Institutional and human resource resource distance on international entry strategies, *JMS,* 46: 1171–1196.

15 P.Y. Li & K.E. Meyer, 2009, Contextualizing experience effects in international business, *JWB,* 44: 370–382.

16 T. Hutzschenreuther & J.C. Voll, 2008, Performance effects of added cultural distance in the path of international expansion, *JIBS,* 39: 53–70.

17 S. Strange, 1996, *The Retreat of the State,* Cambridge: Cambridge University Press; A. Giddens, 1999, *Runaway World,* London: Profile.

18 R. Vernon, 1971, *Sovereignty at Bay: The Multinational Spread of US Enterprises,* New York: Basic Books. J.M. Stopford & S. Strange, *Rival State, Rival Firms,* Cambridge: Cambridge University Press; S. Kobrin, 1997, The architecture of globalization: States sovereignty in a networked global economy, in: J.H. Dunning, ed.: *Government, Globalization and International Business,* Oxford: Oxford University Press; S. Kobrin, 2001, Sovereignty @ Bay: Globalization, multinational enterprise and the international political system, in: A.M. Rugman & T.L. Brewer, eds, *Oxford Handbook of International Business,* Oxford: Oxford University Press; R. Grosse, ed. 2005, ed, *International Business and Government Relations in the 21st Century,* Cambridge: Cambridge University Press.

19 *BBC News,* 2009, EU seal ban challenged by Canada, news.bbc.co.uk, July 27 (accessed July 2009).

20 S. Fellman, M.J. Iversen, H. Sjögren & L. Thue, eds., 2008, *Creating Nordic Capitalism: The Business History of a Competitive Periphery,* Basingstoke: Palgrave-Macmillan; D.J. Snower, A.J.G. Brown & C. Merkl, 2009, Globalization and the welfare state, *JEL,* 47: 136–158.

21 A. Giddens, 1999, *as above* (p. 15).

22 R.G. Rajan & L. Zingales, 2003, *Saving Capitalism from the Capitalists,* New York: Crown; J.N. Bhagwati, 2004, *In Defence of Globalization,* New York: Oxford University Press.

23 T. Levitt 1983. The globalization of markets, *HBR,* May/June; K. Ohmae 1989. Managing in a borderless world, *Harvard Business Review,* May/June 1989;

F. Fukuyama, 1992, *The End of History and the Last Man,* New York: The Free Press.

24 R.S. Tedlow & R. Abdelal, 2004, Ted Levitt's 'The Globalization of Markets': An evaluation after two decades, in: J.A. Quelch & R. Deshpande, eds, *The Global Market,* San Francisco: Jossey-Bass; J.K. Johansson, 2004, *In Your Face: How American Marketing Excess Fuels Anti-Americanism,* Upper Saddle River, NJ: Financial Times/Prentice Hall.

25 M.F. Guillén, 2001, Is globalization civilizing, destructive or feeble? A critique of five key debates in the social science literature, *ARS* 27: 235–60. Similar definitions are used by J. Stiglitz, 2002, *Globalization and Its Discontents* (p. 9), New York: Norton; R. Narula, 2003, *Globalization and Technology,* London: Polity Press.

26 K.J. Moore & D.C. Lewis, 2000, Multinational enterprise in ancient Phoenicia, *BH* 42(2): 17–42.

27 Data in this paragraph and the next are based on G. Jones, 2005, *Multinationals and Global Capitalism: from the Nineteenth Century to the Twenty-first Century,* Oxford: Oxford University Press; also see T.A.B. Corley, 1994, Britain's overseas investments in 1914 revisited, *BH,* 36 (1): 71–88; C. Schmitz, 1995, The world's largest industrial companies of 1912, *BH,* 37 (4): 85–96; A.G. Kenwood & A.L. Longhead, 1999, *The Growth of the International Economy,* Abington: Routledge; D. Hummels, 2007, Transportation cost and international trade in the second era of globalization, *JEP,* 21 (3): 131–154; Fellman, Iversen, Sjögren & Thue, 2008, *as above.*

28 G. Jones, 2005, *as above.*

29 United Nations, 2000, *World Investment Report 2000,* New York and Geneva: United Nations.

30 The term *emerging markets* was probably coined in the 1980s by Antonie van Agtmael, a Dutch officer at the World Bank's International Finance Corporation (IFC). See A. van Agtmael, 2007, *The Emerging Markets Century: How a New Breed of World-class Companies is Overtaking the World,* New York: Simon and Schuster.

31 *The Economist,* 2009, BRICs, emerging markets and the world economy: Not just straw men, June 20.

32 T. London & S. Hart, 2004, Reinventing strategies for emerging markets, *JIBS,* 35: 350–370; S. Hart, 2005, *Capitalism at the Crossroads,* Philadelphia: Wharton School Publishing; C.K. Prahalad, 2005, *The Fortune at the Bottom of the Pyramid,* Philadelphia: Wharton School Publishing; T. London, 2009, Making better investments at the base of the pyramid, *HBR,* May: 106–113.

33 M. Guillén, 2001, *The Limits of Convergence* (p. 232), Princeton, NJ: Princeton University Press;

P. Ghemawat, 2003, Semiglobalization and international business strategy, *JIBS*, 34: 138–152; W. Stanbury & I. Vertinsky, 2004, Economics, demography and cultural implications of globalization, *MIR*, 44: 131–151.

34 S. Leong *et al.*, 2008, Understanding consumer animosity in an international crisis, *JIBS*, 39: 996–1009.

35 Data and quotes in this paragraph are from *Fortune*, 2007, The greatest economic boom ever, July 23.

36 J. Stiglitz, 2010, *Freefall*, New York: Allen Lane; S. Johnson & J. Kwak, 2010, *13 Bankers*, New York: Pantheon.

37 N. Taleb, D. Goldstein & M. Spitznagel, 2009, The six mistakes executives make in risk management, *HBR*, October: 78–81.

38 Narula, 2003, *as above*.

39 On the limitations of using FDI stock as measure of the scope of MNEs see S. Beugelsdijk, J.F. Hennart, A. Slangen & R. Smets, 2009, Measures of multinational activity, working paper, University of Groningen.

40 United Nations, 2009, *World Investment Report 2009* (p. 10), New York and Geneva: United Nations.

41 H. Teegen, J. Doh & S. Vachani, 2004, The importance of nongovernmental organizations (NGOs) in global governance and value creation, *JIBS*, 35: 463–483; M. Yaziyi & J. Doh, 2009, *NGOs and Corporations: Conflicts and Collaboration*, Cambridge: Cambridge University Press.

42 G.G.S. Suder, ed., 2004, *Terrorism and the International Business Environment*, Cheltenham: Elgar; R. Spich & R. Grosse, 2005, How does homeland security affect US firms' international competitiveness? *JIM*, 11: 457–478; M.R. Czinkota, G. Knight, P.W. Liesch & J. Steen, 2010, Terrorism and international business, *JIBS*, 41: 826–843.

43 P. Krugman, 2008, *The Return of Depression Economics and the Crisis of 2008*, London: Penguin; K.E. Meyer, 2009, Thinking Strategically during the Global Downturn, *AIB Insights*, 9: 2–7. *The Economist*, 2006–08, Finance and Economics: Mortgage Lending (16.12.2006), Briefing: Credit derivatives (21.4.2007), Briefing: Securisation (22.9.2007), Briefing: Northern Rock (20.10.2007), Briefing: The City of London's tumble (1.12.2007), Economic Focus: Same as it ever was (12.1.2008), Economic Focus: Chain of Fools (9.2.2008), Briefing: Wall Street's crisis (22.3.2008), Briefing: A short history of modern finance (18.10.2008), Briefing: Hedge funds in trouble (25.10.2008).

44 A. Giddens, 1999, *Ibid*.

45 A. Bird & M. Stevens, 2003, Toward an emergent global culture and the effects of globalization on obsolescing national cultures, *JIM*, 9: 395–407; L. Brimm, 2010, Global Cosmopolitans, Basingstoke: Palgrave Macmillan.

46 J. Pfeffer & C. Fong, 2004, The business school 'business', *JMS*, 41: 1501–1520; K. Starkey, A. Hatchuel & S. Tempest, 2004, Rethinking the business school, *JMS*, 41: 1521–1531; H. von Weltzien Hoivik, 2009, Developing students competence for ethical reflection while attending business school, *JBE*, 88: 5–9.

CHAPTER TWO

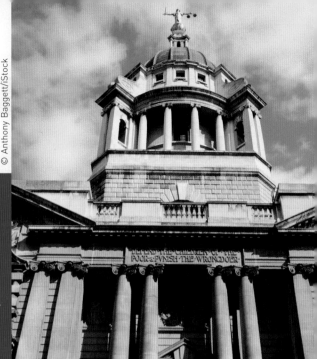

© Anthony Baggett/iStock

FORMAL INSTITUTIONS: ECONOMIC, POLITICAL AND LEGAL SYSTEMS

LEARNING OBJECTIVES

After studying this chapter you should be able to:

1 Explain the concept of institutions and their key role in reducing uncertainty.

2 Explain the basic differences among political systems.

3 Explain the systemic differences among economies.

4 Explain the basic differences between legal systems.

5 Participate in two leading debates on institutions in international business.

6 Draw implications for action.

OPENING CASE

Managing risks in the new South Africa

By Professor Steve Burgess, University of Cape Town.

With a population of 48 million, South Africa represents 10 per cent of Africa's population and 45 per cent of the continent's gross domestic product (GDP). Its GDP is almost as big as the rest of sub-Saharan Africa's 47 countries *combined*. As the engine of growth for Africa, South Africa recently has been growing at 5 per cent annually. It is the largest economy in Africa, and is among the top-ten emerging economies.

Before 1994, South Africa had been ruled by a white minority government that earned notoriety for its apartheid (racial segregation) policy. In 1986, international sanctions led many multinationals to divest their South African operations. In 1994, South Africa accomplished a peaceful transition of power, with a government of national unity led by the African National Congress (ANC) taking over power. ANC's leader, Nelson Mandela, a Nobel peace prize laureate, served as its first post-apartheid president. Since then, South Africa has embarked on a new journey of political reconciliation and economic liberalization.

Yet, doing business in South Africa has always been risky. Although the risks associated with apartheid are well known, managing risks in the post-apartheid era is no less challenging. Since 1994, South Africa has introduced fundamental and comprehensive changes to its 'rules of the game', creating both uncertainties and opportunities. The democratically elected ANC government has adopted a Black Economic Empowerment (BEE) policy aiming to increase blacks' share in the economy. The South African government is committed to protecting property rights, but the BEE rules establish constraints on ownerships rights to achieve certain political objectives.

Few South Africans disagree with basic ideas behind BEE. Yet, there has been much grumbling over the way BEE has been implemented. This is because BEE is setting quotas and timetables in terms of black ownership, executive positions, employment and affirmative action procurement. South African firms, which are predominantly owned and managed by whites, are compelled to sell a substantial percentage (25 per cent to 50 per cent) of their equity to black-owned businesses and investors often at discounted prices. A number of leading South African firms listed on the New York Stock Exchange, such as AngloGold, SAPPI, Sasol and Telkom have disclosed BEE as a risk to shareholders because these firms cannot guarantee that BEE transactions would take place at fair market price. BEE also affects foreign firms. Foreign firms interested in securing government contracts in excess of €10 million are required to invest at least 30 per cent of their sales in local black-owned firms. In the case of defence contracts, the percentage increases to 50 per cent. Firms such as Sasol complain that in a country whose official unemployment rate is stubbornly high at 25 per cent (which may really be as high as 40 per cent), BEE scares away investment and deters foreign firms. Some observers noted that the scheme mainly helps the well-connected black elite in the name of affirmative action, but fails to create jobs for the millions of poor and unemployed blacks, while lowering the quality of some public services. In other words, BEE has sliced up the economic pie differently but has done little to expand it.

Labour regulations are another area attracting business complaints. Unions are given broad power to block layoffs and limit the outsourcing of contracts, making a lot of firms reluctant to hire in the first place. The HIV/AIDS epidemic has reached epic proportions, affecting 5.5 million people, one-ninth of the population. Since laid-off HIV-positive employees will be on government support, the government has made it harder to fire infected employees. The upshot? Skyrocketing absenteeism and healthcare costs.

Despite the risks, many firms – both domestic and foreign – are charging ahead. For large domestic firms, non-compliance with BEE may not be an option in the long run. Yet, they use different strategies to deal with the issue. The first is 'fronting': relying on businesses controlled by blacks to acquire procurement contracts. Second, some cooperate and arrange for the ownership of shares to black people. For example, SABMiller, a London-based global brewer with South African roots announced that in 2010 it will transfer 10 per cent of its equity in its South African operation, valued at Rand 6bn (about €800m), to three main groups: 20 per cent to a new SAB Foundation, 40 per cent to the firm's 9000 workers (of whatever race) and 40 per cent to retailers engaged in selling the firm's beverages. The new shareholders will earn dividends on their special shares and, after ten years, will be able to convert them into shares in the parent firm SABMiller. A third copying strategy has been lobbying to renegotiate the BEE terms. The Chamber

How do legal changes in South Africa since 1994 affect opportunities for business people of all ethnic groups?

of Mines, an industry association for the important mining sector, successfully reduced the targeted ten-year equity quota for black ownership from 51 per cent to 26 per cent. Fourth, many foreign firms find it attractive to form joint ventures (JVs) or merge with black-owned firms. For instance, Tsavliris Salvage Group of Greece formed a JV with Cape Diving & Salvage of South Africa that has a 66 per cent black equity stake. This JV thus is well positioned to go after government contracts in the offshore oil industry.

Sources: We thank Professor Steve Burgess (University of Cape Town) for his insights and assistance on this case. This case is based on (1) S. Burgess, 2003, Within-country diversity: Is it key to South Africa's prosperity in a changing world? *International Journal of Advertising*, 22: 157–182; (2) J. van Wyk, W. Dahmer & M. Custy, 2004, Risk management and the business environment in South Africa, LRP, 37: 259–276; (3) *The Economist*, 2006, The way to BEE, December 23: 99; (4) *The Economist*, 2007, The long journey of a young democracy, March 3: 32–34; (5) R.W. Johnson, 2009, *South Africa's Brave New World: The Beloved Country Since the End of Apartheid*, London: Allen Lane; (6) *Economist Intelligence Unit* (2009): Selling BEE, web-document, www.economist.com (accessed July 2009).

Although South Africa is the country to be in if one wants to do business with Africa, the country's post-apartheid transition presents numerous uncertainties. The rules for business are different than what you might expect, and they are changing frequently. How can businesses play the game when the rules of the game are uncertain and keep changing? How does the government's insistence on BEE affect the costs and benefits of doing business? This chapter explores the variations in the rules of the game that foreign firms face when entering a country they are not familiar with.

Fundamentally, doing business around the globe boils down to 'location, location, location.' As the Opening Case illustrates, different locations have different institutions, popularly known as 'the rules of the game'. Overall, the success and failure of firms around the globe are to a large extent determined by firms' ability to understand and take advantage of the different rules of the game. How firms play the game and win (or lose), at least in part, depends on how the rules are made and enforced. This calls for firms to constantly monitor, decode and adapt to the changing rules of the game. As a result, such an institution-based view has emerged as a leading perspective on international business.[1] This chapter first introduces the institution-based view. Then, we focus on *formal* institutions in political, economic and legal systems. *Informal* institutions (such as culture, ethics and norms) are discussed in Chapter 3.

Institutions
Formal and informal rules of the game.

Institution-based view
A leading perspective in international business that suggests that firm performance is, at least in part, determined by the institutional frameworks governing firm.

AN INSTITUTION-BASED VIEW OF IB

Institutional framework
Formal and informal institutions governing individual and firm behaviour.

Building on the rules of the game metaphor, economic historian Douglass North, a Nobel laureate, more formally defines institutions as 'the humanly devised constraints that structure human interaction'.[2] Firms doing business abroad encounter such rules in their home country, in host countries, and in international and regional organizations such as the World Trade Organization (WTO) and the European Union (EU). The institutional framework governing a particular context is made up of formal and informal institutions governing individual and firm behaviour.

The idea that features of the context influence economic behaviour has a long tradition. The historical school in Germany and Austria, developed since the mid 18th century, taught that economic processes in different countries can only be explained as a consequence of their national histories.[3] In the early 20th century, sociologist Max Weber studied how contextual phenomena such as religion influence economic growth. More recently, German economists of the 'ordo-liberal' tradition such as Walter Eucken have been promoting the idea that the role of the state is to set the rules or legal framework ('Ordnung'), which would then ensure that the market economy functions without major distortion.[4] This idea of an absentee state that established what today is called formal institutions has been underlying the policies that made the German 'economic miracle' of the 1950s possible.

A second intellectual source of the institutional perspective is transaction costs economics as developed by Ronald Coase in the 1930s and Oliver Williamson in the 1970s (both winners of the Nobel prize). Essentially, this work argues that it is costly to use the market mechanism, and as a consequence economic actors organize themselves in less costly ways, notably by establishing firms. The transaction costs, however, are to a large extent influenced by the institutions governing the market. The institutional perspective applied in this book draws in particular on the work of Douglass North, who integrated different lines of thought and emphasized the complementary, and often interdependent, role of formal and informal institutions.

Formal institutions
Institutions represented by laws, regulations and rules.

Shown in Table 2.1, formal institutions include laws, regulations and rules that are set by the authorized bodies. On the national level, this is normally the government, although the authority to set rules may have been delegated to specific bodies within a country (say, a ministry, the competition authority or local councils), or to supra-national bodies such as the European Union (EU) (see Chapter 8). In South Africa, it was the democratically elected government that has explicitly set quotas and timetables for black ownership, executive positions and employment ratios. Domestic and foreign firms failing to meet BEE targets have to pay fines and are disqualified from government contracts (see Opening Case).

Informal institutions
Rules that are not formalized but exist in for example norms and values.

On the other hand, informal institutions are rules that are not formalized but exist in for example norms and values. These concern what behaviours are morally right and wrong, and what is important and what is not within a society. They create pressures on individuals that shape behaviours without being 'cast in iron'. For example, what triggered whistle-blowers to report Enron's wrongdoing were their personal beliefs in right and wrong. However, two conflicting norms were at play. Many employees may have felt uncomfortable with organizational wrongdoing, yet there has also been a norm not to 'rock the boat'. Essentially, whistleblowers had to overcome the norms that encourage silence and follow own personal beliefs.

Regulatory pillar
The coercive power of governments.

Normative pillar
The mechanism through which norms influence individual and firm behaviour.

Institutions can also be classified in three 'pillars' identified by W. Richard Scott, a leading sociologist (Table 2.1).[5] The first regulatory pillar reflects the coercive power of governments and largely corresponds to formal institutions. The normative pillar refers to how the norms, values, beliefs and actions of other

Table 2.1 Dimensions of Institutions

Degree of formality	Examples	Supportive pillars
Formal institutions	• Laws • Regulations • Rules	• Regulatory (coercive)
Informal institutions	• Norms • Cultures • Ethics	• Normative • Cognitive

relevant players influence the behaviour of focal individuals and firms. The cognitive pillar refers to the internalized, taken-for-granted assumptions of how the world works that (usually unconsciously) guide individual and firm behaviour. The financial crises of 2008 revealed that banks made major mistakes in their risk management practices.[6] Probing deeper, it emerged that a combination of cognitive and normative pressures may be at fault.[7] Risk managers widely believed AAA-rated assets to be safe as events that eventually happened were not conceived to be possible – a cognitive limitation. Moreover, the norms of many financial organizations favoured the aggressive attitudes of the traders, who want their money-making transactions approved, rather than the cautious, risk adverse, attitude of the risk department. The norms of the organization however often favoured the traders, a bias that eventually proved fatal for banks such as Bear Stearns and Lehman Brothers.

Cognitive pillar
The internalized, taken-for-granted values and beliefs that guide individual and firm behaviour.

What do institutions do?

Although institutions do many things, their key role, in two words, is to *reduce uncertainty*.[8] Specifically, institutions influence individuals' and firms' decision-making by signalling what conduct is legitimate and acceptable and what is not. Basically, institutions constrain the range of acceptable actions, and thereby reduce uncertainty. Why is it so important to reduce uncertainty? Because uncertainty can be potentially devastating.[9] Political uncertainty such as the possibility of expropriation may render long-range planning obsolete. Economic uncertainty such as fear that a partner may fail to carry out its obligation set out in a contract may result in economic losses. Hence, uncertainty reduces people's willingness to make long term commitments, or any commitments at all. This had a devastating effect during the financial crisis in 2008: After the failure of Lehman Brothers, banks were so worried that another major bank might go bust that they virtually stopped lending to each other, even for short term loans. The institutions of the financial markets stopped working efficiently, and interbank lending dropped dramatically.[10]

Uncertainty increases transaction costs, which are defined as the costs associated with economic transactions. Oliver Williamson refers to frictions in mechanical systems: 'Do the gears mesh, are the parts lubricated, is there needless slippage or other loss of energy?' He goes on to suggest that transaction costs can be regarded as 'the economic counterpart of frictions: Do the parties to exchange operate harmoniously, or are there frequent misunderstandings and conflicts?'[11]

Transaction costs increase if businesses believe that others may behave opportunistically, defined as self-interest seeking with guile. Examples include misleading,

Transaction costs
The costs associated with economic transactions.

Opportunistic behaviour
Seeking self-interest with guile.

Institutional transition
Fundamental and comprehensive changes introduced to the formal and informal rules of the game that affect organizations as players.

cheating and confusing other parties in a transaction. Institutional frameworks can reduce the potential for opportunistic behaviour by explicitly establishing the rules of the game so that violations (such as failure to fulfil a contract) can be mitigated with relative ease (such as through formal arbitration and courts). Other institutional contexts may reduce potential opportunistic behaviour by creating trust between members of a group, or by creating punishments on those who cheat.

Without stable institutional frameworks, transaction costs may become prohibitively high, to the extent that certain transactions simply are not undertaken at all. For example, in the absence of credible institutional framework that protects investors, foreign investors are unlikely to invest in a country,[12] and domestic investors may choose to put their money abroad. Rich Russians may thus purchase foreign assets such as a football club in London or a seaside villa in Cyprus instead of investing in Russia.

Institutions are not static; they evolve over time. Institutional transition, defined as 'fundamental and comprehensive change introduced to the formal and informal rules of the game that affect organizations as players',[13] are common, especially in emerging economies (see Chapter 1 Closing Case). Institutional transition in some emerging economies, particularly those moving from central planning to market competition (such as China, Poland, Russia and Vietnam), has been so pervasive that these countries are simply called 'transition economies' (a *subset* of 'emerging economies').

Such transition can happen gradually, or through a radical change of formal institutions. China and Russia represent examples of these contrasting approaches. China followed an incremental, 'gradualist' approach, whereas Russia pursued a radical, and 'big bang' reform. Both approaches have their merits. On the one hand, radical reforms in Russia may have been necessary to create democratic structures and private ownership in order to prevent falling back on a central plan regime. Such fundamental institutional transition creates both huge challenges and tremendous opportunities for domestic and international firms. For example, a Swedish manager working for IKEA in Russia complained that 'Russia is a bit of a rollercoaster, you don't know exactly what will happen tomorrow'.[14] Such unpredictability did not deter IKEA from investing $2.4 billion to operate eight mega stores in Russia, though in 2009 it put on hold all new investments. On the other hand, China's economic accomplishments suggest that it is possible to achieve major change by initiating substantive but localized reforms, which – if successful – may create an economic and political dynamic that leads to more comprehensive reforms. By most economic measures, China has outperformed Russia over the past two decades.

Two core propositions

Firm behaviours are often a reflection of the formal and informal constraints of a particular institutional framework.[15] In short, institutions matter. How do they matter? The institution-based view suggests two core propositions (Table 2.2). First, managers and firms *rationally* pursue their interests and make choices within institutional constraints. For example, in some countries, labour laws – a formal institution – protect workers from the threat of unemployment by requiring long notice periods and substantial redundancy payment. In an economic downturn, employees are much safer in their job (unless the firm goes bankrupt). However, employers would also be more reluctant to hire new people because hiring implies a long-term commitment to continue employing the person largely irrespective of market fluctuations. This explains why unemployment tends to rise early in a recession in the UK (UK firms find it easy to fire), but is more persistent in Germany when the recession ends (German firms are reluctant to hire).

Table 2.2 Two core propositions of the institution-based view

Proposition 1	Managers and firms *rationally* pursue their interests and make choices within the formal and informal constraints in a given institutional framework.
Proposition 2	Although formal and informal institutions combine to govern firm behaviour, in situations where formal constraints are unclear or fail, informal constraints will play a *larger* role in reducing uncertainty and providing constancy to managers and firms.

The second proposition is that formal and informal institutions combine to govern firm behaviour, but in situations where formal constraints are unclear or fail, informal constraints play a *larger* role in reducing uncertainty and providing constancy to managers and firms.[16] For example, when the formal regime collapsed with the break-up of the former Soviet Union, entrepreneurial firms pursued their ambitions largely relying on informal rules based on personal relationships and connections (called *blat* in Russian) among managers and officials.[17]

Many observers have the impression that relying on informal connections is only relevant to firms in emerging economies and that firms in developed economies only pursue 'market-based' strategies. This is far from the truth. Even in developed economies, formal rules only make up a small (although important) part of institutional constraints, and informal constraints are pervasive. Just as firms compete in product markets, they also fiercely compete in the political marketplace characterized by informal relationships.[18] Basically, if a firm cannot be a market leader, it may still beat the competition in a different area – namely, the non-market, political arena.[19] For example, in September 2008, a rapidly falling Merrill Lynch was able to sell itself to Bank of America for a hefty $50 billion. Supported by US government officials, this mega deal was arranged over 48 hours (shorter than the time most people take to decide on which cars to buy) and the negotiations took place *inside* the Federal Reserve building in New York. In contrast, Lehman Brothers failed to secure government support and had to file for bankruptcy. Overall, the skilful use of a country's institutional frameworks to acquire advantage is at the heart of the institution-based view.

Although there are numerous formal and informal institutions, in this chapter we focus on *formal* institutions (informal institutions will be covered in Chapter 3). Chief among formal institutions are those of the (1) political systems, (2) economic systems and (3) legal systems. Each is briefly described next.

POLITICAL SYSTEMS

A political system refers to the rules of the game on how a country is governed politically. Businesses interact with political systems only indirectly, yet business persons need to understand the political system because it shapes the commercial rules and regulations for business, and it is a major source of risk. At a broad level, there are two primary political systems: (1) totalitarianism and (2) democracy. At a more detailed level, democratic countries vary considerably in how they make and implement rules.

LEARNING OBJECTIVE

2 Explain the basic differences among political systems

Political system
A system of the rules of the game on how a country is governed politically.

Totalitarianism

Totalitarianism (or dictatorship)
A political system in which one person or party exercises absolute political control over the population.

Totalitarianism (or dictatorship) is defined as a political system in which one person or party exercises absolute political control over the population. Although the number of totalitarian regimes has declined, in recent decades, business may still encounter them. In Europe, at present probably only Belarus would qualify as totalitarian. Why do totalitarian regimes persist when democracy has been sweeping around the world? The answer is usually a combination of ideology and control over military and police forces.

An important ideology supporting totalitarian regimes has been communism, which had been embraced throughout Central and Eastern Europe and the former Soviet Union until the late 1980s. It is still the official ideology in China, Cuba, Laos, North Korea and Vietnam. Other totalitarian regimes are motivated by a combination of nationalism, religious motives and a fear of communism. In this nationalist totalitarianism, one political party, typically backed by the military, restricts political freedom, arguing that such freedom would lead to communism or chaos. In the post-war decades, Spain, Portugal and most countries in Latin America and South-East Asia experienced periods of nationalist totalitarianism before becoming democracies

Democracy

Democracy
A political system in which citizens elect representatives to govern the country on their behalf.

Democracy is a political system in which governments derive their legitimacy from their election by their citizens. For example, the citizens of South Africa (Opening Case) elected a parliament, which in turn elected the ANC government in the post-apartheid South Africa (see Opening Case). With the legitimacy of the election, the parliament and the government can issue new rules for business that are considered legitimate and binding (provided they are consistent with the constitution). Democracies however vary considerably in the way they translate the votes of the public into legislation, taxation and other government actions. Like the economy, the political system is governed by institutions. The rules are usually laid down in a constitution, and they determine how elections are organized, how the public vote is translated into seats in parliament, and how much power the elected officials or members of parliament attain. These democratic processes influence the relative influence of different interest groups. Crucial variations among democracies include:[20]

- **Proportional representation versus first-past-the-post:** Most European countries have some form of proportional representation which implies that, essentially, all votes are added up and seats are allocated to political parties proportionately to the number of their votes. This system comes closest to the ideal that all voters are equally important in choosing a country's leaders. Usually, such a system is combined with a minimum threshold share of votes that parties have to attain, such as 2 per cent in Denmark, 4 per cent in Sweden and 5 per cent in Germany. In the absence of such a hurdle, the parliament may become fragmented and unable to support a stable government, as experienced for example in Italy and Israel. In contrast, many Anglo-Saxon countries, including the UK, the USA and India, have a first-past-the-post system, in which each constituency elects *one* representative only. This system tends to favour the relative strongest political parties and gives less influence to smaller parties (apart from regional parties).

- **Direct versus indirect elections of governments:** Most European countries have an indirect democracy where voters elect their representatives in parliament, who on their behalf elect and monitor the government and the most powerful official in the country, normally the prime minister. However, some countries directly elect a president with executive power who then appoints government ministers, notably in France and the USA (see In Focus 2.1).

- **Representative versus direct democracy:** In most countries, voters elect representatives (Members of Parliament) who then act on their behalf. Thus the parliament by majority of the peoples' representatives decides on for example new law, taxation or government spending. However, in some territories, voters can vote directly for certain laws, notably in Switzerland and in several US states. This system gives voters more power, but may lead to inconsistencies and rigidities in the overall legal framework, as experienced recently in California.[21]

- **Centralization of power:** Normally, the national government is the centre of power, but people also elect local representations and in some countries regional assemblies. The power vested in these sub-national parliaments varies considerably. Especially in so-called federal systems such as Australia, Germany and the USA, state-level governments actually wield considerable power, and may even have to approve certain legislative changes at the federal level.

These are just some of the many subtle differences among democratic systems. Beyond politics, these rules also determine what selection processes are considered fair and legitimate in other organizations. For instance, students in continental Europe elect representative in a student parliament by voting for different groups – and each group will receive seats in proportion to their votes. The student union then is elected by this parliament, usually from the largest group. In contrast, students at UK or US universities directly elect individuals to specific posts within the student union.

Why does all this matter for international business? First, political systems determine who sets the rules, and whose interest may be reflected in the rules. For example, in first-past-the-post systems, regionally concentrated interest groups, such as farmers or industries clustered in certain cities or region, tend to have a lot of

Why are political elections – even in other countries – important for business?

IN FOCUS 2.1

Elections around the globe

It can be quite exciting to watch the news from elections around the world and compare how the will of the people translates into the creation of governments. When the people of **France** went to vote in May 2007, they chose their president in a two-stage direct election. At the first stage, Nicolas Sarkozy of the centre-right UMP party won with 31 per cent over Sé-golène Royal of the Socialist party (26 per cent) and centrist candidate François Bayrou (18 per cent). Only the two leading candidates of the first round proceeded the run-off held two weeks later, which Mr Sarkozy won with 53 per cent against 47 per cent for Ms Royal. This system of a run-off election ensures that the president actually is backed by a majority of the electorate, thus avoiding situations where the vote is split among multiple candidates and winner coming home with 40 per cent or less as can easily happen in single-round presidential elections.

When the people of the **USA** went to vote for their president in November 2008, they had already endured over a year of political campaigning. Initially, the race had been on for the presidential candidates of the two main parties, Republicans and Democrats. Over several weeks from January to April 2008, both parties held primary elections across the states of the union. For the Democrats, it became a cliff-hanger; by a narrow margin Barak Obama beat Hillary Clinton. In November, Mr. Obama competed directly with John McCain of the Republicans; other candidates were considered without a realistic chance. The electoral system looks like a direct election, but actually voters are voting for electoral college representatives of their states who then vote for the president, with the (relative) winner in each state receiving all the state's votes. Mr Obama came first across the finishing line with 365 electoral college votes compared to Mr McCain's 173. Obama also received the higher share of the votes with 53 per cent, which is not always the case; and rarely does a president receive over 50 per cent of the popular vote. In 2000, Al Gore actually lost even though he received more popular votes (48.4 per cent) than George Bush (47.9 per cent), because Gore had fewer electoral college votes (266 to 271, after the Florida recount controversy).

When the people of **India** went to vote in May 2009, 714 million voters were eligible to vote – the largest exercise in democracy in the world. The election took place on five dates over four weeks, and about four million officials were involved in managing the process. Voters elected one Member of Parliament in each constituency, a system modelled on the British first-past-the-post system. No party attained an overall majority in parliament, but the Congress Party (the heirs of Jawaharlal Nehru and Indira Ghandi) became the largest party with 206 of 543 seats in the Parliament, while its allies won another 56 seats. Following several rounds of tough negotiations with smaller parties, Congress managed to secure a majority in parliament, and Manmohan Singh was re-elected as prime minister of a coalition government.

When the people of **Germany** went to vote in September 2009, they were choosing between party lists in a system of proportional representation similar to those used in most continental European countries (except France). The parties' share of seats in the parliament represents their share in the direct vote, provided that they attain at least 5 per cent of the popular vote. Five parties passed this threshold, led by the Christian Democrats (33.4 per cent) and the Social Democrats (22.7 per cent). The allocation of seats then follows a complex system with takes into account both the constituency seats that parties obtained directly, and the votes they received in each state. Proportional representation typically leads to coalition governments in which the contributing parties have to negotiate and compromise over their policies. Thus, Chancellor Angela Merkel formed a new coalition government with the Liberal Party, which had received 14.8 per cent of the votes. Such coalitions are rare in first-past-the-post countries such as the **UK** where for example in 2005, 35.3 per cent of the popular votes were sufficient for Tony Blair to achieve a solid parliamentary majority with 356 of 647 seats.

Sources: *BBC News*, 2005–09, (1) Election 2005; (2) France decides 2007; (3) US election results map; (4) India election result 2009; (5) Merkel heading for new coalition, all accessed October 2009.

influence on 'their' representatives in parliament. With an indirect election, a poorly performing prime minister is likely to be ousted by his or her own party, a concern that US President Obama and French President Sarkozy do not need to worry about. In a direct democracy, interests groups and lobbyists may appeal directly to the electorate, which opens opportunities for those with major financial resources. In a centralized country such as France or the UK, the regulations and taxation rates tend to be uniform across the country, while decentralized countries such as the USA may have considerable variations that require adaptation even within the country.

Second, political systems also determine where and how businesses may be able to influence legislative processes through lobbying (mostly legal) or corruption (usually illegal). Third, they influence how frequently the rules of the game for business are changed, a major source of political risk – risk associated with political changes that may negatively impact domestic and foreign firms.[22]

Political risk
Risk associated with political changes that may negatively impact on domestic and foreign firms.

ECONOMIC SYSTEMS

An economic system refers to the rules of the game on how a country is governed economically. The theoretical prototypes are a pure market economy and a command economy, yet between them exists a wide variety of capitalism.

A pure market economy is characterized by the 'invisible hand' of market forces first noted by Adam Smith in *The Wealth of Nations* in 1776. The government takes a hands-off approach known as *laissez faire*. All factors of production are privately owned and individuals are free to engage in all sorts of contracts. The government only performs functions the private sector cannot perform (such as providing roads and defence). A pure command economy is defined by a government taking, in the words of Lenin, the 'commanding heights' in the economy. All factors of production are government- or state-owned and controlled, and all supply, demand and pricing are planned by the government. During the heyday of communism, the former Soviet Union approached such an ideal.

In practice, no country has ever completely embraced Adam Smith's ideal *laissez faire*. It boils down to the relative distribution of market forces versus other forms of coordination. Historically, many countries had a system that came close to the model of a pure market economy in the 19th century, notably the UK and the USA (see Chapter 1). Yet, here is a quiz: at the outset of the 21st century, which economy has the highest degree of economic freedom (the lowest degree of government intervention in the economy)? Hint: It is not the USA. A series of surveys report that it is Hong Kong (notwithstanding that it is under Chinese sovereignty since 1997).[23] The crucial point here is that even in Hong Kong, there is still some noticeable government intervention in the economy. During the aftermath of the 1997 economic crisis when currency speculators short sold the shares of Hong Kong-listed firms to drive down the value of the Hong Kong dollar. The Hong Kong government took the controversial action to use government funds to purchase 10 per cent of the shares of all the 'blue-chip' firms listed under the Hang Seng index.[24] This action prevented the devaluation of the currency, and stabilized the economy by driving off the speculators, but it temporarily placed the blue-chip firms partially into state-ownership.

Likewise, no country has ever practiced a complete command economy despite the efforts of communist zealots throughout the Eastern bloc during the Cold War. Poland never nationalized its agriculture. Many Hungarians were known to have second (and private!) jobs while at the same time working for the state. Black

LEARNING OBJECTIVE

3 Explain the systemic differences among economies

Economic system
Rules of the game on how a country is governed economically.

Market economy
An economy that is characterized by the 'invisible hand' of market forces.

Command economy
An economy in which all factors of production are government- or state-owned and controlled, and all supply, demand and pricing are planned by the government.

markets hawking agricultural produce and small merchandize existed in practically all (former) communist countries.

In the early 21st century, almost all countries have become market economies. In practice, when we say a country has a market economy, it is really a shorthand version for a country that organizes its economy *mostly* (but not completely) by market forces and that still has certain elements of non-market coordination. China, Russia, Sweden and the USA all claim to have a market economy; yet, the ways in which participants in the economy coordinate their activity varies considerably. The varieties-of-capitalism view suggests that economies have different inherent logics of how markets and other mechanisms coordinate economic activity.[25]

In a liberal market economy (LME), the coordination happens predominantly by companies reacting to price signals of the market. Countries such as the USA, the UK and Australia fall into this category. In these LMEs, companies are predominantly financed by issuing shares that are traded on the stock exchanges, while labour markets are flexible and employees enjoy relatively little job protection. At the other end of the spectrum, in a coordinated market economy (CME) such as Italy, Austria, Germany and France, economic actors such as businesses, governments, trade unions and industry associations coordinate their actions through a variety of mechanisms; they are not purely relying on market signals. These countries provide employees with more legal protection – it is not possible to just tell people 'tomorrow you are no longer needed'. At the same time, firms have less opportunity to raise capital through the stock market, or to incentivize managers by linking their salary or bonus to stock market performance. In addition, employees may have representatives on corporate boards, and businesses may be directly involved in the educational system, especially vocational training. For example, the apprenticeship system, which is the backbone of training for crafts and professions in many countries of continental

Varieties of capitalisms view
A scholarly view suggesting that economies have different inherent logics on how markets and other mechanisms coordinate economic activity.

Liberal market economy (LME)
A system of coordination primarily through market signals.

Coordinated market economy (CME)
A system of coordinating through a variety of other means in addition to market signals.

Figure 2.1 Varieties of capitalism

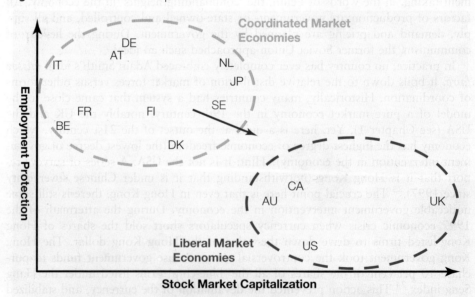

Note: Positing of countries shifts over time, the Figure reflects positions around the year 2000.
Abbreviations: AT = Austria, AU = Australia, BE = Belgium, CA = Canada, DE = German, DK = Denmark, FI = Finland, FR = France, IT = Italy, JP = Japan, SE = Sweden, UK = United Kingdom, US = USA.
Source: P.A. Hall & D. Soskice, eds. 2001, Varieties of Capitalism, Oxford: Oxford University Press, reprinted with permission. Sweden was added by the current authors.

Source: Edited by P.A. Hall & D. Soskice, 2001, *Varieties of Capitalism: The Institutional Foundations of Comparative Advantage*, Oxford: Oxford University Press. Reproduced by permission of Oxford University Press, www.oup.com

Europe, relies on close cooperation between businesses, industry associations and the state, and on long-term commitments of both apprentices and their employers.

The elements of LME and CME are combined in different ways in different countries (Figure 2.1). The Nordic countries combine an extensive welfare state (typical for a CME) with flexible labour markets, strong capital markets and an open trade regime (for an LME). For example, the Danish agricultural industry is organized in cooperatives owned by the farmers, yet they are fiercely competitive internationally, including the largest exporters of meat (Danish Crown) and dairy products (Arla), and they have a long record of advocating free trade, which is rather unusual for farmers.[26] In Southeast Asia, many countries have embraced the principles of an LME, yet with a strong state providing directions and vision regarding the envisaged path of economic development.[27]

Moreover, these economic systems are in constant flux. For example, Sweden had an LME during its early industrialization in the 19th century, and a financial capital driven economy until a major banking crash in 1932. Only thereafter, Sweden developed its well-known welfare economy with a high degree of coordination. However, since the 1970s, the pendulum has been swinging back towards an intermediate position, with the Swedish stock markets gaining in importance for finance and corporate governance.[28] On the other hand, in 2008 several LMEs, notably the USA and the UK were badly hit by bursting housing market bubbles and collapsing banks. They reacted by nationalizing some mortgage banks, and tightening the regulation of the banking sector, which moves them closer to the CME model.

LEGAL SYSTEMS

When you are living or doing business abroad, you are subject to the law of the country in which you operate; your home country's rules do not apply.[29] Thus, you will face a different legal system with its own laws and processes by which these laws are enacted and enforced. By specifying the do's and don'ts, a legal system is the cornerstone of formal institutions. This section first introduces and compares the two main legal traditions, civil and common law before introducing the specific areas of law of particular concern to business: property rights and corporate governance.

Civil law and common law

The biggest and most widespread legal system is civil law (Table 2.3). It is based on written books of law that have been influenced by Roman law, and by the French *code civil* of 1804, which in turn is also partially grounded in Roman law.[30] In civil law countries, the legal text written and approved by the relevant authorities, normally the parliament, is the foundation of law. The law thus derives its legitimacy directly from the elected parliament. Scholarly work on abstract principles and systematic conceptualization also influence both the drafting of legal texts and their interpretation in legal practice. Judges base their decisions on logical reasoning grounded primarily in the text and the spirit and purpose of the law, and on decisions by higher courts. Judicial practice has over time filled gaps in the legal texts, but (contrary to common law) this is a supplementary source.[31]

Common law, which is English in origin, is shaped by statutes as well as precedents and traditions from previous judicial decisions. It gives more weight to customary law, and the courts play a more central role in defining the law, the so-called case law. Statutes passed by legislators cover only specific areas, and tend to be interpreted narrowly.[32] Hence, common law is continuously evolving as judges resolve specific disputes with primary reference to precedents set in previous

LEARNING OBJECTIVE

4 Explain the basic differences between legal systems

Legal system
The rules of the game on how a country's laws are enacted and enforced.

Civil law
A legal tradition that uses comprehensive statutes and codes as a primary means to form legal judgments.

Common law
A legal tradition that is shaped by precedents and traditions from previous judicial decisions.

Case law
Rules of law that have been created by precedents of cases in court.

Table 2.3 Civil and common law

	Civil law	Common law
Historical origins	Roman law and French *code civil* of 1804	English customary law
Primary sources of laws	Codified in books of law, scholarly conceptualization	Statutes, customs, court decisions
Court proceedings	Judges lead the proceedings, including asking questions and deciding.	Judges as arbiters, lawyers dominate proceedings and juries as decision-makers
Business practice	Contracts and codes of practice comparatively brief, traditionally more protection of employees and consumers.	Greater freedom to design contracts and codes of practice; detailed contracts filling gaps in the legal framework; extensive use of lawyers.

Note: These characteristics are stylized, practices varies considerably across countries.

Sources: Based on text in: K. Zweigert & K. Kötz, 1999, *An Introduction to Comparative Law*, 3rd ed., Oxford: Oxford University Press.

cases of similar nature. Such extensions of the law then may give new meaning to the law, which will shape future cases.

Common law may provide businesses with greater freedom to set their own rules, for instance when writing contracts. However, courts will only consider the exact wording of the written contract. This implies that contracts tend to be rather long and detailed, partially substituting for the absence of detailed legal regulations. Corporate lawyers are therefore likely to be essential in business negotiations from the outset to define the terms of the relationship (see In Focus 2.2). The contract freedom tends to benefit those with more bargaining power, i.e. big business. As an unsuspecting consumer, you are more likely to find surprising clauses that you do not like in your mobile phone or credit card service provider's contracts in a common law country. On the other hand, businesses may appreciate civil law because of the greater clarity of rules and the reduced need to negotiate detailed contracts. Many issues are already covered in legal codes, and courts will consider the spirit and intentions of the contracting partners when interpreting a contract. Contracts thus normally cover only the specifics of the transaction and the deviations from the rules in the relevant legal statutes. Moreover, there tends to be less need for industry or corporate 'codes of conduct' to make up for voids in the legal framework in civil law systems (Chapter 10).[33]

Not only does the content of the law differ, but also the processes by which it is enacted. Probably you have seen US law in action in Hollywood movies: lawyers arguing with each other, and juries having to make tricky decisions of fact. American common law is highly confrontational (and thus an attractive setting for movies) because plaintiffs and defendants, through their lawyers, must argue their case in front of judge and jury. Juries of 12 lay persons often have to decide whether a person is guilty, or whether and how much compensation is to be paid. In contrast, you probably have rarely seen a civil law court in action in a movie. That's because it lacks the drama and excitement. Civil law is less confrontational because comprehensive statutes and codes serve to guide judges. Another key difference is that in the USA, each party has to pay its own legal costs. This implies that even if you win a case, you may end up paying out a lot of money. Unsurprisingly,

IN FOCUS 2.2

© binabina/iStock

Spaniards heading across the Atlantic

NaturEner is a Spanish MNE developing and operating wind energy farms in Spain and in North America. A Spanish executive talks of his experiences in dealing with the institutional environment of the USA, and its legal system in particular, comparing it to Spain:

'Developing business in the USA has its own rules, subject to very hard competition without compromise. Respect of private property is absolutely sacred and, apart from environmental restrictions that the authorities may impose, each property owner does what they please with their property or land. On the other hand, there are no particular difficulties when setting up or buying a company. It is true that the presence of lawyers in the daily life of Americans is huge, and the enormous cost of their professional services is not a myth. They influence the lack of regulation, so common in the Anglo-Saxon world, so different to ours. There is much more liberty depending on circumstances,

innumerable legal loopholes. But if you slip it is inevitable you will end up in the courts. In Spain, NaturEner decided to get rid of legal advisors. In the USA on the other hand, it is unavoidable to include a lawyer in the organization. This is the same in Canada. It is a fundamental resource. With our type of operation one can undertake negotiations worth millions between Seattle and New York without the necessity of meeting face to face, by means of faxes and email. But all this, clearly, is always with the direct advice of the lawyers.

One feature is particularly relevant to the activities of NaturEner undertakes [the installation of wind turbine parks]. America is to a large part an empty territory. The population is concentrated in specific areas, but there are millions of hectares where one can put installations of whatever size you like. Another issue is that they don't yet have the electrical power infrastructure necessary, a problem that is evolving in time. The state of Texas, for example, has approved investments of US$5 *billion solely for networks to make it possible to launch more renewable energy projects. The procedure is first to negotiate contracts with the owners of the farms and, subsequently, negotiate with the financial institutions and electrical grid operators to ensure that the energy generated can be sold. There are a series of processes that have to be followed depending on the rules of the particular electricity company, which are regulated by a national committee. A single electricity company cannot do as it pleases, everything is regulated, but the sale of the energy produced and its transmission are negotiated directly with the electricity company in question. And one can sell to an investment*

fund. With foresight, the administration has granted a general environmental approval [of our technology], so that what can take five years here [in Spain] can be resolved there [in Texas] in a third of the time. The Americans won't suffer our rigid bureaucracy; they are much more imaginative, although they have other problems. They are flexible, imaginative, business-oriented and they don't like to waste time.'

Source: R. Sánchez-Castillo Lodares, 2009, Energías renovables: españoles en la pole position, *Claves de la Economía Mundial,* 9, 201–206, translated by Merwyn Manson, University of Bath.

more lawyers are needed in the common law systems – and they tend to be very expensive.

If you are used to common law, you may find civil law countries very bureaucratic because there seem to be fairly detailed rules for almost everything, and not knowing all the rules can easily get you in trouble. On the other hand, if you are used to civil law, you may find common law countries very bureaucratic: each organization has its own rules, and a lot of activities have to be documented in great detail both for independent evaluators (whose criteria are vaguely defined), and as a protection against possible legal action. You may not find as much legal certainty, that is, clarity over the relevant rules that apply in a given situation. The codification of civil law makes it more accessible to everyone. In fact Napoleon himself challenged legislators to produce a 'readable' code back in the early 1800s when the French were drafting their *code civil*.[34] This codification established the unity of the law in its territory, reduced uncertainty and secured equality before the law, as proclaimed by the French Revolution.

Legal certainty
Clarity over the relevant rules applying to a particular situation.

Most countries of the world have adapted legal codes based on civil or common law. In British colonies, the law usually developed along the principles of common law but incorporated local legal traditions, and this mix was retained after gained independence. Countries that at some stage in their history wished to introduce an entirely new and coherent set of rules often adapted civil law to local conditions.[35] For example, many Latin American countries opted for the French *code civil*, while Turkey imported the Swiss civil code (Table 2.4). German civil law is also the foundation of legal codes in East Asia, notably Japan, Korea and Taiwan. Yet, application of the law is quite different in these Asian countries as preference is given to peaceful conciliation and arbitrage rather than public proceedings in court.

Overall, legal systems are a crucial component of the institutional framework. They directly impose do's and don'ts on businesses, and they influence both the political and the economic system. Two aspects of the legal systems tend to be of particular concerns to business: property rights and corporate governance.

Property rights

Property rights
The legal rights to use an economic property (resource) and to derive income and benefits from it.

Regardless of which legal family a country's legal system belongs to, a fundamental economic function of a legal system is to protect property rights – the legal rights to use an economic property (resource) and to derive income and benefits from it.[36] Examples of property include homes, offices and factories as well as intellectual property. Property rights provide the basic economic incentive system

Table 2.4 Legal traditions[1]

Family	Sub-group	Examples
Civil Law	French *code civil*	France, Spain, Italy, Belgium, Netherlands, Poland, Romania, Latin America, French-speaking Africa
	Germanic civil law	Germany, Austria, Switzerland, Hungary, Greece, Turkey, Japan, Korea, Taiwan
	Nordic civil law	Denmark, Finland, Iceland, Norway, Sweden
Common law	English law	England and Wales, Australia, Canada, Ireland, New Zealand
	English law with local customary law	Former British colonies in Africa and Asia
	American common law	USA
	Mixed common and civil law	South Africa, Scotland, Quebec (Canada), Louisiana (USA)
Religious law	Islamic law	Iran, Lybia, Morocco, Saudi Arabia

[1] Most countries have been influenced by multiple legal traditions; the table indicates the main influence on current legal practice.

Sources: Based on text in: K. Zweigert & K. Kötz, 1999, *An Introduction to Comparative Law*, 3rd ed., Oxford: Oxford University Press; R. La Porta, F. Lopez-de-Silvanes, A. Shleifer & R.W. Vishny, 1998, Law and Finance, *JPE* 106: 1113–1155.

that shapes resource allocation. In principle, property rights can be defined by formal arrangements or informal conventions and customs regarding the allocations and uses of property. However, informal conventions are rarely effective beyond clearly defined communities.

What difference do property rights supported by a functioning legal system make? A great deal. Clearly defined property rights enable people and businesses to make contracts over such property, and thus to engage in business – most business transactions concern the transfer of some sort of property, or rights to property. In developed economies, owners of land, buildings or trademarks hold legal titles documenting their rights to derive income and benefits from it and enabling prosecution of violators through legal means. Because of the stability and predictability of such a legal system, tangible property can lead an invisible, parallel life alongside its material existence. It can be used as collateral for credit. For example, the single most important source of funds for new start-ups in the USA is the mortgage of entrepreneurs' houses.

However, if you live in a house but cannot produce a title document specifying that you are the legal owner (which is a very common situation throughout the developing world, especially in 'shantytowns'), no bank will accept your house as collateral for credit. To start up a new firm, you may have to resort to borrowing funds from family members, friends and other acquaintances through *informal* means. But funds through informal means are almost certainly more limited than funds that could have been provided formally by banks. In part because of such under funding, the average firm size in the developing world is smaller than that in the developed world. Such insecure property rights also result in using technologies that employ little fixed capital and do not entail long-term investment. What the developing world lacks and desperately needs is formal protection of property rights to facilitate economic growth.[37]

Although the term *property* traditionally refers to *tangible* pieces of property (such as land), intellectual property specifically refers to *intangible* property that results from intellectual activity (such as writing, creating and inventing). Intellectual property rights (IPRs) are rights associated with the ownership of intellectual property. IPRs primarily include rights associated with (1) patents, (2) copyrights and (3) trademarks.

- Patents are legal rights awarded by government authorities to inventors of new technological ideas, who are given exclusive (monopoly) rights to derive income from such inventions through activities such as manufacturing, licensing or selling.

- Copyrights are the exclusive legal rights of authors and publishers to publish and disseminate their work (such as this book, a photo or a piece of software).

- Trademarks are the exclusive legal rights of firms to use specific names, brands and designs to differentiate their products from others.

The definition of property rights is one issue; their enforcement is an entirely different one. The rise of the internet has created new challenges to the definition and enforcement of IPR, including images, music, texts and movies. On the internet, the enforcement of IPR is technologically difficult, and raises important civil liberties issues.[38] Some countries are also slow in enforcing conventional IPR. In fact, counterfeiting – the production of copied products – is a thriving international business. Some authors suggest that close to 10 per cent of world trade is in counterfeits. Counterfeiting is generally regarded as a by-product of an entrepreneurial boom, such as the boom unfolding in China. A fundamental issue is while most entrepreneurs pursue legitimate business, why do many individuals and firms participate in counterfeiting? Experts generally agree that the single largest determinant lies in institutional frameworks. Clearer definition and stronger enforcement of IPRs may reduce their incentive to do so (see In Focus 2.3).

Corporate governance

A second aspect of the legal framework that is essential for business is corporate governance, that is the rules by which shareholders and other interested parties control corporate decision-makers (typically managers).[39] The rules of corporate governance specify the distribution of rights and responsibilities among different participants in the corporation, such as the board, managers, shareholders and other stakeholders, and spells out the rules and procedures for making decisions on corporate affairs.[40] Corporate governance is important to ensure that managers act in the best interest of the firm, rather than their personal interest. Without effective corporate governance no one would put their money into someone else's firm – and thus firms would remain small.

Variations in corporate governance around the world are closely associated with variations in economic and legal systems. Common law systems have evolved in ways that provide strong protection to financial investors. Thus, shareholders are at the centre of corporate governance. Managers have to serve shareholders' interests, who monitor them through the stock market, while employees and other stakeholders normally have rather little influence. In particular, stock options provide powerful incentives for managers to act in shareholders' interest. Moreover, takeovers provide a mechanism by which widespread equity ownership may rapidly

Intellectual property rights
Rights associated with the ownership of intellectual property.

Patents
Legal rights awarded by government authorities to inventors of new technological ideas, who are given exclusive (monopoly) rights to derive income from such inventions.

Copyrights
Exclusive legal rights of authors and publishers to publish and disseminate their work.

Trademarks
Exclusive legal rights of firms to use specific names, brands and designs to differentiate their products from others.

Corporate governance
Rules by which shareholders and other interested parties control corporate decision-makers.

IN FOCUS 2.3

Protecting intellectual property internationally

Intellectual property rights (IPRs) are usually asserted and protected on a country-by-country basis, which raises a pressing issue internationally: How are IPRs protected when countries have uneven levels of, and willingness associated with, IPR enforcement? IPRs need to be asserted and enforced through a *formal* system, which is designed to provide an incentive for people and firms to innovate and to punish violators. However, the intangible nature of IPRs makes their protection difficult. Around the world, *intellectual piracy* – the unauthorized use of IPRs – is widespread, ranging from unauthorized sharing of music files to deliberate counterfeiting of branded products.

A prerequisite for this to happen is ineffective formal IPR protection. As a WTO member since 2001, China has significantly strengthened its IPR laws in line with the WTO TRIPS Agreement. However, what is lacking is enforcement. In America, convicted counterfeiters face fines of up to €1.5 million and ten years in prison for a *first* offence. In China, counterfeiters will not be criminally prosecuted if their profits do not exceed approximately €7000; few counterfeiters are dumb enough to keep records showing that they make that much money. If they are caught and are found to make less than €7000, they can usually get away with a €700 fine, which is widely regarded as a (small) cost of doing business. In many cases, local governments and police have little incentive to enforce IPR laws, in fear of losing tax revenues and increasing unemployment. China is not alone in this regard. For example, 1000 angry people blocked a attempt of the authorities in Thailand shut down counterfeiters in the year 2000.

To stem the tide of counterfeits, four 'Es' are necessary. The first E, enforcement, even if successful, is likely to be short-lived as long as demand remains high. The other three Es (education, external pressures and economic growth) require much more patient work. Education not only refers to educating IPR law enforcement officials but also the general public about the perils of counterfeits (fake drugs can kill and so can fake auto parts). Educational efforts ideally will foster new norms among a new generation of entrepreneurs who will have internalized the values in favour of more ethical and legitimate businesses.

External pressures have to be applied skilfully. Confronting host governments is not likely to be effective. For example, Microsoft, when encountering extensive software piracy in China, chose to collaborate with the Ministry of Electronics to develop new software instead of challenging it head on. Microsoft figured that once the government has a stake in the sales of legitimate Microsoft products, it may have a stronger interest in cracking down on pirated software.

Finally, economic growth and home-grown brands are the most effective remedies in the long run. In the 1960s, Japan was the global leader in counterfeits. In the 1970s, this dubious distinction passed on to Hong Kong, and later to South Korea and Taiwan. Now it is China's turn. As these countries developed their own industries, local inventors will have interests in protecting their IPR, and they will create pressures for stronger IPR laws. Past experience around the world suggests that China and other leading counterfeiting nations may gradually extend their IPR protection laws and enforcement.

Sources: Based on (1) M.W. Peng, 2001, How entrepreneurs create wealth in transition economies, *AME*, 15: 95–108; (2) T. Trainer, 2002, The fight against trademark counterfeiting, *CBR*, November–December: 20–24; (3) *Business Week*, 2005, Fakes! February 7; (4) D. Clark, 2006, Counterfeiting in China, *CBR*, January–February: 14–15; (5) C.W.L. Hill, 2007, Digital piracy: Causes, consequences and strategic responses, *APJM*, 24: 9–24; (6) *The Economist*, 2007, Counterfeit Goods in China: Mind games, November 10.

become concentrated.[41] Managers act in anticipation of potential hostile takeover and thus aim at keeping the share price high, which is in the interest of shareholders. This focus of the legal framework on shareholders explains why common law countries generally qualify as LME.

In contrast, legislators in civil law countries (especially in French *code civil*) tend to offer less protection to outside shareholders, and hence we see more family and state ownership in these countries. Germanic civil law is strong in protecting creditors, and thus provides a stronger basis for bank financing. Moreover, many Germanic and Nordic civil law countries give stakeholders such as banks and non-managerial employees a formal role in governance. For example, German banks play an important role in the monitoring of firms, as most individual shareholders delegate their voting rights to a bank, which then votes in shareholder meetings on behalf of its clients. Moreover, firms often entertain close relationships with their bank. As lenders, banks have access to inside information and take a central role in monitoring management. These rules reinforce the co-ordination aspect of a CME. Moreover, employee representatives sit on corporate supervisory boards of large firms, and thus directly participate in corporate governance.[42] However, a global trend over the past two decades has led to more legal protection of shareholders, and reduced role of bank governance. For instance, banks in Germany have been divesting their equity stakes in non-bank businesses. Thus corporate governance rules are converging across legal systems.

DEBATES AND EXTENSIONS

LEARNING OBJECTIVE

5 Participate in two leading debates on institutions in international business

Formal institutions such as political, legal and economic systems represent some of the broadest and most comprehensive forces affecting international business. They provoke some significant debates. In this section, we focus on two major debates: (1) drivers of economic development, and (2) political risk.

Institutions and economic development

The differences in economic development around the globe are striking. Based on gross national income (GNI) using official exchange rates, Table 2.5 shows the highest and lowest per capita income countries to be Norway (€55 740) and Burundi (€80), respectively. Why are Northern European countries such as Norway so developed (rich) and Central African countries such as Burundi so underdeveloped (poor)? More generally, what drives economic development in different countries?

Scholars of economic development debate why some countries succeeded in development while others failed.[43] Some argue that accumulation of capital and the productivity of industry are pivotal for development, and hence investment and technological progress are at the best ways to advance development. Yet, for example the Soviet Union had high investment rates while its development stalled from the 1970s onward. Others argue that market-friendly macro-economic policies are essential, including low inflation, stable exchange rates, low government budget deficits and low trade barriers. This certainly plays a role, but cannot be the whole story. A third group of scholars argues that human capital is the key to prosperity, and thus developing countries ought to invest in education.[44] Yet, how do you make sure the educated elite does not just exploit the less lucky ones, or leave the country altogether?

The argument gaining the upper hand in this debate suggests that institutions are the basic determinants of the performance of an economy.[45] Because institutions provide the incentive structure of a society, formal political, legal and economic systems have a significant impact on economic development by affecting the costs of doing business. In short, rich countries are rich because they have developed

Table 2.5 Richest and poorest countries by per capita gross national income (GNI)

Richest ten		Poorest ten	
Norway	€55740	Mozambique	€230
Switzerland	€43660	Rwanda	€230
Denmark	€40040	Niger	€200
Ireland	€35100	Sierra Leone	€190
Sweden	€33580	Malawi	€180
USA	€33570	Eritrea	€170
Netherlands	€33410	Ethiopia	€160
Finland	€32370	Liberia	€110
United Kingdom	€31160	Democratic Republic of Congo	€100
Austria	€31130	Burundi	€80

Source: Adapted from The World Bank, 2009, *World Development Report 2009: Reshaping Economic Geography*, Washington, DC: The World Bank. GNI is gross domestic product (GDP) plus net receipts of primary income (compensation of employees and property income) from non-resident sources. Data refer to 2007.

better market-supporting institutional frameworks. Specifically, several points can be made:[46]

- Institutions ensure that firms are able to make gains from trade. Specifically, they enable firms to enter contracts, and be reasonably sure that partners will honour their contractual obligations, or that they can use the court system to enforce the contract.

- A lack of strong, formal, market-supporting institutions forces individuals to trade on an informal basis with a small neighbouring group and forces firms to remain small, thus foregoing the gains from a sharper division of labour by trading on a large scale with distant partners. For example, most of the transactions in Africa are local in nature, and most firms are small. More than 40 per cent of Africa's economy is reportedly informal, the highest proportion in the world.

- Emergence of formal, market-supporting institutions encourage individuals to specialize and firms to grow in size to capture the gains from complicated long-distance trade (such as transactions with distant, foreign countries).

- When formal, market-supporting institutions protect property rights, they will fuel more innovation, entrepreneurship and thus economic growth.

These arguments, of course, are the backbone of the institution-based view of international business. Championed by Douglass North, the Nobel laureate quoted earlier, this side has clearly won the debate on the drivers of economic development.[47] Considerable empirical evidence supports the view that cognitive skills and economic institutions complement each other in advancing economic development.[48]

Institutions and political risk

Businesses like stable environments, which make it easier to plan for the long term. However, radical changes in the political sphere can cause considerable disruptions including civil wars, riots, protests and breakdowns of public order. Such disruptions can cause major losses to businesses. Yet, even small changes such as changes in the rate of import tariffs constitute a big political risk. For example, in 2009, Libya to the surprise of foreign investors introduced a new requirement that foreign joint ventures must have local chiefs. This created considerable concern among foreign investors operating a subsidiaries as JV, as required by industry regulation in many sectors.[49] The most extreme political risk may lead to nationalization (expropriation) of foreign assets. The last time this happened on a large scale was in the context of the Iranian revolution of 1979.[50]

Firms operating in democracies also confront political risk. However, such risk is lower than in totalitarian states. For example, each election entails the possibility that the opposition wins, and then changes the legal framework to their liking. For example, many supporters of presidential candidate Barak Obama in the USA in 2008 advocated restrictions on free trade or inward investment. From the perspective of foreign businesses doing business in the USA, this represents a political risk – the possibility that such measures are implemented and have negative effect on their business. However, democracies are subject to division of powers: In the USA, not only the president but both Houses of Congress would have to approve new laws; in case of high-level disputes even the Supreme Court may be involved. Hence, policy shifts in a democracy are likely to be less radical and less surprising than in a totalitarian state and hence political risk is typically lower in a democracy.

There is hardly any controversy on the importance of monitoring political risk; yet how can you actually measure political risk? First, you could ask a panel of country experts about their personal views, and you could combine these perceptions into an aggregate country risk index. A number of agencies, such as the Economist Intelligence Unit, Euromoney, and the World Bank (see Chapter 9), produce such rating of political risk. However, great caution must be exercised when using such indices. For example, they failed to provide warning of sudden political changes in Indonesia, Malaysia, South Korea and Thailand triggered by the 1997 East Asian financial crisis. In fact, these had often been rated as the least risky countries: prior to the 1997 crisis, East Asia had been widely regarded as a 'miracle' region, and foreign investors had flocked in. The velocity of the 1997 crisis shocked the vast majority of investors and politicians in these countries as well as international executives and political risk experts. In Indonesia, for example, the authoritarian president was toppled, which led to losses by foreign investors who had closely aligned themselves with the extensive business network of the Suharto family. The underlying political risk in these countries was eventually picked up by the perception-based rankings, but it was too late. Hence, perception-based measures may miss important aspects of political risk![51]

Two complementary approaches thus have been developed. Some commercial providers compile indices based on *symptoms* of political instability such as crime rates, poverty and labour strikes. Additionally, scholars have proposed to look at a country's underlying political system.[52] For example, the political constraint index (POLCON) focuses on the identifiable and measurable number of veto points in a political system, such as multiple branches of the government and judicial independence.[53] The assumption is that a political system with no checks and balances would have no constraints on the leading politicians because nobody possesses the power to veto key decisions. In such a system, political change may become highly unpredictable, thus presenting a lot of risk.

IMPLICATIONS FOR PRACTICE

Focusing on *formal* institutions, this chapter has sketched the contours of an institution-based view of international business, which is one of the two core perspectives we present throughout this book (Chapter 3 will reinforce this view with a focus on *informal* institutions). How does the institution-based view help us answer the fundamental question that is of utmost managerial concern worldwide: What determines the success and failure of firms around the globe? In a nutshell, this chapter suggests that firm performance is, at least in part, determined by the institutional frameworks governing firm behaviour. It is the growth of the firm that, in the aggregate, leads to the growth of the economy. Not surprisingly, most developed economies are supported by strong, effective and market-supporting formal institutions, while most underdeveloped economies are held back by weak, ineffective and market-depressing formal institutions. In other words, when markets work smoothly in developed economies, formal market-supporting institutions are almost invisible and taken for granted. Behind the scenes the formal institutions are reducing the uncertainty facing business.

For managers, this chapter suggests two broad implications for action (Table 2.6). First, managerial choices are made rationally within the constraints of a given institutional framework. Therefore, when entering a new country, managers need to do their homework by having a thorough understanding of the formal institutions affecting their business. Although this is a good start, managers also need to understand *why* Romans do things in a certain way by studying the formal institutions governing Roman behaviour. A superficial understanding may not get you very far and may even be misleading or dangerous. For example, understanding the legal system and codes applying to your industry may help you understand why local firms act the way they do – and how a foreign entrant might gain competitive advantage by doing business differently yet within the scope of what is permitted.

Second, formal institutions are not fixed for all times, they do change. Such change is usually gradual and based on clearly defined processes in the economic, political and legal systems. Thus, business operating in other countries ought to closely follow what is happening in their host country to anticipate possible changes such as a change in tariffs or taxation. Understanding these processes reduces political risk, that is losses from unanticipated changes, and firms may even be able to influence such changes through lobbying at the appropriate places.

Third, although this chapter has focused on the role of formal institutions, managers should follow the advice of the second proposition of the institution-based

Table 2.6 Implications for action

- When entering a new country, do your homework by developing a thorough understanding of the formal institutions governing firm behaviour

- Changes in formal institutions can be anticipated, or even influenced, by engaging in processes in the economic, political and legal systems.

- When doing business in countries with a strong propensity for informal relational exchanges, insisting on formalizing the contract right away may backfire.

view: In situations where formal constraints are unclear or fail, informal constraints (such as relationship norms) will play a *larger* role in reducing uncertainty. This means that when doing business in countries with a strong propensity for informal, relational exchanges, insisting on formalizing the contract right away may backfire. Because these countries often have relatively weak legal systems, personal relationship building is often a substitute for the lack of strong legal protection. Attitudes such as 'business first, relationship afterward' (have a drink after the negotiation) may clash with a norm of 'relationship first, business afterward' (entertainment first, talk about business later). For example, we often hear that Chinese prefer to cultivate personal relationships (*guanxi*) first. In the absence of a strong and credible legal and regulatory regime in China, investing in personal relationships up front may simply be the initial cost one has to pay if interested in eventually doing business together. Such investment in personal relationships is a must in countries ranging from Argentina to Zimbabwe. The broad range of these countries with different cultural traditions suggests that the interest in cultivating what the Chinese call *guanxi*, which is a word found in almost every culture (such as *blat* in Russia and *guan he* in Vietnam), is driven by common institutional characteristics – in particular, the lack of formal market-supporting institutions.

CHAPTER SUMMARY

1 Explain the concept of institutions and their key role in reducing uncertainty:

- Institutions are commonly defined as 'the rules of the game'.

- Institutions have formal and informal components, each with different supportive pillars.

- Their key functions are to reduce uncertainty, curtail transaction costs and constrain opportunism.

- Managers and firms *rationally* pursue their interests and make choices within formal and informal institutional constraints in a given institutional framework.

- When formal constraints are unclear or fail, informal constraints will play a *larger* role.

2 Explain the basic differences among political systems:

- Totalitarianism is a political system in which one person or political party exercises absolute political control.

- In democracies, citizens elect representatives to govern the country, yet the institutions governing this selection vary widely.

3 Explain the systemic differences among economies:

- A pure market economy is characterized by *laissez faire* and total control by market forces.

- In liberal market economies (LMEs), companies are predominantly financed through the stock market, while labour markets are highly flexible.

- In coordinated market economies (CMEs), businesses, governments, trade unions, industry association and other economic actors coordinate their actions not only through markets.

4 Explain the basic differences between legal systems:

- Civil law uses comprehensive statutes and codes as a primary means to form legal judgments.

- Common law is shaped by precedents and traditions from previous judicial decisions.

- Property rights are legal rights to use an economic resource and to derive income and benefits from it.

- Corporate governance systems specify how managers are controlled by other interested parties of the firm.

5 Participate in two leading debates on institutions and international business:

  ● These are (1) What drives economic development? (2) How to best measure political risk?

6 Draw implications for action:

  ● Managers considering working abroad should have a thorough understanding of the formal institutions before entering a country.

  ● In situations where formal constraints are unclear, managers can reduce uncertainty by relying on informal constraints, such as relationship norms.

KEY TERMS

Case law
Civil law
Cognitive pillar
Command economy
Common law
Coordinated market economy (CME)
Copyrights
Corporate governance
Democracy
Economic system
Formal institutions

Informal institutions
Institution-based view
Institutional framework
Institutional transition
Institutions
Intellectual property rights
Legal certainty
Legal system
Liberal market economy (LME)
Market economy
Normative pillar

Opportunistic behaviour
Patents
Political risk
Political system
Property rights
Regulatory pillar
Totalitarianism (or dictatorship)
Trademarks
Transaction costs
Varieties of capitalisms view

CRITICAL DISCUSSION QUESTIONS

1 What are the relative merits of a coordinated market economy (CME) and a liberal market economy (LME)? Would you rather work/study/retire in a CME or an LME?

2 What is in your view the most legitimate way to select student union representatives at your university?

3 As a manager, you discover that your firm's products are counterfeited by small family firms that employ child labour in rural Bangladesh. You are aware of the corporate plan to phase out these products soon. You also realize that once you report to the authorities,

these firms will be shut down, employees will be out of work and families and children will be starving. How would you proceed?

4 Your multinational is the largest foreign investor and enjoys good profits in (1) Sudan, where government forces are reportedly cracking down on rebels and killing civilians, and (2) Belarus, where elections fail to meet normal European standards. As a country manager, you understand that your firm is pressured by activists to exit these countries. The alleged government actions, which you personally find distasteful, are not directly related to your operations. How would you proceed?

CLOSING CASE

The Russia puzzle

By Professor Sheila Puffer and Professor Dan McCarthy, both at North-Eastern University.

  Since the collapse of the former Soviet Union in 1991, Russia has undergone a series of extraordinary

institutional transitions. Russia changed from a communist totalitarian state towards a democracy with regular elections. Its centrally planned economy was transformed into a capitalist economy of mostly private firms. Yet, Russia has remained a huge puzzle to policymakers, scholars and business practitioners both in Russia and abroad, thus provoking a constant debate.

The debate centres on political, economic and legal dimensions. Politically, does Russia really have a democracy? Even before Vladimir Putin's consolidation of presidential power, some critics labelled Russia's democracy 'phoney'. In 2004, Russia was *downgraded* from 'Partly Free' to 'Not Free' – on a 1 to 3 scale of 'Free', 'Partly Free' and 'Not Free'–by Freedom House, a leading nongovernmental organization (NGO) promoting political freedom. This was driven by Russia's recent steady drift toward more authoritarian rule under Putin. Yet, Russia under Putin since 2000 grew 7 per cent annually, whereas Russia under Yeltsin during the 1990s, when it was 'Partly Free', experienced a catastrophic economic decline. Most Russians, who were economically better off in the 2000s, do not seem to mind living in a 'less democratic' country (relative to what Russia was in the 1990s).

Economically, the Russian economy drastically contracted in the early 1990s, by official estimates GDP fell approximately 40 per cent. Some of this decline was cutting inefficient production and official data may have been distorted by reporting biases. Even so, it was a miserable time for many ordinary citizen, when their life expectancy fell. In the late 1990s, the economy picked up again, only to be hit by a major economic crash in 1998 as a result of lax fiscal policy, unsustainable banking practice and capital flight. During the 2000s, however, the Russia economy has been growing at 7 per cent annually, although with a lot of volatility. It remains highly dependent on exports of oil and gas, and thus on the world market prices of these commodities, which are highly volatile. Despite strong human capital in areas such as aerospace engineering and software development, only few modern entrepreneurs have developed prosperous new businesses.

Legally, establishing the rule of law that respects private property is one of the main goals of Russia's institutional transitions. However, in a society where nobody had any significant private property until 1991, how a small number of individuals become super rich oligarchs (tycoons) almost overnight is intriguing. By 2003, the top-ten families or groups owned 60 per cent of Russia's total market capitalization. Should the government protect private property if it is acquired through illegitimate or 'grey' means? Most oligarchs obtained their wealth during the chaotic 1990s. The government thus faces a dilemma: Redistributing wealth by confiscating assets from the oligarchs creates more uncertainty, whereas respecting and protecting the property rights of the oligarchs result in more resentment among the population.

Moscow landscape

© Mikhail Bistrov/iStock

Thus far, the Putin and Medvedyev administration has mostly sided with the oligarchs except when a few oligarchs, notably Mikhail Khodorkovsky, threatened to politically challenge the government. Not surprisingly, oligarchs have emerged as a strong force in favour of property rights protection. In Russia, oligarchs run their firms more efficiently than other types of business owners (except foreign owners). Although the emergence of oligarchs no doubt has increased income inequality and caused mass resentment, on balance, oligarchs are often argued to have contributed to Russia's more recent boom.

Where exactly is Russia heading? Key to solving this puzzle is to understand the government of Prime Minister Putin and his successor as President, Vladimir Medvedyev. Within government, groups of autocrats and reformers are competing for influence. If the reformers gained the upper hand, a stronger, more democratic Russia might emerge that guarantees property rights and facilitates independent entrepreneurs. However, it seems that the autocrats won the battle for the time being. While Russia becomes economically richer and stronger (thanks to high oil prices), the government is bolder and more assertive in foreign affairs, and putting pressures on foreign oil companies, such as BP, to reduce their control over operations in Russia. Yet many Russian citizens argue, if the government delivers economic growth, so what?

With GDP per capita around €6500, Russia in 2008 is at a level similar to that of Turkey and Mexico. Democracies in this income range tend to be rough around the edges. They tend to have corrupt governments, high income inequality, concentrated corporate ownership and turbulent economic performance. In all these aspects, Russia may be quite 'normal'. However, these flaws are not necessarily incompatible with further political, economic and legal

progress down the road. For example, consumers in normal, middle-income countries naturally demand bank loans, credit cards and mortgages, which have only appeared in Russia for the first time and created lucrative opportunities for Russian and foreign firms. Despite some political fluctuation, overall, big political risks, which might deter foreign investors, seem reasonably remote. More and more foreign firms are now rushing into Russia, yet many remain concerned that they would face an 'uneven playing field'.

CASE DISCUSSION QUESTIONS

1   Although a stable legal framework that protects property rights reportedly can remove uncertainty and thus facilitate economic growth, the government's protection of oligarchs is not without controversies. If you were to advise the Russian government on property rights reforms, what would be your advice?

2   If you were managing the funds of a Russia oligarch, where would you invest?

3   If you were a board member at one of the major Western multinational retailers (such as Carrefour, IKEA, Metro or Wal-Mart), would you vote yes or no for a new project to set up your firm's first major store in Russia?

Sources: We thank Professors Sheila Puffer and Dan McCarthy (both at North-Eastern University) for sharing their work on Russia with us. Based on (1) S. Guriev & A. Rachinsky, 2005, The role of oligarchs in Russian capitalism, *JEP*, 19: 131–150; (2) A. Shleifer & D. Treisman, 2005, A normal country: Russia after communism, *JEP*, 19: 151–174; (3) P. Desai, 2005, *Conversations on Russia*, Oxford: Oxford University Press; (4) *The Economist*, 2006, Richer, bolder–and sliding back, July 15; (5) *The Economist*, 2007, Dancing with the bear, February 3; (6) S.M. Puffer & D.J. McCarthy, 2007, Can Russia's state-managed, network capitalism be competitive? *JWB*, 42: 1–13; (7) www.freedomhouse.org, accessed September 2009.

RECOMMENDED READINGS

P.A. Hall & D. Soskice, eds, 2001, *Varieties of Capitalism*, Oxford: Oxford University Press – an introduction and discussion of the varieties of capitalisms view.

D.C. North, 1991, Institutions, *JEP* 5(1): 97–112 – the foundation of contemporary institutional economics.

D.C. North, 2005, *Understanding the Process of Economic Change*, Princeton: Princeton University Press – the Nobel prize winner's recent analysis of institutions supporting economic development and change.

M.W. Peng, D. Wang & Y. Jiang, 2008, *An institution-based view of international business*

strategy, JIBS 39: 920–936 – an introduction to institutional perspectives on international business topics.
K. Zweigert & H. Kötz, 1999, *An Introduction to Comparative Law*, 3rd ed., Translated by

T. Weir, Oxford: Oxford University Press – a systematic overview of the main legal systems around the world.

NOTES:

"FOR JOURNAL ABBREVIATION, PLEASE SEE PAGE XXVI-XXVII."

1 M.W. Peng, D.Y.L. Wang & Y. Jiang, 2008, An institution-based view of international business strategy, *JIBS*, 39: 920–936; M.W. Peng, S. Sun, B. Pinkham & H. Chen, 2009, The institution-based view as a third leg for a strategy tripod, *AMP*, 23: 63–81.

2 D.C. North, 1990, *Institutions, Institutional Change, and Economic Performance* (p. 3), New York: Norton; J. Williamson, 2000, The new institutional economics, *JEL*, 38, 595–613; D.C. North, 2005, *Understanding the Process of Economic Change*, Princeton: Princeton University Press.

3 H.H. Nau & P. Steiner, 2002, Schmoller, Durkheim and the old European institutionalist economics, *JIE*, 36: 1005–1024; B. Sandelin, H.M. Trautwein & R. Wundrack, 2008, *A short history of economic thought*, 2nd ed., London: Routledge.

4 W. Eucken, 1940, *Grundlagen der Nationalökonomie*, Jena: Fischer; P. Koslowski, ed., 2000, *The Theory of Capitalism the German Economic Tradition*, Berlin: Springer; N. Goldschmidt & M. Wohlgemut, eds, 2008, Grundtexte zur Freiburger Tradition der Ordnungsokonomik, Tubingen: Mohr Siebeck.

5 W.R. Scott, 1995, *Institutions and Organizations,* Thousand Oaks, CA: Sage; M. Gelbuda, K.E. Meyer & A. Delios, 2008, International business and institutional development in Central and Eastern Europe, *JIM*, 14: 1–12.

6 A.G. Haldane, 2009, Why Banks failed the stress test, Mimeo, Bank of England, February 13. H.S. Shin, 2009, Reflections on Northern Rock, *JEP*, 23(1): 101–119.

7 *The Economist*, 2009, A personal view of the crisis: Confessions of a risk manager, August 9.

8 M.W. Peng, 2000, *Business Strategies in Transition Economies*, Thousand Oaks, CA: Sage; J. Hooker, 2003, *Working Across Cultures*, Stanford: Stanford University Press.

9 R. Ramamurti, 2003, Can governments make credible promises? *JIM*, 9: 253–269; S. Elbanna & J. Child, 2007, Influences on strategic decision-making, *SMJ*, 28: 431–453; V. Hoffmann, T. Trautmann & J. Hemprecht, 2009, Regulatory uncertainty, *JMS*, 46: 1227–1253.

10 *The Economist*, 2008, Derivatives: A nuclear winter? September 18; *The Economist*, 2008, Rethinking Lehman Brothers: The price of failure, October 2.

11 O. Williamson, 1985, *The Economic Institutions of Capitalism* (pp. 1–2), New York: Free Press.

12 S. Globerman & D. Shapiro, 2003, Governance infrastructure and US foreign direct investment, *JIBS*, 34: 19–34; A. Bevan, S. Estrin & K.E. Meyer, 2004, Institution building and the integration of Eastern Europe in international production, *IBR*, 13: 43–64.

13 M.W. Peng, 2003, Institutional transitions and strategic choices (p. 275), *AMR*, 28: 275–296; see also E. George, P. Chattopadhyay, S. Sitkin & J. Barden, 2006, Cognitive underpinning of institutional persistence and change, *AMR*, 31: 347–365.

14 *The Economist*, 2007, Dancing with the bear, February 3.

15 P. Moran & S. Ghoshal, 1999, Markets, firms, and the process of economic development, *AMR*, 24: 390–412; M. Kotabe & R. Mudambi, 2003, Institutions and international business, *JIM*, 9: 215–217; R. Mudambi & C. Paul, 2003, Domestic drug prohibition as a source of foreign institutional instability, *JIM*, 9: 335–349; T. Ozawa, 2003, Japan in an institutional quagmire, *JIM*, 9: 219–235; A. Parkhe, 2003, Institutional environments, institutional change, and international alliances, *JIM*, 9: 305–316; R. Greenwood & R. Suddaby, 2006, Institutional entrepreneurship in mature fields, *AMR*, 49: 27–46; K.E. Meyer, S. Estrin, S.K. Bhaumik & M.W. Peng, 2009, Institutions, Resources, and Entry Strategies in Emerging Economies, *SMJ*, 31: 61–80; A. Chacar,

W. Newburry & B. Vissa, 2010, Bringing institutional factors into performance persistence research, *JIBS*, 41: 1119–1140.

16 M.W. Peng, 2003, *as above*; A. Dixit, 2004, *Lawlessness and Economics*, Princeton: Princeton University Press.

17 M.W. Peng, 2001, How entrepreneurs create wealth in transition economies, *AME*, 15: 95–108; S.M. Puffer & D.J. McCarthy, 2007, Can Russia's state-managed, network capitalism be competitive? *JWB*, 42: 1–13.

18 A. McWilliams, D. van Fleet & K. Cory, 2002, Raising rivals' costs through political strategy, *JMS*, 39: 707–723; D.A. Schuler, K. Rehbein & R. Cramer, 2002, Pursuing strategic advantage through political means, *AMJ*, 45: 659–672; M.D. Lord, 2003, Constituency building as the foundation for corporate political strategy, *AME*, 17: 112–124; A.J. Hillman & W.P. Wan, 2005, The determinants of MNE subsidiaries' political strategies, *JIBS*, 36: 322–340;.

19 J. Boddewyn & T.L. Brewer, 1994, International-business political behavior, *AMR*, 19: 119–143; J. Crystal, 2003, *Unwanted Company: Foreign Investment in American Industries*, Ithaca: Cornell University Press; J. Bonardi, G. Holburn & R. Bergh, 2006, Nonmarket strategy performance, *AMJ*, 49: 1209–1228; J.P. Lindeque, 2007, A firm perspective of anti-dumping and countervailing duty cases in the United States, *JWT* 41: 559–579.

20 A. Lijphart, 1995, *Electoral Systems and Party Systems: A Study of Twenty-Seven Democracies*, Oxford: Oxford University Press; D.M. Farrell, 2001, *Electoral Systems: A Comparative Introduction*, Basingstoke: Palgrave.

21 B.S. Frey, 1994, Direct democracy, *AER*, 84: 338–348; J.G. Matsuoka, 2005, Direct democracy works, *JEP*, 19, 185–206; *The Economist*, 2009, Charlemagne: The Swiss in the middle, December 5; B.S. Frey, 2009, Letter: Popular politics, *The Economist*, December19; *The Economist*, 2009, Direct democracy: The tyranny of the majority, December 19.

22 T.L. Brewer, 1993, Government policies, market imperfections and foreign direct investment, *JIBS*, 24: 101–120; K. Butler & D. Joaquin, 1998, A note on political risk and the required return on foreign direct investment, *JIBS*, 29: 599–608.

23 Heritage Foundation, www.heritage.org.

24 P. Krugman, 2008, *The Return of Depression Economics and the Crisis of 2008*, London: Penguin.

25 P.A. Hall & D. Soskice, eds, 2001, *Varieties of Capitalism*, Oxford: Oxford University Press; G. Morgan, R. Whitley & E. Moen, 2005, *Changing Capitalism?* Oxford: Oxford University Press; B. Kogut & C. Ragin, 2006, Exploring complexity when diversity is limited, *EMR,* 3: 44–59; M. Carney, E. Gedajlovic & X. Yang, 2009, Varieties of Asian capitalism, *APJM*, 26: 361–380.

26 M. Mordhorst, 2008, Arla from a decentralized co-operation to an MNE, in: S. Fellman, M.J. Iversen, H. Sjögren & L. Thue, eds, *Creating Nordic Capitalism*, Basingstoke: Palgrave-MacMillan.

27 F.B. Tipton, 2009, Southeast Asian capitalism, *APJM*, 26: 401–434; B.K. Ritchie, 2009, Economic upgrading in a state-coordinated, liberal market economy, *APJM*, 26: 435–458.

28 H. Sjögren, 2008, Welfare capitalism: the Swedish economy 1850–2005, in: Fellman *et al.,* eds, 2008, *as above*.

29 M. Dixon, 2007, *A Textbook on International Law*, 7th ed., Oxford: Oxford University Press.; M.N. Shaw, 2009, *International Law*, 6th ed., Cambridge, Cambridge University Press.

30 O.F. Robinson, T.D. Fergus & W.M. Gordon, 1994, *European Legal History*, London: Butterworth; F. Wieacker, 1996, *A History of Private Law in Europe*, Translated by T. Weir, Oxford: Oxford University Press.

31 K. Zweigert & H. Kötz, 1999, *An Introduction to Comparative Law*, 3rd ed., Translated by T. Weir, Oxford: Oxford University Press (Chapters 9 & 18)

32 Zweigert & Kötz, 1999, *as above* (Chapters 15 & 18); V. Bogdanor, 2009, *The new British constitution*, Oxford: Hart.

33 A. Apostolakou & G. Jackson, 2009, Corporate social responsibility in Europe: An institutional mirror or substitute? Working Paper 2009.01, School of Management, University of Bath.

34 Zweigert & Kötz, 1999, *as above*.

35 Zweigert & Kötz, 1999, *as above*. (Chapters 8, 11, 13 & 21).

36 Y. Barzel, 1997, *Economic Analysis of Property Rights*, 2nd ed., Cambridge: Cambridge University Press; R.A. Posner, 2003, *Economic Analysis of Law*, 6th ed., New York: Aspen.

37 H. de Soto, 2000, *The Mystery of Capital*, New York: Basic Books.

38 A. Johns, 2010, *Piracy: The Intellectual Property Wars from Gutenberg to Gates*, Chicago: University of Chicago Press.

39 R.A.G. Monks & N. Minow, 1995, *Corporate Governance*, Oxford: Blackwell.

40 OECD, 2004, *OECD Principles of Corporate Governance*, Paris: OECD; K.E. Meyer, 2005, Privatization and corporate governance in Eastern

Europe, in R. Lang, ed., *The End of Transformation*, Munich: Hampp.

41 LaPorta *et al.*, 1997, *as above*.

42 J.C. Coffee, 2001, The rise of dispersed ownership: the roles of law an the state in the separation of ownership and control, *YLJ*, 111, 1–82; Hall & Soskice, 2001, *as above*.

43 W. Easterly, 2002, The *Elusive Quest for Growth*, Cambridge, MA: MIT Press; G.M. Meier, 2004, *Biography of a Subject*, Oxford: Oxford University Press; M.M. Shirley, 2008, *Institutions and Development*, Cheltenham: Elgar.

44 D.S. Landes, 1998, *The Wealth and Poverty of Nations,* New York: Norton; L.E. Harrison, 2008, *The Central Liberal Truth*. New York: Oxford University Press.

45 De Soto, 2000, *as above*; North, 2005, *as above*; Shirley, 2008, *as above*.

46 A. Sen, 1999, *Development as Freedom*, Anchor Publishing; D. Kaufmann & A. Kraay, 2002, Growth without Governance, World Bank Policy Research Working Paper #2928; D. Rodrik, A. Subramanian & F. Trebbi, 2002, Institutions Rule, IMF Working Paper #02/189.

47 D.C. North, 1994, Economic performance through time, *AER*, 84: 359–368; R. Barro & X. Sala-i-Martin, 2003, *Economic Growth*, Cambridge, MA: MIT Press; G. Roland, 2000, *Transition and Economics*, Cambridge, MA: MIT Press.

48 E.A. Hanushek & L. Woessmann, 2008, The role of cognitive skills in economic development, *JEL* 46: 607–668.

49 H. Saleh, 2009, Libya rules foreign joint ventures must have local chiefs, *Financial Times*, September 4th.

50 R. Click, 2005, Financial and political risks in US direct foreign investment, *JIBS*, 36: 559–575.

51 G.L.F. Holburn & B.A. Zelner, 2010, Political capabilities, policy risk, and international investment strategy, *SMJ*, 31: 1290–1315.

52 P. Vaaler, B. Schrage & S. Block, 2005, Counting the investor vote, *JIBS*, 36: 62–88.

53 The data are available at: www-management.wharton.upenn.edu/henisz/; see also W. Henisz & A. Delios, 2001, Uncertainty, imitation, and plant location, *ASQ*, 46: 443–475; W. Henisz & J. Macher, 2004, Firm and country-level tradeoffs and contingencies in the evaluation of foreign investment, *OSc*, 15: 537–554.

© PeterPhoto/iStock

CHAPTER THREE

INFORMAL INSTITUTIONS: CULTURE, RELIGION AND LANGUAGES

LEARNING OBJECTIVES

After studying this chapter you should be able to:

1 Define what culture is and articulate two of its manifestations: language and religion.

2 Discuss how cultures systematically differ from each other.

3 Explain how language competences shape intercultural interactions.

4 Explain how religions shape cultures.

5 Understand the importance of ethics.

6 Participate in two leading debates on cultures.

7 Draw implications for action.

OPENING CASE

Cartoons that exploded

In September 2005, Danish newspaper *Jyllands-Posten* published a dozen cartoons of the Muslim prophet Muhammad. In a deliberate test of the country's freedom of speech, the newspaper asked cartoonists to feature the prophet Muhammad, knowing that depiction of the prophet is forbidden in Islam. Some of the cartoons were humorous, while others portrayed the prophet in a highly negative, insulting light, including one picturing him with a bomb on his head. A group of ambassadors of Muslim countries asked to meet Danish Prime Minister Anders Fogh Rasmussen over the matter. Yet, contrary to diplomatic practice, he declined to meet, arguing that however distasteful the cartoons were, the government could not apologize on behalf of the newspaper. This was because, in principle, freedom of speech was enshrined in Denmark's constitution, and there was no reason to take action against the newspaper. Debates in Denmark soon moved on to other issues; no-one expected the ferociousness of the explosion these cartoons would ignite *outside* Denmark.

A few weeks after the original publication some Muslim clerics in the Middle East verbally attacked the cartoonists, and hell broke loose. Demonstrators hit the street, even though most of them had never seen the cartoons they were protesting against (and in fact had false ideas of what they depicted). In response, publishers in a total of 22 countries, such as Belgium, France, Germany, the Netherlands, and Norway, reprinted the cartoons in solidarity to make a point about their right to do so in the name of freedom of expression. In some Muslim countries, protests turned to outrage, Danish flags were burned, and Western embassies in Indonesia, Iran, Lebanon, and Syria were attacked. In Khartoum, Sudan, a crowd of 50 000 chanted 'Strike, strike, bin Laden!' At least ten people were killed in protests against the cartoons, as police in Afghanistan shot into crowds besieging Western installations. In addition to mob reactions in the street, Muslim governments took action. In protest against the cartoons, Iran, Libya, Saudi Arabia and Syria withdrew their ambassadors from Denmark. The justice minister of the United Arab Emirates argued: 'This is cultural terrorism, not freedom of expression'.

While acknowledging the importance of freedom of speech, some Western governments expressed sympathy to Muslims. French President Jacques Chirac issued a plea for 'respect and moderation' in exercising freedom of expression. British Foreign Minister Jack Straw called the cartoons 'insensitive'. US President George W. Bush called on world governments to stop the violence and be 'respectful'. Carsten Juste, editor of *Jyllands-Posten*, who received death threats, said that the drawings 'were not in violation of Danish law but offended many Muslims, for which we would like to apologize'.

While Muslim feelings were hurt, Danish firms active in Muslim countries were devastated. Arla Foods, Denmark's largest manufacturing enterprise and one of Europe's largest dairy firms, had been selling to the Middle East for 40 years, and had production in Saudi Arabia for 20 years. They normally sold approximately €400 million a year to the region, including the best-selling brand of butter. As the most prominent Danish business in the Middle East, Arla became the focus of a boycott of Danish products, and lost €4 million in *daily* revenues at the peak of the crisis, and was forced to send home 170 employees. Carrefour, a French hypermarket chain active in the region, pulled Danish products from shelves in its Middle East stores and boasted about it to customers. Arla's CEO Peter Tuborgh publicly distanced the company from the cartoons expressing understanding for the 'humiliation' experienced by Muslims. This however backfired as advocates of free speech in Denmark started to boycott Arla.

In Saudi Arabia, Arla took out full-page newspaper advertizements, reprinting the news release from the Danish Embassy in Riyadh saying that Denmark respected all religions. That failed to stop the boycott. Other Danish firms kept a low profile, or camouflaged their origins. Danish shipping companies, such as Maersk, took down the Danish flag when docking in ports in Muslim countries. Overall, although Muslim countries represented only 3 per cent of all Danish exports, it still proved a substantial blow to some companies.

The crisis has been simmering on. In 2008, new posters appeared on the streets of Jordan calling for a renewed boycott of Danish and Dutch products. In 2009, Anders Fogh Rasmussen's appointment as NATO Secretary General almost failed because of

Why did Muslims gather outside the Danish Consulate in New York City to protest about depictions of the prophet Mohammed printed by a newspapers in Denmark?

opposition from Turkey, NATO's only Muslim member country. Also in 2009, a book about the crisis faced censorship in the USA as the publisher, Yale University Press, removed not only the cartoons but also historical images of the prophet.

Sources: Based on (1) A. Browne, 2006, Denmark faces international boycott over Muslim cartoons, *Times Online*, January 31, http://www. timesonline.co.uk; (2) *The Economist*, 2006, Islam and Free Speech: Mutual incomprehension, mutual outrage, February 11; (3) *The Economist*, 2006, Consumer boycotts: When markets melted away, February 11; (4) M. Mordhorst, 2008, Arla from a decentralized co-operation to an MNE, in: S. Fellman *et al.*, eds, 2008, *Creating Nordic Capitalism*, Basingstoke: Macmillan; (5) T. Seidenfaden & R.E. Larsen, 2007, *Karikaturkrisen: en undersøgelse af baggrund og ansvar*, Copenhagen: Gyldendal; (6) *Information*, 2008, Arla: Vi spiller ikke dobbeltspil i boykottsagen, June 11; (7) *Information*, 2009, Dansk forfatter censuret i USA, August 17.

Publishing the offending cartoons is legal in Denmark, but is it appropriate? Why should many Danish firms, which had nothing to do with the cartoons, suffer major economic losses in Muslim countries? How should companies caught in a cultural conflict handle the situation? How can companies operating abroad avoid tripping themselves over rules that are not even written down? More fundamentally, what informal institutions govern individual and firm behaviour in different countries?

Following Chapter 2, this chapter continues our coverage on the institution-based view by exploring informal institutions, rules that are not formalized but exist in for example norms, values and ethics. Of the two propositions in the institution-based view, the first proposition – managers and firms rationally pursue their interests within a given institutional framework – deals with both formal and informal institutions. The second proposition – in situations where formal institutions are unclear or fail, informal institutions play a larger role in reducing uncertainty – is more important and relevant in this chapter. When formal institutions are effective, then informal institutions complement them, or accommodate different objectives of powerful players – and often they are hardly noticed. However, if formal institutions are not securing effective functioning of the economy,

Informal institutions
Rules that are not formalized but exist in for example norms, values and ethics.

then informal institutions may substitute them, or set up competing systems of economic order.[1] As shown in the Opening Case, this chapter is more than about how to present business cards correctly and wine and dine differently. Informal institutions influence individuals' behaviour in ways that they themselves may not even be aware of. Understanding the often unwritten rules that guide your business partners can make or break your business operations abroad.[2]

WHERE DO INFORMAL INSTITUTIONS COME FROM?

Where do informal institutions come from? They come from socially transmitted information and are part of the heritage that we call culture. They tell individuals in a society what behaviours are considered right and proper, and what would be unacceptable. For instance a person considered rude by his or her peers may not be invited to the next party, or to the next business deal. Typically, cultures have no clearly defined origin, but have evolved over time. Some cultural values have arisen from religious origins – for example what is considered an insult, and how to react to an insult (see Opening Case). Culture is embedded in daily routines, and some aspects are encoded in language.

Those within a society tend to perceive their own culture as 'natural, rational and morally right'.[3] This self-centred mentality is known as ethnocentrism. For example, many US Americans believe in 'American exceptionalism' – that is, the USA is exceptionally well endowed to lead the world. The Chinese call China *zhong guo*, which literally means 'the country in the middle' or 'middle kingdom'. Ancient Scandinavians called their country by a similar name (*midgaard*). Some West Europeans, such as some Danes, passionately believe in their 'freedom of speech' allows them to publish whatever they please. As shown in the Opening Case, those from other societies may feel differently. In other words, common sense in one society may become uncommon elsewhere.[4] This is also a challenge for us as authors writing a textbook for students around the world with diverse cultural backgrounds, and thus different expectations.

Recall from Chapter 2 that formal institutions clearly specifies the do's and don'ts. Informal institutions, by definition, are more elusive. Since they are not written down in law, their enforcement is also informal. Yet, they are no less important.[5] Thus, it is imperative that we pay attention to informal institutions. Here, we are going to first discuss culture and how to compare it across countries, and then we focus on language as a feature of culture, and religion as one source of culture. We round up the chapter by discussing how cultural differences can lead to ethical conflicts.

CULTURES

Culture is probably the most frequently discussed aspect of informal institutions. What is culture? Culture is everywhere, though we notice it especially when we are in unfamiliar territory: people create different arts and architecture, admire different sorts of heroes, eat different foods and follow different sports (see Photo). All this is culture. Yet, it is only the visible surface of culture, also known as artefacts of culture. For example, postcards in tourist destinations depict some of these artefacts, in fact picture postcards themselves are artefacts of culture. Beneath these artefacts, however, are differences in the shared values, norms and assumptions in a society, which are much less visible. However, the underlying differences make up the essence of culture, and create major challenges for international business.

What do tourist postcards tell us about culture?

The concept of culture is complex, and scholars use a variety of different definitions to describe the phenomenon. For example, anthropologist Victor Barnouw defined culture as:

> 'A way of life of a group of people, the configuration of all the more or less stereotyped patterns of learned behaviour, which are handed down from one generation to the next through means of language and imitation'.[6]

Many management scholars prefer more specific definitions such as the one proposed by Geert Hofstede, a Dutch management professor:

> 'Culture is a collective phenomenon that is shared with people who live or lived within the same social environment, which is where it was learned. It is the collective programming of the mind which distinguishes the members of one group or category of people from another.'[7]

Culture thus is shared in a group, connecting members of the group with each other, and with their history. In this chapter, we focus on nation states as the relevant group; other groups are discussed in the section on Debates and Extensions later in this chapter.

Each one of us is a walking encyclopedia of our own culture; most travellers have some anecdotes to tell about cross-cultural experiences or misunderstandings. Sometimes it can be frustrating to feel bombarded with a seemingly random collection of the numerous informal 'rules of the game': Do this in Muslim countries, don't do that in Catholic countries and so on. These are all interesting stories and features, but let us not forget that we are more interested in the overall picture. The point about seeing the overall picture is to understand how cultures are *systematically* different. This section outlines three ways to systematically understand cultural differences: (1) context, (2) cluster and (3) dimension approaches.

The context approach

Context
The underlying background upon which interaction takes place.

Low-context culture
A culture in which communication is usually taken at face value without much reliance on unspoken context.

High-context culture
A culture in which communication relies a lot on the underlying unspoken context, which is as important as the words used.

Of the three main approaches probing into cultural differences, the context approach is the most straightforward because it focuses on a single dimension: context.[8] Context is the underlying background upon which interaction takes place. Figure 3.1 outlines the spectrum of countries along the dimension of low- versus high-context. In low-context cultures (such as in North American and Western European countries), communication is usually taken at face value without much reliance on unspoken context. In other words, yes means yes. In contrast, in high-context cultures (such as Arab and Asian countries), communication relies a lot on the underlying unspoken context, which is as important as the words used. For example, 'yes' does not necessarily mean 'yes, I agree', it might may 'yes, I hear you'.

Why is context important? This is because failure to understand the differences in interaction styles may lead to misunderstandings. For instance, in Japan, a high-context culture, negotiators prefer not to flatly say 'no' to a business request. They may say something like 'We will study it' and 'We will get back to you later'. Their negotiation partners are supposed to understand the context of these responses that lack enthusiasm and figure out that these responses essentially mean no (although the word 'no' is never mentioned). In high-context countries, initial rounds of negotiations are supposed to create the 'context' for mutual trust and friendship. Business activities thus involve frequent social activities, for example in Saudi Arabia and in China (see Closing Case). For individuals brought up in high-context cultures, decoding the context and acting accordingly are their second nature. Straightforward communication and confrontation, typical in low-context cultures, often baffle them. In contrast, people from low-context cultures like to 'get down to business' quickly, focus on the facts, and spell-out what is agreed explicitly in letters of intent, standards of engagements or contracts. This approach, however, may miss (or miscommunicate) the more subtle ways of communicating in high context cultures.

Critics of the context approach argue that the perceived importance of context has a lot to do with the persons familiarity with the context. An American in China may note Chinese making implicit references to context that he or she does not understand; yet, likewise a Chinese may perceive Americans making references to their context – the political, economic and legal system of the USA (see Chapter 2). People operating in their home context may not be aware of such implicit references because they take them for granted. In consequence, critics accuse the context approach of being in 'ethnocentric' in characterizing cultures he least understands as context-specific and those where he grew up as low-context.

Figure 3.1 High-context versus Low-context Cultures

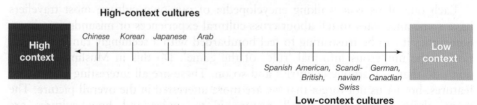

The cluster approach

The cluster approach groups countries that share similar cultures together as one cluster. There are three influential sets of clusters, Table 3.1 illustrates them side by side. Viewing them together can allow us to see their similarities. However, there are also differences.

The first is the Ronen and Shenkar clusters, proposed by management professors Simcha Ronen and Oded Shenkar.[9] These clusters are (1) Anglo, (2) Nordic, (3) Germanic, (4) Latin Europe, (5) Latin America, (6) Near Eastern, (7) Arabic and (8) Far East. The second set of clusters is called the GLOBE clusters, named after the Global Leadership and Organizational Behaviour Effectiveness project led by management professor Robert House.[10] The GLOBE project identifies ten clusters, five of which use identical labels as the Ronen and Shenkar clusters: (1) Anglo, (2) Germanic Europe, (3) Latin America, (4) Latin Europe and (5) Nordic Europe.

Cluster
Countries that share similar cultures together.

Table 3.1 Cultural Clusters

Ronen and Shenkar Clusters[1]	GLOBE Clusters[2]	Huntington Civilizations
Anglo	Anglo	Western
Nordic	Nordic Europe	Western
Germanic	Germanic Europe	Western
Latin Europe	Latin Europe	Western
Israel*	—	Western
Central and Eastern Europe	Eastern Europe	Slavic-Orthodox
Arabic	Middle East	Islamic
Near Eastern[3]	—	—
India*	Southern Asia	Hindu
Sub-Sahara Africa	Sub-Sahara Africa	African
Latin America	Latin America	Latin American
Brazil*	—	Latin American
Far East	Confucian Asia	Confucian (Sinic)
Japan*	—	Japanese

[1] Ronen and Shenkar originally classified eight clusters (in alphabetical order, from Anglo to Nordic), covering 44 countries. They placed Brazil, India, Israel, and Japan as 'independents'. Upon consultation with Oded Shenkar, Peng, Hill and Wang, 2000 (Source (3)), more recently added Central and Eastern Europe and Sub-Sahara Africa as two new clusters.

[2] GLOBE includes ten clusters, covering 62 countries.

[3] Near Eastern includes Turkey, Greece and Cyprus.

Sources: Based on (1) R. House, P. Hanges, M. Javidan, P. Dorfman & V. Gupta (eds.), 2004, *Culture, Leadership, and Organizations: The GLOBE Study of 62 Societies*, Thousand Oaks, CA: Sage; (2) S. Huntington, 1996, *The Clash of Civilizations and the Remaking of World Order*, New York: Simon & Schuster; (3) M. W. Peng, C.W.L. Hill & D.Y.L. Wang, 2000, Schumpeterian dynamics versus Williamsonian considerations, *JMS*, 37: 167–184; (4) S. Ronen & O. Shenkar, 1985, Clustering countries on attitudinal dimension, *AMR*, 10: 435–454.

In addition, GLOBE has (6) Confucian Asia, (7) Eastern Europe, (8) Middle East, (9) Southern Asia and (10) Sub-Sahara Africa, which roughly (but not completely) correspond with the respective Ronen and Shenkar clusters.

The third set of clusters is the Huntington civilizations, popularized by political scientist Samuel Huntington. A civilization is 'the highest cultural grouping of people and the broadest level of cultural identity people have'.[11] Shown in Table 3.1, Huntington divides the world into eight civilizations: (1) African, (2) Confucian (Sinic), (3) Hindu, (4) Islamic, (5) Japanese, (6) Latin American, (7) Slavic-Orthodox and (8) Western. Although this classification shares a number of similarities with the Ronen and Shenkar and GLOBE clusters, Huntington's Western civilization is a very broad cluster that is subdivided into Anglo, Germanic, Latin Europe and Nordic clusters by Ronen and Shenkar and GLOBE. Across the three systems (columns), even though some clusters share the same labels, there are still differences. For example, Ronen and Shenkar's Latin America cluster does not include Brazil (which is regarded as an 'independent'), whereas GLOBE and Huntington's Latin America includes Brazil.

In addition to such an uncontroversial classification scheme, Huntington has advanced a highly controversial idea that the Western civilization will clash with the Islamic and Confucian civilizations in the years to come. Incidents such as 9/11, the Afghanistan war and the Danish cartoons (see Opening Case) have often been cited as evidence of such a clash.

For our purposes, we do not need to debate the validity of Huntington's provocative thesis of the 'clash of civilizations'. We will leave your political science or international relations classes to debate that. However, we do need to appreciate the underlying idea that people and firms are more comfortable doing business with other countries within the same cluster. This is because common history, religion and customs within the same cluster reduce the liability of outsidership when operating abroad (see Chapter 1).

The dimension approach

Although both the context and cluster approaches are interesting, the dimension approach is more influential. The reasons for such influence are probably twofold. First, insightful as the context approach is, context only represents one dimension. What about other dimensions? Second, the cluster approach has relatively little to offer regarding differences among countries *within* one cluster. For example, what are the differences between Italy and Spain, both of which belong to the same Latin Europe cluster according to Ronen and Shenkar and GLOBE? By focusing on multiple dimensions of cultural differences both within and across clusters, the dimension approach has endeavoured to overcome these limitations. While there are several competing frameworks,[12] the work of Hofstede and his colleagues is most widely used[13] and thus is our focus here.

Hofstede and his colleagues have proposed five dimensions (Table 3.2). First, power distance is the extent to which less powerful members within a country expect and accept that power is distributed unequally. For example, in high power distance Brazil, the richest 10 per cent of the population earn approximately 50 per cent of the national income, and most people accept this as 'the way it is'. In low power distance Sweden, the richest 10 per cent only get 22 per cent of the national income.[14] The appreciation of hierarchy is often reflected in the use of titles. For instance, in the USA, subordinates often address their bosses on a first-name basis, which indicates a relatively low power distance. While this boss, Mary or Joe, still has the power to fire you, the distance appears to be shorter than if you have to address this person as Dr. X or Professor Y or Manager Z. Another indication of

Civilization
The highest cultural grouping of people and the broadest level of cultural identity people have.

Power distance
The extent to which less powerful members within a country expect and accept that power is distributed unequally.

Table 3.2 Hofstede's dimensions of culture[1]

	1. Power distance	2. Individualism	3. Masculinity	4. Uncertainty avoidance	5. Long-term orientation
1	Malaysia (104)[2]	USA (91)	Japan (95)	Greece (112)	China (118)
2	Guatemala (95)	Australia (90)	Austria (79)	Portugal (104)	Hong Kong (96)
3	Panama (95)	UK (89)	Venezuela (73)	Guatemala (101)	Taiwan (87)
4	Philippines (94)	Canada (80)	Italy (70)	Uruguay (100)	Japan (80)
5	Mexico (81)	Netherlands (80)	Switzerland (70)	Belgium (94)	South Korea (75)
6	Venezuela (81)	New Zealand (79)	Mexico (69)	El Salvador (94)	Brazil (65)
7	Arab countries (80)	Italy (76)	Ireland (68)	Japan (92)	India (61)
8	Ecuador (78)	Belgium (75)	Jamaica (68)	Yugoslavia (88)	Thailand (56)
9	Indonesia (78)	Denmark (74)	UK (66)	Peru (87)	Singapore (48)
10	India (77)	Sweden (71)	Germany (66)	France (86)	Netherlands (44)
11	West Africa (77)	France (71)	Philippines (64)	Chile (86)	Bangladesh (40)
12	Yugoslavia (76)	Ireland (70)	Colombia (64)	Spain (86)	Sweden (33)
13	Singapore (74)	Norway (69)	South Africa (63)	Costa Rica (86)	Poland (32)
14	Brazil (69)	Switzerland (68)	Ecuador (63)	Panama (86)	Germany (31)
15	France (68)	Germany (67)	USA (62)	Argentina (86)	Australia (31)
16	Hong Kong (68)	South Africa (65)	Australia (61)	Turkey (85)	New Zealand (30)
17	Colombia (67)	Finland (63)	New Zealand (58)	South Korea (85)	USA (29)
18	El Salvador (66)	Austria (55)	Greece (57)	Mexico (82)	UK (25)
19	Turkey (66)	Israel (54)	Hong Kong (57)	Israel (81)	Zimbabwe (25)
20	Belgium (65)	Spain (51)	Argentina (56)	Colombia (80)	Canada (23)
21	East Africa (64)	India (48)	India (56)	Venezuela (76)	Philippines (19)
22	Peru (64)	Japan (46)	Belgium (54)	Brazil (76)	Nigeria (16)
23	Thailand (64)	Argentina (46)	Arab countries (53)	Italy (75)	Pakistan (0)
24	Chile (63)	Iran (41)	Canada (52)	Pakistan (70)	
25	Portugal (63)	Jamaica (39)	Malaysia (50)	Austria (70)	
26	Uruguay (61)	Brazil (38)	Pakistan (50)	Taiwan (69)	
27	Greece (60)	Arab countries (38)	Brazil (49)	Arab countries (68)	
28	South Korea (60)	Turkey (37)	Singapore (48)	Ecuador (67)	
29	Iran (58)	Uruguay (36)	Israel (47)	Germany (65)	
30	Taiwan (58)	Greece (35)	Indonesia (46)	Thailand (64)	

	1. Power distance	2. Individualism	3. Masculinity	4. Uncertainty avoidance	5. Long-term orientation
31	Spain (57)	Philippines (32)	West Africa (46)	Iran (59)	
32	Pakistan (55)	Mexico (30)	Turkey (45)	Finland (59)	
33	Japan (54)	East Africa (27)	Taiwan (45)	Switzerland (58)	
34	Italy (50)	Yugoslavia (27)	Panama (44)	West Africa (54)	
35	Argentina (49)	Puerto Rico (27)	Iran (43)	Netherlands (53)	
36	South Africa (49)	Malaysia (26)	France (43)	East Africa (52)	
37	Jamaica (45)	Hong Kong (25)	Spain (42)	Australia (51)	
38	USA (40)	Chile (23)	Peru (42)	Norway (50)	
39	Canada (39)	West Africa (20)	East Africa (41)	South Africa (49)	
40	Netherlands (38)	Singapore (20)	El Salvador (40)	New Zealand (49)	
41	Australia (36)	Thailand (20)	South Korea (39)	Indonesia (48)	
42	Cost Rica (35)	El Salvador (19)	Uruguay (38)	Canada (48)	
43	Germany (35)	South Korea (18)	Guatemala (37)	USA (46)	
44	UK (35)	Taiwan (17)	Thailand (34)	Philippines (44)	
45	Switzerland (34)	Peru (16)	Portugal (31)	India (40)	
46	Finland (33)	Costa Rica (15)	Chile (28)	Malaysia (36)	
47	Norway (31)	Pakistan (14)	Finland (26)	UK (35)	
48	Sweden (31)	Indonesia (14)	Yugoslavia (21)	Ireland (35)	
49	Ireland (28)	Colombia (13)	Costa Rica (21)	Hong Kong (29)	
50	New Zealand (22)	Venezuela (12)	Denmark (16)	Sweden (29)	
51	Denmark (18)	Panama (11)	Netherlands (14)	Denmark (23)	
52	Israel (13)	Ecuador (8)	Norway (8)	Jamaica (13)	
53	Austria (11)	Guatemala (6)	Sweden (8)	Singapore (8)	

[1] When scores are the same, countries are tied according to their alphabetical order. Arab, East Africa, and West Africa are clusters of multiple countries. Germany and Yugoslavia refer to the former West Germany and the former Yugoslavia, respectively.
[2] Scores reflect relative standing among countries, not absolute positions. They are measures of differences only.

Sources: Adapted from G. Hofstede, 1997, *Cultures and Organizations: Software of the Mind* (pp. 25, 26, 53, 84, 113, 166), New York: McGraw-Hill.

power distance is the practice of addressing people with the formal pronoun '*Sie*' in German, '*Vous*' in French and '*Usted*' in Spanish, which do not have an exact equivalent in modern English.

These cultural differences are reflected in business practice. For instance, managers in high power distance countries such as France and Italy have a greater penchant for centralized authority.[15] Solicitation of subordinate feedback and participation, widely practiced in low power distance Anglo-American countries, is often regarded as a sign of weak leadership and low integrity in high power distance countries such as Egypt, Russia and Turkey.[16]

Second, individualism refers to the perspective that the identity of an individual is fundamentally his or her own, whereas collectivism refers to the idea that the identity of an individual is primarily based on the identity of his or her collective group (such as family, village or company). In individualist societies (led by the USA), ties between individuals are relatively loose, and individual achievement and freedom are highly valued. In contrast, in collectivist societies (such as many countries in Africa, Asia and Latin America), ties between individuals are relatively close, and collective accomplishments are often sought after. We will return to this important dimension later on in this chapter under the 'Debates and Extensions' section.

Third, the masculinity versus femininity dimension refers to the relative importance of values traditionally held by men and women. Masculine societies favour leaders that are assertive, decisive, and 'aggressive' (only in masculine societies does this word carry a positive connotation), along with focus on career progression and material rewards. Such values are commonly associated with traditionally male professions such as politicians, soldiers and investment bankers. Feminine values include compassion, relationships, care for others and job satisfaction – or more generally *quality of life*.[17] The stylized manager in feminine societies thus is 'less visible, intuitive rather than decisive, and accustomed to building consensus'.[18] These values are found in professions traditionally more associated with women such as teaching and nursing, and they also more likely to support social and environmental responsibility. Highly masculine societies (led by Japan) typically maintain a sharp role differentiation along gender lines with most leadership positions taken by men. In contrast, in highly feminine societies (led by Sweden), women increasingly become politicians and soldiers, and men are entitled to, and actually take, paternity leave.[19]

In some masculine societies, it is considered good manners to show appreciation to women in ways that may be misunderstood in more feminine societies: In an example, when a French manager was transferred to a US subsidiary met his American secretary (a woman) the first time, he greeted her with a kiss on the cheek – a practice appreciated as courteous in France. However, the secretary later filed a complaint for sexual harassment.[20] More seriously, Mitsubishi Motors, coming from Japan that leads the world in masculinity, encountered major problems when operating in the USA, where women not only account for a higher share of the labour force but expect to be promoted like their male colleagues. In 1998, its North American division paid $34 million to settle sexual harassment charges.

Fourth, uncertainty avoidance refers to the extent to which members in different cultures accept ambiguous situations and tolerate uncertainty. Members of high uncertainty avoidance cultures (led by Greece) place a premium on job security and retirement benefits. They also tend to resist change, which, by definition, is uncertain. Low uncertainty avoidance cultures (led by Singapore) are characterized by a greater willingness to take risks and less resistance to change. For example, when the swine-flu arrived in Europe, a Danish manufacturer of safety clothing and equipment quickly reported to be sold out because of surging demand from Germany, while sales in Denmark were slow. A customer, a German insurance

Individualism
The perspective that the identity of an individual is fundamentally his or her own.

Collectivism
The idea that the identity of an individual is primarily based on the identity of his or her collective group.

Masculinity
Values traditionally associated with male role, such as assertive, decisive and aggressive.

Femininity
Values traditionally associated with female role, such as compassion, care and quality of life.

Uncertainty avoidance
The extent to which members in different cultures accept ambiguous situations and tolerate uncertainty.

company, explained that Germans like to be prepared for all eventualities[21] – a symptom of high uncertainty avoidance.

Long-term orientation
A perspective that emphasizes perseverance and savings for future betterment.

Finally, long-term orientation emphasizes perseverance and savings for future betterment. China, which has the world's longest continuous written history of nearly 4000 years and the highest contemporary savings rate, leads the pack. On the other hand, members of short-term orientation societies (led by Pakistan) prefer quick results and instant gratification. Unsurprisingly, saving rates are higher in long-term oriented East Asian countries than in short-term oriented USA.

In cultures with a long-term orientation, firms are more likely to nurture long-term ambitions. For instance, Japan's Matsushita has a 250-year plan, which was put together in the 1930s. While this is certainly an extreme case, Japanese and Korean firms tend to focus more on the long term.[22] In comparison, Anglo-American firms often focus on relatively short-term profits (often on a *quarterly* basis).

Overall, there is strong evidence for the importance of culture for running a business.[23] Hofstede's dimensions provide an interesting and informative starting point for interpreting cultural differences.[24] They provide insights into how interactions between members within different groups or nations vary. However, they are not intended to guide the adoption of specific management practices as this requires a more fine grained understanding of the specific organization and its practices. Moreover, it is important to note that Hofstede's dimensions have attracted their share of criticisms (see In Focus 3.1). They are a greatly simplifying analytical tool for complex and evolving phenomena in the real world.[25] Variations of norms and values are prevalent and often hard to observe, and thus require great sensitivity when dealing with people from other countries. Indices such as Hofstede's provide a first indication, like a stereotype. Yet, successful business persons look beyond stereotypes to develop deeper understanding of cultures.[26]

IN FOCUS 3.1

Limitations of Hofstede's framework

Despite the influence of Hofstede's framework, it has attracted a number of criticisms.

- Cultural boundaries are not the same as national boundaries.

- Although Hofstede was careful to remove some of his own cultural biases, 'the Dutch software' of his mind, as he acknowledged, 'will remain evident to the careful reader'. Being more familiar with European cultures, Hofstede might inevitably be more familiar with dimensions relevant to distinguishing European cultures. Thus, crucial dimensions relevant to Asian or African cultures could be missed.

- Hofstede's research was based on surveys of more than 116 000 IBM employees working at 72 national subsidiaries during 1967–1973. This had both pros and cons. On the positive side, it not only took place in the same industry but also in

the same company. Otherwise, it would have been difficult to attribute whether findings were due to differences in national cultures or industrial/organizational cultures. However, because of such a single firm/single industry design, it was possible that Hofstede's findings captured what was unique to that industry or to IBM. In other words, Hofstede's empirical data would reflect the interaction of the IBM organizational culture with local culture, rather than local culture as such. Thus, it was difficult to ascertain whether employees working for IBM were true representatives of their respective national cultures.

- Because the original data are now 40 years old, critics contend that Hofstede's framework would simply fail to capture aspects of cultural change, which have been quite substantive in some countries experiences major social or political upheaval, like transition economies. Moreover, the data for some countries are based on small samples or subsequent studies in other organizations, which makes them imprecise estimates at best.

Hofstede has responded to all four criticisms. First, he acknowledged that his focus on national culture was a matter of expediency with all its trappings. Second, since the 1980s, Hofstede and colleagues relied on a questionnaire derived from cultural dimensions most relevant to the Chinese and then translated it from Chinese to multiple languages. That was how he uncovered the fifth dimension, long-term orientation (originally labelled 'Confucian dynamism'). In response to the third and fourth criticisms, Hofstede pointed out a large number of studies conducted by other scholars using a variety of countries, industries, and firms. Many results were supportive of his original

findings, while others suggest that cultures did indeed change over time. Overall, Hofstede's work is imperfect, but on balance, its values seem to outweigh its drawbacks.

Sources: We thank Professor Tony Fang (Stockholm University) for his assistance. Based on (1) B. McSweeney, 2002, Hofstede's model of national cultural differences and their consequences, *HR*, 55: 89–118; (2) T. Fang, 2003, A critique of Hofstede's fifth national culture dimension, *IJCCR*, 3: 347–368; (3) M. Javidan, R. House, P. Dorfman, P. Hanges & M. Luque, 2006, Conceptualizing and measuring cultures and their consequences, *JIBS*, 37: 897–914; (4) P. Smith, 2006, When elephants fight, the grass gets trampled, *JIBS*, 37: 915–921; (5) G. Hofstede, 2007, Asian management in the 21st century, *APJM*, 24: 411–420; (6) L. Tang & P. Keveos, 2008, A framework to update Hofstede's cultural value indices, *JIBS*, 39: 1045–1063; (7) R. Maseland & A. van Hoorn, 2009, Explaining the negative correlation between values and practices: A note on the Hofstede-GLOBE debate, *JIBS*, 40: 527–532; T. Fang, 2010, Asian management research needs more self-confidence: Reflection on Hofstede 2007 and beyond, *APJM*, 27: 155–170.

LANGUAGES

Among approximately 6000 languages in the world, Chinese is the world's largest in terms of the number of native speakers.[27] English is a distant second, followed closely by Hindi and Spanish (Figure 3.2). How do people across so many languages communicate with each other when negotiating a business deal, or when working together in the same MNE?

LEARNING OBJECTIVE

3 Explain how language competences shape intercultural interactions

Figure 3.2 World population by language

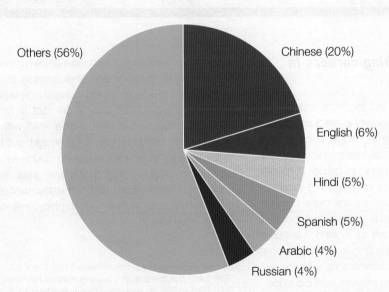

Others (56%)
Chinese (20%)
English (6%)
Hindi (5%)
Spanish (5%)
Arabic (4%)
Russian (4%)

Sources: Authors' estimates based on data in (1) *The Economist Atlas*, 2005, London: The Economist Books; (2) D. Graddol, 2004, The future of language, *Science*, 303: 1329–1331; (3) S. Huntington, 1996, *The Clash of Civilizations and the Remaking of World Order*, New York: Simon & Schuster.

An MNE committed to equal opportunities might consider translating all relevant documents. Yet, this quickly proves highly impractical as demonstrated by the experience of the European Union (EU, see Chapter 8). It has all major documents translated into 23 official languages for 27 member countries, an exercise costing the EU €1.1 billion a year.[28] International managers often have to deal with two, or even three, languages on a daily basis. Knowledge sharing is essential for modern MNEs (see Chapter 15), creating needs for extensive communication across units. To facilitate such communication, many MNE have adopted an (official or unofficial) corporate language (see In Focus 3.2).[29]

Corporate language
The language used for communications between entities of the same MNE in different countries.

Lingua franca
The dominance of one language as a global business language.

English often emerges as the default language of international communication, thus becoming a global business language, known as the lingua franca as many people speak it as a second language (see In Focus 3.2). Hence, non-native speakers of English who can master English, such as the Taiwanese-born Hollywood director Ang Lee, Icelandic-born singer Björk and Colombian-born pop star Shakira (or in fact both authors of this book) have better job and careers prospects. Some foreign investors in places such as China like to hire graduates from language programmes as they consider good communication more important than subject-specific skills to start a career with them. Others invest in training their staff in English.

The dominance of English may give native speakers of English an initial advantage in global business. However, over-reliance on English has also disadvantages. Learning a language helps to develop sensitivity for subtleties of the culture – and for the mistakes non-natives make when speaking English, such as Chinese confusing 'he' and 'she', Russians dropping articles and Germans and Japanese moving verbs to the end of complex sentences. Even basic skills in a foreign language can help to show respect to your host and to build trust. Moreover, they help detecting embarrassing translation errors. For example, Coors Beer translated its slogan 'Turn it loose!' into Spanish as 'Drink Coors and get diarrhoea!' General Motors earned

IN FOCUS 3.2

Languages skills lifting careers in Kone Elevators

Not only top management but technical experts and middle managers have to regularly interact across language barriers when talking to people in other units abroad, or with foreign customers and suppliers. Although companies may have an official corporate language, staff in subsidiaries may speak a local language, and staff in headquarters are more comfortable with yet another language, especially if the MNE is from a small country, such as Finland. Language competences in the corporate language thus are often a precondition for career advancement, while knowledge of other languages can provide a critical edge.

A study of Finish MNE Kone Elevators illustrates these language dynamics: Multi-linguists often become

critical communication intermediaries, which enhance their personal network and their access to knowledge. For example, fluent English speakers in subsidiaries were more likely to be sent to corporate training courses, while headquarter staff with Spanish language competences were sought out by staff in subsidiaries in Spanish-speaking countries as their primary contact. These individuals thus acquired knowledge, reputation and influence well beyond their formal role, which substantially helped their career progression.

Sources: Based on R. Marschan-Piekkari, D.E. Welch & L.S. Welch, 1997, Language: the forgotten factor in multinational management, *EMJ*, 15: 591–598; R. Marschan-Piekkari, D. Welch & L.S. Welch, 1999, In the shadow: the impact of language on structure, power and communication in the multinational, *IBR* 8: 421–440.

IN FOCUS 3.3

Linguistic Skills in the boardroom

English may increasingly be the lingua franca of international business, but some of its vagaries can cause confusion, as Mandarin speaker Zhan Chunxin and Italian speaker Maurizio Ferrari have discovered. Mr. Zhan is chairman and chief executive of Zoomlion, a construction equipment maker that led a € 271m deal for Italian machinery maker Compagnia Italiana Forme Acciaio (CIFA) along with consortium partners Goldman Sachs, Sino-Italian fund Mandarin Capital Partners and Hony Capital, a Chinese private equity firm. Completed in September, the transaction ranks as China Inc's second largest European buy-out and made Zoomlion the world's biggest manufacturer of concrete machinery. Mr. Zhan now works closely with Mr. Ferrari, his counterpart at Cifa. That is no easy task when the two men do not share a common language.

However, Zoomlion and Cifa have taken a more unusual path. Rather than translating between Chinese and Italian, they bridge their linguistic divide using English, which Mr. Ferrari speaks with some difficulty and Mr. Zhan not at all. With Mr. Zhan based at Zoomlion's corporate headquarters in Changsha, capital of central Hunan province, and Mr. Ferrari in Senago, near Milan, much of their interaction is through e-mail. This gives Mr. Zhan's translators and Mr. Ferrari, who taps out his own English-language e-mails, a bit of extra time to craft their messages.

Face-to-face meetings are less forgiving, such as one last September when the issue of 'delocalization' was raised. At issue was whether Cifa might move some functions to Russia. From his Italian vantage point, Mr. Ferrari conceived of this as moving work away from Milan and therefore described the process as 'delocalization'. In China, foreign investors describe a similar process – replacing expensive expatriate staff with Chinese employees in order to save costs – as 'localization'. What, Zoomlion executives wondered, was this 'delocalization'? The prefix 'de' seemed to imply it was the opposite of localization, and it took the two parties some time to figure out that they were talking about the same thing. 'We have lost 30 minutes regarding one word', says Mr. Ferrari.

More than language separates the two companies. State-owned Zoomlion, which is listed on the Shenzhen Stock Exchange, began life in 1992 as the Changsha Hi-Tech Development Area Zoomlion Construction Mechanical Industry Company. Its English moniker was a linguistic accident. 'A colleague who is good at English picked the name [Zoomlion]', Mr. Zhan says. 'It sounded similar to our Chinese name [Zhonglian]. He also said it means 'a roaring lion', although apparently that's not exactly true'.

For now the two companies will continue to use English as their common language but Mr. Ferrari acknowledges that this cannot continue forever. Cifa, he says, is scouring Italian universities for Chinese-language students: 'We must integrate in China – and we must integrate in Italy – [with] people who have the same language'.

Source: 'Linguistic test for a fluent act in the boardroom' by T. Mitchell, *Financial Times*, January 14 2009, copyright © *Financial Times* 2009. Reproduced with permission.

---

ridicule for selling its Nova car in Latin America under that nameplate ('*no va*' means 'no go' in Spanish), as did Rolls-Royce's Silver Mist in Germany ('*mist*' means 'rubbish' in German).[30] More importantly, an expatriate manager not knowing the local language misses a lot of cultural subtleties and can only interact with locals who speak English. Translators can be very helpful, but communicating through a translator can lead to many misunderstandings. For example, many terms do not have an exact expression in other languages: You may find 'noodle soup' and 'dumplings' on restaurant menus in both Vienna, Austria and Hong Kong, China. Yet, the dishes have next to nothing in common. This lack of direct translation is even more challenging for abstract terms such as 'fair' or 'considerate'.[31] For example, what does it mean if you boss describes your work as 'not bad'? In America, it probably means you just survived and better improve next time round. However if your boss is a traditional Chinese, an English gentlemen or a Dane from the rural area of Jutland, this is probably the highest praise you are ever going to get. Last but not least, knowing the local language will make your social life much more fun, as you can participate in more local events (see Closing Case).

In international meetings, people tend to use the language they expect most members of the group to understand at least minimally, which in many contexts is English. Even so, non-native speakers of English often find it easier to understand and relate to other non-native speakers. Some may even resent Britons or US Americans for speaking too fast and for using obscure idioms and slang.[32] Linguistic fluency can be a competitive advantage, but it needs to be handled carefully.

In conclusion, try not to remain monolingual if you have international ambitions. English is the norm in many places, and an additional language (in addition to your native tongue) can give you a critical edge. Hence, you will be better off if you can pick up at least one language – in addition to English – during your university studies.

RELIGIONS

LEARNING OBJECTIVE

4 Explain how religions shape cultures

Religion is a major manifestation of culture, and it is the source of some of the differences in norms and values that we discussed before. The leading religions are (1) Christianity (approximately 1.7 billion adherents), (2) Islam (1 billion), (3) Hinduism (750 million) and (4) Buddhism (350 million), see Figure 3.3. Of course, not everybody claiming to be an adherent actively practices a religion. For instance, some Christians may go to church only once a year – at Christmas. Because religious differences have led to numerous challenges, knowledge about religions is crucial even for non-religious managers. Religious beliefs and activities affect business through (1) religious festivals, (2) daily and weekly routines and (3) activities and objects with symbolic values – positive or negative.

First, religious festivals are focal events of social life, and thus create direct and indirect opportunities for business – as well as periods when businesses and government offices are shut down. For example, in Christian countries, Christmas represents the peak season in shopping and consumption. In the USA, half of the toys are sold in the month before Christmas. Since kids in the USA consume half of the world's toys and virtually all toys are made in Asia, this means 25 per cent of world toy output is sold in one country in one month, thus creating severe production, distribution and coordination challenges. For toy makers and stores, 'missing the boat' from Asia, whose transit time is at least two weeks, can literally devastate an entire season (and probably the entire year). Yet, on December 25 and 26, shops are closed in many European countries. Similar seasonal patterns of demand exist in conjunction with, for example, Diwali in India, Chinese New Year in East Asia and Ramadan in Muslim countries.

Second, daily and weekly routines vary. The monotheistic religions (Christianity, Islam and Judaism) have a lot in common, yet they differ on which day of the week the faithful worship: Christians go to church on Sundays, while Muslims and Jews worship respectively on Fridays and Saturdays. Also daily routines vary. For instance, faithful Muslims interrupt their activities five times a day at specific times for prayer. If you are an expatriate in Indonesia you may experience a driver that stops the car in the middle of the traffic, takes out his prayer carpet and performs his routine. Knowing this practice, a small adjustment of daily work schedules can minimize such disruptions.[33]

Third, religions attach symbolic value to certain objects or activities, which leads to rules on what the faithful are allowed to do, or not to do. Objects or activities

Figure 3.3 Religious heritages of the world

Religions of the World: A Part of Culture

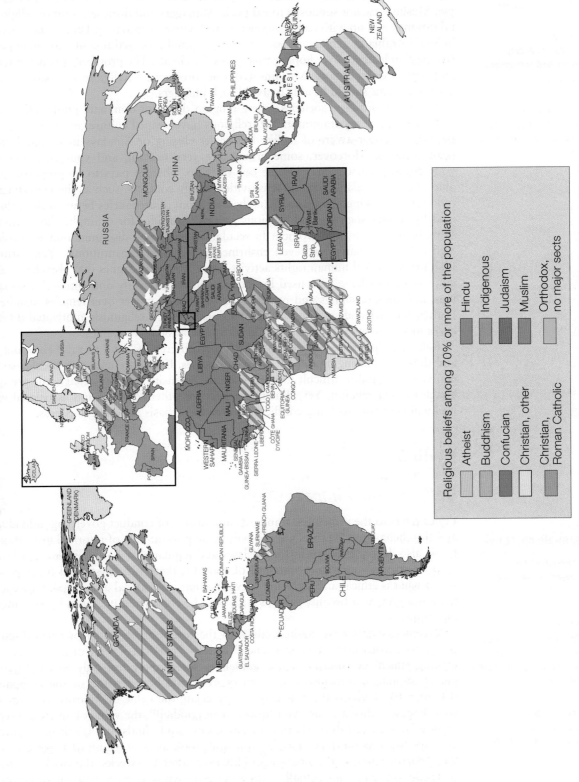

Religious beliefs among 70% or more of the population

- Atheist
- Buddhism
- Confucian
- Christian, other
- Christian, Roman Catholic
- Hindu
- Indigenous
- Judaism
- Muslim
- Orthodox, no major sects

Source: CIA – *The World Factbook 2000*. Note that Confucianism, strictly speaking, is not a religion but a set of moral codes guiding interpersonal relationships.

Holy
An item or activity that is treated with particular respect by a religion.

Taboo
An item or activity considered unclean by a religion.

Secular society
A society where religion does not dominate public life.

considered holy deserve particular respect. For example, cows are holy in Hindu religion, and thus may not be disturbed (let alone be eaten). Other objects are considered taboo or dirty, and thus may not be touched or eaten by the faithful. For example, Muslims are not supposed to eat pork. Managers and firms ignorant of religious taboos may end up with embarrassments, and worse, disasters. A US firm blundered in Saudi Arabia by sending a meticulously prepared proposal bound with an expensive pigskin leather cover hoping to impress the clients. The proposal was never read and soon rejected because Muslims avoid pig products.[34] Religiously sensitive managers and firms should be able to avoid such blunders.

In secular societies, societies where religion does not dominate public life, such concerns are not a paramount. Yet, religions have shaped cultures even where people are no longer aware of it, like businesses closing on Sundays in secular European societies. Moreover, some groups are very faithful, and your customer or your business partner may just be one of them. Thus, it pays to be prepared and able to accommodate religious sensitivities. Many conflicts, such as the Danish cartoon crisis (see Opening Case), actually arise from discrepancies between the values held by secular societies and religious groups. Consider for example, the relationships between man and women: In secular societies non-discrimination is considered a basic human right (even enshrined in national constitutions). Yet, former Irish president and human rights activist Mary Robinson argues that elsewhere religious traditions have been used by those in power to justify and entrench inequalities, including teachings and practices that give men power over females members of their families and societies.[35] Such tensions between religiously motivated differences in values can create a minefield for multinational companies.

Religious differences, more than any other differences, tend to raise emotions – and thus are challenging to handle for businesses. If you are used to a secular society, you may find it difficult to appreciate the intensity of feeling that some groups attach to their religion. Yet, showing respect for other religions and associated values will help you avoiding conflict and creating a basis for doing business.

ETHICS

Definition and impact of ethics

Ethics
The principles, standards and norms of conduct governing individual and firm behaviour.

Code of conduct
A set of guidelines for making ethical decisions.

Ethics refers to the principles, standards and norms of conduct governing individual and firm behaviour.[36] Ethics are not only an important part of informal institutions but is also deeply reflected in formal laws and regulations. To the extent that laws reflect a society's minimum standard of conduct, there is a substantial overlap between what is ethical and legal and between what is unethical and illegal. However, there is a grey area because what is legal may be considered unethical by key interest groups.

Recent scandals have pushed ethics to the forefront of global business discussions. Numerous firms have introduced codes of conduct – a set of guidelines for making ethical decisions.[37] These guidelines often apply not only to employees, but to suppliers, franchisees and others using the brand name of the company (Chapter 10). Perhaps the best way to appreciate the value of ethics is to examine what happens after a crisis. As a 'reservoir of goodwill', the value of an ethical reputation is *magnified* during a time of crisis. One study finds that US firms engulfed in crises (such as the *Exxon Valdez* oil spill) took an average hit of 8 per cent of their market value in the first week. However, after ten weeks, the stock of firms with ethical reputations actually *rose* 5 per cent, whereas those without such reputations dropped 15 per cent.[38] Paradoxically, catastrophes may allow more ethical firms to shine. The upshot seems to be that ethics pays.

Managing ethics overseas

Managing ethics overseas is challenging because what is ethical in one country may be unethical elsewhere.[39] For example, firing staff on short notice to secure profitability is a normal practice in countries such as the USA, yet it is unethical or even illegal in for example France and Germany. It some cases, firms face clear guidelines, or even regulatory restrictions, established in their home countries. On other issues, they have to make decisions 'on the ground' and communicate them to the relevant parties.

How should companies navigate this minefield? There are two schools of thought.[40] First, ethical relativism follows the cliché, 'When in Rome, do as the Romans do'. If women in Muslim countries are discriminated against, so what? Likewise, if industry rivals in China can fix prices, who cares? Is that what the 'Romans' do in 'Rome'? Second, ethical imperialism refers to the absolute belief that 'There is only one set of Ethics (with the capital E), and we have it'. Europeans and US Americans have a reputation for expecting that their ethical values should be applied universally.[41] For example, since sexual discrimination and price fixing are wrong in Europe, they must be wrong everywhere else. In practice, however, neither of these schools of thought is realistic. At the extreme, ethical relativism would have to accept any local practice, whereas ethical imperialism may cause resentment and backlash among locals.

Three 'middle-of-the-road' guiding principles have been proposed by Thomas Donaldson, a business ethicist (Table 3.3). First, respect for human dignity and basic rights (such as those concerning health, safety and the need for education instead of working at a young age) should determine the absolute minimal ethical thresholds for *all* operations around the world.

Second, respect for local traditions suggests cultural sensitivity. If gifts are banned, foreign firms can forget about doing business in China and Japan, where gift giving is part of the business norm. Although hiring employees' children and relatives instead of more qualified applicants is illegal according to European equal opportunity laws, Indian companies routinely practice such nepotism, which would strengthen employee loyalty. What should European companies setting up subsidiaries in India do? Donaldson advises that hiring family members is not necessarily wrong, at least in India.

Let us consider corruption, defined as the abuse of public power for private benefits, usually in the form of bribery (in cash or in kind).[42] It varies greatly across countries (see Table 3.4). In some places, it appears deeply embedded in the culture, while elsewhere it is considered the worst sin a business person might commit. Corruption distorts the basis for competition, thus causing misallocation of resources, slowing economic development and deterring foreign investors.[43] According to Berlin-based Transparency International, an anti-corruption non-governmental

Ethical relativism
A perspective that suggests that all ethical standards are relative.

Ethical imperialism
The absolute belief that 'there is only one set of Ethics (with the capital E), and we have it'.

Corruption
The abuse of public power for private benefits, usually in the form of bribery.

Table 3.3 Managing ethics overseas: three 'middle-of-the-road' approaches

- Respect for human dignity and basic rights
- Respect for local traditions
- Respect for institutional context

Sources: Based on text in (1) T. Donaldson, 1996, *Values in tension: Ethics away from home*, Harvard Business Review, September–October: 4–11; (2) J. Weiss, 2009, 5th *Business Ethics* ed., Cincinnati, OH: Cengage Learning.

Table 3.4 Transparency international rankings of corruption perceptions

Rank	Least corrupt countries of 180	Index: 10 (highly clean) – 0 (highly corrupt)	Rank	Most corrupt countries of 180	Index: 10 (highly clean) – 0 (highly corrupt)
1	New Zealand	9.3	166	Cambodia	1.8
	Denmark	9.3		Kyrgystan	1.8
	Sweden	9.3		Turkmenistan	1.8
4	Singapore	9.2		Uzbekistan	1.8
5	Finland	9.6		Zimbabwe	1.8
	Switzerland	9.1	171	Congo, D.R.	1.7
7	Iceland	8.9		Equatorial Guinea	1.7
	Netherlands	8.9	173	Chad	1.6
9	Australia	8.7		Guinea	1.6
	Canada	8.5		Sudan	1.6
11	Luxembourg	8.3	176	Afghanistan	1.5
12	Austria	8.1	177	Haiti	1.4
	Hong Kong	8.1	178	Iraq	1.3
14	Germany	7.9		Myanmar	1.3
	Norway	7.9	180	Somalia	1.0

Source: Adapted from 'Transparency International', Global Corruption Report 2009, copyright © 2009 Transparency International the global coalition against corruption, published by Cambridge University Press. Reproduced with permission from Cambridge University Press and Transparency International. For more information visit http://www.transparency.org.

organization (NGO), the correlation between a high level of corruption and a low level of economic development is strong. In other words, corruption and poverty go together. On this issue, a broad consensus thus has evolved that MNEs should *not* 'when in Rome do as the Romans do'. Home countries thus try to prevent MNEs from being drawn into corrupt practices (see In Focus 3.4), yet not always do business persons face clear guidelines.

Finally, respect for institutional context calls for a careful understanding of local institutions. Codes of conduct banning bribery are not very useful unless accompanied by guidelines for the scale and scope of appropriate gift giving and receiving. Citigroup allows employees to accept non-cash gifts valued at less than $100. *The Economist* allows its journalists to accept any gift that can be consumed in a single day – a bottle of wine is acceptable, but a case of wine is not.[44] Rhone-Poulenc Rorer, a French pharmaceutical firm, has invited foreign subsidiaries to add locally appropriate supplements to its corporate-wide code of conduct. Overall, these three principles, although far from perfect, can help managers make decisions about which they may feel relatively comfortable.

IN FOCUS 3.4

The OECD Anti-Corruption Convention

How does corruption affect foreign investors? China is an obvious case, where corruption is often reported. Another is Indonesia, where former President Suharto was known as 'Mr. Ten Percent', which refers to the well-known (and transparent!) amount of bribe money foreign firms were expected to pay him or members of his family. Why are these two countries popular FDI destinations? There are two explanations. First, the vast potential of these two economies may outweigh the drawbacks of corruption. Second, overseas Chinese (mainly from Hong Kong and Taiwan) and Japanese firms are leading investors in mainland China and Indonesia, respectively. Hong Kong, Taiwan and Japan may be relatively 'cleaner', in terms of corruption but they are not among the 'cleanest' countries (Table 3.4). It is possible that skills in managing corruption acquired at home helps develop a certain advantages in managing corruption overseas.

Bribery is a criminal offence in most countries, yet prosecution is inconsistent as it is often difficult to prove, or the relevant authorities do not really care. Foreign investors need to be particularly vigilant because catching a foreign briber can be a particularly big scoop for an ambitious local police commissioner – be careful, your conversations may be taped. On the other hand, experienced foreign investors may find ways around this risk by letting local partners do the 'dirty work', and by moving staff out of the country quickly when it gets too hot. The latter approach, however, no longer works.

In 1997, OECD agreed a Convention on Combating Bribery of Foreign Public Officials, which subsequently has been implemented into law in all 30 member countries (essentially all developed econo-

mies). Under this convention, states not only criminalize bribery, but prosecute MNEs and their employees at home for bribery committed *abroad*. The convention departs from the basic principle of international law that prosecution is the responsibility of the country where the crime has been committed. It supports a fairly new precept in international law known as the nationality principle, which states that countries have some jurisdiction (but not unconditional) over their own citizens wherever they may be. In practice, this can be difficult because few countries are willing to extradite their own nationals to other countries (especially those perceived to be corrupt). OECD countries thus established laws with extra-territorial effect that should prevent their firms using corrupt methods abroad. And, the convention is biting: In September 2009, British construction firm Mabey & Johnson was fined £6.6 million for paying bribes in Jamaica and Ghana, and for having broken the UN sanctions of Iraq. At the same time, Britain's (and Europe's) largest defence contractor BAE Systems was investigated for alleged bribes, facing possible fines of over £500 million.

A broader campaign is the UN Convention against Corruption, signed by 106 countries in 2003 and activated in 2005. If every country criminalizes bribery and every investor resists corruption, their combined power will eradicate it. However, this will not happen unless such legislation is institutionalized *and* enforced in every country.

Sources: Based on (1) S. Wei, 2000, How taxing is corruption on international investors? *RES*, 82: 1–11. (2) M. Habib & L. Zurawicki, 2002, Corruption and foreign direct investment (p. 295), *JIBS*, 33: 291–307; (3) *The Economist*, 2009, BAE Systems: see you in court, October 3.

DEBATES AND EXTENSIONS

Informal institutions such as culture, ethics and norms provoke a series of significant debates. In this section, we focus onthree: (1) social groups that share a culture, (2) cultural convergence versus divergence and (3) in-groups versus out-groups in collectivist societies.

LEARNING OBJECTIVE

6 Participate in two leading debates on cultures

Units of culture: social groups

In this chapter, we have focused on national culture, which is the most apparent variation that businesses experience in the global economy. As indicated earlier, this is a simplification, for two reasons. First, although it is customary to talk about French culture or Brazilian culture, there is no strict one-to-one correspondence between cultures and nation states. In most countries, many subcultures co-exist.[45] For example, many Scots, Catalans and Bavarians identify themselves with their regional culture rather than with British, Spanish or German culture. In reverse, non-Bavarian Germans can get quite annoyed when 'German festivals' abroad portray Germany with Bavarian stereotypes such as people wearing lederhosen and eating pork knuckle and sauerkraut. Moreover, groups such as ethnic minorities, religious groups or social strata may develop their own cultures. Likewise, culture in urban centres often varies from rural areas, and young people have different culture than their elders (at least when they are among themselves). Thus, when we talk about national cultures, we are really talking about averages and about informal rules that apply when members of different subgroups interact with each other.

Second, within a firm, one may find a specific organizational culture (such as the 'IKEA culture') that is shared by people working in the organization, and perhaps by customers and suppliers as well.[46] Such shared values and beliefs are often inspired by the founders of a firm, and they help creating a common sense of purpose as well as rules for interacting within the firm. An organizational culture can be shared across a company that transcends national boundaries, and facilitates interaction of individuals originating from different national cultures.

Cultural change: convergence versus divergence

Every culture evolves and changes. A great debate has erupted on the *direction and speed* of cultural change. In this age of globalization, one side of the debate argues that there is a great deal of convergence, especially toward more 'modern' Western values such as individualism and consumerism.[47] As evidence, convergence gurus point out the worldwide interest in Western products and brands such as Levi jeans, Coca-Cola and MTV, especially among the youth. Such an adoption of new, important norms has been particular strong at early stages of economic transition in Eastern Europe. Some commentators described this change as a 'collective culture shock' with Western values replacing socialist values.[48]

However, another side suggests that 'Westernization in consumption' does not necessarily mean 'Westernization in values'. Even if some European brands, such as Arla, are popular in the Middle East, this does not change Muslim values (see Opening Case).[49] Similarly, the increasing popularity of Asian foods and games in Europe does not necessarily mean that Europeans are converging towards 'Asian values'.

The end of the Cold War, the rise of the internet, and the ascendance of English as a common second (and commercial) language all offer evidence of some cultural convergence – at least on the surface and among the urban youth. For example, relative to the average citizens, younger Chinese, Georgian, Japanese and Russian managers are becoming more individualist and less collectivist than the older generation.[50] However, deep down, cultural divergence may continue to be the norm.

Limits of collectivism[51]

A common stereotype is that players from collectivist societies (such as China) are more collaborative and trustworthy, and those from individualist societies (such as

Does the popularity of Chinese food in Europe signal a convergence of culture?

the USA) are more competitive and opportunistic.[52] However, this is not necessarily the case. Collectivists are more collaborative *only* when dealing with their own in-group members – individuals and firms regarded as part of their own collective. The flip side is that collectivists discriminate more harshly against out-group members – individuals and firms not regarded as part of 'us'. It is quite easy, for those not part of an in-group, to wonder what happened to the collective nature of the so-called collective society. On the other hand, individualists, who believe that every person (firm) is on his or her (its) own, make less distinction between in-group and out-group. Therefore, while individualists may indeed act more opportunistic than collectivists when dealing with in-group members (this fits the stereotype), collectivists may be *more* opportunistic when dealing with out-group members. Thus, on balance, the average Chinese is not inherently more trustworthy than the average US American. The Chinese motto regarding out-group members (including other Chinese) is: 'Watch out for strangers. They will screw you!'[53]

This helps explain why the USA, the leading individualist country, is among societies with a higher level of spontaneous trust, whereas there is greater interpersonal and interfirm *distrust* in the large society in China.[54] This also explains why it is so important to establish *guanxi* (relationship) for individuals and firms in China; otherwise, life can be very challenging in a sea of strangers. In another example, one study reported that although Britain and Hong Kong have comparable levels of per capita income, 24 per cent of the internet users shopped online in Britain, whereas only 7 per cent did so in Hong Kong.[55] Of course, numerous factors may be at play (such as the proximity of the next shopping mall), but one crucial point is that shopping online means having some trust in the out-group – the anonymous 'system' that processes payment. Internet users in Hong Kong (most of whom originate from the collectivist Chinese culture) are reluctant to do so.

For example, a professor in Hong Kong asked his MBA students about their use if the internet.[56] Only a couple of students in a class of about 50 had ever purchased anything online, though many had made travel reservations. They simply would not pre-pay, even when told about the online guarantee of the travel website,

In-group
Individuals and firms regarded as part of 'us'.

Out-group
Individuals and firms not regarded as part of 'us'.

© P Narayan/Photolibrary

the travel providers (e.g. hotel) and even their credit card company. Even triple protection was not enough – and this was with well-educated (and well-paid) Hong Kong MBA students. Such is the power of culture. This reluctance to shop online has proven to be an opportunity for the local cable TV company, as Hong Kong and Taiwan consumers have proven very willing to shop and bank through the more secure link of their cable provider – and to be billed for purchases by the cable company.

This insight can help managers and firms deal with one another. Only through repeated social interactions can collectivists assess whether to accept newcomers as in-group members.[57] For example, Russians are said to do business only with people with whom they have become drunk together at least once.[58] If foreigners who, by definition, are from an out-group refuse to show any interest in joining the in-group, then it is fair to take advantage of them. For example, don't refuse a friendly cup of coffee from a Saudi businessman, it might be considered an affront. Most of us do not realize that 'Feel free to say no when offered food or drink' reflects the cultural underpinning of individualism, and folks in collectivist societies do not necessarily view this as an option (also see Closing Case). Watch out for statements like 'it isn't really necessary' or 'do not be influenced by what our company did before'. These are often signals 'it is necessary' or 'you should recall what we did before, and reciprocate accordingly'. Such misunderstanding, in part, explains why many cross-culturally naïve Western managers and firms complain that they have been taken advantage of in collectivist societies. In reality, they are simply being treated as 'deserving' out-group members.

IMPLICATIONS FOR PRACTICE

LEARNING OBJECTIVE

7 Draw implications for action

Cultural intelligence
An individual's ability to understand and adjust to new cultures.

A contribution of the institution-based view is to emphasize the importance of informal institutions as the bedrock propelling or constraining business around the world. How does this perspective answer our fundamental question: What determines the success and failure of firms around the globe? The institution-based view argues that firm performance is, at least in part, determined by the informal cultures, ethics and norms governing firm behaviour.

For managers around the globe, this emphasis on informal institutions suggests two broad implications. First, enhancing cultural intelligence, defined as an individual's ability to understand and adjust to new cultures, is necessary.[59] Nobody can become an expert, the chameleon in Table 3.5 in all cultures. However, a genuine interest in foreign cultures will open your eyes. Acquisition of cultural intelligence passes through three phases: (1) awareness, (2) knowledge and (3) skills.[60] *Awareness* refers to the recognition of both the pros and cons of your 'mental software' and the appreciation of people from other cultures. *Knowledge* refers to ability to identify the symbols, rituals and taboos in other cultures – also known as cross-cultural literacy. Although you may not share (or even may disagree with) their values, you will at least obtain a road map of the informal institutions governing their behaviour. Finally, *skills* are based on awareness and knowledge, plus good practice (Table 3.6). Of course, culture is not everything. It is advisable not to read too much into culture, which is one of many variables affecting global business.[61] However, it is imprudent to ignore culture.

While skills can be taught, the most effective way is total immersion within a foreign culture. Even for gifted individuals, learning a new language and culture to function well at a managerial level will take at least several months of regular study. Many employers do not give their managers that much time to learn before sending them abroad. Thus, many expat managers are inadequately prepared, and the costs

Table 3.5 Five Profiles of cultural intelligence

Profiles	Characteristics
The Local	A person who works well with people from similar backgrounds but does not work effectively with people from different cultural backgrounds.
The Analyst	A person who observes and learns from others and plans a strategy for interacting with people from different cultural backgrounds.
The Natural	A person who relies on intuition rather than on a systematic learning style when interacting with people from different cultural backgrounds.
The Mimic	A person who creates a comfort zone for people from different cultural backgrounds by adopting their general posture and communication style. This is not pure imitation, which may be regarded as mocking.
The Chameleon	A person who may be mistaken for a native of the foreign country. He/she may achieve results that natives cannot, due to his/her insider's skills and outsider's perspective. This is very rare.

Sources: Based on (1) P.C. Earley & S. Ang, 2003, *Cultural Intelligence: Individual Interactions across Cultures*, Palo Alto, CA: Stanford University Press; (2) P.C. Earley & E. Mosakowski, 2004, Cultural intelligence, *HBR*, October: 139–146; (3) P.C. Earley & E. Mosakowski, 2004, Toward culture intelligence: Turning cultural differences into a workplace advantage, *AME*, 18(3): 151–157.

Table 3.6 Implications for action: six rules of thumb when venturing overseas

- Be prepared
- Slow down
- Establish trust
- Understand the importance of language
- Respect cultural differences
- Understand that no culture is inherently superior in all aspects

for firms, individuals and families can be very high (see Chapter 16). This means that you, a student studying this book, are advised to further invest in your own career by picking up at least one foreign language (beyond English), spending a semester (or year) abroad, and reaching out to make some international friends who are taking classes with you (and perhaps sitting next to you). Such an investment during university studies will make you stand out among the crowd and propel your future career to new heights.

Second, managers need to be aware of the prevailing norms and their changes globally. The norms around the globe in the 2010s are more culturally sensitive and ethically demanding than, say, in the 1970s. This is not to suggest that every local norm needs to be followed. However, failing to understand and adapt to the changing norms by 'sticking one's neck out' in an insensitive way may lead to unsatisfactory or disastrous results (see Opening and Closing Cases). The best managers expect norms to shift over time by constantly deciphering the changes in the informal rules of the game and by taking advantage of new opportunities.

In dealing with unfamiliar values, norms and practices, the single most important advice is the need to show respect. Most people are attached to the culture within which they grew up, and they do not take kindly to being told, implicitly or explicitly, that they are wrong. Showing respect for your host's culture, particularly the local cuisine (which locals tend to be very proud of) and an openness to learn, will often go a long way towards establishing trust with those from other cultures and countries.

CHAPTER SUMMARY

1 Define what culture is and articulate two of its manifestations: language and religion:

- Culture is the collective programming of the mind that distinguishes one group from another.
- Managers and firms ignorant of foreign languages and religious traditions may end up making cultural gaffes that harm their business.

2 Discuss how cultures systematically differ from each other:

- The context approach differentiates cultures based on the high- versus low-context dimension.
- The cluster approach groups similar cultures together as clusters and civilizations.
- Hofstede and colleagues have identified five cultural dimensions: (1) power distance, (2) individualism/collectivism, (3) masculinity/femininity, (4) uncertainty avoidance and (5) long-term orientation.

3 Explain how language competences shape intercultural interactions:

- Linguistic competences facilitate communication and access to knowledge, both essential for careers in IB.

4 Explain how religions shape cultures:

- Religions are an important source of variations in norms and values.
- Religious symbols can create strong emotional reactions and sensitivities.

5 Understand the importance of ethics:

- When managing ethics overseas, two schools of thought are ethical relativism and ethical imperialism.
- Three 'middle-of-the-road' principles help guide managers to make ethical decisions.

6 Participate in two leading debates on cultures:

- These are (1) cultural convergence versus divergence, and (2) opportunism versus individualism/collectivism.

7 Draw implications for action:

- It is important to enhance cultural intelligence, leading to cross-cultural literacy.
- It is crucial to understand and adapt to changing norms globally.
- Respect for your hosts will often get you along way.

KEY TERMS

Artefacts of culture
Civilization
Cluster
Code of conduct
Collectivism
Context
Corporate language

Corruption
Cultural intelligence
Culture
Ethical imperialism
Ethical relativism
Ethics
Ethnocentrism

Femininity
High-context culture
Holy
Individualism
Informal institutions
In-group
Lingua franca

Long-term orientation	Out-group	Taboo
Low-context culture	Power distance	Uncertainty avoidance
Masculinity	Secular society	

CRITICAL DISCUSSION QUESTIONS

1 You meet a classmate who has just arrived from a distant country. What are the most important things you want to tell him or her about *your own* country's culture? Would that be issues relating to cultural values, or something simple like 'be careful of staring at people on the bus'.

2 Have a look at the postcards of Valencia (page 69). Do they represent the culture of Valencia as experienced by foreign tourists? Do you think local people of Valencia like to be associated with these images? How can local people and tourist communicate their understanding of Spanish culture?

3 Your new male colleague informs you that he cannot shake hands with female colleagues or clients

because his religion forbids shaking hands (or any physical contact) with women. How do you react?

4 Based on Table 3.5, which best describes your cultural intelligence profile: a Local, Analyst, Natural, Mimic or Chameleon? Why?

5 Assume you work for a Norwegian company exporting a container of salmon to Azerbaijan or Haiti. The customs official informs you that there is a delay in clearing your container through customs, and it may last a month. However, if you are willing to pay an 'expediting fee' of €200, he will try to make it happen in one day. What are you going to do?

RECOMMENDED READINGS

N.A. Boyacigiller, R.A. Goodman & M.E. Philips, eds, 2003, *Crossing Cultures: Insights from the Master Teachers*, London: Routledge – a collection of teaching materials for practical learning about the challenges of cross-cultural management.

G. Hofstede, 1997, *Cultures and Organizations*, New York: McGraw-Hill – introduces and explains Hofstede's five dimensions of culture and their implications for business.

J. Hooker, 2003, *Working Across Cultures*, Stanford: Stanford University Press – explores and explains the multifaceted phenomenon of culture and its implications for business persons.

R. House, P. Hanges, M. Javidan, P. Dorfman & V. Gupta, eds, 2004, *Culture, Leadership, and Organizations: The GLOBE Study of 62 Societies*, Thousand Oaks, CA: Sage – a very comprehensive study developing new constructs to measure cultural variations with focus on leadership styles.

S. Huntington, 1996, *The Clash of Civilizations and the Remaking of World Order*, New York: Simon & Schuster – a very provocative book on the potential for major conflict arising from cultural and political differences.

CLOSING CASE

ALSTOM: Party invitations in Saudi Arabia and in China

The Swiss unit of French engineering giant ALSTOM is building infrastructure projects all over the world,

especially power stations. As is typical for engineering and construction firms, ALSTOM sends their engineers out, often on short term expatriate assignments for a few months. These construction projects are typically in remote locations far away from the major urban hubs, and the engineers have to become accustomed to working with a local workforce and living in the local community. They thus have to learn to adapt – quickly.

Cultural differences often become most evident in the ways people celebrate social events from meeting for lunch to participating in their parties. When working abroad, it is likely that you may be invited to a party, and you may be expected to actively participate. Yet, you may not always know beforehand what is expected of you. A Swiss ALSTOM engineer recalls his experiences from Saudi Arabia:

'Once, there was a farewell for someone from the building site. On this occasion, there was a little celebration. We were told, at midday, after work, there would be a party. We waited and were wondering what would happen, where they would do it, and if they would bring something. There were neither chairs nor tables. Around 2 pm, they came with huge aluminium tablets, the size of a wagon wheel, filled up with rice, and in the middle a huge piece of mutton, grilled mutton. Finally, three or four of these tablets were standing on the floor of the workshop. They just put them on the floor! Of course we had cleaned up before. They came dressed in their celebratory dresses, and we expected some sort of ceremony. But they just sat down on the floor in their white gowns, around the tablets, and started eating.

The [Swiss] colleague who was with me was vegetarian. He said, "Listen, I won't squat on the floor like that, and I won't eat anything either". Everyone had a piece of mutton in his hand – it was incredible. One would hold the mutton, and another pulled out a chunk and passed it to me: "here, mutton, that's good, you must eat". We had no plates and nothing. Everyone grabbed into the bowl, and scooped out a handful of rice. And now, my mate said "I won't squat on the floor like that", and I say, "come on, let's just sit down, you don't have to eat mutton, but you can at least do as if you are".

They were very happy that we were there, and that they could invite us for this meal. It was important to them that we would participate. We had known these people from work, but still, initially the atmosphere was a bit uncomfortable. We didn't know how to behave. But then, after we sat down, and meat was passed around, it got real interesting. We got talking, and relaxed. My mate also sat down and afterwards he said he enjoyed it very much. The English vocabulary of those people was quite limited, so we had to talk "with hands and feet". Even so, we have been chatting about work, and what kind of rice this was, and what was in this rice. It was typical Saudi rice with raisins and the taste was quite fantastic. We couldn't talk much, the language barrier was just there, but then we picked up a few bits of Arabic,

Businessmen in a karoke bar

and the next morning we could say "Good morning" in Arabic. Every day a word more, they had immense joy hearing us speak Arabic.'

No alcohol was served at this party, as you would expect in a Muslim society. Yet this was quite different from the experiences of an Italian engineer who was posted by ALSTOM to China. He was an experienced serial expatriate when he arrived in Foshan, a smaller city in China (1.1 million inhabitants), where he and his team settled down in a local hotel for a couple of weeks. He was responsible for the timely implementation of the building project. But work is not separate from the rest of life in China:

'In China, we knew to party – the staff of the Chinese [JV partner] company, we the ALSTOM people, and all of us together. Parties didn't happen in a regular pattern, but when a party was announced, everyone dressed up, queued at the buffet, and toasted with the glasses. After dinner came the inevitable: Karaoke, or as they call it KTV. We Europeans politely said "no thanks", with one very talented exception. Among the Chinese, however, a group dynamic developed, there was no avoiding: everyone had to accept the microphone at least once. Not even the bosses at the top of the hierarchy could have an exception. I remember how we often had to endure with tightly closed ears three of four horrible performances in a row before a more talented singer took the mike.

It has to be said, we drank a lot. Usually, I don't drink much, but in such places there aren't that many other options to spend your Friday or Saturday evenings. At the banquets, a lot of alcohol came on the table. One morning, I knew that this must have been the case the previous evening. How my colleagues got me back to the hotel, I do not recall. When I met the same Chinese who also were at the party on the construction site, I was showered with congratulations. "You are our hero". Apparently, I must have gone to the highest boss, and had challenged him to "ganbei". Ganbei is a popular game where people challenge each other to drink a glass empty, and those who didn't join were considered ill-mannered. I stood there and didn't know what to think of these compliments. Was it the fact that I had the courage to do that, or did they have an especially good time with their boss that evening?'

Food is a central part of both Italian and Chinese culture. In fact, both love noodles, which reportedly were brought by Marco Polo from China to Italy in the 13th century. Yet, there are also differences that can be quite challenging, which the expatriate describes with Italian flair for illustration:

'The menus of the Chinese cuisine would certainly allow eating for months a different dish every day. That's because there is an incredible diversity in preparation methods and sauces in Chinese cooking. Moreover, it seems that Chinese eat everything that moves, or once has moved: cockroaches, dogs, cats, monkeys, rats, snakes.

I have my own experience with snakes. That was probably the biggest surprise event for me. It started with a bet that I had with the deputy director, a young Chinese. Our deal was that both of us would invite the other to a local meal, and the other had to eat at least one bite. The snakes were still alive when I had to tell the cook my preference, and we could watch the chosen animal being prepared. I did manage to swallow a bit of the fried dish, but the sight of cooked dish already deterred me from trying. The next week we had a revenge. In an international restaurant I ordered a rare steak, well seasoned but without sauce – just the way I like it. After one bite, my Chinese colleague asked me to relieve him of the plate. I can still see his desperate eyes, and hear him saying "I am sorry, but I cannot eat this".'

CASE DISCUSSION QUESTIONS:

1   If you were invited to a party in Saudi Arabia, how would you behave? What would you tell your European colleague who is a vegetarian?

2   Do you think it is appropriate, or necessary, to join the drinking when being invited to a party in China (or Russia)?

3   How would you treat you Saudi Arabian or Chinese colleagues when your company has an official party?

Source: N. Felix, 2007, Dann hat man es gewusst, und dann war gut, pp. 29–37 (p. 30), and L. Etter, 2007, gerostet nicht geröstet, pp. 98–104 (pp. 99–100 & 103–104), both in: M. Spisak & H. Stalder, Eds.: *In der Fremde*, Bern: Haupt. Translated by Klaus Meyer. Copyright © Haupt Bern. Reproduced with permission.

NOTES:

"FOR JOURNAL ABBREVIATION, PLEASE SEE PAGE XXVI–XXVII."

1 G. Helmke & S. Levitsky, 2004, Informal institutions and comparative politics, *PoP*, 2: 725–740; S. Estrin & M. Prevezer, 2010, The role of institutions in corporate governance, mimeo, London School of Economics.

2 J. Salk & M.Y. Brannen, 2000, National culture, networks, and individual influence in a multinational management team, *AMJ*, 43: 191–202; H. Woldu, P. Budhwar & C. Parkes, 2006, A cross-national comparison of cultural value orientations of Indian, Polish, Russian, and American employees, *IJHRM*, 17: 1076–1094.

3 G. Hofstede, 1997, *Cultures and Organizations* (p. xii), New York: McGraw-Hill.

4 S. Michailova, 2002, When common sense becomes uncommon, *JWB*, 37: 180–187.

5 T. Kostova & S. Zaheer, 1999, Organizational legitimacy under conditions of complexity, *AMR*, 24: 64–81; L. Busenitz, C. Gomez & J. Spencer, 2000, Country institutional profiles, *AMJ*, 43: 994–1003.

6 V. Barnouw, 1985, *Culture and Personality*, 4th ed, Homewood, IL: Dorsey Press.

7 Hofstede, 1997, *as above* (p. 5).

8 E.T. Hall & M. Hall, 1987, *Hidden Differences*, Garden City, NY: Doubleday; J. Hooker, 2003, *Working Across Cultures*, Stanford: Stanford University Press (Chapter 2).

9 S. Ronen & O. Shenkar, 1985, Clustering countries on attitudinal dimension, *AMR*, 10: 435–454.

10 R. House, P. Hanges, M. Javidan, P. Dorfman & V. Gupta (eds.), 2004, *Culture, Leadership, and Organizations: The GLOBE Study of 62 Societies*, Thousand Oaks, CA: Sage; V. Taras, P. Steel & B.L. Kirkman, 2010, Negative practice-value correlations in the GLOBE data, *JIBS*, 41: 1330–1338.

11 S. Huntington, 1996, *The Clash of Civilizations and the Remaking of World Order* (p. 43), New York: Simon & Schuster.

12 S. Schwartz, 1994, Cultural dimensions of values, in U. Kim et al. (eds.), *Individualism and Collectivism* (pp. 85–119), Thousand Oaks, CA: Sage; F. Trompenaars, 1993, *Riding the Waves of Culture*, Chicago: Irwin; R. Drogendijk & A. Slangen, 2006, Hofstede, Schwartz, or managerial perceptions, *IBR*, 15, 361–380.

13 K. Sivakumar & C. Nakata, 2001, The stampede toward Hofstede's framework, *JIBS*, 32: 555–574.

14 World Bank, 2004, *World Development Indicators*, http://www.worldbank.org.

15 M.K. Erramilli, 1996, Nationality and subsidiary ownership patterns in multinational corporations, *JIBS*, 27: 225–248.

16 J. Parnell & T. Hatem, 1999, Behavioral differences between American and Egyptian managers, *JMS*, 36: 399–418; C.F. Fey & I. Björkman, 2001, The effect of HRM practices on MNC subsidiary performance in Russia, *JIBS*, 32: 59–75; E. Pellegrini & T. Scandura, 2006, Leader-member exchange (LMX), paternalism, and delegation in the Turkish business context, *JIBS*, 37: 264–279.

17 N.J. Adler & A. Gundersen, 2007, *International Dimensions of Organizational Behaviour*, 5th ed., Cengage Learning.

18 Hofstede, 1997, *Cultures and Organizations* (p. 94).

19 *The Economist*, 2010, Women in the workforce: Female power, January 2.

20 P.C. Earley & E. Mosakowski, 2004, Toward culture intelligence (p. 155), *AME*, 18 (3): 151–157.

21 *Copenhagen Post*, 2009, Company reaps benefits from German flu fears, 24 July ; also see Hooker, 2003, *as above* (Chapter 6).

22 K. Laverty, 1996, Economic 'short-termism', *AMR*, 21: 825–860; L. Thomas & G. Waring, 1999, Competing capitalism, *SMJ*, 20: 729–748; R. Peterson, C. Dibrell & T. Pett, 2002, Long- vs. short-term performance perspectives of Western European, Japanese and US companies, *JWB*, 37: 245–255.

23 G. Van der Vegt, E. Van de Vliert & X. Huang, 2005, Location-level links between diversity and innovative climate depend on national power distance, *AMJ*, 48: 1171–1182; R. Friedman, S. Chi & L. Liu, 2006, An expectancy model of Chinese–American differences in conflict-avoiding, *JIBS*, 37: 76–91; K. Lee, G. Yang & J. Graham, 2006, Tension and trust in international business negotiations, *JIBS*, 37: 623–641; L. Metcalf, A. Bird, M. Shankarmahesh, Z. Aycan, J. Larimo & D. Valdelamar, 2006, Cultural tendencies in negotiation, *JWB*, 41: 382–394.

24 B. Kirkman, K. Lowe & C. Gibson, 2006, A quarter century of culture's consequences, *JIBS*, 37: 285–320; S. Venaik & P. Brewer, 2010, Avoiding uncertainty in Hofstede and GLOBS, *JIBS*, 41: 1294–1315.

25 P.C. Earley, 2007, Leading cultural research in the future, *JIBS,* 37: 922–931; C.S. Ooi, 2007, Unpacking packaged cultures, *EAIQ*, 24: 111–128.

26 Adler & Gundersen, 2008, *as above*.

27 D. Graddol, 2004, The future of language, *Science*, 303: 1329–1331.

28 *The Economist*, 2006, Brussels v the English language: Babelling on, December 16: 50.

29 R. Marschan-Piekkari, D.E. Welch & L.S. Welch, 1999, Adopting a common language, *IJHRM* 10: 377–390.

30 D. Ricks, 1999, *Blunders in International Business*, 3rd ed., Oxford: Blackwell. (p. 31).

31 K.E. Meyer, 2006, Asian management research needs more self-confidence, *APJM, 23:* 119–137.

32 *The Economist*, 2009, Charlemagne: English is coming, February 14.

33 N. Felix, 2007, Dann hat man es gewusst, und dann war gut, in: M. Spisak & H. Stalder, eds, *In der Fremde*, Bern: Haupt, p. 29–37.

34 Ricks, 1999, *as above*.

35 M. Robinson, 2009, Realising rights: the role of religion in human rights and the future, Speech upon receiving honorary degree of doctor of law from the University of Bath (webcast: www.bath.ac.uk/play/video/1253532480, accessed October 2009).

36 A. Crane & D. Matten, 2007, *Business Ethics*, 2nd ed., Oxford: Oxford University Press; L.K. Treviño & K.A. Nelson, 2007, *Managing Business Ethics*, 4th ed., New York: Wiley.

37 I. Maignan & D.A. Ralston, 2002, Corporate social responsibility in Europe and the US, *JIBS*, 33: 497–514; A. Kolk & R. Tulder, 2004, Ethics in international business, *JWB*, 39: 49–60; J. Stevens, H. K. Steensma, D. Harrison & P. Cochran, 2005, Symbolic or substantive document? *SMJ*, 26: 181–195; R. Durand, H. Rao & P. Monin, 2007, Code of conduct in French cuisine, *SMJ*, 28: 455–472.

38 C. Fombrun, 2001, Corporate reputations as economic assets, in M.A. Hitt, R.E. Freeman & J.S. Harrison (eds.), *The Blackwell Handbook of Strategic Management* (pp. 289–312), Cambridge, UK: Blackwell.

39 S.M. Puffer & D.J. McCarthy, 1995, Finding common ground in Russian and American business ethics, *CMR*, 37: 29–46; A. Spicer, T. Dunfee & W. Bailey, 2004, Does national context matter in ethical decision making? *AMJ*, 47: 610–620; K.P. Parboteeah, J. Cullen, B. Victor & T. Sakano, 2005, National culture and ethical climates, *MIR*, 45: 459–519; J.A. Al-Khatib, A. Malshe & N.A. Kader, 2008, Perception of unethical negotiation tactics: A comparative study of US and Saudi managers, *IBR*, 17: 78–102.

40 T. Donaldson, 1996, Values in tension, *HBR*, September–October: 4–11.

41 D. Vogel, 1992, The globalization of business ethics, *CMR*, Fall: 30–49.

42 P. Rodriguez, K. Uhlenbruck & L. Eden, 2004, Government corruption and the entry strategies of multinationals, *AMR*, 30: 383–396; A. Cuervo-Cazurra, 2006, Who cares about corruption? *JIBS*, 37: 807–822; N. Khatri, E. Tsang & T. Begley, 2006, Cronyism, *JIBS*, 37: 61–75; S. Lee & K. Oh, 2007, Corruption in Asia, *APJM*, 24: 97–114; B. Vernard, 2009, Corruption in emerging countries: A matter of isomorphism, *Management*, 12: 1–27.

43 J. Doh, P. Rodriguez, K. Uhlenbruck, J. Collins & L. Eden, 2003, Coping with corruption in foreign markets, *AME*, 17: 114–127; J.G. Lambsdorff, 2003, How corruption affects productivity, *Kyklos*, 56: 457–474; J.H. Zhao, S. Kim & J. Du, 2003, The impact of corruption and transparency on foreign direct investment, *MIR*, 43: 41–62; C. Dirienzo, J. Das, K. Cort & J. Burbridge, 2006, Corruption and the role of information, *JIBS*, 38: 320–332; P.-X. Meschi, 2008, Impact de la corruption d'Etat sur l'évolution des participations européennes dans les coentreprises internationals, *Management*, 11: 1–26.

44 *The Economist*, 2006, The etiquette of bribery: How to grease a palm, December 23.

45 K. Au, 1999, Intra-cultural variation, *JIBS*, 30: 799–813; G. Cheung & I. Chow, 1999, Subcultures in Greater China, *APJM*, 16: 369–387.

46 A.D. Brown, 1998, *Organizational Culture*, 2nd ed., London: FT Prentice Hall; E. Schein, 2004, *Organizational Culture and Leadership*, 3rd ed., San Francisco: Jossey-Bass.

47 T. Levitt, 1983, The globalization of markets, *HBR*, May–June: 92–102; M. Heuer, J. Cummings & W. Hutabarat, 1999, Cultural change among managers in Indonesia? *JIBS*, 30: 599–610.

48 P. Sztompka, 1993, Civilizational incompetence, *ZfS*, 22: 85–95; C. Feichtinger & G. Fink, 1998, The collective culture shock in transition economies, *LDOJ*, 19: 302–324; K.E. Meyer, 2007, Contextualizing organizational learning, *JIBS*, 38: 27–37.

49 M. Bahaee & M.J. Pisani, 2009, Iranian consumer animosity and U.S. products, *IBR*, 18: 199–210.

50 C. Chen, 1995, New trends in allocation preferences, *AMJ*, 38: 408–428; D.A. Ralston, C.P. Egri, S. Stewart, R.H. Terpstra & K. Yu, 1999, Doing business in the 21st century with the new generation of Chinese managers, *JIBS*, 30: 415–428; A. Ardichvili & A. Gasparishvili, 2003, Russian and Georgian entrepreneurs and non-entrepreneurs, *OSt*, 24: 29–46.

51 This section draws heavily on C. Chen, M.W. Peng & P. Saparito, 2002, Individualism, collectivism, and opportunism, *JM*, 28: 567–583.

52 J. Cullen, K.P. Parboteeah & M. Hoegl, 2004, Cross-national differences in managers' willingness to justify ethically suspect behaviors, *AMJ*, 47: 411–421.

53 M.J. Chen, 2001, *Inside Chinese Business*, Boston: Harvard Business School Press.

54 F. Fukuyama, 1995, *Trust*, New York: Free Press; G. Redding, 1993, *The Spirit of Chinese Capitalism*, 2nd ed., Berlin, De Gruyter.

55 K. Lim, K. Leung, C. Sia & M. Lee, 2004, Is e-commerce boundaryless? *JIBS*, 35: 545–559.

56 This example is based on personal communication with Professor David Ahlstrom, Chinese University of Hong Kong.

57 J. Graham & N. Lam, 2003, The Chinese negotiation, *HBR*, 81: 82–91.

58 N. Holden, C.L. Cooper & J. Carr, 1998, *Dealing with the New Russia*: New York: Wiley.

59 P.C. Earley & E. Mosakowski, 2004, Cultural intelligence, *HBR*, October: 139–146; J. Johnson, T. Lenartowicz & S. Apud, 2006, Cross-cultural competence in international business, *JIBS*, 37: 525–543; A. Bartel-Radic, 2009, La competence interculturelle, *MI/IM/GI*, 13 (4): 11–26.

60 Hofstede, 1997, *as above* (p. 230).

61 K. Singh, 2007, The limited relevance of culture to strategy, *APJM*, 24: 421–428.

CHAPTER FOUR

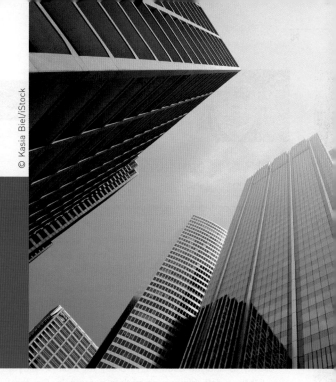

© Kasia Biel/iStock

FIRM RESOURCES: COMPETITIVENESS AND GROWTH

LEARNING OBJECTIVES

After studying this chapter you should be able to:

1 Explain what firms' resources are.

2 Assess the resources of a firm using the VRIO framework.

3 Use benchmarking to consider outsourcing and offshoring decisions.

4 Participate in three leading debates on resources in an international context.

5 Draw implications for action.

OPENING CASE

SAP runs businesses worldwide

In a rare move, Germany's largest software company SAP appointed two co-chairs in 2010 that were neither German nor lived in Germany. This move complemented the remarkable growth of a company only founded in 1972. SAP is world leader for business software programs – that is software that helps other businesses to make best use of their resources. What are the foundations for SAP's success, and why was it struggling in 2010?

SAP was funded by five entrepreneurs in 1972. They had new ideas how to use computers more efficiently to analyze accounting data, yet their employer – IBM – didn't think much of their proposals. So, they established their own company. Already in their first year they generated turnover of about €300 000, and the growth became unstoppable. By 1980, the majority of Germany's top 100 companies were running SAP software on IBM mainframe computers. By 1993, turnover exceed €1 billion, and in 2009 it reached €10.7 billion with a profit margin of 27.4 per cent. The small town of Walldorf (near Heidelberg in south-western Germany) remains to this day the hub of SAP's global operations.

SAP invented and developed the market for enterprise resource planning (ERP) software. Essentially, ERP provides electronic information systems that integrate data from different parts of an organization, such as manufacturing efficiency, inventories, sales and customer feedback. ERP software is like the central nervous system of a company, gathering information, and conveying it in real time to decision-makers in an accessible form – including fancy tables and graphs. SAP designed its software in a modular form that allowed companies to choose elements they needed – and to smoothly upgrade as they grew their own business.

The business model largely works on a combination of products and services: The sale of the software is usually combined with a maintenance contract that includes regular software upgrades, thus generating two income streams – one at the time of the sale, and one spread over several years. As a business-to-business (B2B) supplier, SAP is working closely with many of the world's largest MNEs. This led to early international growth of service operations, including independent business partners that specialize on implementing SAP systems.

SAP was building on German strengths in quality and reliability of engineering, yet at some stage that was not enough. From the 1990s onwards, research and software development have been internationalized with eight centres around the globe. An operation in Palo Alto, California served as an ideas factory and to stay in touch with the latest trends in Silicon Valley. Operations in India focused on the development of specific components and more clearly specified tasks, while Walldorf remained the hub for development and marketing activities. This internationalization allowed SAP to tap into human capital around the world. To stay ahead of the competition, SAP pushed further than most firms by aiming to hire the best software engineers to work for SAP – wherever in the world they are found. Thus, gradually the hub of the development and the top management was shifting away from Walldorf. This internationalization was appreciated by clients and investors outside Germany, but received a mixed response in Walldorf. Disgruntled employees talked in the local media about the 'Americanization' and the loss of traditional values such as commitment to quality and the entrepreneurial spirit of the early years. Having to speak English in internal meetings did not please many of the older engineers.

The industry kept changing fast, and new generations of technology often required new ways of organizing software and its delivery. Oracle and Microsoft became major players in the business software market, but for many years, SAP had the organizational flexibility to redesign its business model. However, new start-up companies with new business models challenged SAPs position. In particular, companies like Salesforce.com developed software for delivery on demand through the internet, and paid by monthly subscription, which allowed more speedy upgrades.

In the early 2000s, Shai Agassi became the rising star of SAP. He had joined SAP when his Israeli software start-up firm was acquired in 2001 for about €400 million. Agassi became head of product development and was appointed to the executive board in 2002, but remained based in California. He pushed to speed up the pace of product development, changing priorities from perfectionist German engineering to

Why is the SAP exhibit an important destination for business persons visiting the world's biggest high-tech fair, CeBIT in Hanover?

getting new ideas to markets quickly. He was widely tipped as successor for CEO Henning Kagermann, yet it was still too early for the firm to accept a non-German head. Agassi resigned in 2007 to set up a new ambitious venture, Better Place, which promises to develop networks of battery exchanges and charging points that would make electrical cars widely available and efficient to use.

During the financial crisis, the IT industry was hit hard. The recession forced many businesses to cut their budgets, especially IT budgets – it is easier to cancel orders for new software than to lay off staff. Thus, IT purchasing managers continued ongoing maintenance and service agreements, but they cut purchases of new software. This hit companies like SAP, but also Microsoft and Oracle. At SAP, a new CEO, Leo Apoteker took over in early 2009, and initiated efficiency improvements – speak budget cuts – that included a reduction of staff from 51 544 to 47 584 by the end of the year. At the same time, SAP tried to secure its revenues by increasing maintenance fees for existing and new customers from 17 per cent of 22 per cent of the purchase price. This led to an uproar among customers, who themselves were stressed by the recession. Eventually, SAP took back its fee increase, but by then a lot of goodwill with its stakeholders had been lost.

In early 2010, the IT industry was coming out of the recession, but at SAP staff morale and customer satisfaction were rock bottom. Leo Apoteker was able to trim excessive slack in the company, yet the way he did it lost him the trust of the employees. The supervisory board acted swiftly and with – by German standards – exceptional speed. Leo Apoteker resigned less than a year after he had taken office, and two successors were appointed: Bill McDermott, a US citizen previously in charge of sales and Jim Hageman Snabe, a Danish former head of product development. The new leaders faced formidable challenges described by the *Financial Times* as 'overseeing a cultural change in a demoralized company'. Meanwhile, German *Manager Magazin* saw the main challenge as reconciliation with the home market and the people who had build and supported the company over many years.

Sources: (1) P. Dvorak & L. Abboud, 2007, Internal revolution, *Wall Street Journal Europe*, May 11; (2) *The Economist*, 2009, Face value: Electric evangelist, April 30; (3) H. Schürmann, 2010, Hohe Erwartungen an neue Führung, *Handelsblatt*, February 2; (4) J. Koenen, 2010, Der Alte ist wieder da, *Handelsblatt*, February 8; (5) *The Economist*, 2010, SAP's chief departs abruptly: Apotekerlypsed, February 8; (6) A. Kaiser, 2010, Abschied vom nationalen Champion, *Manager Magazin*, February 8; (7) M. Palmer, 2010, SAP vows to return to double-digit sales growth, *Financial Times*, March 2; (8) SAP (2010): *Annual Report 2009*; (9) www.sap.com (accessed April 2010).

Why has SAP been able for many years to out compete much larger rivals such as Oracle and Microsoft in its market niche, business software? In an industry that is frequently changing as new generations of software emerge, how can SAP be a leading player with successive technologies? What are the internal sources of success of the firm from Walldorf, a small town in Germany? The answer is that there must be certain resources specific to SAP that are not shared by competitors. This insight has been developed into a resource-based view, which has emerged as one of the two core perspectives on global business.[1]

Resource-based view
A leading perspective in global business that posits that firm performance is fundamentally driven by firm-specific resources.

The resource-based view focuses on the inside of the firm, thus complementing the institutional view, which focuses on firms' external environment. In business, many key decisions concern the alignment of the firm – and its resources in particular – with its environment. Thus, to make the best decisions, you need to understand the inside of the firm as well: Which resources of your firm add value, and how can you systematically assess them? How can you manage your resources to create value, while protecting them from your competitors? How can you develop new resources?

This chapter introduces tools to address these sorts of questions. We first define resources and then introduce classification schemes for resources. Then, we focus on value (V), rarity (R), imitability (I) and organization (O) through a VRIO framework. We apply these concepts in a value chain analysis on the decision whether to keep an activity in-house or outsource it. Finally, debates and extensions follow.

IDENTIFYING RESOURCES

LEARNING OBJECTIVE

1 explain what firms' resources are

A basic proposition of the resource-based view is that a firm consists of a bundle of productive resources. These provide the basis for firms to attain competitive advantages in their markets, and to grow into new activities and markets.[2] Resources come in many different forms. For analytical purposes it is often helpful to distinguish between primary resources as the productive assets of a firm, and capabilities as firms' ability to use them. More precisely we define primary resources as the tangible and intangible assets as well as the human resources that a firm uses to choose and implement its strategies.[3] Such resources can generally be purchased on open markets and customized for use. Individually, they are however insufficient to provide an advantage over competitors, firms have to know how to use them. This knowledge and associated routines and practices are known as capabilities, defined as firm-specific abilities to use resources to achieve organizational objectives. Capabilities are normally developed internally and depend to some degree on tacit knowledge; they are specific to the firm and do not take the form of assets that can be traded or knowledge picked up from a textbook. For example, SAP is able to offer better customer services than its competitors due to its network of specialized business partners helping to implement SAP software. This capability is grounded in specific resources such as the skills of its software engineers and the practical knowledge of its consultants. However, the capability 'comes alive' in the processes by which SAP's employees and partners interact and use these resources to create an unique service.[4]

Primary resources
The tangible and intangible assets as well as human resources that a firm uses to choose and implement its strategies.

Capability
Firm-specific abilities to use resources to achieve organizational objectives.

In practice, primary resources and capabilities are often hard to distinguish or to classify. For convenience we use the simpler term 'resources' to refer to all of them. However, sometimes, you need a more detailed understanding of the firm's resources, for instance, when you want to analyze a firm or to make suggestion over its future strategy. The balance sheet of a company provides some information, but the most important capabilities are usually not evident from the balance sheet. Thus, you need to look deeper inside the company.

Primary resources

On firms' balance sheets, you can find two types of resources: tangible assets and intangible assets. Tangible assets are those items that are observable and quantifiable. They are normally reported on firms' balance sheets in two categories (Table 4.1):

Tangible assets
Assets that are observable and easily quantified.

- **Financial assets** reflect the depth of a firm's financial pockets. They include internal funds such as shareholders' capital and retained profits, as well as external capital, like loans provided by banks.

- **Physical assets** include plants, offices, infrastructure and equipment, as well as inventories of raw materials, components and finished goods. For example, although many people attribute the success of Amazon to its online portal (which makes sense), a crucial reason why Amazon has emerged as the largest bookseller is because it has built some of the largest physical, *brick-and-mortar* book warehouses in key locations around the globe.

Tangible assets are reported on company's balance sheets, but this information is often insufficient to assess their true value for the company's strategy. Many assets are reported at historical costs, that are the original costs that the company paid for it, and depreciated over a number of years. The actual value however depends on their contribution to the products and services that the company can sell in the marketplace: Amazon's warehouses are valuable beyond their resale value because of their role in Amazon's business model.

Table 4.1 Examples of PRIMARY Resources

Tangible Resources	Examples
Financial	Cash, securities, borrowing capacity
Physical	Plants, equipment, sales outlets, land, natural resources
Intangible Resources	**Examples**
Technological	Patents, trademarks, copyrights, trade secrets
Reputational	Brands, relationships, corporate goodwill (e.g. reputation as a quality manufacturer or as a socially responsible corporate citizen)
Human Resources	**Examples**
Skills and know-how	Job-specific skills and know-how held by individual employees
Communication and collaboration abilities	Interpersonal skills and learning capacity for team work and collaboration, emotional intelligence
Organizational Culture	Values, traditions, organizational norms

Sources: Adapted from (1) J.B. Barney, 1991, Firm resources and sustained competitive advantage, *JM*, 17: 101; (2) R. Hall, 1992, The strategic analysis of intangible resources, *SMJ*, 13: 135–144 (3) R.M. Grant, 2010, *Contemporary Strategy Analysis*, 7th ed., Oxford: Blackwell.

Intangible assets
Assets that are hard to observe and difficult (or sometimes impossible) to quantify.

Intangible assets are also found on companies' balance sheets, but they are much harder to value, and they are not always reported. They can be distinguished as technological and reputational resources.

- **Technological resources** include patents, trademarks and copyrights that entitle the firm to intellectual property rights and enable it to generate valuable products.[5] In a broader sense they also include less clearly defined resources such as trade secrets and databases that support the firm's business activity. For example, the value of pharmaceutical companies such as Roche is grounded in their patented medicines, and more recently in biotechnology.[6]

- **Reputational resources** are the firm's goodwill, brand names and business relationships. Goodwill is the value of abilities to develop and leverage the firm's reputation as a solid provider of goods and services, an attractive employer and/or a socially responsible corporate citizen. Reputation can be regarded as an outcome of a competitive process in which firms signal their attributes to constituents.[7] Some firms such as German carmakers BMW and Mercedes Benz focus on quality as the key attribute of their brand. Other aspects of reputation may include quality of customer service, or socially responsible business practices (Chapter 10). For example, British start-up company The Body Shop built a reputation as an 'ethical' cosmetics brand that appealed to many especially young consumers. This made it an attractive acquisition target for French cosmetics giant L'Oreal who aimed to strengthen its position with this important consumer group.[8]

Human resources
Resources embedded in individuals working in an organization.

Some resources are embedded in the individuals working in an organization, and thus known as human resources (or human capital). They are not owned by the firm (and are thus not on the balance sheet) but the firm can use them based on individual contracts. Human resources include:

- individual employees' skills, talent and knowledge, including both knowledge acquired in formal education and through experiential learning on the job, like the workforce assembled by SAP (Opening Case) around the world.

- individual employees' capacity for collaboration and communication, and their abilities for interpersonal interaction that are not captured by the firms' formal systems and structures.[9] For Instance, internet start ups such a Facebook are known for their (relative) youth, technological wizardry and competitive orientation, which enable them to continuously develop new software products.

Organizational culture
Employees' shared values, traditions and social norms within an organization.

- employees' shared values, traditions and social norms within an organization. This organizational culture has been identified as a key factor in explaining superior financial performance in many firms, yet it is notoriously hard to define and value.[10] For example, British chocolate maker Cadbury attributed its success to its unique organizational culture grounded in the founders' Quaker philosophy,[11] which became hard to sustain after Cadbury was acquired by the American food conglomerate Kraft in 2010.

Financial analysts may often take human resources for granted. Yet many MNEs regard them as a foundation of their capabilities, which is evident in the efforts firms put into the management of their human resources (Chapter 16). Moreover, the loss of key people can severely damage a firm. For example, when Italian fashion house Gucci lost both its chairman Domenico De Sole and Vice Chairman Tom

Ford in November 2003, the share price dropped sharply. As a consequence, Gucci was worth about €1 billion less![12]

Capabilities

Capabilities are, by definition, harder to observe and more difficult (or sometimes impossible) to quantify. Yet, it is widely acknowledged that they must be 'there' because no firm is likely to generate competitive advantage by relying on primary resources.[13] How can we make an inventory of capabilities?

The first approach is to look at the value chain, which illustrates how the different activities of a firm come together to add value. In principle, a firm may have capabilities in any of its activities. Shown in Figure 4.1, most goods and services are produced through a chain of vertical activities (from upstream to downstream) that add value – in short, a value chain.[14] For example, a manufacturing process may flow from raw materials, to primary components, to intermediate components, to assembly, to sales and to after sales service. These primary activities are backed up by support activities, such as finance, human resources and research. As an example, a fast-food hamburger may be manufactured in a fairly simple value chain: Farmers grow cows, wheat, tomatoes and other raw materials. These are slaughtered or harvested, processed and aggregated in transportable primary components. Further processes such as baking bread and frying the hamburger creates intermediate components that are delivered to the restaurant. The assembly kicks in when you order, and the sales involves you exchanging money for a meal. The after sales service includes listening any complaints you may have, and cleaning up after you left.

Value chain
A chain of activities vertically related in the production of goods and services.

Each activity along the value chain requires a number of resources. Value chain analysis forces managers to think about firm resources at a very micro, activity-based level.[15] Given that no firm is likely to have enough resources to be good at all primary and support activities, the key is to examine whether the firm has resources to perform a particular activity in a manner superior to competitors. Some companies may have particular capabilities in product development and sales, others are relatively stronger in production. Hence, firms may concentrate on selected stages of the value chain, as we discuss later in this chapter. Fast-food restaurants rarely own slaughterhouses or bakeries, and they may employ specialist cleaning companies to clean up the restaurant every evening.

However, many of the most important capabilities in today's business world relate to abilities to *connect* different stages of the value chain. Thus, value chain analysis is only a first step of an analysis of a firm's capabilities. We can classify capabilities further by the different functions of a company (Table 4.2).

- **Capabilities in innovation** are a firm's assets and skills to (1) research and develop new products and services and (2) innovate and change ways of organizing.[16] Some firms are renowned for innovations. For instance, Sony often pioneers new *classes* of products, such as the Walkman, the Discman and the Aibo (e-pet).

- **Capabilities in operations** are a firm's ability to effectively implement its regular activities, notably the manufacturing process. For example, many German engineering firms such as SAP are known for producing reliable, high quality machines, engines or software. Some firms, such as Dell computers (see Chapter 1, Opening Case) and Zara fashion are better than anyone else in their industry in adjusting operations to changing markets; others, such as Hainan Airlines (In Focus 4.1), excel at delivering consumer service at low costs.

- **Capabilities in marketing** enable firms to develop and sustain brands and to induce consumers to buy these brands. Such capabilities are often grounded in

Figure 4.1 The value chain

Panel A. An Example of Value Chain with Firm Boundaries

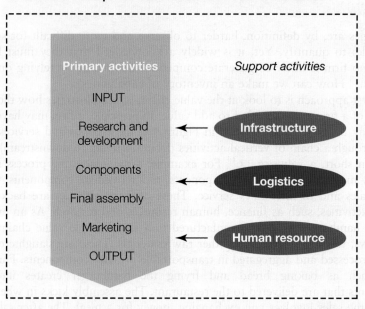

Panel B. An Example of Value Chain with Some Outsourcing

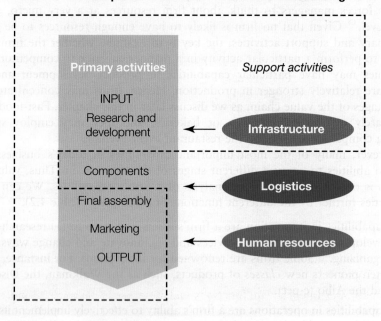

Note: Dotted lines represent firm boundaries

a firm's ability to recognize (potential) consumer demands, develop products to fit this demand and to communicate the benefits of the product to consumers. For example, many popular food brands are owned and managed by a small number of MNEs specialized in brand management, such as Unilever, Procter & Gamble and Mars.

Table 4.2 Examples of Functional Capabilities

Function	Examples of Capabilities	Exemplar companies
Corporate Functions	● Ability to attract and manage financial resources	Exxon Mobil, PepsiCo
	● Strategic management of multiple businesses	General Electric, P&G
	● Strategic innovation	Google, 3M
	● Ability to interact with governments	CNOOC, First Pacific
Research and Development	● Research	Merck, SAP, Rolls-Royce
	● Innovative new product development	3M, Apple
	● Fast-cycle new product development	Zara, Canon
	● Design capability	Nokia, Sony, Samsung
Operations	● Flexibility and speed of response	Four Seasons Hotel, Zara
	● Continuous quality improvement in manufacturing	Toyota, Rolls Royce
	● Efficiency in volume manufacturing	Flextronics, Hon Hai
	● Low cost delivery of customer service	Hainan Airlines, easyJet
Marketing	● Brand management	P&G, Unilever, Carlsberg
	● Reputation for quality	BMW, Mercedes
	● Responsiveness to market trends	MTV, L'Oreal
Sales and distribution	● Efficiency of order processing and distribution	Dell, Amazon
	● Effective distribution management	Wal-Mart, Zara
	● Quality and effectiveness of customer service	Singapore Airlines, SAP

Source: Adapted from R. Grant, 2007, *Corporate Strategy Analysis 6th ed.,* Oxford: Blackwell. Reproduced by permission from Wiley-Blackwell.

- **Capabilities in sales and distribution** enable firms to manage interactions with (potential) customers and in bringing products to the right customer at the right time. Such capabilities are often grounded in efficiency-oriented management processes as well as IT systems and supporting technologies. Wal-Mart is particularly known for its capability to manage complex distribution networks (In Focus 4.2).

- **Capabilities in corporate functions** include a firm's planning, command, and control systems and structures. In general, younger firms tend to rely more on the visions of managers (often founders), whereas more established firms usually have more formalized systems and structures. In emerging economies, corporate functions often include navigating in unstable and incomplete formal institutional frameworks, and the management of relationships with authorities.[17] A related capability, which has proven to be pivotal during the financial meltdown of 2008, is corporate risk management, as those who lack financial foresight were most likely to go under.[18]

IN FOCUS 4.1

Capabilities in low cost operations: Hainan Airlines

By Sunny Li Sun, University of Texas, Dallas.

Until the mid 1980s, China had only one airline company for the entire country, the Civil Aviation Administration of China (CAAC). In the 1980s, CAAC was split up to formed three large airlines known as the Big Three: Air China headquartered in Beijing, China Eastern based in Shanghai and China Southern centred on Guangzhou. At the same time, about two dozen new airlines were permitted to be established, including Hainan Airlines, headquartered in Hainan Island off the Southern coast of China. Surprising to many, Hainan emerged as a winner in an increasingly competitive industry, in part because of its ability to compete on low costs.

What are Hainan Airlines' secrets? First, like its role model, Southwest Airlines in the USA, Hainan specializes in point-to-point flights. Flying point-to-point allows Hainan to turn around flights much faster than hub-and-spoke operators such as the Big Three. The worldwide average ratio of employees per aircraft

is about 170:1. The ratio for China's Big Three is 280:1. In contrast, Hainan's ratio is only 80:1.

Second, Hainan had build a uniform fleet by focusing on the Boeing 737 (for larger markets) and the Dornier 328 regional jet (for smaller markets), thus enjoying great economies of scale in aircraft maintenance. In contrast, the Big Three have a mixture of various types of planes from both Boeing and Airbus, significantly increasing maintenance, components and training costs.

Third, not having any historical baggage associated with CAAC, Hainan from the beginning chose young staff members that fitted its strategy, and emphasized service quality. Moreover, 25 full-time quality inspectors appeared as regular passengers to fly around and 'crack the whip'. Every year, crews rated at the bottom 10 per cent of their peers are automatically fired, quite a ruthless practice for an industry renowned for its 'iron rice bowls' (save jobs).

Sources: We thank Sunny Li Sun (University of Texas at Dallas) for his assistance. Based on (1) D. Li, J. Leong, & M.-J. Chen, 2003, Hainan Airlines: En route to direct competition, Case study, University of Virginia; (3) S.L. Sun & S.R. Cao, 2005, Zhang Da de Xie Zi [Shoes That Fit], Beijing: Chinese Social Sciences Press; (5) http://www.hnair.com.

A resource audit is often the first step for many analyses that you may be doing while studying international business or strategic management. For example, when analyzing the potential for synergies in mergers and acquisitions (Chapter 14), a thorough assessment of the resources of both firms is a crucial first step. Note that firms rarely excel at all these resources, they tend to have strength in some areas and weaknesses in others. For example, Wal-Mart's operational efficiency (In Focus 4.2) comes at the expense of a particularly weak reputation for social responsibility. The list of resources we have provided here gives a starting point for a resource audit. The next step then is to assess them.

LEARNING OBJECTIVE

2 Assess the resources of a firm using the VRIO framework

VRIO framework
The resource-based framework that focuses on the value creation (V), rarity (R), imitability (I) and organizational (O) aspects of resources.

APPRAISING RESOURCES: THE VRIO FRAMEWORK

How can you know how useful your (firm's) resources are? An important line of work on the resource-based view focuses on the value creation (V), rarity (R), imitability (I) and organization (O) aspects of resources, leading to a VRIO framework.[19] Summarized in Table 4.3, these four important questions have a number of ramifications for competitive advantage.

IN FOCUS 4.2

Capabilities in distribution: Wal-Mart

A 120 000 m^2 distribution centre in Bentonville, Arkansas, USA, is the hub of Wal-Mart's North American logistics operation. *New York Times* journalist Thomas Friedman describes how he discovered the capabilities underlying its success:

'… we climbed up to a viewing perch and watched the show. On one side of the building, scores of white Wal-Mart trailer trucks were dropping off boxes of merchandize from thousands of different suppliers. Boxes large and small were fed up a conveyor belt, like streams feeding into a powerful river. Twenty-four hours a day, seven days a week, the suppliers' trucks feed the 12 miles [19 km] of conveyor streams, and the conveyor streams feed into a huge Wal-Mart river of boxed products. But that is just half the show. As the Wal-Mart river flows along, an electric eye reads the bar codes on each box on its way to the other side of the building. There, the river parts again into a hundred streams. Electric arms from each stream reach out and guide the boxes – ordered by particular Wal-Mart stores – off the main river and down its stream, where another conveyor belt sweeps them into a waiting Wal-Mart truck, which will rush these particular products onto the shelves of a particular Wal-Mart store somewhere in the country.

There, a consumer will lift one of these products off the shelf, and the cashier will scan it in, and the moment that happens, a signal will be generated. That signal will go out across the Wal-Mart network to the supplier of that product – whether that supplier's factory is in coastal China or in coastal Maine [USA]. That signal will pop up on the supplier's computer screen and prompt them to make another of that item and ship it via the Wal-Mart supply chain, and the whole cycle will start anew. So no sooner does your arm lift a product off the local Wal-Mart's shelf and onto the checkout counter than another mechanical arms starts making another one somewhere in the world. Call it the "Wal-Mart Symphony" in multiple movements – with no finale. It just plays over and over 24/7/365: delivery, sorting, packing, distribution, buying, manufacturing, reordering, delivery, sorting, packing …

Just one company, Hewlett-Packart, will sell four hundred thousand computers through the four thousand Wal-Mart stores worldwide in

one day during the Christmas season, which will require HP to adjust its supply chain, to make sure that all of its standards interface with Wal-Mart's, so that these computers flow smoothly into the Wal-Mart river, into the Wal-Mart streams, into the Wal-Mart stores …

Wal-Mart today is the biggest retail company in the world, and it does not make a single thing. All it "makes" is a hyperefficient supply chain'.

Source: T.L. Friedman, 2007, *The World is Flat*, 3rd ed., New York: Picador (pp. 151–152).

The question of value creation

The most fundamental question is, do the resources add value?[20] In other words, do they enable a firm to exploit an external opportunity, and/or neutralize an external threat? Machines that convert trees into furniture obviously add value as long as the furniture is more valuable than the trees (that is, the market price of the output is higher than the price of the input). If the value of the trees increases (say because of their carbon capture capacity) or if the value of wooden furniture falls (say, because it is out of fashion), then the machines no longer add value – even if they are technologically still fully operational.

Only value creating resources can possibly lead to competitive advantage, whereas non-value creating capabilities may lead to competitive *disadvantage*. With changes in the competitive landscape, previously value creating resources may become obsolete. The evolution of IBM is a case in point. IBM historically excelled in making hardware, including tabulating machines in the 1930s, mainframes in the 1960s and 1970s and personal computers (PCs) in the 1980s. However, as competition for hardware was heating up, IBM's core capabilities in hardware not

Table 4.3 The VRIO framework

Criterion	Question	Resource 1	Resource 2	Resource 3	Resource 4
Value Creating	Does the resource add value?	No	Yes	Yes	Yes
Rare	How rare is the resource?	—	No	Yes	Yes
Imitability	How difficult is it for others to imitate the resource?	—	No	No	Yes
Organization	Are other policies and procedures organized to support the exploitation of this resource?	No	Yes	Yes	Yes
		↓	↓	↓	↓
Competitive implications		Disadvantage	Parity	Temporary advantage	Sustained advantage

Sources: Adapted from (1) J.B. Barney, 2002, *Gaining and Sustaining Competitive Advantage*, 2nd ed. (p. 173), Upper Saddle River, NJ: Prentice Hall; (2) R.E. Hoskisson, M.A. Hitt, & R.D. Ireland, 2004, *Competing for Advantage* (p. 118), Cincinnati, OH: Thomson South-Western.

only added little value but also increasingly became core rigidities that stood in the way of the firm moving into new areas.[21] Since the 1990s, under two new CEOs, IBM has been transformed to focus on more lucrative software and services, where it has developed new value creating capabilities, aiming to become an on-demand computing *service* provider for corporations. As part of this new strategy, IBM sold its PC division to China's Lenovo in 2004.

The relationship between value creating resources and firm performance is straightforward. Instead of becoming strengths, non-value creating resources, such as IBM's historical expertise in hardware, may become weaknesses. If firms are unable to get rid of non-value creating resources, they are likely to suffer below-average performance.[22] In the worst case, they may become extinct, a fate IBM narrowly skirted during the early 1990s. 'Continuous strategic renewal', in the words of Gary Hamel, a strategy guru, 'is the only insurance against irrelevance'.[23]

The ability to create value, however, is often context-specific. Firms may be highly successful at home, but struggle when they try to transfer their capabilities abroad. For example, Wal-Mart (In Focus 4.2) failed to transfer its business model to Germany, partly because it couldn't achieve the necessary scale, and partly because its work practices were not acceptable to German work forces.

The question of rarity

Simply possessing value creating resources may not be enough. The next question asks: How rare are these resources? At best, value-creating but common resources will lead to competitive parity not to an advantage. Consider SAP software used by businesses worldwide. It certainly creates value by enabling firms to use their resources – people, finances, patents – more efficiently. Yet, it is difficult to derive competitive advantage from the software *alone*. Businesses have to compete on how to use the software most effectively.

Only value creating *and* rare resources have the potential to provide some temporary competitive advantage.[24] Many IT firms exploit their intellectual property (IP) by licensing their patents to others. However, this potentially reduces their rarity. There is always a danger that their licensees (or their licensees' employees) use the technology for purposes other than those originally intended. Although blatant patent infringement is illegal, smart reverse engineering, by inventing 'around' a given patent, is legal. In contrast, Indian IT company Wipro prefer to hold onto their innovations rather than patenting and licensing them. It calls these inventions 'IP blocks', which are bits of software or processes taken from work for one client that it can draw on to serve multiple clients better. Around 10 000 Wipro engineers are involved with such high-end design and development work for numerous clients, but Wipro has fewer than 10 patents.[25] By developing and keeping the technology (mostly) in-house, Wipro protects the rarity of such expertise, and uses it as a competitive advantage when competing for contracts.

Overall, the question of rarity is a reminder of the cliché: If everyone has it, you cannot make money from it. For example, flawless quality may have been a competitive advantage in the automotive industry in the 1970s, yet as competitors have been catching up it is no longer a rare capability. Car manufacturers thus need to differentiate themselves in different ways. In Focus 4.3 reports a story about Hyundai's struggle to develop a 'rare' capability.

The question of imitability

Value creating and rare resources can be a source of competitive advantage but this will disappear quickly if competitors can imitate them. The third question thus is,

IN FOCUS 4.3

Hyundai's uphill battle

Would you be surprised that Hyundai's Genesis was named the North American *Car of the Year* in 2009? Would you believe an authoritative J.D. Power survey which reported that Hyundai has better quality than Toyota and Honda? Trouble is, despite these endorsements, most car buyers don't buy it. Only 23 per cent of all new-car buyers in the USA bother to consider buying a Hyundai. This compares with 65 per cent and 50 per cent for Toyota and Honda, respectively.

Make no mistake: Hyundai is very capable. It was the fastest growing car manufacturer in the US market in the 2000s. Elbowing its way into the entry-level market, Hyundai captured many value-conscious buyers, who appreciated the more *tangible* equipment and performance at lower prices (6 per cent to 10 per cent lower than those of its rivals). However, with the won appreciating 25 per cent against the dollar, the price gap was narrowing between imports of entry-level Hyundai cars from South Korea and more highly regarded brands. Hyundai thus had to go after the higher margin, high-end market. To offset the won appreciation, Hyundai's two-year-old, €700 billion plant

in Montgomery, Alabama, beefed up production. Yet, it turned out cars twice as fast as dealers ordered them. The problem? 'When we don't have a price story', said David Zuchowski, Hyundai's vice president for sales, 'we have no story'. For high-end buyers, it is the *intangible* reputation and mystique that count.

In 2007, Hyundai audaciously compared its newly launched Genesis with both the BMW 5 series and the Lexus ES350. Hyundai created quite a stir when at the height of the 2008/09 recession; it offered its customers a buyback guarantee in case they lost their job within one year of the purchase of the car. Effectively, they offered an insurance policy tied in with the car. This proved quite a successful marketing strategy, and Hyundai grew its sales by 8 per cent while most competitors faced falling sales, and increased its market share in the US from 3.0 per cent to 4.2 per cent in 2009. Yet, will this be enough to create a lasting premium brand reputation?

Sources: Based on (1) *Business Week*, 2007, Hyundai still gets no respect, May 21: 68–70; (2) *The Economist*, 2009, Hyundai's surprising success: Sui genesis, March 5; (3) B. Simnon, 2010, Hyundai moves through gears in US as buyers switch focus, *Financial Times*, January 12; (4) http://www.jdpower.com.

---

how difficult is it for competitors to imitate the resources? It is relatively easy to imitate many *tangible* resources (such as plants), but it is a lot more challenging and often impossible to imitate *intangible* capabilities (such as tacit knowledge, superior motivation and managerial talents).[26] In an effort to maintain a high-quality manufacturing edge, many Japanese firms employ 'super technicians' (or *supaa ginosha*) – an honour designated by the Japanese government – to handle mission-critical work, such as mounting tiny chips onto circuit boards for laptops at Sharp.[27] Although robots can be purchased by rivals, no robots, and few humans elsewhere, can imitate the skills and dedication of the super technicians in Japan.

Causal ambiguity
The difficulty of identifying the causal determinants of successful firm performance.

Imitation is difficult. Why? In two words: causal ambiguity, which refers to the difficulty of identifying the causal determinants of successful firm performance.[28] In an abstract economic model, you can easily establish which variable influences which other variable. However, in the real world, organizations have complex internal patterns and processes that escape systematic modelling. For example, why do Italian fashion houses stay ahead in the world of fashion for decades? Is it the training that designers and tailors received in their apprenticeship? Is it the close-knit networks of small firms in Northern Italy? Is it the experience of designers growing up in a fashion-oriented culture? Or, is simply that people elsewhere associate Italian names with 'fashionable'? Outsiders usually have a hard time understanding what a firm – or a network of firms – does inside its boundaries. We can try, as many rival luxury

© webphotographeer/iStock

How do Italian designers stay ahead in the volatile business of fashion?

goods manufacturers have, to identify the Italian recipe for success by drawing up a long list of possible reasons labelled as 'capabilities' in our classroom discussion. But in the final analysis, as outsiders, we are not sure.[29]

What is even more fascinating for scholars and students and more frustrating for rivals is that often managers of a successful firms do not know exactly what contributes to their success. But to make matters more confusing, different managers of the same firm may have different lists. When probed as to which capability is 'it', they usually suggest that it is all of the above in *combination*. This is probably one of the most interesting and paradoxical aspects of the resource-based view: If insiders have a hard time figuring out what explains their firm's performance, it is not surprising that outsiders' efforts in understanding and imitating these capabilities usually fail.[30]

The difficulties of imitation are related to a phenomenon known as social complexity, which refers to the socially complex ways of organizing typical of many firms. Many MNEs consist of thousands of people scattered in many different countries. How they overcome cultural differences and are organized as one corporate entity and achieve organizational goals is profoundly complex.[31] Often, it is their invisible relationships that add value.[32] Such organizationally embedded capabilities are thus very difficult for rivals to imitate. This emphasis on social complexity refutes what is half-jokingly called the 'Lego toy' view of the firm, in which a firm can be assembled (and disassembled) from modules of technology and people (à la Lego toy blocks). By treating employees as identical and replaceable blocks, this view fails to realize that the social capital associated with complex relationships and knowledge permeating many firms can be a source of competitive advantage.[33] The social complexity underlying many capabilities, especially in knowledge-intensive industries, also has implications for crisis management: Laying off people in difficult times may imply losing capabilities for good that cannot be recreated by hiring new people when the economy picks up again. Such capabilities based on social complexity thus are valuable, rare, and *hard-to-imitate* and can provide the basis for a sustained competitive advantage.

Social complexity
The socially complex ways of organizing typical of many firms.

The question of organization

Even value creating, rare and hard-to-imitate resources may not give a firm sustained competitive advantage if the firm is not properly organized. For example, internet companies developing news, social networking or online games have some of the most valuable, rare and hard-to-imitate resources, many of them fail to deliver profits for the firms that created the service. More generally, the question of organization asks: Are other policies and procedures of the firm (such as an internet service provider) organized to enable and support the exploitation of its value creating, rare and costly-to-imitate resources? In economics, the question is known as appropriability, the ability of the firm to appropriate the values for itself. This depends on (1) revenues received from customers, and (2) expenses paid to suppliers.

First, how do you ensure that customers pay for the goods or services they benefit from. This question is particular challenging for many online service providers that are used by many people who don't pay. How do social networking websites such as Linkedin, Xing or Facebook survive financially? The (main) answer is advertising revenues, a secondary answer is premium services such as special database search functions (Linkedin, Xing) or online games (Facebook). Second, firms have to ensure that they keep a large share of the revenues, and don't overpay their suppliers. This is challenging for firms where 'star performers' are a crucial element in their resource mix, for example, football clubs, movie studios or TV stations. These star performers tend to have a large bargaining power that they can use to attain a share of the revenues generated by the firm.

Overall, only valuable, rare, and hard-to-imitate resources that are organizationally embedded and exploited can lead to sustained competitive advantage and persistently above-average performance.[34] Because resources cannot be evaluated in isolation, the VRIO framework presents four interconnected and increasingly difficult hurdles for them to become a source of sustainable competitive advantage (see Table 4.3 above).

Appropriability
The ability of the firm to appropriate the values for itself.

APPLYING RESOURCE ANALYSIS: BENCHMARKING

A key tool for analyzing resources is benchmarking.[35] The essence of benchmarking is to compare your resources against those of your competitors on the basis of two questions: (1) Which resources are most important in conferring sustainable competitive advantage in your industry? (2) Where are your strengths and weaknesses as compared to your competitors? Benchmarking then involves four steps:

LEARNING OBJECTIVE

3 use benchmarking to consider outsourcing and offshoring decisions

Benchmarking
An examination of resources to perform a particular activity compared against competitors.

1 **Choose a benchmark organization** to compare yourself with. To assess your own competitiveness you have to benchmark against your competitors, in particular the 'best in class'. If you are facing a single more important competitor, you may learn most from benchmarking directly against that competitor, rather than an industry average. Alternatively, you can benchmark against the industry leader in another country to explore your potential for further improvement.

2 **Identify the relevant resources.** A good staring point is often the balance sheet where you will find tangible and intangible assets. Then look for indications of human resources and explore the company's operations and track record for capabilities in particular functions or activities (see Table 4.1 and Table 4.2 above).

3 **Assess the importance of your resources.** As decision-maker, you need to focus on those resources that are most relevant to compete *in your industry*.

R&D, manufacturing and marketing can – and often should – be moved outside',[47] what is left for workers at home? Labour Unions are concerned about offshoring competition driving down wages and benefits in the industrial heartlands of, for example, the UK or France. Factories and workers thus need to continuously upgrade their capabilities to justify their higher wages. But also some business scholars are concerned that offshore outsourcing nurtures rivals.[48] Why are Indian IT/BPO firms emerging as strong rivals challenging EDS and IBM? It is in part because they built up their capabilities doing work for EDS and IBM in the 1990s.

Offshoring service providers are gradually moving up the value chain. In manufacturing, many Asian firms, which used to be original equipment manufacturers (OEMs) executing design blueprints provided by Western firms, now want to have a piece of action in design by becoming original design manufacturers (ODMs) (see Figure 4.5). Having mastered low-cost and high-quality manufacturing, Asian firms such as BenQ, Compal, Flextronics, Hon Hai, HTC and Huawei are indeed capable of capturing some design function from Western firms such as Dell, HP, and Nokia.[49] In Eastern Europe, companies like Videoton of Hungary are following in their footsteps. They tend to start with small design changes that facilitate the production process, and gradually upgrade to adding new features and creating entirely new products.

As they upgrade, however, OEM manufacturers become a competitive threat to their former masters. A number of Asian OEMs/ODMs, have openly announced that their real ambition is to become original brand manufacturers (OBMs). For example, HTC from Taiwan has for many years build mobile phones as an ODM for Western operators such as Verizon and Orange. Based on this experience, it set out to develop its own brand, initially in Asia, to challenge Apple and Nokia.[50] For the time being, it seems that the main value added of new products is still in the development and marketing offices located in, for example, California or Scandinavia

Original equipment manufacturer (OEM)
A firm that executes the design blueprints provided by other firms and manufactures such products.

Original design manufacturer (ODM)
A firm that both designs and manufactures products.

Original brand manufacturer (OBM)
A firm that designs, manufactures and markets branded products.

Figure 4.5 From Original *Equipment* Manufacturer (OEM) to Original *Design* Manufacturer (ODM)

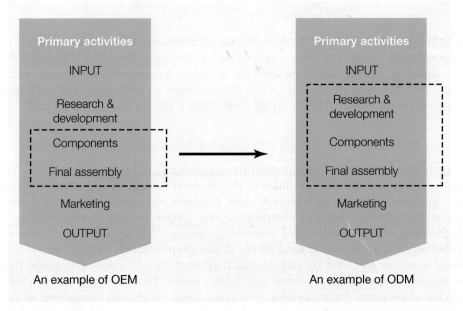

Note: Dotted lines represent organizational boundaries. A further extension is to become an original *brand* manufacturer (OBM), which would incorporate brand ownership and management in the marketing area. For graphic simplicity, it is not shown here.

IN FOCUS 4.4

How much does China benefit from outsourcing?

The Chinese government has been running a television advertising campaign over the past month to improve the international image of China-made products. At one point the camera focuses on an Apple iPod and a caption written on the back that says: 'Made in China with software from Silicon Valley',

There are many potential landmarks for the surge in the Chinese economy over the past decade – the bulging foreign exchange reserves now worth more than $2000bn (£1250bn, €1386), the endless energy investments in far-flung lands or the longest sea bridge in the world in Hangzhou Bay. But in many ways the iPod is the most appropriate symbol for the surge because it encapsulates both the great advances that have been made as well as the long road ahead.

Since 2000, China has graduated from making a large part of the world's low-end products – think socks or cigarette lighters – to making the most sophisticated, design-led consumer electronic goods.

Apple contracts out the manufacture of iPods and much of the work is done at the Shenzhen factory of

Hon Hai, a Taiwanese company that also uses the trade name Foxconn. Many of the country's strengths are contained within Hon Hai's vast facility, which employs at least 200 000 people and also churns out Sony PlayStations and Nokia cell phones. To create such a production line demands a mixture of infrastructure, logistics and trained staff that no other developing country can match.

Yet the iPod also highlights the limitations of the Chinese economy. Researchers at the University of California at Irvine examined which countries garnered the economic value from iPod production. The conclusion was that only about 5 per cent of the value is retained in China, with the bulk going to the designers, retailers and suppliers of sophisticated components.

Their research encapsulates the task China faces – to create more companies that move up the value chain from contract manufacturing and to boost the spending power of Chinese staff who have not benefited from the boom as might be expected.

Source: 'iPod points to struggle ahead' by G. Dyer, *Financial Times*, 30 December 2009, copyright © *Financial Times* 2009. Reprinted with permission.

(see In Focus 4.4). Similarly, with the increasing emphasis in electronics on digital (as opposed to analogue) products, countries such as Germany, the UK and the USA that are strong in software development have been able to reassert themselves in industries, such as consumer electronics that were thought to have been 'lost' to foreign competition (as indicated in the Apple story below). But for how much longer?

Long-term competition with dynamic capabilities

Dynamic capabilities
Higher level capabilities that enable an organization to continuously adapt to new technologies and changes in the external environment.

Capabilities help firms to gain competitive advantages, and to beat their rivals. Yet, how do they stay ahead in an industry that is always changing and where competitors continuously come up with new ideas, products and capabilities? Some authors argue that staying ahead of competitors over longer periods of time requires a higher level of capabilities called dynamic capabilities.[51] Essentially, operational capabilities such as those discussed earlier in this chapter enable firms to attain competitive advantages. Yet to stay ahead, they need to continuously upgrade their operational capabilities. Dynamic capabilities enable firms not only to develop a stream of products, but to develop new operational capabilities to compete in ever changing environments.[52] It is not good enough to compete in today's market, firms need to anticipate and adapt to markets of the future. For example, Apple has reinvented itself several times, reorganizing the company's capabilities to lead in new generations of technologies – from PCs to iPods and to iPhones. Apple's dynamic capability to reinvent itself is closely associated with CEO Steve Jobs and his core management team, which effectively builds off its excellent consumer designs and strength in digital technology and software. In the business software industry, Oracle, Microsoft and SAP (Opening Case) similarly managed to continuously reorganize themselves around new generations of technology.

Sceptics of the dynamic capabilities approach argue that dynamic capabilities are impossible to identify because they are so diverse and abstract. Looking back, it may be possible to say what made a firm successful over a long period of time (such as Steve Jobs' leadership style). Yet, no one knows what dynamic capabilities will allow firms to thrive in the future. In theory, it makes sense to distinguish operational and dynamic capabilities, but it is hard to derive specific managerial tools from this insight.

IMPLICATIONS FOR PRACTICE

How does the resource-based view answer the big question in global business: What determines the success and failure of firms around the globe? The answer is straightforward: Fundamentally, why some firms outperform others is because winners possess some value creating, rare, hard to imitate and organizationally embedded resources that competitors do not have.[53] This insight raises two fundamental questions for managers 1) how can we best exploit our current resources, and 2) how should we build resources that we can exploit tomorrow. Likewise, students should develop capabilities as the foundation for their career (Table 4.4).

First, there is nothing very novel in the proposition that firms 'compete on resources'. The subtlety comes when managers attempt, via the VRIO framework, to distinguish resources that are value creating, rare, hard to imitate and organizationally embedded from those that do not share these attributes. Managers, who cannot pay attention to every resource, must have some sense of what really matters, and what is likely to matter in the future. Benchmarking and the VRIO framework help managers to evaluating their firms' capabilities relative to rivals, and thus to provide a basis for strategic decisions. Increasingly, what really matters is not primary resources that are relatively easy to imitate, but knowledge-based capabilities that are harder for rivals to lay their arms around. This is a crucial reason that we increasingly label the new global economy as a 'knowledge-based economy'. Therefore, managers need to focus on the identification, development and leveraging of VRIO-capabilities.

Second, managers need to continuously upgrade their resources to remain competitive in rapidly changing environments. Benchmarking plays an important part in this as firms aim to catch up in functions and activities where they are lagging,

Table 4.4 Implications for action

- Managers need to understand their resources based on the VRIO framework to optimize their resource exploitation.
- Managers need to continuously create new resources, in part by benchmarking against the best, and in part by developing entirely new capabilities that go beyond the competitors' state-of-the-art.
- Students are advised to make themselves 'untouchables' whose jobs cannot be offshored.

while preventing others to catch up where they are leading. However, imitation of best practice may not be enough. Follower firms that meticulously replicate every resource possessed by winning firms can hope to attain competitive parity, though by the time they catch up to the leader, the leader may already have moved on.[54] To achieve competitive advantage, firms need to develop their own unique capabilities. The best performing firms often create new ways of adding value.

Leaders, on the other hand, need to be aware that no competitive advantage lasts forever in the global competition of the 21st century. Over time, all advantages may erode. As noted earlier, each of IBM's product-related advantages associated with tabulating machines, mainframes and PCs was sustained for a period of time. But eventually, these advantages disappeared. Therefore, the lesson for all firms, including current market leaders, is to develop strategic *foresight* – 'over-the-horizon radar' is a good metaphor – that enables them to anticipate future needs and move early to identify and develop resources for future competition.[55]

Finally, here is a very personal and relevant implication for action. As a student who is probably studying this book in a developed (read: high-wage and thus high-cost!) country in Western Europe, you may be wondering: What do I get out of this? How do I cope with the frightening future of global competition? There are two lessons you can learn. First, the whole debate on offshoring, a part of the larger debate on globalization (Chapters 1 and 9), is very relevant and directly affects your future as a manager, a consumer and a citizen. So do not be a couch potato. Be active, become informed, get involved and be prepared because it is not only *their* debate; it is *yours* as well. Second, be very serious about the advice of the resource-based view. Although this view has been developed to advise firms, there is no reason you cannot develop that into a resource-based view of the *individual*. That is, you should develop your personal capabilities to prepare your career.

CHAPTER SUMMARY

1 Explain what firm resources are:

- Resources include primary resources and capabilities that provide the basis for firms to attain competitive advantages, and to grow.

- Primary resources include tangible and intangible assets, as well as human resources.

- Capabilities can be classified by their stage of the value chain, or their function within the organization.

2 Assess the resources of a firm using the VRIO framework:

- A VRIO framework suggests that only resources that are value creating, rare, hard to imitate and organizationally embedded will generate sustainable competitive advantage.

3 Use benchmarking analysis outsourcing and offshoring decisions:

- Benchmarking is a technique of comparing a firm's capabilities to its rivals.

- Outsourcing is defined as turning over all or part of an organizational activity to an outside supplier.

- Offshoring is defined as relocating an activity to another country, either in house or with outsourcing, to take advantage of locational advantages in that country.

4 Participate in two debates on cross-border capabilities and offshoring:

- In the long run, is offshoring beneficial or detrimental for Western firms and economies?

- In the long run, how can dynamic capabilities helps firms to stay ahead in ever-changing industries?

5 Draw implications for action:

- Managers need to understand their resources based on the VRIO framework to optimize their resource exploitation.

- Managers need to continuously create new resources, in part by benchmarking against the best, and in part by developing entirely new capabilities that go beyond the competitors' state-of-the-art.

- Students are advised to make themselves 'untouchables' whose jobs cannot be offshored.

KEY TERMS

Appropriability	Intangible assets	Outsourcing
Benchmarking	Nearshoring	Primary resources
Capability	Offshore outsourcing	Resource-based view
Captive offshoring	Offshoring	Social complexity
Causal ambiguity	Organizational culture	Tangible assets
Domestic outsourcing	Original brand manufacturer (OBM)	Value chain
Dynamic capabilities	Original design manufacturer (ODM)	VRIO framework
Human resources	Original equipment manufacturer (OEM)	

CRITICAL DISCUSSION QUESTIONS

1 Pick any pair of rivals (such as Samsung/Sony, Nokia/Motorola, and Boeing/Airbus) and explain why one outperforms another. Apply both a benchmark analysis (Figure 4.2) and a VRIO framework (Table 4.3) to the resources of the chosen pair.

2 Conduct a VRIO analysis of your business school or university in terms of (1) perceived reputation (such as rankings), (2) faculty strength, (3) student quality, (4) administrative efficiency, (5) IT and (6) building maintenance relative to the top-three rival schools/universities. If you were the dean with a limited budget, where would you invest scarce financial resources to make your school number one over its rivals? Why?

3 One reason why outsourcing service providers have lower costs is that their labour force may not be unionized. Would it be appropriate for an established industry leader to outsource to such a company?

4 Since firms read information posted on competitors' websites, is it ethical to provide misleading information on resources on corporate websites? Do the benefits outweigh the costs?

CLOSING CASE

Avon perfects direct selling

When numerous mighty, masculine companies in the banking and automobile industries fell left and right during the recent recession, Avon Products, a self-styled 'company for women', rose to new heights around the world. Avon is a leading global beauty products company with 42 000 employees and with €7 billion in annual turnover. As the world's largest direct seller, Avon markets 'smart value' products to women in more than 100 countries through 5.8 million

How did Avon make the most of its resources and capabilities when entering China?

independent sales representatives affectionately known as 'Avon Ladies'. Today, not all Avon representatives are women, and Avon has officially dropped the 'Lady' title for them. They are simply called 'representatives', because Avon has been increasingly recruiting men to hawk its products. While numerous companies in most industries lost money in 2008, Avon's revenue grew 5 per cent (in local currencies), to a record €7.3 billion. The growth continued in 2009, reaching 7 per cent (in local currencies) in the third quarter. The number of active representatives jumped 10 per cent worldwide. In the USA alone, Avon recruited 200 000 more representatives during an aggressive recruitment drive in March 2009. Investors acknowledged Avon's enviable performance, pushing up its share price from March to November by 150 per cent, more than doubling the value of the company!

Founded in 1886, Avon pioneered direct selling. In its long history, Avon has its fair share of ups and downs. So why has its performance been so outstanding lately? Obviously, the severity of the 2008/09 recession has rewritten a number of taken-for-granted 'rules of the game' concerning job security, employment, and careers. Direct selling has always been a way (mostly for women) to supplement their income. During the recession, it became all the more important for an increasingly large number of both women and men who lost their jobs. Even people holding a regular job increasingly joined direct selling, in case their jobs disappear. Burned

by the recession, individuals who felt the need to 'recession-proof' their income found direct selling to be a great new line of work. According to Richard Berry, director of the UK Direct Selling Association:

> 'Direct selling is almost uniquely immune to economic trends. When you have a recession and people want a low-cost way of making an extra income, direct selling is a great option. The reason our members tend not to suffer from a drop in consumer demand is that the products they sell are low-cost household and personal products, all of which are the last thing to suffer a downturn in demand.'

On the other hand, with essentially no entry barrier, laid-off bankers and stay-at-home moms were rushing in. Competition is tough. Why has Avon been doing so well? Avon's iconic brand certainly helps. Its massive army of Avon representatives ensures unrivalled reach around the globe. Another reason is that a new generation of representatives find that they do not have to go door-to-door if they do not want to. Instead, they take catalogues to social events, or they operate on the 'party-plan' model, pitching their wares at neighbourhood potlucks and dessert parties. They are typically networked, using Facebook, Twitter and Blackberry to creatively expand their business. Direct selling is not a get-rich-quick scheme. Representatives have to work hard. In the USA, the average revenue for a party is €300, of which the representative makes

25 per cent. So to earn a good living, a lot of parties are needed.

In addition, direct selling can be a low-risk way of experimenting with entrepreneurial ideas, even for those who eventually move away from direct selling. This is because direct selling gives individuals an idea of how they like selling, how good they are at it and how they manage their time, inventory and finances to maximize profit – without necessarily having to quit current jobs. Avon's chairperson and CEO, Andrea Jung, proudly noted in her message to Avon's website visitors that Avon is 'a true force for good, improving and changing the lives of others as we continue to fulfil our vision as the company for women'.

CASE DISCUSSION QUESTIONS:

1 Applying the VRIO framework, what are the sources of Avon's success?

2 How sustainable is Avon's success in the long run?

3 Why was Avon doing relatively well during the global recession of 2008/09?

Sources: Based on (1) *Business Week*, 2009, Door-to-door sales revive in Britain, July 8; (2) *Business Week*, 2009, The entrepreneurs born of recession, March 13; (3) *Shanghai Daily*, 2009, Avon Lady ranks boom in downturn, June 28; (4) *The Telegraph*, 2009, Avon Lady reborn in the USA, July 5; (5) www.avoncompany.com (accessed on December 18, 2009).

RECOMMENDED READINGS

J.B. Barney, 1991, Firm resources and sustained competitive advantage, *JM*, 17: 99–120 – The original paper that explained and popularized the resource-based view.

R.M. Grant, 2010, Contemporary strategy analysis, 7th ed., Oxford: Blackwell – A strategy textbook that is grounded in the resource-based view, see especially Chapters 5 and 6.

G. Hamel & C.K. Prahalad, 1994, *Competing for the Future*, Boston: Harvard Business School Press – A management guru book using resource-based thinking.

M.W. Peng, 2001, The resource-based view and international business, *JM*, 27: 803–829 – A paper applying resource-based reasoning to the international sphere.

C.E. Helfat, S. Finkelstein, W. Mitchell, M. Peteraf, H. Singh, D. Teece & S.G. Winter, 2007, *Dynamic Capabilities: Understanding Strategic Change in Organizations*, Oxford: Blackwell – Leading scholars discuss the state-of-the-art of the resource based view and of dynamic capabilities research.

NOTES:

"FOR JOURNAL ABBREVIATION, PLEASE SEE PAGE XXVI-XXVII."

1 B. Wernerfelt, 1984, A resource-based view of the firm, *SMJ*, 5: 171–180; J.B. Barney, 1991, Firm resources and sustained competitive advantage, *JM*, 17: 99–120; M.W. Peng, 2001, The resource-based view and international business, *JM*, 27: 803–829.

2 E. Penrose, 1959, *The Theory of the Growth of the Firm*, London: Blackwell; M. Pettus, 2001, The resource-based view as a developmental growth process, *AMJ*, 44: 878–896; K.E. Meyer, 2006, Globalfocusing: From domestic conglomerate to global specialist, *JMS,* 43, 1109–1144; C. Pitelis & A. Verbeke, 2007, Edith Penrose and the future of the multinational enterprise, *MIR*, 47: 139–149; J. Steen & P. Liesch, 2007, A note on Penrosian growth, resource bundles, and the Uppsala model of internationalization, *MIR*, 47: 193–206; H. Greve, 2008, A behavioral theory of firm growth, *AMJ*, 51: 476–494.

3 J.B. Barney, 2001, Is the resource-based view a useful perspective for strategic management research? (p. 54), *AMR* 26: 41–56.

4 R.M. Grant, 1991, The resource-based theory of competitive advantage, *CMR*, 33, 114–135; J. McGee, H. Thomas & D. Wilson, 2005, *Strategy Analysis & Practice*, Maidenhead: McGraw Hill.

5 A. Phene, K. Fladmoe-Lindquist & L. Marsh, 2006, Breakthrough innovations in the US biotechnology industry, *SMJ*, 27: 369–388; E. Danneels, 2007, The process of technological competence leveraging, *SMJ*, 28: 511–533; M. Reitzig & P. Puranam, 2009, Value appropriation as an organizational capability, *SMJ*, 30: 765–789.

6 *The Economist*, 2009, Roche digests Genentech: Back to the lab, December 12.

7 N. Gardberg & C. Fombrun, 2006, Corporate citizenship, *AMR*, 31: 329–346; V. Rindova, T. Pollock & M. Hayward, 2006, Celebrity firms, *AMR*, 31: 50–71.

8 *The Economist*, 2006, Ethical Business: The body beautiful, March 25.

9 N. Hatch & J. Dyer, 2004, Human capital and learning as a source of competitive advantage, *SMJ*, 25: 1155–1178.

10 C.F. Fey & D.R. Denison, 2003, Organizational culture and effectiveness, *OSc*, 14: 686–706; D.R. Denison, S. Haaland & P. Goelzer, 2004, Corporate culture and organizational effectiveness, *OD*, 33, 98–109;

11 N. O'Regan & A. Ghobadian, 2009, Successful strategic re-orientation: Lessons from Cadbury's experience, *JSM*, 2, 405–412.

12 R.M. Grant, 2010, *Contemporary Strategy Analysis*, 7th ed., Oxford: Blackwell (p. 139).

13 H. Itami & T. Roehl, 1987, *Mobilizing Invisible Assets*, Cambridge, MA: Harvard University Press; A. Carmeli & A. Tishler, 2004, The relationships between intangible organizational elements and organizational performance, *SMJ*, 25: 1257–1278; S. Dutta, O. Narasimhan & S. Rajiv, 2005, Conceptualizing and measuring capabilities, *SMJ*, 26: 277–285;

14 M.E. Porter, 1985, *Competitive Advantage*, New York: Free Press; C. Stabell & O. Fjeldstad, 1998, Configuring value for competitive advantage, *SMJ*, 19: 413–437.

15 G. Johnson, L. Melin, & R. Whittington, 2003, Micro strategy and strategizing, *JMS*, 40: 3–22; A. Parmigiani, 2007, Why do firms both make and buy? *SMJ*, 28: 285–311.

16 J. Birkinshaw, R. Nobel, & J. Ridderstråle, 2002, Knowledge as a contingency variable, *OSc*, 13: 274–289; S. McEvily, K.E. Eisenhardt, & J. Prescott, 2004, The global acquisition, leverage, and protection of technologies competencies, *SMJ*, 25: 713–722; K.G. Smith, C.J. Collins, & K.. Clark, 2005, Existing knowledge, knowledge creation capability, and the rate of new product introduction in high-technology firms, *AMJ*, 48: 346–357; M. Subramaniam & M. Youndt, 2005, The influence of intellectual capital on the types of innovative capabilities, *AMJ*, 48: 450–463.

17 W. Henisz, 2003, The power of the Buckley and Casson thesis, *JIBS*, 34: 173–184; M.W. Peng, 2003, Institutional transitions and strategic choices, *AMR*, 28: 275–296.

18 T. Holcomb, M. Holmes & B. Connelly, 2009, Making the most of what you have, *SMJ*, 30: 457–485; N. Taleb, D. Goldstein & M. Spitznagel, 2009, The six mistakes executives make in risk management, *HBR*, October: 78–81.

19 Barney, 1991, *as above*; J.B. Barney & W.S. Hesterly, 2008, *Strategic Management and Competitive Advantage*: 2nd ed., Upper Saddle River: Pearson Prentice-Hall.

20 S. Lippman & R. Rumelt, 2003, A bargaining perspective on resource advantage, *SMJ*, 24: 1069–1086; R. Adner & P. Zemsky, 2006, A demand-based perspective on sustainable competitive advantage, *SMJ*, 27: 215–239; J.C. Anderson, J.A. Narus & W. Van Rossum, 2006, Customer value propositions in business markets, *HBR*, March: 91–99; J. Morrow, D. Sirmon, M.A. Hitt & T. Holcomb, 2007, Creating value in the face of declining performance, *SMJ*, 28: 271–283.

21 D. Leonard-Barton, 1992, Core capabilities and core rigidities, *SMJ*, 13: 111–125; B. Vissa & A. Chacar, 2009, Leveraging ties, *SMJ*, 30: 1179–1191.

22 N. Siggelkow, 2001, Change in the presence of fit, *AMJ*, 44: 838–857; G. P. West & J. DeCastro, 2001, The Achilles heel of firm strategy, *JMS*, 38: 417–442; D. Lavie, 2006, Capability reconfiguration, *AMR*, 31: 153–174.

23 G. Hamel, 2006, Management innovation (p. 78), *HBR*, February: 72–84.

24 N. Carr, 2003, *Does IT Matter?* Boston: Harvard Business School Press.

25 *The Economist*, 2005, Patents and Technology: Thinking for themselves, October 22; S. Ethiraj, P. Kale, M.S. Krishnana, & J.V. Singh, 2005, Where do capabilities come from and how do they matter? *SMJ*, 26: 25–45.

26 R. Schroeder, K. Bates, & M. Junttila, 2002, A resource-based view of manufacturing strategy, *SMJ*, 23: 105–118; A. Knott, D. Bryce & H. Posen, 2003, On the strategic accumulation of intangible assets, *OSc*, 14: 192–208; D. Miller, 2003, An asymmetry-based view of advantage, *SMJ*, 24: 961–976; G. Ray, J.B. Barney & W. Muhanna, 2004, Capabilities, business processes, and competitive advantage, *SMJ*, 25: 23–37; B. Skaggs & M. Youndt, 2004, Strategic positioning, human capital, and performance in service organizations, *SMJ*, 25: 85–99.

27 *Business Week*, 2005, Better than robots, December 26.

28 A.W. King, 2007, Disentangling interfirm and intrafirm causal ambiguity, *AMR*, 32: 156–178; T. Powell, D. Lovallo, & C. Caringal, 2006, Causal ambiguity,

management perception and firm performance, *AMR*, 31: 175–196; S. Jonsson & P. Renger, 2009, Normative barriers to imitation, *SMJ*, 30: 517–536.

29 M. Lieberman & S. Asaba, 2006, Why do firms imitate each other? *AMR*, 31: 366–385.

30 A. Lado, N. Boyd, P. Wright & M Kroll, 2006, Paradox and theorizing within the resource-based view, *AMR*, 31: 115–131.

31 S. Tallman, 1991, Strategic management models and resource-based strategies among MNEs in a host market, *SMJ*, 12: 69–82; J. Birkinshaw & N. Hood, 1998, Multinational subsidiary evolution, *AMR*, 23: 773–795.

32 T. Kostova & K. Roth, 2003, Social capital in multinational corporations and a micro-macro model of its formation, *AMR*, 28: 297–317; P. Moran, 2005, Structural vs. relational embeddedness, *SMJ*, 26: 1129–1151.

33 K.E. Meyer & M.W. Peng, 2005, Probing theoretically into Central and Eastern Europe, *JIBS*, 36, 600–621.

34 S. McEvily & B. Chakravarthy, 2002, The persistence of knowledge-based advantage, *SMJ*, 23: 285–305; S. Zahra & A. Nielsen, 2002, Sources of capabilities, integration and technology commercialization, *SMJ*, 23: 377–398; J. Fahy, G. Hooley, J. Beracs, K. Fonfara & V. Gabrijan, 2003, Privatization and sustainable advantage in the emerging economies of Central Europe, *MIR*, 43: 407–428.

35 Grant, 2010, *as above* (140–144).

36 *The Economist*, 2009, Briefing: Toyota: Losing its shine, December 12; D. Pilling, 2010, How Toyota engineered its own downfall, *Financial Times*, February 11.

37 J. Barthelemy, 2003, The seven deadly sins of outsourcing, *AME*, 17 (2): 87–98; F. Rothaermel, M.A. Hitt, & L. Jobe, 2006, Balancing vertical integration and strategic outsourcing, *SMJ*, 27: 1033–1056.

38 M. Jacobides & S.G. Winter, 2005, The co-evolution of capabilities and transaction costs (p. 404), *SMJ*, 26: 395–413; M. Kang, J. Mahoney, & D. Tan, 2009, Why firms make unilateral investments specific to other firms? *SMJ*, 30: 117–135.

39 A.L. Ranft & M.D. Lord, 2002, Acquiring new technologies and capabilities, *OSc*, 13: 420–441.

40 S. Beugelsdijk, T. Pedersen & B. Petersen, 2009, Is there a trend towards global value chain specialization? *JIM*, 15: 126–141; S. Chen, 2009, A transaction cost rationale for private branding and its implications for the choice of domestic versus offshore outsourcing, *JIBS*, 40: 156–175; J. Doh, K. Bunyaratavej & E. Hahn, 2009, Separable but not equal, *JIBS*, 40: 926–943; M. Kotabe & R. Mudambi, 2009, Global sourcing and value creation, *JIM*, 15: 121–125.

41 S. Bottler, 2010, Wenn Unternehmen nach Deutschland zurückkehren, *Handelsblatt*, February 4.

42 K. Coucke & L. Sleuwaegen, 2008, Offshoring as a survival strategy, *JIBS*, 39: 1261–1277; D. Gregorio, M. Musteen, & D. Thomas, 2009, Offshore outsourcing as a source of international competitiveness of SMEs, *JIBS*, 40: 969–988; R. Javalgi, A. Dixit, & R. Scherer, 2009, Outsourcing to emerging markets, *JIM*, 15: 156–168; M. Kenney, S. Massini, & T. Murtha, 2009, Offshoring administrative and technical work, *JIBS*, 40: 887–900; B. Kedia & D. Mukherjee, 2009, Understanding offshoring, *JWB*, 44: 250–261; K. Kumar, P. van Fenema, & M.A. von Glinow, 2009, Offshoring and the global distribution of work, *JIBS*, 40: 642–667; F. Contractor, V. Kumar, S. Kundu & T. Pedersen, eds, 2010, *Outsourcing and Offshoring of Business Activities*, Cambridge: Cambridge University Press.

43 T. Mayer, 2006, Nearshoring to Central and Eastern Europe, *Deutsche Bank Research*, August 14.

44 J. Doh, 2005, Offshore outsourcing, *JMS*, 42: 695–704.

45 J. Lamont, 2009, India taps into riches as the west's back office, *Financial Times*, December 30.

46 D. Farrell, 2005, Offshoring, *JMS*, 42: 675–683.

47 M. Gottfredson, R. Puryear, & S. Phillips, 2005, Strategic sourcing (p. 132), *HBR*, February: 132–139.

48 C. Rossetti & T. Choi, 2005, On the dark side of strategic sourcing, *AME*, 19 (1): 46–60.

49 A. van Agtmael, 2007, *The Emerging Market Century*, New York: Simon & Schuster.

50 *The Economist*, 2009, Face value: Upwardly mobile, July 11.

51 C.E. Helfat & M. Peteraf, 2003, The dynamic resource-based view, *SMJ*, 24: 997–1010; D. Teece, G. Pisano, & A. Shuen, 1997, Dynamic capabilities and strategic management, *SMJ*, 18: 509–533; K.M. Eisenhart & J.A. Martin, Dynamic Capabilities: What are they? *SMJ*, 21: 1105–1121; G. Lee, 2008, Relevance of organizational capabilities and its dynamics, *SMJ*, 29: 1257–1280; S.E. Dixon, K.E. Meyer & M. Day, 2010, Stages of Organizational Transformation in Transition Economies: A Dynamic Capabilities Approach, *JMS*, 47: 416–436.

52 C.E. Helfat & M.B. Lieberman, 2002, The birth of capabilities, *ICC*, 12, 725–760.

53 W. DeSarbo, C. Nenedetto, M. Song, & I. Sinha, 2005, Revisiting the Miles and Snow strategic framework, *SMJ*, 26; 47–74; G.T. Hult, D. Ketchen, & S. Slater, 2005, Market orientation and performance, *SMJ*, 26: 1173–1181.

54 G. Hamel & C.K. Prahalad, 1994, *Competing for the Future*, Boston: Harvard Business School Press.

55 Hamel & Prahalad, 1994, *as above*.

PART TWO

BUSINESS ACROSS BORDERS

BUSINESS ACROSS BORDERS

© Ranplett/iStock

CHAPTER FIVE

TRADING INTERNATIONALLY

LEARNING OBJECTIVES

After studying this chapter you should be able to:

1   Use the resource-based and institution-based views to explain why nations trade.

2   Understand classical and modern theories of international trade.

3   Appreciate how economic and political institutions influence international trade.

4   Participate in two leading debates on international trade.

5   Draw implications for action.

OPENING CASE

Port of Rotterdam: gateway to the world

The Netherlands are one of the richest countries of the world, and the area around the estuary of the rivers Rhine and Maas is the richest area of the Netherlands. Yet, this area is not rich in any particular natural resources. The Netherlands may be famous for tulips and windmills – but that alone cannot explain their wealth. What then explains the economic success of the Netherlands over the centuries?

The answer is international trade. The Netherlands has long been a nation of traders, from the Dutch East India Company in the 17th century to modern day merchants and bankers. The hub of trade is the Port of Rotterdam, Europe's largest. It stretches over 40 kilometres and covers over 10 000 hectares of land. Over one million tones of goods are loaded, unloaded and distributed in Rotterdam *every day* – more than twice the turnover of the next largest European ports, Antwerp and Hamburg. Worldwide, Rotterdam ranks

fourth behind the East Asian hubs of Shanghai, Ningbo and Singapore. All kinds of cargo pass through Rotterdam, including oil, chemicals, ores, bulk goods like cars, and refrigerated cargo such as fruit. Every year, 33 000 ocean going ships call in the port, 6.5 million containers are transferred and 120 million m^3 crude oil arrive to be refined and distributed throughout Europe. The transportation businesses in the port add €6.6 billion to Dutch GDP, while other industries located in the vicinity add another €5.0 billion.

By volume, 90 per cent of world trade is transported by ship, making seaports key nodes of international trade. The Port of Rotterdam is, as the main hub for sea-bound transportation in and out of Europe, a market of over 500 million consumers. Containers arrive from Asia on Mega ships that are too large even for medium size ports such as Hamburg or Le Havre. Thus, containers are transferred in Rotterdam to smaller ships sailing to ports along the Atlantic coast into the North and Baltic Seas, up the river Rhine and

A container ship in Rotterdam Harbour

across to the UK. More than 500 liner services connect Rotterdam with over 1000 ports worldwide.

Huge investments have expanded the port, and more are planned for the future. The infrastructure is build around the Nieuwe Waterweg (New Channel), which opened in 1870 and connects the city of Rotterdam directly to the North Sea. It has been continuously widened and deepened, while far out in the North Sea a man-made channel allows easy access even for the largest ships of the world. Maasvlakte 1, which contains the largest container terminals, was reclaimed from the estuary 30 years ago. A new expansion of the port, called Maasvlakte 2, is to extend the port further into the North Sea, creating 1000 hectares of industrial land directly on deep water by the year 2030.

Globalization has accelerated the growth of ports like Rotterdam as shipments of goods have consistently been growing faster than GDP, with a temporary but substantive set-back during the 2008/9 recession. The fastest growing businesses of the Port of Rotterdam, and of maritime transport worldwide, is container shipping. Containers are standardized and allow a much faster transfer over different modes of transport. In Rotterdam, over 100 mega-cranes are working day and night to unload containers arriving from overseas, and reloading them to regional container ships, inland boats, trains and trucks. Experts forecast a tripling of container transportation by the year 2020 – if new terminals can be built fast enough.

The Dutch government has heavily invested in transportation infrastructure to connect Rotterdam with its hinterland, including regional shipping lines, inland waterways (especially the Rhine connecting to Germany, France and Switzerland), oil-pipelines, roads and railways – with strategically located transhipment points between different transport modes. Many goods from the German industrial heartlands of the Ruhr region are loaded on riverboats or direct trains in Duisburg, and then shipped downstream to Rotterdam, and from there out into the world. Yet, traffic jams hold up trucks, and the regional and national authorities are under pressure to invest in upgrading the infrastructure connecting Rotterdam with Duisburg and other secondary hubs.

The port has attracted many businesses relying on imported goods, especially petroleum refining and chemicals processing plants. Rotterdam also has the largest depots of oil and oil products in Europe with tank storage of 28.4 million m^3. Many Japanese and American MNEs have set up their European distribution centres in the South-West of the Netherlands, making the region a hub in the European distribution networks of many multinational firms. Businesses seek efficient infrastructure such as the Port of Rotterdam to be able to trade and compete around the world.

Sources: (1) R. Wrights, 2007, Rotterdam struggles to contain its enthusiasm as demand surges ahead, *Financial Times*, December 5; (2) A. Granzow & R. Reichstein, 2008, Alle Wege führen über Duisburg, *Handelsblatt*, April 11; (3) Port of Rotterdam, 2009, *Port Statistics*, mimeo, (4) www.portofrotterdam.com (accessed October 2009).

Why does trading make the Netherlands one of the richest nations in the world? What are the underlying economic forces that make it beneficial for nations to trade – even if intermediaries such as the Port of Rotterdam take a substantial share of the benefits? International trade is the oldest and still the most important building block of international business. It is a major driving force of globalization and been growing faster than GDP in recent decades. Figure 5.1 shows that world trade growth (averaging about 6 per cent during 1998–2008) routinely outpaces GDP growth (averaging 3 per cent during 1998–2008). Even in 2008, a very difficult year, trade growth (2.2 per cent) still exceeded GDP growth (1.8 per cent). Yet trade growth has been more volatile than GDP growth; for example the recession of 2009, world trade dropped by about 10 per cent.

Unsurprisingly, international trade is also a hot topic in politics as the benefits of trade are often unevenly distributed. Debates on international trade tend to be very ferocious, because so much is at stake. This chapter will help you to participate in such debates. We start by outlining the theoretical foundations for international trade. These theories provide a structured way of thinking and analyzing issues that are central to both businesses and government policy. We begin by outlining how the two core perspectives introduced in earlier chapters – namely, resource-based

Figure 5.1 Growth in world trade outpaces growth in world GDP

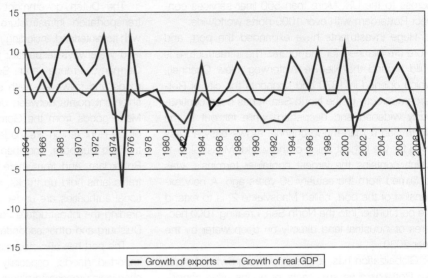

(ANNUAL % CHANGE)

Note: Data for 2009 are preliminary estimates.

Source: *Overview of developments in the international trading environment, Annual Report* by the Director-General, WTO document # WT/TPR/OV/12, November 18 (www.wto.org), copyright © World Trade Organization, 2009. Reproduced with permission.

and institution-based views – can help us understand the crucial issue of why nations trade. The remainder of the chapter deals with (1) theories and (2) institutions shaping international trade. As before, debates and implications for action follow.

WHY DO NATIONS TRADE?

Most nations actively participate in international trade – consisting of exporting (selling abroad) and importing (buying from abroad). Table 5.1 provides a snapshot of the top-ten exporting and importing nations in the two main sectors: goods and services. In goods exports, Germany has for many years been the world champion, though China took the lead during the recession of 2009. In imports of goods, Germany is the second largest importer behind the USA. In services, the USA is both the largest exporter and the largest importer. Britain and Germany come second as service exporter and importer, respectively.

Relative to domestic trade, international trade entails much greater complexities. So why do nations go through these troubles to trade internationally? Without getting into details, we can safely say that there must be economic gains from trade. More important, such gains must be shared by *both* sides; otherwise, there would be no willing exporters and importers. In other words, international trade is a *win-win* deal. Why are there gains from trade? How do nations benefit from such gains? The remainder of the chapter will answer these questions.

Before proceeding, it is important to clarify that 'nations trade' is a misleading statement. A more accurate expression would be: 'firms from different nations trade'.[1] Unless different governments directly buy and sell from each other (such as arms sales), the majority of trade is conducted by firms, which pay little attention to country-level ramifications. For example, oil majors such as Shell and BP import oil to Europe (often Rotterdam) and do not export much. They thus directly

LEARNING OBJECTIVE

1 use the resource-based and institution-based views to explain why nations trade

Exporting
Selling abroad.

Importing
Buying from abroad.

Table 5.1 Leading trading nations

	Top 10 Exporters of goods	Value (€ billion)	World share (%)		Top 10 Importers of goods	Value (€ billion)	World share (%)
1	Germany	1 000	9.1%	1	USA	1 479	13.2%
2	China	975	8.9%	2	Germany	823	7.3%
3	USA	888	8.1%	3	China	773	6.9%
4	Japan	534	4.9%	4	Japan	520	4.6%
5	Netherlands	433	3.9%	5	France	483	4.3%
6	France	416	3.8%	6	United Kingdom	431	3.8%
7	Italy	369	3.3%	7	Netherlands	392	3.5%
8	Belgium	326	3.0%	8	Italy	380	3.4%
9	Russia	322	2.9%	9	Belgium	321	2.9%
10	United Kingdom	313	2.8%	10	South Korea	297	2.7%
	World total	11 010	100%		World total	11 207	100%

	Top 10 Exporters of services	Value (€ billion)	World share (%)		Top 10 Importers of services	Value (€ billion)	World share (%)
1	USA	356	14.0%	1	USA	249	10.5%
2	United Kingdom	193	7.6%	2	Germany	195	8.2%
3	Germany	160	6.3%	3	United Kingdom	136	5.7%
4	France	104	4.1%	4	Japan	113	4.8%
5	Japan	98	3.9%	5	China	104	4.4%
6	Spain	98	3.8%	6	France	94	3.9%
7	China	94	3.7%	7	Italy	90	3.8%
8	Italy	84	3.3%	8	Spain	74	3.1%
9	India	72	2.8%	9	Ireland	70	3.0%
10	Netherlands	70	2.7%	10	South Korea	63	2.7%
	World total	2 546	100%		World total	2 369	100%

Source: Adapted from *World Trade Report 2009* (Appendix Table 5 and Table 3). All data from 2008, copyright © World Trade Organization, 2009.

Trade deficit
An economic condition in which a nation imports more than it exports.

Trade surplus
An economic condition in which a nation exports more than it imports.

Balance of trade
The aggregation of importing and exporting that leads to the country-level trade surplus or deficit.

contribute to the trade deficit (a surplus of imports over exports) of countries like France and Spain, which is something their government may not like. However, in most countries, governments cannot tell firms, such as Shell or BP, what to do (and not to do) unless firms engage in illegal activities. Therefore, we need to be aware that when we ask 'Why do nations trade?' we are really asking 'Why do firms from different nations trade?' When discussing imbalance of trade where Germany and China run a trade surplus (a surplus of exports over imports), we are really referring to thousands of firms buying from and selling to Germany and China, which also have thousands of firms buying from and selling to other countries. The aggregation of such buying (importing) and selling (exporting) by both sides leads to the country-level balance of trade – namely, whether a country has a trade surplus or deficit.

Having acknowledged the limitations of statements such as 'nations trade', we will still use them. This is not only because these expressions have been commonly used but also because they serve as a shorthand version of the more accurate but more cumbersome ones such as 'firms from different nations trade'. This clarification does enable us to use the two *firm-level* perspectives introduced earlier – namely, the resource- and institution-based views – to shed light on why nations trade.

Recall from Chapter 4 that resources and capabilities determine the competitive advantage of a firm. Applied to international trade, this insight suggests that firms use their resources and capabilities to produce goods and services that have a competitive advantage in markets abroad, and hence they export. Firms abroad have different resources and capabilities, and thus export different products – which leads to mutually beneficial flows of exports and imports. Theories of international trade explore in more detail why this is so.

Further, recall from Chapters 2 and 3 that numerous politically and culturally derived rules of the game, known as institutions, constrain individual and firm behaviour. In international trade, various regulations in form of both tariffs and non-tariff barriers (NTBs) that create trade barriers around the world. On the other hand, we also see the rise of rules that facilitate trade, such as those promoted by the World Trade Organization (WTO – see Chapter 9). Explanations of the actual flows of trade thus need to consider these institutions.

The remainder of this chapter expands on these two perspectives.

Classical trade theories
The major theories of international trade that were advanced before the 20th century, which consist of mercantilism, absolute advantage and comparative advantage.

Modern trade theories
The major theories of international trade that were advanced in the 20th century, which consist of product life cycle, strategic trade and national competitive advantage.

Theory of mercantilism
A theory that holds the wealth of the world (measured in gold and silver) is fixed and that a nation that exports more and imports less would enjoy the net inflows of gold and silver and thus become richer.

THEORIES OF INTERNATIONAL TRADE

Theories of international trade provide one of the oldest, richest and most influential bodies of economics. In this section, we briefly review major theories of international trade in the order in which they evolved: (1) mercantilism, (2) absolute advantage, (3) comparative advantage, (4) product life cycle, (5) strategic trade and (6) national competitive advantage. The first three are often regarded as classical trade theories, and the last three are viewed as modern trade theories.

Mercantilism

In the 1600s and 1700s, international trade was widely regarded as a zero-sum game. Politicians like French statesman Jean-Baptiste Colbert believed in the theory of mercantilism, which suggests that the wealth of the world (measured in gold and silver at that time) was fixed and that a nation that exported more and imported less would enjoy the net inflows of gold and silver and thus become richer. On the other hand, a nation experiencing a trade deficit would see its gold and silver flowing out and, consequently, would become poorer. The implication? Exports are good; imports are bad.

Although mercantilism is largely discredited by scholars, it is not an extinct dinosaur. Very much alive, mercantilism is the direct intellectual ancestor of modern-day protectionism, which is the idea that governments should actively protect domestic industries from imports and vigorously promote exports. During the recession of 2009, many politicians advocated mercantistic policies to (in the short run) protect jobs in their own country.

Absolute advantage

The theory of absolute advantage, advocated by Adam Smith in his *The Wealth of Nations* in 1776, opened the floodgates of the free trade movement that is still going on today. Smith argued that in the aggregate, it is the 'invisible hand' of markets, rather than governments, that should determine the scale and scope of economic activities. Thus the principles of a market economy (Chapter 2) should apply for international trade as they apply for domestic trade. By trying to be self-sufficient and to (inefficiently) produce a wide range of goods, mercantilist policies *reduce* the wealth of a nation in the long run. Smith thus argued for free trade, which is the idea that free market forces should determine how much to trade with little (or no) government intervention.

Specifically, Smith proposed a theory of absolute advantage: Under free trade, each nation gains by specializing in economic activities in which a nation has absolute advantage. What is absolute advantage? It is the economic advantage one nation enjoys that is absolutely superior to other nations. For example, Smith argued that because of better soil, water and weather, Portugal enjoyed an absolute advantage over England in the production of grapes and wines. Likewise, England had an absolute advantage over Portugal in the production of sheep and wool. England could grow grapes at a greater cost and with much lower quality. Smith suggested that England should specialize in sheep and wool, Portugal should specialize in grapes and wines, and they should trade with each other. Smith's greatest insights were in the argument (1) that by specializing in the production of goods for which each has an absolute advantage, both can produce more, and (2) that by trading, both can benefit more. In other words, international trade is not a zero-sum game as suggested by mercantilism. It is a *win-win* game.

How can this be? Let us use an example with hypothetical numbers (Figure 5.2 and Table 5.2). For the sake of simplicity, assume there are only two nations in the

Protectionism
The idea that governments should actively protect domestic industries from imports and vigorously promote exports.

Free trade
Trade uninhibited by trade barriers.

Theory of absolute advantage
A theory suggesting that under free trade, each nation gains by specializing in economic activities in which it has absolute advantage.

Absolute advantage
The economic advantage one nation enjoys that is absolutely superior to other nations.

Figure 5.2 Absolute advantage

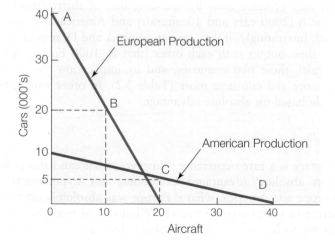

Table 5.2 Absolute advantage

Each country has 800 resources		Europe	America	Total
	resources for 100 cars	20	80	
	resources for 1 aircraft	40	20	
1. Production and consumption with no specialization and without trade (each country devotes half of its resources to each activity) (Points B and C respectively)	cars	20 000	5 000	25 000
	aircrafts	10	20	30
2. Production with complete specialization at point A and D respectively	cars	40 000	0	40 000
	aircraft	0	40	40
3. Consumption after each country trades one-fourth of its output	cars	30 000	10 000	40 000
	aircraft	10	30	40
4. Gains from trade	cars	+10 000	+5 000	+15 000
	aircraft	0	+10	+10

world: 'Europe' and 'America'. They produce only two products: cars and aircraft. Production of cars or aircraft, naturally, requires resources such as labour, land and technology. Assume that both are equally endowed with 800 units of resources. Between the two activities, America has an absolute advantage in the production of aircraft – it takes 20 resources to produce an aircraft (for which Europe needs 40 resources) and the total American capacity is 40 aircraft if it does not produce cars (point D in Figure 5.2). Europe has an absolute advantage in the production of cars – it takes 20 resources to produce 100 cars (for which the America needs 80 resources) and the total European capacity is 4000 cars if it does not make aircraft (point A). It is important to note that America can build cars and Europe can build aircraft, albeit inefficiently. But because both nations need cars and aircraft, without trade, they produce both by spending half of their resources on each – Europe at point B (2000 cars and 10 aircraft) and America at point C (500 cars and 20 aircraft). Interestingly, if they stay at points A and D, respectively, and trade one-quarter of their output with each other (that is, 1000 European cars with 10 American aircraft), these two countries, and by implication the global economy, both produce more and consume more (Table 5.2). In other words, there are *net* gains from trade based on absolute advantage.

Comparative advantage

Absolute advantage is a rare occurrence. However, what can nations do when they do *not* possess absolute advantage? Continuing our hypothetical two-country example of Europe and America, what if Europe was absolutely inferior to America in the production of both cars and aircraft? What should Europe do? What should America do? Obviously, the theory of absolute advantage runs into a dead end.

Figure 5.3 Comparative advantage

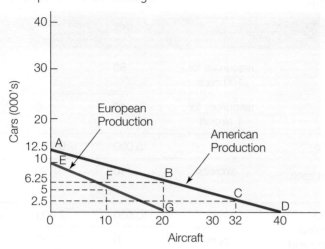

In response, British economist David Ricardo developed a theory of comparative advantage in 1817. This theory suggests that even if America has an absolute advantage over Europe in both cars and aircraft, as long as Europe is not equally less efficient in the production of both goods, Europe can still choose to specialize in the production of one good (such as cars) in which it has comparative advantage – defined as the relative (not absolute) advantage in one economic activity that one country enjoys in comparison with other country. Figure 5.3 and Table 5.3 show that Europe's comparative advantage lies in its *relatively less inefficient* production of cars: If Europe devotes all resources to cars; it can produce 10 000 units, which is four-fifths of the 12 500 cars American can produce. However, at a maximum, Europe can produce only 20 aircraft, which is merely one-half of the 40 aircraft America can make. By letting Europe specialize in the production of cars and importing some cars from Europe, America is able to leverage its strengths by devoting its resources to aircraft. For example, if (1) America devotes four-fifths of its resources to aircraft and one-fifth to cars (point C of Figure 5.3), (2) Europe concentrates 100 per cent of its resources on cars (point E) and (3) trading with each other, both countries produce and consume more than what they would produce and consume if they devote half of their resources to each activity (see Table 5.3).

Again, there are net gains from trade, this time from comparative advantage. One crucial concept here is opportunity cost – given the alternatives (opportunities), the cost of pursuing one activity at the expense of another activity. For America, the opportunity cost of concentrating on cars at point A in Figure 5.3 is tremendous relative to producing aircraft at point D, because it is only 25 per cent more productive in cars than Europe but is 100 per cent more productive in aircraft.

The theory of comparative advantage may seem counterintuitive, compared to absolute advantages. However, this theory is far more realistic and useful to explain the patterns of trade in the real world. It may be easy to identify an absolute advantage in a highly simplified, two-country world, as in Figure 5.2, but how can each nation decide what to specialize in when there are more than 200 nations in the world? It is simply too complex to ascertain that one nation is absolutely better than all others in one activity. The theory of comparative advantage suggests that even without an absolute advantage, America can still profitably specialize in aircraft as long as it is *relatively* more efficient than others. The message of comparative advantage is that is may pay to import products from countries that are

Theory of comparative advantage
A theory that focuses on the relative (not absolute) advantage in one economic activity that one nation enjoys in comparison with other nations.

Comparative advantage
Relative (not absolute) advantage in one economic activity that one nation enjoys in comparison with other nations.

Opportunity cost
Given the alternatives (opportunities), the cost of pursuing one activity at the expense of another activity.

Table 5.3 Comparative advantage

Each country has 800 resources		Europe	USA	Total
	resources for 100 cars	80	64	
	resources for 1 aircraft	40	20	
1. Production and consumption with no specialization and without trade (each country devotes *half* of its resources to each activity), at point F and B respectively	cars	5 000	6 250	11 250
	aircrafts	10	20	30
2. Production with specialization (Europe devotes all resources to cars, and America devotes one-fifth of its resources to cars and four-fifths to aircraft), at point E and C respectively	cars	10 000	2 500	12 500
	aircraft	0	32	32
3. Consumption after Europe trades 4 000 cars for 11 US aircraft	cars	6 000	6 500	12 500
	aircraft	11	21	32
4. *Gains* from trade	cars	+1 000	+250	+1 250
	aircraft	+1	+1	2

absolutely inferior in the production of these products, just as it may pay for you to delegate some of your work (see In Focus 5.1). Hence, comparative rather than absolute advantages explains the pattern of international trade.

Where do absolute and comparative advantages come from? In one word, productivity. Smith looked at *absolute* productivity differences, and Ricardo emphasized *relative* productivity differences. In this sense, absolute advantage is really a special case of comparative advantage. But what leads to such productivity differences? In the early 20th century, Swedish economists Eli Heckscher and Bertil Ohlin argued that absolute and comparative advantages stem from different resource endowments – namely, the extent to which different countries possess various resources, such as labour, land and technology. These resources are in economics known as 'factors of production'. The factor endowment theory (or Heckscher-Ohlin theory) thus suggests that nations tend to export goods whose production requires a lot of those resources that the country has a lot of. In other words, nations develop comparative advantage based on their *locally abundant* factors.[2] Numerous examples support the theories of comparative advantage and resource (factor) endowments. For instance, Brazil is blessed by its abundant resources of land, water, and weather that enable it to become an agricultural powerhouse (see In Focus 5.2). For another example, when Indian firms set up call centres to service Western clients, they use human labour, a resource that is very abundant in India, to replace some automation functions when answering the phone. In Europe and North America, labour shortage has driven the development of telephone automation technology. However, many people still prefer talking with a live person rather than buttons on a machine (press 1 for this, press 2 for that). This creates opportunities for trade in call centre services.

IN FOCUS 5.1

Comparative advantage and YOU

Despite the seemingly abstract reasoning, the theory of comparative advantage is very practical. Although you may not be aware of it, you have been a practitioner of this theory almost *every day*. How many of you grow your own food, knit your own sweaters and write your own software? Hardly any! You probably buy most you consume. By doing this, you are actually practicing this theory. This is because buying your food, sweaters and software from producers frees up the time it would have taken you to grow your own food, knit sweaters and write software – even assuming you are multi-talented and capable of doing all of the above. As students, you are probably using this time wisely to study a subject (ranging from accounting to zoology) in which you may have some comparative advantage. After graduation, you will trade your skills (via your employer) with others who need these skills from you. By specializing and trading, rather than producing everything yourself, you help channel the production of food, sweaters and software to more efficient producers. Some of them may be foreign firms. You and these producers mutually benefit because they can produce more for everyone to consume, and you can concentrate on your studies and build your tradable skills.

Let's assume that at your school, you are the best student. At the same time, you also drive a cab at night to earn enough money to put you through school. In fact, you become the best cab driver in town, knowing all the side streets, never getting lost and making more money than other cab drivers. Needless to say, by studying during the day and driving a cab at night, you don't have a life. However, your efforts are handsomely rewarded when the best company in town hires you after graduation, and very soon, as a fast tracker, you become the best manager in town. Of course, you quit driving a cab after joining the firm. The best cab driver can earn about €50 000 a year, whereas the best manager can make €500 000, so your choice would be obvious. One day, you leave your office and jump into a cab to rush to the airport. The cab driver misunderstands your instruction, gets lost, and is unnecessarily stuck in a bad traffic jam. As soon as you become irritated because you may miss your flight, you start to smile because you remember today's lecture. 'Yes, I have an absolute advantage both in driving a cab and being a good manager compared with this poor cab driver. But by focusing on my comparative advantage in being a good manager', you remember what your professor said, 'this cab driver, whose abilities are nowhere near my cab driving skills, can tap into his comparative advantage (funny, he has one!), trade his skills with me, and can still support his family'. With this pleasant thought, you end up giving the driver a big tip when arriving at the airport.

In summary, *classical* theories, (1) mercantilism, (2) absolute advantage and (3) comparative advantage (which includes resource endowments), evolved from approximately 300 years ago to the beginning of the 20th century. More recently, three *modern* theories, outlined next, emerged.

Product life cycle

Up to this point, classical theories all paint a *static* picture: If England has an absolute or comparative advantage in textiles (mostly because of its resource endowments such as favourable weather and soil), it should keep producing them. However, this assumption of no change in resource endowments and trade patterns does not always hold in the real world. In Adam Smith's time, over 200 years ago, England was a major exporter of textiles; today England's textile industry is insignificant. So what happened? One may argue that in England, weather has changed

IN FOCUS 5.2

Brazil's comparative advantage in agriculture

A pine tree in a forest in Finland needs 50 years before it can be felled to make paper. A eucalyptus tree in coastal Brazil is ready in seven. Grapes in France can only be harvested once a year. Grapes in northeastern Brazil can bear fruit twice a year. Chicken and hog farmers in Canada have to consume energy to heat the barns. Their competitors in Brazil need no energy to heat their animals' dwellings. Blessed by an abundant supply of sun, soil and water, Brazil is a pre-eminent player in agricultural products such as beef, coffee, rubber, Soya and sugar. Brazil's agricultural prowess may be the envy of many less so well-endowed countries, in Brazil it has become a source of frustration. For much of the 20th century, the Brazilian government sought to deviate from Brazil's dependence on agriculture-based commodities and to industrialize, often with little regard to comparative or competitive advantage. Their favourite policy was protectionism, which often did not succeed.

Brazil's market opening since the 1990s has let more Brazilians to realize that the country's comparative advantage indeed lies in agriculture. One commodity that can potentially transform the low prestige associated with agricultural products is sugar cane-based ethanol. Brazil is a world leader in the production of ethanol, which has been mandated as an additive to gasoline used in cars since the 1970s. A system to distribute ethanol to gas stations, an oddity in the eyes of the rest of the world until recently, now a national treasure that is the envy of the world. At present, no light vehicle in Brazil is allowed to run on pure gasoline. Since 2007, the mandatory blend for car fuels is at least 25 per cent ethanol. Brazil currently produces 18 billion litres of ethanol, of which it exports 4 billion – more than half of worldwide exports. Ethanol accounts for 40 per cent of the fuel used by cars in Brazil. As the global ethanol trade is estimated to rise 25-fold by 2020, Brazil's comparative advantage in agricultural products is destined to shine more brightly.

Sources: Based on (1) *Economist*, 2007, The economy of heat, April 14: 8–9; (2) World Bank, 2008, Biofuels: The promise and the risks, in *World Development Report 2008* (pp. 70–71), Washington: World Bank; (3) M. Jaeger, 2009, Brazil 2020, *Deutsche Bank Research*, www.dbresearch.com, November 27.

---

and soil has become less fertile, but it is difficult to believe that weather and soil have changed so much in 200 years, which is a relatively short period for climatic changes. For another example, since the 1990s, Japan turned from a net exporter to a net importer of personal computers (PCs), while Malaysia transformed itself from a net importer to a net exporter – and this example has nothing to do with weather or soil change. Why do patterns of trade in PCs change over time? Classic theories would have a hard time answering this intriguing question.

Product life cycle theory
A theory that accounts for changes in the patterns of trade over time by focusing on product life cycles.

In the 1960s, Raymond Vernon of Harvard and Seev Hirsch of Tel Aviv developed the product life cycle theory, which was the first *dynamic* theory to account for changes in the patterns of trade over time.[3] Vernon divided the world into three categories: (1) lead innovation nation (which, according to him, is typically the USA), (2) other developed nations and (3) developing nations. Further, every product has three life cycle stages: new, maturing and standardized. In the first stage, production of a new product that commands a price premium will concentrate in the USA, which exports to other developed nations. In the second, maturing stage, demand and ability to produce grow in other developed nations (such as Australia and Italy) so it is now worthwhile to produce there. In the third stage, the previously new product is standardized (or commoditized). Therefore, much production will now move to low-cost developing nations, which export to developed nations. In other words, comparative advantage may change over the lifetime of a product.

While this theory was first proposed in the 1960s, some later events (such as the migration of PC production) have supported its prediction. However, this theory has been criticized on two accounts. First, it assumes that the USA will always be the lead innovation nation for new products. This was probably true in the immediate post-WWII period, but that was an exceptional period. For example, the fanciest cell phones are now routinely pioneered in Asia and Europe. Second, this theory assumes a stage-by-stage migration of production that takes at least several years (if not decades). The reality of the 21st century, however, is an increasing number of firms now *simultaneously* launching new products (such as iPods or game consoles) around the globe.

Strategic trade theory

Except for mercantilism, all the theories that have been discussed have nothing to say about the role of governments. Since the days of Adam Smith, government intervention is usually regarded by economists as destroying value because it allegedly distorts free trade. However, government intervention is extensive and is not going away. Can government intervention actually add value? Since the 1970s, a new theory, strategic trade theory, has been developed to explain why.[4]

Strategic trade theory suggests that strategic intervention by governments in certain industries can enhance their odds for international success. What are these industries? They have high up-front costs of entry, notably investments in research and in capability development and they tend to be highly capital-intensive, which creates high entry-barriers. In consequence, these industries feature substantial first-mover advantages – namely, advantages that first entrants enjoy and do not share with late entrants. Typical examples are the jet engine industry (see Integrative

Strategic trade theory
A theory that suggests that strategic intervention by governments in certain industries can enhance their odds for international success.

First-mover advantage
Advantage that first entrants enjoy and do not share with late entrants.

© MACIEJ NOSKOWSKI/iStock

How did strategic trade policy contribute to the creation of the Airbus A380?

case 'Rolls Royce') and the aircraft industry. Founded in 1915 and strengthened by large military orders during World War II, Boeing has long dominated the commercial aircraft industry. In the jumbo jet segment, Boeing's first-mover advantages associated with its 400-seat 747, first launched in the late 1960s, are still significant today. Alarmed by such US dominance, in the late 1960s, European governments realized that if they do not intervene in this industry, individual European aerospace firms on their own would be driven out of business by US rivals. Therefore, British, French, German and Spanish governments joined together to launch and subsidize Airbus. In four decades, Airbus has risen from nowhere to a position where it now has a 50–50 split of the global market with Boeing.

How do governments help Airbus? Let us use a recent example: the very large, superjumbo aircraft, which is larger than the Boeing 747. Both Airbus and Boeing are interested in entering this market. However, the demand in the next 20 years is only about 400 to 500 aircraft, and a firm needs to sell at least 300 just to break even, which means that only one firm can be profitably supported. Shown in Figure 5.4 (panel A), if both enter, the outcome will be disastrous because each will lose €5 billion (cell 1). If one enters and the other does not, the entrant will make €20 billion (cells 2 and 3). It is possible that both will enter and clash (see Chapter 11). Airbus is promised a subsidy of, say, €10 billion if it enters, then the picture changes to panel B. Regardless of what Boeing does, Airbus finds it lucrative to enter. In cell 1, if Boeing enters, it will lose €5 billion as before, whereas Airbus will make €5 billion (€10 billion subsidy minus €5 billion loss). So Boeing has no incentive to enter. Therefore, the more likely outcome is cell 2, where Airbus enters and enjoys a profit of €30 billion. Thus, the subsidy has given Airbus a *strategic*

Figure 5.4 Entering the Superjumbo aircraft Market?

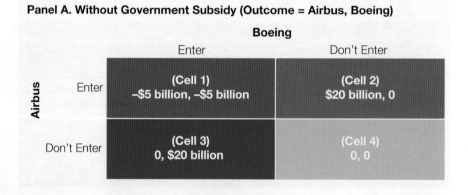

Panel A. Without Government Subsidy (Outcome = Airbus, Boeing)

		Boeing	
		Enter	Don't Enter
Airbus	Enter	(Cell 1) –$5 billion, –$5 billion	(Cell 2) $20 billion, 0
	Don't Enter	(Cell 3) 0, $20 billion	(Cell 4) 0, 0

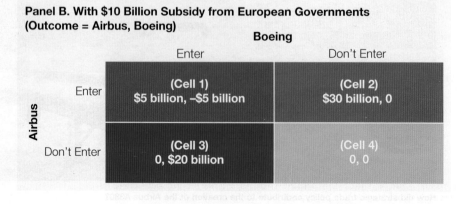

Panel B. With $10 Billion Subsidy from European Governments (Outcome = Airbus, Boeing)

		Boeing	
		Enter	Don't Enter
Airbus	Enter	(Cell 1) $5 billion, –$5 billion	(Cell 2) $30 billion, 0
	Don't Enter	(Cell 3) 0, $20 billion	(Cell 4) 0, 0

advantage, and the policy to assist Airbus is known as a strategic trade policy.[5] This has indeed been the case, as the 550-seat A380 will enter service when this book is published.

Strategic trade theorists do not advocate a mercantilist policy to promote all industries. They only propose to help a few strategically important industries. However, this theory has been criticized as impractical on two accounts. First, the argument assumes that governments have very detailed information about cost structures in an industry, and can make rational decisions. What if governments are not sophisticated and objective enough to do this job? Second, a lot of industries claim that they are strategically important. For instance, farmers in many countries successfully argued that agriculture would be a strategic industry (guarding food supply against foreign dependence or terrorists) to justify more subsidies. Overall, where to draw the line between strategic and nonstrategic industries is tricky.

Strategic trade policy
A trade policy that conditions or alters a strategic relationship between firms.

National competitive advantage of industries

The most recent theory is known as the theory of national competitive advantage of industries. This is popularly known as the 'diamond' model because its principal architect, Harvard strategy professor Michael Porter, presents it in a diamond-shaped diagram[6] (Figure 5.5). This theory focuses on why certain *industries* (but not others) within a nation are competitive internationally. For example, although Japanese electronics and automobile industries are global winners, Japanese service industries are notoriously inefficient. Porter is interested in finding out why.

Porter argues that the competitive advantage of certain industries in different nations depends on four aspects that form a 'diamond'. First, he starts with resource endowments, which refer to the natural and human resource repertoires noted by the Heckscher-Ohlin theory. For example, the coal and steel industry historically developed where coals and iron ore were found, for example in England and Wales as well as in Northern France and Western Germany. The paper industry is flourishing in Scandinavia where forests are plentiful and thus timber is readily available.

Theory of national competitive advantage of industries (or 'diamond' model)
A theory that suggests that the competitive advantage of certain industries in different nations depends on four aspects that form a 'diamond'.

Figure 5.5 National Competitive Advantage of Industries: The Porter Diamond

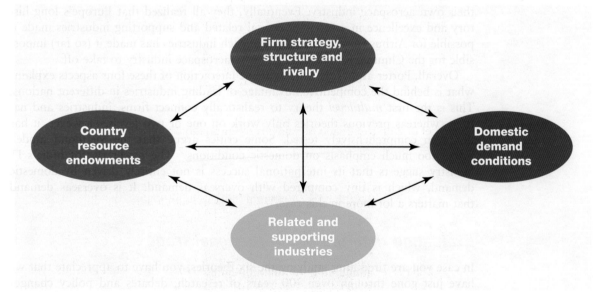

High-tech clusters are developing around university cities such as Munich or Cambridge because scientists and graduates – both scarce human resources – are readily available in these areas. The resource endowment element of the diamond thus builds on insights from previous theories. Yet, Porter argues that resource endowments are not enough.

Second, tough domestic demand propels firms to scale new heights. Why are Japanese consumer electronics firms so competitive worldwide? One reason is that Japanese consumers demand the most novel technology and the highest standards of quality for items such as mobile phones, i-Pods and games consoles. Endeavouring to satisfy such domestic demand, manufacturers are driven to satisfy these most demanding customers, which then provide them with a quality product they can also sell in other markets. In other words, abilities to satisfy a tough domestic crowd may make it possible to successfully deal with less demanding overseas customers.

Third, domestic firm strategy, structure and rivalry in one industry plays a huge role in its international success or failure. Historically, world leaders in many industries have emerged from close geographic proximity, driven by the intense rivalry between two firms. The most famous example is probably Puma and Adidas who both hail from Herzogenaurach, a small town in Germany. Another example is the Japanese electronics industry, which is driven by a *domestic* rivalry that is probably the most intense in the world. When shopping for digital cameras or camcorders, if you are tired with some 20 models in an average European electronics store, you will be more exhausted when shopping in Japan: The average store there carries about 200 models (!). Most firms producing such a bewildering range of models do not make money. However, the few top firms (such as Canon) that win the tough competition domestically may have a relatively easier time when venturing abroad because overseas competition is less demanding.

Finally, related and supporting industries provide the foundation upon which key industries can excel. In the absence of strong related and supporting industries such as engines, avionics and materials, a key industry such as aerospace cannot become globally competitive. Each of these related and supporting industries requires years (and often decades) of hard work. For instance, emboldened by the Airbus experience, Chinese, Korean and Japanese governments poured money into their own aerospace industry. Eventually, they all realized that Europe's long history and excellence in a series of crucial related and supporting industries made it possible for Airbus to succeed. A lack of such industries has made it (so far) impossible for the Chinese, Korean and Japanese aerospace industry to take off.

Overall, Porter argues that the dynamic interaction of these four aspects explains what is behind the competitive advantage of leading industries in different nations. This is the first *multilevel* theory to realistically connect firms, industries and nations, whereas previous theories only work on one or two levels. However, it has not been comprehensively tested. Some critics argue that the 'diamond model' places too much emphasis on domestic conditions.[7] The recent rise of India's IT industry suggests that its international success is not entirely driven by domestic demand, which is tiny compared with overseas demand. It is overseas demand that matters a lot more in this case.[8]

Evaluating theories of international trade

In case you are tired after studying the six theories, you have to appreciate that we have just gone through over 300 years of research, debates and policy changes around the world in about ten pages (!). As a student, that is not a small accomplishment. Table 5.4 enables you to see the 'forest'.

Table 5.4 Theories of international trade: a summary

Classical theories	Main points	Strengths and influences	Weaknesses and debates
Mercantilism (Colbert, 1600s–1700s)	• International trade is a zero-sum game – trade deficit is dangerous • Governments should protect domestic industries and promote exports	• Forerunner of modern-day protectionism	• Inefficient allocation of resources • Reduces the wealth of the nation in the long run
Absolute advantage (Smith, 1776)	• Nations should specialize in economic activities in which they have an absolute advantage and trade with others • By specializing and trading, each nation produces more and consumes more, wealth increases	• Birth of modern economics • Forerunner of the free trade movement • Defeats mercantilism, at least intellectually	• When one nation is absolutely inferior to another, the theory is unable to provide any advice • When there are many nations, it may be difficult to find an absolute advantage
Comparative advantage (Ricardo, 1817; Heckscher, 1919; Ohlin, 1933)	• Nations should specialize in economic activities in which they have a comparative advantage and trade with others • Even if one nation is absolutely inferior to another, the two nations can still gainfully trade • Factor endowments underpin comparative advantage	• More realistic guidance to nations (and their firms) interested in trade but having no absolute advantage • Explains patterns of trade based on factor endowments	• Relatively static, assuming that comparative advantage and factor endowments do not change over time
Modern theories			
Product life cycle (Vernon, 1966)	• Comparative advantage first resides in the lead innovation nation, which exports to other nations • Production migrates to other advanced nations and then developing nations in different product life cycle stages	• First theory to incorporate dynamic changes in patterns of trade • More realistic with trade in industrial products in the 20th century	• Many innovations originate outside the USA. • Many new products are now launched simultaneously around the world

Modern theories

Strategic trade (Brander, Spencer, Krugman, 1980s)	• Strategic intervention by governments may help domestic firms reap first-mover advantages in industries with high barriers to entry • First-mover firms may have better odds at winning internationally	• More realistic and positively incorporates the role of governments in trade • Provides direct policy advice	• Ideological resistance from many 'free trade' scholars and policymakers • Invites many industries to claim they are strategic
National competitive advantage of industries (Porter, 1990)	• Competitive advantage of different industries in different nations depends on the four interacting aspects of a 'diamond' • The four aspects are (1) factor endowments, (2) domestic demand, (3) firm strategy, structure, and rivalry, and (4) related and supporting industries	• Most recent, most complex and most realistic among various theories • As a multilevel theory, it directly connects research on firms, industries and nations	• Has not been comprehensively tested • Overseas (not only domestic) demand may stimulate the competitiveness of certain industries

Today, the classical pro-free trade theories seem like common sense. However, we need to appreciate that they were *revolutionary* in the late 1700s and early 1800s in a world of mercantilism. These theories attracted numerous attacks. But eventually, they defeated mercantilism, at least intellectually. Influenced by these classic theories, England in the 1830s dismantled its protectionist Corn Laws, which contributed to the surge of international trade during the first wave of globalization in the late 1800s (see Chapter 1).

All theories simplify to make their point. Classical theories rely on highly simplistic assumptions of a model consisting of only two nations and two goods. They also assume perfect resource mobility – that is, one resource removed from cars production can be moved to make aircraft. In reality, both industries require highly specialized skills. Further, classical theories assume no foreign exchange complications and zero transportation costs. So, in the real world of many countries, numerous goods, imperfect resource mobility, fluctuating exchange rates, high transportation costs and product life cycle changes, is free trade still beneficial as Smith and Ricardo suggested? The answer is still yes, as worldwide data support the *basic* arguments of free traders such as Smith and Ricardo.[9] (See the section on Debates and Extensions for disagreements.)

Instead of relying on simple factor analysis, modern theories rely on more realistic product life cycles, first-mover advantages and the 'diamond model' to explain and predict patterns of trade. Overall, classical and modern theories have significantly contributed to today's ever deepening trade links. Yet, international trade takes place in a web of national and international institutions, created by complex political processes that do not always favour the overall best arrangements.

Resource mobility
The ability to move resources from one part of a business to another.

NATIONAL INSTITUTIONS AND INTERNATIONAL TRADE

Many international institutions, such as the WTO (see Chapter 9), have been established to facilitate international trade. However, institutions created by nation states imply that as 'rules of the game', trade barriers are a persistent reality of international trade. Although some have dismantled in recent years, many remain, and new ones are invented. The global recession of 2008/09 led to an increase in protectionist actions in a number of countries.[10] Let us examine how they affect international trade, and why they have been created.

LEARNING OBJECTIVE

3 appreciate how economic and political institutions influence international trade

Tariff barriers

There are two broad types of trade barriers: (1) tariff barriers and (2) nontariff barriers (NTBs). As a major tariff barrier, an import tariff is a tax imposed on imports. A simple analysis shows how import tariffs distort international trade – and why consumers loose out.[11] Figure 5.6 uses rice tariffs in Japan as a hypothetical example to show that there are *unambiguously* net losses – known as deadweight loss.

Tariff barrier
Trade barriers that rely on tariffs to discourage imports.

Nontariff barrier (NTB)
Trade barriers that rely on nontariff means to discourage imports.

Import tariff
A tax imposed on imports.

Deadweight loss
Net losses that occur in an economy as the result of tariffs.

- Panel A: In the absence of international trade, the domestic price is P_1 and domestic wheat farmers produce Q_1, determined by the intersection of domestic supply and demand curves.
- Panel B: Because the domestic rice price P_1 is higher than world price P_2, foreign farmers export to Japan. In the absence of tariffs, Japanese farmers reduce output to Q_2. Japanese consumers enjoy more rice at Q_3 at a much lower price P_2.
- Panel C: The government imposes an import tariff, effectively raising price from P_2 to P_3. Japanese farmers increase production from Q_2 to Q_4, and consumers pay more at P_3 and consume less by reducing consumption from Q_3 to Q_5. Imports fall from Q_2Q_3 in panel B to Q_4Q_5 in panel C.

Who is better or worse off with tariffs? The gains are represented by areas in Panel C. Farmers sell more rice at a higher price, they gain area A. The governments pockets tariffs on the imports, area C. However, consumer are worse off

Figure 5.6 Tariff on Rice Imports in Japan

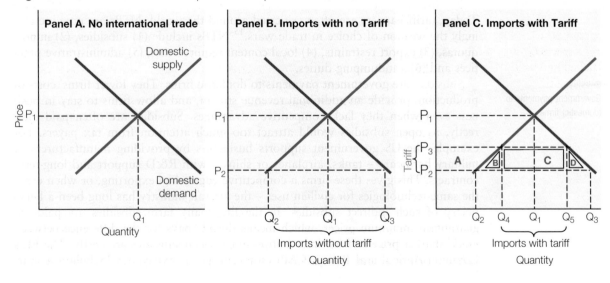

Panel A. No international trade

Panel B. Imports with no Tariff

Panel C. Imports with Tariff

having to pay higher prices, and some of them not buying rice at all, represented by the area consisting of A, B, C, and D. Hence, we can calculate the deadweight loss.

$$
\begin{aligned}
\text{Deadweight loss} \quad &= \text{Loss to consumer} - \text{Gains to farmers} \\
\text{government} \quad &\quad -\text{Tariff revenues to government} \\
&= \text{Area } (A + B + C + D) - \text{Area } (A) - \text{Area } (C) \\
&= \text{Area } (B + D)
\end{aligned}
$$

The deadweight loss (areas B and D) represent unambiguous economic inefficiency to the nation as a whole. Tariffs such as these are common around the world, not only for agricultural produce: A Microsoft Xbox 360 console that retails for about €250 in the USA costs about €750 in Brazil, after adding import tariffs.[12] In 2009, the USA slapped a 35 per cent import tariff on tyres made in China. Brazilian Xbox gamers and American tyre buyers have to pay more, and some may be unable to afford the products. While not being able to lay your arms around an Xbox will have no tangible damage, some economically struggling US drivers who should have replaced their worn-out tyres may delay replacing their tyres, which increases the possibility of fatal accidents.[13]

Given the well-known net losses, why are tariffs imposed? The answer boils down to politics. Although almost every consumer in a country is hurt because of higher import prices, it is very costly, if not impossible, to politically organize geographically scattered individuals and firms to advance the case for free trade.[14] On the other hand, certain special interest groups tend to be geographically concentrated and well organized to advance their interest. Farmers tend to be particularly powerful around the world. In Europe, they represent 2 per cent of the population, but they had a strong impact on the original design of EU rules since the 1950s, and these rules are slow to change (see Chapter 8). In Japan, although farmers represent less than 5 per cent of the population, they represent disproportionate votes in the Diet (Japanese parliament). Why? Diet districts were drawn up in the aftermath of World War II, when most Japanese lived in rural areas. Such districts were never rezoned, although the majority of the population now lives in urban areas. Likewise, in the USA, each state has two representatives in the Senate, which gives a large political weight to thinly-populated rural states such as Kansas or Wisconsin. Thus, when the powerful farm lobby speaks, governments listen.

Nontariff barriers (NTBs)

Today, tariff barriers are often criticized around the world. NTBs are now increasingly the weapon of choice in trade wars.[15] NTBs include (1) subsidies, (2) import quotas, (3) export restraints, (4) local content requirements, (5) administrative practices and (6) antidumping duties.

Subsidy
Government payments to (domestic) firms.

Subsidies are government payments to domestic firms. They lower firms' costs of production, provide an additional revenue stream, and allow firms to stay in business even when they lack competitive advantages. Subsidies are often paid indirectly, as open subsidies would attract too much attention from tax payers. For example, the US government supports businesses by providing manufacturers of military hardware – tanks, airplanes or ships – with R&D support and long-term contracts. This gives these firms a competitive edge when exporting, or when using the same technologies for civilian uses – the aircraft industry has long been a beneficiary of such indirect subsidies. In the EU, many farm subsidies are paid via guaranteed minimum prices, which means the EU pays for the difference between world market price and its 'intervention price'. Such subsidies are costly: The EU's Common Agricultural Policy (CAP) costs European taxpayers €35 billion a year, eating up 40 per cent of the EU budget.[16] European taxpayers may complain about CAP, yet the main losers are probably farmers in developing countries who cannot export their foodstuffs to the EU.

Import quotas are restrictions on the quantity of imports. Import quotas are worse than tariffs because with tariffs, foreign goods can still be imported if tariffs are paid. By constraining the volume of trade, quotas have a similar effect as a monopoly: supply is constrained and prices go up, producers earn higher rents and consumers pay more. The main difference to tariffs is that governments do not earn tariff revenues.[17] Quotas are thus the most straightforward denial of absolute or comparative advantage. For example, the textile industry in developed economies had been 'temporarily' protected by quotas for about 40 years – until 2005.[18] As soon as the protectionist Multifiber Agreement (MFA) was phased out and textile quotas were lifted on January 1, 2005, China's comparative (and probably absolute) advantage in textiles *immediately* shone. In the first quarter of 2005, the number of Chinese trousers exported to the USA rose 1573 per cent, T-shirts 1277 per cent and underwear 318 per cent.[19] In the second quarter of 2005, both the USA and European Union said 'Enough!' and slapped quotas on Chinese textiles again.

Because import quotas are protectionist pure and simple, there are political costs that countries have to shoulder in today's largely pro-free trade environment. In response, voluntary export restraints (VERs) have been developed to show that on the surface, exporting countries *voluntarily* agree to restrict their exports. VERs in essence are export quotas. One of the most (in)famous examples is the VERs that the Japanese government agreed upon in the early 1980s to restrict US-bound automobile exports. This, of course, was a euphemism because the Japanese did not volunteer to restrict their exports. Only when faced with concrete threats did the Japanese agree. Later, empirical studies of these VERs suggested that VER raised prices in *both* Japan and the US, some Japanese firms benefited from higher profits, US authorities lost tariffs revenues and US consumers were the biggest losers.[20] In part, this is because Japanese companies established production facilities in the USA and thus 'jumped over' the trade barriers (yet they still were subject to regulation, so-called local content requirements – see Chapter 6).

Import quota
Restrictions on the quantity of imports.

Voluntary export restraint (VER)
An international agreement in which exporting countries voluntarily agree to restrict their exports.

Local content requirement
A requirement that a certain proportion of the value of the goods made in one country originate from that country.

Was the EU right to slam quotas on imports of clothing from China?

Administrative practices
Bureaucratic rules that make it harder to import foreign goods.

Administrative practices refer to bureaucratic rules that make it harder to import foreign goods. Since 2008, Indonesia and Malaysia have limited imports to certain (not all) ports. India has banned Chinese toys, citing safety concerns. Argentina has revised the import licensing regime.[21] The USA tightened requirements to label the origin of pigs and pork products imported from Canada, and caused Canada to appeal to the WTO. Such apparently innocent regulation hidden in domestic legislation can have substantive impact on the (opportunity) costs of importing (see Closing Case).

Antidumping duty
Costs levied on imports that have been 'dumped' (selling below costs to 'unfairly' drive domestic firms out of business).

Finally, the arsenal of trade warriors also includes antidumping duties levied on imports that have been sold at less than a 'fair' price – or 'dumped' – and thus harm domestic firms. The argument is that foreign competitors may sell at low price until domestic firms go out of business, and then ratchet up their prices to recover losses from their aggressive market entry strategy. Although there is little economic basis for the use of anti-dumping duties, they are a frequent and powerful instrument in international trade. Once allegations of dumping have been filed, potential importers have to prove their innocence, which creates a huge administrative burden for them – and deters all but the most savvy importers (see In Focus 5.3).[22]

Taken together, trade barriers reduce or eliminate international trade. Although certain domestic industries and firms benefit, the entire country – or at least a majority of its consumers – tends to suffer. Given these well-known negative aspects, why do people make arguments against free trade? The next two sections outline economic and political arguments against free trade.

Economic arguments against free trade

Prominent among economic arguments against free trade include (1) the need to protect domestic industries and (2) the necessity to shield infant industries. The oldest and most frequently used economic argument against free trade is the urge to protect domestic industries, firms and jobs from 'unfair' foreign competition – in short, protectionism. The following excerpt is from an 1845 petition of the French candle makers to the French government:

'We are subject to the intolerable competition of a foreign rival, who enjoys such superior capabilities for the production of light, that he is flooding the domestic market at an incredibly low price. From the moment he appears, our sales cease, all consumers turn to him and a branch of French industry whose ramifications are innumerable is at once reduced to complete stagnation. This rival is nothing other than the sun. We ask you to be so kind as to pass a law requiring the closing of all windows, skylights, shutters, curtains and blinds – in short, all openings, holes, chinks and fissures through which sunlight penetrates ...'[23]

Although this was a hypothetical satire written by a French free trade advocate Fredric Bastiat over 150 years ago, similar points are often heard today. Such calls for protection are not limited to commodity producers like candle makers in the 19th century. At the height of the recession in 2009, British workers at the Lindsey oil refinery went on strike to protest against IREM, an Italian construction company, bringing its Italian and Portuguese workers into the country to conduct expansion work. British unions claimed the Italians were undercutting their wages (though no evidence was provided, and under EU rules they are bound by British law), and the issue triggered sympathy-strikes at power stations across the country.[24] On this occasion, they could not push the government into action. Yet gradually barriers to non-EU workers have been rising in the UK, like elsewhere in the developed countries.

IN FOCUS 5.3

US antidumping against Chinese apple juice concentrate producers

By Professor Lianlian Lin, California State Polytechnic University, Pomona

The US Commerce Department (in short, 'Commerce') frequently initiates anti-dumping investigations of Chinese imports. In most cases, Chinese producers were found to be guilty of dumping in the USA and had to suffer high punitive tariffs. However, tides turned in 2004 when Chinese agricultural product firms claimed victory in a case on non-frozen apple juice concentrate (AJC).

Commerce's probe into AJC production in China started in June 1999 in response to a petition filed by American apple juice producers. They requested a 92 per cent anti-dumping rate and then dropped to 52 per cent after they heard that Chinese AJC producers started to fight by responding. If the Chinese respondents did not respond to the investigation, they would obviously lose. If they chose to respond, their chances of winning the case was estimated to be 25 per cent.

China was the world's largest producer of AJC, exporting about 90 per cent of its AJC production. In 2003, AJC exports reached 417 000 tons worth US$ 254 million. The proposed anti-dumping rate of 52 per cent, if imposed, would have devastated Chinese AJC producers and apple growers. Among about 30 Chinese AJC producers involved in the US antidumping investigation, 15 companies agreed to respond and then 11 companies collectively hired experienced American lawyers with one firm dropping out later. The case took four and a half years (1999–2004) and cost about US$ 3.6 million in legal fees for the Chinese respondents.

A key point of contention was how much it would cost to produce AJC in a market economy. Since China was not considered a 'market economy', Commerce chose India and other surrogate factors of production for valuation purpose. Commerce concluded that Chinese AJC exports were sold at less than 'fair market value' and the US International Trade Commission determined that the Chinese dumping materially injured US industry. As a result, an anti-dumping rate of 15 per cent was imposed on the Chinese exporters

with one firm receiving zero tariff, while the 52 per cent rate remained the same for Chinese firms that had not responded.

Nine Chinese respondents appealed the case to the US Court of International Trade, challenging the selection of India as a surrogate country and Indian prices for juice apple and calculation of expenses. Unusually, the Court did not support Commerce's decision, and the Chinese AJC producers won. When choosing India as a surrogate country, Commerce relied on the data in a private market study prepared for US petitioners by a paid consultant because there were no official countrywide data about AJC production in India. According to the Court, secondary information might not be entirely reliable and could be used if it had probative value – serving as proving evidence. The burden of verifying secondary information such as the market study from independent sources fell squarely on Commerce. Commerce failed to adequately explain how the data in the market study could serve as substantial evidence of the Indian AJC industry as a whole and thus led to its conclusion that India was a significant producer of comparable merchandize (AJC) to be a proper surrogate country.

Accordingly, Commerce observed the Court's decisions and used Turkey as the surrogate country. It then amended the weighted average dumping margins to 1.5 per cent (3.83 per cent for four Chinese respondent firms and 0 per cent for six firms), while the same rate (52 per cent) was maintained to other Chinese AJC exporters that did not respond. To the ten Chinese respondents, reducing the punitive tariff first from 92 per cent to 52 per cent, then to 15 per cent, and finally to 1.5 per cent on average was regarded as a major victory in the US anti-dumping game whose rules were typically stacked against them.

Sources: This In Focus was prepared by Professor Lianlian Lin (California State Polytechnic University Pomona). It was based on (1) A-570-855, Department of Commerce, International Trade Administration, 2004, Certain non-frozen apple juice concentrate from the People's Republic of China: Notice of amended final determination and amended order pursuant to final court decision, *Federal Register*, 69 (30), February 13; (2) X. Wang, 2004, Taking four and a half years, Chinese agricultural product firms won US Commerce Department for the first time, *Economic Information Newspaper*, February 12, http://news.xinhuanet.com.

Infant industry argument
The argument that temporary protection of young industries may help them to attain international competitiveness in the long run.

Another argument is the infant industry argument. If domestic firms are as young as 'infants', in the absence of government intervention, they stand no chance of surviving and will be crushed by mature foreign rivals. Thus, it is imperative that governments level the playing field by assisting infant industries. This argument has been advanced in the 19th century by John Stuart Mills in Britain and Friedrich List in Germany and it periodically reappears in public debates. From a theoretical perspective, it is feasible that with the *temporary* protection by trade barriers, a young industry can develop its capabilities to a level where it can compete with more established competitors elsewhere.[25]

There is plenty of evidence of temporary tariffs seemingly helping an industry, from the US tin industry in the 19th century to machinery and electronics in Korea and Taiwan in the 1960s. More recently, the Danish windmill industry arguably got a head start because of infant industry support from the Danish government.[26] Unfortunately governments have a tendency of prolonging such tariffs when companies fail to achieve international competitiveness. For example, Latin America replied heavily on protectionism in the 1960s and 1970s invoking the infant industry argument. Yet, the tariffs remained in place for decades, seriously hampering economic development. The infant industry argument only works when firms are exposed to competition – and tariffs indeed are temporary. In reality, they rarely are quickly abandoned.

Political arguments against free trade advance a nation's political, social and environmental agenda regardless of possible economic gains from trade. These arguments include (1) national security, (2) consumer protection, (3) foreign policy and (4) environmental and social responsibility. In practice, it is often difficult to assert if these are the true reasons for government interventions, or if vested interests from the local industry are the true motivation behind these arguments. Such cases are thus often referred to the WTO for arbitration.

First, national security concerns are often invoked to protect defence-related industries. Many nations fear that if they rely on arms imports, their national security may be compromised if there are political or diplomatic disagreements between them and the arms-producing nation. The largest buyer of military hardware, the US military, is subject to strict regulations requiring that a major part of the manufacturing is done in the US even when buying from non-US suppliers. Even so, it is rare that a non-US supplier actually receives a major order. For example, in February 2008 the US Air Force selected a consortium of Northrop Grumman and EADS to supply 179 tanker aircraft. Boeing complained and politicians in Washington went into an overdrive, reasons to cancel the contract were found, and a new tender was announced in September 2009.[27] Similarly, France has always insisted on maintaining an independent defence industry, even though arguably it would be cheaper to procure from large US and British suppliers.

Second, consumer protection has frequently been used as an argument for nations to erect trade barriers. In the 1990s, many countries – even within the EU – banned British beef for fears that mad cow disease might spring over to humans. Likewise, any incidence of diseases in cattle tends to trigger swift reaction from trading partners to protect their farmers' livestock, and their consumers. In the early 2000s, a single case of mad cow disease in Canada led the USA to completely ban beef imports from Canada. For another example, American hormone-treated beef was banned by the EU because of alleged health risks. The WTO 1998 ruled against the EU in 1998 on the grounds of insufficient scientific evidence, but the EU failed to allow hormone treated beef in, and conflict dragged on until 2009.

Trade embargo
Politically motivated trade sanctions against foreign countries to signal displeasure.

Third, foreign policy objectives are often sought through trade intervention. Trade embargoes are politically motivated trade sanctions against foreign countries to signal displeasure. Many Arab countries maintain embargoes against Israel.

During the cartoon incident in 2006, a number of Muslim countries initiated embargoes against Denmark (see Chapter 3 Opening Case). The USA has trade embargos against countries like Burma, Cuba, Iran, North Korea, Syria and Sudan. Sanctions are popular even though there is little evidence that a trade embargo would be effective.[28] The only successful case was probably the anti-Apartheid sanctions against South Africa before 1994. But sanctions hurt businesses: in 2009, DHL paid a record fine of $9.4 million because it violated US embargoes and sent shipments to Iran, Sudan and Syria. Specifically, DHL, according to a US Treasury Department statement, 'may have conferred a significant economic benefit to these sanctioned countries that potentially created extraordinarily adverse harm'. What are such dangerous shipments? Condoms, Tiffany jewellery and radar detectors for cars, according to the same Treasury Department statement.[29]

Finally, environmental and social responsibility can be used as political arguments to initiate trade intervention against certain countries. Developed countries tend to have sophisticated standards that apply to all aspect of manufacturing, such as labour standards and limits on environmental emissions. Some interests groups argue that imported goods ought to be manufactured by the same standards, even where the local regulations and standards are fundamentally different. The producing countries may see such interference in their internal matters as an illegitimate trade barrier. For example, in the 'shrimp turtle case', the USA banned shrimp imports from India, Malaysia, Pakistan and Thailand because shrimp were caught in their waters using a technique that also accidentally trapped sea turtles, an endangered species protected by the USA. These nations were upset and brought the case to the WTO, who ruled in their favour, and the USA eventually complied (see Chapter 9).

DEBATES AND EXTENSIONS

As has been shown, international trade has a substantial mismatch between theories and realities, resulting in numerous debates. This section highlights two leading debates: (1) trade deficit versus surplus and (2) classic theories versus new realities.

LEARNING OBJECTIVE

4 participate in two leading debates on international trade

Trade deficit versus trade surplus

Smith and Ricardo would probably turn in their graves if they heard that one of today's hottest trade debates still echoes the old debate between mercantilists and free traders 200 years ago. Nowhere is the debate more ferocious than in the USA, which runs the world's largest trade deficit. In 2006, it reached a record US$ 759 billion (6 per cent of GDP). Then it dropped during the recession to US$ 699 billion in 2008 and US$ 375 billion in 2009, before increasing again in 2010. Should this level of trade deficit be of concern? Free traders argue that this is not a grave concern. They suggest that the USA and its trading partners mutually benefit by developing a deeper division of labour based on comparative advantage. The 2008 Nobel laureate in economics Paul Krugman argued in an earlier article in 1993:

'International trade is not about competition, it is about mutually beneficial exchange … Imports, not exports, are the purpose of trade. That is, what a country gains from trade is the ability to import things it wants. Exports are not an objective in and of themselves: the need to export is a burden that a country must bear because its import suppliers are crass enough to demand payment'.[30]

Critics disagree. They argue that international trade *is* about competition between nations – about markets, jobs and incomes. The debate in the USA tends to focus on a particular country with which the country runs the largest deficit: Japan in the 1980s and 1990s and China in the 2000s. The USA run trade deficits with all of its major trading partners – Canada, the EU, Japan and Mexico – and is in trade disputes with them most of the time (see Closing Case). Nevertheless, the China trade debate is by far the most emotionally charged and politically explosive, perhaps fuelled by the political and cultural barriers between the two countries. Table 5.5 summarizes major arguments and counterarguments in this debate.[31] Two things seem certain: (1) Given Americans' appetite for imports, the US trade deficit is difficult to eliminate. (2) Drastic measures proposed by some protectionist members of US Congress (such as slapping Chinese imports with 20 per cent to 30 per cent tariffs if the Yuan does not appreciate 'satisfactorily') are unrealistic and would violate US commitments to the WTO. As China's export drive continues, according to The *Economist*, China will be the 'scapegoat of choice' for the economic problems of USA for a long time.[32] (We will discuss the currency issue in Chapter 7.) Similar tensions have arisen within the eurozone as Germany persistently generates a large export surplus, while other countries have structural trade deficits and wish the Germans would buy more of their produce.

Classical theories versus new realities

While the first debate (mostly on China) is primarily about *merchandize* trade and unskilled manufacturing jobs that classical theories talk about, the second debate (mostly on India) is about *service* trade and high-skill jobs in high technology such as IT. Economic theorists in the 19th century certainly could not have dreamed about using the internet to send *this* manuscript to India to be typeset and counted as India's service exports.

Classical theorists and their modern-day disciples argue that the USA and India trade by tapping into each other's comparative advantage. India leverages its abundant, high-skill and low-wage labour. Americans will channel their energy and resources to higher skill, higher paying jobs. Regrettably, certain Americans will lose jobs, but the nation as a whole benefits, so the theory goes.[33]

But not so fast, argued retired MIT Economics Professor Paul Samuelson. In an influential paper, Samuelson suggested that in a more realistic world, India can innovate in the area that the USA traditionally enjoys comparative advantage, such as IT.[34] Indian innovation can reduce the price of US software exports and curtail the wage of US IT workers. Despite the availability of cheaper goods (which is a plus), the net effect may be that the USA is *worse* off as a whole. Samuelson is not an anti-globalization ideologue. Rather, he won a Nobel Prize for his research on the gains from international trade,[35] and his economics textbook has trained generations of students. Now, even Samuelson is not so sure about one of the founding pillars of modern economics, comparative advantage.

The reaction has been swift. Jagdish Bhagwati, an Indian-born, Columbia University trade expert, and his colleagues countered Samuelson by arguing that classical pro-free trade theories still hold.[36] Bhagwati and colleagues wrote:

'Imagine that you are exporting aircraft, and new producers of aircraft emerge abroad. That will lower the price of your aircraft, and your gains from trade will diminish. You have to be naïve to believe that this can never happen. But you have to be even more naïve to think that the policy response to the reduced gains from trade is to give up the remaining gains as well. The critical policy question we must address is: When external developments,

Table 5.5 Debate on the US trade deficit with China[1]

US trade deficit with China is a huge problem	US trade deficit with China is not a huge problem
Naive trader versus unfair protectionist	*Market reformer versus unfair protectionist*
• The USA is a 'naive' trader with open markets. China has 'unfairly' protected its markets	• China's markets are already unusually open. Its trade volume (merchandise and services) is 75% of GDP, whereas the US volume is only 25% – so is Japan's
Greedy exporters	*Eager foreign investors*
• Unscrupulous Chinese exporters are eager to gut US manufacturing jobs and drive US rivals out of business	• Two-thirds of Chinese exports are generated by foreign-invested firms in China, and numerous US firms have invested in and benefited from such operations in China
The demon who has caused deflation	*Thank China for low prices*
• Cheap imports sold at 'the China price' push down prices and cause deflation	• Every consumer benefits from cheap prices brought from China by US firms such as Wal-Mart
Intellectual property (IP) violator	*Inevitable step in development*
• China is a blatant violator of IP rights, and US firms lose $2 billion a year	• True, but (1) the US did that in the 19th century (to the British), and (2) IP protection is improving in China
Currency manipulator	*Currency issue is not relevant*
• The Yuan is severely undervalued (maybe up to 40%), giving Chinese exports an 'unfair' advantage in being priced at an artificially low level	• The Yuan may be somewhat undervalued, but (1) US and other foreign firms producing in China benefit, and (2) Yuan appreciation will not eradicate US trade deficit
Trade deficit will make the USA poorer	*Trade deficit does not cause a fall in the US standard of living*
• Since imports have to be paid, the USA borrows against its future with disastrous outcomes	• As long as the Chinese are willing to invest in the US economy (such as Treasury bills), what's the worry?
Something has to be done	*Remember the gains from trade argued by classical theories?*
• If the Chinese don't do it 'our way', the USA should introduce drastic measures (such as slapping 20% to 30% tariffs on all Chinese imports)	• Tariffs will not bring back US jobs, which will simply go to Mexico or Malaysia, and will lead to retaliation from China, a major *importer* of US goods and services

[1] This table is a representative sample—but not an exhaustive list—of major arguments and counterarguments in this debate. Other issues include (1) statistical reporting differences, (2) environmental damage, (3) human rights, and (4) national security, which are not discussed to make this table manageable.

Sources: Based on (1) L. Tyson, 2003, The folly of slapping quotas on China, *Business Week*, December 8; (2) *Business Week*, 2006, The runaway trade giant, April 24; (4) *The Economist*, 2005, China and the world economy: From T-shirts to T-bonds, July 28; (5) *The Economist*, 2005, America and China: The dragon comes calling, September 1; (6) O. Shenkar, 2005, *The Chinese Century*, Philadelphia: Wharton School Publishing; (7) *South China Morning Post*, 2007, US visit aims for progress on Yuan, July 30.

such as the growth of skills in China and India, for instance, do diminish the gains from trade to the US, is the harm to the US going to be reduced or increased if the US turns into Fortress America? The answer is: The US will only increase its anguish if it closes its markets'.[37]

In any case, according to Bhagwati and colleagues, the 'threat' posed by Indian innovation is vastly exaggerated, and offshoring is too small to matter much. Although approximately 3.4 million US jobs may be offshored by 2015, we have to realize that in any given year, the US economy destroys 30 million jobs and creates slightly more, thus dwarfing the effect of offshoring. Further, Bhagwati argues that higher level jobs will replace those lost to offshoring.

However, here is a huge problem: Where are such newer and higher-level jobs? Will there be enough of such jobs in Western Europe and the USA? Bhagwati has no concrete answer. For example, as Amazon launched its fanciest new product, the Amazon Kindle e-reader, no US-based producer was able to make it, and the jobs went to China, South Korea and Taiwan.[38] Ultimately, countries with a persistently high trade deficit face the question, how can we develop new capabilities that make our businesses internationally competitive – and enable us to sustain our standard of living?

IMPLICATIONS FOR PRACTICE

LEARNING OBJECTIVE

5 draw implications for action

How does this chapter answer the big question in global business adapted for the context of international trade: What determines the success and failure of firms' exports around the globe? The two core perspectives lead to two answers. Fundamentally, the various economic theories underpin the resource-based view, suggesting that successful exports are generated by firms endowed with resources and capabilities that give them a competitive edge over their foreign rivals. However, the political realities stress the explanatory power of the institution-based view: As rules of the game, institutions such as laws and regulations promoted by various special interest groups can protect certain domestic industries, firms and individuals, erect trade barriers, and make the nation as a whole worse off.

As a result, three implications for action emerge (Table 5.6). First, location, location, location! In international trade, savvy managers' job number one is to leverage comparative advantage of world-class locations. For instance, as managers aggressively tapped into Argentina's comparative advantage in wine production, its wine exports grew from $6 million in 1987 to $500 million in 2008.

Second, comparative advantage is not fixed. Managers need to constantly monitor and nurture the current comparative advantage of a location and take advantage of new promising locations. Managers who fail to realize the departure of

Table 5.6 Implications for action

- Discover and leverage comparative advantage of world-class locations
- Monitor and nurture the current comparative advantage of certain locations and take advantage of new locations
- Be politically aware to demonstrate, safeguard and advance the gains from international trade.

comparative advantage from certain locations are likely to fall behind. For instance, numerous German managers have moved production elsewhere, citing Germany's reduced comparative advantage in basic manufacturing. However, they still concentrate top-notch, high-end manufacturing in Germany, leveraging its excellence in engineering.[39]

Third, managers need to be politically active if they are to gain from trade. Although managers at many uncompetitive firms have long mastered the game of twisting politicians' arms for more protection, managers at competitive firms, who tend to be pro free trade, have a tendency to shy away from 'politics'. They often fail to realize that free trade is *not* free – it requires constant efforts and sacrifices to demonstrate, safeguard and advance the gains from such trade.

CHAPTER SUMMARY

1 Use the resource- and institution-based views to explain why nations trade:

- The resource-based view suggests that nations trade because some firms use their unique resources and capabilities to produce goods in demand in other nations.

- The institution-based view suggests that national and international 'rules of the game' influence the actual flows of international trade.

2 Understand classical and modern theories of international trade:

- Classical theories include (1) mercantilism, (2) absolute advantage and (3) comparative advantage.

- Modern theories include (1) product life cycles, (2) strategic trade and (3) the 'diamond model'.

3 Appreciate how economic and political institutions influence international trade:

- The net impact of various tariffs and NTBs is that the whole nation is worse off while certain special interest groups (such as certain industries, firms and regions) benefit.

- Economic arguments against free trade centre on (1) protection from 'unfair' competition and (2) infant industries.

- Political arguments against free trade focus on (1) national security, (2) consumer protection, (3) foreign policy and (4) environmental and social responsibility.

4 Participate in two leading debates on international trade:

- The first debate deals with whether persistent trade deficit is of grave concern or not.

- The second deals with whether service trade will benefit or hurt rich countries.

5 Draw implications for action:

- Discover and leverage comparative advantage of world-class locations.

- Monitor and nurture current comparative advantage of certain locations and take advantage of new locations.

- Be politically engaged to demonstrate, safeguard, and advance the gains from international trade.

KEY TERMS

Absolute advantage
Administrative practices
Antidumping duty
Balance of trade
Classical trade theories

Comparative advantage
Deadweight loss
Exporting
Factor endowment theory
    (or Heckscher-Ohlin theory)

First-mover advantage
Free trade
Import quota
Import tariff
Importing

Infant industry argument
Local content requirement
Modern trade theories
Nontariff barrier (NTB)
Opportunity cost
Product life cycle theory
Protectionism
Resource (factor) endowments

Resource mobility
Strategic trade policy
Strategic trade theory
Subsidy
Tariff barrier
Theory of absolute advantage
Theory of comparative advantage
Theory of mercantilism

Theory of national competitive
    advantage of industries
    (or 'diamond' model)
Trade deficit
Trade embargo
Trade surplus
Voluntary export restraint (VER)

CRITICAL DISCUSSION QUESTIONS

1 After the 2008–09 crisis, is the trade policy of your country's government turning into more protectionist? Why?

2 What is the ratio of total volume of international trade (exports + imports) to GDP in your country? How about the ratio for the following: the USA, the European Union, Japan, Russia, China and Singapore? Do these ratios help you answer question 1?

3 As a foreign policy tool, trade embargoes, such as US embargoes against Cuba, Iraq (until 2003) and

North Korea, are meant to discourage foreign governments. But they also cause a great deal of misery among the population (such as shortage of medicine and food). Are embargoes ethical?

4 Although the nation as a whole may gain from free trade, there is no doubt that certain regions, industries, firms and individuals may lose their jobs and livelihood due to foreign competition. How can the rest of the nation help the unfortunate ones cope with the impact of international trade?

CLOSING CASE

Canada and the USA fight over pigs

by Professor Stephen Globerman, Western Washington University.

Sharing the world's longest undefended border, Canada and the USA are the best of friends. Their bilateral trading relationship is the world's largest, with $560 billion in volume. The two-way traffic that crosses the Ambassador Bridge between Windsor, Ontario, and Detroit, Michigan, equals all US exports to Japan. About 76 per cent of Canada's exports (approximately ¼ of its GDP) go to its southern neighbour, making it the largest exporter to the USA. Canadian products command approximately 20 per cent of the US import market share. In comparison, China, the second largest exporter to the USA, commands slightly over 10 per cent. Canada is also the largest importer of US products, absorbing about ¼ of US exports. The USA runs a sizeable trade

deficit with Canada, at $78 billion in 2008. Despite such a close relationship, they fight like 'cats and dogs' in trade disputes. Most recently, they have traded blows over pigs.

In an effort to tighten food labelling, the outgoing Bush Administration issued Mandatory Country of Origin Labelling (COOL) legislation. New rules published on August 1, 2008 and January 15, 2009 require US firms to track and notify customers the country of origin of meat and other agricultural products at each major stage of production, including at the retail level. Unfortunately, such a seemingly innocent move in the name of protecting consumers provoked fierce protests from the Canadian government, hog farmers and other agricultural producers. In a normal year, Canada would export approximately US$3 billion hogs (live pigs) to the USA. In the first three quarters of 2009, such exports suffered a 60 per cent drop.

The reason is that many young Canadian pigs are exported to the USA, and they are mixed and raised

Pigs in a pen at market

with indigenous US pigs for fattening and slaughter. After several months, separating the (immigrant) Canadian pigs from the (native born) US pigs is challenging and costly. The US Department of Agriculture estimates that it will cost the food industry US$2.5 billion to comply with the new rules. When facing such hassles, several major US pork producers, including the top five that account for more than half of all pork sold in the USA (Cargill, Hormel, JBS SA, Seaboard and Smithfield), simply stopped buying hogs from Canada or gradually phased out such purchases. In addition to damaging livestock exports, processed meat products from Canada, including the legendary Canadian bacon, were also broadly affected.

In December 2008, Canada requested consultation with the US governments, and they negotiated in May and June 2009 with the new Obama administration. While the USA modified some rules to alleviate Canadian concerns, the negotiations eventually broke down. Canada's frustrated Trade Minister Stockwell Day said in October 2009:

'The US requirements are so onerous that they affect the ability of our hog and cattle exporters to compete fairly in the US market. The US law leaves

the Canadian government with no choice but to escalate its first formal trade dispute with the Obama Administration by pressing charges at the WTO'.

In response, US Trade Representative Ron Dirk and Agriculture Secretary Tom Vilsack in a joint statement in October 2009 argued:

'We believe that our implementation of COOL provides information to consumers in a manner consistent with our WTO commitments. Countries have agreed since long before the existence of the WTO that country-of-origin labelling is a legitimate policy. It is common for other countries to require that goods be labelled as to their origin'.

The COOL pig fight is not the only dispute between Canada and the USA. The list of Canada's trade grievances includes 'Buy American' purchasing rules and generous US biofuel tax breaks for paper mills.

While Canada and the USA fight over item by item in their long list of trade grievances, a useful mental exercise is to ask: What if these two friendly countries stopped trading all together? Normally, scholars studying this intriguing question would have to use simulation methods based on hypothetical data to entertain what would happen if they stopped trading. Such an unthinkable scenario did take place in 2001. Immediately after the terrorist attacks on September 11, 2001, the USA panicked and closed all airports, seaports and land crossings with Canada (and Mexico). The world's largest bilateral trading relationship literally shut down. When the borders reopened days later, US officials undertook intensive inspections of commercial traffic that, among other things, delayed truck carriers for up to 18 hours. An exhaustive study found that Canadian exports to the USA in the fourth quarter of 2001 were 20 per cent lower than they would have been in the absence of the border security consequences of 9/11. Even by 2005, exports from Canada were $12 billion less than they would otherwise have been, had 9/11 and the US security responses not occurred. By the same time (2005), US exports to Canada resumed their 'normal' level. In other words, Canadian exporters will suffer disproportionate damage due to any unilateral tightening of the border by the USA – whether for security reasons or for food safety reasons. As Canadian hog producers struggle with the recession, the high Canadian dollar, a spike in feed costs and widespread swine flu fears, it remains to be seen whether cool heads will prevail when fighting over COOL.

CASE DISCUSSION QUESTIONS:

1   Why do Canada and the USA have the largest bilateral trading relationship in the world?

2   Why do Canadian products have such a large market share in the USA?

3   While 98 per cent of Canada-US trade flows smoothly, trade disputes only affect the remaining 2 per cent. Some argue that the Canadians have over-reacted in this case. What do you think?

Sources: We thank Professor Steven Globerman (Western Washington University) for his assistance. It is based on (1) I. Fergusen, 2006, *United States-Canada Trade and Economic Relationship*, Washington: Congressional Research Service; (2) *Globe and Mail*, 2009, Canada turns to WTO over US label law, October 8: B7; (3) S. Globerman & P. Storer, 2008, *The Impacts of 9/11 on Canada-US Trade*, Toronto: University of Toronto Press; (4) *Pig Progress*, 2009, US-COOL dispute proceeds by WTO, October 8, www.pigprogress.net; (5) United States – certain country of origin labelling (COOL) requirements – request for the establishment of a panel by Canada, WTO document #WT/DS38418, www.wto.org.

RECOMMENDED READINGS

J.N. Bhagwati, A. Panagariya, & T. Sribivasan, 2004, The muddles over outsourcing, *Journal of Economic Perspectives*, 18, 93–114 – A recent statement of the benefits of free trade, applied to the question of outsourcing.

R.C. Feenstra, 2004, *Advanced International Trade: Theory and Evidence, Princeton*: Princeton University Press – A specialized textbook that explains the theories and institutions of international trade.

P.R. Krugman & M. Obstfeld, 2009, *International Economics: Theory and Practice*, 7th ed, Boston: Pearson. – A textbook that covers international trade extensively.

P. Rivoli, 2005, *The Travels of a T-shirt in the Global Economy*, Hoboken: Wiley – An economist is tracing and explaining the interdependencies of international trade using the case of a T-shirt.

P. Samuelson, 2004, Where Ricardo and Mill rebut and confirm arguments of mainstream economists supporting globalization, *Journal of Economic Perspectives*, 18, 135–146 – An esteemed international trade economists outlining some concerns regarding free trade.

NOTES:

"FOR JOURNAL ABBREVIATION, PLEASE SEE PAGE XXVI-XXVII."

1 J. Baggs & J.A. Brander, 2006, Trade liberalization, profitability and financial leverage, *JIBS*, 37: 196–211; also see A.B. Bernard, J.B. Jensen, S.J. Redding & P.K. Schott, 2007, Firms in international trade, *JEP*, 31(3); 105–130.

2 B. Ohlin, 1933, *Interregional and International Trade*, Cambridge, MA: Harvard University Press. In this work, Ohlin summarized and extended E. Heckscher's research first published in 1919. Another implication of this theory is that trade does not benefit everyone in an economy, but only those who own the relatively abundant resources.

3 R. Vernon, 1966, International investments and international trade in product life cycle, *QJE*, May: 190–207; S. Hirsch, 1975, The product cycle model of international trade, *OBES*, 37, 305–317.

4 J.A. Brander & B. Spencer, 1985, Export subsidies and international market share rivalry, *JIE*, 18: 83–100; P. Krugman (ed.), 1986, *Strategic Trade Policy and the New International Economics,* Cambridge, MA: MIT Press; J.A. Brander, 1995, Strategic trade policy, NBER Working Paper #W5020.

5 P. Krugman, 1994, *Peddling Prosperity*, New York: Norton.

6 M. Porter, 1990, *Competitive Advantage of Nations*, New York: Free Press.

7 J. Dunning, 1993, *The Globalization of Business*, London: Rutledge; H. Moon, A. Rugman & A. Verbeke, 1998, A generalized double diamond approach to the global competitiveness of Korea and Singapore, *IBR*, 7: 135–151; H. Davies & P.D. Ellis, 2001, Porter's *Competitive Advantage of Nations*: Time for the final judgment? *JMS*, 37: 1189–1215.

8 D. Kapur & R. Ramamurti, 2001, India's emerging competitive advantage in services, *AME*, 15 (2): 20–32.

9 R.E. Baldwin, 1992, Measureable dynamic gains from trade, *JPE*, 100, 162–174; D.M. Bernhofen & J.C. Brown, 2005, An empirical assessment of the comparative advantage gains from trade, *AER*, 95: 208–225.

10 *The Economist*, 2009, Globalisation and trade: The nuts and bolts come apart, March 28; *The Economist*, 2009, World trade: unpredictable tides, July 15.

11 R.C. Feenstra, 1992, How costly is protectionism, *JEP,* 6, 159–178.

12 *Business Week*, 2009, Seeking the next billion gamers, July 6: 54.

13 Tire Industry Association (TIA), 2009, Tire Industry Association expresses disappointment with President's decision concerning Chinese tire tariff, September 14, Bowie, MD: TIA, www.tireindustry.org.

14 J.N. Bhagwati, 2004, *In Defense of Globalization*, New York: Oxford University Press.

15 D. Hanson, 2010, *Limits to Free Trade*, Cheltenham: Elgar.

16 *The Economist*, 2005, Special Report: The EU's agricultural policy, December 10; *The Economist*, 2009, Charlemagne: Milk and other stupidies, February 14.

17 R.C. Feenstra, 1992, *as above*.

18 H. Nordas, 2004, The global textile and clothing industry beyond the Agreement on Textiles and Clothing (p. 34), Discussion paper no. 5, Geneva: WTO Secretariat.

19 *The Economist*, 2005, The textile industry: The great stitch-up, May 28.

20 S. Berry, J. Levinsohn & A. Pakes, 1999, Voluntary export restrains on automobiles, *AER*, 8, 400–430.

21 *The Economist*, 2009, Globalisation and trade: The nuts and bolts come apart, March 28.

22 T. Klitgaard & K. Schiele, 1998, Free trade vs fair trade, *CIEF*, 4, 1–6; J.P. Lindeque, 2007, A firm perspective of anti-dumping and countervailing duty cases in the United States of America, *JWT*, 41, 559–579.

23 F. Bastiat, 1964, *Economic Sophisms*, A. Goddard (ed. and trans.), New York: Van Nostrand.

24 *The Economist*, 2009, Industrial action: Discontents, wintry and otherwise, February 19.

25 P. Dasgupta & J. Stiglitz, 1988, Learning-by-doing, market structure and industrial and trade policies, *OEP*, 40, 246–268.

26 J.D. Hansen, C. Jensen & E.S. Madsen, 2003, The establishment of the Danish windmill industry, *RWE*, 139: 329–1347.

27 *The Economist*, 2008, Boeing v Airbus: This time it's war, January 31; *The Economist*, 2009, Airbus and Boeing resume the feud: Hard pounding, June 18.

28 G. Hufbauer, J. Schott & K. Elliott, 2007, *Economic Sanctions Reconsidered*, 3rd ed., Washington, DC: Peterson Institute for International Economics.

29 *USA Today*, 2009, DHL will pay $9.4M fine to settle shipping dispute, August 7: 2A.

30 P. Krugman, 1993, What do undergrads need to know about trade? (p. 24), *AER*, 83: 23–26.

31 O. Shenkar, 2005, *The Chinese Century*, Philadelphia: Wharton School Publishing; M. Feldstein, 2008, Resolving global imbalance, *JEP*, 22(3), 113–125.

32 *The Economist*, 2003, China and the world economy: Tilting at dragons, October 25; *The Economist*, 2007, Trade and the economy: America's fear of China, May 17; The Economist, 2010, How to stop a currency war, October 16.

33 C. Mann, 2003, *Globalization of IT Services and White Collar Jobs*, Washington, DC: Institute for International Economics.

34 P. Samuelson, 2004, Where Ricardo and Mill rebut and confirm arguments of mainstream economists supporting globalization, *JEP*, 18 (3): 135–146.

35 P. Samuelson, 1962, The gains from international trade once again, *EJ*, 72: 820–829.

36 J.N. Bhagwati, A. Panagariya, & T.N. Srinivasan, 2004, The muddles over outsourcing, *JEP*, 18 (4): 93–114.

37 J.N. Bhagwati & A. Panagariya, 2004, Trading opinions about free trade (p. 20), *Business Week*, December 27.

38 G. Pisano & W. Shih, 2009, Restoring American competitiveness, *HBR*, July–August: 114–125.

39 B. Venohr & K.E. Meyer, 2009, Uncommon common sense, *BSR*, 20, 38–43.

CHAPTER SIX

INVESTING ABROAD DIRECTLY

© Terraxplorer/iStock

LEARNING OBJECTIVES

After studying this chapter you should be able to:

1   Understand the vocabulary associated with foreign direct investment (FDI).

2   Explain how ownership, location and internalization (OLI) advantages lead to FDI.

3   Explain how home and host country institutions affect FDI.

4   Appreciate the benefits and costs of FDI to host and home countries.

5   Participate in two leading debates on FDI.

6   Draw implications for action.

OPENING CASE

Spanish MNEs enter the global stage

Spanish Multinational Enterprises (MNEs) have been a relative latecomer to international business. Yet by 2008, Spain had become the 6th largest recipient of foreign direct investment (FDI), and the 8th largest source of FDI. Foreign firms' stock of FDI in Spain had grown from €201 billion in 2001 to €454 billion in June 2009, while Spanish firms owned €455 billion of FDI stock abroad, up from €264 billion in 2001.

Spain was a relatively closed and less advanced economy during its years of dictatorship, which ended only in 1975. With the introduction of democracy, liberalization and opening of the economy progressed, and Spain started to catch up with the rest of Western Europe. Since the early 1980s, liberalization and privatization increased competition from foreigners enter-ing Spain, but also propelled Spanish enterprises to compete abroad. EU membership in 1986, the EU common market in effect from 1993 and the adoption of the euro in 1999 further levelled barriers to trade and investment.

In the 1990s, Spanish MNEs expanded abroad. Some entered other European countries to benefit from the easier access of the EU common market, while many focusing especially in Latin America exploiting the similarities of language, culture and development process. Moreover, Latin America was undergoing privatization and liberalization processes not unlike Spain's experience a decade earlier. Hence, business leaders, especially in the banking and utilities industries, saw opportunities to enter new markets that were not too different from Spain, and to contrib-

How did Spanish bank Santander become a common sight on British high streets?

© ICP/Alamy

ute their experiences and competences to the industrial development of their hosts. This drive into Latin America was led by six of the largest companies in Spain who accounted for over 90 per cent of all Spanish FDI in that region: Banco Santander and BBVA in banking, Endesa and Iberdola in public utilities, Repsol in oil and gas as well as Telefónica, Spain's main telephone operator. Telefónica alone spend about €70 billion, though the value of this investment suffered substantial losses in the early 2000s before the business turned profitable towards the end of the decade. In the years 1999 and 2000, Spanish firms invested more than US firms in Latin America, while Spain accounted for more than half of the EU's investment in Latin America.

In the early 2000s, Spanish MNEs refocused their attention to Western Europe, exploiting the opportunities of market integration and expansion in the EU. Especially consumer goods and tourism businesses expanded from Spain to other parts of Europe. For example, the entrepreneurial start-ups in the fashion industry like Inditex (owner of Zara), successfully entered the international stage by pioneering new concepts of fast fashion, expanding first across Europe, and then to other parts of the world. Thus, the pattern of FDI from Spain became more geographically diversified by reducing the strong focus on Latin America (Figure 6.1).

The leading Spanish MNEs are concentrated in several industries. In Banking, BBVA and Santander have become market leaders in many countries of Latin America. Starting the 1990s with little international experience, they became the largest foreign banks in Latin America through some 20 acquisitions. More recently, Santander made several acquisitions in the UK, Abbey National in 2004 followed in 2009 by two mortgage banks who faltered during the financial crisis. These acquisitions made Santander one of the largest retail banks in the UK, serving about 25 million customers through its 1300 branches. Meanwhile, Santander acquired Sovereign Bankcorp to build a bridgehead in the USA, the world's largest financial market.

In the energy sector, privatized companies are leading the international expansion. FDI in this sector is often in form of acquisitions, which are driven by opportunities such as the privatization of the local electricity industry. For example, Endesa, an electric utilities operator started its international acquisition spree with a major investment in 1997 in Chile, which was first Latin American country to create a legal framework for FDI that reduced the business risk to acceptable levels. Endesa subsequent became market leader in Chile, Argentina and Peru. By 2009, Endesa derived 42 per cent of its turnover from Latin America. More recently, entrepreneurial private firms

Figure 6.1 Spanish outward FDI flows

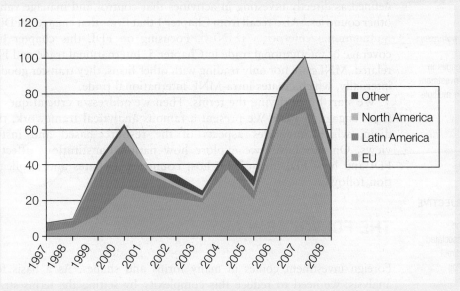

such as NaturEner have become major players in renewable energies, in particular operating wind parks.

In the construction sector, companies like Ferrovial, ACS and Sacyr Vallehermoso have grown on the back of the construction boom, while expanding into the operation of infrastructure such as motorways or airports, moving away from construction and into services. In the 2000s, Ferrovial in particular has embarked in a major acquisition drive abroad with two objectives: (1) to reduce its dependence on the Spanish market, and (2) to reduce the volatility of its revenues, which previously were derived mainly from the very cyclical construction industry. Across Europe, Ferrovial acquired construction businesses such as Amey in the UK and Budimex in Poland as well as airport operators such as Swissport in Switzerland and BAA in the UK. Many UK airports such as Heathrow and Gatwick are thus run by this Spanish MNE. In fact, the UK authorities are so concerned about Ferrovial's market power that they put it under pressure to sell some of the airports.

At the same time, Latin American business such as Mexican cement maker CEMEX, use Spain as a spring board to European markets. CEMEX originally established it Spanish operations as a means to access European capital markets and thus to lower its capital costs. Since then, CEMEX has used Spain as a basis to expand across Europe, and it still uses Spain as basis for its regional headquarters. Itself a foreign investor in Spain, CEMEX thus is also a major outward foreign investor from Spain.

Sources: (1) J.I. Galan, J. Gonzáles-Benito & J.A. Zuñiga, 2007, Factors determining the location decisions of Spanish MNEs, *JIBS*, 38, 975–997; (2) P. Ghemawat, 2007, *Redefining Global Strategy*, Cambridge, MA, Harvard Business School Press; (3) *The Economist*, 2007, Spanish business: Conquistadores on the beach, May 5; (4) P. Toral, 2008, The Foreign Direct Investments of Spanish Multinational Enterprises in Latin America, *JLAS*, 40, 513–544; (5): N. Puig & P.F. Pérez, 2009, A silent revolution: The internationalization of large Spanish family firms, *BH*, 51, 462–483; (6) *The Economist*, 2009, Spanish companies in Latin America: A good bet? May 2; (7) Bank of Spain website (www.bde.es, accessed December 2009).

Foreign direct investment (FDI)
Investment in controlling and managing value-added activities in other countries.

Multinational enterprise (MNE)
A firm that engages in foreign direct investment and operates in multiple countries.

Why are Spanish firms increasingly interested in investing in FDI in Latin America and Europe? Is it because of the push of high labour costs at home? The pull of low labour costs and lucrative markets abroad? Or both? Why do they choose direct investment rather than trade (Chapter 5) or financial investment (Chapter 7) when operating abroad? Why are these particular firms investing abroad, while other domestically successful firms are not? Recall from Chapter 1 that foreign direct investment (FDI) is defined as directly investing in activities that control and manage value creation in other countries.[1] Also recall from Chapter 1 that firms that engage in FDI are known as multinational enterprises (MNEs). Focusing on FDI, this chapter builds on our coverage of international trade in Chapter 5. International trade and FDI are closely related. MNEs are not only trading with other firms, they transfer goods and services internally, which creates intra-MNE international trade.

We start by clarifying the terms. Then we address a crucial question: Why do firms engage in FDI? We present a famous analytical framework, the OLI paradigm, which integrates aspects of the resource-based and institution-based views. On this basis, we explore how national institutions affect the flow of FDI and how FDI impacts on host countries. Debates and implications for action follow.

LEARNING OBJECTIVE

1 understand the vocabulary associated with foreign direct investment (FDI)

THE FDI VOCABULARY

Foreign investment comes in many forms and shapes. As a basis for systematic analysis, we need to reduce this complexity by setting the terms straight. Specifically, we will discuss (1) the key word is D, (2) horizontal versus vertical FDI, (3) FDI flow and stock and (4) MNE versus non-MNE.

The key word is D

There are two primary kinds of international investment: FDI and foreign portfolio investment (FPI). FPI refers to investment in a portfolio of foreign securities such as stocks and bonds that do not entail the active management of foreign assets. Essentially, FPI is 'foreign *indirect* investment'. In contrast, the key word in FDI is D (direct) – namely, the direct hands-on management of foreign assets. Undertaking FPI is normally not a full time job. If you own foreign stocks and bonds, you don't need to do anything else – just collect your dividends or interest. In contrast, engaging in FDI requires substantial resource commitments – including managerial time to oversee the operations – you have to 'get your feet wet' by actively managing foreign operations. In other words, foreign direct investors participate in the strategic decision-making of the local firm.

For statistical purposes, FDI is defined by the United Nations as involving an equity stake of 10 per cent or more in a foreign-based enterprise.[2] Hence, FDI includes joint-ventures, that is operations with shared ownership by several domestic or foreign companies. Larger equity stakes, ideally 100 per cent, give foreign investor more control over the operation. However, investors like to share control under certain circumstances, for example when both partners contribute intangible resources to the business, as we shall discuss in Chapter 12.

Horizontal and vertical FDI

FDI establishes a new operation that can stand up in various relationships to the existing company. Recall the value chain introduced in Chapter 4, through which firms perform value-adding activities stage by stage in a vertical fashion (from upstream to downstream). Horizontal FDI *duplicates* its home country-based activities at the same value chain stage in a host country through FDI (see Figure 6.2). For example, Endesa generates and distributes electricity in Spain. Through horizontal FDI, it does the same type of activity in host countries in Latin America.

If a firm through FDI moves upstream or downstream in different value chain stages in a host country, we label this vertical FDI (Figure 6.3). For instance, if VW (hypothetically) only assembles cars and does not manufacture components in Germany, but in Spain, it enters into components manufacturing through FDI (an upstream activity), this would be upstream vertical FDI. Likewise, if VW does not engage in car distribution in Germany but invests in car dealerships in France or Italy (a downstream activity), it would be downstream vertical FDI. In practice, many FDI projects have horizontal and vertical elements, yet the horizontal – vertical terminology helps to describe how different operations stand to each other, go.

FDI flow and stock

How much FDI is there? There are two ways to look at this question: by flow and by stock. FDI flow is the amount of FDI moving in a given period (usually a year) in a certain direction. FDI inflow refers to inbound FDI moving into a country, and FDI outflow refers to outbound FDI moving out of a country. Figures 6.4 and 6.5 illustrate the top ten economies receiving inflows and generating outflows of FDI. Note the position of Spain (Opening Case) as a major recipient and source of FDI.

FDI stock is the value of foreign-owned firms operating in a country, or controlled by a country's firms abroad. Hypothetically, between two countries A and B, if firms from A undertake €10 billion of FDI in B in year 1 and another €10 billion in year 2, then we can say that in each of these two years, B receives annual

Foreign portfolio investment (FPI)
Investment in a portfolio of foreign securities such as stocks and bonds.

Joint-venture
An operation with shared ownership by several domestic or foreign companies.

Horizontal FDI
A type of FDI in which a firm duplicates its home country-based activities at the same value chain stage in a host country.

Vertical FDI
A type of FDI in which a firm moves upstream or downstream in different value chain stages in a host country.

Upstream vertical FDI
A type of vertical FDI in which a firm engages in an upstream stage of the value.

Downstream vertical FDI
A type of vertical FDI in which a firm engages in a downstream stage of the value chain in two different countries.

FDI flow
The amount of FDI moving in a given period (usually a year) in a certain direction.

FDI stock
The total accumulation of inbound FDI in a country or outbound FDI from a country across a given period of time (usually several years).

Figure 6.2 Horizontal FDI

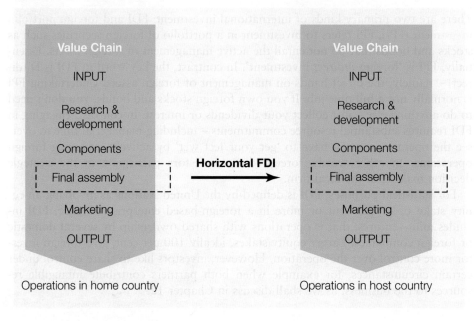

Figure 6.3 Vertical FDI

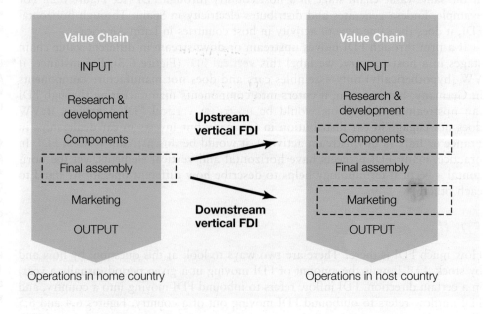

FDI *inflows* of €10 billion and, correspondingly, A generates annual FDI *outflows* of €10 billion. If we assume that there was no revaluation (for instance due to currency fluctuations), then this investment added €20 billion to the *stock* of FDI in B by the end of year 2.

Figure 6.4 Top 10 recipients of FDI inflows

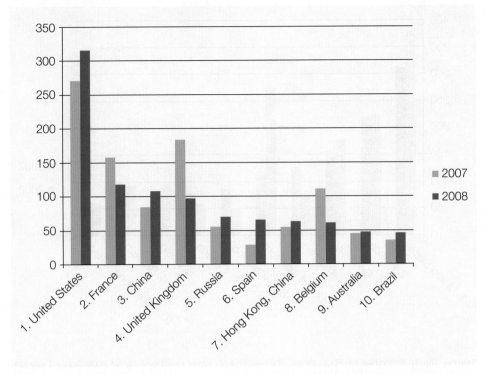

The differences between flow and stock are important. Figure 6.6 shows the fluctuation of annual FDI inflows, which have dropped during the recession of 2008/09. Emerging economies as a group attracted 43 per cent of the FDI inflows in 2008, of which Brazil, Russia, India and China (BRIC) as a group attracted 16 per cent. Firms from some emerging economies, such as those from India and China, have also become major players on the global stage, generating 20 per cent of FDI outflows worldwide. Figure 6.7 shows that the inward FDI stock had been rising until 2007. Essentially, flow is a snapshot of a given point in time, and stock represents cumulating volume.

MNE versus non-MNE

An MNE, by definition, is a firm that engages in FDI. Note that non-MNE firms can also do business abroad by (1) exporting and importing, (2) licensing and franchising, (3) outsourcing, (4) engaging in FPI or other means. What sets MNEs apart from non-MNEs is FDI. An exporter has to undertake FDI to become an MNE. In other words, Zara would not be an MNE if it manufactured all its clothes in Spain and exported them around the world. Zara became an MNE only when it started to directly invest abroad, for instance in shops and distribution centres.

MNEs existed for a long time, and they experienced an earlier peak in activity around the year 1900 (see Chapter 1). Since the 1950s, MNEs have experienced significant growth. In 1970, there were approximately 7000 MNEs worldwide. In

Figure 6.5 Top 10 economies for FDI outflows, 2007–2008

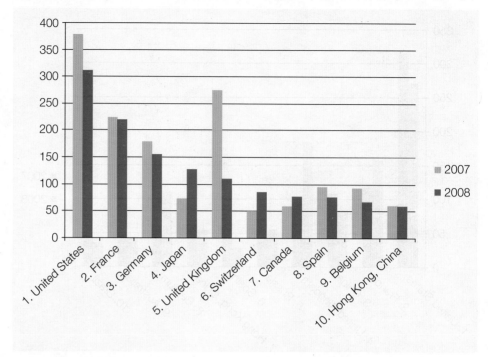

Figure 6.6 Annual FDI inflows, 1990–2008 (billions of dollars)

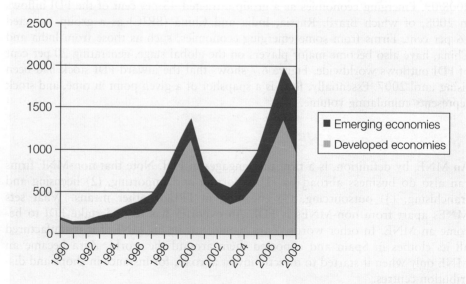

Figure 6.7 Inward FDI stock, 1990–2008 (billions of dollars)

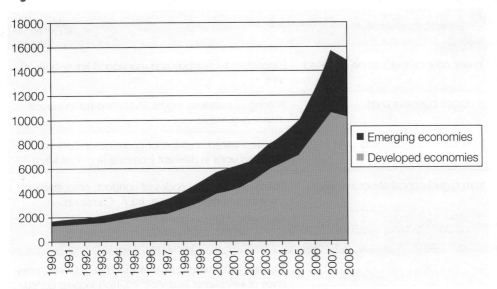

1990, there were 37 000 MNEs, with 170 000 foreign affiliates. By 2009, more than 82 000 MNEs (*more than double* the 1990 number) managed about 810 000 foreign affiliates (*almost five times* the 1990 number).[3] Clearly, there has been a proliferation of MNEs lately.

WHY DO FIRMS BECOME MNES BY ENGAGING IN FDI?

Having set the terms straight, we need to address a fundamental question: Why do so many firms become MNEs by engaging in FDI? There must be economic gains for these firms from using FDI rather than other forms of international business. What are the sources of such gains? British international business scholar John Dunning developed a frame work known as OLI paradigm, which proposes that FDI is the most appropriate form of international business if three conditions are met (Table 6.1):[4]

1 The firm possesses ownership advantages (O-advantages), defined as resources of the firm that are transferable across borders, and that enable the firm to attain competitive advantages abroad. Firms are at a natural disadvantage when competing in a foreign country, what we call the liability of outsidership (Chapter 1). O-advantages enable MNEs to overcome this liability when competing abroad.

2 The local context provides some sort of locational advantage (L-advantages), that is operation at that location allows the MNEs to create value it would not be able to create at home. L-advantages include in particular access to local markets and to resources, such as human capital and raw materials.

LEARNING OBJECTIVE

2 explain how ownership, location and internalization (OLI) advantages lead to FDI

OLI paradigm
A theoretical framework positing that ownership (O), locational (L) and internalization (I) advantages combine to induce firms to engage in FDI.

Ownership advantages
Resources of the firm that are transferable across borders, and enable the firm to attain competitive advantages abroad.

Location advantages
Advantages enjoyed by firms operating in certain locations.

Table 6.1 Oli Paradigm

Types of O-advantages	Examples
• Resources created in one country that can be exploited in other countries	• Proprietary technology and managerial know-how (e.g. VW)
• Sharing of resources across business units	• Sharing of business model and brand name across stores (e.g. IKEA)
• Capabilities arising from combining business units in multiple countries	• Logistics based on superior coordination between business units in different locations (e.g. Wal-Mart)
• Capabilities arising from organizational structures and culture	• Operation manuals, codes of conduct. organizational norms and practices (e.g. IKEA, Carrefour)
Types of L-Advantages	**Examples**
• Markets	• Size and growth consumer demand (e.g. China), presence of key clients (e.g. Antolin), high income consumers (e.g. Haier in the USA)
• Location-bound resources	• Human capital, such as a skilled labour force, natural resources, such as oil and gas deposits (e.g. Shell, BP) and agriculture (e.g. land in Africa)
• Agglomeration	• Geographic cluster of potential customers and suppliers (e.g. cars in Slovakia)
• Institutions	• Incentive schemes to attract FDI (e.g. Hungary)
I-Advantages: Types of Market Failure	**Examples**
• Asset specificity	• FDI versus exports (e.g. aluminium industry)
	• FDI versus outsourcing (e.g. Flextronics, Wipro)
• Information asymmetry	• FDI versus exports where assessing the quality of the goods is difficult (e.g. database access in consultancy)
	• FDI versus outsourcing where monitoring of the actual process is important (e.g. Nike, adidas)
• Dissemination risk	• FDI versus licensing of technology (e.g. automotive components)
	• In-house versus outsourcing of complex manufacturing processes (e.g. consumer electronics manufacturing)
• Tacit knowledge transfers	• FDI versus licensing/franchising of complex knowledge (e.g. Marks & Spencer)
• Strategic control	• FDI versus licensing as market entry strategy (e.g. Starbucks)

Source: Based on *Multinational Enterprises and the Global Economy*, 2nd ed, by J.H. Dunning & S. Lundan, 2008, Reproduced with permission from Edward Elgar Publishing Ltd and Professor S. Lundan.

3 The activities in both locations are better organized within a multinational firm rather than using a market transaction, a condition known as internalization advantages (I-advantages). They arise for example from the transaction costs of international markets. Firms may be able to organize certain activities more effectively internally. Such internalization replaces cross-border markets (such as exporting and importing) with one firm (the MNE) locating in two or more countries.

Overall, firms become MNEs because FDI provides ownership, location and internalization advantages that they otherwise would not obtain. We employ our two core perspectives introduced earlier, resource- and institution-based views, to explore the OLI paradigm.

OWNERSHIP ADVANTAGES

Do firms that are successful domestically have what it takes to win internationally? Not necessarily. In fact, domestic focus is common in a business that you probably encounter almost daily: retailing. In France, you may shop at E. Leclerc or Géant, in Germany; you may go to Tengelmann or Edeka, while in Spain your first choice might be El Corte Inglés. Few outside the country will have heard of these names. Why is that? Knowledge of local customers and suppliers along with a network of outlets are key capabilities in the business of retailing. Yet, these capabilities are difficult to transfer across borders. They are location-bound resources tied to the location. Firms with such location-bound resources are likely to grow domestically, for instance by branching out in related industries.

The essence of O-advantages is that they are *not* location-bound, but they enable a firm to compete abroad, where they face the natural disadvantage of being an outsider. In other words, O-advantages are internationally transferable, and enable the firm to achieve competitive advantages abroad. Successful retailers must have some other capabilities that indeed are transferable. These are usually managerial capabilities related to managing large stores and in coordinating complex supply chains (recall In Focus 4.2 'Wal-Mart'). For example, Swedish furniture retailer IKEA has found that its Scandinavian style of furniture combined with do-it-yourself flat packaging is very popular around the globe. IKEA thus has become a cult brand in many countries.

O-advantages can take many forms, including capabilities that the MNE has created at home and transferred abroad, capabilities arising from the multinational operations as such, and capabilities embedded in the organizational structures and culture of an MNE. For example, proprietary technological and management know-how initially enabled VW to compete abroad; nowadays these capabilities are reinforced by a global network of operations that enable VW to enter further markets. Mature MNEs usually combine these types of O-advantages, which gives them additional competitive advantages over single-country firms that only have access to resources of a single country.

LOCATION ADVANTAGES

Foreign direct investors are by definition outsiders in the location where they invest. Given the liability of outsidership, foreign locations must offer compelling advantages to doing business.[5] We may regard the continuous expansion of international business, such as FDI, as an unending saga in search of location-specific

Internalization advantages
Advantages of organizing activities within a multinational firm rather than using a market transaction.

Internalization
The replacement of cross-border markets (such as exporting and importing) with one firm (the MNE).

Location-bound resources
Resources that cannot be transferred abroad.

advantages. They come in many forms, including (1) markets, (2) resource endow-ments, (3) agglomeration and (4) institutions. This section outlines these types of locational advantages, in Chapter 12 we discuss more specifically how firms inter-act with them when choosing where and how to enter.

Markets as L-advantages

Many foreign investors are primarily pursuing access to foreign markets. Hence, they invest where they expect future demand for their products, looking for both large markets and fast growing markets. Thus, many businesses have been investing in sales operations in China, attracted by the prospect of potentially over a billion consumers, and high growth rates in recent years. Yet, why do they need to estab-lish FDI close to their markets – can't they just export? Five different reasons en-courage firms to set up operations close to their markets.

- **Protectionism** in the form of tariffs or non-tariff barriers may inhibit exports (Chapter 5). However, MNEs can quite literally jump over such protectionist barriers by setting up local production.

- **Transportation costs** continue to be a major barrier to trade in some industries, despite their drastic decline over the past century. However, products are still costly to transport over long distances if they are perishable (e.g. fresh fruit), breakable (e.g. sheet glass for windows), heavy (e.g. cement) or bulky (e.g. certain construction materials). In these industries, local production often allows serving a market at lower costs. For example Mexican CEMEX has build or acquired cement factories geographically distributed across the countries where it competes to be close to all major construction sites.

- **Direct interaction with the customer** is essential in industries where associated services such as just in-time delivery or after sales services are an essential part of the product offering. For example, the suppliers to the automotive industry need to produce near the brand manufacturers to integrate in their supply chain, which has motivated FDI by automotive suppliers such as Grupo Antolin (In Focus 6.1).

- **The production and sale of some services** cannot be physically separated, for example in hotels, banking or consultancy. The delivery of such services thus normally requires a local presence. For example, Spanish banks use local branches to serve clients in Latin America, as well as Spanish MNEs operating in the region (see Opening Case).

- **Marketing assets** may be important for a fast entry strategy. FDI enables MNEs to acquire local firms that control sought-after assets such as distribution networks and brand names. For example, Wal-Mart entered the UK by acquiring local supermarket chain ASDA, which provided an established brand name and a network of sales outlets.

Markets are important even in low-income/low-cost locations. Grupo Antolin is building factories in China *not* because it is cheap to make car seats in China (In Focus 6.1). The country's inefficiencies in advanced engineering and transportation costs of bring seats back to Europe would more than offset the savings brought by cheap labour. Antolin has one clear goal: seeking greater access to car manufac-turers in China. In reverse, Chinese household goods manufacturer Haier invested in high-cost USA to be close to its consumers and develop products suitable for North America (In Focus 6.2).

IN FOCUS 6.1

Grupo Antolin pursues OLI advantages

Grupo Antolin is a Spanish family-owned manufacturer of automotive components that emerged in Burgos, a small city in Northern Castille in the 1950s. By 2008 it had sales of €2.2 billion and over 10 000 employees and operations in 22 countries. The industry has gone through major changes in recent years as suppliers are not only delivering parts, but designing, developing and manufacturing entire 'modules'. Grupo Antolin developed into a full service supplier for interior modules, including overhead systems, door functions and seat functions. It developed unique ownership advantages in the development and manufacturing of such modules, integrating multiple technologies and materials, including in particular electronics, and associated services. Normally, modules are delivered just-in-time and just-in-sequence into the clients' assembly line.

The shift in the industry has triggered major changes in the international activities of Antolin. Traditionally, Antolin has mainly supplied VW's Spanish affiliate SEAT, and then production sites of the VW group worldwide, such as Wolfsburg (Germany) and Made Boleslaw (Czech Republic). However, dependence on one key client is risky. Antolin thus diversified its clients to include all major car manufacturers, while developing its specialization in the area of interior components. This strategy allowed strengthening of its ownership advantages in the deliver of complex modules, and exploiting these in a wider arrange of markets. Hence, Antolin invested in production facilities, logistics centres and technical-commercial offices at the locations of clients' production sites (to integrate in their supply chain) and development centres (to collaborate on product development). The location advantages sought thus were both attractive markets

(i.e. presence of key customers) and availability of technical competences.

By 2009, Antolin has been supplying all major car manufacturers, with the biggest clients being VW (28 per cent of sales), Ford (15 per cent), Peugeot-Citroën PSA (15 per cent) and Renault (13 per cent). In emerging economies, Antolin has been supplying foreign investors' assembly plants as well as emergent local firms such as Tata and Mahindra in India. At the same time, Antolin could tap into new skilled workforces, for example with its Design Centre in Pune, India. The FDI took many different forms, dependent on the local conditions, including greenfield plants, acquisitions of local companies, joint ventures and, though rarely, licensing of specific technologies to local firms. Internalization advantages in many cases suggested taking full ownership of the foreign operation to maintain control over the technology transferred.

Recent FDI projects include, for example, the acquisition of a headliner plant in Leamington Spa (UK), a greenfield plant manufacturing seat systems in Jarney (France) aimed to supply Renault, and a new plant in Ostrava (Czech Republic) to supply Hyundai. In China, Antolin established in 2008 a 50:50 joint venture with Ningbo Huaxing. This joint venture gives Antolin access to Ningbo Huaxing's clients, which includes the biggest foreign producers in China, VW and General Motors, as well as Isuzu and Honda. As a consequence of this aggressive expansion strategy, in 2009, Antolin has been operating 86 plants and 20 technical-commercial offices in 22 countries, employing over 10 000 people worldwide.

Sources: (1) M.H. Antolin-Raybaud, 2009, Antolin company presentation, EIBA conference, Valencia, December; (2) *Business Week*, 2008, Grupo Antolin Irausa enters into joint venture with Ningbo Huaxing Electronic Co, June 7; (3) www.grupoantolin.com.

Resources as L-advantages

For most of this book, we talk about resources controlled by the firm. Yet, location-bound resources are tied to a specific country, and form part of a country's L-advantages. These include natural resources like raw materials, agricultural land and geography but also created assets such as human capital and infrastructure.[6] Foreign investors try to tap into these resources and use them for their objectives.

IN FOCUS 6.2

Haier invests in the USA

Haier is China's largest and the world's fifth largest appliance maker. Since the early 1990s, Haier has launched an export push. Although Haier manufactures 250 product lines at home, its US entry, starting in 1994, sidestepped market leaders such as GE and Whirlpool by focusing on a very narrow segment – small (sub-180 litre) refrigerators that serve hotel rooms and dorms. Incumbents had dismissed this segment as peripheral and low margin. Since then, the Haier brand has successfully penetrated nine of the ten largest US retail chains, including Wal-Mart and Target.

Haier has also become a foreign direct investor by setting up factories in India, Indonesia and Iran. Since 2000, it has invested more than $30 million to build a factory in Camden, South Carolina. One wonders why a Chinese multinational, blessed with a low-wage work force at home, would want to open a plant in high-wage USA. Haier officials suggest that shipping refrigerators across the Pacific is costly and can take 40 days, thus offsetting China's wage advantage. Better to build close to the customer and place the 'Made-in-USA' tag on the product, which is a tie-breaker among US consumers. The factory brings other less tangible benefits as well. It shows a commitment to the US market, which increases retailers' confidence in carrying the brand. Also, it is 'politically correct' when Chinese exports are being criticized for taking away American jobs.

Sources: Based on (1) R. Crawford & L. Paine, 1998, The Haier Group (A), Harvard Business School case 9-398-101; (2) B. Wysocki, 2002, Chinese firms aim for global market, *Asian Wall Street Journal*, January 29; (3) M. Zeng & P.J. Williamson, 2003, The hidden dragons, *HBR*, 81 (10): 92–104.

For example, oil majors like Shell and BP invest in oil exploration at many inhospitable places around the world. More recently, Chinese MNEs have joined the quest for natural resources, not only oil and gas, but also in agriculture (In Focus 6.3).

Some of these resources are controlled by local firms, others are available on local markets, and a few may even be free (such as the sunshine that a solar energy plant might exploit). If resources are controlled by local firms, such as research teams or brand names, then FDI is likely to be undertaken as JV or acquisition (see Chapter 12 for details). For example, many MNEs from emerging economies such as India and China are investing abroad to access resources that they need to compete on the global stage, in particular technology and brand names. They can enhance their competitiveness by combining their own with such resources acquired by taking over firms in Europe or North America.[7]

Agglomeration as L-advantages

Agglomeration
The location advantages that arise from the clustering of economic activities in certain locations.

L-advantages also arise from the clustering of economic activities in certain locations – referred to as agglomeration.[8] Many investors, especially those seeking innovations, like to locate in clusters of related businesses. The basic idea dates back at least to Alfred Marshall, a British economist who first published it in 1890. Advantages of locating in a cluster stem from (1) knowledge spillovers among closely located firms that attempt to hire individuals from competitors, (2) industry demand that creates a skilled labour force whose members may work for different firms without having to move out of the region and (3) industry demand that facilitates a pool of specialized suppliers and buyers to also locate in the region.[9]

IN FOCUS 6.3

Land rush in Africa

If you believe FDI only involves manufacturing and services, welcome to FDI in agriculture. Recently, many countries that export capital but import food are offshoring production to countries that need capital but have land to spare. FDI in foreign farms is nothing new. The term 'banana republics' refers to exactly this phenomenon in an earlier era: US firms like United Fruit invested in banana plantations in Central America. What is unusual is the scale of recent land deals. Since 2005, 20 million hectares (48 million acres) – an area as big as France's farmland or 20 per cent of the EU's farmland – has been acquired by capital exporting countries such as Saudi Arabia, Kuwait, United Arab Emirates, South Korea and China. They buy or lease millions of acres, grow staple crops or biofuels and ship output back home. The countries doing the selling include the world's least developed ones, such as Congo, Ethiopia, Madagascar, Malawi, Mali and Sudan.

A triggering event seems to have been the skyrocketing oil prices several years ago, which resulted in spikes of food prices around the world. In an effort to combat food price hikes, governments in major food exporting countries such as Argentina, India and Ukraine restricted food exports. Although more recently oil and food prices came down and food export restrictions were removed, food importing countries were alarmed, reaching the conclusion that the OLI advantages associated with FDI outweigh the beauty of relying on international food trade. Critics argue that these land deals are neo-colonialist 'land grabs' that are detrimental to host countries. Defenders claim these deals represent new opportunities to tap into the comparative advantages of both home and host countries.

Sources: Based on (1) *The Economist*, 2009, Buying farmland abroad: Outsourcing's third wave, May 23; (2) United Nations, 2009, *World Investment Report 2009: Transnational Corporations, Agricultural Production, and Development*, New York: UN.

Agglomeration explains why certain cities and regions, in the absence of obvious geographic advantages, can attract businesses. In particular, suppliers follow downstream manufacturers, and industry newcomers locate near industry leaders.[10] For instance, the Netherlands grows and exports two-thirds of the worldwide exports of cut flowers. Slovakia produces more cars per capita than any other country in the world, thanks to the quest for agglomeration benefits by global automakers (In Focus 6.4). Overall, agglomeration advantages stem from:

- Knowledge spillovers (knowledge diffused from one firm to others) among closely located firms that attempt to hire individuals from competitors.

- Industry demand that creates a skilled labour force whose members may work for different firms without having to move out of the region.

- Industry demand that facilitates a pool of specialized suppliers and buyers also located in the region.[11]

Knowledge spillover
Knowledge diffused from one firm to others among closely located firms.

Institutions as L-advantages

The institutional environment can also be an L-advantage, or a locational disadvantage. Countries that offer free access and equal opportunities for foreign investors are obviously more attractive to invest in than those who create barriers to foreign investors. Hence, clear and simple rules, low levels of corruption and an efficient

IN FOCUS 6.4

Car manufacturers cluster in central Europe

After the fall of the Iron Curtain in 1989, car makers in Central and Eastern Europe (CEE) faced an uphill struggle to survive in a market economy (see Chapter 8). Their workforce had strong technical skills, but they lacked managerial competences and their models were outdated. The transformation started when Volkswagen (VW) acquired an equity stake in Czech car manufacturer Skoda. Since then, automakers have pumped in more than €20 billion FDI, transforming the region into the world's newest car cluster. Fiat, Hyundai, Kia, Opel, Peugeot-Citroën, Renault, Suzuki – everybody who wants to be somebody in this industry has come. Automotive suppliers have followed brand name manufacturers, thus creating an entire network of automotive related industries in a corridor from Warsaw to Budapest. Slovakia, whose population is only 5.4 million, was forecast to produce close to one million cars annually by 2010, or about one for every six residents. About one third of Slovak exports were cars or car components.

The advantages for such agglomeration are enormous. First, hourly labour costs were €4.59 in Slovakia and €6.56 in the Czech Republic in 2006, which is significantly cheaper than the average of €25 an hour in Western Europe. Second, work ethic is stronger and rules more flexible in the east. At VW's plants on both sides of the former Iron Curtain, Slovaks work 40 hours a week, whereas Germans put in only 28 hours. In Slovakia, if automakers need to meet a surge in demand, new shifts can be arranged overnight. In Germany, negotiations with unions to boost hours may take several *months*. Thanks to low labour costs and motivated workers, VW's Bratislava factory in Slovakia is the most profitable of 42 VW plants worldwide (though low corporate taxes and transfer priceing also may have contributed to the achievement). Finally, the rise of CEE has given automakers a powerful hand to deal with unions in Western Europe. Although large-scale plant closures have not (yet) happened in Western Europe, trade unions will be reluctant to push for big pay raises when faced with such a credible threat.

Sources: Based on (1) K.E. Meyer, 2000, International production networks and enterprise transformation in Central Europe, *CES*, 42, 135–150; (2) *Economist*, 2004, European carmaking: Going east, March 26; (3) M. Jakubiak, P. Kolesar, I. Izvorski & L. Kurekova, 2008, *The Automobile Industry in Slovakia*, Commission on Growth and Development Working paper No. 29, Washington, DC: World Bank.

bureaucracy make a country more attractive to invest in.[12] We discuss these issues further when considering the institutional view in the next section.

Location-specific advantages are not constant; they grow, evolve and/or decline. If policymakers fail to maintain the institutional attractiveness (for example, by raising taxes) or if companies overcrowd and bid up factor costs such as land and talents, some firms may move out of certain locations previously considered advantageous.[13] For example, Hungary was particularly welcoming to international business in the early 1990s as many state-owned enterprises were sold directly to foreign investors. However, a decade later *The Economist* reported a change in policy. In 2009, two foreign-owned national radio stations saw their licenses reallocated to local businesses, while French utilities company Suez Environnement was locked out of their offices after alleged irregularities (but without legal process). Meanwhile, the opposition party blamed foreign investors for the country's ills and promised to review all recent deals once they are in office. Consequently, *The Economist* recommended that foreign investors think twice before committing to Hungary.[14] Hungarian economists thought this reporting to be unfair as in other cases the authorities had intervened on behalf of foreign investors – yet, who are investors going to trust?

INTERNALIZATION ADVANTAGES

A key advantage of FDI over other modes is the ability to replace ('internalize') external market relationships with one firm (the MNE) owning, controlling and managing activities in two or more countries. This is important because, compared with domestic transaction costs, international transaction costs tend to be higher. For example, obtaining information and verifying a business partner's reputation is both more costly and more time-consuming. Likewise, costs of monitoring performance are higher where language and other communication barriers arise. Enforcing a contract when a partner behaves opportunistically is more complex because laws and regulations are typically enforced on a nation-state basis. Suing the other party in a foreign country is not only costly but also uncertain (Chapter 2). In the worst case, such imperfections are so grave that markets fail to function.

High transaction costs can result in market failure – imperfections of the market mechanisms that make some transactions prohibitively costly and sometimes prevent transactions from taking place. In response, MNEs emerge as an alternative organizational form that does not rely on these imperfect (external) markets.[15] This section outlines how internalization enables MNEs to overcome market failure by discussing three types of decisions (1) FDI versus exporting, (2) FDI versus licensing and (3) FDI versus outsourcing.

Market failure
Imperfections of the market mechanism that make some transactions prohibitively costly.

FDI versus exporting

How do MNEs overcome market failure through internalization? Let us consider a simple example:[16] an aluminium smelting firm in Europe, and a bauxite mine in Latin America. The bauxite is transformed by aluminium smelters into aluminium, a critical component in many products, such as cars. Thus, the two companies may engage in international trade; the bauxite mine exports and the aluminium smelter imports the bauxite. However, the markets for bauxite are subject to market failure because the aluminium smelting plant needs to be adapted to the specific properties of the bauxite. Thus, aluminium smelters need to make an investment in their plants that is specific to the mine supplying the bauxite, a problem known as asset specificity. The specificity of the relationship between the bauxite mine and the aluminium smelter creates a dependence that could be exploited opportunistically by the bauxite mine. For example, *after* the deal is signed, the bauxite mine may demand higher than agreed upon prices, citing a variety of reasons such as inflation, natural disasters or simply rising prices. The aluminium smelter thus has to either (1) pay more than the agreed upon price or (2) refuse to pay and suffer from the huge costs of keeping expensive facilities idle. In other words, the bauxite mine's opportunistic behaviour can cause the aluminium smelter to lose a lot of money.

Asset specificity
An investment that is specific to a business relationship.

FDI overcomes such market failure through internalization. By replacing an external market relationship with a single organization spanning both countries, the MNE thus reduces cross-border transaction costs and increases efficiencies.[17] In theory, there can be two possibilities: (1) The aluminium smelter undertakes upstream vertical FDI by owning bauxite mines in Latin America, or (2) The bauxite mine undertakes downstream vertical FDI buying aluminium smelting assets in Europe (Figure 6.8, Panel A). FDI essentially transforms the international trade between two independent firms in two countries to intra-firm trade between two subsidiaries in two countries controlled by the same MNE.[18] The MNE is thus able to coordinate cross-border activities better, an I-advantage. However, in other industries, such as tin, where no such specific investments are required, firms are less likely to integrate vertically (Figure 6.8, Panel B).

Intra-firm trade
International trade between two subsidiaries in two countries controlled by the same MNE.

Figure 6.8 Overcoming market failure through FDI

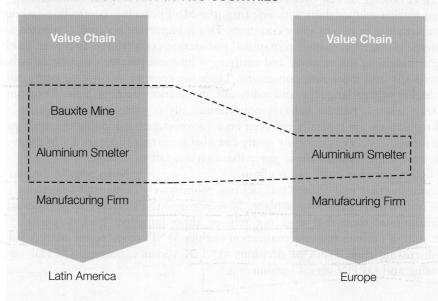

PANEL A: ONE COMPANY IN TWO COUNTRIES

Value Chain

Bauxite Mine

Aluminium Smelter

Manufacuring Firm

Latin America

Value Chain

Aluminium Smelter

Manufacuring Firm

Europe

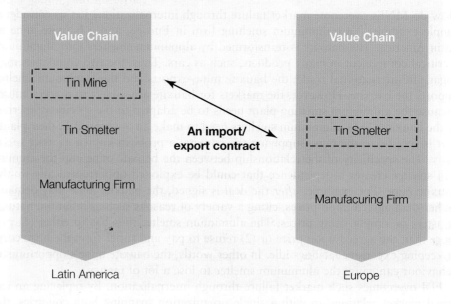

PANEL B: A MARKET TRANSACTION

Value Chain

Tin Mine

Tin Smelter

Manufacuring Firm

Latin America

An import/ export contract

Value Chain

Tin Smelter

Manufacuring Firm

Europe

FDI versus licensing

Licensing
Firm A's agreement to give Firm B the rights to use A's proprietary technology or trademark for a royalty fee paid to A by B.

In some cases, exporting is not feasibly to enter a foreign market, for example, when transportation costs are too high. The company may then face the choice between licensing the technology to a local firm and FDI establishing its own production facilities. How to choose between these two options? Three reasons may compel firms to prefer FDI to licensing.

First, FDI affords a high degree of direct management control that reduces the risk of firm-specific resources and capabilities being opportunistically taken advantage of. A key risk abroad is dissemination risk, defined as the risk associated with unauthorized diffusion of firm-specific know-how. If a foreign company grants a license to a local firm to manufacture or market a product, 'it runs the risk of the licensee, or an employee of the licensee, disseminating the know-how or using it for purposes other than those originally intended'.[19] Owning and managing proprietary assets through FDI does not completely shield firms from dissemination risks (after all, their employees can quit and join competitors), but FDI is better than licensing that provides no such management control. Consequently, FDI is extensively used in knowledge-intensive, high-tech industries, such as automobiles, electronics, chemicals and IT.[20]

Second, even if there is no opportunism on the part of licensees and if they are willing to follow the wishes of the foreign firm, certain types of knowledge may be too difficult to transfer to licensees without FDI.[21] Knowledge has two basic categories: (1) explicit and (2) tacit (implicit). Explicit knowledge is codifiable (that is, it can be written down and transferred without losing much of its richness). Tacit knowledge, on the other hand, is non-codifiable, and its acquisition and transfer require hands-on practice. For instance, a driving manual represents a body of explicit knowledge. However, mastering this manual without any road practice does not make you a good driver. Tacit knowledge is evidently more important and harder to transfer and learn; it can only be acquired through learning by doing (in this case, driving practice supervized by an experienced driver). Likewise, operating a department store chain like French Carrefour's stores entails a great deal of knowledge, some explicit (often captured in an operational manual) and some tacit. However, simply giving foreign licensees a copy of the Carrefour operational manual will not be enough. Foreign employees will need to learn from Carrefour personnel side by side (learning by doing). From a resource-based standpoint, it is Carrefour's tacit knowledge that gives it competitive advantage (see Chapter 4). Carrefour owns such crucial tacit knowledge, and it wants to ensure that its competences are properly deployed to protect its reputation and to maximize its return on investment. Therefore, properly transferring and controlling tacit knowledge calls for FDI.[22]

Finally, FDI provides more direct and tighter control over foreign operations. Even when licensees (and their employees) have no opportunistic intention to take away 'secrets', they may not follow the wishes of the foreign firm that provides the know-how. Without FDI, the foreign firm cannot order or control its licensee to move ahead. For example, Starbucks entered South Korea by licensing its format to ESCO. Although ESCO soon opened ten stores, Starbucks felt that ESCO was not aggressive enough in growing the chain. But there was very little Starbucks could do. Eventually, Starbucks switched from licensing to FDI, which allowed Starbucks to directly call 'the shots' and promote the aggressive growth of the chain in South Korea.

FDI versus offshore outsourcing

Internalization advantages also arise for offshoring though that is a very different sort of transaction. Rather than transferring a technology, it involves the transfer of activities to be delivered back to the parent firm. Recall from Chapter 4 that outsourcing to a foreign location becomes 'offshore outsourcing', whereas FDI – that is, performing an activity in-house at an overseas location – is in-house offshoring (see Figure 4.4). Like licensing, this involves a complex relationship between the two operations, and the question arises: can this transaction be handled using the market, or should it be internalized? Three types of problems may arise when offshoring is handled at arm's-length by outsourcing (1) hold-up problems due to asset

Dissemination risks
The risks associated with unauthorized diffusion of firm-specific know-how.

Tacit knowledge
Knowledge that is non-codifiable, and whose acquisition and transfer require hands-on practice.

© david pearson/Alamy

How does tacit knowledge help Carrefour operate stores in Middle East?

specificity, (2) unauthorized dissemination of technology and (3) costs of monitoring quality and standards.

First, if the activity would require substantial specific investment by the service provider, the problem of asset specificity arises. This may lead to one sided dependence of one partner on the other, and market failure is likely. Hence, you rarely see outsourcing of activities that are unique to a firm. Typically, firms outsource activities that are common across several industries, where there is scope for other firms to develop complementary specialist capabilities for that activity. For example, Flextronics is a specialist for assembly of electronics products, while Wipro specializes in IT services. They know how to manage these operations, and enable their customers to focus on product development and marketing.

Second, the outsourcing service provider may use knowledge of the firm's technology for other purposes, for instance helping competitors or entering the industry itself. Thus, offshore outsourcing requires safeguards on the use of technology. For instance, it is standard practice that service providers may not simultaneously provide similar services to a competitor. But even such safeguards may not suffice when latest and non-patented knowledge is involved. In such a situation, a firm may prefer to operate its offshore manufacturing plant itself, i.e. in-house offshoring.

Third, for some activities companies may find it necessary to monitor the actual manufacturing process, rather than simply buying the finished products. For example, considerable concern has been raised that suppliers of textile and footwear in developing countries are using child labour or other work practices deemed unethical by consumers in Europe. In consequence, companies such as Nike and Adidas have developed detailed codes of conduct as well as training for their suppliers.[23] However, ownership of the relevant production facilities as in-house offshoring would provide even better control over labour practices.

NATIONAL INSTITUTIONS AND FDI

Host country institutions

The establishment of FDI, like any strategic decision, is motivated by firms' desire to exploit or develop their resources. Yet, these decisions are influenced by a range of institutions that have been created by both host and home countries.[24] Most countries nowadays expect that, at least in principle, FDI leads to a win-win situation for both home and host countries. Since the 1980s, many countries have thus adopted more FDI-friendly policies. However, most countries have retained some institutions that either (1) restrict the presence of FDI or (2) regulate the operations of FDI. Restrictive institutions come in three forms:

LEARNING OBJECTIVE

3 explain how home and host country institutions affect FDI

- **Outright bans on FDI** rule out FDI completely, either for the entire economy or for specific sectors. Complete bans on FDI were common in developing economies, though they have become rare by the last decade of the 20th century. Governments hostile to FDI have in the past nationalized MNE assets, and banned new investment. Between the 1950s and the early 1980s, such policies were common throughout Africa, Asia, Eastern Europe and Latin America.[25] More recent examples include the nationalization of the oil industry by the Chavez government in Venezuela.

- **Case-by-case approvals of FDI** substitute for outright bans of FDI, and make every FDI subject to a registration and approval process. In practice, this often means that governments can impose a wide range of conditions that are subject to negotiation with the foreign investors. Such approval procedures are common in emerging economies. For instance, at early stages of their economic opening, China and Vietnam would vet every investor, only gradually did they move to automatic approval for most industries.

- **Ownership requirements** are a specific form of restriction that disallow full foreign ownership, but allow foreign investors to operate in a county if they establish a joint venture with a local firm. For example, Vietnam did not allow the acquisition of local firms until about 2001, thus forcing foreign investors who wanted to access local firms to establish a joint venture. Even in developed economies, foreign investors face such restrictions in selected industries. For example, the USA does not allow foreign majority ownership in domestic air transportation and other sectors deemed sensitive because of national security.

Even when foreign investors are free to set up their operations, they are not necessarily free to do as they like, they are subject to the institutional setting of the host economy. The regulation of FDI comes in two parts:

- **General regulatory institutions of business:** From the perspective of a host country, a FDI establishes a new firm that – like any firm – is subject to the laws and regulations of the country. Thus, the operations of a foreign investor are subject to the host country's institutional framework, which may be quite different than what the investor is used to at home. For example, foreign investors may have to comply with specific regulation such as restrictions on advertising or the pricing of utilities.

- **FDI specific regulation:** Some countries make the operation of FDI subject to specific regulations. For example, local content requirements require a certain proportion of the value of the goods made in the country to originate from that country.[26] The Japanese automobile VERs discussed in Chapter 5 are a

Local content requirements
These requirements state that a certain proportion of the value of the goods made in the country should originate from that country.

case in point here. Starting in the mid-1980s, because of VERs, Japanese automakers switched to producing cars in the USA through FDI. However, initially, such factories were 'screwdriver plants' because a majority of components were imported from Japan and only the proverbial screwdrivers were needed to tighten the screws. To deal with this issue, many countries impose local content requirements, mandating that a 'domestically produced' product will still be treated as an 'import' subject to tariffs and NTBs unless a certain fraction of its value is produced locally.

Restrictions on FDI are common in developing countries, yet they also exist in Western Europe and North America. In the 1960s, Europeans were concerned about the massive US FDI in Europe. In the 1980s, Americans were alarmed by the significant Japanese FDI inroads into the USA. Over time, such concerns subsided. More recently, in 2006, a controversy erupted when Dubai Ports World, a Dubai government-owned company, purchased US ports from another *foreign* firm, Britain's P&O. This entry gave Dubai Ports World control over terminal operations at the ports of New York/New Jersey, Philadelphia, Baltimore, Miami and New Orleans. Although Dubai has been a US ally for three decades, then Senator Hillary Clinton argued, 'Our port security is too important to place in the hands of foreign governments'. She was not alone; many politicians, journalists and activists opposed such FDI. In this 'largest political storm over US ports since the Boston Tea Party',[27] Dubai Ports World eventually withdrew. A similar reaction prevented high-profile acquisition attempts by Chinese investors in the USA (such as CNOOC's bid for Unocal) and Australia (such as Chinalco's bid for Rio Tinto).

On the other hand, some governments provide positive incentives for some foreign investors, including tax holidays, provision of infrastructure or even outright

Why was the sale of US ports to Dubai Ports World controversial?

subsidies.[28] For example, the Czech Republic ran a scheme that offered new foreign investors tax relief for up to ten years and duty-free importing. In addition, in areas with high unemployment, job creation subsidies and training grants for up to 25 per cent of training costs were available. For some foreign investors, these incentives played a role in their decision to locate a plant in the Czech Republic rather than any of the neighbouring countries.[29] Also, tariffs can be used to attract foreign investors: if you can't export to a country, you might consider setting up a local factory. However, international agreements, such EU competition policy (see Chapter 8), constrain the extent to which governments are allowed to provide such subsidies.

Home country institutions

Home countries generally do not have specific policies to encourage or discourage FDI. However, some see MNEs as vital to achieving national economic objectives such as the transformation of an economy or a means to access scarce resources. For example, the Japanese government since the 1960s has encouraged companies to move labour intensive operations overseas to enable the technological upgrading of the Japanese economy.[30] The Chinese government in the early 2000s actively supports companies investing overseas in natural resources, as China is scarce in resources like minerals or agricultural produce (see In Focus 6.4).[31] Such support is especially crucial at early stages of countries' outward FDI.

   Others are concerned that the transfer of capital or jobs may be detrimental to the home economy, and thus oppose some forms of FDI. On the one hand, efficiency considerations suggest that in many cases relocation of labour-intensive parts of the value chain may actually enhance competitiveness and thus benefit the company and the home country in the long run. On the other hand, the relocation of production is often opposed by trade unions fearing the loss of jobs, but it is rare that governments publicly intervene to dissuade MNEs not to establish production overseas. A rare exception happened in January 2010 when Renault announced its intention to relocate production of the Clio to Turkey. French government ministers issued strong statements condemning the action, and – with reference to the state's 15 per cent equity stake in Renault – put pressure on Renault to cancel its plans.[32]

BENEFITS AND COSTS OF FDI

Why do countries restrict or regulate FDI? Many economists and managers argue that MNEs generally are good for society; yet there are also widespread concerns. Even leading economists acknowledge that at least some forms of MNE activity may be harmful to host economies.[33] These perceptions of potential negative effects shape political views of FDI and thus the institutional environment in different countries. Hence, to understand why institutions offer a mix of incentives and obstacles, we need to analyze the benefits and costs associated with FDI. Foreign direct investors interact in many ways with firms and individuals in their host country, which makes the assessment of their costs and benefits very complex.[34] Table 6.2 provides a simplified overview of some potential benefits and costs from the perspective of local people, firms, government and the environment.

LEARNING OBJECTIVE

4 appreciate the benefits and costs of FDI to host and home countries

- **Consumers** generally appreciate foreign investors that bring new consumer goods at better quality and/or lower prices. Some may, however, mourn the disappearance of traditional local producers that are no longer able to compete.

Table 6.2 Possible Benefits and Costs of FDI for Host Countries

	Possible benefits of FDI	Possible negative effects of FDI
Consumers	• Access to international quality products and brands • Lower prices due to scale economies and competition	• Reduces variety of traditional local brands (if local firms are crowded out)
Suppliers	• Technology transfer enhancing productivity • Opportunity to become an international supplier	• Crowding out by international sourcing
Competitors	• Technology spillovers enable learning • Competition may trigger upgrading and innovation	• Crowding out by overwhelming competition
Workers	• Employment opportunities • Typically higher labour standards than local firms • Training and knowledge transfer	• Often less labour intensive production (thus less work places) than local firms
Government	• Tax revenues • Economic growth	• Costs of subsidies and other incentives
Natural environment	• MNEs often have higher environmental standards than local firms	• MNEs may locate highly polluting activities in places with less stringent regulation

Note: These are possible effects that vary across FDI projects.

Sources: (1) 'Perspectives on Multinational Enterprises in Emerging Economies', K.E. Meyer, 2004, *Journal of International Business Studies*, 34, pp. 259–277, Palgrave Macmillan; (2) 'When and where does foreign direct investment generate positive spillovers?' K.E. Meyer and E. Sinani, 2009, *Journal of International Business Studies*, 40, pp. 1075–1094, Palgrave Macmillan; (3) 'Multinational corporations and spillovers' Blomström M. and Kokko, A., *Journey of Economic Surveys*, 12, pp. 247–277, 1998, Blackwell; (4) Editors' Introduction in: *Multinational Enterprises and Host Economies*, K.E. Meyer, ed., 2008, Edward Elgar Publishing. Reproduced with permission of Palgrave Macmillan, Wiley-Blackwell and Edward Elgar Publishing Ltd.

- **Suppliers** to the foreign investors may benefits from new orders and from training in modern production and supply chain management practice.[35] These benefits, however, occur only if the foreign investors actually source locally; some foreign investors prefer to import their components from their established suppliers, and thus offer few opportunities for local firms.

- **Competitors** have a very ambiguous relationship with foreign entrants. On the one hand, they may learn by observing the advanced technologies and management practices. These knowledge spillovers may enable some local firms to upgrade their own practices, and thus increase sales and even increase their exports.[36] However, knowledge spillovers are difficult to realize if the gap between locals and foreign investors is too big. Weaker local firms may be overwhelmed by the foreign competition and thus forced to close down.

- **Workers** benefit from new jobs created directly or indirectly by the FDI. Direct benefits arise when MNEs employ individuals locally, training them in latest technologies and management practices. For example, more than 50 per cent of the Irish manufacturing employees work for MNEs.[37] Indirect benefits include jobs created when local suppliers increase hiring and when MNE employees spend money locally resulting in more jobs. For instance, in 2006, Toyota directly employed 32 000 employees in the USA. Indirectly, it created an estimated 386 000 jobs. On the other hand, foreign-owned production facilities in emerging economies are often more capital intensive and thus create fewer job than local firms using more traditional production processes.

- **Host governments** benefit from increased tax revenues, provided they have not agreed to extensive tax holidays, or other financial incentives for the investors. Moreover, if foreign investors stimulate growth in the local economy, this has indirect positive effects for the society and government revenues.

- **The natural environment** may be negatively affected if foreign investors establish polluting industrial plants, or destroy natural habitats. However, arguably, this is more of a side-effect of industrialization than of FDI as such. Foreign investors typically use more environmentally friendly technologies than comparable local firms because it allows them to standardize their operations and to satisfy interest groups back home.[38]

The actual benefits and costs of FDI thus vary greatly across FDI projects, and across various aspects of the relationship between foreign investors and the local society. Political proponents can easily find positive or negative examples supporting their particular view: Some FDI projects are undoubtedly beneficial for the hosts, while some are harmful for some constituents. Empirical research suggests that suppliers and employees typically are better off because of the presence foreign investors, but the actual benefits and costs depend on the specific characteristics of the FDI projects.

DEBATES AND EXTENSIONS

MNEs are widely regarded as the embodiment of globalization (see Chapter 1). Not surprisingly, they have stimulated a lot of debates. Despite the general trend towards friendlier policies to facilitate inbound FDI, debates continue in various host countries. At the heart of these debates is the age-old question: Can we trust foreigners and foreign firms in making decisions important to our economy? This section discusses (1) the interaction between MNEs and host governments, and (2) sovereign wealth funds.

LEARNING OBJECTIVE

5 participate in two leading debates on FDI

How MNEs and host governments bargain

For small firms, institutions and government policies are largely 'given', and the firms have to adjust. However, larger firms – and small firms acting together – may have some power to influence institutions and political processes, or at least the application of particular rules in a particular case. Governments tend to be interested in some of the benefits of FDI, for example the creation of jobs or the upgrading of technology. Hence, the actual FDI and the regulations applying to it are to some degree the outcome of a bilateral negotiation process. Hence, the relationship between MNEs and host governments is shaped by their relative bargaining power – their ability to extract a favourable outcome from negotiations due to one party's strengths.[39] MNEs typically prefer to minimize the interventions from host governments and maximize the incentives provided by host governments. Host governments usually want to ensure a certain degree of control and minimize the incentives provided to MNEs. Sometimes, host governments try to induce MNEs to undertake activities that they would otherwise not do, such as investing in advanced R&D or locating in less prosperous regions. However, host governments have to use incentives because MNEs have options to invest elsewhere. Different countries, in effect, are competing with each other for precious FDI dollars. The upshot is that despite a variety of conflicts, there are conditions within which the interests of both sides may converge on an outcome that makes each side better off.[40]

The bargaining between MNEs and FDI is characterized by the 'three Cs': common interests, conflicting interests and compromises.[41] It does not end with the initial investment decision, but often it continues over the entire lifetime of an FDI operation. A well-known phenomenon is the obsolescing bargain, a renegotiation of a deal *after* the initial FDI entry when the relative bargaining positions have changed.[42] This is a concern in particular for projects that require large, non-recoverable up-front investment (called sunk-costs) and long pay back periods, as in natural resource exploration and infrastructure operations.[43] For example, foreign oil companies frequently run into difficulties after having 'sunk' their investments in places such as Russia or Venezuela. Likewise, investors in power plants, telecommunication networks, bridges or airports are very concerned about the regulatory regime *after* the initial construction has been completed. In such situations, a government may opportunistically take advantage of the shifting bargaining power by renegotiating in three stages:

- In stage one, the MNE and the government negotiate a deal that involves assurances of property rights and incentives.

- In stage two, the MNE makes its investment by building the bridge or power plant, in the expectation of recovering the investment from future revenue streams.

- In stage three, the MNE sells its services, and thus recovers its investment and, after a while, may earn handsome profits. Observing such profits along with perceived high prices for electricity or bridge tolls (and perhaps less than perfect service), domestic political groups may pressurize the government to renegotiate the deal that seems to yield 'excessive' profits to the foreign firm (which, of course, regards these as 'fair' return on their risky investment). The previous deal, therefore, becomes obsolete. The government's tactics include changing rules applying to pricing of electricity or bridge tolls, demanding a higher share of profits and taxes or even confiscating foreign assets – in other words, expropriation.

At this time, the MNE has already invested substantial resources that it cannot recover and often has to accommodate some new demands. Otherwise, it may face expropriation or exit at a huge loss. Not surprisingly, MNEs do not appreciate the risk associated with such obsolescing bargains, and they seek long-term guarantees from host government to reduce their exposure. Unfortunately, recent actions in Venezuela and Bolivia suggest that obsolescing bargains are not necessarily becoming obsolete.[44] The political stability of a country thus is a major concern for MNEs in mining, oil exploration, infrastructure and other capital intensive industries.

Bargaining power
The ability to extract a favourable outcome from negotiations due to one party's strengths.

Obsolescing bargain
Refers to the deal struck by MNEs and host governments, which change their requirements after the initial FDI entry.

Sunk cost
Up-front investments that are non-recoverable if the project is abandoned.

Expropriation
Governments' confiscation of private assets.

Sovereign wealth fund investments

A sovereign wealth fund (SWF) is 'a state-owned investment fund composed of financial assets such as stocks, bonds, real estate or other financial instruments funded by foreign exchange assets'.[45] Investment funds that we now call SWFs were first created in 1953 by Kuwait. Most SWFs are based in countries in the Middle East and Asia that generated current account surpluses, for instance from oil and gas revenues (Table 6.3). The only major European SWF is Norway's Government Pension Fund, which is investing the nation's saving from oil revenues for future generations. These SWFs undertake FDI, yet they operate differently than

Sovereign wealth fund (SWF)

A state-owned investment fund composed of financial assets such as stocks, bonds, real estate or other financial instruments.

Table 6.3 The 15 Largest Sovereign Wealth Funds

Sovereign wealth fund	Country	Assets (€ billion)	Origins	Foundation	Transparency Index *
Abu Dhabi Investment Authority	United Arab Emirates	437	Oil & gas	1976	3
Government Pension Fund of Norway	Norway	310	Oil & gas	1990	10
SAMA Foreign Holdings	Saudi Arabia	300	Oil & gas	n/a	2
SAFE Investment Company	China	242	Other	n/a	2
China Investment Corporation	China	201	Other	2007	6
Government of Singapore Investment Corporation	Singapore	172	Other	1981	6
Kuwait Investment Authority	Kuwait	141	Oil & gas	1953	6
National Welfare Fund	Russia	124	Oil & gas	2008	5
National Social Security Fund	China	102	Other	2000	5
Hong Kong Monetary Authority Investment Portfolio	China (Hong Kong)	97	Other	1998	8
Temasek Holdings	Singapore	85	Other	1974	10
Libyan Investment Authority	Libya	49	Oil & gas	2006	2
Qatar Investment Authority	Qatar	45	Oil & gas	2005	5
Australian Future Fund	Australia	34	Other	2004	9
Revenue Regulation Fund	Algeria	33	Oil & gas	2000	1

Notes:* scale from 1 (Fund provides contact information) to 10 (Fund provides details of investment strategy, origins of wealth, ownership structure etc); n/a = data not available.

Source: 'The 15 Largest Sovereign Wealth Funds' from Current news, 2009, www.swfinstitute.org copyright © Sovereign Wealth Fund Institute. Reproduced with permission.

conventional MNEs: (1) they are state-owned or controlled, (2) they typically acquire equity stakes sufficient to influence target forms, yet they do not get involved in day-to-day management or integrate operations.

While most SWFs make relatively passive FPI, some have become more active, direct investors as they hold larger stakes in recipients. During the financial crisis, SWFs came to the rescue. In November 2007, the Abu Dhabi Investment Authority injected $7.5 billion (4.9 per cent of equity) into Citigroup. In early 2008, China Investment Corporation (CIC) invested $5 billion for a 10 per cent equity stake in Morgan Stanley. In November, British bank Barclays sold 31 per cent of its outstanding shares to SWFs in Abu Dhabi and Qatar.[46]

Such large-scale investments have ignited considerable debate. On the one hand, SWFs have brought much needed cash to desperate Western firms. On the other hand, concerns are raised by host countries, which are typically developed economies. A primary concern is national security in that SWFs may be politically (as opposed to commercially) motivated. Another concern is SWFs' inadequate transparency. Governments in developed economies like the USA, in fear of the 'threats' from SWFs have thus created measures to defend their companies from SWF takeovers.

As discussed earlier, FDI certainly has both benefits and costs to host countries. However, in the absence of any evidence that the costs outweigh benefits, the rush to erect anti-SWF barriers is indicative of protectionist sentiments. For executives at hard-pressed Western firms, it would not seem sensible to ask for government bailouts on the one hand, and to reject cash from SWFs on the other hand. Most SWF investment is essentially capital investment with few strings attached. For example, CIC, which acquired 10 per cent of Morgan Stanley equity, did not demand a board seat or a management role. Commenting on inbound Chinese investment in the USA (including SWF investment), two experts note:

> 'It seems feckless on the part of US policymakers to stigmatize Chinese investment in the USA based upon imprecise and likely exaggerated estimates of the relevant costs and risks of that investment'.[47]

Thanks to the worsening financial crisis in 2008–09, some SWF suffered major losses from their investments.[48] Such a 'double whammy' – both the political backlash and the economic losses – has severely discouraged government officials and SWFs. To reassure host countries, major SWFs at a summit in Santiago, Chile, agreed to a voluntary code of conduct known as the Santiago Principles. These principles are designed to alleviate some of the concerns in host countries and to enhance the transparency and the commercial (non-political) viability of such investment.

IMPLICATIONS FOR PRACTICE

LEARNING OBJECTIVE

6 draw implications for action

The big question in global business, adapted to the context of FDI, is: What determines the success and failure of FDI around the globe? The answer boils down to two components. First, from a resource-based view, some firms are very good at FDI because they leverage ownership, location and internalization advantages in a way that is value-creating, rare, and hard to imitate by rival firms. Second, from an institution-based view, institutions in home and host countries either enable or constrain FDI from reaching its full economic potential. Therefore, the success and failure of FDI also significantly depend on institutions governing FDI as 'rules of the game'.

As a result, three implications for action emerge (Table 6.4). First, carefully assess whether FDI is justified in light of other possibilities such as exporting,

Table 6.4 Implications for Action

- Carefully assess whether FDI is justified in light of other foreign entry modes such as outsourcing and licensing
- Pay careful attention to the location advantages in combination with the firm's strategic goals
- Be aware of the institutional constraints and enablers governing FDI and enhance legitimacy in host countries

outsourcing and licensing. This exercise needs to be conducted on an activity-by-activity basis as part of the value chain analysis (see Chapter 4). If internalization advantages are deemed not crucial, then FDI is not recommended.

Second, once a decision to undertake FDI is made, pay attention to the old adage: 'Location, location, location!' The quest for location advantages has to create a fit with the firm's strategic goals. For example, if a firm is searching for the best 'hot spots' for innovations, this location shortlist is likely to be limited for a few firms in that particular industry (see Chapter 12).

Finally, given the political realities around the world, be aware of the institutional constraints. Recent events suggest that MNE managers should not take FDI-friendly policies for granted. Setbacks are likely. In the long run, MNEs' interests in home and host countries can be best safeguarded if they accommodate rather than neglect or dominate national interests. In practical terms, contributions to local employment, job training, education, pollution control and financial support for local infrastructure, schools, research and sports will demonstrate MNEs' commitment to the countries in which they operate.[49] These actions will reduce liabilities of outsidership and enhance MNEs' legitimacy in the eyes of governments and the public.

CHAPTER SUMMARY

1 Understand the vocabulary associated with FDI:

- FDI refers to directly investing in activities that control and manage value creation in other countries.
- MNEs are firms that engage in FDI.
- FDI can be classified as horizontal FDI and vertical FDI.
- Flow is the amount of FDI moving in a given period in a certain direction (inflow or outflow).
- Stock is the total accumulation of inbound FDI in a country or outbound FDI from a country.

2 Explain how ownership, location and internalization (OLI) advantages explain the emergence of FDI:

- Ownership refers to MNEs' resources that are internationally transferable and enable firms to attain competitive advantages abroad.
- Location refers to certain locational advantages that can help MNEs attain their strategic goals.
- Internalization refers to the replacement of cross-border market relationship with one firm (the MNE) locating in two or more countries. Internalization helps to overcome market imperfections.
- Exporting, licensing and outsources provide alternatives to FDI when market failures are unlikely to affect the operation.

3 Explain how home and host country institutions affect FDI:

- Host countries may restrict FDI by outright bans, case-by-case approval or limits on foreign ownership, but such restrictions have become less common in recent years.

- Foreign investors are subject to the same regulatory institutions as local firms, plus in some countries special regulations for foreign investors.

- Home countries rarely adopt a specific policy on outward FDI.

4 Appreciate the benefits and costs of FDI to host and home countries:

- Foreign direct investors interact with a variety of stakeholders in the host economy, each of which many benefit directly or indirectly, while some may be worse off.

5 Participate in two political debates on FDI:

- The first debate concerns the 'obsolescing bargain' in the relationship between MNEs and host governments.

- The second debate concerns the role of sovereign wealth funds (SMEs).

6 Draw implications for action:

- Carefully assess whether FDI is justified, in light of other options such as outsourcing and licensing.

- Pay careful attention to locational advantages in combination with the firm's strategic goals.

- Be aware of the institutional constraints governing FDI and enhance legitimacy in host countries.

KEY TERMS

Agglomeration	Horizontal FDI	Market failure
Asset specificity	Internalization advantages	Multinational enterprise (MNE)
Bargaining power	Internalization	Obsolescing bargain
Dissemination risks	Intra-firm trade	OLI paradigm
Downstream vertical FDI	Joint-venture	Ownership advantages
Expropriation	Knowledge spillover	Sovereign wealth fund (SWF)
FDI flow	Licensing	Sunk cost
FDI stock	Local content requirements	Tacit knowledge
Foreign direct investment (FDI)	Location advantages	Upstream vertical FDI
Foreign portfolio investment (FPI)	Location-bound resources	Vertical FDI

CRITICAL DISCUSSION QUESTIONS

1 Identify the top-five (or top-ten) *source* countries of FDI into your country. Then identify the top-ten (or top-20) foreign MNEs that have undertaken inbound FDI in your country. Why do these countries and companies provide the bulk of FDI into your country?

2 Identify the top-five (or top-ten) *recipient* countries of FDI from your country. Then identify the top-ten (or top-20) MNEs headquartered in your country that have made outbound FDI elsewhere. Why do these countries attract FDI from the top MNEs in your country?

3 Worldwide, which countries were the largest recipient and source countries of FDI *last year*? Why? Will this situation change in five years? Ten years? How about 20 years down the road? Why?

4 MNEs are bargaining with host governments that – in many countries – are elected by the population. Is it legitimate to pressure governments to make concessions that the voting public would not agree with? Should agreements between MNEs and governments always be made public?

CLOSING CASE

Bharti Airtel acquires resources and companies

By Dr. Ajit Nayak, University of Bath.

In March 2010, Bharti Airtel announced that it will acquire Zain Africa BV for $10.7 billion. Zain Africa is one of the leading mobile telecom companies in Africa with operations in 18 countries. Sunil Mittal, the charismatic entrepreneur and founder of Bharti Airtel stated:

'This agreement is a landmark for global telecom industry ... a pioneering step towards South–South cooperation and strengthening of ties between India and Africa. With this acquisition, Bharti Airtel will be transformed into a truly global telecom company with operations across 18 countries fulfilling our vision of building a world-class multinational'.

This deal comes hotly on the heels of Bharti Airtel's acquisition of a 70 per cent stake in Bangladesh's Warid Telecom International, a subsidiary of UAE's Dhabi Group, in January 2010.

Few people in Europe or the USA would have heard of these companies. Bharti Airtel is India's largest mobile network operator and the fifth largest in the world by subscription base. Its customer base has grown by around 68 per cent *every year* from 2001–2009. The Zain Africa and Warid deals demonstrate Bharti Airtel's ambition and capability to raise capital globally in difficult times to finance global deals. It also signals, as Sunil Mittal stated, Bharti Airtel's 'intent to further expand our operations to international markets where we can implant our unique business model and offer quality and affordable telecom services'. Is the Bharti Airtel case evidence of new confidence of emerging economies MNEs as they attempt to become the new kids on the global stage?

Sunil Mittal may have been inspired by his namesake L.N. Mittal and the Arcelor-Mittal deal or by the

How did Airtel become a major player in mobile telephony across a wide range of emerging economies?

Tata-Corus deal both in 2006. But this was different. This was an Indian firm going global by looking at strategically prioritizing other emerging economies. Whereas the Mittal-Arcelor and the Tata-Corus deals in the steel industry were motivated by acquiring production capacity, strategic assets and technology, and access to western markets, Bharti Airtel aimed to expand its successful low-cost business model in other emerging economies. The similarities to the Indian markets enabled Bharti Airtel to use and build on its existing capabilities. However, as with the Mittal-Arcelor deal, the role and significance of governments in protecting their largest firms and determining cross-border acquisitions is apparent. In contrast, the Bangladeshi government was very keen to attract the $300 million investment into its telecom industry through the Warid deal. As Manoj Kohli the outgoing CEO remarked, 'The Government of Bangladesh, the regulator, telecom minister, all senior government officials have supported and encouraged us to complete this deal expeditiously'. The Zain acquisition poses significant hurdles in terms of getting support from the various African countries which are yet to be resolved. For example, the government of Gabon has objected to the deal.

Bharti Airtel's growth story is remarkable. Started in 1995 by Sunil Mittal, it has grown to become a major player on the world telecom stage and now acts as a beacon for Indian firms looking to expand globally. Bharti Airtel is much more global than it looks at first glance. The Zain and Warid deals means that Bharti Airtel now operates in 18 countries. Prior to 2010 it only operated in India, Sri Lanka and the Seychelles. But a closer look reveals the global scope of this firm in terms of its value chain, leadership and mind-set. First, in stark contrast to India's outsourcing destination for call centre services tag, Bharti Airtel counter-intuitively outsourced several parts of its value chain, including IT to IBM and network equipment to Nokia, Siemens (now merged) and Ericsson. Imagine that! An Indian company outsourcing its activities to Western multinationals.

Second, Bharti Airtel has had significant global presence on its board of directors since 1997. The British telecom giant BT had a 44 per cent stake in Bharti until 1999. Donald Cameron, BT's former Director (New Ventures), joined the Bharti board in 1999. Sunil Mittal also invited P.M. Sinha, President & CEO of Pepsi, N. Kumar, Vice-Chairman of the Sanmar Group, Wong Hung Khim, Group Chairman & CEO of DelGro Group of Companies, Singapore and Pulak Prasad, Managing Director, Warburg Pincus. In announcing these appointments, the company emphasized the importance of people with global exposure and global mindsets:

'We welcome the new independent directors, who come into Bharti with their vast wealth of professional expertise … These corporate leaders will help us to further focus sharply on shareholder value, guide us in ensuring the best of corporate governance and assist us in making Bharti a company that is managed by leading edge, world class values, processes and practices'.

SingTel, Singapore's largest telecom company, holds the majority stake in Bharti Airtel and its CEO (Chua Sock Koong) and nominees are represented on the board of directors of Bharti Airtel. Another major shareholder is Warburg Pincus, who invested US$ 292 million to finance Bharti's growth, and had continuous representation on the Bharti board. One would be hard pressed to find other MNEs with such an internationally diverse board, let alone an Indian company.

Third, a consistent mark of Mittal's and Bharti's entrepreneurship is the disruption of established wisdom and models. Akhil Gupta, one of the architects of Bharti Airtel's strategy highlights the need for clarity and simplicity in communicating strategic issues. On the issue of outsourcing to western MNEs, he stated three key principles:

'First, who has the better domain knowledge, is it us or somebody else, and forget about core and non-core; second, who can attract better human capital; and third, who has better economies of scale. If the answer to all three was somebody else, then we definitely outsourced'.

Irrespective of established norms and international reputations, Bharti Airtel aimed to simplify and innovate in terms of the business model to grow. By outsourcing to major international players, and developing business models that incentivized all parties to improve and grow the mobile network services, Airtel has created a new low-cost – high-growth – business model. The hallmark of entrepreneurs and firms from emerging economies is that they have to improvise and innovate from a low cost base, inferior technology and under-developed home markets. By turning all three negatives into opportunities, Airtel his aiming to write the rules of the game globally.

To what extent is Bharti Airtel's model unique to emerging economy MNEs?

CASE DISCUSSION QUESTIONS

1   From a resource based view, what are Bharti Airtel's main resources? How were these resources built, and how do they shape its ongoing path of growth?

2   From an institution based view, how are the challenges of entering emerging economies such as Bangladesh and Africa different from entry in Western European economies?

3   Compare Bharti Airtel's approach to internationalization with that of European MNEs.

4   What are the implication of the rise of emerging economy MNEs such as Bharti Airtel for globalization?

Sources: This case was written by **Dr Ajit Nayak** (University of Exeter) based on personal interviews with the company and (1) *Economic Times* (India), Zain, Bharti Airtel to ink Africa deal on Tuesday, 29 March 2010; (2) N. Karmali, 2010, Sunil Mittal Seals Zain Deal, Forbes, March 30; (3) N. Karmali, 2010, Bharti Airtel Dials Bangladesh, Forbes, January 12; (4) *Economic Times* (India), 2010, Airtel will make a strong mark in Bangladesh, January 12; (5) www.airtel.in; (6) www.bharti.com (both accessed January–April 2010). Reproduced with permission.

RECOMMENDED READINGS

J.H. Dunning, 2000, The eclectic paradigm as an envelope for economic and business theories of MNE activities, *IBR*, **12, 141–171** – A summary of the OLI paradigm.

J.H. Dunning & S. Lundan, 2008, *Multinational Enterprises and the Global Economy*, **2nd ed., Cheltenham: Elgar** – The most comprehensive book on the multinational enterprise, including theoretical foundations, empirical evidence and policy issues.

M. Forsgren, 2008, *Theories of the multinational firm*, **Cheltenham: Elgar** – A monograph critically reviewing five alternative theoretical perspectives on MNEs.

R. Grosse, ed., 2005, *International Business and Government Relations in the 21st Century*, **Cambridge: Cambridge University Press** – A collection of articles examining institutions and politics surrounding multinational enterprises.

K.E. Meyer, ed., 2008, *Multinational Enterprises and Host Economies* **(2 vols), Cheltenham: Elgar** – A collection of articles on the theme of benefits of costs of FDI.

UNCTAD, annual, *World investment Report*, **Geneva: United Nations** – A rich source of FDI data and analysis of current trends.

NOTES:

"FOR JOURNAL ABBREVIATION, PLEASE SEE PAGE XXVI-XXVII."

1   R.E. Caves, 1996, *Multinational Enterprise and Economic Analysis*, 2nd ed., Cambridge: Cambridge University Press.

2   United Nations, 2009, *World Investment Report 2009*, New York and Geneva: United Nations.

3   United Nations, 2009, *as above*.

4   J.H. Dunning, 1993, *Multinational Enterprises and the Global Economy*, Reading, MA: Addison-Wesley; J.H. Dunning & S. Lundan, 2009, *Multinational Enterprises and the Global Economy*, 2nd ed., Cheltenham: Elgar.

5   P.J. Buckley & N. Hashai, 2004, A global system view of firm boundaries, *JIBS*, 35: 33–45; J. Dunning, 1998, Location and the multinational enterprise, *JIBS*, 29: 45–66; R. Grosse & L.K. Trevino, 2005, New institutional economics and FDI location in Central and Eastern Europe, *MIR*, 45: 123–145.

6 R. Narula & J.H. Dunning, 2000, Industrial Development, Globalisation and Multinational Enterprises, *ODS*, 28: 141–167.

7 R. Ramamurti & J.V. Singh, eds, 2009, *Emerging Multinational from Emerging Markets*, Cambridge: Cambridge University Press; A. Cuervo-Cazurra, 2009, The multinationalization of developing county MNEs, *JIM*, 14: 138–154; D. Tan & K.E. Meyer, 2010, Business groups' outward FDI, *JIM*, 16: 154–164.

8 W. Chung & A. Kalnins, 2001, Agglomeration effects and performance, *SMJ*, 22: 969–988; E. Maitland, S. Nicholas, W. Purcell & T. Smith, 2004, Regional learning networks, *MIR*, 44: 87–100; J.M. Shaver & F. Flyer, 2000, Agglomeration economies, firm heterogeneity and foreign direct investment in the United States, *SMJ*, 21: 1175–1193.

9 S. Tallman, M. Jenkins, N. Henry & S. Pinch, 2004, Knowledge, clusters and competitive advantage, *AMR*, 29: 258–271; L. Canina, C.A. Enz & J.S. Harrison, 2005, Agglomeration effects and strategic orientations, *AMJ*, 48: 565–581; E. Maitland, E. Rose & S. Nicholas, 2005, How firms grow, *JIBS*, 36: 435–451; L. Nachum & C. Wymbs, 2005, Product differentiation, external economies and MNE location choices, *JIBS*, 36: 415–434.

10 Shaver & Flyer, 2000, as above.

11 A. Kalnins & W. Chung, 2004, Resource-seeking agglomeration, *SMJ*, 25: 689–699; L. Nachum, 2000, Economic geography and the location of TNCs, *JIBS*, 31: 367–385; M.E. Porter, 1998, *On Competition*, Boston: Harvard Business School Press; Tallman et al., 2004, as above.

12 S. Globerman & D. Shapiro, 2003, Governance infrastructure and US foreign investment, *JIBS*, 34: 19–39; A. Bevan, S. Estrin & K.E. Meyer, 2004, Institution Building and the Integration of Eastern Europe in International Production, *IBR*, 13, 43–64; K.E. Meyer & H.V. Nguyen, 2005, Foreign Investment Strategies and Sub-national Institutions in Emerging Markets, *JMS*, 42, 63–93; Grosse & Trevino, 2006, as above.

13 N. Driffield & M. Munday, 2000, Industrial performance, agglomeration, and foreign manufacturing investment in the UK, *JIBS*, 31: 21–37; Kalnins & Chung, 2004, as above.

14 *The Economist*, 2009, Foreign investors in Hungary: Less welcome, November 7.

15 P.J. Buckley & M.C. Casson, 1976, *The Future of the Multinational Enterprise*, London: Macmillan; J.F. Hennart, 1982, *A Theory of Multinational Enterprise*, Ann Arbor: University of Michigan Press.

16 This example is inspired by J.F. Hennart, 1988, Upstream vertical integration in the aluminium and tin industries, *JEBO*, 281–199.

17 J. Campa & M. Guillén, 1999, The internalization of exports, *MS*, 45: 1463–1478; P. Buckley & M. Casson, 2009, The internalization theory of the multinational enterprise, *JIBS*, 40, 1563–1580.

18 L. Eden, L. Juarez & D. Li, 2005, Talk softly but carry a big stick, *JIBS*, 36: 398–414; L. Eden & P. Rodriguez, 2004, How weak are the signals? *JIBS*, 35: 61–74; I. Filatotchev, R. Strange, J. Piesse & Y. Lien, 2007, FDI by firms from new industrialized economies in emerging markets, *JIBS*, 38: 556–572.

19 C.W.L. Hill, P. Hwang & C. Kim, 1990, An eclectic theory of the choice of international entry mode (p. 124), *SMJ* 11: 117–128.

20 J. Denekamp, 1995, Intangible assets, internalization, and foreign direct investment in manufacturing, *JIBS*, 26: 493–504; M. Cannice, R. Chen & J. Daniels, 2004, Managing international technology transfer risk, *MIR*, 44: 129–139.

21 B. Kogut & U. Zander, 1993, Knowledge of the firm and the evolutionary theory of the multinational corporation, *JIBS*, 24: 625–646.

22 X. Martin & R. Salomon, 2003, Tacitness, learning and international expansion, *OSc*, 14: 297–311.

23 S. Frenkel & D. Scott, 2002, Compliance, collaboration and codes of labour practice, *CMR*, 45, 29–49; L. Hartman, D.G. Arnold & R.E. Wokutch, eds., 2003, *Rising above Sweatshop*, New York: Praeger.

24 Grosse, ed., 2005, *as above*.

25 T. Poynter, 1982, Government intervention in less developed countries, *JIBS*, 13: 9–25; R. Vernon, 1977, *Storm over the Multinationals*, Cambridge, MA: Harvard University Press.

26 S. Lall & R. Narula, 2004, Foreign direct investment and its role in economic development, *EJDR* 16, 447–464.

27 *The Economist*, 2006, America's ports and Dubai: Trouble on the waterfront, February 25.

28 C. Oman, 2000, *Competition Policy for Foreign Direct Investment*, Paris: OECD; R. Grosse, ed., 2003, *International Business and Government Relations*, Cambridge: Cambridge University Press.

29 T.J.S. Mallya, A. Kukulka & C. Jensen, 2004, Are incentives a good investment for the host country? *TNC*, 13, 109–148.

30 K. Kojima, 1985, Japanese and American direct investment in Asia, *HJE* 26, 1–36. T. Ozawa, 1979, International investment and industrial structure, *OEP*, 31, 72–92.

31 X. Yang, Y. Jiang, R. Kang & Y. Ke, 2007, A comparative analysis of the internationalization of Chinese and Japanese firms, *APJM*, 26, 141–162; S. Globerman & D. Shapiro, 2009, Economic and strategic considerations surrounding Chinese FDI in the United States, *APJM*, 26: 163–183.

32 E. Bembaron, 2010, L'État contre la délocalisation de la Clio en Turquie, *Le Figaro*, January 11; *Le Monde*, 2010, Le gouvernement s'insurge contre la délocalisation de la Clio en Turquie, January 11.

33 R.E. Caves, 1996. *Multinational Enterprise and Economic Analysis*, 2nd ed., Cambridge: Cambridge University Press; L.T. Wells, 1998, Multinationals and the developing countries, *JIBS*, 29, 101–114; D. Rodrik, 1999. The new global economy and developing countries, Policy Essay nr. 24, John Hopkins University Press, Washington, DC.

34 Blomström M. & Kokko, A. 1998. Multinational corporations and spillovers, *JES,* 12, 247–77; K.E. Meyer, 2004, Perspectives on multinational enterprises in emerging economies, *JIBS*, 35: 259–276.

35 S. Lall, 1980, Vertical inter-firm linkages in LDCs: An empirical study, *OBES* 42, 203–226. R. Belderbos, G. Capannelli & K. Fukao, 2001, Backward vertical linkages of foreign manufacturing affiliates, *WD,* 29, 189–208.

36 B. Aitken & A. Harrison, 1999, Do domestic firms benefit from direct foreign investment? *AER*, 89: 605–618; S.E. Feinberg & S.K. Majumdar, 2001, Technology spillovers from foreign direct investment in the Indian pharmaceutical industry, *JIBS*, 32: 421–437; H. Görg & E. Strobl, 2001, Multinational companies and productivity spillovers, *EJ*, 111: 723–739; P.J. Buckley, J. Clegg & C. Wang, 2002, The impact of inward FDI on the performance of Chinese manufacturing firms, *JIBS*, 33: 637–655; B.S. Javorcik, 2004, Does foreign direct investment increase the productivity of domestic firms? *AER*, 94: 605–627; Y. Wei & X. Liu, 2006, Productivity spillovers from R&D, exports, and FDI in China's manufacturing sector, *JIBS*, 37: 544–557; K.E. Meyer & E. Sinani, 2009, When and where does foreign direct investment generate positive spillovers? *JIBS*, 40, 1075–1094.

37 F. Barry & C. Kearney, 2006, Multinational enterprises and industrial structure in host countries, *JIBS*, 37: 392–406.

38 L. Zarsky, 1999, Havens, halos and spaghetti: Untangling the evidence about FDI and the environment, conference paper, Paris: OECD, January, (http://www.olis.oecd.org/olis/1998doc.nsf/LinkTo/CCNM-EMEF-EPOC-CIME(98)5); P. Christmann, 2004, Multinational companies and the natural environment: Determinants of global environmental policy standardization, *AMJ,* 47, 747–760.

39 D. Lecraw, 1984, Bargaining power, ownership and profitability of transnational corporations in developing countries, *JIBS*, 15: 27–43; T. Murtha & S. Lenway, 1994, Country capabilities and the strategic state, *SMJ*, 15: 113–129; A.M. Rugman & A. Verbeke, 2001, Multinationals and public policy, In: A.M. Rugman & T.L. Brewer, *Oxford Handbook of International Business*, Oxford: Oxford University Press. 818–842; J. Nebus & C. Rufin, 2010, Extending the bargaining power model, JIBS, 41: 996–1015.

40 M.W. Peng, 2000, Controlling the foreign agent, *MIR*, 40: 141–165.

41 J. Boddewyn & T.L. Brewer, 1994, International business political behavior, *AMR*, 19: 119–143; T. Agmon, 2003, Who gets what, *JIBS*, 34: 416–427; H. Aswicahyono & H. Hill, 1995, Determinants of foreign ownership in LDC manufacturing, *JIBS*, 26: 139–158.

42 T.L. Brewer, 1992, An issue-area approach to the analysis of MNE-government relations, *JIBS*, 23: 295–309; R. Ramamurti, 2001, The obsolescing 'bargain model', *JIBS*, 32, 23–39; L. Eden, S. Lenway & D.A. Schuler, 2005, From obsolescing bargain to the political bargaining model, in: R. Grosse, ed., *International Business and Government Relations in the 21st Century*, Cambridge: Cambridge University Press.

43 J. Doh & R. Ramamurti, 2003, Reassessing risk in developing country infrastructure, *LRP*, 36: 337–353.

44 *Business Week*, 2006, Venezuela: You are working for Chavez now, May 15; *The Economist*, 2006, Bolivia: Now it's the people's gas, May 6.

45 SWF Institute, 2009, About sovereign wealth fund, www.swfinstitute.org.

46 T.A. Hemphill, 2009, Souvereign wealth funds, *TIBR,* 51: 551–566.

47 Globerman & Shapiro, 2009, as above (p. 180).

48 *The Economist*, 2009, Banks and sovereign wealth funds: Falling knives, December 12.

49 E. Iankova & J. Katz, 2003, Strategies for political risk mediation by international firms in transition economies, *JWB*, 38: 182–203.

CHAPTER SEVEN

EXCHANGE RATES

© AlandJ/iStock

LEARNING OBJECTIVES

After studying this chapter you should be able to:

1 Understand the determinants of exchange rates.

2 Track the evolution of the international monetary system.

3 Identify firms' strategic responses to deal with exchange movements.

4 Participate in three leading debates on exchange movements.

5 Draw implications for action.

OPENING CASE

The economic crisis upsets exchange rates

The year 2009 has been a difficult year for many businesses and citizens in Central and Eastern Europe. Countries across the region had embarked on capitalism in the early 1990s from fairly similar starting points; yet, they have evolved quite differently in recent years. A key difference has been their exchange rate regime, the rules that determine the price of their currency. This had major implications on their ability to cope with the global economic crisis in 2008/09 – and how individual citizens were affected. Let's have a brief look at four countries that joined the EU in 2004: Poland, Hungary, Latvia and Slovakia (see Table 7.1).

Poland and Hungary had adopted flexible exchange rates. **Poland** had been most radical in its economic stabilization and market-oriented reforms in the early 1990s, and became the fastest growing country in the region in the late 1990s. The healthy growth continued in the 2000s, with GDP growth of 6.8 per cent in 2007. When the crisis reached Europe in 2008, Poland suffered only a mild slow downturn of growth at 4.9 per cent, and in the crisis year of 2009 achieved a positive growth of 1.3 per cent, a rare achievement at that time. The banking system remained relatively stable, and with a large domestic economy, Poland was less affected by the downturn of world trade.

However, not all is well in Poland: The Polish zloty lost 28 per cent of its value from mid 2008 to February 2009. Thus, Poles found it more difficult to pay for their travels abroad, and prices of imported goods

went up. Moreover, home owners with a mortgage faced stiff challenges. Before the crisis, interest rates on mortgages in euro of Swiss francs were considerably lower than those in Polish zloty. Thus, 40 per cent of mortgages were in foreign currencies, equivalent to about 12 per cent of Polish GDP, according to IMF estimates. Most of these borrowers had their assets (notably heir house) and their income (salary) in zloty. With the depreciation of the zloty – unexpected by most borrowers – they needed more zlotys to pay their euro or Swiss francs debt. Unable to afford the higher mortgage payments, many people lost their home. In a way, these home buyers were acting like a hedge fund – but often without understanding the risks they were taking when signing their mortgage.

Hungary, too, had a flexible exchange rate, but it faced considerably more challenges. The economy has been growing steadily at around 4 per cent or higher until 2006, but slowed down in 2007. In addition, Hungary had for a long time been burdened with relatively high debt, which made it more vulnerable. When the crisis hit, Hungary had to negotiate a special financing programme with the IMF and the EU for €18 billion in October 2008. The programme committed Hungary to stabilize its macroeconomy, which required cuts in budget spending and higher interest rates. The Hungarian forint depreciated by 22 per cent from summer 2008 to February 2009. Like in Poland, businesses and individuals faced steep increases in their debt payments for loans taken out in foreign currencies. In addition they faced the consequences of a recession at home, which reduced their ability to earn the money to service their debt.

Table 7.1 Economic Crisis in Selected CEE Countries

Country	Exchange Rate Regime	GDP per capita 2008, billion €	GDP Growth 2009 (EBRD projection)	Foreign currency mortgages, % of total
Poland	Floating	12 432	1.3%	40%
Hungary	Floating	10 198	−6.5%	70%
Latvia	Fixed	9 459	−16.0%	83%
Slovakia	Euro	10 501	−7.8%	1%

How did Poland's exchange rate regime affect its people during the financial crisis?

Other countries had fixed exchange rates, and they faced different sorts of challenges. The Baltic States Estonia, Latvia and Lithuania had adopted a fixed exchange rate based on a 'currency board' as a centrepiece of their economic policy since the early 1990s. For many years, it served them well. They emerged from the Soviet Union to implement radical market oriented reforms, achieved economic growth far above European average, and joined the EU in the first wave of new members from the transition economies in 2004.

However, the economic crisis tested their resolve. Without the flexibility of floating exchange rates, defence of the exchange rate became first policy priority during the crisis – and that almost failed.

Latvia was particularly hard hit. Extensive bank lending, particular for construction and consumer loans had fuelled an economic boom with over 10 per cent of annual GDP growth in 2005 to 2007. However, the crisis came suddenly and severely. First, the housing bubble burst. Then, the main locally-owned bank, Parex, went bust and had to be nationalized. In December 2008, Latvia had to ask the IMF for a €7.5 billion bailout. To get that money the Latvian government had to commit to a tight fiscal policy: government budgets were cut and interest rates were raised. The economy shrank by 4.6 per cent in 2008, and by a staggering 16.0 per cent in 2009.

With the expectation of joining the euro soon, even more Latvian borrowers – over 80 per cent of all mortgages – had taken out their mortgages in foreign currencies: the interest rates were lower, and with pegged exchange rates, what was the risk? If the government maintained the peg, indeed, home owners saved a lot of money that way. However, with the economy in a deep recession and local construction firms going bust, many borrowers struggled keeping their earnings up. The Latvian government faced a dilemma. Devaluation of the Latvian currency would help exports and thus help boost the economy – yet, it risked bankrupting a large number of its own people. Hence, the government opted for a very tough adjustment economic programme.

Two countries had entered the eurozone before the crisis hit, courtesy of their strong economic record in the early 2000s: Slovakia and Slovenia. Henceforth, they enjoyed the full protection of the currency union, which helped them to get through the recession relatively well.

Slovakia attracted billions of FDI, especially in the car industry (see Chapter 6), and these direct investors were more resilient than financial investors: They couldn't easily shut down when economic prospects became more uncertain. However, due to the strong euro, Slovakia – like Greece or Spain – faced challenges to its competitiveness because it could not devalue its currency when some key competitors had done so. On the other hand, Slovak home buyers had no reason to consider a currency other than the euro, and compared to their neighbours they were relatively save.

Sources: (1) *The Economist*, 2009, Ex-communist economies: the whiff of contagion, February 28; (2) *The Economist*, 2009, Foreign-currency mortgages: The bills are alive, October 10; (3) D.M. Nuti, 2009, Eastern Europe: from slowdown to nosedive, Blog, http://dmarionuti.blogspot.com, May 10; (4) EBRD, 2009, *Transition Report 2009*, London: European Bank of Reconstruction and Development.

Why is the exchange rate regime so important? What determines exchange rates? How do exchange rates affect trade and investment? How do firms manage their exposure to volatile exchange rates? Continuing from our two previous chapters on trade (Chapter 5) and foreign direct investment (FDI) (Chapter 6), this chapter addresses these crucial questions regarding financial flows in international business.

Exchange rate
The price of one currency in another currency.

An exchange rate is the price of one currency in another currency. The exchange rates between the world's major currencies are constantly on the move. Some of them are highly volatile, as illustrated in the Opening Case. Figures 7.1A and 7.1B show the volatility in two of the worlds most important exchange rates, $/€ and £/€. We use the terms appreciation and depreciation to describe shifts in the values of currencies. An appreciation is always described as an increase in the value of the currency, that is foreigners have to pay more for one unit, while a depreciation is a

Appreciation
(of a currency)
An increase in the value of a currency.

Depreciation
(of a currency)
A decrease in the value of a currency.

Figure 7.1A Exchange rate: US$/€ from 2005 to 2009

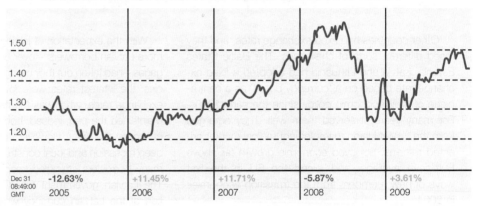

| | -12.63% | +11.45% | +11.71% | -5.87% | +3.61% |
| Dec 31 08:49:00 GMT | 2005 | 2006 | 2007 | 2008 | 2009 |

Source: *Financial Times*, www.ft.com/currencydata, accessed 31 December 2009, copyright © *Financial Times* 2009. Reproduced with permission.

Figure 7.1B Exchange rate: £/€ from 2005 to 2009

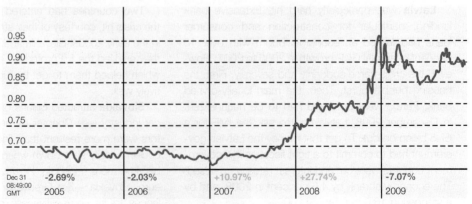

| | -2.69% | -2.03% | +10.97% | +27.74% | -7.07% |
| Dec 31 08:49:00 GMT | 2005 | 2006 | 2007 | 2008 | 2009 |

Note: The graphs show the price of 1 € in $ or £. A high value thus indicates a strong € and a weak $ or £.

Source: *Financial Times*, www.ft.com/currencydata, accessed 31 December 2009, copyright © *Financial Times* 2009. Reproduced with permission.

Table 7.2 Examples of key currency exchange rates

	€	¥	£	$
1.00 euro (€)	--	133.060	0.88790	1.44040
1.00 Chinese yuan	0.10165	13.5338	0.09028	0.14650
1.00 Indian rupee	1.49540	1.99070	0.01328	0.02156
100 Japanese yen (¥)	0.00751	--	0.00667	0.01082
1.00 Polish zloty	0.24330	0.32475	0.21649	0.35135
1.00 Russian rouble	0.02289	3.04760	0.02036	0.03299
1.00 Swedish krone	0.09750	12.9840	0.08656	0.14050
1.00 Swiss franc	0.67380	89.6500	0.59830	0.97090
1.00 Turkish lira	0.46423	0.61801	0.41200	0.66770
1.00 British pound (£)	1.12570	149.810	--	1.62230
1.00 US dollar ($)	0.69390	92.3600	0.61590	--

Source: 'Currency rates are constantly fluctuating' published on www.ft.com/currencydata 31 December 2009, copyright © 2010 Thomson Reuters. All Rights Reserved. Reproduced with permission.

loss of value of the currency. The price of the euro (€) in dollars ($) moved from $1.20 = €1 in early 2006 to almost $1.60 = €1 in summer of 2008, before falling back to $1.25 = €1 in the next winter.[1] Hence, the euro appreciated vis-à-vis the dollar from 2006 to 2008, and depreciated sharply in autumn 2008. Seen from the perspective of the dollar, it first depreciated over two years, before appreciating in 2008. As another example, the British pound (£) was worth £0.65 = €1 at the beginning of 2007, it then depreciated (the euro appreciated) to £0.95 = €1 at the end of 2008 before regaining some value in 2009.

Some other exchange rates are less volatile because of various form of government intervention (Table 7.2). For example, the Chinese yuan has for many years been pegged to the dollar, and then moved within narrow bands, due to government intervention. We discuss these issues taking the institution-based view as our primary starting point. Essentially, the institution-based view suggests that the 'rules of the game', domestic and international institutions (such as the IMF) influence exchange rates and affect capital movements. We start with a basic question: What determines exchange rates? Then, we track the evolution of the international monetary system and explain how different exchange rate regimes work. How firms strategically respond is outlined next. We conclude with some discussion on debates and extensions.

MARKETS FOR CURRENCIES

The currency exchange market is a market where individuals, firms, governments and banks buy and sell foreign currencies. Unlike a stock exchange, the currency exchange market has no central physical location. This market is truly global and transparent. Buyers and sellers are geographically dispersed but constantly linked (quoted prices change as often as 20 times a minute).[2] The market opens on Monday morning first in Tokyo and then Hong Kong and Singapore. Gradually,

LEARNING OBJECTIVE

1 understand the determinants of exchange rates

Currency exchange market
A market where individuals, firms, governments and banks buy and sell foreign currencies.

Frankfurt, Zurich, Paris, London, New York, Chicago and San Francisco 'wake up' and come online.

Operating on a 24/7 basis, the currency market is the largest and most active market in the world. On average, the worldwide volume exceeds $2 trillion a *day*. To put this mind-boggling number in perspective, the amount of one single *day* of currency exchange transactions is roughly double the amount of entire worldwide FDI outflows in one *year* and roughly equals close to one-quarter of worldwide merchandize exports in one *year*. What drives the prices in these currency markets?

The concept of an exchange rate as the price of a commodity – one country's currency – helps us understand its determinants. Basic economic theory suggests that the price of a commodity is most fundamentally determined by its supply and demand. Strong demand will lead to price hikes, and oversupply will result in price drops. Of course, we are dealing with a most unusual commodity here, money, because currency transactions are often an indirect outcome of other transactions. Yet, the basic underlying principles still apply.

First, when France sells products to the UK, French exporters often demand that they be paid in euros because that is more convenient to them. Likewise, British tourists need to buy euros to pay for their hotels, restaurants and other expenses in France (which are technically speaking French service exports). British importers of French products will somehow have to generate euros to pay for their imports. The easiest way to generate euros is to *export* to France (or other countries using the euro), and be paid in euros. In this example, the euro is the common transaction currency involving both French imports and French exports. Hence, the British importer of French goods would buy euros from their bank, that in turn buys them on international currency markets. On the other hand, British exporters receive euros as payments for their goods; they would thus sell their euros. This first source of supply and demand on currency markets is international trade in goods or services (Chapter 5).

The second source of demand and supply of foreign currency is foreign direct investment (Chapter 6). When a company builds a factory or buys another company abroad, it needs to buy foreign currency to pay for the expense. This creates a demand for the host country's currency. On the other hand, when overseas affiliates repatriate profits that creates a demand for the home country's currency. The third source of supply and demand is financial investors who buy a portfolio of assets such as shares or bonds in another country purely for financial reasons. These financial investors account by far for most transactions in financial markets.

Because currencies are such unique commodities, their markets are influenced not only by economic factors but also by a lot of political and psychological factors. We next explore five underlying forces that contribute to the supply and demand for currencies: (1) relative price differences, (2) inflation and monetary supply, (3) interest rates; (4) productivity and balance of payments and (5) investor psychology.

Relative price differences and purchasing power parity

Purchasing power parity (PPP) hypothesis
Hypothesis suggesting that, in the long run, baskets of goods would cost the same in all currencies ('law of one price').

Some countries (such as Switzerland) are famously expensive, and others (such as the Philippines) are known to have cheap prices. How do these price differences affect exchange rate? An answer is provided by the purchasing power parity (PPP) hypothesis, which is essentially the 'law of one price'. The theory suggests that in the absence of trade barriers (such as tariffs), the price for identical products sold in different countries must be the same. Otherwise, arbitragers may 'buy low' and 'sell high', eventually driving different prices for identical products to the same level around the world. The PPP hypothesis suggests that in the long run, exchange rates should move toward levels that would equalize the prices of an identical basket of goods in any two countries.[3]

You can test the PPP hypothesis yourself by buying the same product in several countries as you travel. If it is a tradeable product, and there are no differences in taxation and no tariff barriers it should – in theory – cost the same in every country. The *Economist* magazine does this exercise regularly using a McDonald's Big Mac hamburger. In March 2010, a Big Mac cost $3.58 in the USA and – at market exchange rates – $4.62 in the eurozone.[4] According to this calculation, the euro was 29 per cent 'overvalued' against the dollar. However, the Big Mac is not really a tradable good – it is largely made from local ingredients and with local labour. Hence, it is domestic demand and supply that determine the price of a Big Mac.[5] To truly test the PPP hypothesis, you have to use a tradable good such as a t-shirt, an IPod or a car (and you have to deduct value added tax). Thus, the answer to the question 'why is Switzerland much more expensive than the Philippines?' is that goods are not perfectly free to trade across countries.

Inflation and money supply

The PPP in its strict interpretation may at best apply in the long term – the Big Mac index has for many years suggested that the Swiss Franc is overvalued and various emerging economy currencies are undervalued. However, a weaker version of PPP, known as relative PPP hypothesis, suggests that *changes* in prices should be the same in both countries, after considering the exchange rate. Thus, when prices rise faster (the inflation is higher) in Britain than in euroland, then the British pound should depreciate relative to the euro proportional to the difference in the inflation rate.

> **Relative PPP hypothesis**
> Hypothesis suggesting that changes in exchange rates will be proportional to differences in inflation rates.

Inflation is closely associated with amount of money in circulation. A high level of inflation is essentially too much money chasing too few goods in an economy – technically, an expansion of a country's money supply. The more money people have in their purse, the higher the prices they are able to pay. A government, when facing budgetary shortfalls, may choose to print more currency to increase the money supply, which tends to stimulate inflation. In turn, this would cause its currency to depreciate. This makes sense because as the supply of a given currency (such as the British pound) increases while the demand stays the same, the per unit value of that currency (such as one pound) goes down. Therefore, the exchange rate is very sensitive to changes in monetary policy. It responds swiftly to changes in money supply. The depreciation of the pound relative to the euro during the financial crisis of 2008/09 may thus have been caused by the Bank of England's more loose monetary policy aimed to stimulate domestic demand.

> **Inflation**
> The (average) change of prices over time.

Interest rates, and interest rate parity

Financial investors are not so much interested in the prices of Big Macs, or other goods they might buy in either country; they focus on their return on investment. In the short run, variations in interest rates have a powerful effect. A basic consideration is this: Should I invest my money at home, or should I invest abroad? If markets are efficient, then these two investment alternatives should yield the same outcome. This is known as interest rate parity. It suggests that the return should be the same for the following two transactions:

> **Interest rate parity**
> Hypothesis suggesting that the interest rate in two currencies should be the same after accounting for spot and forward in exchange rates.

a Invest in a one year government bond in your own country.

b (1) Buy foreign currency at today's rate (the spot market rate), (2) invest in a one year foreign currency government bond and (3) sell foreign currency for delivery in one year's time.

> **Spot market rate**
> The exchange rate for immediate payment.

Forward transaction
A currency exchange transaction in which participants buy and sell currencies now for future delivery, typically in 30, 90 or 180 days, after the date of the transaction.

You can actually sell currency for delivery at specified days in the future, typically 30, 60, 90 or 180 days, a forward transaction. This means you commit yourself to deliver the currency at that time at that price (the forward exchange rate) – independent of where the current exchange rate is in the future. The forward exchange rate reflects market participants' expectations of the future exchange rate. This expectation may be driven by, for example, the differences in inflation rates, and thus the relative PPP hypothesis discussed above. *Before proceeding, make a little experiment!* Pick up the latest issue of the *Financial Times* or another financial newspaper and find current rates for the following: (1) today's exchange rate, (2) forward exchange rates one year from today and (3+4) interest rates for money market investment in the two currencies. Can you demonstrate that interest rate parity holds? (If you look at a shorter time period, you will need to adjust the interest rate earned, for example 90/360 for three months).

Forward exchange rate
The exchange rate for forward transactions.

Since investors have these two investment alternatives, logically, exchange rates and interest rates are very closely related. If one country increases its interest rate while the other does not, then either the current exchange rate or the forward exchange rate has to adjust. If the inflation rates are the same (and expected to stay the same), then the forward exchange rate is likely to stay stable, and the current exchange rate is likely to appreciate. If increases in interest rates also affect inflation expectations, then the main adjustment may be in the forward exchange rate.

Productivity and balance of payments

In international trade, the rise of a country's productivity, relative to other countries, will improve its competitive position – this is a basic proposition of the theories of absolute and comparative advantage discussed in Chapter 5. Productivity fuels exports, which in turn increases demand for a country's currency. One recent example is China. All the China-bound FDI inflows in dollars, euros and pounds have to be converted to local currency, boosting the demand for the yuan. Hence, the yuan would appreciate unless the government was neutralizing the effect by buying massive amounts of US government bonds. Other examples are not hard to find. The rise in relative Japanese productivity over the past three decades led to a long-run appreciation of the yen, which rose from about ¥310 = $1 in 1975 to ¥118 = $1 in 2007.

Balance of payments (BoP)
A country's international transaction statement, including merchandize trade, service trade and capital movement.

Recall from Chapter 5 that changes in productivity will change a country's balance of trade. A country that is highly productive in manufacturing may generate a surplus in trade in goods, whereas a country that is less productive in manufacturing may end up with a deficit on its trade account. These have ramifications for the balance of payments (BoP) – officially known as a country's international transaction statement. Table 7.3 illustrates the components of the BoP for the UK in the year 2009. In that year, the UK imported more goods than its exported, leading to a deficit of £81.8 billion on the 'trade balance'. In services, the UK generated an export surplus of £49.3 billion, the biggest contributor being financial services (despite the financial crisis in that year). The UK also earned a surplus on income, most of which arose from foreign direct investment undertaken by British firms in the past. The UK paid more in transfer overseas than it received; this category included payments to and from the EU as well as for example development aid. The sum of all these transactions, known as current account, lead to a deficit of £18.4 billion in the UK in 2009.

Current account (of the BoP)
Exports and imports of goods and services.

Capital and financial account (of the BoP)
Sales and purchases of financial assets.

This deficit was financed by a variety of financial flows recorded in the capital and financial account. Net inflows of FDI of £17.5 billion, hence more foreign investors were investing in the UK than British MNEs investor overseas, which is a reversal from a long term trend – note in the current account that British MNEs generate more income than foreign MNE operating in the UK – and of transfers, which are mainly from individuals working abroad. The balance of financial investments is

Table 7.3 The UK Balance of Payments, 2009 (billion pound)

	Current Account	Export (income)	Import (payments)	Balance
1	Trade in Goods	227.670	309.460	−81.790
2	Trade in Services	161.168	111.855	49.313
3	Income	175.571	146.915	28.656
4	Transfers	16.998	31.612	−14.614
5	Current Account Balance (line 1+2+3+4)			−18.435

	Capital and Financial Account	Foreign investment in the UK	UK investment abroad	Balance
6	Capital Transfers	5.854	2.225	3.629
7	Direct Investment	29.320	11.852	17.468
8	Financial Investment	−191.693	−190.213	−1.480
9	Reserve Assets		5.763	−5.763
10	Capital and Financial Account Balance (line 6+7+8+9)			13.854
11	Net errors and omissions (line 10−5)			−4.581

very small, at a deficit of £1.5 billion, although the financial flows in and out of the country have been very large indeed during the year. Other countries with a substantial current account deficit, such as the USA, had to finance it by selling government bonds to foreign investors, which also showed up in the BoP line. In the UK in 2009, the central bank increased its position of foreign reserve assets by £5.8 billion, which also showed up as investment abroad in the BoP. These numbers added up to the capital and financial account of £13.9 billion. In theory, the capital and current account should balance – in practice however, they don't. There is quite a substantial measurement error in these data because the Central bank never knows details of all transactions and needs to make estimates for some of the numbers.

To make a long story short, a country experiencing a current account surplus will see its currency appreciate; conversely, a country experiencing a current account deficit will see its currency depreciate. This may not happen overnight, but it will happen in a span of years and decades. Going back to the 1950s and 1960s, the rise of the dollar was accompanied by a sizable US surplus on merchandize trade. By the 1970s and 1980s, the surplus gradually turned into a deficit. By the 1990s and 2000s, the US current account deficit became ever increasing, forcing the dollar to depreciate relative to other currencies, such as the euro, the Japanese yen and the Chinese yuan. Broadly speaking, the value of a country's currency is an embodiment of its economic productivity and balance of payments positions.

Investor psychology

Although theories on price differences (PPP), interest rates, inflation and money supply and balance of payments policies predict long-run movements of exchange rates, they often fall short of predicting short-run movements. It is investor psychology, some of which is fickle and thus very hard to predict, that largely determines short-run movements. Professor Richard Lyons at the University of California, Berkeley, is an expert on exchange rate theories. However, he was baffled when he was invited by a friend to observe currency trading first hand:

> 'As I sat there, my friend traded furiously all day long, racking up over $1 billion in trades each day. This was a world where the standard trade was $10 million, and a $1 million trade was a "skinny one". Despite my belief that exchange rates depend on macroeconomics, only rarely was news of this type his primary concern. Most of the time he was reading tea leaves that were, at least to me, not so clear … It was clear my understanding was incomplete when he looked over, in the midst of his fury, and asked me: "What should I do?" I laughed. Nervously'.[6]

Bandwagon effect
The result of investors moving as a herd in the same direction at the same time.

Capital flight
A phenomenon in which a large number of individuals and companies exchange domestic currencies for a foreign currency.

Investors – currency traders (such as the one Lyons observed), foreign portfolio investors, and average citizens – may move as a 'herd' at the same time in the same direction, resulting in a bandwagon effect. The bandwagon effect seemed to be at play in the second half of 2008, when the Icelandic krona lost more than half of its value against key currencies such as the dollar and the euro. Essentially, a large number of individuals and firms exchanged the krona for the key foreign currencies in order to minimize their exposure to Iceland's financial crisis – a phenomenon known as capital flight. This would push down the demand for, and thus the value of, domestic currencies. Then, more individuals and companies joined the herd, further depressing the exchange rate and setting off a major economic crisis.

Overall both economics and psychology are involved in determining exchange rates. However, so far we have discussed currency markets *as if* they are freely driven by supply and demand. Of course, that is not entirely true. The markets for some

© Alex Segre/Alamy

What drives the day to day activities of currency traders?

currencies are heavily influenced by governments (more precisely, by Central Bank interventions). To understand how and why, we first need to make a historical excursion.

INSTITUTIONS OF THE INTERNATIONAL MONETARY SYSTEM

Three eras are commonly distinguished in the evolution of the institutions governing currency exchange markets, known as the international monetary system, over the past 150 years. They are (1) the gold standard, (2) the Bretton Woods system and (3) the post – Bretton Woods system.

The gold standard (1870–1914)

The gold standard was a system in place between the 1870s and 1914, when the value of most major currencies was maintained by fixing their prices in terms of gold. Gold was used as the common denominator for all currencies. This was essentially a global fixed rate system, with little volatility and every bit of predictability and stability. To be able to redeem its currency in gold at a fixed price, every central bank needed to maintain gold reserves. The system provided powerful incentives for countries to avoid run current account deficits, as that would quickly deplete their reserves of gold.

The gold standard was severely undermined in 1914 when World War I broke out and several combatant countries printed excessive amounts of currency to finance their war efforts. After World War I, many countries re-joined the gold standard. However, during the Great Depression (1929–1933), countries engaged in competitive devaluations in an effort to boost exports at the expense of trading partners. But no country could win such a 'race to the bottom', and the gold standard eventually had to be abandoned.

Gold standard
A system in which the value of most major currencies was maintained by fixing their prices in terms of gold, which served as the common denominator.

The bretton woods system (1944–1973)

Towards the end of World War II, at an allied conference in Bretton Woods, New Hampshire, USA, a new system – known as the Bretton Woods system – was agreed upon by 44 countries. The Bretton Woods system was centred on the US dollar as the new common denominator. All currencies were pegged at a fixed rate to the dollar, and changes in exchange rates were rare. The USA became the anchor of the system by promising that other countries could at any time convert their dollars to gold at $35 per ounce.

At the Bretton Woods conference, two institutions were created that were to secure the stability of this new monetary system, and the world economy more generally. Both continue to play an important role in the globally integrated economy of the 21st century (see Chapter 9). The International Monetary Fund (IMF) provides financial assistance to countries experiencing temporary imbalances in their balance of payment, and helps countries to secure macroeconomic stability. The World Bank provides loans for specific projects in developing countries to support their economic development, for example construction of airports, reforms of the education system or administration of privatization programmes.

In the Bretton Woods system, the dollar was given a pivotal role in the global economy, making it the most used reserve currency of countries around the world. This was appropriate at the time because the US economy had the highest levels of productivity and contributed approximately 70 per cent of the global GDP in the late 1940s. The system was sustained by the large US trade surplus with the rest of the world; the USA was the export engine of the world when the rest of the

Bretton Woods system
A system in which all currencies were pegged at a fixed rate to the US dollar.

International Monetary Fund (IMF)
International organization that provides financial assistance to countries experiencing temporary imbalances in their balance of payment, and helps securing macroeconomic stability.

World Bank
International organization that provides loans for specific projects in developing countries.

world recovered from World War II. Overall, the system served the world well for about 25 years.

By the late 1960s and early 1970s, a combination of rising productivity elsewhere and US inflationary policies put pressures on Bretton Woods. First, West Germany and other countries got caught up in productivity and exported more, and the USA ran its first post-1945 trade deficit in 1971. This pushed the German mark to appreciate and the dollar to depreciate – a situation very similar to the yen – dollar relationship in the 1980s and the yuan – dollar relationship in the 2000s. Second, in the 1960s, to finance the Vietnam War, the USA increased government spending not by additional taxation but by increasing the money supply. These actions led to rising inflation levels and strong pressures for the dollar to depreciate.

As currency traders bought more German marks, Germany's central bank, the Bundesbank, had to buy billions of dollars to maintain the dollar/mark exchange rate fixed by Bretton Woods. Being stuck with massive amounts of the dollar that was worth less now, Germany allowed its currency to float in May 1971.

Likewise, the Bretton Woods system became a pain in the neck for the USA because it was not allowed to unilaterally change the exchange rate of the dollar. Per Bretton Woods agreements, the US Treasury was obligated to dispense one ounce of gold for every \$35 brought by a foreign central bank such as the Bundesbank. Consequently, when other countries realized that the \$35 rate was no longer realistic, gold started flowing from the USA into the coffers of other central banks. In August 1971, to stop this loss of its reserves, the US government unilaterally announced that the dollar was no longer convertible into gold, effectively defaulting on its earlier promise. After tense negotiations, major countries collectively agreed to hammer in the coffin nails of the Bretton Woods system by allowing their currencies to float in 1973. In retrospect, the Bretton Woods system had been built on two conditions: (1) the US inflation rate had to be low and (2) the US could not run a substantial trade deficit. When both these conditions were violated, the demise of the system was inevitable.

The post – bretton woods system (1973 – present)

Post – Bretton Woods system
A system of flexible exchange rate regimes with no official common denominator.

As a result, today we live in the post – Bretton Woods system. This system is essentially built around floating exchange rates between the world's major currencies (dollar, euro, yen), with a diversity of exchange rate regimes described earlier for other currencies, ranging from various floating systems to various fixed rates. Its main drawback is turbulence and uncertainty. Since the early 1970s, the US dollar is no longer the official common denominator. However, it has retained a significant amount of 'soft power' as a key currency, accounting for about 65 per cent of the reserve currencies held by central banks. The leading role is unlikely to change in the near future as dollar denominated financial markets are most liquid.[7]

Floating (or flexible) exchange rate policy
The willingness of a government to let the demand and supply conditions determine exchange rates.

Since 1973, countries can choose between three major exchange rate policies: (1) floating rate, (2) a pegged rate or (3) adoption of another (or common) currency. Governments adopting the floating (or flexible) exchange rate policy tend to be free market believers, willing to let the demand and supply conditions determine exchange rates – usually on a daily basis via the currency exchange market. However, few countries adopt a free float, which would be a pure market solution. Most countries practice a managed float, with selective government interventions. Of the major currencies, the US, Canadian and Australian dollars, the yen, and the pound have been under managed float since the 1970s (after the collapse of the Bretton Woods system). Since the late 1990s, several developing countries, such as Brazil, Mexico and South Korea, have also joined the managed float regime, as did Hungary and Poland (see Opening Case). The severity of intervention is a matter of degree. Heavier intervention moves the country closer to a fixed exchange rate policy,

Free float
A pure market solution to determine exchange rates.

Managed float
The practice of influencing exchange rates through selective government intervention.

and less intervention enables a country to approach the free float ideal. A main objective of intervention is to prevent the emergence of erratic fluctuations that may trigger macroeconomic turbulence.

An alternative exchange rate regime is the pegged exchange rate policy – countries 'peg' the exchange rate of their currencies relative to another currency, typically the dollar or the euro. This means that the currency is allowed to fluctuate only within a more or less narrow band relative to that other currency. For example the Danish krone (DKK) is pegged to the euro. Even in 2009 – a year with high volatility in international currency markets – the DKK/€ rate only fluctuated between 7.47 and 7.42. Others choose a continuously adjusting exchange rate – known as crawling band – which may be suitable for a country that wishes to allow for a slightly higher inflation than the currency it is pegged to. China has at times adopted a crawling band to gradually adjust its exchange rate.

Pegged exchange rate
An exchange rate of a currency attached to that of another currency.

Crawling bands
A policy of keeping the exchange rate within a specified range, which may be changing over time.

There are two benefits for a peg policy. First, a peg stabilizes the import and export prices for smaller economies that otherwise may experience high volatility in their exchange rate. Second, many developing countries with high inflation have pegged their currencies to the dollar or the euro (currencies with relatively low inflation) to restrain domestic inflation. However, there are two drawbacks of pegging an exchange rate. First, interest rates have to be set to support the pegged exchange rate (remember interest rate parity) and cannot be used for other economic policy objectives. Second, the peg has to be credible. Currency exchange traders are likely to attack a currency if they believe that a pegged rate is not sustainable, for example because the inflation rate is too high or Central Bank does not have enough reserves. The expectation that the currency will be devalued creates a big profit opportunity for those selling the currency just before the devaluation. This expectation can be so powerful that it overwhelms even the most esteemed central banks. The UK experienced such a devaluation in 1992, which severely disrupted business and ultimately led to the downfall of the Thatcher government.

An extreme case of a pegged exchange rate is a fixed exchange rate, which allows no movements of the currency at all. Such fixed rates have become rare since the 1970s. The most extreme fixed rate policy is a currency board, which is a monetary authority that issues notes and coins convertible into a key foreign currency at a *fixed* exchange rate. Usually, the fixed exchange rate is set by law, making changes to the exchange rate politically very costly for governments. To honour its commitment, a currency board must back the domestic currency with 100 per cent of equivalent foreign currencies. In the case of Hong Kong's currency board, every HK$7.8 in circulation is backed by US$1. By design, a currency board is passive. When more US dollars flow in, the board issues more Hong Kong dollars and interest rates fall. When more US dollars flow out, the board reduces money supply and interest rates rise. The Hong Kong currency board has been jokingly described as an Asian outpost of the US Federal Reserve. This is technically accurate because interest rates in Hong Kong are essentially determined by the US Federal Reserve. While the Hong Kong currency board was a successful bulwark against speculative attacks on the Hong Kong dollar in 1997 and 1998, a currency board is not necessarily a panacea, as evidenced by Argentina's experience (In Focus 7.1).

Fixed exchange rate
An exchange rate of a currency relative to other currencies.

Currency board
A monetary authority that issues notes and coins convertible into a key foreign currency at a fixed exchange rate.

The third option is to give up your own monetary policy entirely, and thus rely on another country, or a common Central Bank, to manage inflation and exchange rate. Such a common currency is used for example in West Africa where 14 countries use the 'CFA franc', which in turn is fixed to the euro. Thus, monetary policy for these countries in Africa is effectively determined by the European Central Bank in Frankfurt. Of course, the euro itself is a common currency shared by 16 countries in 2010, as we will discuss in greater detail in the next chapter. Some small

Common currency
Currency shared by a number of countries

IN FOCUS 7.1

Hong Kong and Argentina: A tale of two currency boards

Hong Kong is usually cited as an example that has benefited from a currency board. In the early 1980s, Hong Kong had a floating exchange rate. As Britain and China intensified their negotiations over the colony's future, the fear that the 'Hong Kong way of life' might be abandoned after 1997 shook business confidence, pushed down real estate values and caused panic buying of vegetable oil and rice. The result was 16 per cent depreciation in the Hong Kong dollar against the US dollar. In 1983, the Hong Kong government ended the crisis by adopting a currency board that pegged the exchange rate at HK$7.8 = US$1. The currency board almost immediately restored confidence. The second major test of the currency board came in 1997, in the first autumn after Hong Kong was returned to Chinese sovereignty. During the Asian financial crisis of 1997–1998, Hong Kong's currency board stood like a rock, successfully repelled speculative attacks, and maintained its peg to the US dollar.

In Argentina, hyperinflation was rampant in the 1980s. Prices increased by more than 1000 per cent (!) in both 1989 and 1990. In 1991, to tame its tendency to finance public spending by printing pesos,

Argentina adopted a currency board and pegged the peso at parity to the US dollar (1 peso = US$1). At first, the system worked, as inflation was brought down to 2 per cent by 1995. However, by the late 1990s, Argentina was hit by multiple problems. First, appreciation of the dollar made its exports less competitive. Second, rising US interest rates spilled over to Argentina. Third, depreciation of Brazil's real GDP resulted in more imports from Brazil and fewer exports from Argentina to Brazil. To finance budget deficits, Argentina borrowed dollars on the international market, as printing more pesos was not possible under the currency board. When further borrowing became impossible in 2001, the government defaulted on its $155 billion public debt (a world record), ended the peso's convertibility, and froze most dollar-denominated deposits in banks. In 2002, Argentina was forced to give up its currency board. After the delink, the peso plunged, hitting a low of 3.5 to the dollar. Riots broke out as people voiced their displeasure with politicians.

Sources: Based on (1) F. Gunter, 2004, Why did Argentina's currency board collapse? *The World Economy*, May: 697–704; (2) R. Carbaugh, 2007, *International Economics*, 11th ed. (p. 492–495), Cincinnati, OH: Thomson South-Western.

countries, have one-sidedly adopted another currency, for example the dollar is used in Panama and the euro is used in Montenegro.

Pegged versus floating exchange rates

With the blending of pegged and floating exchange rate regimes, the debate has never ended on which would be better. Proponents of pegged exchange rates argue that these rates impose monetary discipline by preventing governments from engaging in inflationary monetary policies (essentially, printing more money). Proponents also suggest that pegged exchange rates reduce uncertainty and thus encourage trade and FDI, not only benefiting the particular economy but also helping the global economy.[8]

Proponents of floating exchange rates believe that market forces should take care of supply and demand and thus the price of any currency.[9] Under a pegged (or fixed) exchange rate, central banks have to continuously intervene to guarantee the exchange rate. A trade deficit would result in diminishing of currency reserves, which is not sustainable over longer periods of time. Floating exchange rates create an automatic adjustment mechanisms where trade surpluses lead to currency appreciation that then increases the prices of exports, and thus reduces the trade surplus. In other words, flexible exchange rates may help avoid the sudden crises that occur under fixed exchange rates when expectations of an impending devaluation arise. For example, Thailand probably would not have been devastated so suddenly in July 1997 (generally regarded as the triggering event for the 1997 Asian financial crisis) had it operated a floating exchange rate system. In addition, floating exchange rates allow each country to make its own monetary policy. A major problem of the Bretton Woods system was that in the late 1960s, other countries were not happy about fixing their currencies to the currency of a country, the USA, which conducted inflationary monetary policies.

MANAGING EXCHANGE RISKS

Firms engaging in international business are almost always exposed to exchange rate movements. Thus, they face exchange rate risk (or currency risk), that is the possibility of financial losses because of unexpected changes in exchange rates. Whenever a foreign currency transaction involves a payment to be made at a later time – such as payment for goods upon delivery – firms are exposed to exchange rate risks. In volatile markets, this exchange rate risk can potentially undermine the profitability of a business transaction; in extreme cases it has driven companies into bankruptcy (for example, in the Thai crisis of 1997).

The fundamental principle for minimizing exchange rate risk is to ensure that future revenue streams and future expenses are in the same currency. Whenever expected financial flows are in different currencies, companies are exposed to currency risk.[10] In a flexible exchange rate regime, the exchange rate risk is evident from the volatility of the exchange rates in the past (see Figures 7.1a and 7.1b above). In a fixed exchange rate regime, the risk is more difficult to assess. There is a large probability that the exchange rate stays the same. However, there is also a small probability that the fixed exchange rate breaks down – and then a very substantial adjustment may occur. Companies can address this risk in two ways, (1) by strategically structuring their business in such a way that revenues are in the same currencies as expenses, or by (2) using financial market instruments to manage risk exposure (Table 7.4).

LEARNING OBJECTIVE

3 identify firms' strategic responses to deal with exchange movements

Exchange rate risk (or currency risk)
The risk of financial losses because of unexpected changes in exchange rates.

Table 7.4 Managing Exchange Rate Risk

Strategic	Financial
• Invoicing in your own currency	• Spot market transaction plus investing or borrowing in foreign currency
• Strategic hedging by balancing currencies of cost and revenue streams	• Forward market transactions
• Diversification by trading in multiple currencies	• Swap market transactions

Strategic responses

Companies can reduce their exposure to exchange rate risk in three ways, (1) by invoicing in their own currency, (2) by strategic hedging or (3) by risk diversification. The most basic way to reduce exchange rate risk is to invoice customers in your own currency, and to only accept payment in your own currency. This may sound very simple, but it is actually the most powerful way to protect yourself (In Focus 7.2). In practice, the currency of invoicing is subject to negotiation, and you may have to agree to a slightly less favourable price. Invoicing in your own currency is a low risk option, but it is not completely risk free: you still face the (normally small) possibility that your business partner goes bankrupt in a financial market upheaval, and thus is unable to pay up.

Second, a more sophisticated strategy is strategic hedging, which involves organizing activities in such a way that currencies of expenditures and revenues match. For example, a British firm receiving a major export order from France may in return order some components in France. It can then use the euro received for its export order to pay for its own imports. Or, companies may establish a local production facility. If part of the production occurs locally, then some of the costs are in local currency, which reduces the exchange rate exposure.[11] Strategic hedging was one of the key motivations behind Toyota's 1998 decision to set up a new factory in France instead of expanding its existing British operations (which would cost less in the short run). France is in the euro zone that the British refused to join. Strategic hedging refers to arranging your operations such as to reduce your exposure to exchange rate risk – through sourcing or FDI. This is more strategic because it established long-term structures that reduce the need for complex financial management, and it involves managers from many functional areas (such as production, marketing and sourcing) in addition to those from finance.

Third, companies may diversify their exchange rate risk by engaging with a number of countries using different currency zones to offset the currency losses in certain regions through gains in other regions.[12] Such currency risk diversification reduces exposure to unfavourable exchange movements from any one currency. For example, a European firm selling to a wide range of countries (and invoicing in local currency) in 2008 may have experience substantial losses on its orders from Iceland but made gains on orders to the USA. This strategy however does not work if your own country experiences a major crisis. Imagine a (hypothetical) British company in early 2007 ordering construction of a building to be completed and paid in a mix of euros and dollars at the end of 2008. Since the pound sharply depreciated in 2008 (see Figure 7.1B), this company would have struggled to pay the agreed amount of euro and dollars. A different sort of strategy is required, and that's where financial markets can help.

Strategic hedging
Organizing activities in such a way that currencies of revenues and expenditures match.

Currency risk diversification
Reducing overall risk exposure by working with a number of different currencies.

Financial management responses

How can companies use financial markets to manage their exchange rate risks? There are three primary types of exchange transactions: (1) spot transactions, (2) forward transactions and (3) swaps. Spot transactions are the classic single-shot exchange of one currency for another. For example, through spot transactions, Russian tourists may buy several thousand euros with their roubles and will get their euros from a bank right away. A Russian business expecting an invoice in euro in a year's time could in principle also buy the euros on the spot market, and then invest them in German government bonds until the invoice arrives. In practice, however, the company may not have the money available at this earlier time.

The second option is to use forward markets. Recall that forward transactions allow participants to buy and sell currencies now for future delivery, typically

IN FOCUS 7.2

Irish exporters cope with currency fluctuation

A member of the euro area, Ireland has strong exporters that sell not only throughout Europe but also in many other parts of the world. The downside of selling around the world is the complication of having to deal with currency fluctuation. Approximately 50 per cent of the Irish export invoicing is done in either British pound sterling or US dollars, which have fluctuated substantially during the 2008/09 crisis. While hedging using forward contracts is an obvious coping strategy, many smaller exporters cannot afford the expenses. In addition, hedging is not risk-free. Wrong bets may end up burning firms big time.

To better cope with currency fluctuation, a straightforward mechanism is to insist on payment in euros. As

a growing number of buyers of Irish exports have agreed, this strategy seems to have worked. A survey in late 2008 conducted by the Irish Exporters Association found that 38 per cent of buyers in the UK, 18 per cent in North America, 48 per cent in the Middle East, 45 per cent in Asia, 67 per cent in Latin America and 83 per cent in non-euro area European countries were willing to pay Irish exporters in euros, thus eliminating the problem of currency fluctuation for Irish exporters. Although this is a small piece of evidence, it does help paint a picture of the euro's rising popularity as a major currency for international trade around the world.

Sources: Based on (1) The Euro Information Website, 2009, www .ibiblio.org/theeuro/InformationWebsite.htm; (2) *The Independent*, 2009, Exporters get resourceful to fight currency fluctuation, November 21, www.independent.ie; (3) Irish Exporters Association, 2009, http://www.irishexporters.ie.

© PSL Images/Alamy

How can Irish exporters, such as Guinness, minimize their exchange rate risk exposure?

in 30, 90 or 180 days, after the date of the transaction. The primary benefit of such transactions is to protect investors from exposure to the fluctuations of the spot rate, an act known as currency hedging. Currency hedging is essentially a way to minimize the exchange rate risk inherent in all non-spot transactions. Traders and investors expecting to make or receive payments in a foreign currency in the future are concerned whether they will have to make a greater payment or receive less in

Currency hedging
A transaction that protects traders and investors from exposure to the fluctuations of the spot rate.

terms of the domestic currency should the spot rate change. For example, if the forward rate of the euro (€/$) is exactly the same as the spot rate, the euro is 'flat'. If the forward rate of the euro per dollar is *higher* than the spot rate, the euro has a forward discount. If the forward rate of the euro per dollar is *lower* than the spot rate, the euro then has a forward premium.

Hypothetically, assume that (1) today's exchange rate of €/$ is 1, (2) a US firm expects to be paid €1 million six months later and (3) the euro is at a 180-day forward discount of 1.1. The US firm may take out a forward contract now and convert euro earnings into a dollar revenue of $909 091 (€1 million/1.1) after six months. Does such a move make sense? There can be two answers. Yes, if the firm knew in advance that the future spot rate would be 1.25. With the forward contract, the US firm would make $909 091 instead of $800 000 (€1 million/1.25) – the difference is $109 091 (14 per cent of $800 000). However, the answer would be no if the spot rate after six months was below 1.1. If the spot rate remained at 1, the firm could have earned $1 million, *without* the forward contract, instead of only $909 091. This simple example suggests a powerful observation: Currency hedging may lead to a win or loss compared to a strategy of 'wait and buy on the sport market' (see Closing Case). However, the waiting strategy exposes the firm to a currency risk – exchange rates can go up as well as down. Remember, that the best bet available for the future exchange rate is the rate in the forward market. Only if you believe that you are smarter than the market would it make sense to bet against the market (and there are a lot of smart people active in that market). Of course, *afterwards* a lot of people will say 'you should have …' – but with hindsight advice is always cheap!

A third major type of currency exchange transaction is a swap. A currency swap is the conversion of one currency into another in Time 1, with an agreement to revert it back to the original currency at a specific, Time 2, in the future. Deutsche Bank may have an excess balance of pounds but needs dollars. At the same time, Union Bank of Switzerland (UBS) may have more dollars than it needs at the moment but is looking for more pounds. They can negotiate a swap agreement in which Deutsche Bank agrees to exchange with UBS pounds for dollars today and dollars for pounds at a specific point in the future.

The primary participants of the currency exchange market are large international banks such as Deutsche Bank and UBS that trade among themselves. How do these banks make money by trading money? They make money by capturing the difference between their offer rate (the price to sell) and bid rate (the price to buy) – the bid rate is *always* lower than the offer rate. The difference of this 'buy low, sell high' strategy is technically called the spread. For example, Deutsche Bank may quote offer and bid rates for the Swiss franc at $0.5854 and $0.5851, respectively, and the spread is $0.0003. That is, Deutsche Bank is willing to sell 1 million francs for $585 400 and buy 1 million francs for $585 100. If Deutsche Bank can simultaneously buy and sell 1 million francs, it can make $300 (the spread of $0.0003 × 1 million francs). Given the instantaneous and transparent nature of the electronically linked currency exchange market around the globe (one new quote in London can reach New York before you finish reading this sentence), the opportunities for trading, or arbitrage, can come and go very quickly. The globally integrated nature of this market leads to three outcomes:

- Razor-thin spread.
- Quick (often literally split-second) decisions on buying and selling (remember Professor Lyons's observation earlier).
- Ever increasing volume to make more profits (recall the daily volume of $2 trillion). In the earlier example, $300 is obviously just a few 'peanuts' for

Forward discount
A condition under which the forward rate of one currency relative to another currency is higher than the spot rate.

Forward premium
A condition under which the forward rate of one currency relative to another currency is lower than the spot rate.

Currency swap
A currency exchange transaction between two firms in which one currency is converted into another in Time 1, with an agreement to revert it back to the original currency at a specific Time 2 in the future.

Offer rate
The price offered to sell a currency.

Bid rate
The price offered to buy a currency.

Spread
The difference between the offered price and the bid price.

Deutsche Bank. Do a little math: How much trading in Swiss francs does Deutsche Bank have to do to make $1 million in profits for itself?

Overall, the importance of currency management cannot be overstressed for firms of all stripes interested in doing business abroad. Firms whose performance is otherwise stellar can be devastated by unfavourable currency movements.

From a resource-based view, it seems imperative that firms develop resources and capabilities that can combat currency risks in addition to striving for excellence in, for example, operations and marketing.[13] MNE subsidiary managers in certain countries may believe that there are lucrative opportunities to expand production. However, if these countries suffer from high currency risks, it may be better – for the multinational as a whole – to curtail such expansion and channel resources to other countries whose currency risks are more manageable. Developing such expertise is no small accomplishment because, as noted earlier, prediction of currency movements remains an art or a highly imprecise science. Because of such challenges, financial market capabilities are essential for firms to profit from (or at least avoid being crushed by) unfavourable currency movements.

DEBATES AND EXTENSIONS

In the highly uncertain world of exchange rate movements, stakes are high, and debates are numerous. We review two major debates here: (1) a strong versus a weak dollar, (2) hedging versus not hedging.

A strong dollar versus a weak dollar

The debate on the US trade deficit is part of a larger debate on the value of the US dollar. Under the Bretton Woods system (1944–1973), the US dollar was the only common denominator. Since the demise of Bretton Woods in 1973, the importance of the US dollar has been in gradual decline. This does not mean that the US dollar is no longer important; it still is. It is the dollar's relative importance – in particular, its value – that is at the heart of this debate.

As noted earlier in the section on the determinants of exchange rates, the value of a currency is a broad reflection of a country's economic strengths. During the boom years of 2005–2008 the dollar has been loosing about 25 per cent of its value reaching almost $1.60 per euro in mid 2008 (see Figure 7.1A). At the onset of the financial crisis, the trend sharply reversed as investors took refuge in the dollar as the traditional currency of stability, raising the dollar to below $1.30 per euro. After a few months, however, the euro bounced back and the dollar fell back and fluctuated around $1.40 to $1.50 per euro. At the same time, the dollar is still strong compared to the Chinese yuan, which is pegged to the dollar despite the two countries experiencing very different economic conditions.[14]

What are the implications of a weak dollar for the rest of the world? Although a weak dollar hurts exporters in Asia and Europe, it helps remedy the US balance of payments and results in more global balancing. As the US economy slows down and thus is unable to absorb more imports (the USA already has by far the world's largest current account deficit), a weak dollar forces Asian and European economies to boost their domestic demand. Thus, the world economy may become less unbalanced with a gradual slide of the dollar.

However, the rest of the world has two reasons to support a strong dollar. First, the rest of the world holds so many dollars as currency reserves that most countries

LEARNING OBJECTIVE

4 participate in three leading debates on exchange movements

fear the capital loss they would suffer if the dollar falls too deep. China leads the world by holding €1.7 trillion of foreign reserves, two thirds of which are in US dollars.[15] A devaluation of the dollar would result in a huge loss for those holding US$-denominated assets. Second, many countries prefer to keep the value of their currencies down to promote exports. Unfortunately, the more and the longer they pile up dollars, the bigger the eventual losses in the event of a dollar depreciation. How to manage the dollar's slide without causing too much pain remains a 'trillion-dollar' question.

Currency hedging versus not hedging

Given the unpredictable nature of exchange rates (at least in the short run), it seems natural that firms that deal with transactions in foreign currencies would engage in currency hedging (see Closing Case). Firms that fail to hedge are at the mercy of the spot market. In 1997, Siam Cement, a major chemicals firm in Thailand, had $4.2 billion debt denominated in foreign currencies and hedged none of it. When the Thai baht sharply depreciated against the US dollar in July 1997, Siam Cement had to absorb a $517 million loss, which wiped out all the profits it made during 1994–1996.[16] This was a common occurrence during the Asian crisis, and in several of the financial crises that followed, from Russia 1998 to Iceland 2008, as well as in Hungary and Poland (see Opening Case).

Hedging your currency in financial markets has a similar effect as an insurance. If everything went well, you wonder whether it was worth the effort. However, there are costs and risks that are easily overlooked: (1) bank fees, (2) counter party risk and (3) uncertainty in the underlying business transaction.

First, hedging is not free, after all, banks do charge for their services and for the risk that they may assume in the transaction. This cost can be quite substantial if you want to hedge over long time periods, unusual contract length, or in less traded currencies.

Second, counter party risk is the risk that your bank with which you have a hedging contract goes bankrupt. Usually, this possibility is seen as remote and many finance texts may not bother to mention it in the context of currency exchange markets. However, when Lehman Brothers went down in autumn of 2008, some business suddenly found themselves with claims that they could do realize.

Third, what happens if the underlying transaction does not take place as expected, and thus future revenues or expenses do not materialize? For example, when the oil price soared in 2007, many airlines anticipated having to pay a much higher price (in dollars) for fuel in the future – fuel always being a major cost factor in this industry. Thus, they expected to need a lot of dollars in the future, and bought them using forward contracts. However, in 2008 the oil price collapsed, while demand for air travel grew slower than expected – hence, airlines needed fewer dollars than expected. However, having entered forward contracts at a time when the dollar was relatively expensive, they had to sell those dollars at a lower price in the spot market. In consequence Cathay Pacific Airways had to write off close to $1 billion, while Ryanair, Air France-KLM and Southwest also made substantive losses.[17]

Given the overwhelming theoretical arguments in favour of hedging, it may be surprising that in 2008 only about 55 per cent of large firms engaged in financial hedging, up from 45 per cent in the previous year.[18] Among America's largest firms, about two thirds do not use financial hedging, including many large firms, such as 3M, Deere, Eastman Kodak, ExxonMobil and IBM. Managers argue that currency hedging eats into profits. A simple forward contract may cost up to half a percentage point per year of the revenue being hedged. More complicated transactions and longer time horizons may cost more. As a result, many firms believe that the ups and downs of various currencies balance out in the long run. Some, such as IBM, focus on strategic hedging and risk diversification but refrain from currency hedging. Such a strategy may be viable for larger firms that have only a small part of their costs and revenues in foreign currencies, and that have diversified their risk exposure (typical for big US firms). However, for small firms with a large share of international business, for firms exposed to a small number of currencies, and for firms originating from a small country that is subject to substantial exchange rate uncertainty, such a strategy can be fatal – as the Siam Cement example illustrates!

IMPLICATIONS FOR PRACTICE

The big question in global business, adapted to the context of exchange rate movements, is: What determines the success and failure of currency management around the globe? The answer boils down to two components. First, from an institution-based standpoint, the changing rules of the game – economic, political and psychological – enable or constrain firms. Wal-Mart's low-cost advantage from made-in-China products stems at least in part from the Chinese government's policy to peg its yuan at a favourable level against the dollar. Consequently, Wal-Mart's low-cost advantage may be eroded as the yuan appreciates. Second, from a resource-based perspective, firms' capabilities in currency management may make or break them. As illustrated in the Closing Case, Markel's wrong bets on the currency movements resulted in painful pay cuts for its employees.

As a result, three implications for action emerge (Table 7.5). First, managers must be aware of their currency risk exposure, which arises from differences in the currencies of their expected revenues and expenditures. This requires constant monitoring of the firms' financial data, and of contractual commitments and claims that are expected to result in payments at a later time.

Second, risk analysis of any country must include its currency risks. Previous chapters have advised managers to pay attention to the political, regulatory and cultural feature of various countries. Here, a crucial currency risk dimension is added. To assess currency risks, they need not only pay attention to the broad long-run movements informed by PPP, productivity changes and balance of payments, but also to the fickle short-run fluctuations triggered by interest rate changes and investor mood swings. An otherwise attractive country may suffer from high inflation, resulting in devaluation of its currency on the horizon. Countries in Southeast Asia prior to 1997 and in Central and Eastern Europe prior to 2008 represented such scenarios. Numerous firms ignoring such a currency risk dimension were burned badly in these financial crises.

Finally, a country's high currency risks do not necessarily suggest that this country needs to be totally avoided. Instead, it calls for a prudent currency risk management strategy via strategic or financial hedging. Not every firm has the stomach or

LEARNING OBJECTIVE

5 draw implications for action

Table 7.5 Implications for Action

- Managers must at all times be aware of their currency risk exposure.
- Risk analysis of any country must include an analysis of its currency risks.
- A currency risk management strategy is necessary via currency hedging, strategic hedging, or both.

capabilities to do both. Smaller, internationally inexperienced firms (such as Markel) may outsource currency hedging to specialists in their bank. Strategic hedging may be unrealistic for such smaller firms without operations abroad. On the other hand, many larger, internationally experienced firms choose not to touch currency hedging, citing its costs. Instead, they focus on strategic hedging and risk diversification. Although there is no fixed formula, firms not having a well-thought-out currency management strategy may be caught off guard when currency movements take a wrong turn.

CHAPTER SUMMARY

1 Understand the determinants of exchange rates:

- An exchange rate is the price of one currency expressed in another.

- Basic determinants of exchange rates include (1) relative price differences and PPP, (2) inflation, (3) interest rates, (4) productivity and balance of payments, (4) exchange rate policies and (5) investor psychology.

2 Track the evolution of the international monetary system:

- The international monetary system evolved from the gold standard (1870–1914), to the Bretton Woods system (1944–1973), and eventually to the current post-Bretton Woods system (1973–present).

- The current system is characterized by a mix of managed floats between major currencies and pegged exchange rates for many other currencies.

3 Identify firms' strategic responses to deal with exchange risk exposure:

- Firms' strategic responses include (1) invoicing in their own currency, (2) strategic hedging or (3) risk diversification.

- Financial markets can be used to manage exchange rate risk by using (1) spot transactions, (2) forward transactions and (3) currency swaps.

4 Participate in three leading debates on exchange movements:

- These are: (1) fixed a strong versus a weak dollar, and (2) currency hedging versus not hedging.

5 Draw implications for action:

- Managers must at all times be aware of their currency risk exposure.

- Risk analysis of any country must include an analysis of its currency risks.

- A currency risk management strategy is necessary via currency hedging, strategic hedging, or both.

KEY TERMS

Appreciation (of a currency)
Balance of payments (BoP)
Bandwagon effect
Bid rate
Bretton Woods system
Capital and financial account
  (of the BoP)
Capital flight
Common currency
Counter party risk
Crawling bands

Currency board
Currency exchange market
Currency hedging
Currency risk diversification
Currency swap
Current account (of the BoP)
Depreciation (of a currency)
Exchange rate
Exchange rate risk
  (or currency risk)
Fixed exchange rate

Floating (or flexible) exchange
  rate policy
Forward discount
Forward exchange rate
Forward premium
Forward transaction
Free float
Gold standard
Inflation
Interest rate parity
International Monetary Fund (IMF)

Managed float
Offer rate
Pegged exchange rate
Post–Bretton Woods system

Purchasing power parity (PPP)
  hypothesis
Relative PPP hypothesis

Spot market rate
Spread
Strategic hedging
World Bank

CRITICAL DISCUSSION QUESTIONS

1 Identify the currencies of the top-three trading partners of your country in the last ten years. Find the exchange rates of these currencies, relative to your country's currency, ten years ago and now. Explain the changes. Then predict the movement of these exchange rates ten years from now.

2 Should China revalue the yuan against the dollar? If so, what impact may this have on (1) US balance of payments, (2) Chinese balance of payments, (3) relative competitiveness of Mexico and Thailand, (4) European firms importing from China and (5) European retail consumers?

3 As a finance manager in a European company (accounting in euros), one of your sales managers proudly tells you that he has just signed a contract for a sale to Russia due in two years time, to be paid in Russia roubles. How do you react?

4 The English Premier League earns £250 million annually arising from broadcasting contracts abroad, of which 16 per cent arises from Southeast Asia. Contracts are usually signed for three-year periods after a competitive tender.[19] As manager of a television company in South East Asia, you want a share of the cake and prepare a bid for a contract for broadcast rights in your country. Tender conditions specify payment in British pound spread over the three-year period. How do you manage the associated exchange rate risk?

CLOSING CASE

Markel corporation fights currency fluctuations

Markel Corporation is a family-owned tubing maker based in Plymouth Meeting, Pennsylvania. Its tubing and insulated lead wire are used in appliances, automobiles, and water purifiers. Approximately 40 per cent of its $30 million sales are exported, mainly to Europe. To protect itself from currency fluctuations, Markel has two strategies: (1) charge customers stable prices in their own currencies and (2) use forward contracts.

Markel executives believe that their strategy of setting prices in foreign currencies, mainly the euro, has helped it attain 70 per cent of the world market share in its specialty market. But this also means that Markel signs contracts that will be paid in a lot of euros months or even years down the road. There is always the danger that the value of these euros in dollars may be much less than what it is when contracts are signed.

To combat the uncertainty associated with exchange rates, Markel purchases forward contracts from PNC Financial Services Group in Pittsburgh. Markel agrees to pay PNC, for example, one million euros in 30 (or 90 or 180) days, and PNC guarantees a certain amount of dollars regardless of what happens to the exchange rate. When Markel's chief financial officer (CFO) believes that the dollar would appreciate against the euro, he may hedge his entire expected euro earnings with a forward contract. If he feels that the dollar would depreciate, he may hedge, for example, half of the euro earnings and take a chance that Markel will make more dollars by doing nothing with the other half of the euro earnings. Unfortunately, the CFO does not always make the right bet. In April 2003, for instance, Markel had to pay PNC 50 000 euros from a contract that Markel purchased three months earlier. PNC paid $1.05 per euro or $52 500. If Markel had waited, it could have made an additional $1 500 by selling at the going rate, $1.08.

© Marco Hegner/iStock

Why do manufacturers of industrial products, such as cables, need to understand principles of exchange rate management?

How an export-intensive firm such as Markel deals with exchange rates can directly make or break its bottom line. In 1998, Markel signed a five-year export deal with a German firm and set the sales price assuming the euro would be $1.18 by 2003, about the same level as the euro was traded when introduced officially in 1999. But the euro declined sharply, hitting a low of 82 cents in 2000. Thus, each euro Markel received was worth far less in dollars than anticipated. During 2000–2002, Markel had to swallow more than $650 000 in currency losses, which contributed to its overall losses. Consequently, Markel employees had to endure pay cuts, and the firm had to redouble its efforts to boost efficiency and cut costs.

By 2003, Markel signed most of its currency deals assuming that the euro would be valued between 90 and 95 cents. When the euro soared to $1.08, helped by the war in Iraq and nervousness about the US trade deficit, Markel began to reap windfalls.

Executives estimated that if the euro remained between $1.05 and $1.07, the company would profit from $400 000 to $500 000 in currency gains in 2003, significantly recovering from the losses in 2000–2002.

CASE DISCUSSION QUESTIONS

1   Some argue that given the complexity and unpredictability, currency hedging is not worth it. Is currency hedging worth it for Markel?

2   Can Markel improve the performance of its currency hedging?

3   Other than currency hedging, what other currency management strategies can Markel choose?

Sources: Based on (1) R. Carbaugh, 2007, *International Economics*, 11th ed. (pp. 381–382), Cincinnati, OH: Thomson South-Western; (2) http://www.markelcorporation.com. © Courtesy of Markel Corporation.

RECOMMENDED READINGS

S. Y. Cross, 1998, *The Foreign Exchange Market in the United States*, **New York: Federal Reserve Bank of New York** – A clear exposition of the institutions and practice in currency markets.

C. Henderson, 2006, *Currency Strategy*, **2nd ed., New York: Wiley** – A comprehensive though somewhat theoretical treatment of a variety aspects of currency exchange markets.

M. Taylor, 1995, The economics of exchange rates, *JEL* **33, 13–47** – A comprehensive review of the economics underlying the formation of exchange rates.

J. Williamson, 1998, *Crawling Bands or Monitoring Bands: How to Manage Exchange Rates in a World of Capital Mobility*, **Washington, DC, Institute of International Economics** (www.iie.com/publications/papers/paper.cfm?ResearchID=319) – A review of the alternative ways for countries to manage their currencies.

NOTES:

"FOR JOURNAL ABBREVIATION, PLEASE SEE PAGE XXVI-XXVII."

1   In this chapter, we follow financial markets in using $ sign to denote the US$ unless otherwise specified. This is a simplification as Australia, Canada, Hong Kong, Singapore and Taiwan also call their currency 'dollar'.

2   R. Carbaugh, 2007, *International Economics*, 11th ed. (p. 360), Cincinnati, OH: Thomson South-Western.

3   A. Taylor & M. Taylor, 2004, The purchasing power parity debate, *JEP*, 18: 135–158.

4   *The Economist*, 2010, The Big Mac index: Exchanging blows, The Economist Online (www.economist.com), March 16.

5   D.M. Nuti, 2009, The Economist's burgernomics, Blog, dmarionuti.blogspot.com, August 14.

6   R. Lyons, 2001, *The Microstructure Approach to Exchange Rates* (p. 1), Cambridge, MA: MIT Press.

7   R.N. Copper, 2009, *The Future of the dollar*, Washington, DC: Peterson Institute of International Economics.

8   e.g. R.I. McKinnon, 1988, Monetary and exchange rate policies for international financial stability, *JEP*, 2(1), 82–103.

9   e.g. J. Williamson, 2006, *Choosing monetary arrangements for the 21st Century*, Washington, DC, Peterson Institute of International Economics.

10 F. Carrieri & B. Majerbi, 2006, The pricing of exchange risk in emerging stock markets, *JIBS*, 37: 372–391;

L. Jacque & P. Vaaler, 2001, The international control conundrum with exchange risk, *JIBS*, 32: 813–832.

11 K.D. Miller & J.J. Reuer, 1998, Firm strategy and economic exposure to foreign exchange rate movements, *JIBS*, 29, 493–514.

12 B. Kogut & N. Kulatilaka, 1994, Operating flexibility, global manufacturing, and the option value of a multinational network, *MS*, 40: 123–139; C. Pantzalis, B. Simkins & P. Laux, 2001, Operational hedges and the foreign exchange exposure of US multinational corporations, *JIBS*, 32: 793–812.

13 R. Faff & A. Marshall, 2005, International evidence on the determinants of foreign exchange rate exposure of multinational corporations, *JIBS*, 36: 539–558; R. Weiner, 2005, Speculation in international crises, *JIBS*, 36: 576–587.

14 *The Economist*, 2009, Banyan: Currency contortions, December 19.

15 J. Anderlini, 2010, China's foreign reserves hit $2399bn, *Financial Times*, January 15.

16 Carbaugh, 2007, *as above* (p. 380).

17 *The Economist*, 2009, Corporate hedging gets harder: The perils of prudence, June 18.

18 *The Economist*, 2009, Corporate hedging ..., *as above*.

19 H. Richards, 2010, Dealmaking skill adds to the score, *Financial Times*, April 21.

PART THREE

GLOBALIZATION

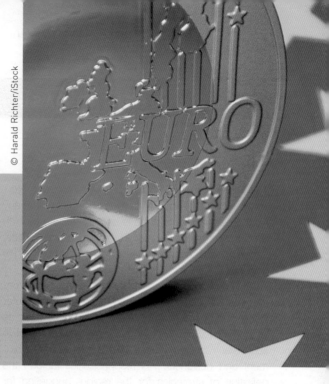
© Harald Richter/iStock

CHAPTER EIGHT

EUROPEAN INTEGRATION

LEARNING OBJECTIVES

After studying this chapter you should be able to:

1 Explain the origins and the evolution of the EU.

2 Explain the evolution of the institutional environment in transition economies.

3 Explain how and why the institutional framework created by the EU is pivotal for business.

4 Outline the political institutions of the EU.

5 Participate in debates over the future of the EU.

6 Draw Implications for Action.

OPENING CASE

A day in European business

It is Tuesday morning 5 a.m., a nearly empty motorway lies ahead of Marcus as he is driving his company Audi on a familiar route: he is heading for the Munich airport. As a manager with European responsibilities, travelling and engaging with other cultures is his daily job.

Marcus is Vice President Northern Europe of an entrepreneurial software company providing computer aided design software for use in businesses such as large architectural firms, municipalities, automotive suppliers, aviation manufacturers, media and entertainment and designers. His responsibilities include the definition of strategies for the region, budgeting for several European countries, negotiations with new potential business partners and business reviews with his own local teams, suppliers and partners.

After leaving the car on deck 12 of the spacious car deck and writing down the exact location (important!), he heads for the security check and his gate at International Departures. Lufthansa has sent him his check-in details via barcode on the display of his mobile phone to jump the queue at the gate. Early in the morning departure times are quite reliable and the flight departs on time: two hours to read the morning news, to get an update on worldwide financials, to enjoy a cup of tea or two and an unspectacular sandwich.

Arriving in Warsaw airport, there is less border security that in the past. Since Poland became a member of the EU and the Schengen Agreement, there are no passport controls any longer. Business travellers try to avoid check-in luggage to save time, and ten minutes later he is greeted by his local Country Manager. Unfortunately, he can not take advantage of the EU's monetary union, and still has to use five different purses. In addition to the 'Euro purse', he needs one for Swedish krones, one for Romanian leu, one for British pounds and finally one for Polish zloty, which is what he is carrying today. It's quite a challenge to grab the right one when leaving home at 4:30 in the morning.

While an experienced driver takes Marcus and his Country Manager through Warsaw's rush hour traffic, they discuss the latest development at the Polish office. Since joining the EU, the level of professionalism has significantly increased at all levels of management in Poland, and English has become the norm for conversations with local staff. This was not the case when Marcus started doing business in Poland in 2001. Initially, he could communicate only with the Country Manager directly in English. For the first year, all employees were enrolled in English language training every Friday afternoon. Now this training has paid off, and Marcus can easily communicate directly with everyone in the office.

This time, his first appointment is with a major supplier in the centre of Warsaw to review the business development and discuss opportunities for the coming months. After three hours of PowerPoint presentations, financial reports and marketing reviews, he is invited for a quick business lunch at a Chinese restaurant. Another two hours in the car on the way to his company's Polish office in Łodz are followed by an internal staff meeting with updates by all business unit managers. Channel partners are a precious asset to the company, and their development, financial strength and ability to close deals at end-customers are topics that need to be reviewed by the local teams. It is the VP's job to make sure the right mindset is present everywhere, service levels are met and staff's compensation schemes keep them hungry to do more and develop the business to the next level.

Marcus' visits to a country office typically take three days packed with meetings and events to justify the expenses of the journey. Modern technology allows video conferencing at high quality, yet it can not replace the extremely important 'human' factor in business negotiations. However, Marcus prefers face-to-face discussions where recognizing subtle expressions on the other's face can make a difference between closing a deal and coming home empty handed.

Doing business in different European countries, Marcus faces differences in bureaucracy on almost every step. In Poland, for example, it seems that everything needs to be filed in several copies, stamped and signed. Notaries hold 'the license to print money' because more or less everything related to the administration of a limited company (called 'Sp. z o.o.') needs to be signed in the presence of a notary. The easiest way to discover this is by having a dinner – Why? If you would like to use the receipt of the restaurant as a proof for expenses related to a business you have to ask the waiter for that. After ten minutes

IN FOCUS 8.1

Common agricultural policy

Probably the most controversial EU policy is the **common agricultural policy (CAP)**. In the late 1950s, Europe was still concerned about its ability to generate enough food for its rapidly growing population. Thus, the CAP became one of the first areas for European integration. It was designed to encourage and secure food supplies, ensure a high quality of life for farmers, stabilize markets and ensure reasonable prices for consumers. The CAP used a system of subsidies and market intervention, and initially made good progress towards these aims.

Over the next decades, however, the economics of agriculture shifted; Europe no longer experienced widespread food shortages. The CAP, however, was slow to adapt to changing realities, and thus generated undesirable side-effects such as overproduction. The EU bought excess supplies at guaranteed prices, which encouraged production beyond what was needed. The CAP thus built up inventories that European consumers didn't need, the so-called 'butter mountains' and 'milk lakes'. These were sold on world markets, often at prices considerably below internal prices, which caused distortions that may have inhibited farmers in the developing world.

Since the early 1990s, the CAP has slowly been reformed, though at every stage insiders (mainly farmers) tried to protect their vested interests. Initial reforms deliberately withdrew a proportion of farm land from production. Later, subsidies have been decoupled from the amount of production. Farmers thus are treated as guardians of nature and of traditional landscapes rather than merely as economic producers of agricultural products. The CAP however continues to be one of the most disputed area of EU policy where national interests collide, due to the wide variation of products and organizational forms in the agricultural sector, itself an outcome of diversity of social, climatic and geological differences.

Sources: Based on: (1) R. Fennel, 1997, *The common agricultural policy: Continuity and Change*, Oxford: Clarendon Press; (2) A.J. Greer, 2003, *Agricultural policy in Europe*, Manchester: Manchester University Press; (3) A. Swinbank & C. Daugbjerg, 2006, The 2003 CAP Reform: Accommodating WTO Pressures, *CEP*, 4: 47–64.

© Marcelo Silva/iStock

Cows waiting to start the milking process

market grew in size and the union gained political weight in world politics. As early as 1960, the UK, Ireland, Norway and Denmark applied for membership. Yet, their entries were delayed by French objections until 1973 (Table 8.2). Norwegian voters, however, rejected membership in a referendum in 1972 (and again in 1994),

Table 8.2 Countries of the union

Country	Member of EEC/EU since	Member of Schengen area since	Member of Eurozone since (b)
Belgium	1958	1995	2002
France	1958	1995	2002
Germany	1958	1995	2002
Luxembourg	1958	1995	2002
Netherlands	1958	1995	2002
Italy	1958	1997	2002
Denmark	1973	2001	Opt out
Ireland	1973	Partial 2002 (a)	2002
United Kingdom	1973	Partial 2000 (a)	Opt out
Greece	1981	2000	2002
Portugal	1986	1995	2002
Spain	1986	1995	2002
Austria	1995	1997	2002
Finland	1995	2001	2002
Sweden	1995	2001	Not implemented
Cyprus	2004	Not yet implemented	2008
Czech Republic	2004	2007	Not implemented
Estonia	2004	2007	Not implemented
Hungary	2004	2007	Not implemented
Latvia	2004	2007	Not implemented
Lithuania	2004	2007	Not implemented
Malta	2004	2007	2008
Poland	2004	2007	Not implemented
Slovakia	2004	2007	2009
Slovenia	2004	2007	2007
Bulgaria	2007	Not yet implemented	Not implemented
Romania	2007	Not yet implemented	Not implemented
Iceland	EEA only (c)	2001	Not member
Norway	EEA only	2001	Not member
Switzerland	Not member	2008	Not member
Lichtenstein	EEA only	2009	Not member

Country	Member of EEC/EU since	Member of Schengen area since	Member of Eurozone since (b)
Turkey	Candidate	Not member	Not member
Croatia	Candidate	Not member	Not member
FYR Macedonia	Candidate	Not member	Not member

Notes: (a) Ireland and the UK implemented police and judicial cooperation rules only, and are not committed to removing border controls.
(b) Year from when Euro notes officially became sole currency; the Euro has also been adopted in Montenegro, Kosovo, Andorra, Monaco, San Marino and the Vatican;
(c) EEA = European Economic Area, an extension of the single market to nonmembers.

Sources: Based on: (1) D. Dinan, 2004, *Europe Recast: A History of Europen Union*. Palgrave-Macmillan; (2) *BBC News*, 2001, EU glossary: Jargon, (http://news.bbc.co.uk, accessed July 2009).

mainly because they wished to retain control over their national fishing grounds. In the 1980s, Spain, Portugal and Greece joined after replacing their totalitarian governments by democracies. In 1990, former East Germany joined the EU by joining the Federal Republic of Germany (West Germany). Finland, Sweden and Austria joined in 1995.

The process of accepting new members has been formalized in 1993 with the establishment of the Copenhagen Criteria. These criteria require that new members have a stable democracy and a fully functioning market economy. Moreover, they must demonstrate a good record on human rights, the ability to cope with the competitive pressures of the common markets and the ability take on obligations of membership, also known as *acquis communautaire*.[3] Under these new rules, ten countries, most of them transition economies, joined in 2004, followed by Bulgaria and Romania in 2007.

> **Copenhagen Criteria**
> Criteria the new members have to fulfil to be admitted as members of the EU.

Continuous deepening

After a trip to Europe in 1986, the conservative American humorist P.J. O'Rourke told his compatriots about his experiences 'Among the Euro-Weenies'. He joked about 'dopey little countries', 'pokey borders', 'itty-bitty' languages and 'Lilliputian' drink measures. Most poignantly, he claimed 'you can't swing a cat without sending it through customs'.[4] How arrogant! Yes, but there was a grain of truth in this. However, by the time of O'Rourke's visit, Europeans were well on their way to overcoming their historical divisions and fragmented markets.

The process of overcoming divisions of the union can be traced by the succession of treaties and agreements between the Member States (Table 8.1). Many of them are known by the cities where crucial meetings took place, including the Treaties of Maastricht, Amsterdam and Lisbon. In the 1970s and early 1980s, the progress towards a single market slowed down as European economies were struggling with their competitiveness, being held back by rigid institutional frameworks and small, fragmented markets. Policy initiatives, notably the Single European Act (SEA) adopted in 1986, aimed to reinvigorate the integration process along with economic liberalization. This act reformed the institutions and prepared for the single market to come into effect on January 1, 1993. Crucially, it introduced weighted majority decision-making in selected policy areas to facilitate reaching agreements; before 1986 national vetoes had frequently inhibited change. In

> **Single European Act (SEA)**
> The agreement that established the basis for the single European market.

preparation for the single market, the EU adopted nearly 280 separate items of legislation in the period 1986 to 1992.[5] This legislation aimed to open hitherto closed national markets, and to reduce the complexity and costs for business selling their goods and services in other countries of the union.

The next big step has been the Maastricht Treaty of 1993, which both deepened and broadened the scope of the union.[6] In addition to further economic integration, the treaty set the foundations for common foreign and security policy, and for cooperation in police and judicial matters. In the economic sphere, it established the timeline and the criteria of the establishment of the monetary union, and thus the introduction of the euro as a common currency. Moreover, it introduced the new name European Union (EU), which reflects the higher degree of integration.

The treaties of Amsterdam (1999) and Nice (2003) revised the procedures of decision-making aiming to reduce the power of national vetoes and increasing the power of the parliament. Moreover, they created further areas of policy coordination, such as asylum seekers and law enforcement. The legal foundations of the EU continued, however, to be based on an amalgam of treaties rather than a coherent set of rules. This abnormality was supposed to be addressed by the European Constitution, which had been prepared in 2002–03 by the European Convention, which was comprised of representatives of national parliaments, national governments, the European Parliament and the European Commission. It aimed to facilitate decision-making in the union, create new and simpler institutional structures and to integrate fundamental human rights in the EU's legal foundations.[7] However, voters in both France and the Netherland voted against this partly because they were concerned about further losses of national sovereignty, and partly because they wished to penalize their national politicians promoting the constitution. After the European Constitution went nowhere, the Lisbon Treaty signed in 2007 was designed to substitute it, but with somewhat less ambitious reforms.[8] This series of treaties thus advanced European integration and the shared institutions of the EU, while opening for new members.

THE OTHER EUROPE: TRANSITION AND ACCESSION

Central planning and real socialism[9]

Central and Eastern Europe (CEE) experienced a very different 'integration' in the 20th century. During the Cold War, Eastern and Western Europe followed diverging trajectories of political and economic development. While Western Europe established market economies, CEE developed a system of central planning under the guidance (and military pressure) of the Soviet Union. The political ideology of the ruling Communist parties grounded in Marxism–Leninism idealized collective values and the rising working class. Yet, the economy was coordinated by a central plan that left little scope for individual initiative.

The central plan determined which factory would produce what, with which inputs, and delivered to whom. The plan focused on quantitative output targets with few incentives for quality and customer service. Thus, firms in a supply chain would not interact directly, and firms would not be compelled to adapt their products to consumer demand, nor would they be free to choose their suppliers. This created huge inefficiencies in allocating resources. Moreover, this system provided no incentives for firms or individuals to innovate; thus technologically business in CEE fell far behind the west. The lack of adequate hotels in places like Łodz (see Opening Case) is typical for CEE during that time.

Maastricht Treaty
A major treaty deepening integration in Europe.

European Constitution
An ambitious project to create a new legal foundation for the EU, which failed.

Lisbon Treaty
A major treaty integrating earlier treaties of the EU, and changing the institutional structures of the EU.

LEARNING OBJECTIVE

2 Explain the evolution of the institutional environment in transition economies

Central and Eastern Europe
The common name used for the countries east of the former Iron Curtain.

International trade within CEE took place in the context of the Comecon, an economic integration scheme that, like the national economies, was grounded on the principles of central planning. The countries traded largely with each other, while only small volumes of East–West business conduced on the basis of counter-trade negotiated with state-trade monopolies.

Comecon
The pre-1990 trading bloc of the socialist countries.

From plan to market[10]

In 1990, the economic system of central planning collapsed. The nations of CEE thus entered a painful process of economic transition to replace their defunct economic systems by a market economy. Initial reform programmes followed three primary aims: liberalization, stabilization and privatization.[11] Liberalization should enable individuals and businesses to take their own decisions and initiatives, and thus to set free entrepreneurial spirits. Stabilization had to combat macroeconomic imbalances, notably external debt and hidden inflation that emerged when price controls were removed. Privatization was to transfer ownership from the state to private shareholders, and thus to give private owners appropriate incentives to make the best of the firms.

Economic transition
The process of changing from central plan to a market economy.

Liberalization
The removal of regulatory restrictions on business.

However, these reforms did not kick-start an economic miracle. Several economies quite literally collapsed, with GDP dropping at an unprecedented rate. In Russia, the output drop continued for seven years, by which time the level of GDP had fallen by 47 per cent from its 1990 level. Central European economies turned their economies around quicker. Even so, Hungary, Poland and the Czech Republic experienced two to three years of recession and lost 15 per cent to 18 per cent of their GDP. How could this happen?

Stabilization
Policies to combat macroeconomic imbalances.

Privatization
The change of ownership from state to the private owners.

The reforms were slow to implement a fourth aspect of transition, the creation of institutions that secure the effective functioning of a market economy.[12] You may find this surprising because you have read Chapters 2 and 3, and know about the importance of formal and informal institutions. Many Western advisers of the 1990s had developed their understanding of economic crises in for example Latin America, where the main concern was macroeconomic instability. However, economic transition is more than sorting out an economic crisis – it is about shifting out the entire set of rules by which an economy functions. Thus, one set of institutions governing economic activity (central plan) is replaced by a different one (market).

Yet, new institutions cannot be created overnight. The formal structures of the old system disintegrated before the institutions supporting a market economy were in place. Hence, businesses in CEE started life in a market economy by facing extensive market failure. They lacked, for example, legal institutions to enforce contracts and information systems to provide market data (Chapter 2). This created extensive information asymmetries and opportunities for opportunistic behaviour.[13] State bureaucrats were made business leaders, yet they lacked experience of working in a market economy. Moreover, the existing institutions could not be relied on for long-term decisions because they were unstable, and at times inconsistent. Businesses thus had to act on markets that did not yet exist; and they lacked the (often tacit) knowledge on how to use the market mechanism.[14] At the same time, the informal institutions of the old system such as norms and values formed during the socialist period were still peoples' minds.[15] To manage this complexity, businesses often fell back on informal networks that had helped overcoming shortages in the old regime.[16]

Policy choices made during the period of radical change in the early 1990s created new institutions. Decisions during this 'window of opportunity', and the inheritances from the previous regime continue to shape the institutional framework in

IN FOCUS 8.2

Privatization in central and eastern Europe

Privatization has been a pivotal element of transition, and it has shaped many of the formal and informal institutions that evolved in Central and Eastern Europe (CEE) since 1990. Handing over large numbers of firms to new owners is a complex and time consuming challenge. Moreover – contrary to for example the UK in the 1990s – the region lacked efficient capital markets and domestic savings that could be invested. These obstacles were overcome by novel routes of mass privatization, most notably voucher schemes. More conventional modes included direct sales to outside investors, management–employee buy-outs and restitution to former owners. Often, the political processes surrounding privatization gave managers (and in some countries, workers) considerable influence. This resulted in, for example, many Polish firms having employees as minority or even majority shareholders.

Voucher schemes have been a popular means of mass privatization because they were allowed to redistribute the wealth of the post-socialist society to its citizens, and to create widespread ownership of industrial equity. This was hoped to generate popular support for reform. For example, the Czech scheme – the first and most publicised – privatized a major share of the country's assets in several waves of multiple-auction bidding processes. Many individuals handed over their vouchers to investment funds that accumulated them and made bids on behalf of individuals. However, this pattern created complex agency relationships between dispersed owners, funds and managers.

The privatization process laid the basis for new owners guiding firms and was hoped to create more efficient, and profitable, operations. Yet, privatization was often insufficient to trigger the necessary enterprise restructuring. Many of the new ownership structures failed to establish appropriate incentives structures that would guide managers in transforming firms, a problem known as corporate governance conflicts. The different approaches of privatization in the early 1990s explain some of the variations in ownership structures, corporate governance and firm performance across the region.

Sources: Based on: (1) World Bank, 1996, *World Development Report 1996*, Washington, DC: Oxford University Press; (2) M. Bornstein, 1997, Non-standard Methods in the Privatization Strategies of the Czech Republic, Hungary and Poland, *EoT* 5: 323–338; (3) S. Estrin, 2002, Competition and Corporate Governance in Transition, *JEP* 36: 1947–1982.

each transition economy. The development of institutions is path dependent, and radical change is, in a historical perspective, rare.[17] As a result, the economies of CEE two decades after the fall of the Berlin Wall vary considerably, and they are different from a typical western European country.

EU accession

Despite the challenges of institution building, transition economies opened up to international trade and FDI early in the transition process. Within a few years, trade pattern realigned, FDI surged and the structure of industry adapted to new pan-European patterns of international business.[18] Western businesses started selling in some countries well ahead of EU membership; for example, Marcus' software firm established its Polish office in Łodz in 2001. Arguably, the external liberalization made a major contribution to the path of transition and the transformation of enterprises.

A key feature of this external opening has been the aspiration to join the EU. The process went through several stages of agreements with the EU, political reforms and changes in the legal framework. The EU provided a mix of financial support and pressures for regulatory reform, notably a push to adopt aspects of the EU regulatory frame as a precondition for market access. On the route to EU membership, the requirements of the Copenhagen Criteria were a major hurdle. However, the first wave of CEE countries joined the EU (see Table 8.2) in 2004, followed by Bulgaria and Romania in 2007. Two countries soon also joined the common currency: Slovenia (2007) and Slovakia (2009).

THE EU AS INSTITUTIONAL FRAMEWORK FOR BUSINESS

Over the past half century, the EU has created an institutional framework that establishes many of the rules by which businesses compete. New members and associated countries have adopted parts of this framework, often ahead of membership. These institutions have succeeded in removing most internal trade barriers. For example, EU now has a single market for aviation, which means that all European carriers compete on equal terms across the EU (including domestic routes in foreign countries). This deregulation has allowed discount airlines such as Ryanair and easyJet to build major market shares on intra-European routes, and it facilitated mega-mergers in the industry, such as Air France-KLM. On the ground, it used to take Spanish lorry drivers 24 hours to cross the border into France due to numerous paperwork requirements and checks. Since 1992, customs controls have been disbanded, and since 1996 even passport controls have been abolished. Border checkpoints between the two countries are no longer manned as people no longer need to show their passport. Now Spanish lorry drivers can move from to Barcelona to Paris – and on as far as the Arctic Circle – just like they would travel from Barcelona to Granada. This new freedom of movement, however, is only made possible by a complex political and legal framework.

A prime focus of the EU has been to secure the 'four freedoms' of the EU single market, namely the freedom of movement of people, goods, services and capital. Everyone in the union can benefit from these four freedoms:[19] As an individual citizen, you have the right to live, work, study or retire in another EU country. As a consumer, you benefit from lower prices and a wider choice of things to buy, which are the result of increased competition and scale economies. As a business, you can obtain easier and cheaper access to markets and suppliers in other countries of the union.

The institutional framework of the EU thus governs not only the relationship between its Member States, but directly impacts on the activities of businesses. The shared institutional framework is both complex and controversial due to the diversity of legal traditions, commercial interests and political ideologies across the continent. It continues to evolve in inter-governmental agreements and decisions by supranational bodies such as the Council and the Parliament. Next, we explore four aspects of this complex institutional framework that are particularly relevant to international businesses in Europe: (1) the single market, (2) the free movement of people, (3) the euro and (4) European competition policy.

The single market[20]

The single market is about free movements of goods, capital, people and services within the union. It complements the customs union, which secures application of a common external tariff on all imported goods. Such a single market can, however, not be created by a simple stroke of a pen. It is a complex process of bringing down barriers and simplifying rules.

The basic principle underlying most EU institutions is that the free movement of goods may only be restricted in special cases, for instance when there are risks

Four freedoms of the EU single market
Freedom of movement of people, goods, services and capital.

related to public health, environment or consumer protection. In these areas, national regulations in the nation states have been replaced by a common European rules. On the other hand, sectors that are not subject to such concerns are generally not subject to EU legislation. They are regulated by the principle of 'mutual recognition', introduced by the SEA in 1986. This implies that products that meet the necessary laws and technical standards in any one country may also be sold throughout the EU. Trade in this 'non-harmonized sector' accounts for about half of the trade in goods within the EU, while the other half is accounted for by the 'harmonized sector'.[21]

When is a common regulation better, and when should national laws plus 'mutual recognition' prevail? The Maastricht Treaty introduced the subsidiarity principle, which establishes a priority for decentralization. Thus, the EU is supposed to take action only if it is more effective than actions taken at national, regional or local level (in addition to areas which are defined as the EU exclusive competence). This principle was to prioritize the rights of national and local governments, though it does give the EU more power in areas where national differences may inhibit free trade.[22]

In sectors, where the EU sees higher risks for customers, it aims to harmonize technical regulations to increase transparency, minimize risks and to ensure legal certainty. In consequence the regulation of, for example, pharmaceuticals is based on a two tier structure: (1) a centralized procedure across all Member States for drug authorization for specified groups of medications governed by the European Agency for the Evaluation of Medicinal Products (EMEA) (see also Integrative Case 'Novo Nordisk'); (2) a decentralized procedure applying for the majority of conventional medicinal products governed by national authorities, but providing EU-wide marketing authorization.[23] The harmonization often implies higher costs, for example in the food industry, where harmonization raised safety standards, and thus increased compliance costs for companies. These costs often affect smaller firms disproportionately as the same procedures and documentation requirements apply to all firms.[24]

The creation of a harmonized framework is a complex and politically hotly disputed process. For example, in 2008, the EU discussed a new Directive to regulate the use of pesticides in agriculture; their use would affect consumers of foods anywhere in the single market. The harmonization has however been controversial as some national politicians feel it would infringe their sovereignty. Thus, scientists, farmers, the food industry and consumer organizations joined the debate on the Pesticides Directive. Some argued that the proposed regulation would unduly restrict the industry and raise costs, while others accused the EU of failing to protect consumers.[25] Journalists and politicians joined in, some demanding all of the above and ignoring the fact that political decisions such as these require sensitive trade-offs. It is a tough job to be a European law maker – be it in the Commission, or in the Parliament (See Closing Case).

The single market for services has been more difficult to implement than the single market for goods, for two reasons.[26] First, many service sectors have very complex regulatory regimes, for example, banking or telecommunications. Second, most services need some form of local delivery because you cannot pack them up and send by mail or freight the way you might do with a chocolate bar, a pair of shoes or even a car. Self-employed persons may in principle move between Member States to provide services on a temporary or permanent basis. Yet, to be able to sell your services, you need to be sure that your professional qualifications will be recognized. Service providers thus are subject to both home country and host country regulations. The EU saw a need to harmonize these regulations for many service sectors. This has profound implications even for businesses operating only

Mutual recognition
The principle that products recognized as legal in one country may be sold throughout the EU.

Harmonized sector
Sectors of industry for which the EU has created common rules.

Subsidiarity
The EU takes action only if it is more effective than actions taken at lower levels.

nationally because EU directives trigger major legal changes in national law. In Germany, for example, EU service sector liberalization forced radical liberalization of traditional regulation in a wide range of sectors, from the opening of electricity and telecommunications industries to fundamental reform of the crafts sector.[27]

Even with this harmonization, the single market for services is not yet really a single market. A study by the EU Commission identified a large gap between its vision of an integrated EU economy and the reality in service sectors.[28] Residual barriers increase costs and lower quality of services provided in other countries. In particular, SMEs are inhibited because they are particularly affected by complex administrative and legal requirements. A new Services Directive aims to eliminate obstacles to trade in services, thus allowing the development of cross-border operations.[29]

An area of particular sensitivity is the free movement of capital. In principle, EU citizens should be able to conduct their financial transactions in any country of the union, including opening bank accounts, buying shares in companies or purchasing real estate. However, this principle requires mutual liberalization of capital markets, and – especially in the wake of the financial market crash of 2008 – coordination of financial market regulation and supervision.[30] Some of the rules affecting these types of transactions, however, remain governed by national regulators, and may thus vary between countries. For example, Icelandic bank Landisbanken operated in the UK through an Internet bank, attracting savers by promising higher interest rates. Yet, when it went bankrupt in 2008, a major row broke out between the British and Icelandic governments over who should pay for reimbursing those who had deposited large funds with the bank.[31]

If EU-wide harmonization is making life so much easier for businesses and consumers, why don't we see enthusiastic support for it across Europe? First, European laws are usually a compromise between national legislators who tend to prefer principles already in use in their own country. Political compromises between such positions, however, appear to add to the complexity of the legislation. Second, any new legislation may affect different countries and interest groups differently; and those facing major adjustments or protecting vested interests mobilize political support. EU harmonization often implies liberalization and thus opening of markets, which players protected under national rules are afraid of. Thus, with benefits widely shared and costs falling of specific groups, building and retaining political support for such reforms is challenging.

Free moving people

The freedom of movement for goods and services is complemented by the freedom for persons to freely move between Member States. The Single European Act of 1986 for the first time established the right of individuals to move freely in the EU to live, work, study or retire. This right initially focused on opening European labour markets. Yet, over the years, it has been extended to cover all citizens, thus fulfilling a dream of the founders in the 1950s. However, many obstacles and uncertainties still prevent people from relocating across Europe.[32]

If you are thinking of moving to another country, a major concern may be the recognition of your professional qualification – for example your university degree. Traditionally, many countries would only recognize qualifications obtained under their own jurisdiction. The EU has thus introduced rules to guarantee mutual recognition of qualifications. These rules include:[33]

- the harmonization of training requirements which allow for automatic recognition of selected professional qualifications, in particular in the health sector and for architects;

- the mutual recognition of all other professions that require a qualification;
- the automatic recognition of professional experience for professions of craft, commerce and industry sectors.

Erasmus Programme
An EU programme encouraging student mobility in Europe.

The EU has also instigated a number of programmes that actively encourage mobility of people across borders. The Erasmus Programme launched in 1987 has helped 1.4 million students to spend part of their studies in another European country. Erasmus provides scholarships and regulates the credit transfer and supports networking between universities. Similarly, the *Grundvig* programme supports individuals in adult education, while vocational training is supported by the *Leonardo-da-Vinci* scheme. *Marie Currie* scholarships help conducting research in other countries, while *Jean Monnet* Scholars receive support for teaching Europe-related themes. In parallel, EU countries participate in the Bologna Process, which aims to advance higher education across Europe (see In Focus 8.3).

Bologna Process
A political process aimed at harmonizing European higher education.

For many people, the most visible aspect of the freedom of movement of persons has been the abolition of border controls. Until 1995, travellers still had to show their passports each time they crossed a border within the EU (except between the

IN FOCUS 8.3

Mobile students: The Bologna Process

For students, an important aspect of the free movement of people is the so-called Bologna Process. It was initiated in 1999 with the Bologna Declaration by Ministers of Education from 29 European countries at the University of Bologna, Italy. It has profound implications for how university education is organized in Europe and beyond. The main aim is to facilitate the mobility of students and professionals within Europe by making the standards of academic degrees more comparable and compatible throughout Europe. The expected improvements of higher education are expected to strengthen Europe's knowledge base, and to ensure the further development of cutting-edge research in Europe. Moreover, the Bologna Process is hoped to attract more students from outside Europe, and to facilitate the convergence of university systems in Europe and the USA.

The Bologna Process is not an EU initiative and does not have the status of EU legislation, though EU institutions help with its implementation. The Bologna agreement is a separate arrangement involving both EU members and non-members. Moreover, it is not a treaty or convention, and thus it does not create legal obligations for the signatory states; the extent of participation is voluntary.

A cornerstone of the Bologna Process is a common course structures based on ECTS credits, and a degree structure with Bachelor, Master and PhD degrees. This common structure helps exchange students to fit their semester or year abroad into their degree programme, and it makes it easier to move to a university in another country. The basic structure is an academic year of 60 ECTS-credits that are equivalent to 1500–1800 hours of study. A Bachelor degree typically requires 180–240 ECTS credits (three to four years of study). A master degree builds on a completed bachelor degree and encompasses typically 90–120 ECTS credits (18 to 24 months). A doctoral degree builds on a Master degree and is expect to take another three years. Beyond the basic guidelines, however, individual countries have considerable freedom to design their educational programmes. Notably, the UK has adopted only a few aspects of this framework, and most British universities continue to offer three-year Bachelor degrees and one-year Master degrees.

Sources: Based on: (1) B. Wächter, 2004, The Bologna Process: Developments and prospects, *EJE*, 39: 265–273; (2) C. Tauch, 2004, Almost half-time in the Bologna Process: Where do we stand? *EJE* 39: 275–288; (3) I. Bache, 2006, The Europeanization of higher education: Markets, politics or learning? *JCMS*, 44: 231–248; (4) P. Ravinet, 2008, From voluntary participation to monitored coordination: why European countries feel increasingly bound by their commitment to the Bologna Process, *EJE* 43: 353–367.

Benelux countries). The basis for the removal of border controls has been the 'Schengen Agreement', originally a separate agreement signed by five countries in the town of Schengen in Luxemburg in 1985.

The abolition of passport controls, desirable as it is for travellers, does however require a closer coordination in a number of other areas. In particular, the police and judicial systems had to cooperate more closely, and the external borders of the so-called Schengen Area needed to be managed more tightly. Consequently, the Schengen Agreement coordinates procedures and policies regarding a number of judicial matters such as entry into and short stays in the area by non-EU citizens, police cooperation, political asylum seekers, and combating cross-border drugs-related crime.[34]

The implementation of these rules has not been easy, and thus, it took ten years from the signing of the agreement to the actual removal of border controls on March 26, 1995. All members of the EU have since joined the agreement, though some have yet to implement it (see Figure 8.2.), and it was absorbed into the legal framework of the EU with the Amsterdam Treaty in 1999. However, the UK and Ireland only adapted the police and judicial cooperation; they continue their passport controls at their intra-EU borders. The Schengen Area of free travel extends beyond the EU to Iceland, Lichtenstein, Norway and Switzerland.

The Schengen arrangement also benefits visitors from other parts of the world. They are normally given a 'Schengen visa' which permits stay in the Schengen

Schengen Agreement
The agreement that laid the basis for passport-free travel.

Schengen Area
The area covered by the Schengen Agreement.

Schengen Visa
Visa giving non-citizens access to the Schengen Area.

Figure 8.2 The Schengen Area

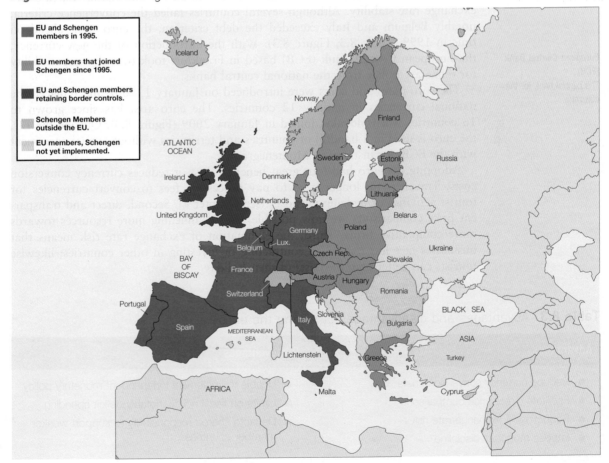

Area and travel between Schengen states as long as the conditions for entry are still fulfilled.[35] The visa can be obtained at the embassies of any Schengen country. Yet, this simplification comes at the expense of a more complex application process.

The euro as a common currency[36]

Eurozone
The countries that have adopted the euro as their currency.

As an economic union, the EU's proudest accomplishment has been the introduction of a common currency, the euro (€). The economies using the euro, known as the eurozone, account for about 21 per cent of world GDP. The euro was introduced in two phases. In 1999, it became 'virtual money' in 12 countries, used only for financial transactions but not in circulation. Exchange rates with national currencies were fixed at that point. In 2002, the euro was introduced as banknotes and coins. To meet the cash needs of over 300 million people, the EU printed 14.25 billion banknotes and minted 56 billion coins – with a total value of € 660 billion. The new banknotes would cover the distance between the earth and the moon five times![37] Overall, the introduction of the euro was an amazing logistical achievement.

Maastricht Criteria
Criteria that countries have to fulfil to join the eurozone.

In the Maastricht Treaty of 1992, Member States had legally committed themselves to introduce a monetary union no later than January 1, 1999. The treaty established criteria, known as Maastricht Criteria, that countries had to fulfil to be accepted into the monetary union: Countries were required to have annual budget deficits not exceeding 3 per cent of GDP, public debt under 60 per cent of the GDP, inflation rates within 1.5 per cent of the three lowest rates in the EU, long-term interest rates within 2 per cent of the three EU countries with the lowest rate and exchange rate stability. Although several countries failed the convergence criteria, notably Belgium and Italy exceeded the debt criterion, the euro went ahead on time in 1999 (Table 8.3, Figure 8.3). With the introduction of the new currency, the European Central Bank (ECB) based in Frankfurt took over the responsibility for monetary policy from the national central banks.

European Central Bank (ECB)
The central bank for the eurozone.

The euro notes and coins were introduced on January 1, 2002 and replaced the national currencies in initially 12 countries. The euro area has since grown to 16 countries when Slovakia joined in January 2009 (Figure 8.3). Outside the EU, the euro is used in a handful of countries and territories without formal agreement with the ECB, for instance in Montenegro.

Adopting the euro had four great benefits. First, it reduces currency conversion costs. Travellers no longer need to pay processing fees to convert currencies for tourist activities or hedging purposes (see Chapter 7). Second, direct and transparent price comparisons are now possible, thus channelling more resources towards more competitive firms. Third, the elimination of exchange rate risk means that businesses face less risk when contracting or investing in other countries; likewise tourists can better plan the costs of their holiday.

Table 8.3 Advantages and disadvantages of joining the euro

Advantages	Disadvantages
● Reduce currency conversion costs	● Unable to implement independent monetary policy
● Facilitate direct price comparisons	● Limits on fiscal policy, notably deficit spending
● Reduction of exchange rate risk	● De facto shared responsibility to support weaker member countries
● Impose monetary discipline	

Figure 8.3 The Euro zone

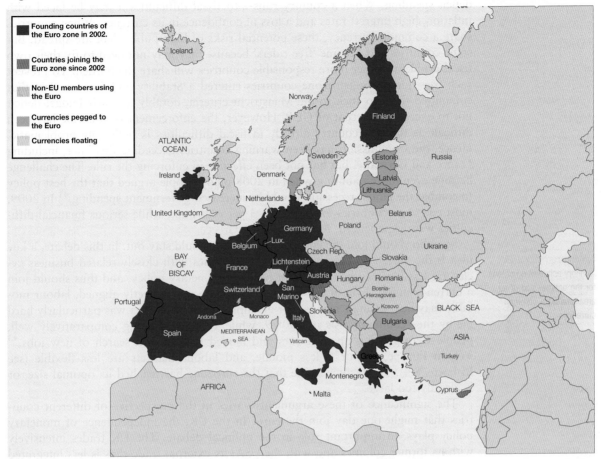

Fourth, adopting the euro imposes macroeconomic discipline on participating governments. Prior to adopting the euro, different governments independently determined exchange rates. Italy, for example, sharply devalued its lira in 1992 and in 1995. Although Italian exports became cheaper and more competitive overseas, other EU members, especially France, were furious.[38] Also, when confronting recession, governments often printed more currency and increased spending. Such actions cause inflation, which may spill over into neighbouring countries. By adopting the euro, eurozone countries agreed to abolish national monetary policy as a tool to solve macroeconomic problems. These efforts provided much needed stability, especially for countries with a less than impressive record in this area in the past. Overall, the euro has boosted intra-EU trade by approximately 10 per cent. Commanding 27 per cent of global currency reserves (compared to 19 per cent in 1999), the euro has also established itself as the only competitor to the US dollar.[39]

However, there are also significant costs involved. The first, noted earlier, is the loss of the ability to implement independent monetary policy. This is a serious concern when business cycles or production costs developed differently across the eurozone. For example, over the 2000s, labour cost have been rising faster in Spain, Italy and Greece compared to Germany, which contributed to rising trade deficits in these countries, while Germany accumulated trade surpluses. The need to agree on a common monetary policy under such circumstance is challenging.[40]

The second is the lack of flexibility in implementing fiscal policy in areas such as deficit spending. When a country runs into fiscal difficulties it may be faced with inflation, high interest rates and a loss of confidence in its currency. When countries share a common currency, these potential risks of high public debt are spread. But some countries can become 'free riders' because they may not need to fix their own fiscal problems; other more responsible countries will share the burden. To prevent such free riding, the eurozone countries entered a Stability and Growth Pact that committed them to stick to the Maastricht criteria, notably for their budget deficit not to exceed 3 per cent of GDP. However, the enforcement of this rule has been difficult as fining a country already in fiscal difficulties is politically problematic. Hence, the Commission has been warning countries exceeding this limit, including France and Germany, but has not been effective in enforcing the rule. The challenge became even more daunting when in 2008 many people argued that the best policy to combat the global recession would be increased government spending.[41] In 2009, most eurozone countries exceeded the 3 per cent limit, while serious financial difficulties were experienced, for example, by Greece.

So, who should join the eurozone, and who should stay out. In this debate, a key idea is the 'optimum currency area'.[42] Economies with closely related business cycles are less likely to have different needs in monetary policy, and thus should join a currency union. Even if the business cycles are not perfectly aligned, labour mobility may help easing tensions. For example, when California was particularly hard hit by the economic crisis in 2008/9, while Texas was doing comparatively well, people were packing up their cars and moved Eastward in search of new jobs.[43] Yet, in Europe, labour is less mobile, and labour markets are less flexible (see In Focus 8.4). Thus, some argue that the eurozone has reached its optimal size, or is already too large.

The significance of these arguments varies in the perspective of different countries that might one day join the euro. In the UK, the independence of monetary policy plays an important role in the political debate. The UK trades intensively with its former colonies and with the USA; its external trade thus is less integrated with the rest of the EU than most continental countries (see Chapter 1). Moreover, the UK industry has structural differences to the rest of Europe, such as a smaller agricultural sector, a bigger financial services sector, and oil reserves in the North Sea. These structural differences imply that the British economy may be subject to different business cycles, and thus in need of a different monetary policy than continental Europe. Moreover, the UK has more private home ownership financed by variable rate mortgages, which makes ordinary people directly dependent on the central bank interest rate.[44] These arguments suggest the Britain may in fact be outside the 'optimal currency area'.

These arguments are less applicable for other countries. For example, Denmark is economically more integrated with the rest of the EU, and its industry structure more similar to its neighbours. Hence, it is hard to argue that Denmark would be outside the optimal currency area. The domestic political debate prior to the referendum in September 2000, when Denmark rejected joining the euro, focused primarily on issues of national sovereignty. As Denmark had a solid track record in macroeconomic policy and the exchange rate of the Danish Crown had been pegged to the euro anyway, it made little substantive difference, apart from Danes paying slight higher interest rates on their mortgage due to the residual currency risk. Lithuania is also a small country that is strongly integrated in European trade. However, Lithuania had only a short period of solid macroeconomic policy, and the Litas continued to be seen as less solid than the Danish crown. Thus, Lithuanians were very keen on joining the euro when in 2007 they missed the Maastricht criteria only by a tiny margin.

Optimal currency area
A theory establishing criteria for the optimal size of an area sharing a common currency.

IN FOCUS 8.4

Boom and bust in Spain

Spain joined the euro from the outset, and enjoyed a decade of very successful economic growth. GDP grew by an annual average of 3.7 per cent over the decade to 2006, compared to 2.1 per cent in the remainder of the eurozone, thus creating over five million new jobs, and attracting waves of immigration. The euro contributed to this success story: The euro lowered Spain's costs of servicing government debt, and confidence in the stability of the currency attracted foreign investment – not to mention heightened self-esteem of Spaniards feeling that they now had taken their rightful place in Europe. This prosperity was strengthened by prudent fiscal policy running budget surpluses when times were good, and a comparatively robust banking sector.

However, the prosperity had side-effects. Private consumers and businesses took advantage of the combination of a solid currency and low interest rates, and went on a spending spree. This led to a current account deficit of 10 per cent in 2007, and rapidly rising property prices (similar to the UK and Ireland). A major part of the economic growth happened in the housing market: the house building industry increased its share to as much as 7.5 per cent of GDP. When the economic crisis hit, credit flows dried up and the housing bubble burst. Construction projects were stopped, and unemployment surged. The tourism sector, which contributes 11 per cent of employment in Spain, was particularly hit as foreign visitors spend less money, or remained home. Especially the British recession affected Spain: a quarter of tourists come from Britain, and their visits fell by 16 per cent in the first half of 2009. With the British pound loosing over 25 per cent of its value in 2008/09 (See Chapter 7), a holiday in Spain became unaffordable for many Brits.

What options did the Spanish government have to tackle the crisis? Monetary policy had been transferred to the ECB, and thus devaluation of the currency was not an option. Thus, the Spanish economy needed other sources of flexibility to get back on its feet. Prudent fiscal policy gave the government some leverage to increase government spending

which softened the impact somewhat. One might also expect pressure on wages to keep costs down and thus maintain international competitiveness of Spanish exports, yet this did not happen. The Spanish labour market had developed a two-tier structure. Two thirds of workers enjoyed safe long-term employment, while the rest were on short-term contracts. The recession hit the two parts of the labour markets unequally. Those in long-term contracts were even able to negotiate pay rises of 3 per cent in real terms, while those in short-term employment bore the brunt of rising unemployment. While the drop of Spanish GDP was a notch below the EU average, its increase in unemployment from 11 per cent in 2007 to 18 per cent in 2009 was among the sharpest increases. Under flexible exchange rates, wage increases above the rate of productivity increase are normally compensated by devaluation of the currency. Spanish multinationals with a global strategy however did quite well by leveraging their international operations across Europe and Latin America (See Chapter 6).

While the Euro has undoubtedly helped Spain in its long run of above average economic growth, it is hard to say whether staying out of the eurozone would have eased the impact of the global crisis. Hypothetically, what would have happened? First, the Spanish peseta might have devalued in 2008, similar to the British pound, which might have stimulated exports, thus allowing the Spanish economy to recover quicker albeit from a lower level of real income. Second, wild speculation and high volatility of the exchange rates within Europe might have further accelerated the disruptive effects of economy, possibly even leading to an Iceland style collapse.

Sources: Based on: (1) C. Giles & (2) V. Mallet, 2009, Britain and Spain: A tale of two housing bubbles, *Financial Times*, January 11; (2) V. Mallet, 2009, Spain's recession: After the fiesta: *Financial Times*, February 17; (3) *The Economist* (2009): Unemployment in Spain: Two-tier flexibility, July 11; (4) J. Pérez-Campanero, 2009, Diez años del euro: Evaluación y perspectivas tras las crisis financiera, *Claves de la Economía Mundial*: 09: 293–298; (5) J. Rodriguez Lopez, 2009. Proceso de crisi inmobilaria en Europa y Estados Unidos: El caso de España, *Claves de la Economía Mundial*: 09: 299–306; (6) *Frankfurter Allgemeine Zeitung*, 2009, Aktienmarkt Spanien: Sonniger Optimismus sorgt für Kursauftrieb, August 20.

EU competition policy

Markets are probably the best way to ensure efficient allocation of goods and services, and to create incentives for businesses to constantly improve their offerings. However, these functions of the market only work well if everyone plays by the rules, and no one attains so much power as to control the market. An important aspect of the institutional framework thus is competition policy. Competition regulators aim to ensure that competition is not distorted by dominant players in the market, or by illegal collusion.

In the EU, the European Commission takes this regulatory role for cases affecting multiple countries, and national authorities such as the Office for Fair Trading (OFT) in the UK and the Kartellamt in Germany for cases affecting national markets. The Commission thus acts as a regulatory authority with respect to anti-trust issues and is working for economic liberalization and preventing state aid.[45] Businesses wishing to merge their operations in Europe thus need to notify the Commission if the business exceeds certain size thresholds. The Commission will then evaluate if the merger would create substantial impediment to effective competition. This policy has implications beyond Europe. For example, when US firms GE and Honeywell wished to merge in 2001, the Commission intervened because it feared market concentration.[46] Similarly, competitors coordinating their pricing can expect an intervention from the EU that may lead to a massive fine of up to 10 per cent of their global turnover.[47] The EU competition policy thus sets the formal institutional framework for competitive dynamics and for mergers and acquisitions, as we will discuss in, respectively, Chapter 13 and 14.

EU competition policy regulates not only companies, but also national governments. Local or national governments sometimes want to subsidize companies, for example to secure jobs in a local area. However, the EU has placed tight constraints on 'state aid' that the nation states, and their sub-entities, are allowed to provide to businesses. This is considered important to avoid national or local authorities competing with each other, for example to attract a major production plant. The main beneficiary of such 'subsidy competition' would be the MNE choosing an investment location. If the Commission finds that aid has been given in violation of its rules, it may demand repayment as in privatization of Automobile Caiova (Romania) and the Gdynia and Szczecin shipyards in Poland, or airline companies Olympic Airways (Greece) and Al Italia (Italy).[48]

However, there are numerous exemptions from the prohibition of state aid, including support for research and development, renewable energy and energy efficiency, broadband networks and the development of designated disadvantaged regions. The financial crisis of 2008/9 tested the EU's anti-subsidy commitment as many national governments bailed out firms in liquidity crisis, especially in the banking sector. The EU approved aid and broader schemes to support the financial sector in many countries of the EU, but it is expected that such support would not be approved under normal circumstances.

THE POLITICAL SYSTEM OF THE EU[49]

LEARNING OBJECTIVE

4 Outline the political institutions of the EU

Like the rules and regulations in a nation state, the EU institutions are constantly evolving. However, institutional change is more complex than in most nation states because of the decentralized and coordinated modes of decision-making. The president does not have the power to determine the overall direction, and the parliament is not empowered to create and pass laws. The member states continue to dominate decision-making in Brussels. Imagine, if the governors of the states of the USA were to convene in Washington twice a year to haggle over all major policies to be implemented during the next half year. Sounds crazy? Well, it is approximately like that in the EU – because the EU is not a nation state but an association of sovereign nation states.

Formal structure

The formal structure of the EU has some similarities with the structures in nation states, yet the actual lines of power are quite different. The Lisbon Treaty aimed to reduce the apparent inefficiencies of the system by reducing the power of national vetos and creating new positions of the President of the European Council and the Foreign Policy Representative. Even so, the political structures of the EU remain complex; the main institutions are the Commission, the Parliament, the Council and the Court of Justice.

The most important body policy making in the EU is the European Council (not to be confused with the Council of Europe). It defines the general political directions and priorities for the EU, which are decided by consensus. The European Council is chaired by the President of the European Council (a position newly created with the Lisbon Treaty) and consists of the heads of government of the Member States and the President of the Commission. Herman van Rumpoy of Belgium was appointed as the first President in December 2009. The EU High Representative for Foreign Affairs and Security Policy, another important new position created by the Lisbon Treaty, participates in the work of the council.

The highest formal decision-making body is the Council of the European Union, which consists of the ministers of the Member States. Depending on the issue on the agenda, each country is represented by the minister responsible for that subject (foreign affairs, finance, social affairs, transport, agriculture, etc.). The Council of the EU takes decisions by qualified majority voting, with votes for each country weighted by its population size ranging from 29 votes for UK, Germany, France and Italy to 3 votes for Malta. The presidency of the Council of the EU is held for six months by each Member State on a rotational basis.

The European Commission is the EU's executive arm with a role similar to that of a national government with responsibility for the day-to-day running of the EU. Most legislation is initially discussed in the Commission where different national positions are debated at length with the aim to find mutually agreeable rules (See Closing Case 'Nokia goes to Brussels'). The Commission is based in Brussels and organized in departments known as 'Directorate General' (DG), each headed by a Commissioner. It is composed of 25 commissioners, each from a different country[50] and each with his or her specific area of responsibility. The President of the Commission is nominated by the European Council, and thus by consensus between the governments of the Member States. The parliament formally has to confirm the appointment of the Commission, which it usually does. In 2004, Jose Manuel Baroso of Portugal succeeded Romano Prodi of Italy as President of the Commission, and he was reappointed for another five years in 2009.

The European Parliament in Strasbourg is elected every fifth year since 1979 directly by the citizens of Member States in a unique exercise in multi-national democracy. The parliament has gradually increased its power and responsibilities. It has to approve European law, it monitors the growing EU bureaucracy, and it shares the control over the EU budget. The parliament discusses all forthcoming legislation, and it is thus of critical importance to businesses that wish to anticipate changes in its framework. Most Members of the European Parliament (MEPs) belong to one of the European parties, which are associations of the national parties that are usually

European Council
The assembly of heads of governments setting overall policy directions for the EU.

President of the European Council
The person chairing the meetings of the European Council.

Council of the European Union
The top decision-making body of the EU, consisting of ministers from the national governments; it decides by qualified majority voting.

European Commission
The executive arm of the EU, similar to a national government.

Directorate General (DG)
A department of the commission, similar to a ministry of a national government.

President of the Commission
The head of the EU's executive, similar to a national prime minister.

European Parliament
The directly elected representation of European citizens.

© Ziutograf/iStock

Why is the European Parliament important for business?

better known to voters. In debates members typically vote along party lines, though they are more independent than in most national parliaments, and on occasion national concerns dominate voting behaviour. For instance, in 2001 the proposed Takeover Directive was voted down by MEPs from countries fearing to be disadvantaged by the way the Takeover Directive would interact with corporate governance systems in their country.[51] The parliament has important monitoring and co-decision rights, yet it does not hold all the powers of a typical national parliament, notably it cannot initiate legislation, it cannot raise revenues and it cannot choose a head of government. In other words, its is shaping the rules, but not selecting the people.

The EU also has its own judicial system with the European Court of Justice (ECJ) based in Luxembourg and a General Court. The General Court mainly deals with cases taken by individuals and companies directly before the EU's courts, while the Court of Justice primarily deals with cases taken up by the Commission and cases referred to it by the courts of Member States. In addition national courts are required to enforce the treaties that their country has ratified, and thus the laws enacted under them.

European Court of Justice (ECJ)
The court system of the EU.

Democratic processes

The European elections may appear a bit peculiar because they receive much less attention in the media than national elections. Yet the election is for one of the most influential political bodies in the world, and the election is probably the second largest election in the world (after India). Especially for businesses, most of the relevant rules are decided in the European Parliament – when legislation comes down to national parliaments, they are constrained by what has been decided already in Strasbourg and Brussels. Equally crucial, the European Parliament scrutinizes the budget of the EU, and thus the Commission. Hence, it does its best to minimize money wasted. National politicians may not admit it, but in many areas of politics, true power has slipped away from national parliaments a long time ago. But they won't tell you – except when they need a scapegoat.

However, not all is well with European democracy. Many voters feel disenfranchised because they do not see how they can influence decisions made in Brussels. This is partly due to the complexity of the process, not to mention the many translations, and partly because national newspapers rarely discuss the legislative process in Brussels. Moreover, the larger a group that tries to reach a common policy, the more compromises have to be made – in the EU, the representatives of almost 500 million citizens have to agree. Many voters also fail to understand why decisions cannot be made closer to them at national or even local level. The principle of 'subsidiarity' feels rather abstract and does not seem to work in practice. The bureaucrats in Brussels seem a far way off, not unlike voices in Scotland or Galicia complaining about bureaucrats in London and Madrid. Various parties have been arguing for more democracy in Europe, yet for some this implies securing veto rights wielded by (democratically elected) national governments, whereas for others it means more power to the (democratically elected) European Parliament, possibly including the right for the Parliament to elect the Commission. When politicians join this debate it is helpful to ask where they have their own powerbase; national governments are as likely to vote for strengthening the European Parliament as turkeys to vote for Christmas.

DEBATES AND EXTENSIONS

The EU is subject to ongoing political debates that may eventually lead to changes in its political or economic institutions or in its membership. It is important for businesses to be aware of such debates as they may create threats or opportunities for business. Here we discuss (1) the consequences of possible further enlargement, and (2) relationship of the UK to the rest of the EU.

LEARNING OBJECTIVE

5 Participate in debates over the future of the EU

Consequences of enlargement

EU enlargement has accelerated in the 2000s, yet there are significant concerns about pushing it further. The EU's largest expansion took place in 2004, with ten new members. Although this was a political triumph, it created an economic burden. The ten new members added 20 per cent to the population but only 9 per cent to the GDP, with 46 per cent of the average GDP per capita relative to the 15 old members of the EU.[52] While CEE displayed the strongest economic growth rates within the EU and provided low-cost production sites, the richer old member countries had to provide billions of euros in aid to bring CEE up to speed.

In the same spirit, of the old members, only Britain, Ireland and Sweden immediately opened their labour markets to citizens from the new member countries. Others were experiencing unemployment of 9 per cent or more and were fearful of an onslaught of job seekers from CEE taking away scarce jobs. There are good reasons to fear. In two years (2004–2006), approximately 200 000 CEE job seekers came to Ireland and about 600 000 (including half a million Poles) showed up in Britain – the biggest single wave of migration in British history.[53] Despite the relatively vibrant growth of the British and Irish economies, there is a limit to the absorptive capacity of their labour markets, resulting in second thoughts on the wisdom of such an open-door policy.[54] When Bulgaria and Romania joined the EU in 2007, Britain joined its partners in Western Europe and restricted immigration from these two countries.

Another major debate regarding enlargement is Turkey, whose average income is similar to Romania.[55] Turkey has a customs union with the EU since 1996, but membership negotiations have repeatedly been delayed. In addition, its large

Muslim population is a concern for a predominantly Christian EU. If Turkey were to join, its population of 73 million would make it the second most populous EU country behind only Germany, whose population is 83 million. Given the current demographic trends (high birth rates in Turkey and low birth rates in many current member countries), by 2020, Turkey, if it were to join the EU, would become the most populous and thus one of its most powerful members. It is not surprising that existing members of the club are anxious.

Half in, half out: the British[56]

While many are queuing to get into the EU, one nation sometimes wishes she had never come in. In 1998, the *Financial Times* summarized the British relationship with 'Europe' (which in Britain often means 'The Rest of Europe'), as follows:

> *'Britain lives with its history. The post-war relationship with its European neighbours has been one infused with misery and missed opportunities. To come to terms with what is now the European Union is to come to terms with the retreat from past glory. The nation's leaders have shunned the challenge.'*[57]

This quotation from 1998 still rings true over a decade later. Essential to understanding the ambivalent relationship of the British, or more precisely their political leaders, towards Europe is to understand that most British politicians of the 20th century never appreciated the EU as a political project, but rather focused on the economic benefits. In the 1950s, the United Kingdom stayed out of the union as it still prioritized relationships with its (former) colonies in the Commonwealth over relationships with its European neighbours. It first applied for membership in the 1960s, but was then vetoed by French leader, General De Gaule. Eventually, the UK joined along with Denmark and Ireland in 1973. Psychologically, many people of Britain see themselves as an independent nation with a major role on the world stage rather than a part of Europe, to which they geographically belong.

Thus, the UK has been reluctant to engage in the deepening of the union. When the SEA laid out the path to the Single Market in 1986, the British went along because the basic principles – widespread liberalization – reflected Anglo-Saxon principles of a free market economy, strongly promoted at the time by Prime Minister Margaret Thatcher. However, she negotiated rebates and exceptions for Britain, which won her support at home, but few friends elsewhere. When the Maastricht Treaty introduced coordination of environmental and social issues, she negotiated an opt-out from the social chapter. British firms thus could get away with lesser social standards and shorter notice periods in case they wished to lay-off staff. Many people in the rest of Europe – not just trade unions – thought this gave British firms a rather unfair competitive advantage. After a change in government, Britain surrendered this opt-out with the Amsterdam Treaty. Britain also stayed out of the eurozone, and the passport free travel of the Schengen Area.

Arguably, many of the conflicts over the appropriate form of EU regulation are grounded in the differences between civil and common law (see Chapter 2). The continental approach of detailed regulation sits uneasily with the British tradition that gives more weight to interpretation and case law. However, British businesses are often more euro-friendly than politicians from the two main political parties. While they may see European legislation as overly intrusive, the costs of staying out and thus missing market opportunities on the continent are even higher. On the other side of the channel, some are getting fed up with British obstinacy. Especially for the political left, the single market project reflects Anglo-Saxon values of free enterprise, and thus an Anglo-Saxon ideological take-over of Europe. Most Brits certainly don't see it that way. It will take many more years until the British and their partners develop a common understanding of what Europe is really about.

IMPLICATIONS FOR PRACTICE

LEARNING OBJECTIVE

6 Draw Implications for Action

Businesses operate in a context where the rules and regulations issued by the institutions of the EU (Commission, Council, and Parliament) and are central to what is permitted, and what is not. (Table 8.4) In other words, the EU is probably more important in shaping the institutional environment for business in Europe than national governments. Businesses thus need to keep their eyes on what is going in Strasbourg and Brussels.

First, you need to know the rules, and to identify advantages that your business may achieve within this institutional context. The provisions, stipulations and legal requirements attached to the different EU policy areas require careful audit from businesses operating in the union. You need to know what rights you have when operating in another country, and how to comply with existing regulation in your industry.

Second, you need to think forward and anticipate future changes in rules. At times, policy developments can be quite rapid, and only by staying in touch with discussions in the European sphere, you will be able to stay ahead of your competitors in adapting to institutional change. In the same way, you may recognize opportunities and threats early by following the debates on possible further expansion of the union. To be able to anticipate changes in the institutional framework of the EU, you need to monitor the discussion in the EU, especially the EU parliament.

Third, as a concerned citizen or as a business leader, you may direct your efforts of lobbying towards the institutions of the EU.[58] Lobbying is about making your voice heard and known to decision-makers with the aim to influencing political processes. As a lobbyist you may be able to influence preferences at an early stage, influence the positions taken by national governments, and – by working with the media – influence public perceptions of European issues. Business lobbies have shifted their attention from national capitals to Brussels and Strasbourg, where decision-makers are seeking information and qualified opinions on issues relevant to business. The Commission and various associated institutions are working on a wide range of regulations likely to affect businesses some day in the future. Any piece of legislation needs to clear three hurdles: the Commission, the Council and the Parliament. All three bodies are involved in the decision-making, and may thus be relevant for lobbyists. Once new legislation reaches national parliaments it is usually too late to effect major changes, even though the media may only pick up issues at that stage.

Lobbying
Making your voice heard and known to decision-makers with the aim of influencing political processes.

Table 8.4 Implications for practice

- Know the rules that apply to your industry in the EU
- Anticipate future changes in the rules by monitoring decision-making processes in the EU
- Direct your efforts of lobbying towards the institutions of the EU

CHAPTER SUMMARY

1 Explain the origins and the evolution of the EU:

- European Integration started with the Treaties of Rome aiming to overcome the historical divisions of Europe.

- The EU has continuously been enlarged, starting with the UK, Denmark and Ireland in 1973.

- The integration in the EU has continuously been deepened through a series of intergovernmental treaties often known by the cities where they were signed. Most important are the Single European Act (1986), the Maastricht Treaty (1992) and the Lisbon Treaty (2007).

2 Explain the evolution of the institutional environment in transition economies:

- Before 1990, CEE countries had an economic system organized around a central plan.

- The processes of transition in the 1990 focused on liberalization, stabilization, privatization and, crucially, the creation of a new institutional framework.

- Having met the Copenhagen Criteria of the EU, ten CEE countries became members of the EU in 2005 and 2007.

3 Explain how and why the institutional framework created by the EU is pivotal for business:

- The single market is based on the four freedoms of movement of goods, capital, people and services. It is implemented though harmonization of regulation in some sectors, and mutual recognition of national regulation in other sectors.

- The EU aims to facilitate free movement of people within the union, notable to enable people to take up a job in another country. This idea is supported by the Schengen Agreement for passport-free travel and the Bologna Process for European higher education.

- The euro has become a common currency in 16 countries that have transferred their monetary policy to the European Central Bank. Other countries are waging the costs and benefits of joining this eurozone.

- EU competition policy aims to ensure that a competitive environment is maintained in cases of mergers and acquisitions, cartels and collusion and state aid.

4 Outline the political institutions of the EU:

- The formal political structures of the EU resemble a government, yet national governments wield considerable power through the Council.

- The decision-making processes in the EU are based on democratic principles, yet they often are far removed from the individual citizens in member countries.

5 Participate in debates over the future of the EU:

- Enlargement creates not only benefits but also costs for existing EU members, who thus may be less enthusiastic to admit further members.

- The UK has an ambiguous relationship with the EU grounded in its history and its political culture.

6 Draw Implications for Action:

- With major institutional changes being decided at European level, businesses need to be informed about current rules and expected future change, and they may direct their lobbying to Brussels and Strasbourg.

KEY TERMS

Bologna Process
Central and Eastern Europe
Comecon
Common agricultural policy (CAP)
Common market

Copenhagen Criteria
Council of Europe
Council of the European Union
Customs union
Directorate General (DG)

Economic transition
Economic union
Erasmus Programme
Euro
European Central Bank (ECB)

European Coal and Steel Community
   (ECSC)
European Commission
European Constitution
European Convention on Human
   Rights
European Council
European Court of Human Rights
European Court of Justice (ECJ)
European Parliament
European Union
Eurozone

Four freedoms of the EU single
   market
Free trade area
Harmonized sector
Liberalization
Lisbon Treaty
Lobbying
Maastricht Criteria
Maastricht Treaty
Members of the European Parliament
   (MEPs)
Mutual recognition
Optimal currency area

Political union
President of the Commission
President of the European Council
Privatization
Schengen Area
Schengen Agreement
Schengen Visa
Schuman plan
Single European Act (SEA)
Single market
Stabilization
Subsidiarity
Treaties of Rome

CRITICAL DISCUSSION QUESTIONS

1 When should the EU issue regulation that is binding for all businesses in all countries, and when should it instead leave regulation to the nation states?

2 Some trade unions fear that the free movement of people depresses wages of ordinary workers because immigrants from other European countries are willing to work for lower wages. Should the free movement of people thus be restricted for some countries, or for certain time periods?

3 Given the importance of the European Parliament in shaping the institutional framework of the EU, why is voter participation in European elections often rather low?

4 Is it appropriate for bureaucrats in the EU Commission to communicate directly with businesses likely to be affected by a new set of rules?

CLOSING CASE

The Eco-Design Directive: Nokia goes to Brussels

In August 2007, a new EU Directive came into force that harmonized regulation of environmental standards with respect to energy using products. This 'Directive on the Eco-design of Energy-using Products' (EuP) aims to lower negative environmental impact over the entire life cycle of products. It is gradually being applied to an increasing range of products, and has profound implications for manufacturers and importers of, for example, mobile handsets. Yet, it did not come as a surprise to industry leaders such as Nokia of Finland.

Since the beginning of the millennium, Nokia had been a market leader for mobile phone handsets, having pulled ahead of its arch rival Ericsson of Sweden. Nokia emphasized not only technological features but

design and image in its product development and marketing. Being positioned in the premium segment of a pan-European market, Nokia invested in building a brand that appealed to its young and upwardly mobile customers. This included taking a lead on social and environmental sustainability issues.

Environmental policy debates were shifting from focus on environmentally friendly production to environmentally friendly products. Traditionally, environmental pressure groups would, for example, focus on the emissions from a specific production plant. However, around the year 2000, this was shifting to a product focus. Thus, manufacturers were challenged to consider the environmental impact of their products over the entire life cycle, including the disposal of the product when consumers would eventually discard it. For example, the car industry has been pressured in

© Alex Segre/Alamy

What is the best route to navigate through Brussels politics?

some countries to assume costs associated with the scrappage of cars. This pressure led firms to change their designs to reduce the use of materials that were costly to recycle. In the mobile phone sector, such issues were a potential issue because of the use of metals in the electronics that, if disposed of inappropriately, could lead to environmental hazard.

The EU Commission took the initiative for new environmental regulation that would harmonize national regulations. New proposed directives aimed, first, to ensure that new environmental standards would not vary across countries in ways that inhibit free trade in the union, and, second, to raise the environmental standards. Two initiatives were discussed from September 2000 among the departments (DGs) of the Commission. The DG Enterprise drafted a Directive on the impact on the environment of electrical and electronic equipment (EEE), while the DG Transport and Energy was working on a Directive on energy efficiency requirements for end-use equipment (EER).

The discussions were of concern to companies like Nokia, which were following closely the policy debates both nationally and in Brussels. Nokia had established a representative office in Brussels specifically to deal with EU related matters. In the debate over new environmental standards for electronics products, several issues were of concern to Nokia. First, would national governments be allowed to enact stricter require-

ments within their boundaries? As a company selling in many markets, Nokia naturally preferred a standardized approach with little variation of laws across countries. Second, should there be a full-scale life cycle assessment? This would not only be costly and time-consuming, but require assessing potential impacts that are simply not known, such as pollution arising from discarded mobile phones. Third, should small and medium-sized businesses be given simplified requirements? If this was the case it might make it difficult to source components from such firms. Fourth, should the EU's own environmental management system be mandatory for all firms? Nokia preferred to continue using ISO 14001, which is also recognized outside the EU.

Nokia principally had several venues through which it could aim to influence policy decision-making processes in Brussels. First, it might approach its national government, which might aim to influence decisions in the Council of Ministers. In this case, the Finish government acknowledged the responsibility of the Commission, and thus the national politics route was not given priority. Second, Nokia might work through industry associations that it is a member of, and that have established communication channels to the relevant DGs of the Commission and to the Parliament. In this case, Nokia worked with the European Information, Communications and Consumer Electronics

Technology Industry Association (EICTA). A drawback of this approach is that industry associations normally represent what all members can agree on as a common position, i.e. the lowest common denominator. This is not necessarily in the interest of those players in an industry that have already established above-average standards.

Third, companies may form ad hoc coalitions with other companies with similar interests, thus sharing each others' lobbying resources. Fourth, a large company like Nokia might aim to directly influence the Commission via the relevant DGs. At the time, Erkki Liikanen from Finland was Commissioner for Enterprise and Information Society, and Nokia had a good relationship with him and his team. Nokia worked with industry associations as well as ad hoc coalitions of leading players in the industry to develop such direct channels, including bilateral meetings on issues where industry associations found it difficult to build a consensus.

The legislative process progressed in multiple iterations of discussions within the Commission. In November 2002, the two separate legislative processes were merged, and in August 2003 the new 'Directive on Establishing a Framework for the Setting of Eco-design Requirements for **E**nergy-**u**sing **P**roducts' (EuP) was formally proposed. Following further consultations and negotiations it was formally approved as Directive 2005/32/EC by the Council and the Parliament in April 2005 and came into force in August 2007. Nokia found its interests reasonably well accommodated, though the data collection and reporting requirements established by the new directive are quite substantial. However, a harmonized regulation helps those businesses already operating across Europe, while high standards help businesses that have already established competences in managing to a high standard.

The new Directive led to industry specific regulation, so-called Integrated Product Policy (IPP), which establishes the best available practice and the standards thus to be used. The development of IPPs was initiated by a series of pilot studies, and Nokia volunteered to lead the pilot study for mobile phones. With a collaborative approach to working with the Commission and a reputation for being an environ-mentally responsible company, Nokia found that its views were heard and respected by policy makers. The pilot study on mobile handsets found that the environmental impact would be less than in other industries, and it thus did not become a priority for the Commission to regulate this industry.

Nokia continues to build its environmental reputation, not only by compliance with the regulatory requirements, such as this directive, but by acting proactively. This enhances its image among young consumers, and is acknowledged for instance by its inclusion in Dow Jones Sustainability Index and FTSE4Good index on corporate sustainability. An element of this environmental strategy is to anticipate new requirements, and thus to lead in their implementation. An ear on the ground in Brussels helps anticipating future requirements that may translate into new EU Directives, or that may be promoted by influential NGOs.

CASE DISCUSSION QUESTIONS:

1 How can companies get into the discussions on new legislation at an early stage when the major direction is likely to be decided?

2 What are the merits of using the alternative venues for lobbying: (1) national governments, (2) industry associations, (3) ad hoc coalitions and (4) direct approach to the Commission?

3 What are the merits of using a cooperative approach to working with the Commission (or a national government)?

4 Watch the set of Video presentations at http://www.eup-ecodesign.com/webcasts/eupDirective/. If you were manager in a company manufacturing or importing energy-using products, what measures should you be taking?

Sources: Based on: (1) P. Kautto, 2007, Industry-government Interaction in the preparation of a new directive: Nokia, Industry Associations and EuP, *European Environment*, 17: 79–91; (2) P. Kautto, 2009, Nokia as an environmental policy actor: Evolution of collaborative corporate political activity in a multinational company, *JCMS*, 47: 103–125. (3) European Commission, no date, *Eco-Design of Energy-Using Products*, (http://ec.europa.eu); (4) Nokia, no date, *Environmental Strategy* (http://www.nokia.com).

RECOMMENDED READINGS

D. Dinan, 2004, Europe Recast: *A History of European Union*. **Palgrave-Macmillan** – A detailed historical account of the EU.

M. Lavigne, 1999, *Economics of Transition*, **2nd ed., Basingstoke: Macmillan** – An analysis of the failures of the socialist system in CEE and of the transition process of the 1990s.

R. Mercado, S. Welford, K. Prescott, 2000, *European Business*, **4th ed., London: Pearson** – A textbook covering both the political development of the EU and the challenges for business in the EU.

J. Pelkmans, 2006, *European Integration: Methods and Economic Analysis* **London: Prentice Hall** – An economics perspective on how the EU works.

G. Suder, 2008, *Business in Europe*, **Los Angeles: Sage** – A textbook covering the institutional context of the EU and business practice in the EU.

H. Wallace, W. Wallace, M. Pollack, 2005. *Policy-Making in the European Union*, **5th ed., Oxford: Oxford University Press** – A collection of articles describing and analyzing political processes in the EU.

NOTES:

"FOR JOURNAL ABBREVIATION, PLEASE SEE PAGE XXVI-XXVII."

1   D. Dinan 2004. *Europe Recast: A History of European Union*. Palgrave Macmillan. S.S. Nello 2005. *The European Union: Economics, Policies and History*, McGraw Hill; M.J. Dedman, 2009, *The Origins and Development of the European Union 19451995: A History of European Integration*, 2nd ed., London: Routledge.

2   Original document available at: http://eur-lex.europa.eu/en/treaties/index.htm (last accessed June 2009).

3   H. Grabbe, 2002, European Union conditionality and the acquis communautaire, *IPSR*, 23: 249–268.

4   *The Economist*, 2009, Holding together: A special report on the euro area, supplement (16 pages), June 13.

5   European Commission, no date, Historical overview (http://ec.europa.eu, accessed June 2009).

6   *BBC News*, 2001, Euro-glossary: Maastricht Treaty (www.bbc.co.uk, accessed June 2009).

7   D. Phinnemore, 2004, *Treaty establishing a constitution for Europe*, Chatham House Briefing Paper, London: Chatham House; A. Moravcsik, 2005, A too perfect union? Why Europe said 'No', *CH*, 104: 355–359; A. Hurrelmann, 2006, European Democracy, 'Permissive consensus' and the collapse of the EU constitution, *ELJ*, 13: 343–359.

8   C. Reh, 2009, The Lisbon Treaty: De-constitutionalizing the European Union? *JCMS*, 47: 635–650.

9   A. Nove, 1969, *An Economic History of the Soviet Union*, London: Penguin; D.H. Alcroft & S. Morecroft, 1995, *Economic Change in Eastern Europe since 1918*, Aldershot: Elgar; M. Lavigne 1999. *The Economics of Transition*, 2nd ed., Basingstoke: Macmillan (Chapters 1 to 5); B. Kogut and U. Zander, 2000, Did socialism fail to innovate? *AJS*, 65: 169–190.

10 World Bank 1996. *World Development Report 1996: From Plan To Market*, New York: Oxford University Press; Lavigne, 1999, *as above* (Chapters 7 & 8); K.E. Meyer 2001. Transition Economies, in: T.K. Brewer & A.M. Rugman, eds.: *Oxford Handbook of International Business*, Oxford: Oxford University Press, 715–759; D. Gros & A. Steinherr, 2004, *Economic Transition in Central and Eastern Europe*, Cambridge: Cambridge University Press.

11 V. Corbo, F. Coricelli & J. Bosak, eds, 1991, *Reforming Central and Eastern European Economies*, Washington, DC: The World Bank; C. Clague & G.C. Rausser, eds 1992, *The Emergence of Market Economies in Eastern Europe*, Oxford: Blackwell.

12 S. Estrin, 2002, Competition and corporate governance in transition, *JPE*, 36: 1947–1982.

13 W. Swaan, 1997, Knowledge, transaction costs and the creation of markets in post-socialist Economies, in: P.G. Hare & J. Davis, eds, *Transition to the Market Economy*, Vol. II, London: Routledge, 53–76.

14 M.W. Peng, 2003, Institutional transition and strategic choices, *AMR*, 28: 275–296.

15 C. Vlachoutsicos, 1998, *Russian Communitarianism*. Working paper #120, William Davidson Institute,

University of Michigan Business School; T. Buck, 2005, Modern Russian corporate governance, *JWB*, 38: 299–313.

16 A.V. Ledeneva, 1998, *Russia's Economy of Favours*, Cambridge: Cambridge University Press; K.E. Meyer & M.W. Peng, 2005, Probing theoretically into Central and Eastern Europe, *JIBS*, 36: 600–621; M. Gelbuda, K.E. Meyer & A. Delios, 2008, International business and institutional development in Central and Eastern Europe, *JIM*, 14: 1–11; S.M. Puffer & D.J. McCarthy, 2007, Can Russia's state-managed, network capitalism be competitive? *JWB*, 24: 1–13.

17 D.C. North, 2005, *Understanding the process of economic change*, Princeton: Princeton University Press.

18 K.E. Meyer, 1995, Direct foreign investment in the early years of economic transition, *EoT*, 3: 301–320; N. Crespo & M.P. Fontoura, 2007, Integration of CEES into EU market, *JCMS*, 45: 611–632.

19 Citizen of new member countries may benefit from the full freedom of movement only after a transition period of often several years.

20 S. Mercado, R. Welford & K. Precott, 2000, *European Business*, 4th ed., London: Pearsons (Chapter 3); J. Pelkmans, 2006, *European Integration: Methods and Economic Analysis*, 3rd ed., Harlow: Pearsons (Chapter 5 to 10).

21 European Commission, no date, A single market for goods (http://ec.europa.eu, accessed June 2009).

22 *BBC News*, 2001, Euro-glossary: Maastricht Treaty, (http://news.bbc.co.uk, accessed September 2009).

23 Mercado, Welford & Precott, *as above*, 2000 (Page 93–94).

24 D. Smallbone, A. Cumbers, S. Syrett & R. Leigh, 1999, The single European market and SMEs: A comparison of its effects in the food and clothing sectors in the U.K. and Portugal, *RegP*, 33: 51–62.

25 *The Economist*, 2008, Regulating pesticides: A balance of risk, July 3.

26 J.S. Knudsen, 2005, Breaking with tradition: Liberalisation of services trade in Europe, in: A. Verdun & O. Groci, eds, *The European Union in the Wake of Eastern Enlargement*, Manchester: Manchester University Press; European Commission, no date, Freedom to provide services/Freedom of establishment (http://ec.europa.eu, accessed June 2009).

27 S. Schmidt, 2005, Reform in the shadow of community law: Highly regulated economic sectors, *GP*, 14: 157–173.

28 European Commission, 2002, The state of the internal market for services, Report to the Council and the Parliament (http://eur-lex.europa.eu, accessed July 2009).

29 European Commission, no date, A single market for services (http://ec.europa.eu, accessed July 2009).

30 L. Quaglia, R. Eastwood & P. Holmes, 2009, The financial turmoil and EU policy cooperation in 2008, *JCMS*, 47: 63–87; J. Chung, J. Grant, N. Tait & A. van Duyn, 2009, Plea for dialogue on regulation of financial sector, *Financial Times*, February 4; J. Hughes, 2009, City looks nervously at focus on financial sector crackdown, *Financial Times*, April 1; J. Hughes, 2009, In death do we part, *Financial Times*, July 8.

31 U. Elleman-Jensen, 2010, Island melder sig ud af verden, *Berlingske Tidende*, January 6; M. Huden, 2010, Iceland can refuse debt servitude, *Financial Times*, January 6.

32 Mercado, Welford & Prescott, *as above*, 2000 (Chapter 6); European Commission, no date, Living and working in the single market (http://ec.europa.eu, accessed June 2009); European Commission, no date, Your Europe (http://ec.europa.eu, accessed June 2009).

33 European Commission, no date, Professional qualifications (http://ec.europa.eu, accessed June 2009).

34 Auswärtiges Amt (German Foreign Ministry), no date, The Schengen Agreement and the Convention Implementing the Schengen Agreement (www.auswaertiges-amt.de, accessed June 2009).

35 Auswärtiges Amt, no date, *as above*.

36 D. Currie, 1998, *Will the Euro work?* London: Economist Intelligence Unit; Mercado, Welford & Prescott, 2000, *as above* (Chapter 4); D. March 2009. *The Euro: The Politics of the New Global Currency*, Yale University Press; *The Economist*, 2009, Holding together: A special report on the euro area (supplement, 16 pages), June 13; P. De Grauwe, 2009, *Economics of the Monetary Union*, 8th ed., Oxford: Oxford University Press.

37 G. Zestos, 2006, *European Monetary Integration: The Euro* (64), Cincinnati, Ohio: Cengage South-Western.

38 *The Economist*, 2005. A survey of Italy (16 pages), November 25.

39 S. Ruhkamp, 2009. Der Euro gewinnt weltweit an Gewicht, *Frankfurter Allgemeine Zeitung*, July 9.

40 *The Economist*, 2008, The ECB at ten: A decade in the sun, June 7. *The Economist*, 2009, The euro at ten: Demonstrably durable, January 3.

41 T. Barber, 2008, Fiscal rules reform allows budget deficits to rise, *Financial Times*, November 4; B. Benoit, 2009, Germany set to suffer record deficit, *Financial Times*, May 14.

42 R. Mundel, 1961, A theory of optimum currency area, *AER*, 51: 657–65.

43 *The Economist*, 2009, California's budget crisis: Meltdown on the ocean, July 11.

44 M. Bainbridge, B. Burkitt & P. Whyman, 1998, *Is Europe ready for EMU?* Bruges Group Occasional Paper #30.

45 S. Bishop & M. Walker, 1999, *Economics of E.C. Competition Law*, London: Sweet & Maxwell; Mercado, Welford & Prescott, 2000, *as above* (Chapter 4); M. Furse, 2008, *Competition law of the EC and UK*, 6th ed., Oxford: Oxford University Press; X. Vines, ed., 2009, *Competition Policy in the EU*, Oxford: Oxford University Press.

46 E.J. Morgan & S. McGuire, 2004, Transatlantic divergence: GE-Honeywell and the EU's merger policy, *JEPP* 11: 39–56; Y. Akbar & G. Suder, 2006, The new EU merger regulation, *TIBR*, 48, 667–686.

47 A. Wigger & A. Nölke, 2007, Enhanced roles of private actors in EU business regulation and the erosion of Rhenish capitalism: The case of antitrust enforcement, *JCMS* 45: 487–513; E.J. Morgan, 2009, Controlling cartels – Implications of the EU policy reforms, *EMJ*, 27: 1–12.

48 European Commission, 2009, *Report on Competition Policy 2009*, Brussels: EU.

49 S. Hix, 2005, *The Political System of the European Union*, 2nd ed., Basingstoke: Palgrave MacMillan; J. Peterson & M. Shackleton, eds, 2006, *The Institutions of the European Union,* 2nd ed., Oxford University Press; H. Wallace, W. Wallace & M. Pollack, 2005, *Policy-Making in the European Union,* 5th ed, M. Nugent, 2003, *The Government and Politics of the European Union*, 5th ed., Basingstoke: Palgrave Macmillan.

50 Countries whose nationals hold position of President of the European Council or of High Representative for Foreign Affairs do not appoint Commissioners.

51 J.S. Knudsen, 2005, Is the single European Market an Illusion? Obstacles to reform of EU takeover regulation, *ELJ*, 11: 507–524.

52 *The Economist*, 2004, The future of Europe: A club in need of a new vision, May 1.

53 *The Economist*, 2006, A survey of Poland, May 13.

54 *The Economist*, 2006, Migration from eastern Europe: Second thoughts, August 26.

55 H. Arikan, 2006, *Turkey and the EU: An awkward candidate for EU membership*, Aldershot: Ashgate; F. Nowak-Lehman, D. Herzer, I. Martinez-Zarzoso & S. Vollmer, 2007, The impact of a customs union between the Turkey and the EU on Turkey's exports to the EU, *JCMS* 45: 719–743. E. Largo & K. Jørgensen, eds, 2007, *Turkey and the European Union*, Basingstoke: Palgrave-Macmillan.

56 D. Gowland and A. Turner, eds, 1998, *Reluctant Europeans: Britain and European Integration 194–1998: A documentary history*; London: Pearson; D. Watts & C. Pilkington, 2005, *Britain in the European Union Today*, 3rd ed., Manchester: Manchester University Press; S. Wall, 2008, *A Stranger in Europe: Britain and the EU from Thatcher to Blair*, Oxford: Oxford University Press; *The Economist*, 2009, Charlemagne: Those exceptional British, March 28.

57 P. Stephens, 1998, UK's view of Europe obscured by past glories, *Financial Times*, January 4.

58 P. Bouwen, 2002, Corporate lobbying in the EU, *JEPP*, 9, 365–390; Y. Taminiau & A. Wilts, 2006, Corporate lobbying in Europe, *JPA*, 122–130; D. Coen, 2007, Empirical and theoretical studies in ERU lobbying, *JEPP*, 14: 333–345. G. Suder, 2008, *Business in Europe*, Los Angeles: Sage (Chapter 9).

CHAPTER NINE

GLOBAL INTEGRATION AND MULTILATERAL ORGANIZATIONS

LEARNING OBJECTIVES

After studying this chapter you should be able to:

1 Explain the multilateral institutions of global trade system, and their current challenges.

2 Explain the multilateral institutions of global monetary system, and their current challenges.

3 Describe the advantages and disadvantages of regional and bilateral economic integration in the Americas, Asia Pacific and Africa.

4 Participate in two debates on further multilateral policy forums and institutions contributing to economic integration.

5 Draw implications for action.

OPENING CASE

WTO mediates between Airbus and Boeing

Two of the mightiest companies in the world have been battling for leadership of the global market for large and very large aircraft. Yet, this is not only a battle between two firms, but between governments backing their respective champions. Caught in the middle, the World Trade Organization (WTO) is tasked with creating a level playing field for international competition.

Boeing was founded in 1916 and emerged as the world's leading aircraft manufacturer in the 1950s, exploiting its capabilities of building military aircraft during World War II. In the next decade, Boeing developed ever larger aircraft, launching the 707 in 1957, the 737 in 1967 and the 747 in 1969. At that time Boeing still had two domestic competitors; yet Lockheed Martin exited the large aircraft market in 1986, and McDonnell Douglas was acquired by Boeing in 1997. Since that time, the world market for large civil aircraft has been a duopoly of Boeing and Airbus.

Airbus was created in 1970 as a Franco-German joint venture with government backing and the explicit objective to challenge the monopoly of US manufacturers. The A300 launched in 1974 and the A320 launched in 1988 became Airbus' flagship products, and challenged the dominance of the USA. In 2001, Airbus for the first time won more new orders than its US rival. In the same year, it became an independent company wholly owned by EADS, a European air, space and military conglomerate (but with far smaller military operations that Boeing).

The European governmental support displeased Boeing and American politicians. Initially, the subsidies were tolerated because of the 'infant industry' nature of the support, and the small market share of Airbus. At the same time, European observers felt that Boeing gained an unfair advantage from its close association with the US air force, by far the world's largest buyer of military aircraft and technology. In 1992, the EU and the USA signed an agreement defining and limiting the support provided to their aircraft manufacturers. In particular, they banned direct production and sales subsidiaries, but allowed certain forms of launch aid in the form of state-guaranteed loans and spillovers from military to civil aviation research and product development.

However, the 1992 agreement was widely considered as unsatisfactory because it legitimized subsidies – and

How do Boeing and Airbus fight their competitive battle for leadership in the global market?

© ROUX Olivier/SAGAPHOTO.COM/Alamy

thus transfers from taxpayers to businesses. In 2004, Boeing convinced the US government to terminate the 1992 agreement, and to lodge a formal complaint against the EU for subsidies allegedly in violation of WTO regulation. The EU responded in kind and submitted a complaint against the US government support for Boeing. Ever since, the WTO has been trying to negotiate peace between the two potent adversaries and their powerful political supporters.

The US complaint focuses on so-called launched aid provided by European governments for the next generation aircraft, the A380. This launch aid comes as loans (according to the USA) at interest rates below market rates that only need to be repaid in line with sales of the commercialized aircraft (Table 9.1). Secondary complaints focus on infrastructure investments and research contracts benefiting Airbus. EU maintains that interest rates on launch aid loans are at market rates, and do not distort competition. Moreover, other support mentioned in the US complaint is available to all businesses and the travelling public (in case of the airport extension in Hamburg).

The EU complaint focuses on the close relation between Boeing and the US military. Boeing participates in major research contracts with the defence ministry, NASA and other institutions to develop new technologies for military and space applications. Yet, new knowledge in one part of Boeing directly benefits other areas, namely civil aviation and the development of the 787 Dreamliner in particular. A major concern is that these relationships lack transparency, which inhibits assessment of the financial benefits received by Boeing. Yet, the call for more transparency conflicts with the US concern about secrecy in national security matters.

The WTO handles both complaints in separate procedures. Many observers predict that both complaints were likely to be upheld to a large extent. Hence, both Boeing and Airbus are likely to loose because they may be asked to repay subsidies. Moreover, the complexity of supply chains with Boeing suppliers in Europe and Airbus suppliers in the USA make it very difficult to assess which national economies really benefit from the current regime. In addition, both sides spend substantial legal costs and top management

Table 9.1 Claims and Counterclaims (simplified)

	Boeing's Complaints against Airbus	Airbus' Complaints against Boeing
Complaints	• 'Launch aid' loans by European governments distort competition by lowering the financing risk for Airbus. • Interest rates paid by Airbus for government guaranteed loans are below market rates. • Government supported construction of infrastructure, for example for the extension of the runway of Hamburg airport. • Direct capital injections by governments as shareholders. • Research contracts for the European aviation and space industry.	• Indirect subsidization of the civil arm of Boeing via R&D contracts from the defence ministry, NASA and other government institutions, with a lack of transparency. • Tax concession and financial support from US States, in particular Washington. • Export promotion via tax advantages for export oriented companies and loans from the Export–Import bank • Launch aid from the government of Japan for the development of major components of the 787.
Responses	• Launch aid is effectively granted at market interest rates, and aims to correct for inefficiencies in long-term capital markets. • Infrastructure investment benefits all businesses and individuals in the area. • Military research links are much smaller than in the US.	• Research contracts are awarded based on competitive bidding that is in principle open to all businesses. • Demand for transparency would endanger national security. • Export promotion schemes have been discontinued following an earlier WTO ruling.

time, while Chinese competitors are plotting their entry into the industry.

In March 2010, the formal ruling of the WTO regarding the US complaint was notified to the participating parties. The public relations departments of both firms went into overdrive to 'spin' the outcome and to claim victory. Unsurprisingly, the US media reported victory for Boeing, while the European media emphasized the large number of aspects where Airbus' position was upheld. Meanwhile, everyone was awaiting the ruling on the European complaint against

the USA. Together, these rulings may provide a basis for new negotiations. Yet, few observers expect the conflict to be resolved any time soon.

Sources: Based on: (1) N. Pavcnik, 2002, Trade disputes in the commercial aircraft industry, *WE*, 25: 733–751; (2) E. Heyman, 2007, Boeing v Airbus, *Deutsche Bank Research*, Frankfurt: Deutsche Bank; (3) *The Economist*, 2009, Boeing and Airbus argue about subsidies, August 15; (4) C. Drew & N. Clark, 2010, W.T.O. Affirms Ruling of Improper Airbus Aid, *New York Times*, March 23; (5) P. Clark, 2010, Airbus claims WTO win over Boeing, *Financial Times*, March 24.

Global economic integration
Efforts to reduce trade and investment barriers around the globe.

Regional economic integration
Efforts to reduce trade and investment barriers within one region.

Multilateral organizations
Organizations set up by several collaborating countries.

When companies – such as Boeing and Airbus – have a disagreement about the rules of the game, how do they sort out their differences? What if even their two (or more) governments don't agree? There must be some place where countries can discuss their differences, resolve their conflicts and agree on common rules. Since the 1940s, continuous processes of global economic integration have created common rules and organizations aiming to facilitate international trade and investment. In addition, regional economic integration, such as the European Union (EU, Chapter 8), has facilitated international business within region of the world.

In these processes, multilateral organizations have attained a central role in setting rules and in helping resolve disputes between countries. The word 'multilateral' here indicates that they are based on an agreement between many countries, as opposed to bilateral agreements between two countries. In the area of international trade, the World Trade Organization (WTO) is designed to resolve trade disputes, while the International Monetary Fund (IMF) is the guardian of the global monetary system and helps countries in financial distress. For businesses, the question is how these supra-national institutions affect the institutional frameworks under which they operate. Specifically, how do changes in the rules of the game via global and regional economic integration, as emphasized by the institution-based view, enable firms to better develop and leverage their capabilities, as highlighted by the resource-based view? This chapter focuses on the role of multilateral institutions in international trade and monetary system, followed by a discussion of regional and bilateral economic integration. This chapter is full of debates over the merits of institutional arrangements. The Debates and Extensions section extends the debates to other areas of international policy coordination: economic development, climate change and financial sector regulation.

THE MULTILATERAL TRADE SYSTEM

Benefits of global integration by trade

Recall from Chapters 5 and 6 that, theoretically, there are economic gains when firms from different countries freely trade and invest. However, in the 1920s and 1930s, virtually all governments imposed protectionist policies through tariffs and quotas trying to protect domestic industries. Collectively, these beggar-thy-neighbour policies triggered retaliation that further restricted trade (Figure 9.1), which worsened the Great Depression and eventually contributed to World War II. In the late 1940s, the world community, mindful of the mercantilist trade

Figure 9.1 Down the tube: Contraction of world trade during the great depression (1929–1933, millions $)

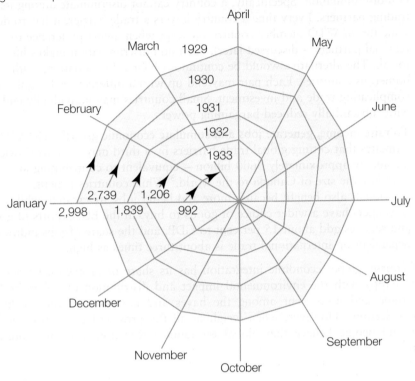

Source: Charles P. Kindleberger, 1986, 'The Contracting Spiral of World Trade' in *The World in Depression* (Figure 10 p.170). Copyright © 1986 by Charles P. Kindleberger. Published by the University of California Press. Reproduced with permission.

wars during the 1930s, initiated several developments aimed to foster economic and political integration, including the foundation of the United Nations, the creation of the Bretton Woods institutions (IMF and World Bank) and the General Agreement on Tariffs and Trade (GATT), the predecessor of the World Trade Organization (WTO).

The WTO is now the main multilateral organization establishing rules for international trade, and resolving trade-related conflicts between nations worldwide. The WTO focuses on economic benefits of trade. Yet, the underlying process of global economic integration is *political* in nature.[1] These political objectives have been important especially in the 1950s and 1960s, while economic benefits have been emphasized in more recent debates:

World Trade Organization (WTO)
The organization underpinning the multilateral trading system.

- **To handle disputes constructively.** This is especially evident in the WTO's dispute resolution mechanisms (discussed later in this chapter). Although there is an escalation in the number of disputes brought to the WTO, such an increase, according to the WTO, 'does not reflect increasing tension in the world. Rather, it reflects the closer economic ties throughout the world, the WTO's expanding membership, and the fact that countries have faith in the system to solve their differences.'[2] In other words, bringing disputes to the WTO is so much better than declaring war on each other.

- **To make life easier for all participants.** A common set of rules applying to all trading partners makes live easier for businesses because they don't have to learn about new institutions for each market to which they export. The goal

Principle of non-discrimination
A principle that a country cannot discriminate among its trading partners (a concession given to one country needs to be made available to all other GATT/WTO members).

of common rules is promoted by the WTO through its principle of non-discrimination. Specifically, a country cannot discriminate among its trading partners. Every time a country lowers a trade barrier, it has to do the same for *all* WTO member countries (except when giving preference to regional partners – discussed later). Such non-discrimination makes life easier for all. The alternative would be continuous bilateral negotiations with numerous countries. Each pair may end up with a different deal, significantly complicating trade and investment. Small countries may individually end up with substantially reduced bargaining power.

- **To raise income, generate jobs and stimulate economic growth.** The WTO estimates that cutting global trade barriers by a third may raise worldwide income by approximately $600 billion – equivalent to contributing an economy the size of Canada to the world.[3] While countries benefit, individuals also benefit because more and better jobs are created, while consumers have a wider choice of goods to buy. In the EU, exports of goods and services add about 15 per cent to GDP, and the share of jobs indirectly dependent on international trade is about three times as high.

Of course, global economic integration has its share of problems. Critics may not be happy with the environmental impact and distribution of the fruits from more trade and investment among the haves and have-nots in the world (see Debates Section). However, when weighing all the pros and cons, most governments and people believe that global economic integration generates enormous benefits.

Multilateral trade institutions

General Agreement on Tariffs and Trade (GATT)
A multilateral agreement governing the international trade of goods (merchandize).

The origins of today's World Trade Organization (WTO) are in the General Agreement on Tariffs and Trade (GATT), created in 1948. It was technically an agreement but *not* an organization. Its major contribution was to reduce the level of tariffs by sponsoring 'rounds' of multilateral negotiations. As a result, the average tariff in developed economies dropped from 40 per cent in 1948 to 3 per cent in 2005. In other words, the GATT facilitated some of the highest growth rates in international trade recorded in history. Between 1950 and 1995 (when the GATT was phased out to become the WTO), world GDP grew about five-fold, but world merchandize exports grew about 100 times (!). During the GATT era, trade growth consistently outpaced GDP growth (see Chapter 5).

Despite the GATT's phenomenal success in bringing down tariff barriers, by the mid-1980s when the Uruguay Round was launched, it was clear that reforms would be necessary. Such reforms were triggered by three concerns. First, because of the GATT's focus on merchandize trade, neither trade in services nor intellectual property protection was covered. Both of these areas were becoming increasingly important, especially to developed economies. Second, in merchandize trade, there were a lot of loopholes that called for reforms. The most (in)famous loophole was the Multifibre Arrangement (MFA) designed to *limit* free trade in textiles, which was a direct violation of the letter and spirit of the GATT. Finally, the GATT's success in reducing tariffs, combined with the global recessions in the 1970s and 1980s, led many governments to invoke nontariff barriers (NTBs), such as subsidies and local content requirements (see Chapter 5). Unlike tariff barriers that were relatively easy to verify and challenge, NTBs were subtler but pervasive, thus triggering a growing number of trade disputes. The GATT, however, lacked effective dispute resolution mechanisms. Thus, participating countries agreed in 1994 to upgrade the GATT and to launch the WTO.

World Trade Organization: 1995–present

Established on January 1, 1995, the WTO has become the GATT's successor. This transformation turned the GATT from a provisional treaty serviced by an ad hoc secretariat to a full-fledged international organization, headquartered in Geneva, Switzerland. One interesting question is: What happened to the GATT? Did it 'die'? Not really, because the GATT is still in existence as part of the WTO. But this is confusing. A straightforward way to distinguish the new GATT (as part of the WTO) from the original GATT is to identify the new one as 'GATT 1994' and the old one as 'GATT 1947'.

Significantly broader than the GATT, the WTO has six main areas (Figure 9.2):

- An umbrella agreement, simply called the Agreement Establishing the WTO.
- An agreement governing the international trade of goods, still using the old title as the General Agreement on Tariffs and Trade (GATT) – technically, as noted, it is GATT 1994.
- An agreement governing the international trade of services, the General Agreement on Trade in Services (GATS). The GATS aims to open up markets in service industries such as insurance, telecommunications, tourism and transportation, which requires member countries to liberalize these traditionally tightly controlled sectors to let foreign companies compete.

> **General Agreement on Trade in Services (GATS)**
> A WTO agreement governing the international trade of services.

- An agreement governing intellectual property rights, the Trade-Related Aspects of Intellectual Property Rights (TRIPS). This agreement establishes rules regarding intellectual property rights used in international trade, which were a particular concern to MNEs in developed countries wishing to exploit their copyrights, patents, trademarks and geographic names. It was not popular among developing countries that now faced more payments for e.g. urgently needed medicines first developed by Western MNEs.

> **Trade-Related Aspects of Intellectual Property Rights (TRIPS)**
> A WTO agreement governing intellectual property rights.

- Trade dispute settlement mechanisms, which allow for the WTO to adjudicate trade disputes among countries in a more effective and less time-consuming way (discussed next).
- Trade policy reviews, which enable the WTO and other member countries to 'peer review' a country's trade policy (In Focus 9.1).

Figure 9.2 Six main areas of the WTO

Umbrella	Agreement Establishing the WTO		
Three main areas	Goods (GATT)	Services (GATS)	Intellectual Property (TRIPS)
Conflict resolution	Dispute Settlement Mechanism		
Transparency	Trade Policy Reviews		

Source: 'Six Main Areas of the WTO' adapted from Understanding the WTO p.22, 2003, copyright © World Trade Organization, 2003.

IN FOCUS 9.1

China's first decade in the WTO

China became a new member of the WTO in 2001 and went through its first trade policy review in 2006. The review focused on three areas: trade, services and intellectual property rights (IPRs). In terms of trade (GATT 1994), fellow members commended China's efforts to revise over 2000 laws and regulations to comply with its WTO commitments. The average tariff was reduced from 16 per cent in 2001 to 10 per cent in 2005. Import quotas were virtually eliminated. In terms of services (GATS), members acknowledged that commitments undertaken by China were more extensive than those of other developing countries. However, liberalization of key service sectors, such as banking and insurance, was slower than other sectors. In terms of IPRs (TRIPS), many members expressed concern that, despite China's efforts, enforcement remained problematic. Overall, China's record of WTO implementation was generally considered good, despite some room for improvement.

By most statistical measures, China's first years in the WTO were very successful. China's GDP growth averaged 9 per cent. It became the world's third largest trading nation (after the USA and Germany) and one of the largest recipients of FDI (averaging $55 billion annually). China is now the largest exporter to the EU and the fourth largest market for EU exports (after USA, Russia and Switzerland). China's share in EU trade is growing: Its share in EU imports grew from 12.5 per cent in 2004 to 16.0 per cent in 2008, while its share in EU exports grew from 5.1 per cent to 6.0 per cent over the same time period. In reverse, the EU buys 21 per cent of Chinese exports (ahead of the USA with 19.0 per cent), and it supplies 11.7 per cent of Chinese imports, second only to Japan (13.5 per cent).

Overall, several experts noted that China on the whole met the letter, if not the full spirit, of its WTO commitments. In particular, commitments that were easy to implement, such as tariff reductions, were largely met. In more difficult areas such as IPRs,

implementation fell short. In a critical published statement, US Trade Representative Susan Schwab wrote: 'it is apparent that China has not yet fully embraced the key WTO principles of non-discrimination and national treatment'. In theory, foreign banks could open branches in most parts of the country as of 2006. But here is a catch: They could open only one branch a year, and each branch must have operating capital of $50 million, a burden that local banks do not have to shoulder.

Meanwhile, internal Chinese debates centre on two issues. First, is China now too dependent on trade, especially exports? Strong export growth often leads to foreign resentment and antidumping actions. During the WTO's first decade (1995–2005), Chinese exporters were the most frequent targets for antidumping actions worldwide, with approximately 15 per cent of all such cases. China complained to the WTO, in its official report as part of the trade policy review, that 'discriminatory measures against a particular member is contrary to the spirit of free trade and the principle of non-discrimination enshrined in the multilateral trading system'. Second, do foreign-invested enterprises (FIEs) benefit too much? In 2005, FIEs accounted for more than 60 per cent of Chinese exports. FIEs enjoy lower tax rates than domestic firms. Taxpayers in a developing country such as China are effectively subsidizing FIEs, many of which come from developed countries. To many Chinese, this does not seem fair and calls for equalization in taxation between FIEs and domestic firms.

Sources: Based on (1) *Business Week*, 2006, How Beijing is keeping banks at bay, October 2; (2) K. Lieberthal, 2006, Completing WTO reforms, *China Business Review*, September: 52–58; (3) S. Schwab, 2006, A message from the US Trade Representative, *China Business Review*, September: 30; (4) Y. Wang, 2006, China in the WTO, *China Business Review*, September: 42–48; (5) WTO, 2006, *Trade Policy Review Report by the People's Republic of China*, Geneva: WTO; (6) WTO, 2006, *Trade Policy Review Report by the Secretariat: People's Republic of China*, Geneva: WTO (7) European Commission, 2009, Trade Statistics China, trade.ec.europa.eu, accessed January 2010.

To the disappointment of developing countries, the WTO did not require developed countries to open up their agricultural sectors. However, overall, the WTO has a far wider scope, bringing into the multilateral trading system – for the first time − trade in services, intellectual property, dispute settlement and peer review of policy.[4] The next two sections outline two of its major initiatives: dispute settlement and the Doha Round.

Trade dispute settlement

One of the core activities of the WTO is its dispute settlement mechanism, which aims to resolve conflicts between governments over trade-related matters. Before the WTO, the old GATT mechanisms experienced (1) long delays, (2) blocking by accused countries and (3) inadequate enforcement. The WTO dispute settlement mechanism addresses these three problems. The preferred approach is to facilitate negotiations between the two countries to help them to settle the dispute themselves. When a country submits a formal complaint to WTO, the first stage thus is a period of mandatory bilateral consultations. If this consultation fails, the WTO establishes a panel of experts that investigates the case, hears the opinions of the two parties and eventually issues a report. This report is the basis for the ruling of the WTO. As it can only be rejected by consensus, it generally is the same as the final ruling. The whole process follows a tight time line for each stage, and lasts about 12 months (or 15 months if a country appeals). This process avoids the long delays of the old GATT system, and it makes it impossible for countries to bloc rulings against them. WTO decisions will be final.

In terms of enforcement, the WTO does *not* have its own enforcement capability. The WTO simply recommends that the losing countries change their laws or practices and, if they do not do so, may authorize the winning countries to use tariff retaliation to compel the offending countries' compliance with the WTO rulings. That is more than the old GATT would do, yet still lacks real enforcement 'teeth'. A country that has lost a dispute case can choose its own options: (1) change its laws or practices to be in compliance or (2) defy the ruling by doing nothing and be willing to suffer trade retaliation by winning countries known as 'punitive duties'. Trade sanctions are of course a dubious measure because it involves raising tariffs and imposing additional costs on the winning country's own importers. It can be effective if used strategically to hit the other country in a sensitive area. Yet, for small countries in dispute with a big country, it can be mainly symbolical.[5]

Fundamentally, a WTO ruling is a *recommendation* but not an order; no higher level entity can order a sovereign government to do something against its wishes. In other words, the offending country retains full sovereignty in its decision on whether or not to implement a panel recommendation. Most of the WTO's trade dispute rulings indeed are resolved without resorting to trade retaliation. As shown in the 'shrimp-turtle' case (In Focus 9.2), even some of the most powerful countries, such as the USA, have lost cases and have painfully adjusted their own laws and practices to be in compliance with the WTO rulings. However, certain 'big' cases, such as the conflict between Airbus and Boeing (Opening Case), have been in dispute for decades. The WTO tends to condemn subsidies, but as long as both the EU and US support their aircraft makers, and favour their own firms in military procurement, no end is in sight.

The Doha Round: The 'Doha Development Agenda'

A new round of trade negotiations was initiated at the WTO in Doha, Qatar, in November 2001. This 'Doha Round' is significant because it was the first round in the history of GATT/WTO to specifically aim at promoting economic development in developing countries. This would make globalization more inclusive and help the

Dispute settlement mechanism
A procedure of the WTO to resolve conflicts between governments over trade-related matters.

The Doha Round
A round of WTO negotiations started in Doha, Qatar, in 2001 − Officially known as the 'Doha Development Agenda'.

IN FOCUS 9.2

The WTO's 'Shrimp–Turtle' case

In 1997, India, Malaysia, Pakistan and Thailand brought a joint complaint to the WTO against a US ban on shrimp imports from these countries. The protection of sea turtles was at the heart of the ban. Shrimp trawlers from these countries often caught shrimp with nets that trapped and killed an estimated 150 000 sea turtles each year. The US Endangered Species Act, enacted in 1989, listed as endangered or threatened five species of sea turtles and required US shrimp trawlers to use turtle excluder devices (TEDs) in their nets when fishing in areas where sea turtles may be found. It also placed embargoes on shrimp imports from countries that do not protect sea turtles from deadly entrapment in nets. The complaining countries, unwilling to equip their fleets with TEDs, argued that the US Endangered Species Act was an illegal trade barrier. The WTO panel ruled in favour of the four Asian countries and provoked a firestorm of criticisms from environmentalists, culminating in some violence in the Seattle protests against the WTO in 1999. The USA appealed but lost again. In its final ruling, the WTO Appellate Body argued that the USA lost the case *not* because it sought to protect the environment but because it violated the principle of non-discrimination. It provided countries in the Western Hemisphere, mainly in the Caribbean, technical and financial assistance to equip their fishermen with TEDs. However, it did not give the same assistance to the four complaining countries. The WTO opined:

'We have not decided that the protection and preservation of the environment is of no significance to members of the WTO. Clearly, it is. We have not decided that the sovereign nations that are members of the WTO cannot adopt effective measures to protect endangered species, such as sea turtles. Clearly, they can and should ... What we decided in this appeal is simply this: although the measure of the United States in dispute in this appeal serves an environmental objective that is recognized as legitimate ... this measure has been applied by the United States in a manner which constitutes arbitrary and unjustifiable discrimination between members of the WTO ... WTO members are free to adopt their own policies aimed at protecting the environment as long as, in so doing, they fulfil their obligations and respect the rights of other members under the WTO Agreement.'

After its appeal failed, the USA reached agreements with the four complaining countries to provide technical and financial assistance on TEDs to be implemented on their shrimp boats.

For advocates of free trade and of developing countries' rights, this case demonstrates that even relatively weak countries can win against superpowers in the WTO. In contrast, environmental NGOs saw this case as evidence that the WTO rules aimed at promotion of international trade would constrain individual countries ability to implement policies aimed at protecting the natural environment.

Sources: Based on (1) WTO, 2003, *Understanding the WTO* (pp. 68–69), Geneva: WTO; (2) R. Carbaugh, 2005, *International Economics*, 10th ed. (pp. 186–187), Cincinnati, OH: Cengage South-Western; (3) A. Walter & G. Sen, 2009, *Analyzing the Global Political Economy*, Princeton: Princeton University Press.

world's poor. Consequently, the official title of the Doha Round was the 'Doha Development Agenda'. The agenda was ambitious: It would (1) reduce agricultural subsidies in developed countries to facilitate exports from developing countries, (2) slash tariffs, especially in industries that developing countries might benefit (such as textiles), (3) free up trade in services and (4) strengthen intellectual property protection. The first two items were pushed primarily by developing countries (and several NGOs), the other two by developed economies (led by the USA and the EU). In these negotiations, the EU is representing all its member countries, such that Europe speaks with one voice – though it is often difficult for the members to agree what the EU voice should say.[6]

Unfortunately, in the Cancún meeting in September 2003, numerous countries failed to deliver what they had signed up for two years before in Doha. The 'hot potato' turned out to be agriculture (see Closing Case). Australia, Argentina and most developing countries demanded that Japan, the EU and the USA reduce farm subsidies. The EU and Japan rejected proposals to significantly reduce agricultural tariffs or farm subsidies. The USA actually *increased* farm subsidies. On the other hand, many developing countries, led by India, refused to tighten protection for intellectual property, citing their needs for cheap generic drugs to combat diseases such as HIV/AIDS. Overall, developing countries refused to offer concessions in intellectual property and service trade in part because of the failure of Japan, the EU and the US to reduce farm subsidies.

After the failed Cancún meeting, member countries continued talking until in Geneva in July 2006, it was evident that they were still miles apart. The Doha Round was thus officially suspended, to the disappointment of virtually all countries involved.[7] The sheer complexity of an agreement on 'everything' among 149 member countries (as of 2006) in the Doha Round had proven to be a challenge to far. However, multilateral trade negotiations are notoriously challenging. In 1990, the Uruguay Round was similarly suspended, only to rise again in 1994 with a far-reaching agreement that launched the WTO. Whether history will repeat itself remains to be seen. On the other hand, although a global deal might be lost, regional and bilateral deals are moving 'at twice the speed and with half the fuss'.[8] One upshot of Doha's failure is stagnation of multilateralism and acceleration of regionalism. At the same time, new issues are added to the agenda: Europe and North America are increasingly paying attention to issues such as labour and environmental standards, and as they are increasing requirements at home, they also want to make sure imported goods live up to the same standards (Chapter 10). Emerging economies, in contrast, often see a lot of this 'CSR agenda' as a new form of protectionism.

THE MULTILATERAL MONETARY SYSTEM

Recall from Chapter 7 that after World War II, a fixed exchange rate system was created with the US dollar as the anchor currency. Along with this Bretton Woods system the International Monetary Fund (IMF) was created to help countries maintaining the fixed exchange rate.[9] Since the 1970s, the IMF no longer acts to secure stable exchange rates, but its mandate shifted to promoting international monetary cooperation and providing temporary financial assistance to member countries to help overcome balance of payments problems. The IMF performs three primary activities on behalf of its 184 member countries: (1) monitoring the global economy, (2) providing technical assistance to developing countries and (3) lending to countries in financial difficulties.

The lending activity of the IMF is focused on helping countries experiencing severe balance of payments problems. The IMF can be viewed as a lender of last resort to assist member countries should they get into financial difficulty. By definition, the IMF's lending refers to loans, not free grants. IMF loans usually have to be repaid in one to five years. Although there are some extensions for payments, no member country has defaulted. The ideal scenario for the IMF to make a difference is that when a country suffers from a balance of payments crisis (for example, rapid outflow of capital) that may trigger a financial crisis, the IMF can step in and inject funds in the short term.

While an IMF loan provides short-term financial resources, it also comes with strings attached – policy reforms that the recipient country must undertake as

LEARNING OBJECTIVE

2 explain the multilateral institutions of global monetary system, and their current challenges

International Monetary Fund (IMF)
A multilateral organization promoting international monetary cooperation and providing temporary financial assistance to countries with balance of payments problems.

IMF conditionality
Conditions that the IMF attaches to loans to bail out countries in financial distress.

condition for receiving the loan. The aim of this IMF conditionality is to fight the sources of macroeconomic imbalances, notably inflation and government deficits – and should ensure the country is *able* to repay the loan. Thus, the IMF typically imposes conditions that require belt-tightening by pushing governments to embark on reforms that they probably would not have undertaken otherwise. The details – where to cut government expenditure – are normally negotiated with the government of the country. For instance, when the IMF provided a $30 billion loan to Brazil in 2002, the Brazilian government agreed to maintain a budget surplus of 3.75 per cent of GDP or higher to pay for government debt. In the 1990s, the IMF has often gone into action in emerging economies, such as Mexico (1994), Russia (1996 and 1998), Asia (Indonesia, South Korea and Thailand, 1997) followed by Turkey (2001) and Brazil (2002). After a few years of relative calm, the IMF became again the 'global economic fireman' in the global crisis of 2008/09. The IMF provided rapid-fire bailouts to ten countries, mostly in Europe, between September 2008 and March 2009 (see Figure 9.3). While the bailouts required painful adjustments, they helped the economies to recover by 2010.[10] In the Greek budget crisis of 2010, the IMF worked with the EU to create a rescue package.

While the IMF comes to the rescue in times of crisis, it is not necessarily popular in the countries it is helping. That is because the conditions attached to bailout loans are often unpopular among those concerned. MIT Professor Simon Johnson, formerly a senior economist with the IMF, observes that as an IMF adviser, 'you're never at the top of anyone's dance card' because, essentially, 'IMF specializes in telling its clients what they don't want to hear'. The advice that political and financial leaders don't like to hear boils down to this: Desperate economic situations are often caused by elites overreaching themselves – and the necessary reforms involve cutting the financial wealth as well as the political influence of these elites. In Johnson's words:

> 'Eventually, as the oligarchs in Putin's Russia now realize, some within the elite have to lose out before recovery can begin. It's a game of musical chairs: there just aren't enough currency reserves to take care of everyone, and the government cannot afford to take over private-sector debt

Figure 9.3 The IMF's bailouts of 2008/09 (as percentage of GDP and in US$ billion)

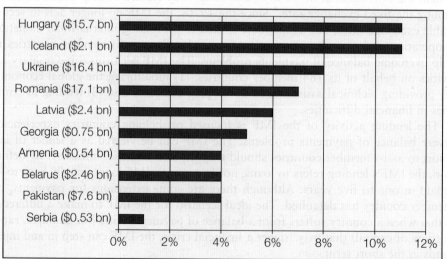

Source: Data taken from the International Monetary Fund www.inf.org (accessed September 2009). Reproduced with permission.

completely. So the IMF staff looks into the eyes of the minister of finance and decides whether the government is serious yet. The fund will give even a country like Russia a loan eventually, but first it wants to make sure Prime Minister Putin is ready, willing and able to be tough on some of his friends.'[11]

The complexity of the IMF's actions means that it cannot please everyone. One line of criticism centres on the IMF's lack of accountability.[12] On average, there are only about 11 officials to deal with crucial economic decisions in each country, and the IMF has a staff of fewer than 1000. These officials are not democratically elected, and some of them lack deep knowledge of the host country. Consequently, IMF-induced adjustment programmes can be politically explosive. For example, in 1998, the IMF forced the Indonesian government to drastically cut back on food subsidies for the poor. People rioted in the streets, and hundreds were killed. Some observers blamed the IMF for having triggered the riots, while others saw the riots as a reaction to three decades of unsustainable economic policy and suppression by the authoritarian Suharto regime.

A second and perhaps more challenging criticism is that the IMF's 'one-size-fits-all' strategy may be inappropriate.[13] Since the 1930s, to maintain more employment, most Western governments have abandoned the idea of balancing the budget. Deficit spending has been used as a major policy weapon to pull a country out of an economic crisis. Yet, the IMF often demands governments in more vulnerable developing countries, in the midst of a major economic crisis, to balance their budgets by slashing spending (such as cutting food subsidies). Arguably, these actions often make the crisis far worse than it needs to be. After the IMF came to 'rescue' countries affected by the 1997 Asian financial crisis, the unemployment rate was up threefold in Thailand, fourfold in South Korea and tenfold in Indonesia. Some scholars criticize the IMF for sticking to its policies in the absence of conclusive research and with the knowledge of repeated failures. However, demonstrating the success or failure of an IMF rescue package is difficult: you would have to know what would have happened without the rescue package. Obviously, times are tough when the IMF arrives – but is it because of excessive and unsustainable spending before the crisis, or because the IMF is 'too tough'? Some critics actually argue that the IMF is too soft – allowing countries to run deficits that are not sustainable in the medium- to long-term.

The IMF has continuously modified its approach based on experiences and analyses of various crises over the past three decades.[14] Since no two countries – or two crises – are identical, the IMF constantly faces a dilemma when going into action: How to design a programme that brings the country back to economic stability, while limiting social disruptions? The financial crisis of 2008 has led to renewed debates around the pros and cons of IMF conditionality, has led to some reform initiatives (In Focus 9.3). A limitation of IMF policy that became obvious in this crisis is that the IMF has no power over those countries that do not need its loans even when running major budget deficits or current account deficits – notably the USA and the EU.

REGIONAL AND BILATERAL ECONOMIC INTEGRATION

LEARNING OBJECTIVE

3 describe the advantages and disadvantages of regional and bilateral economic integration in the Americas, Asia Pacific and Africa

Some integration and coordination is taking place world wide, yet other initiatives of great practical relevance to business occur on a regional level. In particular, there is now a proliferation of regional trade deals. Except for Mongolia, all WTO members are involved in some regional trade arrangement. In Chapter 8, we discussed

IN FOCUS 9.3

The IMF's actions and criticisms

The momentum of the criticisms, the severity of the global crisis of 2008/09, and the desire to better serve the international community have triggered a series of IMF reforms. Some of these reforms represent a total (180 degrees) change from its previous directions, resulting in an 'IMF 2.0' dubbed by *Time* magazine. For example, the IMF now starts to promote more fiscal spending in order to stimulate the economy and to ease money supply and reduce interest rates, given the primary concern for the global economy now is deflation and recession, but not inflation. Obviously, the IMF's change of heart is affected by the tremendous stimulus packages unleashed by developed economies since 2008, which result in skyrocketing budget deficits. If the developed economies can (hopefully) use greater fiscal spending and budget deficits to pull themselves out a crisis, the IMF simply cannot lecture developing economies that receive its loans to balance their budgets in the middle of a crisis. Further, given the stigma of receiving IMF loans and listening and then implementing IMF lectures, many countries avoid the IMF until they run out of options. In response, in April 2009, the IMF unleashed a new Flexible Credit Line (FCL), which would be particularly useful for crisis prevention by providing the flexibility to draw on it at any time, with no strings attached – a radical contrast to the requirement to be in compliance with IMF-imposed targets as in traditional IMF loans. Mexico is the first country that has requested and been approved to tap the FCL for up to $47 billion, which is the largest financial arrangement in IMF's history.

Further, the IMF 2.0 is likely to become three times bigger – leaders in the G20 Summit in London in April 2009 agreed to enhance the IMF's funding from $250 billion to $750 billion. Of the $500 billion new funding (technically Special Drawing Rights [SDRs]), the US, the EU and Japan each is expected to contribute $100 billion. China has signed up for $40 billion. However, this is still not a done deal, because it is possible that US Congress may veto the $100 billion spending on 'other countries' problems' at a time when the American economy is hurting. Further, injection of substantial funding from emerging economies has led the finance ministers of Brazil, Russia, India and China (BRIC) who met in March 2009 to call for better representation of these countries. However, enhancing voting rights for emerging economies would result in reduced shares for developed economies. Even with the IMF's new proposed change to vote shares, Brazil, with 1.72 per cent of the votes (up from the current 1.38 per cent), will still carry less weight than Belgium (with 1.86 per cent, down from the current 2.09 per cent). Such points of contention continue to rage throughout IMF discussions. Therefore, IMF reforms will be a long-term undertaking that will not stop any time soon.

Sources: Based on text from (1) *The Economist*, 2009, Mission possible, April 11: 69–71; (2) *The Economist*, 2009, New fund, old fundamentals, May 2: 78; (3) A. Ghosh, M. Chamon, C. Crowe, J. Kim, & J. Ostry, 2009, Coping with the crisis: Policy options for emerging market countries, IMF staff position paper, Washington: IMF; (4) *Time*, 2009, International Monetary Fund 2.0, April 20.

Free trade area (FTA)
A group of countries that remove trade barriers among themselves.

European Integration, yet regional integration is not limited to Europe, it is also a common feature in other parts of the world. In particular, trade liberalization in the form of free trade areas (FTAs) has proliferated. Here, we review the experiences in North and South America, Asia and Africa.

Regional economic integration in North America

North American Free Trade Agreement (NAFTA)
A free trade agreement among Canada, Mexico and the USA.

The North American Free Trade Agreement (NAFTA), consisting of Canada, Mexico and the USA has been labelled 'one of the most radical free trade experiments in history because of the very different levels of economic development'.[15]

Politically, the Mexican government was interested in cementing market liberalization reforms by demonstrating its commitment to free trade. Economically, Mexico was interested in securing preferential treatment for 80 per cent of its exports. Consequently, by the stroke of a pen, Mexico declared itself a *North* American country. In the USA, when unemployment was 7 per cent in the early 1990s, many Americans thought it did not seem to be the best time to open up borders.

As NAFTA went into effect in 1994, tariffs on half of the exports and imports among members were removed immediately. Remaining tariffs would be phased out by 2010. Companies adapted to these changes in the rules of the game, to take advantage of new opportunities to disaggregate their value chains across North America, and to serve larger markets.[16]

By most statistical measures, NAFTA was a great success. In its first decade, trade between Canada and the USA grew twice as fast as it did before NAFTA. Expanding even faster, US exports to Mexico grew threefold, from $52 billion to $161 billion. US FDI in Mexico averaged $12 billion a year, three times what India took in. Mexico's US-bound exports grew threefold, and its GDP rose to become the ninth in the world, up from 15th in 1992. Mexico's GDP per capita rose 24 per cent during 1993–2003 to over $4000.[17]

What about jobs? In Mexico, *maquiladora* (export assembly) factories blossomed under NAFTA, with jobs peaking at 1.3 million in 2000. Beyond *maquiladoras*, the export boom NAFTA caused reportedly accounted for more than half of the 3.5 million jobs created in Mexico after 1994. However, there has been no sign of a substantial loss of jobs in the USA. Studies estimate that about 300 000 US jobs were lost due to NAFTA, which, on the other hand, added about 100 000 jobs. This net loss was small since the US economy generated 20 million new jobs during the first decade of NAFTA. NAFTA's impact on job destruction versus creation in the USA was minimal. However, a hard count on jobs misses a pervasive but subtle benefit. NAFTA has allowed US firms to *preserve* more US jobs because 82 per cent of the components used in Mexican assembly plants are US-made, whereas factories in Asia use far fewer US parts. Without NAFTA, entire industries might be lost rather than just the labour-intensive portions.[18]

Although economic theory suggests that trade benefits all partners (see Chapter 5), the impact of trade is different among members. More than 85 per cent of Canadian and Mexican exports go to the USA, but only 40 per cent of US exports go to NAFTA partners (about 22 per cent to Canada and 18 per cent to Mexico). Despite the explosion in trade, US imports from Mexico amount to less than 1.5 per cent of US GDP, and consequently, their impact was relatively small. Low-priced Mexican imports helped hold down inflation but only modestly, shaving about 0.1 per cent off the annual inflation rate in the USA.[19]

After its initial success, NAFTA faces new challenges. Opponents of globalization in both Canada and the USA no longer focus on the negative impact of competition from Mexico but rather on China and India. Despite the impressive gains, many Mexicans feel betrayed by NAFTA. Because of Chinese competition, Mexican real wages in manufacturing have stagnated. Many US, Canadian, European and Japanese multinationals are shifting some of their factory work to China, which replaced Mexico as the second largest exporter to the USA (after Canada).[20] About 1000 *maquiladora* factories have closed down since 2000. One reason many Mexicans are disappointed is that the deal might have been oversold by its sponsors as a cure-all for Mexico to become the next South Korea. If NAFTA has disappointed, it may be in part because the Mexican government has not capitalized on the opportunities NAFTA has offered. There is only so much free trade can do; other reforms in infrastructure and education need to keep up.[21]

Complementing NAFTA, the USA signed a similar deal with several smaller neighbours. The USA-Dominican Republic-Central America Free Trade Agreement (CAFTA), which took effect in 2005, brought together 'a whale and six minnows' (five Central American countries – Guatemala, Honduras, El Salvador, Nicaragua and Costa Rica – plus the Dominican Republic).[22] Although small, the six CAFTA countries collectively represent the second largest US export market in Latin America (behind only Mexico). Globally, CAFTA is the 10th largest US export market, importing more than Russia, India and Indonesia *combined*.[23]

USA-Dominican Republic-Central America Free Trade Agreement (CAFTA)
A free trade agreement between the USA and five Central American countries and the Dominican Republic.

South America: Andean Community, Mercosur and UNASUR

Whatever NAFTA's imperfections, it is much more effective than the two customs unions in South America: Andean Community and Mercosur. Members of the Andean Community (launched in 1969) and Mercosur (launched in 1991) are mostly countries on the *western* and *eastern* sides of the Andean mountains, respectively (Figure 9.4). There is much mutual suspicion and rivalry between both organizations as well as within each of them. Mercosur is relatively more protectionist and suspicious of the USA, whereas the Andean Community is more pro-free trade.[24] When Colombia and Peru, both Andean Community members, signed trade deals with the USA, Venezuela, led by President Hugo Chavez, pulled out of the Andean Community in protest and joined Mercosur in 2006. At the same time, Uruguay, a Mercosur member, demanded permission from the group to sign a separate trade deal with the USA; otherwise, it threatened to quit Mercosur.[25]

Andean Community
A customs union in South America that was launched in 1969.

Mercosur
A customs union in South America that was launched in 1991.

Figure 9.4 Regional Economic Integration in South America

Both regional initiatives have not been effective, in part because only about 5 per cent and 20 per cent of members' trade is within the Andean Community and Mercosur, respectively. Their largest trading partner, the USA, lies outside the region. It is a free trade deal with the USA, not among themselves, that would generate the most significant benefits. Emboldened by NAFTA, in 1998, all Latin American countries (except Cuba) launched negotiations with Canada and the USA for a possible Free Trade Area of the Americas (FTAA). However, by 2005, Argentina, Brazil, Paraguay, Uruguay and Venezuela changed their mind and announced that they opposed FTAA, thus undermining the chances of free trade from Alaska to Patagonia.[26] Instead of pursuing FTAA, Andean Community and Mercosur countries in 2008 agreed to form the Union of South American Nations (commonly known by its Spanish acronym, UNASUR, which refers to *Unión de Naciones Suramericanas*). Inspired by the EU, UNASUR announced its intention to eventually adopt a common currency, parliament, and passport. A functioning union similar to that of the EU is envisaged for 2019, but uncertain given the political disunity on the continent.

Free Trade Area of the Americas (FTAA) A proposed free trade area for the entire Western Hemisphere.

Union of South American Nations (UNASUR) An initiative to further economic and political integration in South America.

Regional economic integration in Asia Pacific

In the Asia Pacific region, integration is taking place at multiple levels and speeds (Figure 9.5). Founded in 1967, the Association of South-East Asian Nations(ASEAN) had not been economically active until 1992. Encouraged by the EU, ASEAN in 1992 set up the ASEAN Free Trade Area (AFTA), which accelerated intra-ASEAN trade, despite a temporary setback after the 1997 Asian economic crisis. In addition to the free trade agreement, ASEAN members have signed a number of further cooperation agreements regarding investment, trade in services, a single aviation market as well as cultural and sport events. ASEAN has the ambition of moving from a FTA to a common market with the creation of the ASEAN Economic Community by 2015.[27]

Association of South-east Asian Nations (ASEAN) The organization underpinning regional economic integration in Southeast Asia.

Although internal trade is growing, ASEAN suffers from a similar problem that Latin American countries face: ASEAN's traditional main trading partners, the USA, the EU, Japan and China, are outside the region. Intra-ASEAN trade accounts for on average 27.6 per cent of exports of ASEAN countries, though this percentage varies from 7.1 per cent for Cambodia and 14.4 per cent for the Philippines to 58.2 per cent for Myanmar and 87.5 for Laos.[28] The benefits of AFTA, thus, may be unequally distributed. Moreover, ASEAN is subject to considerable internal political tensions and cultural diversity. Most member countries have experienced authoritarian regimes in the recent past but have moved towards democracy in recent decades. In contrast, Myanmar (Burma) is run by an authoritarian military regime that is subject to trade boycotts from many countries outside the region. Moreover, economic cultural and religious diversity is considerably higher in ASEAN compared to the EU: Per capita GDP in 2008 varied from €33 882 in Singapore and €32 892 in Brunei to €1303 in Cambodia and €796 in Myanmar. Hence people in Singapore earn more than 40 times as much as those in Myanmar.

Despite this internal diversity and reluctance to interfere in each others domestic politics, economic integration is progressing. ASEAN is also acting as a group in negotiating trade agreements with other countries, including agreements and regular summits with the EU. ASEAN is an important trading partner of the EU, accounting for 5.1 per cent of EU imports, and 4.3 per cent of EU exports. ASEAN has signed bilateral free trade agreements with Korea (in effect 2007), Japan (2008), India (2010) and Australia and New Zealand. Politically most significant may be the ASEAN China Free Trade Agreement (ACFTA), which was signed in 2002 and came into effect in 2010 to create the largest free trade area among emerging economies. Given the strong competition from China, ACFTA may potentially turn rivalry into a partnership. ACFTA was predicted to boost ASEAN's exports to

ASEAN-China Free Trade Agreement (ACFTA) An agreement to establish a free trade area encompassing ASEAN and China.

Figure 9.5 Regional Economic Integration in Asia Pacific

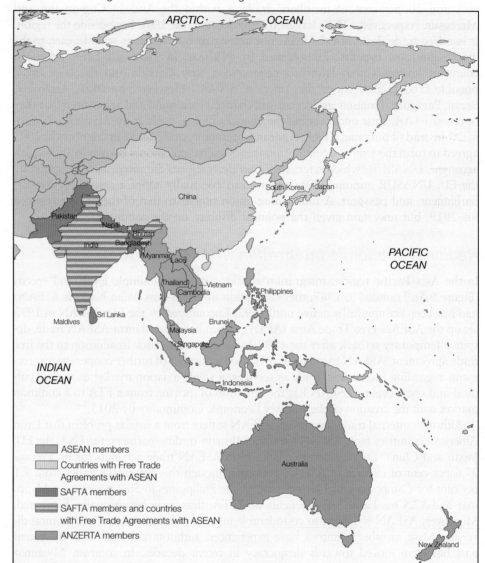

ARCTIC   OCEAN

China

South Korea   Japan

PACIFIC
OCEAN

Pakistan

Nepal

Bhutan

India   Bangladesh

Myanmar

Laos

Thailand   Vietnam

Cambodia   Philippines

Sri Lanka

Maldives

Brunei

Malaysia

Singapore

INDIAN
OCEAN

Indonesia

ASEAN members

Countries with Free Trade
Agreements with ASEAN

SAFTA members

SAFTA members and countries
with Free Trade Agreements with ASEAN

ANZERTA members

Australia

New Zealand

China by 48 per cent and China's exports to ASEAN by 55 per cent, thus raising ASEAN's GDP by 0.9 per cent and China's by 0.3 per cent.[29]

Another important regional free trade agreement in Asia includes the South Asian Free Trade Area (SAFTA) that brings together India, Pakistan, Bangladesh, Sri Lanka, the Maldives, Nepal and Bhutan, which was agreed in 2004 and is scheduled for full implementation in 2016. In the Middle East, the Gulf Cooperation Council (GCC) has created a political and economic integration that dates back to 1981, involving Saudi Arabia, Kuwait, Bahrain, Oman, Qatar and the United Arab Emirates.

Regional economic integration in Africa

Regional integration initiatives in Africa are both numerous and ineffective. A case in point is the fact that because one country often has memberships in multiple regional deals, a map using one colour to indicate one country's membership in one regional deal will be difficult. Consequently, Figure 9.6 draws a 'spaghetti bowl' to capture the various African regional deals. This complicated diagram also suggests that no sane professor will want to quiz students on the membership of these different deals in your exam (!). While various African countries are interested in reaping the benefits from regional economic integration, there is relatively little trade within Africa (amounting to less than 10 per cent of the continent's total trade), because protectionism often prevails. Frustration with a current regional deal often leads to a new deal, usually with a different set of countries, eventually leading to the 'spaghetti bowl' in Figure 9.6.

Most African countries share similar same kinds of comparative advantages, namely in exports raw materials (oil, minerals, precious metals) or agricultural produce (coffee, cacao, fruit). Hence, they would benefit most from access to European or North American markets, while the gains from regional trade are comparatively small. The challenge noted in Asia and Latin America thus applies even more so for Africa: The potential main potential trading partners are outside Africa.

Figure 9.6 Regional economic integration in Africa

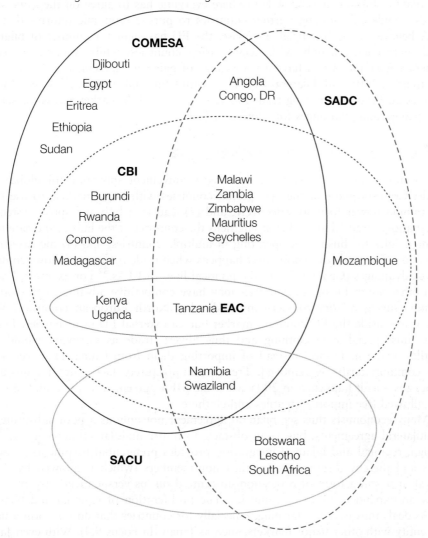

Source: Based on: (1) J.N. Bhagwati, 2002, *Free Trade Today* (p. 115), Princeton, NJ: Princeton University Press. CBI–Cross Border Initiative; (2) COMESA–Common Market for Eastern and Southern Africa; EAC–Commission for East Africa Co-operation; (3) SADC–Southern African Development Community; SACU–Southern African Customs Union.

Bilateral trade agreements

After the failure of the Doha Round of trade negations, the world has seen a proliferation of bilateral FTAs. Traditionally, bilateral agreements existed mainly on a regional basis. For example, the Australia-New Zealand Closer Economic Relations Trade Agreement (ANZCERTA or CER), launched in 1983, it turned the rivalry between Australia and New Zealand into a partnership. As an FTA, the CER over time removed tariffs and NTBs. For example, both countries agreed not to charge exporters from the other country for 'dumping'. Citizens from both countries can also freely work and reside in the other country. Mostly due to the geographic proximity and cultural homogeneity, CER has become a very successful FTA.

Since the suspension of the Doha round of trade negotiations, bilateral deals have proliferated. The USA has been leading this trend. Starting with Israel in 1985, the USA signed 17 bilateral free trade and investment agreements with countries as diverse as Australia, Singapore, Peru, Oman and Jordan, while three more are in the process of ratification.[30] US policy makers see bilateral agreements as an opportunity to push trade liberalization further than what could be achieved in multilateral forums like the WTO (where everyone has to agree on the same standards), while encouraging partner countries to pursue economic reforms that the USA believes to be beneficial. Likewise, the EU has signed a number of bilateral trade agreements, mainly with neighbouring countries; while countries in Latin America Asia and Africa have a wide range of pair-wise agreements. China joined the trend in 2005 with bilateral FTA deals with Chile and Pakistan.[31] Some of these treaties go beyond removing trade barriers, and establish market access for service companies, and guarantees for protecting FDI.

Trade creation or trade diversion?

Advocates of bilateral FTAs see them as a convenient substitute for global free trade. Critics argue that they (1) permit countries with large markets to use their bargaining power to more effectively, and (2) lead to a hub and spoke system of international trade that further strengthens the countries at the hubs, (3) create fragmented rules for businesses operating in multiple countries, and (4) increase trade diversion. The trade diversion effect happens when trade no longer follows comparative advantages (Chapter 5) but the political lines of FTAs.[32] For example, France and other South European countries may have competitive advantages in clothing manufacturing *relative to* Germany and other North European countries. With free trade inside the EU common market but an external EU tariff barrier, France may thus specialize in clothing and thus 'divert' trade as Germany would buy textiles 'made in France' instead of importing them from China. However, once the common tariffs is removed, French manufacturers face painful adjustment processes – as it happened in 2005 when the MFA agreement expired and thus the EU allowed free import of textiles and clothing.

Many economists thus see bilateral agreement not only as a poor substitute for multilateral agreements, but as an obstacle to future multilateral agreements.[33] By design, regional and bilateral integration provides preferential treatments to members and thereby *discriminates* against non-members (which is allowed by WTO rules). It is still a form of protectionism centred on 'us versus them', except 'us' is now an expanded group of countries. The proliferation of regional and bilateral FTAs deals thus may be alarming, especially for countries that do not form a natural entity with other major markets, such as Japan (In Focus 9.4). With even Japan joining FTAs, the only Asian economies left 'out in the cold' are Taiwan (blocked by China) and North Korea (lacking friends).

Australia-New Zealand Closer Economic Relations Trade Agreement (ANZCERTA or CER)
A bilateral trade agreement between Australia and New Zealand.

Trade diversion
A change in trade pattern away from comparative advantages due to trade barriers.

IN FOCUS 9.4

Is Japan being left out?

As of 2002, Japan was one of the only four WTO members not a party to any preferential regional trade agreement. Since then, Japan has concluded bilateral agreements with Singapore and Mexico, and negotiations are currently underway with ASEAN and South Korea. Japan's sudden interest in preferential regional trade agreements, after two decades of shunning the trend, suggests that the country might be worried about being left out. This raises an important question: How have the major preferential trade agreements of which Japan is not a member affected Japan's trade? The map presents some estimates of six major trade groups' effects on Japan's trade (Figure 9.7). For each group, the figure indicates two percentage changes: the change in Japan's exports to a trade group's

members calculated as a percentage of Japan's trade with that group and Japan's imports from group member countries also calculated as a percentage of Japan's trade with that group. Most of the numbers are negative, indicating that trade groups tended to *reduce* members' imports from and exports to Japan. The major exception is the large increase in Japanese imports from the EU. So far, the Asian economic integration group, AFTA, has had the smallest effect on Japanese trade.

Sources: Adapted from B. Yabrough & R. Yabrough, 2006, *The World Economy* (pp. 275–276), Cincinnati, OH: Cengage South-Western. Reprinted with permission. Data are from H. Wall, 2003, NAFTA and the geography of North American trade, *Federal Reserve Bank of St. Louis Review*, 85 (March–April): 13–26. AFTA—ASEAN Free Trade Area; ANZCERTA—Australia and New Zealand Closer Economic Relations Trade Agreement.

Figure 9.7 Japan trade effects

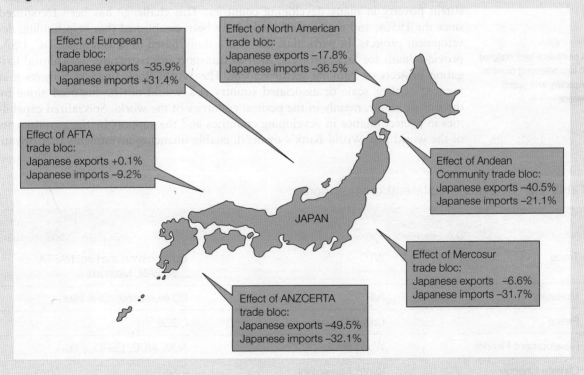

Critics such as esteemed trade economist Jagdish Bhagwati argue that rather than walking on two legs (global and regional), 'we have wound up on all fours' – crawling with slow progress.[34] This sorry state is triggered by the pursuit of countries' individual interest in a globally uncoordinated fashion. As FTAs proliferate, non-members feel that they are squeezed out and begin plotting their own regional and bilateral deals.

DEBATES AND EXTENSIONS

The WTO and the IMF are probably the most important multilateral organizational for global business. However, global integration and coordination is also taking place in many other areas, and political leaders of the world continuously see the need to address the challenges of the global economy, and societies in general. Thus, lots of political meetings and multilateral organizations aim to facilitate the way we live together on this globe.

The largest and most ambitious multilateral organization is certainly the United Nations (UN), whose mission is to secure world peace. Here we extend the discussion on global integration with three more specific agendas of political negotiations and collaboration: (1) economic development, (2) stopping climate change and (3) securing stability of the banking system (Table 9.2).

The development agenda

A major challenge for the global economy is the inequality among nations, and persistent poverty in many developing countries. This challenge has been recognized since the 1950s, and multilateral banks have been established that help funding development projects. In particular, the World Bank based in Washington, DC, USA, provides loans for large projects, such as transport infrastructure, agricultural irrigation projects or banking sector reform. The World Bank finances projects that because of their scale or associated country risk would not be financed alone by the private sector, mainly in the poorest countries of the world. Specialized capabilities in project finance in developing countries and the support by the governments of the world (the World Bank's owners), enable financing investments that private

World Bank
A multilateral bank designed to help developing countries, especially with project finance.

Table 9.2 Selected multilateral organizations

Policy Agenda	Global	Regional
Trade	WTO	EU (common market), NAFTA, ASEAN, Mercosur
Monetary	IMF	EU (eurozone), CFA franc
Peace	United Nations	OSCE
Development Finance	World Bank	ADB, AfDB, EBRD, IDB
Climate Change	Kyoto Agreement, Copenhagen Accord	–
Financial Sector Regulation	Basel Committee	–

investment bankers may consider as too risky. Recipients of the loans are normally the respective country's governments, or projects secured by government guarantees.[35]

In addition, the World Bank has a large pool of economic advisors who assess projects, and otherwise advise governments on a wide range of issues such as how to facilitate economic growth, or run an effective government administration – a critical contribution in countries that only recently attained independence. Moreover, the World Bank and the IMF are running major research projects on economic development, and compile and publicize economic data. Some observers see these research, advisory and information collection functions as even more important than the underlying lending activities. As a student, you can benefit from this activity directly: When preparing a term paper or dissertation you may find databases such as the *World Development Indicators* or the *International Financial Statistics* valuable and up-to-date sources of information (and more reliable than data found in newspapers).

However, talking of the World Bank, it is important to remember that it is a bank, and not a charity. Banks give loans, not gifts (though the slightly lower interest rate charged may be considered as a gift). Hence, money received from the World Bank (like IMF loans) need to be repaid, and projects thus need to generate more in revenues than they cost. In contrast, charities, national governments or multilateral organizations like UNDP or UNCTAD may provide money or services for free – as a gift. Such official or private development aid is a gift from generous donors wishing to help societies suffering extreme poverty or the consequences of a major disaster, such as the Indian Ocean tsunami in 2004 or the Haitian earthquake in 2010.

Development aid
A gift from generous donors wishing to help developing countries.

The World Bank is complemented by regional development banks such as the Asian Development Bank (ADB) based in Manila, the African Development Bank (AfDB) headquartered in Abidjian, Côte d'Ivoire and the Inter-American Development Bank (IDB) based in Washington, DC, USA. In Europe, the European Bank for Reconstruction and Development (EBRD) based in London serves transition economies. It was established in 1991 when the economies of Central and Eastern Europe broke away from central and planning and embraced the market economy. The EBRD is heavily involved in the restructuring of former state-owned enterprises, and (differently from the World Bank) the EBRD is temporarily taking small equity stakes in selected privatized companies.

European Bank for Reconstruction and Development (EBRD)
A multilateral bank designed to help transition economies.

For businesses, development projects funded by the World Bank or other development bank provide opportunities to engage in infrastructure development projects. The backing of the World Bank reduces the risks normally associated with such projects in developing countries. In transition economies, the EBRD may also become a partner for a foreign investor, for example when acquiring an equity stake in a joint venture.

The climate change agenda

A major concern at the outset of the 21st century is the environmental impact of human activity.[36] International agreements cover a wide range of issues from the conservation of rainforests to the protection of whales. A major focus of the environmental discussion has become the warming of the Earth's atmosphere as a result of green house gases (GHG) emissions. The scale of the problem requires extraordinary ingenuity and cooperation among governments, firms and consumers around the world. Since the United Nations Framework Convention on Climate Change (UNFCCC) was signed in 1992, global emissions of CO_2, the most potent GHG, have *risen* by a third.

Kyoto Agreement
An agreement committing developed countries to limit their greenhouse gas emissions.

Building on the UNFCCC, the Kyoto Protocol signed in 1997 was an attempt to do something immensely difficult. Under Kyoto, developed countries pledged to cut emissions by 6 per cent from 1990 levels by 2012. Each country was thus allowed to emit a certain quantity of CO_2. Governments issue emission permits to polluting firms within their borders, and such permits (essentially rights to pollute) can be bought and sold by firms worldwide. Through this emissions trading system, polluting firms can pay someone else (at home or in other participating countries) to cut emissions and claim credit.

While the EU and Japan took Kyoto most seriously, the USA, which had been the world's number one emitter of GHG until recently, refused to ratify it during the Bush presidency. Developing countries, who were not leading polluters at the time, were not asked to commit to limits on emissions. They argued that the developed countries had caused the problem and thus needed to resolve it – and moreover developing countries ought to be given a chance to develop first. Kyoto had a substantial impact on European businesses where emissions trading schemes stabilized pollution. However, the worldwide effects were limited because Kyoto did not cover the world's top emitting country, the USA, and placed no limits on India and China who developed faster than anticipated over the next decade, making the China the biggest source of GHG.

To address these shortcomings, world leaders met in December 2009 in Copenhagen, aiming to negotiate a more effective, more inclusive and more equitable global deal. By that time, the scientific evidence about climate change became stronger, showing for example that the average temperature on Earth had increased by 1°C since the Industrial Revolution. Over a decade after Kyoto, GHGs in the atmosphere were still increasing. Worse, they were increasing at an accelerating rate. Because GHGs stay in the atmosphere for decades (and often centuries), continuous creation of GHGs is predicted to lead to global warming of as much as 5°C by the end of this century, with disastrous ramifications. In addition to more volatile weather conditions, storms and heat waves, it would cause rising sea levels that result in the permanent flooding of many low-lying coastal areas (including whole countries and major ports), famine and possibly wars. Clearly, climate change is a global problem. The solution has to be global.

While the global community convening in Copenhagen, in principle, agreed with the necessity to do something (the goal was to control the level of global warming to 2°C by the century's end), countries strongly disagreed what each of them needed to do. Since there is no 'free environmental lunch', the debate boils down to who has to give up most to stop global warming. In the past, developed countries have created most GHGs on a per capita and cumulative basis, while 1.6 billion people in the developing world still suffer from poverty and lack access to electricity, which will most likely be generated by old, high-carbon technologies. The World Bank in the *World Development Report 2010*, released before the Copenhagen conference, urged developed countries to take aggressive action to reduce their own emissions, which 'would free some "pollution space" for developing countries, but more importantly, it would stimulate innovation and the demand for new technologies so they can be rapidly scaled up'.[37]

A crucial bone of contention is coal-fired power plants. Relative to oil, gas, nuclear, wind, solar and biofuel sources, coal is not only the cheapest and the dirtiest, but also the most widely used energy source in countries such as China. New sources of energy such as wind, solar and biofuel are still more expensive, such that they stand little chance in the absence of subsidies (or taxes on 'old' technologies). Not surprisingly, few politicians in the coal-dependent countries advocate the aggressive displacement of coal in power plants.

Proposals are numerous but solutions are few, because every new proposal generates new loopholes. Extending the emissions certificate scheme created in Kyoto (and implemented in Europe) would create a major allocation problem. A key stick-ing point in the debate on tradable emission certificates is the allocation of certifi-cates: should every one of six billion people in the world receive the same quantity of certificates or should past pollution be the benchmark – that latter implies that those who polluted most in the past also get the rights to polluting more in the fu-ture. In the USA, emissions trading schemes were discussed in 2009/10 but political opposition remained strong.[38] Critics argued that this would be a stealth tax that would be a job killer, encouraging US firms to shift more production abroad. Then, the next proposal called for import duties on goods from countries that have laxer rules on emissions. Not surprisingly, China and other developing coun-tries vehemently opposed such 'climate protectionism'.

It is clear that with so much at stake, no solution will be perfect and trade-offs will be inevitable. The *Economist* suggests that climate change 'is a prisoner's di-lemma, a free-rider problem and the tragedy of the commons all rolled into one'.[39] However, inaction was not an option for the Copenhagen conference. In an attempt to bring in emerging economies, the US delegation agreed with leaders of Brazil, China, India, South Africa, on the last day of the conference, a very weak, non-binding Copenhagen Accord.[40] The Accord agreed to limit the level of global warming to no more than 2°C by the century's end. Developed countries committed to reducing their GHG emissions by 80 per cent by 2050, while no targets were set for developing countries. In essence, countries agreed to keep talking. While some politicians such as US President Obama called the Copenhagen Accord 'a meaning-ful first step', most European governments – and even more so NGOs – were deeply disappointed by the a lack of a binding agreement.

Copenhagen Accord
A declaration by developed and developing countries to combat climate change.

For businesses, this state of affairs implies that standards and incentive schemes are likely to continue to vary across countries, and that the expected stimulus for new technologies remained weak and uncertain. Energy intensive industries, on the other hand, face fewer pressures for urgent (costly) adjustment then might have happened under more stringent commitments.

The financial sector regulation agenda

Banks take in savings and invest them in a variety of assets from loans to businesses to government bonds. Banks are private businesses. Yet, in contrast to most other businesses, the bankruptcy of a bank can have major consequences for large numbers of people – if not the entire economy. Throughout the last two hundred years, several major recessions around the world have been triggered by 'bank runs' – people queu-ing outside the banks trying to take their savings out because they suddenly believe it is no longer safe.[41] In consequence, countries have created regulatory frameworks that aim to guarantee the stability of the financial sector. They require banks, for ex-ample, to hold minimum capital levels, report activities in great detail and participate in insurance schemes. This regulation has reduced the frequency of major banking crises and scandals – but it has not eliminated them. In 2008, UK mortgage bank Northern Rock collapsed, soon to be followed by Icelandic Landisbanken and US in-vestment bank Lehman Brothers. Others were rescued through emergency take-overs like Bear Stearns in the US and HBOS in the UK. However, the consequences of these banking collapses were felt far beyond the countries concerned. Hence, a key concern on the international policy agenda became, do we need international coordination of bank regulation and supervision?

Basel Committee
A group of central bankers establishing standards for banking supervision.

We already have some international standards for banks, which have been cre-ated by the Basel Committee for Banking Supervision (in short, Basel Committee), a group of central bankers from the major economies of the world. This committee starts from the basic premise that national regulators in the home country of a bank

Basel II
The name of a set of rules
for banking regulation.

have the primary responsibility for the supervision and liquidity of the banks, including their foreign subsidiaries.[42] However, host countries have the right to constrain the activities of foreign banks, and some supervisory powers over subsidiaries. Moreover, the Basel Committee agreed and disseminated minimum regulatory standards, which have been revised in 2004 and are known as 'Basel II'. In particular, these rules establish minimum capital requirements for banks – how much equity they need to have relative to the investments they make. Basel II also introduced procedures for 'risk metrics' that relate the capital requirements to the riskiness of the portfolio of investments of a bank.[43] For example, government bonds are less risky than shares in companies, or loans to small businesses. Moreover, a portfolio of different types of investment is less risky than putting 'all your eggs in one basket'. While banks may use their own methods for assessing risks, in practice, risk rating agencies such as Moody and Finch play an important role. They assign ratings (such as AAA, AA, A) to different assets, and these ratings then (indirectly) determine how much equity banks need to hold.

These risk metrics in particular have come in for considerable criticism in the aftermath of the financial crisis of 2008, as they apparently failed to secure banking stability in countries traditionally believed to have the most developed financial markets – USA and UK.[44] In particular, risk management practices failed to capture rare events that occur only once in a generation and they underestimated systemic risk arising from the interdependence of banks.[45] Moreover, the rating agencies have been criticized for changing their ratings only after a major crisis had broken out.[46] Debates on reforms of the systems in the aftermath of the financial crash of 2008 thus focused on two issues: raising the basic capital requirements and reforming the procedures of assessing the risk of banks' investment portfolios.[47]

Beyond the discussion on the appropriate standards, a big debate is evolving whether national regulation of international banks is enough.[48] Do we need a global bank supervisor? Obviously, this debate raises major questions about who should be in charge of the supervision, and what action they should take when problems appear – and who pays for consequences? National sovereignty is at stake, as is the stability of the global economy. This is likely to become one of the big political debates in the global economy in the 21st century.

IMPLICATIONS FOR PRACTICE

LEARNING OBJECTIVE

5 draw implications for
action

Of the two major perspectives on global business (institution- and resource-based views), this chapter has focused on the institution-based view. To address the question, 'What determines the success and failure of firms around the globe?' the chapter has been devoted to introducing the rules of the game as institutions governing global and regional economic integration. How does this knowledge help managers? Managers need to combine the insights from the institution-based view with those from the resource-based view to come up with strategies and solutions to capitalize on opportunities presented by global and regional economic integration. Three broad implications for action emerge (Table 9.3).

First, managers need to understand the rules of the game at both global and regional levels. Changes in the rules induced by for example FTAs change the viability of business models, and may force firms to rethink their strategies. Although trade negotiations involve a lot of politics that many managers think they can hardly care less about, managers ignore these rules and their transitions at their own peril. When the MFA was phased out in 2005, numerous managers at textile firms who had become comfortable under the MFA's protection complained about their lack of preparation.

Table 9.3 Implications for action

- Managers need to understand the rules of the game at both global and regional levels to assess challenges and opportunities.
- Firms ought to make the most of their home region as they are often better prepared to compete on regional as opposed to global levels.
- Managers need to be aware and possibly engaged in the political discussions as they are likely to shape the business environment of the future.

In fact, they had 30 years to prepare for this event. When the MFA was signed in 1974, it was agreed that it would be phased out by 2005. The attitude that 'we don't care about (trade) politics' can lead to a failure in due diligence. In another example, firms that developed 'green' technologies early may benefit from new government policies aimed to address climate change – even though the Copenhagen Accord does not spell out mandatory policies. The best managers expect their strategies to shift over time in response to changes in the 'big picture', taking advantage of new opportunities brought by global and regional integration.

Second, the accelerated regionalism suggests that firms ought to make the most of their home region. The majority of international trade by EU countries is with other EU countries (Chapter 1). Likewise, the majority of the multinational enterprises (MNEs) generate most of their revenues in their home markets or their home region.[49] The largest MNEs may have a presence all over the world, but their centre of gravity (measured by revenues) is often still close to home. Regional strategies make sense because most countries within a region share some cultural, economic and geographic similarities – as well as FTAs. From a resource-based standpoint, most firms are better prepared to compete on regional as opposed to global levels. Managers, in short, need to think both local and global to create the best local solution based on resources that they may be able to access anywhere in the world.[50]

Third, managers need to be aware and possibly engaged in the political discussions as they are likely to shape the business environment of the future. In the broadest sense, these debates are about capitalism as a unifying worldwide economic system. In theory (Chapter 5), the economic benefits of international trade are evident. Yet, so are numerous conflicts over the distribution of these benefits, and over undesirable side-effects of rapid economic growth. The discussion of multilateral institutions has highlighted the political nature of many of the rules governing international trade and investment. The widespread perception that the burden of the global economic crisis – caused by rich bankers in rich countries – falls strongly on the poor and the unskilled has given new impetus to those dismissing the whole structure of global integration as unfair. Even *The Economist* is concerned:

> 'For Western liberals, even ones who believe in open markets as unreservedly as this paper, that means facing up to some hard facts about the popularity of their creed. Western capitalism's victory over its rotten communist rival does not ensure it an enduring franchise with voters. As Karl Marx pointed out during globalization's last great surge forward in the 19th century, the magic of comparative advantage can be wearing – and cruel. It leaves behind losers in concentrated clumps (a closed tyre factory, for instance), whereas the more numerous winners (everybody driving cheaper cars) are disparate. It makes the wealthy very wealthy: in a global market, you will hit a bigger jackpot

than in a local one. And capitalism has always been prone to spectacular booms and busts.'[51]

Businesses acting on this global stage of international trade, investment and finance are at the forefront of many of these debates. They thus face pressures to explain their role and their contributions to society to enhance their legitimacy, as well as the legitimacy of the system that allows them to prosper.

The global debates raised in this chapter – from international trade to climate change – suggest that societies around the world face major challenges that governments alone are not able to address satisfactorily. MNEs have power and influence that enable them to make contributions to some of these issues. Increasingly, they face pressures to do so. How and why companies assume responsibility that goes beyond generating profits for their shareholders, we discuss in the next chapter.

CHAPTER SUMMARY

1 Explain the multilateral institutions of global trade system, and their current challenges:

- There are both political and economic benefits for global integration by trade.

- The GATT (1948–1994) significantly reduced tariff rates on merchandize trade.

- The WTO (1995–present) was set up not only to incorporate the GATT but also to cover trade in services, intellectual property, trade dispute settlement and peer review of trade policy.

- The Doha Round to promote more trade and development thus far failed to accomplish its goals.

2 Explain the multilateral institutions of global monetary system, and their current challenges:

- The IMF promotes monetary cooperation and provides temporary financial assistance with balance of payments problems.

- IMF loans are usually conditional on macro-economic or financial reforms, which is often controversial in the countries concerned.

3 Describe the advantages and disadvantages of regional and bilateral economic integration in the Americas, Asia Pacific and Africa:

- Despite problems, NAFTA has significantly boosted trade and investment among members.

- In South America, the prominent regional deals are Andean Community and Mercosur.

- Regional integration in Asia Pacific is taking place in ASEAN, SAFTA and the GCC.

- Regional integration deals in Africa are both numerous and ineffective.

- Bilateral agreements allow further trade liberalization, but can lead to a fragmentation of rules and trade flows.

4 Participate in two debates on further multilateral policy forums and institutions contributing to economic integration:

- Development banks such as the World Bank provide loans for projects such as infrastructure in developing countries.

- The Kyoto Agreements and the Copenhagen Accord aim to combat climate change.

- International banking standards promoted by the Basel Committee are being revised in view of the experiences of the global financial crisis.

5 Draw implications for action:

- Managers need to understand the rules of the game at both global and regional levels to assess challenges and opportunities.

- Firms ought to make the most of their home region as they usually are better prepared to compete on regional as opposed to global levels.

- Managers need to be aware and possibly engaged in the political discussions as they are likely to shape the business environment of the future.

KEY TERMS

Andean Community
ASEAN-China Free Trade Agreement (ACFTA)
Association of Southeast Asian Nations (ASEAN)
Australia-New Zealand Closer Economic Relations Trade Agreement (ANZCERTA or CER)
Basel II
Basel Committee
Copenhagen Accord
Development aid
Dispute settlement mechanism
European Bank for Reconstruction and Development (EBRD)

Free trade area (FTA)
Free Trade Area of the Americas (FTAA)
General Agreement on Tariffs and Trade (GATT)
General Agreement on Trade in Services (GATS)
Global economic integration
IMF conditionality
International Monetary Fund (IMF)
Kyoto Agreement
Mercosur
Multilateral organizations
North American Free Trade Agreement (NAFTA)

Principle of non-discrimination
Regional economic integration
The Doha Round
Trade diversion
Trade-Related Aspects of Intellectual Property Rights (TRIPS)
Union of South American Nations (UNASUR)
USA-Dominican Republic-Central America Free Trade Agreement (CAFTA)
World Bank
World Trade Organization (WTO)

CRITICAL DISCUSSION QUESTIONS

1 The Doha Round collapsed because many countries believed that no deal was better than a bad deal. Do you agree or disagree with this approach? Why?

2 Critics argue that the WTO single-mindedly promotes trade at the expense of the environment (In Focus 9.2). Therefore, trade, or more broadly, globalization, needs to slow down. What is your view on the relationship between trade and the environment?

3 Who should be in charge of regulating and supervising banks that operate internationally? What principles should guide such regulation?

4 You are an IMF official going to a country whose export earnings are not able to pay for imports. The government has requested a loan from the IMF. Which areas would you recommend the government to cut: (1) education, (2) salaries for officials, (3) food subsidies and/or (4) tax rebates for exporters?

CLOSING CASE

The future of globalization: Wärtsilä power scenarios

Wärtsilä Corporation is a Finnish MNE developing, manufacturing and servicing very large scale engines in particular for ships and power stations. It prides itself on delivering 'complete lifecycle power solutions' and aims to 'offer innovative products, services and solutions, based on constantly better and environmentally compatible technologies'. Following a sequence of acquisitions of manufacturers and service providers around the world over the past decade,

Wärtsilä has become a global leader in this sector of the energy industry with a turnover of €2.6 billion and 19 000 employees in 70 countries around the world.

The future of the energy industry is highly uncertain, and contingent on changes in consumer behaviour, politics and technology. How can a company in such an uncertain environment plan for the future? Wärtsilä decided look into the future using a scenarios approach. It brought together experts inside and outside the company to develop essentially stories describing the future *might* look like. Their primary goal was to develop insights into the changes that they and their customers may face in the future.

The scenario team developed three scenarios that explore how the tensions between living standards of a growing population and climate change may shape the paths of globalization, and the energy sector in particular. In order to develop a broad perspective, an international and cross-functional team spend about 8000 hours of work to discuss issues such as macroeconomics, geopolitics and the natural environment. Top managers from Wärtsilä thus engaged in discussions with academics, NGOs, business leaders, government representatives and other experts. A key theme of the scenarios throughout the scenarios was power – not only in the sense of energy, but influence: who can influence events and why?

The first scenario was named the 'green earth'. It envisages a consumer driven cultural change that is based on a general awareness of the scarcity of resources and of the causes of climate change. This process leads to the adoption of energy conserving technologies and behavioural changes, for example in the use of transportation. In parallel, governments adopt stringent environmental standards for the life-cycle of products and services. In consequence, for example, mass transportation and electrical vehicles become the preferred modes of transport; the demand for oil is reduced, and the demand for natural gas and renewable energy sources increases. The geopolitical situation remains stable and the world economy grows at a modest pace.

The second scenario, called blue globe, predicts major changes in technology that enable economic growth while curbing emission. World leaders make substantive commitments to reducing greenhouse gas emissions, which spurs innovation in the energy sector. Technologies such as carbon-capture and storage, nuclear power and large-scale wind parks thus support continued economic growth. At the same time, transportation is electrified, which reduces its impact on the environment, and stops the rise of the price of oil. The reduced demand for oil leads to changes of geopolitics with reduced political tensions.

The third scenario, called grey world, is more pessimistic. It envisages increased scarcity of resources, with energy security becoming the pivotal issues driving international business and politics. Research into new technologies does not lead to viable new solutions, while public opinion prevents the construction of new nuclear power stations. With leading economies dependent on imported energy, the bargaining power of oil and gas exporting countries increases. Energy production is largely based on fuels available locally, or traded based on bilateral trade agreements. Political tensions run high, and regional wars over energy and raw materials are a distinct possibility. Lack of inter-governmental agreements thus undermines the potential for economic prosperity.

© Paolo Patrizi/Alamy

Will hybrid cars be the solution for the world's energy shortage?

Wärtsilä shared the scenarios with its business partners to stimulate discussions on future business opportunities – and treats. Often, these discussions triggered by the scenarios were the most interesting outcome. None of these scenarios was expected to come true exactly as described, but the future was likely to be a blend of all three. In this sense, the scenarios challenged conventional modes of thinking, and support strategic planning and decision-making.

CASE DISCUSSION QUESTIONS

1 From a resource-based perspective, how is technological change likely to influence future paths of globalization?

2 From an institution-based perspective, how are national and international politics likely to influence future paths of globalization?

3 If you were an executive in the energy sector, how would you prepare your business for the future?

Sources: (1) Wärtsilä Corporation, 2008, *Powerscenarios 2023*, Mimeo, Helsinki; (2) V. Riihimaki (Vice President of Wärtsilä Power Plants), 2009, *Keynote Speech*, 10th Vaasa International Business Conference; (3) Wärtsilä Corporation, 2009, Corporate Website www.wartsila.fi (Accessed October 2009); www.facebook.com/pages/Power-scenarios-2023/189333649301 (accessed November 2011).

RECOMMENDED READINGS

B.M. Hoekman & M.M. Kostecki, 2009, *The Political Economy of the World Trading System*, **3rd ed., Oxford: Oxford University Press** – A book explaining how the WTO has evolved and how it works in practice.

A.O. Krueger, 1997, Wither the World Bank and the IMF? *JEL,* **36, 1983–2020** – A review and evaluation of the activities and policies of the financial multilateral institutions from the 1940s to the 1990s.

J. Stiglitz, 2002, *Globalization and its Discontents*, **New York: Norton** – A Nobel prize winning economist formerly associated with the IMF gives a critical account of the state of globalization with a special focus on the role of the IMF.

A. Walter & G. Sen, 2009, *Analyzing the Global Political Economy*, **Princeton: Princeton University Press** – Explains how the global economy works with focus on political forces and the role of multilateral institutions.

NOTES

1 World Trade Organization, 2005, *10 Benefits of the WTO Trading System*, Geneva: WTO.

2 World Trade Organization, 2005, *as above* (p. 3).

3 *10 Benefits of the WTO Trading System* (p. 8). However, some argue that these estimates may be too optimistic. See J. Stiglitz & A. Charlton, 2005, *Fair Trade for All* (p. 46), New York: Oxford University Press.

4 R. Carbaugh, 2005, *International Economics*, 10th ed. (p. 181), Cincinnati, OH: Cengage South-Western.

5 M.L. Busch & E. Reinhardt, 2002, Developing countries and GATT/WTO dispute settlement, *JWT*, 37: 719–735.

6 S. Meunier & K. Nicolaïdis, 1999, Who speaks for Europe? *JCMS*, 37, 477–501.

7 *The Economist*, 2006, The future of globalization, July 29; World Trade Organization, 2006, Talks suspended, news release, July 24, http://www.wto.org (accessed July 24, 2006).

8 *Economist*, 2006, In the twilight of Doha (p. 63), July 29.

9 P. Kenen, 1985, Macroeconomic theory and policy: how the closed economy opened, in: P. Kenen & R.W. Jones, *Handbook of International Economics*, Amsterdam: North Holland.

10 *The Economist*, 2010, East European economies: Fingered by fate, March 20.

11 S. Johnson, 2009, The quiet coup, *The Atlantic*, May.

12 J. Stiglitz, 2002, *Globalization and Its Discontents*, New York: Norton.

13 S. Edwards, 1989, The International Monetary Fund and developing countries, North Holland: Carnegie Rochester Series on Public Policy 31, 7–68; S. Radelet & J. Sachs, 1998, The onset of the East Asian financial crisis, NBER working paper #6680; P. Krugman, 2008, *The Return of Depression Economics and the Crisis of 2008*, London: Penguin.

14 A.O. Krueger, 1998, Whither the World Bank and the IMF, *JEL*, 36, 1983–2020.

15 *Business Week*, 2003, Mexico: Was NAFTA worth it? December 22.

16 A.M. Rugman & J. Kirton, 1998, Multinational enterprise strategy and the NAFTA trade and environment regime, *JWB*, 33: 438–454.

17 *Business Week*, 2003, Mexico: Was NAFTA worth it? December 22.

18 *Business Week*, 2001, NAFTA's scorecard: So far, so good, July 9.

19 *Business Week*, 2001, NAFTA's scorecard, *as above*; L.G. Kletzer, 2004, Trade-related job loss and wage insurance, *RIE*, 12-724-748.

20 J. Sargent & L. Matthews, 2006, The drivers of evolution/upgrading in Mexico's maquiladoras, *JWB*, 41: 233–246.

21 Stiglitz & Charlton, 2005, *as above* (p. 23).

22 *The Economist*, 2005, Another such victory, July 30: 66.

23 US Trade Representative, 2005, *The Case for CAFTA*, February, www.ustr.gov, accessed October 2006.

24 *The Economist*, 2006, Trade in South America, August 26.

25 *The Economist*, 2006, Mercosur's summit: Downhill from here, July 29.

26 United Nations, 2006, *World Investment Report 2006* (p. 75), Geneva: UNCTAD.

27 ASEAN, 2008, *ASEAN Economic Community Blueprint*, www.aseansec.org (accessed February 2010); *The Economist*, 2010, Banyan: Asia's never-closer union, February 6.

28 ASEAN, 2009, *Intra- and extra-ASEAN trade 2008*, www.aseansec.org (accessed February 2010).

29 ASEAN Secretariat, 2002, *Southeast Asia: A Free Trade Area*.

30 Office of the US Trade Representative, no date, Free Trade Agreements, www.ustr.gov (accessed January 2010).

31 World Trade Organization, 2006, *Trade Policy Review Report by the People's Republic of China*, Geneva: WTO.

32 M. Fratanni & C.H. Oh, 2009, Expanding RTAs, trade flows, and the multinational enterprise, *JIBS*, 40: 1206–1227.

33 P.I. Levy, 1997, A Political-Economic Analysis of Free-Trade Agreements, *AER*, 87, 506–519; D.K. Brown, A.V. Deardorff & R.M. Stern, 2003, Multilateral, regional and bilateral trade-policy options for the United States and Japan, *WE*, 26, 803–826.

34 J.N. Bhagwati, 2002, *Free Trade Today* (p. 119), Princeton, NJ: Princeton University Press.

35 M. Gavin & D. Rodrik, 1995, The World Bank in a historical perspective, *AER*, 85, P&P 329–334; Krueger, 1998, *as above*.

36 K.P. Gallagher, ed., 2008, *Handbook on Trade and the Environment*, Cheltenham: Elgar; E. Christie, 2009, *Finding Solutions for Environmental Conflicts*, Cheltenham: Elgar; D. Helm & C. Hepburn, 2009, *The Economics and Politics of Climate Change*, Oxford: Oxford University Press.

37 World Bank, 2009, *World Development Report 2010*, Washington: World Bank; *The Economist*, 2009, The grass is always greener, April 24.

38 *The Economist*, 2010, Lexington: A fresh dose of honesty, February 6.

39 *The Economist*, 2009, A special report on climate change and the carbon economy: Getting warmer, December 5;

40 *New York Times*, 2009, Climate deal announced, but falls short of expectations, December 18; *The Guardian*, 2010, various articles: Low targets, goals dropped (December 19); If you want to know who's to blame for Copenhagen, look to the US Senate (December 21), How do I know China wrecked the Copenhagen deal? (December 22), Blame Denmark, not China (December 28).

41 K. Galbraith, 1957, *The Great Crash* (reprinted: 1992, London: Palgrave); P. Krugman, 2007, *as above*.

42 E.B. Kapstein, 1994, *Governing the Global Economy*, Cambridge, MA: Harvard University Press.

43 F. Heid, 2007, The cyclical effects of the Basel II capital requirements, *JBF*, 31, 3885–3900.

44 A. Walter & G. Sen, 2009, *Analyzing the Global Political Economy*, Princeton: Princeton University Press.

45 A.G. Haldane, 2009, Why Banks failed the stress Test, mimeo, Bank of England, February; R.M. Stulz, 2009, 6 ways companies mismanage risk, *HBR*, 87(3): 86–94.

46 H.O. Henkel, 2009, *Die Abwracker: Wie Zocker und Politiker unsere Zukunft verspielen*, München: Heyne.

47 *The Economist*, 2010, Reforming banking: Base camp Basel, January 23.

48 I. Begg, 2009, Regulation and supervision of financial intermediaries in the EU, *JCMS*, 47, 1107–1128.

49 A.M. Rugman, 2005, *The Regional Multinationals*, Cambridge, UK: Cambridge University Press; A.M. Rugman & A. Verbeke, 2004, A perspective on regional and global strategies of multinational enterprises, *JIBS*, 35: 3–18.

50 C.K. Prahalad & M.S. Krishnan, 2008, *The New Age of Innovation*, New York: McGraw Hill.

51 *The Economist*, 2009, So much gained, so much to lose, November 7.

© Serhiy Zavalnyuk/iStock

CHAPTER TEN

CORPORATE SOCIAL RESPONSIBILITY

LEARNING OBJECTIVES

After studying this chapter you should be able to:

1 Articulate a stakeholder view of the firm.

2 Articulate CSR challenges faced by firms operating in the global economy.

3 Explain how institutions influence firms' corporate social responsibility activities.

4 Participate in two leading debates concerning corporate social responsibility.

5 Draw implications for action.

Starbucks: standards in the spotlight

Founded in 1971, Starbucks took off in 1987 after being purchased by Howard Schultz, who is its present chairman. Starting with a single store in Seattle, USA, Starbucks grew to 16 635 restaurants in 2009, of which 5507 were outside USA. It generated worldwide revenues of about €7.0 billion, of which close to €2.0 billion came from overseas operations. Around the world, Starbucks has created coffee houses where people feel comfortable to relax. Even in China, young people feel homely in an atmosphere that integrates Chinese and American cultures.

Since its 1987 (re)birth, Starbucks has tried to position itself as a company that, in the words of Schultz, 'puts people first and profits last'. In the 1990s, Starbucks developed an environmental mission statement, created a corporate social responsibility (CSR) department, named a senior vice president for CSR, and began working with non-governmental organizations (NGOs). However, even so, NGOs frequently criticize Starbucks for failing social obligations.

In 2000, Global Exchange, an NGO promoting the idea of 'Fair Trade', launched a campaign against Starbucks. The Fair Trade movement advocated a minimum 'fair' price of US$1.26 per pound to ensure a 'living wage' for coffee producers – regardless of the highly volatile market price, which was only 64 cents per pound in 2000. In early 1999, TransFair USA, a third-party licensing organization, launched the Fair Trade Certified label. In November 1999, TransFair and Starbucks met to discuss Fair Trade coffee. While discussion were in progress, Global Exchange turned up the heat on Starbucks in February 2000 by demonstrating in front of a San Francisco store after a local TV station aired a clip on child labour on Guatemalan coffee farms. A few days later, during the open forum portion of the Starbucks shareholders meeting, Global Exchange activists took the microphone and demanded that Starbucks offer Fair Trade coffee. Things got heated and these activists were physically removed from the meeting.

Why did Global Exchange target Starbucks rather than any other company – certainly there must have been firms with lower standards? From the perspective of an NGO seeking publicity, Starbucks presented an ideal target: (1) the firm itself claimed to be highly responsible, but appeared to fall short of other organizations' standards, (2) its popularity among the middle classes and intellectuals means it is directly relevant to the NGOs' the most likely supporters and (3) its geographic spread means that customers around the world care about it – and might join campaigns against it. Protests might not only damage Starbucks' image but would also make it *physically* difficult for customers to enter and leave stores. Financially, buying Fair Trade coffee ($1.26 per pound) would not be prohibitively expensive, since Starbucks was already paying a premium price of $1.20 per pound. However, the price wasn't the key issue for Starbucks: The main obstacle was that Fair Trade co-ops do not deliver the consistent volume and quality of coffee beans that Starbucks requires to consistently serve the same quality of drinks throughout its restaurants.

Starbucks could have ignored Global Exchange, fought back or capitulated. However, Starbucks chose a middle ground, agreeing to sell Fair Trade coffee in its domestic company-owned stores. Soon, Starbucks became the largest US purchaser of Fair Trade coffee purchasing 653 000 pounds in 2001, which increased by 2007 to 20 million pounds, or 6 per cent of its coffee purchases. Starbucks thus accounts for 10 per cent of all Fair Trade certified coffee worldwide (and 20 per cent of Fair Trade certified coffee imported to the USA). However, the Fair Trade movement continues to face challenges as overall demand for Fair Trade remains low. Of the coffee produced by Fair Trade producers, only 20 per cent was marketed as Fair Trade coffee, and the rest had to be sold at the lower, world market price due to lack of demand.

In addition to purchasing Fair Trade coffee, Starbucks in 2001 has launched its own Coffee and Farmer Equity (CAFE) guidelines to:

'ensure the sustainable supply of high quality coffee, achieve economic accountability, promote social responsibility within the coffee supply chain and protect the environment.'

By 2009, Starbucks had a fleet of CAFE practices 'verifiers' (inspectors) and purchased 77 per cent of its coffee from CAFE practices suppliers.

Since 2001, Starbucks has been publishing a *Corporate Social Responsibility Annual Report*, starting with a letter from Schultz to 'Dear stakeholders'. The report for the financial year 2008 (published in 2009) lists collaborations with 13 NGOs ranging from Trans Fair USA to Conservation International and Save the Children. The reports cover a wide range of issues apart from labour practices, in particular environmental aspects of growing coffee and of running restaurants. It proclaims:

'It has always been, and will always be, about quality. We're passionate about ethically souring the finest *coffee beans, roasting them with great care and improving the lives of people who grow them. We care deeply about all of this, our work is never done.'*

However, not everyone agrees what 'ethically sourcing' really means.

Sources: Based on (1) P. Argenti, 2004, Collaborating with activists, *California Management Review*, 47: 91–116; (2) D. Vogel, 2005, The low value of virtue, *Harvard Business Review*, June: 26; (3) *Business Week*, 2007, Saving Starbucks' soul, April 9: 56–61; (4) Starbucks, 2009, *FY2008 Global Responsibility Report*, http://www.starbucks.com; (5) M. Venkatraman & T. Nelson, 2009, From servicescape to consumptionscape: a photo-elicitation study of Starbucks in the New China, *JIBS*, 1010–1026; (6) http://www.globalexchange.org.

Do Starbuck's customers really care where the coffee is coming from?

Although many regard Starbucks as one of the most socially responsible firms, the Opening Case raises crucial questions: Should firms assume responsibility for social issues of the world? How should companies react to pressures to take responsibilities beyond their legal obligations? Why did major coffee producers follow the lead by Starbucks and develop their own codes of conduct?[1] There are no easy answers to these questions. This chapter helps you answer these and other questions concerning corporate social responsibility (CSR), defined as:

'The firm's consideration of, and response to, issues beyond the narrow economic, technical and legal requirements of the firm to accomplish social benefits along with the traditional economic gains which the firm seeks.'[2]

Globalization has created new challenges for CSR, placing it into many debates on international business. Single country firms usually do fairly well by following

Corporate social responsibility (CSR)
The consideration of, and response to, issues beyond the narrow economic, technical and legal requirements of the firm to accomplish social benefits along with the traditional economic gains which the firm seeks.

the laws of their country; this will prevent them from getting into too much trouble. However, once firms cross borders they not only have to deal with the formal and informal rules of each host country, they may also be subjected to pressures at home with respect to their activities abroad – think of journalists investigating the practices of sub-suppliers in distant locations. Thus, globalization is creating new challenges in terms of both the moral complexity of the issues – what is 'right' to do where? – and the operational complexity of implementing consistent CSR practices throughout a global operation. CSR thus is part of the corporate response to the social and environmental issues brought to the fore by globalization (Chapters 1 and 9).

A key concern is – sustainability, which is defined as the ability 'to meet the needs of the present without compromising the ability of future generations to meet their needs'.[3] Globalization as discussed in Chapter 1 and 9 contributes in several ways to the urgency of sustainability in the 21st century.[4] First, rising levels of population, poverty and inequity associated with globalization call for new solutions. Second, the power of national governments has declined in the wake of globalization relative to both MNEs and non-governmental organizations (NGOs), have increasingly assumed the role of monitor and in some cases enforcer of social and environmental standards.[5] Third, the global interconnectedness through travel and internet communications creates a greater awareness of social or environmental issues arising in other parts of the world. Finally, industrialization has created some irreversible effects on the environment.[6] As firms contribute to many of these problems, many citizens believe that firms should also take on at least some responsibility for solving them. These expectations translate into pressures on firms to engage in CSR. Yet, the drivers underpinning global sustainability are complex and multi-dimensional. Several multilateral organizations have developed statements expressing these multi-dimensional expectations, summarized in Table 10.1. Firms have responded by developing triple bottom line strategies that take into account their *economic, social* and *environmental* performance.

The remainder of this chapter first introduces a stakeholder view of the firm to explain the evolution of CSR before looking at CSR issues arising specifically in the global operations of multinational enterprises (MNEs). Then we discuss how the institution-based view can explain international variations in CSR practices and communications, and apply the resource-based view to explore how companies may benefit from CSR. Debates and extensions follow.

sustainability
The ability to meet the needs of the present without compromising the ability of future generations to meet their needs.

Triple bottom line
Firms' economic, social and environmental performance.

STAKEHOLDERS OF THE FIRM

LEARNING OBJECTIVE

1 Articulate a stakeholder view of the firm

Stakeholder
Any group or individual who can affect or is affected by the achievement of the organization's objectives.

At the heart of CSR is the concept of stakeholder, which is 'any group or individual who can affect or is affected by the achievement of the organization's objectives'.[7] Shown in Figure 10.1, while shareholders are an important group of stakeholders, other stakeholders include managers, non-managerial employees (hereafter 'employees'), suppliers, customers, communities, governments and social and environmental groups. A major debate on CSR is whether managers' efforts to promote the interests of these stakeholders are at odds with their fiduciary duty to safeguard shareholder interests.[8] As firms are not social agencies and that their primary function is to serve as economic enterprises, it is certainly true that they are unable to resolve all the social problems of the world. Yet, on the other hand, failing to heed certain CSR imperatives may be self-defeating in the long run. Therefore, the key is how to prioritize.[9]

Table 10.1 CSR for MNEs: Recommendations from International Organizations

MNEs and Host Governments

- Should not interfere in the internal political affairs of the host country (OECD, UN)
- Should consult governmental authorities and national employers' and workers' organizations to ensure that their investments conform to the economic and social development policies of the host country (ICC, ILO, OECD, UN)
- Should reinvest some profits in the host country (ICC)

MNEs and Laws, Regulations and Politics

- Should respect the right of every country to exercise control over its natural resources (UN)
- Should refrain from improper or illegal involvement in local politics (OECD)
- Should not pay bribes or render improper benefits to public servants (OECD, UN)

MNEs and Technology Transfer

- Should develop and adapt technologies to the needs of host countries (ICC, ILO, OECD)
- Should provide reasonable terms and conditions when granting licenses for industrial property rights (ICC, OECD)

MNEs and Environmental Protection

- Should respect the host country laws and regulations concerning environmental protection (OECD, UN)
- Should supply to host governments information concerning the environmental impact of MNE activities (ICC, UN)

MNEs and Consumer Protection

- Should preserve the safety and health of consumers by disclosing appropriate information, labelling correctly and advertising accurately (UN)

MNEs and Employment Practices

- Should cooperate with host governments to create jobs in certain locations (ICC)
- Should give advance notice of plant closures and mitigate the adverse effects (ICC, OECD)
- Should respect the rights for employees to engage in collective bargaining (ILO, OECD)

MNEs and Human Rights

- Should respect human rights and fundamental freedoms in host countries (UN)

Sources: Based on (1) ICC: *The International Chamber of Commerce Guidelines for International Investment*, http://www.iccwbo.org; (2) ILO: *The International Labour Office Tripartite Declarations of Principles Concerning Multinational Enterprises and Social Policy*, http://www.ilo.org; (3) OECD: *The Organization for Economic Cooperation and Development Guidelines for Multinational Enterprises*, http://www.oecd.org; (4) UN: *The United Nations Code of Conduct on Transnational Corporations*, http://www.un.org.

Primary and secondary stakeholder groups

The stakeholder view of the firm propagates that companies should take a broader view on whom they are responsible to. Instead of only pursuing an economic bottom line such as profits and shareholder returns, firms are expected to simultaneously address the demands of all stakeholder groups.[10]

To be able to do that effectively, primary and secondary stakeholders, their interests and their powerbases must be identified.[11] Primary stakeholder groups are constituents on which the firm relies for its continuous survival and prosperity.[12] Shareholders, managers, employees, suppliers, customers – together with governments and communities whose laws and regulations must be obeyed and to whom taxes and other obligations may be due – are typically considered primary stakeholders.

Secondary stakeholder groups are defined as 'those who influence or affect, or are influenced or affected by, the corporation, but they are not engaged in transactions with the corporation and are not essential for its survival.'[13] Environmental groups (such as Greenpeace) often take it upon themselves to promote

Primary stakeholder groups
The constituents on which the firm relies for its continuous survival and prosperity.

Secondary stakeholder groups
Those who influence or affect, or are influenced or affected by, the corporation, but they are not engaged in transactions with the corporation and are not essential for its survival.

Figure 10.1 A Stakeholder view of the firm

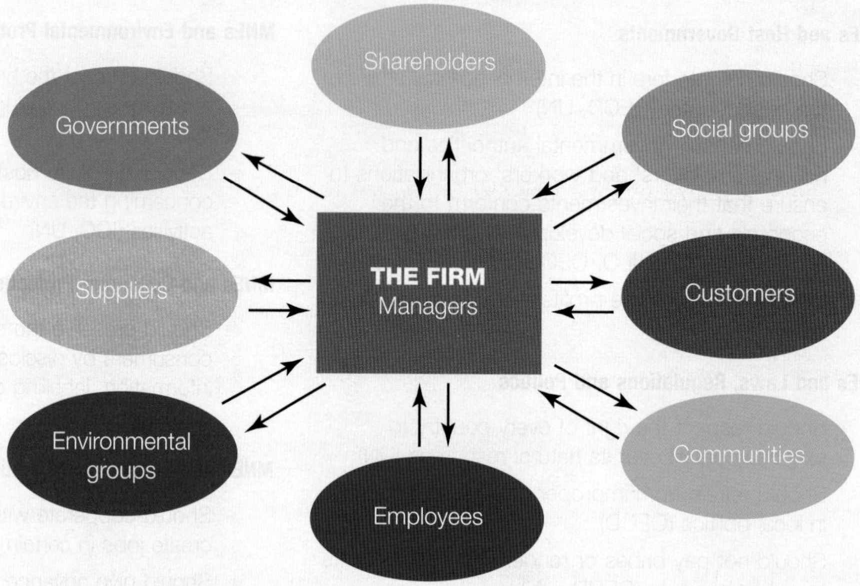

Source: Adapted from 'The stakeholder theory of the corporation: Concepts, evidence, and implications' by T. Donaldson & L. Preston, 1995 (p. 69), *Academy of Management Review*, 20: pp.65–91, permission conveyed through Copyright Clearance Centre.

pollution-reduction technologies. Trade unions and organization concerned about labour practices (such as the Fair Labor Association) frequently challenge firms that allegedly fail to provide decent labour conditions for employees at home and abroad.[14] Although firms do not depend on secondary stakeholders for their survival, such groups may have the potential to cause significant embarrassment and damage to a firm – as illustrated by the confrontation between Starbucks and Global Exchange (Opening Case).

TWO PERSPECTIVES ON WHY SHAREHOLDERS MATTER

Who are the most important stakeholders? At a recent meeting of CSR managers at Copenhagen Business School, these managers were asked 'who is your most important audience?' The almost unanimous answer was: 'employees and future employees'.[15] In other words, *you* as a potential future employee are perhaps the most important target of CSR initiatives. Why? Most of the firms present at the meeting were operating in high technology industries where the attraction and retention of the most talented young people is key to their success. One way to attract highly motivated young people is to offer a work environment which they appreciate – and that includes shared values that they can identify with. Hence, CSR is, at least in Denmark, an important means to recruit the best graduates from business schools and universities.

Two different lines of argument have evolved as to why firms ought to pay attention to their stakeholders. First, the instrumental view suggests that treating stakeholders well may indirectly help the financial performance of the firm.[16] For example, good environmental practice may reduce wastage, well-treated employees are more productive and a reputation for social responsibility may strengthen a

Instrumental view
A view that treating stakeholders well may

brand and thus attract more customers; all of which can enhance revenues. Hence, proponents of this argument suggest that good ethics may be a useful instrument to help make good profits. They thus advocate only CSR initiatives believed to enhance profitability.

In contrast, the normative view suggests that firms *ought* to be self-motivated to 'do it right' because they have societal obligations. Scholars developing their arguments out of moral philosophy or religious value systems tend to assert a moral duty for firms that goes beyond respecting the law and generating profits. [17] Hence, they argue that firms ought to be self-motivated to 'do it right' independent of a direct link to financial performance. Codes of conduct thus ought to express values that organizational members view as central and enduring.[18] Proponents of this view may prefer a narrower definition of CSR that only includes activities that are not aimed at increasing profits: a new recycling facility counts as CSR only to the extent that sales of the recycled products do not cover the additional costs.

Normative view
A view that firms ought to be self-motivated to 'do it right' because they have societal obligations.

Stakeholder conflicts

While some CSR debates pitch shareholders against other stakeholders, different stakeholder groups also disagree with each other (Figure 10.2). Hence, the challenge is not only to balance between shareholders and other stakeholders, but between different groups of stakeholders. For example, producing food for millions of people certainly addresses a social concern that CSR should be advocating – who would want to be responsible for widespread famine? However, food production also uses a lot of environmental resources. Cattle in particular eat a lot of grains and Soya – which in turn require land that otherwise could be used for human food production. Cattle also emit large amount of methane, a gas contributing to global warming. With rising incomes, many people in emerging economies are increasing the meat content of their diets, which aggravates the environmental problems of cattle farming. Some advocate vegetarianism as a solution, yet few are really willing to forego meat.

Figure 10.2 An example of conflicting objectives

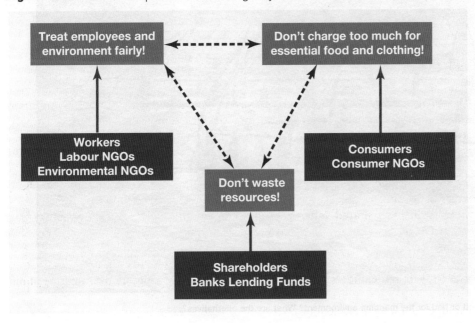

Similar controversies surround fish: For a long time, over-fishing of the oceans was seen as a major environmental problem, and fish farming ('aquaculture') was seen as a solution. Yet, it gradually emerged that aquaculture too can be a source of environmental damage (see In Focus 10.1). Different stakeholders disagree with

IN FOCUS 10.1

Salmon: chicken of the sea

There has been an explosion in the global supply of salmon recently. This rising supply is not due to an increase of wild salmon catch, which has been in steady decline for decades because of dams, pollution and over-fishing. As the wild Atlantic salmon disappear (wild Pacific salmon are still relatively safe), salmon farming (aquaculture) has been on the rise.

Starting in Norway as a cottage industry in the late 1960s, salmon farming spread to Britain, Canada, Iceland and Ireland in the 1970s, the USA in the 1980s, and Chile in the 1990s. Farm-raised salmon live in sea cages. They are fed pellets to speed their growth (twice

as fast as in the wild), pigments to replicate the pink wild salmon flesh, and pesticides to kill the lice that go hand in hand with an industrial feedlot. Atlantic salmon farming (still dominated by Norwegian firms and followed by Chilean companies) has exploded into a €1.5 billion a year global business that produces approximately 700 000 tons of fish annually. In comparison, the wild salmon catch in the Atlantic (only allowed by Britain and Ireland) is only 3000 tons a year. In essence, it is Atlantic salmon farming companies that have brought you all the delicious and nutritious salmon, which has been transformed from a rare, expensive seasonal delicacy to a common chicken of the sea to be enjoyed year

© Lee Torrens/iStock

Is salmon farming good or bad for the maritime environment? What are the alternatives?

round. In addition, salmon farming took commercial fishing pressure off wild salmon stocks and provides employment to maritime regions. For example, in economically weak western Scotland, salmon aquaculture employs approximately 6400 workers.

But here is the catch: Farm-raised salmon have (1) fouled the nearby sea, (2) spread diseases and sea lice and (3) led to a large number of escaped fish. Each of these problems has become a growing controversy. First, heavy concentration of fish in a tiny area – up to 800 000 in one floating cage – leads to food and faecal waste that promotes toxic algae blooms, which in turn have led to closure of shell-fishing in nearby waters. Second, sea lice outbreaks at fish farms in Ireland, Norway and Scotland have devastating effects on wild salmon and other fish. The third and probably most serious problem is the escaped salmon. Many salmon have escaped when seals chewed through pens, storms demolished cages or fish were spilled during handling. In Scotland, for example, nearly 300 000 farmed fish escaped in 2002. Research has found that escaped salmon interbreed with wild salmon. In Norwegian rivers that are salmon spawning grounds, 10 per cent to 35 per cent of the 'wild' fish are found to be escaped salmon.

Wild salmon are an amazing species, genetically programmed to find their spawning grounds in rivers after years of wandering in the sea. Although at present, only one egg of every 4000, after maturing to become a fish, is likely to complete such an epic journey, salmon have been magical fish in the legends of Iceland, Ireland, Norway and Scotland. These legends are threatened by the escaped farm-raised salmon and the hybrid they produce with wild salmon because genetically homogeneous salmon, descended from aquaculture fish, are ill suited to find these rivers and could also leave the species less able to cope with threats such as disease and climate change. In short, the biodiversity of the wild salmon stocks, already at dangerously low levels, is threatened by fish farming. Defenders of fish farming, however, argue that *all* farming alters, and sometimes damages, the environment. They argue that there is no reason that the emerging aquaculture industry needs to be held to higher standards.

Sources: Based on (1) *Business Week*, 2006, Fished out, September 4; (2) *Economist*, 2003, A new way to feed the world, August 9; (3) *Economist*, 2003, The promise of a blue revolution, August 9; (4) F. Montaigne, 2003, Everybody loves Atlantic salmon: Here's the catch, *National Geographic*, 204 (1): 100–123.

each other how best to address these issues. Another area of conflict between stakeholders concerns the production of garments. Many consumers chase low prices, either because they are too poor to afford products produced at higher social standards, or because they are not concerned about the conditions under which the products were made. These consumers 'voting with their purse' are at odds with the advocates of higher labour standards. In fact, empirical evidence suggests that consumers around the world may support ethical product when asked in opinion polls, but act quite differently when they make their own purchasing decisions.[19]

Other conflicts concern the indirect consequences of transferring rules across countries. For example, NGOs in Europe and North America expect firms not to employ child labour, work by persons under the age of 16. Yet, are the children really better off without a job?[20] There is an implicit assumption in this argument that children would spend their time in meaningful education and that they have enough food to eat – in developing countries these assumptions may not hold. Children that have work may well be better off than those that do not. When the US stopped garment imports from Bangladesh in the mid 1990s due to child labour, about 50 000 children lost their job. However, many of them depended on the income; some even were the main breadwinner of the family. In consequence families lost their home, while poverty, social disintegration, crime and even child prostitution increased in the local areas.[21] A better solution for the children would have been to combine work and education. In another example, a study of the long-term implications of the campaign to abolish child labour in the manufacture of footballs in the Sialkot district of Pakistan found that the campaign benefited MNEs and NGOs, yet many poor women and children were worse off as they no

Child labour
Working persons under the age of 16.

longer have access to work.[22] Issues are even more complex in the pharmaceuticals industry (see Integrative Case 'Novo Nordisk').

Assessing the merits of different stakeholder claims is further complicated by the fact that some vocal groups inside or outside the firm may pursue opportunistic goals of their own. Even the process of developing a CSR strategy can be captured by organizational politics and interest groups within the firm. [23] Moreover, the interests of stakeholders 'at home' may conflict with the interest of stakeholders abroad: Expanding overseas, especially toward emerging economies, may provide employment to people in host countries and develop these economies at the 'base of the pyramid', all of which have noble CSR objectives. However, this is often done at the expense of domestic employees and communities. To prevent such a possible fate, in 2004, Daimler's German unions had to accept a pay freeze and an increase of work hours from 35 to 39 hours per week with no extra pay in exchange for promises that 6000 jobs would be kept in Germany for eight years. Otherwise, their jobs would have gone to the Czech Republic, Poland or South Africa. People in these countries would probably have appreciated the new opportunities, yet, employees and communities in developed economies fear that those laid off may end up on social welfare programmes. Thus, some media, unions and politicians may argue that MNEs' actions shirk their CSR by increasing the social burdens of their home countries.

The conflicting stakeholder objectives and interests come to the fore when the media put their spotlight on a specific issue, such as pollution of a local river, or complaints by disgruntled former employees that may or may not have merit.[24] Rarely do journalistic reports provide a comprehensive and balanced assessment of a firm's overall positive and negative contributions to society. Handling of the media thus is a challenging task for companies that aspire to build a reputation as a responsible company.

CSR IN THE GLOBAL ECONOMY

Acting on the global stage exposes MNEs to more complex ethical issues that increase the importance of creating appropriate CSR policies. One important area is corruption, which we have already discussed in chapter 3. Recall that for companies originating in OECD countries, legislation in home countries penalizes those who bribe overseas. This is an unusual case of legislation extending beyond national borders. On many other issues, MNEs have to figure out themselves what is 'right', considering formal and informal institutions in *both* home and host countries. We next discuss two areas where these issues are particular pertinent: (1) environmental standards and (2) labour standards.

Environment: arbitraging or raising standards?

MNEs are running some of the largest industrial operations around the world, and hence they are also among the biggest polluters. However, are they to blame for pollution around the world? One side of the debate argues that because of heavier environmental regulation in developed economies, MNEs may have an incentive to arbitrage on differences in environmental costs. Thus, they would shift pollution-intensive production to 'pollution havens' in developing countries, where environmental standards may be lower. This argument suggests that MNEs in highly polluting industries relocate production to locations with less stringent regulations, or they might use the threat of such relocation to pressure politicians not to raise

Table 10.2 Pressures on standards

Pressures on MNEs to Lower Standards	Pressures on MNEs to Raise Standards
• Lowering costs by standards arbitrage, i.e. producing where regulations imposes least costs • Using the threat of relocation to prevent governments from raising legal requirements ('race to the bottom')	• Closer monitoring by stakeholders at home and abroad • Scale advantages of common practices and standards throughout the organization • Opportunities for first mover advantages in new technologies and practices • Lower risk of catastrophic disruptions

environmental standards.[25] To attract foreign direct investment, developing countries may thus enter a 'race to the bottom' by lowering (or at least not tightening) environmental standards.[26]

The other side argues that MNEs may actually have positive effects on the environment in developing countries, for four reasons (Table 10.2). First, MNEs are likely to adopt higher CSR standards than local firms because they are more closely monitored by various stakeholders in their home and host countries. Second, they may gain scale advantages from implementing common standards across operations in different countries. It is easier to manage a global operation if everyone follows the same standards and procedures. This implies that standards are likely to be higher than the local requirements at any specific location. Third, firms exposed to higher environmental regulations may become early movers into new technologies, which may translate into long-term competitive advantages when other countries follow in upgrading their standards.[27] Fourth, higher standards reduce risk of catastrophic events such as a fire destroying production facilities, or a high profile media report detecting pollution the firm itself was not aware of. Such events can settle firms with major liabilities and lawsuits.

Some MNEs go even beyond their own operations and work with local governments to raise environmental standards in the country in general, for example by advising on legislation or contributing to training officials (In Focus 10.2). Such action may actually be in the interest of the MNEs: Tighter law enforcement will hit in particular local competitors with a low cost strategy. Hence, many MNEs have several economic reasons to *voluntary* apply environmental standards higher than those required by host countries.[28]

The empirical evidence is stronger for the standardization argument as MNEs typically outperform local firms in environmental management.[29] One study of environmental standards found that governmental pressures lead to harmonization of performance standards, industry pressures lead to standardization of processes, while consumer pressures mainly affect firms' communications.[30] Another study finds that US capital markets significantly reward environmental practices, thus refuting the perspective that being green constitutes a liability that depresses market value.[31] However, MNEs are often associated with industrialization (which host countries appreciate), and industrialization increases pollution.[32] Hence, MNEs as a group do not appear to substantially add to the environmental burden in developing countries, though there may be exceptions in particularly sensitive industries.

Race to the bottom
Countries competing for foreign direct investment by lowering environmental standards.

IN FOCUS 10.2

Dow chemical company in China

Dow Chemical Company is a leading US-based MNE operating in more than 175 countries. Since 1999, Dow has advocated the Guiding Principles of Responsible Care, a voluntary initiative within the global chemical industry to safely handle its products from inception to ultimate disposal.

China naturally has become an increasingly important market for Dow. However, beyond Dow's immediate market reach, the general deterioration of the environment in China, an unfortunate by-product of the strong economic growth, is visible and getting worse. As a result, China's leadership is increasingly considering environmental sustainability as a key national policy.

Recognizing an opportunity to demonstrate its CSR commitment, Dow partnered with the State Environmental Protection Administration (SEPA) of China to launch a SEPA-Dow National Cleaner Production Pilot Project in 2005, to which Dow agreed to contribute US$ 750 000 over the first three years. The project aims to develop an integrated preventive environmental strategy for industrial processes, products and services to increase efficiency and reduce risks and possible damage to humans and the environment. The pilot project has focused on training local environmental protection agencies and officials as well as managers at small- and medium-sized enterprises

(SMEs), a category of firms in China that, on average, tends to be less professional and more reckless in environmental management.

In the pilot project's first year, 19 SMEs from seven provinces in the chemical, dyeing, electronics, brewery and food industries participated. The project generated a combined reduction of wastewater by 3.3 million cubic meters, of exhaust gas emission by 554 tons, and of solid waste by 487 tons. This resulted in 538 cleaner production measures and an annual economic profit of approximately US$ 130 000 for the 19 participating firms. Overall, these achievements, in Dow's own words:

'... confirm Dow's belief that cleaner production not only reduces waste in the production processes, it also increases the efficiency of energy resources and ultimately improves competitiveness of enterprises.'

Further, through environmental audits, case studies and further dissemination, Dow intends to diffuse such best practices to more firms in China and beyond.

Sources: Based on (1) *China Business Review*, 2007, Dow partners with China's SEPA, May–June: 17; (2) Dow, 2006, SEPA-Dow Cleaner Production National Pilot Project achieves strong start and outstanding results, http://news.dow.com (accessed June 3, 2007); (3) M.W. Peng, 2006, Dow Chemical in America and China, in M.W. Peng, *Global Strategy* (pp. 511–512), Cincinnati, OH: Cengage South-Western.

Labour: How to treat those who work for you abroad?

Workers around the world complain about their working conditions. While some may have exaggerated expectations on the privileges they ought to enjoy, at the other end there are undoubtedly many who live and work under unimaginably poor conditions (see In Focus 10.3). Often this is an outcome of the poverty of the country. The working poor may live under horrible conditions in the eyes of a Western idealist. Yet, they may still be better off with the job than unemployed and begging in the slums.

MNEs are confronted with low labour standards when they are sourcing from developing countries. The 1980s and 1990s saw an acceleration of extended supply chains to poorer countries, and initially MNEs were not particularly fuzzed about how their shoes or T-shirts were manufactured, as long as the quality and the price were right. Major publicity campaigns targeting well-known brands such as Nike put an end to such a naïve approach to international sourcing.

IN FOCUS 10.3

Working poor

The miserable working conditions in some parts of the world are periodically highlighted in news reports and in scholarly studies. The following quotations illustrate some of the worst examples. In El Salvador, a government study of maquiladora factories found that:

> '... in the majority of companies, it is an obligation of the personnel to work overtime under the threat of firing or some other kind of reprisal. This situation, in addition to threatening the health of the workers, causes family problems in that [the workers] are unable to properly fulfil obligations to their immediate family. On some occasions, because the work time is extended into the late hours of the night, the workers find themselves obligated to sleep in the factory facilities, which do not have conditions necessary for lodging of personnel.' (source 2)

The conditions become alive in the recollections of individual workers, such as the following statement by a 26 year old worker in a maquiladora factory in Mexico:

> 'We have to work quickly with our hands, and I am responsible for sewing 20 steering wheel covers per shift. After having worked for nine years at the plant, I now suffer from an injury in my right hand. I start out the shift okay, but after about three hours of work, I feel a lot of sharp pains in my fingers. It gets so bad that I can't hold the steering wheel correctly. But still the supervisors keep pressuring me to reach 100 per cent of my production. I can

only reach about 70 per cent of what they asked for. These pains began a year ago and I am not the only one who suffered from them. There are over 200 of us who have hand injuries and some have lost movement in their hands and arms. The company has fired over 150 people in the last year for lack of production. Others have been pressured to quit' (source 1).

Another source emphasizes the working conditions are below what ordinary newspaper readers even can imagine:

> 'The manner in which these women lived, the squalidness and unhealthy location and nature of their habitations, the impossibility of providing for any of the slightest recreations or moral or intellectual culture or of educating their children can be easily imagined: but we assure the public that it would require an extremely active imagination to conceive this reality.' (source 3)

Actually, this report is referring to textile factories in New York, and it was published in the New York Daily Tribune in the year 1845. It illustrates that poor treatment of workers is not specific to certain cultures, if anything it is a typical of early stages of industrialization.

Sources Based on: (1) P. Varley, C. Mathiasen & M. Voorhes, 1998, The Sweatshop Quandry: Corporate Responsibility on the Global Frontier. Washington, DC: Investor Responsibility Research Center (p. 68); (2) D.G. Arnold & N.E. Bowie, 2003, Sweatshops and Respect for Persons, *BEQ*, 13, 221–242 (p. 230); (3) Hartman, L.P., B. Shaw & R. Stevenson, 2003, Exploring the Ethics and Economics of Global Labor Standards, *BEQ*, 13, 193–220 (p. 195).

The economics of labour standards are similar to those of environmental standards (Table 10.2). There are gains from producing where costs are lowest, but there are countervailing pressures for MNEs to raise standards above local norms. However, there are crucial differences. The typical environment polluter is a big plant in the chemicals or paper industry, which requires large capital investments and is stuck at its location once the construction of the plant is completed. This reduces the bargaining power of such firms negotiating with regulators. In contrast, many labour intensive operations are 'footloose plants' that require little set-up costs (apart from staff training) and can easily relocate when regulations change. Thus, the pressures to lower standards (left column in Table 10.2) are relatively strong.

Footloose plant
Plants that can easily be relocated.

IN FOCUS 10.4

Implementing standards at Adidas

Like other sportswear manufacturers, Adidas faced major challenges in the mid 1990s from NGOs regarding labour practices in its the supply chain. Adidas responded by hiring a prominent activist, David Husselbee, to develop and implement its CSR strategy. He initiated a process of consultation with the company's internal and external stakeholders, and developed codes of conduct for the company and its suppliers.

These standards available on the internet cover a wide range of issues including forced labour, child labour, discrimination, wages and benefits, hours of work, freedom of association and collective bargaining, disciplinary practices, environmental requirements and community involvement. The standards have been developed through discussions with stakeholders in Europe and North America (Adidas' most important markets) and in the countries of its main manufacturing sites. The American side contributed especially on the labour side, which Europeans tend to treat as given (that is, defined by law), whereas the European side has been leading the development of codes for health, safety and the environment (HSE).

In 2000, Adidas implemented a comprehensive inspection programme for its suppliers, and found many incidences of standards not being kept, such as maximum work hours ignored, poor age documentation, wages below minimum wages and working rules not publicly displayed in the work place. Unusually, Adidas made this report public. The violations identified varied considerably across countries due to different emphasis of laws, law enforcement and informal norms. Informed by this report, Adidas launched several initiatives to spread its standards of engagement, including identification of suppliers further down the supply chain, development of auditing tools and procedures and hiring staff to support these activities. Audit teams visited factories not only to monitor compliance, but to train the management in the use of the standards of engagement and to explain the likely benefits of higher standards for the business itself.

The inspection reports are very detailed with dozens of criteria on which HSE and labour conditions are monitored. Every incidence of a suspected non-compliance is documented, including for example presence of appropriate security for specific chemicals and accident reports even for minor injuries. This exercise is both costly and time consuming for both the monitoring team and for the management of the factory visited who have to be available to answer questions from the monitors. The inspection report then rates each factory on a scale from 1 to 5 on several criteria. At the same time, it aims to engage in a constructive dialog to provide solutions to problems that occur.

An important element of the CSR policy is transparency, which led Adidas to publish a list of its suppliers online complete with address. In July 2009, the list contained 1044 suppliers, many of which are based in emerging countries like China (261), Vietnam (65), India (62), Indonesia (55) and Korea (56). However, some plants remain in advanced economies like the USA (60), Japan (58), Italy (24), UK (18), Spain (17) and Germany (16). Adidas also annually publishes 'performance data' on its website containing details such as (aggregate) supplier ratings from audit reports, number of warning letters send to suppliers, and suppliers terminated – of which there were six in 2007, one in 2008 and none in 2009.

The introduction of new standards of engagement led to improvements in supplier firms, especially in those firms that chose a pro-active approach. An independent study found rising product quality, fewer accidents, lower staff turnover and rising productivity in a pro-active supplier firm, while reluctant adoption of the code in another supplier firm led to inferior economic performance. As another example, HSE concerns in a garment factory in Thailand indicated frequent injuries to the hands of the women operating the fast moving sewing machines. The installation of needle guards not only reduced the number of such accidents, but increased the speed and efficiency of workers no longer worried about needle wounds.

Adidas is cooperating with the Fair Labor Association (FLA), which provides external, independent monitoring, complaints procedures and public reporting. The FLA has accredited Adidas after extensive review of its compliance programme. Other recognition for Adidas' efforts in the area CSR come from industry organizations. Most notably, Dow Jones Sustainability Index (DJSI) has included Adidas every year since 2000, recognized it as industry leader since 2003, and named it 'Global Supersector Leader' 2009/2010 for the sector 'Personal & Household Goods' for the second consecutive time.

Sources Based on: (1) Adidas-Salomon, 2000, *Our World: Social and environmental report 2000*, Herzongenaurach: Adidas-Salomon; (2) S. Frenkel & D. Scott, 2002, Compliance, Collaboration, and Codes of Labor Practice: The Adidas connection, *CMR*, 45, 29–49 (3) L.P. Hartman, R.E. Wokutch & J.L. French, 2003, Adidas-Salomon, in: L.P. Hartman, D.G. Arnold & R.E. Wokutch, eds, *Rising Above Sweatshops*, Westport: Praeger. 191–248; (4) www. adidas-group.com (accessed March 2010).

In their own operations in developing countries, MNEs often provide professional training, higher wages and better working conditions than local competitors.[33] They try to attract some of the best people, and after investing in their training, they are keen to keep them. Even so, MNEs are being criticized: local firms may complain that the best people do not want to work for them because MNEs pay 'too high' wages. Meanwhile, trade unions back home may complain about the 'too low' wages paid in developing countries that put pressures on wages in developed countries.

The real challenges, however, emerge when MNEs buy products or components from local firms. In Europe, many consumers – and NGOs – expect that their shoes and their clothes are made by people being paid and treated fairly. This raises two questions: Are MNEs responsible for what happens in other firms, and how can they be sure what actually happens in a sub-suppliers' plant?

The first question is often answered differently from a legal and a normative perspective. Legally, firms are responsible for their operations, not those of other firms. Moreover, the relevant laws applying to each plant are normally those of the country where it is located – not those of the country of origin of the MNE. Such a legalistic view was adopted by many firms in the 1970s and 1980s, but it less common now. MNEs concerned with their brand reputation accept that normative pressures are also relevant in defining the appropriate standards in both their own operations, and the operations of their suppliers and sub-suppliers.[34] These pressures for introducing labour charters arise from a variety of sources, including legal requirements, industry self-regulation and NGOs. MNEs have reacted to such pressures by introducing 'standards of engagement' (also known as 'codes of conduct' or 'standards of ethics') that they impose on suppliers. These establish minimum standards for working hours, age of workers, health and safety, wages and other aspects of operating a manufacturing plant. With these standards come monitoring and enforcement regimes that should help suppliers achieve higher standards, while – after appropriate warnings – discontinuing relationships with non-compliant suppliers.

These monitoring and enforcement procedures are quite costly and time-consuming as they require detailed record keeping, reporting and attention from top management (In Focus 10.4). Even so, these processes have become the focus of attacks by NGOs. They allege that monitors are insufficiently independent and don't publish all their reports, and that unsatisfactory suppliers are not kicked out rigorously enough.[35] One recent study interviewed workers outside their place of work in Southern China, and presents allegations that suppliers not only fail to meet the standards they have committed to, but have developed tactics to systematically mislead monitoring teams.[36] More progress has been achieved by MNEs that shift from a focus on compliance with the standards of engagement to a commitment approach that involves joint problem solving, information exchange and the diffusion of best practices.[37]

Standards of engagement (code of conduct, code of ethics)
Written policies and standards for corporate conduct and ethics.

INSTITUTIONS, STAKEHOLDERS AND CSR

Institutional differences

Debates and practices of CSR vary across countries and they change over time. The roots of such differences are often differences in formal and informal institutions.[38] In fact, international debates over CSR sometimes suffer miscommunication due to differences in cultural values. People in liberal market economies (LMEs) and coordinated market economies (CMEs) have different understandings of what firms are, and what their role in the society is. Yet, if we don't agree about the purpose of the firm, it is difficult to agree on its obligations.

Recall from Chapter 2 that in LMEs like the USA and the UK, firms are unambiguously considered an economic enterprise that exists to serve the shareholders' interest. In line with this view, Milton Friedman, a University of Chicago economist, eloquently suggested: 'The social responsibility of business is to increase its profits'.[39] This line of thought draws upon the idea that pursuit of economic self-interest (within legal constraints) promotes the welfare of society as a whole. Hence, firms' first and foremost stakeholders are shareholders, whose interests managers have a legal duty to look after. With this primacy of shareholders and a strong belief in the efficiency of the market mechanism comes strong support for the instrumental view of CSR: 'It is good if it helps profits'. Economists such as Milton Friedman extend the argument to suggest that if firms attempt to attain social goals, such as providing employment and social welfare, managers will lose their focus on profit maximization (and its derivative, shareholder value maximization) and thus cause greater harm than good.[40] Some even argue that workers would be worse off if firms unilaterally raised standards because the firm would loose competitiveness and in consequences workers would loose their job.[41]

In the USA, the leading LME, firms have a high degree of discretion over their activities since regulations are less constraining, and markets are to a large degree self-organized by businesses rather than regulated by the state. At the same time, the financial system requires a high degree of transparency, the education system is largely private, the cultural system values individual freedom but also 'giving back to society' that is sharing the wealth with others. These features of the institutional context induce firms to voluntarily assume responsibilities for societal concerns (Table 10.3, Figure 10.3).[42] This explicit CSR includes issues that might be covered by government activities in CMEs, such as support for universities, health care or employee training. It may be strategic in the sense that the CSR activity aims to achieve certain specified benefits for society as well as for the firm itself.[43] Explicit CSR is supported by a culture that simultaneously appreciates people who make a lot of money, and people who voluntarily help others. Thus, philanthropy, donations for cultural, environmental, scientific or other benefits of the wider society, has a long tradition in the USA (see Closing Case).[44]

In CMEs like those in Western Europe, most firms are also owned by private shareholders. Managers have to act in the interest of the shareholders, yet a wide range of formal and informal constraints impose other obligations on firms. Cooperative arrangements such as standards set by industry association and collective bargaining with trade unions establish standards and processes that firms have to accommodate. Interest groups, political parties and the media often implicitly adopt a normative view when discussing CSR, though they may disagree what the relevant norms are. Shareholders' rights are thus constrained. At the same time, the state has a far more active role in a CME. Regulations of many aspects of business are more specific and the state is supplying a wide range of services to society,

Explicit CSR
Voluntarily assuming responsibilities of societal concerns.

Philanthropy
Donations for purposes that benefit the wider society.

Table 10.3 Explicit and implicit CSR compared

Explicit CSR	Implicit CSR
Describes corporate activities that assume responsibility for the interests of society	Describes corporations' role within the wider formal and informal institutions for society's interests and concerns
Consists of voluntary corporate policies, programmes, and strategies	Consists of values, norms, and rules that result in (often codified and mandatory) requirements for corporations
Incentives and opportunities are motivated by the perceived expectations of different stakeholders of the corporation	Motivated by the societal consensus on the legitimate expectations of the roles and contributions of all major groups in society, including corporations

Source: 'Implicit and Explicit CSR' by D. Matten and J. Moon, Academy of Management, 32, 2008, pp.404–424, permission conveyed through Copyright Clearance Centre.

Figure 10.3 Implicit and explicit CSR, and varieties of capitalism

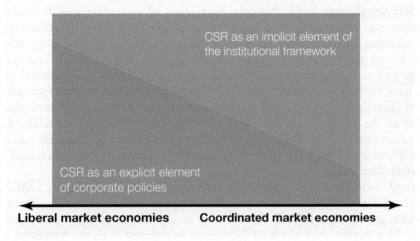

CSR as an implicit element of the institutional framework

CSR as an explicit element of corporate policies

Liberal market economies   **Coordinated market economies**

Source: 'Implicit and Explicit CSR' by D. Matten and J. Moon, Academy of Management, 32, 2008, pp.404–424, permission conveyed through Copyright Clearance Centre.

financed by taxes raised from individuals and firms. This is supported by cultures that consider many aspects of the welfare state as the responsibility of the state, and expect firms and individuals to help the state with its responsibilities by first paying taxes (that are higher than in the USA) and by obeying laws and regulations.

In this institutional context, firms see much less reason to engage in explicit CSR by voluntarily doing *more* than what they are expected to do. Rather, they engage in implicit CSR, that is participation in the wider formal and informal institutions for the society's interests and concerns.[45] Hence, they take into consideration the interests of other stakeholders by following the formal and informal rules of the society for such interaction with stakeholders. Hence, they do good things for society, but not on a voluntary basis as an explicit CSR. Firms pursuing implicit CSR would

Implicit CSR
Participating in the wider formal and informal institutions for the society's interests and concerns.

not be inclined to claim special credit for doing so, and they would not be able to gain any special reputation because all firms in the same context follow the same rules. Thus, European observers shake their head about some CSR initiatives in the US: even the highlighted 'responsible' practices may fall short of legal requirement in many European countries, especially on labour issues such as employee representation within the firm, working time or redundancy procedures. For example, Starbucks (Opening Case) announced in 2004 a CSR initiative to pay health care benefits for all those they employed for more than 20 days per month. In many European countries they would be obliged to do so by law, even for part-time employees.[46]

The differences in institutional pressures are reflected in standards of engagements used by firms around the world; they vary considerably across firms, industries and countries.[47] US codes of conduct tend to focus on secondary stakeholder issues, such as labour standards in the supplier network and welfare of the community. European codes concentrate more on production activities, such as quality management and the environmental footprint. Hong Kong codes tend to focus on corruption prevention but pay less attention to broader CSR issues because corruption is perceived to be a major concern.

In recent years, the institutional context for CSR has changed in two ways (1) CSR has moved up the corporate agenda around the world, and (2) there has been some degree of convergence between CMEs and LMEs. First, why have so many stakeholder groups become more vocal, and been able to influence corporate agendas? On the one hand, this may be a result of increasing wealth. Social and environmental concerns become important to people once their basic needs such as food, clothing and accommodation, have been met. In a way, caring for others is like a luxury good that rich people can afford. Less affluent people and societies tend to be less fuzzed about that. On the other hand, formal and informal institutions have evolved over time. Since the 1970s, the world has seen an increasing focus on 'shareholder value', and government policies have actively promoted the market as the predominant (or only) coordination mechanism, especially during the Reagan years in the USA and the Thatcher years in the UK. The CSR movement of the 1990s and 2000s can be seen as countermovement to firms' increased focus on shareholder value.

Second, why are LMEs and CMEs converging? On the one hand, LMEs have introduced more regulation on a number of issues such as the environment, and corporate governance. In fact, the UK may be located at an intermediate point of Figure 10.3 in part as a result of legislation introduced with the European social charter (Chapter 8). On the other hand, firms in CMEs realized that obeying by the rules may not be enough when operating across borders. As local rules in host countries vary, and may be below those of the home country, MNEs face social pressures not unlike those in LMEs to explicitly state how they manage, for example, labour issues in supplier firms. Thus, US firms have started the trend of introducing explicit corporate standards of engagement, yet this practice has quickly spread to MNEs based in Europe.

Institutions and CSR strategies

How do companies react to institutional pressures to engage in CSR? We can distinguish four broad types of strategic responses: (1) reactive, (2) defensive, (3) accommodative and (4) proactive strategies (see Table 10.4).

A reactive strategy is passive. When problems arise, denial is usually the first line of defence. In the absence of formal regulation, the need to take necessary action is neither internalized through cognitive beliefs, nor becoming any norm in practice.

Reactive strategy
A strategy that would only respond to CSR causes when disasters and outcries break out.

Table 10.4 Strategic responses to ethical challenges

Strategic responses	Strategic behaviours	Examples in the text
Reactive	Deny responsibility, do less than required	*Ford Pinto fire (the 1970s)*
Defensive	Admit responsibility but fight it, do the least that is required	*Nike (the early 1990s)*
Accommodative	Accept responsibility, do all that is required	*Ford Explorer roll-overs (the 2000s)*
Proactive	Anticipate responsibility, do more than is required	*BMW (the 1990s)*

The reactive strategy is indicated by relatively little or no support of top management to CSR causes. Firms do not feel compelled to act unless they are forced by law or the courts. For example, Ford marketed the Pinto car in the early 1970s, knowing that its gas tank had a fatal design flaw that could make the car susceptible to exploding in rear-end collisions. Citing high costs, Ford decided not to recall the Pinto and add an improvement. For several years, frequent accidents happened and people were killed and burned in Pintos. Only in 1978, under intense pressures from the government, the media and consumer groups, Ford belatedly recalled all 1.5 million Pintos.[48]

A defensive strategy focuses on regulatory compliance while rejecting informal pressures from the media and activists to do 'more'. In the early 1990s, Nike was charged for running 'sweatshops', while these incidents took place in its contractors' factories in Indonesia and Vietnam. As Nike did not own or manage these factories, it initially argued, essentially, that they don't make shoes and what happens inside another firm is not their responsibility. However, consumer pressures mounted and legislators considered legal changes that would force the industry to act. Thus, Nike started acknowledging an ethical responsibility that extends beyond the legal boundaries of the firm. A defensive strategy is often based on an attitude of viewing CSR as an added cost or nuisance. Firms acknowledge a narrowly defined responsibility but fight any extensions beyond legal requirements.

An accommodative strategy accepts responsibility to apply norms and standards advocated by NGOs but not (yet) enshrined in law. It requires some support from top managers, who may increasingly view CSR as a worthwhile endeavour and a social obligation.[49] Recently, Nike and the entire sportswear industry became more accommodative. For example, in 2000, when Ford Explorer vehicles equipped with Firestone tyres had a large number of fatal roll-over accidents, Ford evidently took the painful lesson from its Pinto fire fiasco in the 1970s. It initiated a speedy recall, launched a media campaign featuring its CEO, and discontinued the 100-year-old relationship with Firestone. However, cynics argued that Ford's motivation was to place blame squarely on Firestone. Even if Ford's public relations campaign was mainly 'window dressing', publicizing a set of ethical criteria against which it can be judged opens doors for more scrutiny by concerned stakeholders. It probably is fair to say that Ford became a better corporate citizen in 2000 than what it was in 1975.

Defensive strategy
A strategy that focuses on regulatory compliance with little top management commitment to CSR causes.

Accommodative strategy
A strategy that is characterized by some support from top managers, who may increasingly view CSR as a worthwhile endeavour.

© Owen Price/iStock

Should car manufacturers be obligated to take back used cars?

Proactive strategy
A strategy that endeavours to do more than is required in CSR.

Finally, a proactive strategy involves doing more than is required, constantly anticipating responsibility and endeavouring to 'go beyond the call of duty'. This approach to CSR is particularly attractive to firms that view CSR as a source of differentiation and branding. For example, in 1990, BMW anticipated new responsibilities associated with initiatives by the environmental movement to require the car industry to 'take-back' cars at the end of their life time for recycling. BMW not only designed easier-to-disassemble cars, but also signed up the few high-quality dismantler firms as part of an exclusive recycling infrastructure. Further, BMW actively participated in public discussions and succeeded in establishing its approach as the German national standard for automobile disassembly. Other automakers were later required to follow BMW's lead, and had to develop the necessary technologies and infrastructure from scratch.[50]

Proactive strategies may cover three areas of activities. First, like BMW, they actively participate in regional, national and international policy discussions. To the extent that policy discussions today may become regulations in the future, it seems better to get involved early and (ideally) steer the course toward a favourable direction (see Chapter 8, Closing Case 'Nokia goes to Brussels'). One might suspect that such lobbying is mainly used to convince policy-makers *not* to raise standards. However, for firms that already pursue high standards, it is actually levelling the competition as competitors may be forced to raise their standards and thus loose their cost advantage.

Second, proactive firms often build alliances with stakeholder groups, for example with NGOs.[51] Because of historical tension and distrust, these 'sleeping-with-the-enemy' alliances are not easy to handle. The key lies in identifying relatively short-term, manageable projects of mutual interest. For instance, Unilever Indonesia commissioned Oxfam, a UK based charity, to comprehensively explore and document its impact on poverty and development. The report provided a basis for both Unilever and local stakeholders to improve their practices. It showed for example that Unilever paid a lot of taxes to the Indonesian government, provides employment and shares best practices in the local economy. It treated its employees better than local firms, paying entry-level employees 123 per cent of the minimum wage, spending US$ 254 million of local supplies, and reinvesting profits of US$ 182 in the local economy. Even so, it contributed little to people living in poverty, the prime concern of Oxfam.[52]

Third, proactive firms often engage in *voluntary* activities that go beyond what is required by law.[53] While there are numerous examples of industry-specific self-regulation,[54] an area of intense global interest is the pursuit of the International Organization for Standardization (ISO) 14001 certification of environment management systems. Headquartered in Switzerland, ISO consists of national standards bodies of 111 countries. Launched in 1996, ISO 14001 has become the gold standard for CSR-conscious firms.[55] Although not required by law, many MNEs have adopted ISO 14001 standards in all their facilities worldwide. Moreover, firms such as GM, Toyota and Siemens demanded all of their top-tier suppliers be ISO 14001 certified.

DEBATES AND EXTENSIONS

The subject of CSR is full of debates. Probably, most of you as readers find something in the previous pages that you would like to debate. In corporate board rooms, CSR has become a hot issue that needs to be balanced with the quest for profit, which is why we consider this chapter to be a central part of this book. Here, we discuss three questions: (1) is an active CSR good for the firm itself, notably its financial performance? (2) is CSR good for the stakeholder that are object of this policy? and (3) should companies be politically neutral in their CSR overseas?

LEARNING OBJECTIVE

4 participate in two leading debates concerning corporate social responsibility

Is CSR good for financial performance?

The link between CSR and financial performance is a major area of ongoing research. Yet, there still is no conclusive evidence of a direct link between CSR and economic performance such as profits and shareholder returns.[56] Although some studies indeed report a positive relationship,[57] others find a negative relationship or no relationship.[58] A meta-analysis (a study that aggregates findings of earlier studies) suggests that social responsibility and, to a lesser extent, environmental responsibility are on average associated with better financial performance.[59]

There can be a number of explanations for these inconsistent findings. A resource-based explanation suggests that a good reputation may be a value-creating, rare, hard to imitate and organizationally-embedded (VRIO) resource, especially in industries with a poor reputation. A reputation takes a long time to build – consumers are not impressed by fancy announcement, but they look for a track record of activity as shown for example by Novo Nordisk (see Integrative Case: On the other hand, because of capability constraints discussed earlier, many firms are not cut out for a CSR-intensive (differentiation) strategy. Hence, some companies benefit from CSR policies, while others do not. For example, companies like Wal-mart or Aldi competing in very price-sensitive market segments are less likely to benefit from proactive CSR than companies like Morrisons or Marks and Spencers that compete on the basis on their brand image.

More detailed studies suggest that consistent CSR policies over long time periods have a positive effect, while short-term or temporary initiatives do not. This is because CSR benefits a firm when it can build a credible reputation as a responsible firm – and that does not happen overnight. Thus, 'it takes time for being socially responsible to translate into higher financial returns and ... it is the consistent application of a strategy of social responsibility that ultimately pays off in financial terms'.[60] Moreover, too much of the good thing may not be good for firms' performance: Some firms may be 'overdoing their goodness' in ways that actually harms their financial performance. In summary, because each firm is different (a basic assumption of the resource-based view), not every firm's economic performance is likely to benefit from CSR.

Is CSR good for society?

Some critics describe CSR activity as mere 'window dressing', and assert that the firms only do what is good for themselves. In other words, CSR is seen mainly as a public relations exercise, with few benefits for workers in sub-supplier plants or for the natural environment they claim to be protecting. These critics point to the efforts that companies spend on communicating their activities and on converting CSR into brand value – and thus into market share and profits.[61] We can understand these debates as a conflict between the instrumental view and the normative view. The *instrumental view* asserting that CSR is good *if* it helps corporate performance is a dominant norm in corporate boardrooms, many business schools and university departments of economics. In other words, good initiatives are those that helps firms '*doing well by doing good*', as suggested by the 2007 conference theme of the (American) Academy of Management.[62]

In contrast, many NGOs, journalists and politicians have adopted a *normative view* asserting that firms also have other obligations to their stakeholders. These critics often do not appreciate initiatives by managers doing CSR with an eye on financial performance to satisfy their obligation to shareholders and their own share option plans. Since this conflict is essentially about values, there is no 'right or wrong' answer to it. However, *if* there is a link between CSR, corporate reputation, and consumers buying the products, *and if* the reputation depends on outcomes of CSR rather than on public relations, *then* we would expect that even instrumentally motivated CSR is creating benefits for the stakeholders that consumers care about. The empirical evidence on this complex linkages is, however, inconclusive.

Some CSR initiatives indeed do *not* create value for the stakeholders. Good intentions are not sufficient to create positive impact on stakeholders. Creating impactful CSR initiatives requires in fact a good understanding of how initiatives of the firm interact with the local context. We earlier mentioned children losing their job as a result of anti-child-labour campaigns. For another example, a study of local community development projects organized by oil 'multis' in local areas where they operate in Nigeria found that they made many mistakes that governmental aid agencies made decades ago, due to naïve understanding of the social structure of the local society, which led to low impact of their contributions.[63] Such incidences, however, should be an exception as observers would quickly point out such flaws, which would harm the expected positive reputation effect.

Other critics suggest that CSR is mainly making up for damage caused previously by the same MNEs. For example, a left-leaning German magazine reported on the publicity about Fair Trade chocolate in the UK by pointing out that it really is a response to problems the firms themselves have created:

> '*Five giants control about 80 per cent of international cacao trade. Especially during the 1990s, they pressed the prices to such an extent that it was*

impossible for farmers to invest in better crops, plant protection and new tools. In the past 12 month, the harvest was the worst in 14 years due to heavy rainfalls, pest and fungal diseases.'[64]

As a result, cacao prices have been surging and manufacturers are concerned about the long-term security of their supplies. By investing in cacao production and paying farmers a higher price, they hope to secure their supplies, and this also helps to attain 'Fair Trade' certification.

A similar link has been suspected behind Wal-Mart's recent drive to increase environmental standards in its production. Wal-Mart has become a target of many NGOs due to the combination of its sheer size (and thus bargaining power) and its relentless focus on 'everyday low prices' which induced suppliers to cut corners whenever they could. In the words of a Chinese expert cited in the *Washington Post*:

'They are the rule setters. Before Wal-Mart only cared about price and quality, so that encouraged companies to race to the bottom of environmental standards. They could lose contracts because competition was so fierce on price. [Now, they changed.] Wal-Mart says if you're over the compliance level, you're out of business. That will set a powerful signal.'[65]

Wal-Mart did take action, for example by suspending 126 suppliers for a year due to unsatisfactory compliance, and permanently halted purchasing from 35 – out of about 10 000 suppliers in China. However, Wal-Mart itself faces conflicting institutional pressures; in the words of an executive: *'Our customers care, they just don't want to pay more'.* [66]

Local norms versus hypernorms

In the 1990s, Shell was harshly criticized for 'not lifting a finger' when the Nigerian government brutally cracked down on rebels in the Ogoni region in which Shell operated. However, such well-intentioned calls for greater engagement in the local community are in direct conflict with a longstanding principle governing the relationship between MNEs and host countries: non-intervention in local political affairs (see the *first* bulleted point in Table 10.1).

The call to respect local norms and political sovereignty originated from concerns that MNEs might engage in political activities against the national interests of the host country. Chile in the 1970s serves as a case in point. Before a national election for the presidency in 1970, ITT (a US-based MNE) had channelled millions of US$ to opponents of socialist candidate Salvador Allende. However, Allende won the election and pursued a policy that included nationalization of the assets of foreign investors such as ITT. Later, ITT together with the US secret service CIA allegedly promoted the coup that killed President Allende on September 11, 1973. Consequently, the idea that MNEs should not interfere in the domestic political affairs of the host country has been enshrined in a number of codes of MNE conduct.[67]

An alternative view suggests that there are certain hypernorms – norms considered valid anywhere in the world – that MNEs ought to respect wherever they operate.[68] The norms advocated by international organizations (Table 10.1) fall in this category. Conflicts between local norms and hypernorms are common but rarely as evident as during the apartheid era in South Africa, when local laws required racial segregation of the workforce. Following the idea of hypernorms, some MNEs such as BP deliberately bypassed or ignored these local laws to challenge, breach and seek to dismantle the apartheid system. Emboldened by the

Hypernorms
Norms considered valid anywhere in the world.

successful removal of the apartheid regime in South Africa in 1994, CSR advocates have unleashed a new campaign, stressing the necessity for MNEs to promote hypernorms (or 'universal values'), in particular, in the human rights area. Shell, after its widely criticized (lack of) action in Nigeria, has explicitly endorsed the United Nations Declaration on Human Rights and supported the exercise of such rights 'within the legitimate role of business' since 1996.

But when exactly should hypernorms dominate over local norms? Almost every country has local laws and norms that some foreign MNEs may find objectionable. In Malaysia, ethnic Chinese are discriminated against by law. In many Arab countries, women are expected to 'cover up' in public places. In Asian countries such as China, independent trade unions are illegal. At the heart of this debate is whether foreign MNEs should spearhead efforts to remove some of these discriminatory practices or conform to host country laws and norms. This obviously is a nontrivial challenge.

IMPLICATIONS FOR PRACTICE

LEARNING OBJECTIVE

5 Draw implications for action

While CSR is subject to many debates, our discussion points to three implications for practice (Table 10.5). First, managers need to understand not only the formal rules of the game, but the informal pressures emanating from a variety of social groups that influence consumer behaviour and political processes and thus possible future legislation. For example, at the Copenhagen Climate Summit in December 2009, many businesses were demonstrating how their technologies may help in addressing the issues politicians were debating, for example by improving the efficiency of energy use (e.g. more fuel efficient cars), efficiency improvements in energy generation (e.g. changes in existing power plants), power generation from renewable sources (e.g. wind and solar energy), bio-combustibles, nuclear and carbon capture (i.e. putting carbon created in power station underground).[69]

Second, managers need to match their CSR publicity with the CSR capabilities. Although your competitors may engage in high-profile CSR activities allowing them to earn a lot of bragging rights about their triple bottom line, blindly imitating these practices while not knowing enough about their own firm may lead to some disappointment. Instead of always chasing the newest best practices, firms are advised to select CSR practices that fit with their *existing* resources, capabilities, and especially, complementary assets,[70] while building the capabilities to achieve higher goals in the future. In particular, firms only benefit from CSR statements if they can actually live up to their standards, and demonstrate progress towards their stated goals. Failed standards and un-achieved goals invite attacks from NGOs.

Third, given the increasingly inescapable responsibility to be good corporate citizens, managers may want to integrate CSR as part of the core activities and processes of the firm – instead of 'faking it' and making cosmetic changes.[71] For

Table 10.5 Implications for action

- Managers should understand the institutions affecting CSR, anticipate changes, and seek to influence such changes.
- CSR publicity should match CSR capabilities.
- CSR should be an integral part of the core activities and processes of a firm.

example, instead of treating NGOs as threats, firms like sportswear manufacturer Adidas (In Focus 10.4) have its sourcing policies certified by NGOs. Dow Chemical (In Focus 10.2) has established community advisory panels in most of its locations worldwide. Traditionally, many managers may have treated CSR as a nuisance, involving regulation, added costs and liability. Such an attitude may underestimate potential business opportunities associated with CSR.

What determines the success and failure of firms around the world? No doubt, CSR will increasingly become an important part of the answer. The best performing firms are likely to be those that can integrate CSR activities into the core economic functions of the firm while addressing social and environmental concerns.[72] The globally ambiguous and varying CSR standards, norms and expectations make many managers uncomfortable. As a result, many managers continue to relegate CSR to the backburner. However, this does not seem to be the right attitude for current and would-be managers who are studying this book – that is, *you*. It is important to note that we live in a dangerous period of global capitalism. Managers, as a unique group of stakeholders, have an important and challenging responsibility to safeguard and advance the world economy. From a CSR standpoint, this means building more humane, more inclusive and fairer firms that not only generate wealth and develop economies but also respond to changing societal expectations concerning CSR around the world.[73]

CHAPTER SUMMARY

1 Articulate a stakeholder view of the firm:

- A stakeholder view of the firm urges companies to consider not only shareholders but other interested parties.

- An instrumental view advocates attention to stakeholders if that helps financial performance; in contrast a normative view believes in the moral obligation of companies to treat stakeholders responsibly.

- Stakeholders often disagree with each other, creating complex moral challenges and needs for effective communication.

2 Articulate CSR challenges faced by firms operating in the global economy

- MNEs face opposing economic incentives to produce where environmental regulation is less tight, and to implement standards higher than the legal minimum.

- Labour standards in foreign subsidiaries and supplier networks are subject to scrutiny by NGOs as well as by the MNEs themselves.

3 Explain how institutions influence firms' corporate social responsibility activities:

- Institutional differences explain why American firms are more likely to pursue voluntary, 'explicit CSR', while European firms pursue 'implicit CSR'.

- When confronting institutional pressures for CSR, firms may employ (1) reactive, (2) defensive, (3) accommodative and (4) proactive strategies.

4 Participate in three leading debates concerning corporate social responsibility:

- These are: (1) CSR and financial performance, (2) CSR and benefits for society and (3) political neutrality in CSR engagement overseas.

5 Draw implications for action:

- Managers should understand the institutions affecting CSR, anticipate changes and seek to influence such changes.

- CSR publicity should match CSR capabilities.

- CSR should be an integral part of the core activities and processes of a firm.

KEY TERMS

Accommodative strategy
Child labour
Corporate social responsibility
  (CSR)
Defensive strategy
Explicit CSR
Footloose plant
Global sustainability

Hypernorms
Implicit CSR
Instrumental view
Normative view
Philanthropy
Pollution haven
Primary stakeholder groups
Proactive strategy

Race to the bottom
Reactive strategy
Secondary stakeholder groups
Stakeholder
Standards of engagement (code of
  conduct, code of ethics)
Triple bottom line

CRITICAL DISCUSSION QUESTIONS

1 In your opinion, how should MNEs act when legal
requirements on labour or environmental issues vary
between the different countries in which they operate?
Should they remain politically neutral and adopt
practices and laws of the host country, or should they
stick to the rules that would apply to the same
operation back home?

2 Some argue that investing in emerging economies
greatly increases the economic development and
standard of living of the base of the global economic
pyramid. Others contend that moving jobs to low-cost
countries not only abandons CSR for domestic
employees and communities in developed economies
but also exploits the poor in these countries and
destroys the environment. How would you participate
in this debate if you were (1) CEO of an MNE

headquartered in a developed economy moving
production to a low-cost country, (2) the leader of a
labour union in the home country of the MNE that is
losing lots of jobs or (3) the leader of an environmental
NGO in the low-cost country in which the MNE
invests?

3 You find out that one of your suppliers, contrary to
your standards of engagement, is employing persons
aged 14 to 16 years of age. How do you react?

4 You are the PR officer of a major MNE in the chemicals
industry. A national environmental committee in your
home country alleges that your company is covering
up an environmental disaster caused by your
subsidiary in India, in which several people died. How
do you react?

CLOSING CASE

Different ethics: naming your school

Construction is progressing on a hill overlooking the
campus of the Hong Kong University of Science and
Technology (HKUST) for a new building for the business school. Established in 1991, HKUST has rapidly
become an intellectual powerhouse highly regarded
well beyond the territory especially in sciences, engineering and management. Its existing campus, built
with funds of the (then still British controlled) Hong
Kong government and local businesses, is located
on a hill slope on the Eastern side of Hong Kong,
and its state of the art facilities are the envy of

academics and students across Asia. The new Lee
Shau Kee Business Building is located in the new
Lee Shau Kee Campus. It is named in honour of Dr
Lee Shau Kee, who contributed HK$ 400 million
(about €38 million) to the construction costs, and,
aged 82, personally participated in the ground breaking ceremony in 2010. Who is Dr Lee? He is believed
to be the second richest man in Hong Kong, and
made his millions in property development, hotels
and internet businesses.

Universities in Hong Kong already have many buildings or libraries named after Li Ka Shing, head of the
richest family business in the territory, and the same

© Stuart Robertson/Alamy

How can Universities like Hong Kong University of Science and Technology manage the relationships with their sponsors?

name graces the library of Singapore Management University and a building of the National University of Singapore. These Asian universities have perfected an art developed by American universities: Get rich people to cough up really large amounts of money, and in return honour them by naming a building – or even an entire school – in their name.

Would that be feasible in Continental Europe? No way! The notion of naming a building, a street, a university or the like after a *living* person is considered unethical, if not illegal. The idea of bestowing an honour to a person in return for a cash payment, moreover, is considered a corrupt practice in many places. History explains why. It used to be common practice that rulers give their name to universities they founded, thus many German universities are named after long dead dukes or kings. However, today's students often don't know these names – thus Universitas Georgia Augusta (named after George II (1683–1760), king of England and elector of Hanover) is usually known as University of Göttingen. In the 20th century, the practice of naming places after living people went amok, and led to repeated re-naming of places. In Germany, local councils were busy renaming streets, buildings or even entire cities after the fall of the Nazi regime, making sure to eradicate a symbolism that the Nazi's had intended to stay forever. For example, the cities of Wolfsburg and Salzgitter – both founded in the 1930s – acquired their now established names only after 1945. Likewise, after 1989, local councils in Eastern Germany faced similar challenges, including the citizens of Karl-

Marx-Stadt who eagerly reverted back to their more mundane – but less controversial – name of Chemnitz. In Russia, St. Petersburg (named after Tsar Peter the Great) was first renamed Petrograd and then Leningrad, before reverting back St. Petersburg after the fall of communism. This historical experience explains the aversion to naming places after living people. Some countries even have laws that prohibit it.

How then can universities in Europe attract and acknowledge corporate sponsorship? When Copenhagen Business School opened its new building, all the major lecture halls were named after major Danish companies – in fact the list of rooms reads almost like the who-is-who of Danish businesses. At the same time, Copenhagen's new opera house, funded by Denmark's richest businessman Mærsk McKinney Møller (of the Mærsk shipping company), bears no formal acknowledgement. Yet, it is popularly known as 'Mærsk's mausoleum', pronounced with an ambiguous mix of admiration and cynicism.

Naming yourself after your sponsors carries risks, as a number of American universities experienced over the years. Living people may fall from grace, or fail to pay up, and what do you do then? Universities such as Georgia Tech and Thunderbird in Arizona had to drop the names of benefactors from buildings when the promised donations failed to materialize. In the UK, the business school of Imperial College thought they had stroke luck big time when in 2000 they attracted £27 million of funding from Gary Tanaka, a Japanese-American businessman, and renamed themselves

Tanaka Business School in the process. However, Mr Tanaka became embroiled in a scandal, and in 2005 faced fraud charges for having stolen money from the company he chaired. Following a lengthy trial that kept his name in the news, a New York court eventually send him to jail for five years in 2010. This development raised a major ethical dilemma for the Tanaka Business School: should they change their name and return the money? They chose a compromise by reverting back to the name Imperial College Business School in 2008, but kept the name Tanaka Building.

CASE DISCUSSION QUESTIONS:

1   In your country, should universities actively solicit donations from wealthy individuals and private business? Are you concerned about possible conflicts of interest?

2   What is the appropriate form of acknowledging private donations? Should this include commitments to name a building or an organizational unit after the company, the person, or a person related to the donor?

3   What should businesses ask for in return for handing over large amounts of cash to universities? Should shareholders support such donations to universities?

4   How should a university react when a donor's reputation is damaged due to activities unrelated to the university?

Note: In China and other Asian countries, family names are followed by the given names. When in Europe or America, many people invert their name for the convenience of their hosts. Thus, European newspapers may mention Mr. Ka-Shing Li and Mr. Shau-Kee Lee, when Asian news talks of Mr. Li Ka Shing and Mr. Lee Shau Kee.

Sources Based on: (1) D. Bradshaw, 2008, Imperial drops Tanaka name, *Financial Times*, August 20; (2) *HKUST Business School Newsletter*, 2010, New Campus Kick-off, issue 39, January; (3) *The Telegraph*, 2010, Gary Tanaka, fund manager thanked by the Queen, given five-year jail term for fraud, February 6.

RECOMMENDED READINGS

J.H. Dunning, ed., 2004, *Making Globalization Good: The Moral Challenges of Global Capitalism*, Oxford: Oxford University Press – A collection of essays by scholars as well as political and religious leaders about the moral challenges of global capitalism.

L.P. Hartman, D.G. Arnold & R.E. Wokutch, 2003, *Rising above Sweatshops: Innovative Approaches to Global Labor Challenges*, Westport, CT: Praeger – A study that investigated several initiatives by firms and industry organizations to raise labour standards in firms supplying Western MNEs.

D. Matten & J. Moon, 2009, 'Implicit' and 'Explicit' CSR: A conceptual framework for a comparative understanding of corporate social responsibility, *AMR*, 33, 404–424 – A theoretical articles that explains why the driving forces of CSR differ between Europe and North America.

A.G. Scherer & G. Palazzo, eds., 2008, *Handbook on Research on Global Corporate Citizenship*, Cheltenham: Elgar – A collection of essays outlining and reflecting over the state of the art in research on CSR in a global context.

R. Van Tulder & A. van der Zwart, 2006, *International Business-Society Management*, Abington: Routledge – A textbook that explores the role of companies' CSR practices within the conflicting pressures of markets, state and civil society.

M. Yaziyi & J. Doh, 2009, *NGOs and Corporations: Conflicts and Collaboration*, Cambridge: Cambridge University Press – Analyzes the relations between firms and NGOs from both sides, exploring the potential (and limits) for mutually beneficial interaction.

NOTES

1 A. Kolk, 2005, Corporate social responsibility in the coffee sector, *EMJ*, 23: 228–236; I.A. Davies, B. Doherty & S. Knowx, 2009, the rise and stall of a fair trade pioneer, *JBE*, 92: 127–147.

2 K. Davis, 1973, The case for and against business assumption of social responsibilities (p. 312), *AMJ*, 16: 312–322. See also A. McWilliams, D. Siegel & P. Wright, 2006, Corporate social responsibility, *JMS*, 43: 1–18.

3 World Commission on Environment and Development, 1987, *Our Common Future* (p. 8), Oxford: Oxford University Press.

4 P. Shrivastava, 1995, The role of corporations in achieving ecological sustainability, *AMR*, 20: 936–960; S. Hart & M. Milstein, 2003, Creating sustainable value, *AME*, 17: 56–67.

5 H. Teegen, 2003, International NGOs as global institutions, *JIM*, 9: 271–285; J. Doh & T. Guay, 2006, CSR, public policy, and NGO activism in Europe and the United States, *JMS*, 43: 47–73; M. Yaziyi & J. Doh, 2009, *NGOs and Corporation*, Cambridge: Cambridge University Press.

6 P. Romilly, 2007, Business and climate change risk, *JIBS*, 38: 474–480.

7 E. Freeman, 1984, *Strategic Management: A Stakeholder Approach* (p. 46), Boston: Pitman.

8 P. David, M. Bloom & A. Hillman, 2007, Investor activism, managerial responsiveness and corporate social performance, *SMJ*, 28: 91–100.

9 J. Coombs & K.M. Gilley, 2005, Stakeholder management as a predictor of CEO compensation, *SMJ*, 26: 827–840; S. Sharma & I. Henriques, 2005, Stakeholder influences on sustainability practices in the Canadian forest products industry, *SMJ*, 26: 159–180; B. Husted & D. Allen 2006, CSR in the MNE, *JIBS*, 37: 838–849; G. Kassinis & N. Vafeas, 2006, Stakeholder pressures and environmental performance, *AMJ*, 49: 145–159.

10 T. Donaldson & L. Preston, 1995, The stakeholder theory of the corporation, *AMR*, 20: 65–91.

11 R. Mitchell, B. Agle, & D. Wood, 1997, Toward a theory of stakeholder identification and salience, *AMR*, 22: 853–886; C.E. Eesley & M. Lenox, 2006, Firm responses to secondary stakeholder action, *SMJ*, 27: 765–781.

12 T. Kochan & S. Rubinstein, 2000, Toward a stakeholder theory of the firm, *OSc*, 11: 367–386; R. Wolfe & D. Putler, 2002, How tight are the ties that bind stakeholder groups? *OSc*, 13: 64–80.

13 M. Clarkson, 1995, A stakeholder framework for analyzing and evaluating corporate social performance (p. 107), *AMR*, 20: 92–117.

14 T.J. Palley, 2002, The child labor problem and the need for international labor standards, *JEI*, 36: 601–615; D. O'Rourke, 2003, Outsourcing Regulation: Analyzing nongovernmental systems of labor standards and monitoring, *PSJ*, 31: 1–29.

15 Klaus Meyer, participant observation.

16 T. Jones, 1995, Instrumental stakeholder theory, *AMR*, 20: 404–437; M. Orlitzky, F.L. Schmidt & S.L. Reyes, 2003, Corporate social responsibility and financial performance, *OSt*, 24: 403–441.

17 A.G. Scherer & M. Smid, 2000, The downward spiral and the US model business principles, *MIR*, 40: 351–371; D.G. Arnold, 2003, Philosophical foundations, In: L.P. Hartman, D.G. Arnold & R.E. Wokutch, *Rising above Sweatshops: Innovative Approaches to Global Labor Challenges*, Westport, CT: Praeger; L.P. Hartmann, B. Shaw & R. Stevenson, 2003, Exploring the ethics and economics of global labor standards, *BEQ* 13, 193–220; J.H. Dunning, ed., 2004, Making Globalization Good, Oxford: Oxford University Press.

18 C. Robertson & W. Crittenden, 2003, Mapping moral philosophies, *SMJ*, 24: 385–392; J. van Oosterhout, P. Heugens, & M. Kaptein, 2006, The internal morality of contracting, *AMR*, 31: 521–539.

19 T.M. Devinney, P. Auger & G.M. Eckhardt, 2010, *The Myth of the Ethical Consumer*, Cambridge: Cambridge University Press.

20 J.L. French, 2009. Children's labor market involvement, household work and welfare, *JBE*, 92: 63–78.

21 Hartman, Arnold & Wokutch, 2003, *as above* (p. 227).

22 F.R. Khan, 2004. Hard times recalled: The child labour controversy in Pakistan's soccer ball industry, In: F. Bird, E. Raufflet & J. Smucker, *International Business and the Dilemmas of Development*, Basingstoke: Palgrave-Macmillan, 132–156.

23 S.B. Banerjee, 2007, *Corporate Social Responsibility*, Cheltenham: Elgar; K. Bondy, 2008, The paradox of power in CSR, *JBE*, 82: 307–323.

24 D.L. Spar, 1998, The spotlight and the bottom line, *FA*, 77: 7–12.

25 H.J. Leonard, 1988, *Pollution and the Struggle for a World Product*, Cambridge, UK: Cambridge University Press; N. Mabey & R. McNally, 1998, *Foreign direct investment and the environment*, WWF-UK Report, (www.wwf-uk.org/filelibrary/pdf/fdi.pdf); L. Zarsky,

1999. *Havens, halos and spaghetti: Untangling the evidence about FDI and the environment*, conference paper, Paris: OECD, January 28–29.

26 D.L. Spar & D. Yoffie. 1999. Multinational enterprises and the prospect for justice, *JIA*, 52: 557–581.

27 M.E. Porter, 1990, *The Competitive Advantage of Nations*. New York: Free Press; M.E. Porter & C. van der Linde, 1995, Toward a new conception of the environment-competitiveness relationships, *JEP*, 9: 97–118.

28 A.M. Rugman & A. Verbeke, 1998, Corporate strategy and international environmental policy, *JIBS*, 29: 819–833; P. Christmann & G. Taylor, 2006, Firm self-regulation through international certifiable standards, *JIBS*, 37: 863–878.

29 A.A. King & J.M. Shaver, Are aliens green? *SMJ*, 22, 1069–1085; M.W. Hansen, 2003, Managing the environment across borders, *TNC*, 12: 27–52; J. Child & T. Tsai, 2005, The dynamic between MNC strategy and institutional constraints in emerging economies, *JMS*, 42: 95–126; R. Hoffmann, C.G. Lee, B. Ramasamy & M. Yeung, 2005, FDI and pollution, *JID*, 17: 311–317.

30 P. Christmann, 2004, Multinational companies and the natural environment, *AMJ*, 47: 747–760.

31 G. Dowell, S. Hart, & B. Yeung, 2000, Do corporate global environmental standards create or destroy market value? *MS*, 46: 1059–1074.

32 J. He, 2006, Pollution haven hypothesis and environmental impacts of foreign direct investment, *EE*, 60: 228–245.

33 B. Aitken, A. Harrison & R.E. Lipsey, 1997, Wages and foreign ownership, *JIE* 43: 103–132. N. Driffield & S. Girma, 2003, Regional foreign direct investment and wage spillovers, *OBES*, 65: 453–474; F. Heyman, F. Sjöholm & P.G. Tingvall, 2007, Is there really a foreign ownership wage premium, *JIE* 73: 355–376.

34 E. Lee, 1997, Globalization and Labour Standards, *ILR*, 136: 173–188.

35 O'Rourke, 2003, *as above*.

36 N. Egels-Zandén, 2007. Suppliers' compliance with MNCs' codes of conduct, *JBE*, 75, 45–62.

37 S. Frenkel & D. Scott, 2002, Compliance, collaboration, and codes of labor practice: The adidas connection', *CMR*, 45, 29–49; R. Locke, M. Amengual & A. Mangla, 2009, Virtue out of necessity, *P&S*, 37: 319–351.

38 S. Charreine Petit & J. Surply, 2008, Du whistleblowing à l'americaine à l'alerte éthique à la française, *Management*, 11: 113–135; A. Temple & P. Walgenbach, 2007, Global standardization of organizational forms and practices? *JMS*, 44, 1–24.

39 M. Friedman, 1970, The social responsibility of business is to increase its profits, *New York Times Magazine*, September 13 (Reprinted in: K.E. Meyer, ed. 2009, *Multinational Enterprises and Host Economies*, Cheltenham: Elgar).

40 M. Jensen, 2002, Value maximization, stakeholder theory, and the corporate objective function, *BEQ* 12: 235–256.

41 D. Henderson, 2001, *Misguided Virtue*, London: Institute for Economic Affairs; *The Economist*, 2001, Curse of the Ethics Executive, November 17. Note that his argument implicitly assumes (as is common in economics) that markets are efficient. In other words, consumer goods markets competition is based on price (and not, for example, reputation), labour markets with free entry and exit from contracts, full information of workers signing an employment contract, and no imbalanced bargaining power. If these assumptions are substantially violated the argument collapses.

42 D. Matten & J. Moon, 2009, 'Implicit' and 'Explicit' CSR, *AMR*, 33, 404–424; A. Apostolakou & G. Jackson, 2010, Corporate social responsibility in Western Europe, *JBE*, in press.

43 M.E. Porter & M.R. Kremer, 2006, Strategy and society, *HBR*, 84 (December), 78–92.

44 S.J. Brammer & S. Pavlin, 2005, Corporate community contributions in the United Kingdom and the United States, *JBE*, 56, 15–26; S.J. Brammer, S. Pavelin & L.A. Porter, 2009, Corporate charitable giving, multinational companies and countries of concern, *JMS*, 46: 575–596.

45 Matten & Moon, 2008, *as above*.

46 Matten & Moon, 2008, *as above*.

47 G. Weaver, 2001, Ethics programs in global businesses, *JBE*, 30: 3–15; A. Kolk & R. van Tulder, 2004, Ethics in international business, *JWB*, 39: 49–60; I. Maignan & D.A. Ralston, 2002, CSR in Europe and the US, *JIBS*, 33: 497–514.

48 D. Gioia, 2004, Pinto fires, in L.K. Trevino & K.A. Nelson, 2004, *Managing Business Ethics* (105–108).

49 S.B. Banerjee, 2001, Managerial perceptions of corporate environmentalism, *JMS*, 38: 489–513; D. Matten & A. Crane, 2005, Corporate citizenship, *AMR*, 30: 166–179.

50 S. Hart, 2005, *Capitalism at the Crossroads*, Philadelphia: Wharton School Publishing.

51 D.L. Spar & L.T. LaMure, 2003, The power of activism, CMR, 45(3): 78–101; C. Hardy, T. Lawrence & D. Grant, 2005, Discourse and collaboration, *AMR*, 30: 58–77; J. Selsky & B. Parker, 2005, Cross-sector partnerships to address social issues, *JM*, 31: 849–873; B. Arya & J. Salk, 2006, Cross-sector alliance learning

and effectiveness of voluntary codes of CSR, *BEQ*, 16: 211–234; S. Vachani, J.P. Doh & H. Teegen, 2009, NGO's influence on MNE's social development strategies in varying contexts, *IBR*, 18: 446–456.

52 Yaziji & Doh, 2009, *as above*.

53 P. Bansal & K. Roth, 2000, Why companies go green, *AMJ*, 43: 717–737.

54 A.A. King & M. Lenox, 2000, Industry self-regulation without sanctions, *AMJ*, 43: 698–716.

55 R. Jiang & P. Bansal, 2003, Seeing the need for ISO 14001, *JMS*, 40: 1047–1067; A.A. King, M. Lenox & A. Terlaak, 2005, The strategic use of decentralized institutions, *AMJ*, 48: 1091–1106.

56 J.S. Harrison & R.E. Freeman, 1999, Stakeholders, social responsibility, and performance, *AMJ*, 42: 479–487; J.D. Margolis & J.P. Walsh, 2003, Misery loves companies, *ASQ*, 268–305; M. Barnett & R. Salomon, 2006, Beyond dichotomy, *SMJ*, 27: 1101–1122; A. Lockett, J. Moon & W. Visser, 2006, CSR in management research, *JMS*, 43: 115–136; D.A. Schuler & M. Cording, 2006, A corporate social performance-corporate financial performance behavioral model for consumers, *AMR*, 31: 540–558; V. Strike, J. Gao & P. Bansal, 2006, Being good while being bad, *JIBS*, 37: 850–862.

57 M. Russo & P. Fouts, 1997, A resource-based perspective on corporate environmental performance and profitability, *AMJ*, 40: 534–559; S. Waddock & S. Graves, 1997, The corporate social performance-financial performance link, *SMJ*, 18 303–319; S. Berman, A. Wicks, S. Kotha, & T. Jones, 1999, Does stakeholder orientation matter? *AMJ*, 42: 488–506.

58 B. Agle, R. Mitchell & J. Sonnenfeld, 1999, What matters to CEOs? *AMJ*, 42: 507–525; A. McWilliams & D. Siegel, 2000, CSR and financial performance, *SMJ*, 21: 603–609.

59 Orlitzky, Schmidt & Reyes, 2003, *as above*.

60 S.J. Brammer & A.I. Millington, 2008, Does it pay to be different? *SMJ*, 29: 1325–1343.

61 Banerjee, 2007, *as above*.

62 http://meeting.aomonline.org/2007/ (accessed March 2010).

63 G. Frynas, 2005, The false developmental promise of corporate social responsibility, *IA*, 81, 581–598.

64 *Der Spiegel*, 2010, Warum Schokogiganten auf politisch korrekten Kakao setzen, January 3, translated by Klaus Meyer.

65 S. Mufson, 2010, In China, Wal-Mart presses suppliers on labor, environmental standards, *Washington Post*, February 28.

66 Mufson, 2010, *as above*. A similar message arises from the study by Devinney *et al.*, 2010, *as above*.

67 J.M. Kline, 2003, Political activities by transnational corporations, *TNC*, 12: 1–26.

68 T. Donaldson & T.W. Dunfee, 1994, Toward a unified conception of business ethics, *AMR*, 19: 252–284; G.G. Brenkert, 2009, ISCT, hypernorms and business, *JBE*, 88: 645–658; T. Donaldson, 2009, Compass and dead reckoning, *JBE*, 88: 659–664.

69 *El País*, 2009, Gran negocio verde en Copenhague, December 13.

70 A. McWilliams & D. Siegel, 2001, Corporate social responsibility, *AMR*, 26: 117–127.

71 S. Sharma, 2000, Managerial interpretations and organizational context as predictors of corporate choice of environmental strategy, *AMJ*, 43: 681–697; Yaziji & Doh, 2009, *as above*.

72 B. Husted & J. Salazar, 2006, Taking Friedman seriously, *JMS*, 43: 75–91.

73 Dunning, 2004, *as above*; N. Gardberg & C. Fombrun, 2006, Corporate citizenship, *AMR*, 31: 329–346; A. Peredo & J. Chrisman, 2006, Toward a theory of community-based enterprise, *AMR*, 31: 309–328.

THE FIRM ON THE GLOBAL STAGE

THE FIRM ON THE GLOBAL STAGE

© Anton Seleznev/iStock

CHAPTER ELEVEN

STARTING INTERNATIONAL BUSINESS

LEARNING OBJECTIVES

After studying this chapter you should be able to:

1 Explain the different options for firms to start engaging in international business.

2 Explain how firms develop resources for international business.

3 Explain how institutions influence exporting behaviour.

4 Participate in two leading debates on early stage internationalization.

5 Draw implications for practice.

OPENING CASE

Kaspersky lab is scaling the globe

By Dr. Anna Gryaznove, Moscow State University, Russia and Olga Annushkina, SDA Bocconi School of Management.

Kaspersky Lab, the fourth largest antivirus software vendor in the world with 2008 revenues that exceeded US$0.3 bn, was founded in Moscow in 1997 by four young and ambitious software engineers, among which were a young married couple, Natalya and Eugene Kaspersky. Back in 1994, Natalya, a graduate of Moscow Institute of Electronic Engineering, started working in KAMI Information Technologies centre, where she was a manager of the antivirus software development group set up by Eugene. The couple established Kaspersky Lab three years later: Eugene was in charge of antivirus software development, while Natalya, the company's chief executive, was responsible for definition and implementation of the business model. At that time, this required strenuous digging for clients – corporate clients, dealers and distributors that would help the company to reach private clientele.

In mid 1990s the market for antivirus software was at its very beginning in Russia and worldwide, and at that time in Russia Kaspersky Lab was not very lucky in finding many clients willing to pay for something they couldn't touch (software). The start of the company in 1997 was a very big challenge. Kaspersky Lab had 19 staff, and revenues were insufficient to survive. At that time, attracting external investments in Russia for a software start-up was impossible. Help came from an unexpected source. In 1996, they had entered OEM agreements by licensing its AV engine to two of their competitors – Finnish, F-Secure and German, G Data. In late 1997, Natalya went to Finland and agreed with F-Secure that they would pay advanced royalties to Kaspersky Lab on a monthly basis.

How can an anti-virus software start-up develop its international business activities?

Intermediaries are more common for standardized products and commodities (such as textiles, woods and meats), where competition focuses primarily on price.[9]

Export via intermediaries not only enjoys the economies of scale in domestic production (similar to direct exports), but it is also relatively worry-free because the intermediary handles cross-cultural communication, international payments and other activities that small firms may find rather burdensome. However, they have some drawbacks because of the introduction of third parties with their own agendas and objectives that are not necessarily the same as the exporter's.[10] The primary reason exporters choose intermediaries is because of information asymmetries concerning risks and uncertainties associated with foreign markets. Intermediaries with international contacts and knowledge essentially make a living by taking advantage of such information asymmetries. They may have a vested interest in making sure that such asymmetries are not reduced.

If exporters are interested in learning more about how their products perform overseas, they may employ their own local agent or distributor. The difference is that sales agents receive a commission on sales, while distributors trade on their own account; in other words, they buy the products and then sell them on in the local market at their own risk and using their own channels.[11] Such local intermediaries normally provide knowledge of the local market and network relationships with local customers, thus facilitating both access to customers and after-sales service. However, this kind of arrangement entails the risk that the distributor effectively controls the local market and shares information only selectively. Distributors may, for example, repackage products under their own brand and monopolize the communication with customers. For example, Nilfisk, a Danish producer of commercial vacuum cleaners, worked successfully for many years with its Spanish Distributor Nilfisk Aspiradoras. Yet, the distributor acted fiercely independently, and Nilfisk found it difficult to integrate the operations more tightly. In an industry where after-sales service is essential, local customers had build loyalty with the distributor rather than with the manufacturer. This gave the distributor considerable bargaining power when it came to rearranging the distributor agreements.[12]

Some firms with negative experiences with intermediaries subsequently moved back to direct exports. This is likely to be appropriate in particular for exporters that deal with a small number of customers and with products that require a high degree of direct interaction between the manufacturer and the user. Direct exports may thus be used for instance by manufacturers of technologically complex machines, or producers of customized intermediate products. A particular challenge for such firms may be after-sales service: how do you fix a defective machine at the other end of the world? The internet helps to deliver many aspects of after-sales service, for example performance analysis and error identification. Yet, customers may still develop more confidence to a supplier with a local operation, which may necessitate establishment of a sales subsidiary (see Chapter 12).

The opposite coin of exporting is importing. Many textbooks focus on the exporter as the primary decision-maker, but importers are equally important in driving international trade. In many ways, the activities are the same, yet from a buyer's perspective. Initially, firms may engage in sporadic imports by ordering from a supplier they met at a trade fair, or via the internet. For small transactions with a trustworthy source, they may simply pay in advance using their credit card. You can also do that as an individual, but remember that you will be liable to pay customs and duties when the products arrive in your country (unless it is an intra-EU transaction and value-added tax has been paid in the country of origin, see Chapter 8). For larger transactions, a letter of credit (Figure 11.1), guarantees importers that

Sales agent
An intermediary receiving commission for sales.

Distributor
An intermediary trading on their own account.

their payment is only released when they have received the goods. For regular imports, firms would develop supplier relationships that involve extensive exchange of knowledge and, usually, a firmer contractual arrangement.

Alternatively, importers may employ specialized intermediaries to find suitable suppliers, and to negotiate appropriate terms of delivery. Trading houses such as Li & Fung of Hong Kong have taken on the role of trade intermediary to coordinate the entire supply chain for their customers. For instance, a European department store may order shirts to a particular specification, and Li & Fung would source all the components across Asia, arrange for their assembly at a low cost location, organize transportation and customs clearance, and deliver the finished shirts to a warehouse in Europe.[13]

Managing international services

Traditionally, international trade meant sending goods across borders. Yet, globalization – especially advances in communication and transport technologies – has changed that. Countries like Greece and Cyprus earn more through exports of services than through exports of goods, mainly due to their shipping and tourism industries. The UK, the largest exporter of services among the EU countries, earned €215 billion in 2008 through export of services, compared to exports of goods of €317 billion.[14] Traditionally, services had to be produced at the site of delivery – serving a meal normally requires a cook and a kitchen at the site where the customer wants to eat. However, regulatory and technological changes facilitate trade in services, taking two different forms: (1) cross-border services, and (2) servicing foreign residents.

First, cross-border services are services that are sent across national borders. A wide range of services fall in this category, and they have been growing fast in recent years. Airlines transport people around the globe; courier companies deliver parcels and letters, while maritime shipping companies coordinate fleets of cargo and containerships on the world's oceans. Some forms of cross-border supply involve persons travelling to another country on a temporary basis, for example a university sends a teacher, a hospital sends a specialist doctor or a group of musicians gives a concert. Similarly, construction engineers, architects and other consultants may design a bridge or write a report in their main office with occasional visits to see the site. Such transactions count as exports in the balance of payment because they earn money for the national economy. For example, if the government of Vietnam hires a Sweden-based professor to prepare a report on ecological changes in the Mekong Delta, this counts as a service export from Sweden. If, however, a Swedish aid organization pays for the report, then it does not count as export, even if the field research is conducted in Vietnam.

Other cross-border supplies of services do not require a physical movement of people: a software application can be send over the internet, and a call centre can counsel clients by phone. The internet has created entirely new opportunities for such cross-border supply of services based on web-application such as online learning or offshoring of back-office services including data entry, processing of financial transactions or proofreading of documents (such as this book).

Second, servicing foreign visitors involves delivery of services to people living in other countries. This form of service export is driving the internationalization of, for example, tourism, education and health care businesses. In tourism, every firm is a potential exporter, even your neighbourhood take-away and your local bed and breakfast (B&B). However, it is only really meaningful to talk about international

Cross-border services
Supplying services across national borders.

Servicing foreign visitors
Supplying services to customers coming from abroad.

business when businesses systematically target international customers. A hotel may for instance offer English language menus, a souvenir shop and tourist guides trained in cross-cultural communication. The internet offers inexpensive opportunities for small firms, such as B&Bs, to increase their exposure to potential clients around the world, and thus to compete with larger hotel chains.[15] Beyond advertising, they may accept bookings online, backed-up with online credit card payments systems. Larger tourism businesses, such as entertainment parks or hotel chains, may systematically target international customers by advertising in magazines abroad or cooperating with travel agents (see In Focus 11.1).

The internationalization of education is driven by individuals' desire to tap into knowledge and experience available abroad.[16] Educational institutions recruit potential students by marketing in target countries, and by activating their international Alumni networks. Language schools have been leading the trend: scores of continental European teenagers come to England every Easter and every summer to brush up their English – and to have a good time. Others, from boarding schools to senior management executive training, have been developing programmes aimed at international audiences. For example, British universities market their programmes through the government-backed British Council and specialized agencies to potential students around the globe.

In the health care sector, international clients are still a relatively new phenomenon. Traditionally, internationalization was inhibited by high travel costs, information asymmetries and the national structure of health insurance systems. Yet, hospitals in some emerging economies offer treatments at much lower costs than in the USA or in Western Europe, and they attract patients not covered by health insurance.[17] For example, 1000-bed Narayana Hrudayala Hospital in Bangalore, India has developed a cost efficient business model that allows surgeons to focus and build experience in very specific areas by performing large numbers of operations of a similar type. Their lower costs attract some of the estimated six million US citizens seeking affordable medical care outside of the USA.[18] Similarly, South African hospitals have specialized in beauty treatment: tell your friends you are off on a Safari and out of sight, and return mystically rejuvenated three weeks later.[19]

Managing international contracts

Most international business transactions are not one-off transactions, but they are embedded in longer term contractual relationships. A wide range of contracts have been developed that combine exports and imports of goods and services, transfer of rights, define of contributions and allocate profits and risk of a business operation. This section provides a brief glance at some of them: (1) licensing, (2) franchising, (3) turnkey and build-own-operate projects, (4) subcontracting and (5) management contracts.

Manufacturers may earn revenues on their capabilities without physically producing the goods by licensing or franchising. The basic idea of these contracts is to transfer property rights (see Chapter 2) for a royalty fee but without necessarily becoming involved in the local operation. Contract Licensing refers to an agreement in which Firm A (called the licensor) gives Firm B (called the licensee) the rights to use A's proprietary technology (such as a patent) or trademark (such as a corporate logo) for a royalty fee paid to A by B. For example, a software developer like SAP, Microsoft or Kapersky Lab (Opening Case) may licence its software to other firms. These other firms are then allowed to use the software under terms defined in the

Contract Licensing
Firm A's agreement to give Firm B the rights to use A's proprietary technology (such as a patent) or trademark (such as a corporate logo) for a royalty fee paid to A by B.

Licensor
The company granting a license.

Licensee
The company receiving a license.

IN FOCUS 11.1

Tourism: exporting experiences

Selling to tourists is like exports in reverse: rather than sending goods to your customer, the customers come to the goods. Yet, what is it that this industry sells: hotel beds, fine dinners and bus rides? People can get these services in a lot of locations, even at home. What are they looking for when on holiday? The distinctive quality – or competitive advantage – lies in the 'experiences' that particular activities offer at the location. Tourists thus vary in their appreciation of tourist activities, each with their own personal experience of interacting with the local context.

This reverse nature of tourism 'exports' creates challenges for those who provide the services. An important aspect is the communication of the values and unique experience associated with the event or location. Thus, tourism service providers often collaborate to create and market brand values associated with a city, a region or a country, for example 'Wonderful Copenhagen', 'Greece A Masterpiece you can Afford' or 'Malaysia truly Asia'.

Another challenge is to deliver experiences that the tourists appreciate. Tourists come from different cultures and thus normally lack understanding and appreciation of the local culture, yet many seek to experience local culture as part of their holiday. They would like to participate in the activities of the locals, but do tourists experience the event in the same way? Or does the event itself change its nature because of the presence of tourists? Some tourism operators thus create staged authenticity with events adapted to perspectives 'native folk dances' or, in Britain, 'medieval banquets'. Tourism service providers are acting as mediators of culture helping foreigners to interpret and appreciate what they are experiencing. They thus face a creative tension between the demand for authenticity and the barriers to communicating cultural values and traditions.

Tourists in London: What are they "buying"?

© btrenkel/iStock

Sources: We thank Can-Seng Ooi (Copenhagen Business School) for helping us with this In Focus. Based on: C.S. Ooi, 2002, *Cultural Tourism & Tourism Culture*, Copenhagen: CBS Press; T. O'Dell & P. Billing, ed., 2005, *Experiencescapes*, Copenhagen: CBS Press; J.C. Holloway & N. Taylor, 2006, *The Business of Tourism*, 7th ed., Harlow: Pearson.

Franchising
Firm A's agreement to give Firm B the rights to use a package of A's proprietary assets for a royalty fee paid to A by B.

contract, yet they may (normally) not share it with other users. Franchising represents a similar idea, but typically covers entire business concepts: not only the product, service and trademark, but also the marketing strategy, operation manuals and quality control procedures. Many world famous brands such as McDonalds, Starbucks or Bennetton are managed as franchise chains. Thus the relationship between the giver of the franchise (the franchisor) and the recipient (the franchisee) involves extensive training and continuing communication.[20]

A great advantage is that licensors and franchisors can expand abroad with relatively little capital of their own.[21] Entrepreneurs interested in becoming licensees/franchisees have to put their own capital up front. Thus, the licensor/franchisor does not have to bear the full costs and risks associated with foreign expansion. For example, Bang & Olufsen runs most sales outlets for its designer consumer electronics as franchise operations. Their UK subsidiary employs only 40 people who provide training and support to franchisees in the UK, Ireland and the Benelux countries.[22]

On the other hand, the licensor/franchisor does not have tight control over production and marketing, and thus how their technology and brand names are used.[23] If a foreign licensee was producing substandard products that damage the brand and refuses to improve quality, the franchisor would be left with the difficult choices of (1) suing its licensee in an unfamiliar court abroad or (2) discontinuing the relationship, both of which are complicated and costly. For example, Starbucks franchised its coffee shop concept to a joint venture with German department store chain Karstadt. The venture lost both partners a lot of money before Starbucks could make a fresh start with new partners.[24]

Becoming licensees or franchisees of foreign brands is an opportunity for entrepreneurs to build their business. Foreign licensors and franchisors will provide training and technology transfer – for a fee, of course. The entrepreneur consequently can learn a great deal about how to operate at world-class standards. Further, they do not have to be permanently under the control of licensors and franchisors. If enough learning has been accomplished and enough capital has been accumulated, it is possible to discontinue the relationship and to reap greater

Franchisor
The company granting a franchise.

Franchisee
The company receiving a franchise.

How can companies cooperate to jointly implement major construction projects such as power stations or bridges?

entrepreneurial profits. For example, in Thailand, Minor Group, which had held the Pizza Hut franchise for 20 years, broke away from the relationship. Its new venture, The Pizza Company, is now the market leader in Thailand.[25] Most franchise contracts would however rule out direct competition.

Third, turnkey projects refer to projects in which clients pay contractors to design and construct new facilities. At project completion, contractors will hand clients the proverbial 'key' to facilities ready for operations – hence the term *turnkey*. This form of contracting is particular common in the construction and civil engineering industries. Companies like ALSTOM with core competences in designing and implementing large projects such as power stations, motorways or airports would thus manage the entire design and construction process on site, in part through expatriate experts (see Chapter 3, Closing Case).

For larger projects, the tasks get more complex, more specialized competences have to be combined, and long-term risks have to be shared. The contract thus is often more than a simple construction order, but for example a design and build contract, which includes architectural work as well as the physical construction. Infrastructure projects often designed as build–operate–transfer (BOT) agreements, include the management of the facility after the construction has been completed. After completion of the project, the consortium would operate the facility and collect user fees over a specified period of time (for instance 20 years) before ownership is transferred to the local party, typically the host government. Such complex contracts increasingly replace the traditional 'build-transfer' type of turnkey projects. Often several firms get together to establish a consortium, that is a project focused temporary business owned and management jointly. Consortia may then jointly bid for contracts and implement the work (See In Focus 11.2). Some construction companies have moved into the operation of large infrastructure projects. For example, Ferrovial of Spain is operating London Heathrow and other British airports.

Fourth, subcontracting combines the export of raw materials with the import of finished goods. Firms use subcontracting to outsource an intermediate stage of their value chain to a location where this particular activity can be done more cheaply. The subcontractor would work to the exact specification of the main manufacturer. Subcontracting is also increasingly used when offshoring back office services such as data processing.[26] The advantage is that this allows saving costs on labour intensive processes, such as sewing in garments manufacture. The disadvantage is the limited control over what is going on inside the subcontractors' plant. For instance, it has become a major concern to NGOs that subcontractors in developing countries are not maintaining international labour standards; companies thus have to create special training and monitoring procedures to ensure high standards (see Chapter 10).[27] Skilful use of sub-contracting allows small firms, such as Danish publisher Skandinavia A/S, to leverage their resources (In Focus 11.3).

Some firms have taken the idea of subcontracting from labour intensive processes to outsourcing design and development work. Such R&D contracts allow firms to tap into the best locations for certain innovations at relatively low costs, such as IT work in India and aerospace research in Russia.[28] However, three drawbacks may emerge. First, given the uncertain and multidimensional nature of R&D, these contracts are often difficult to negotiate and enforce. Although delivery time and costs are relatively easy to negotiate, quality is often difficult to assess. Second, such contracts may nurture competitors. A number of Indian IT firms, nurtured by

Turnkey project
A project in which clients pay contractors to design and construct new facilities and train personnel.

Design and build (DB) contract
A contract combining the architectural or design work with the actual construction.

Build–operate–transfer (BOT)
A contract combining the construction and temporary operation of a project eventually to be transferred to a new owner.

Consortium
A project based temporary business owned and managed jointly by several firms.

Subcontracting
A contract that involves outsourcing of an intermediate stage of a value chain.

R&D contract
A subcontracting of R&D between firms.

IN FOCUS 11.2

Building bridges

Construction is big business – in more than one sense! One of the largest bridges the world has ever seen is currently being constructed between the countries of Qatar and Bahrain in the Arabian Gulf. The Qatar-Bahrain Causeway connecting the two countries will be 40 km long coast-to-coast with 18km of embankments where the sea is shallow and 22 km of viaducts and bridges over deep water, including two arch bridges over shipping channels. It is expected to cut the travel time by car from six hours to just 30 minutes. The construction is expected to take five years to build and cost in the range of €3 billion. No single company would be able to handle all the design, construction and commission of such a big project: A wide range of different capabilities need to be brought together and integrated. Moreover, the construction of such a mega infrastructure project creates complex interfaces between the public sector and the private sector as many governmental agencies become involved, and many businesses from around the world compete for a share of the work. Businesses thus use a complex net of contracts to codify their contributions, their obligations, and their share in the risk.

At an early stage of this project, Danish consultants COWI conducted preliminary engineering and environmental investigations in 2001/02. They carried out surveys and investigated on land and at sea, compared alternative alignments, conducted costs and environmental impact assessments and presented a preliminary conceptual design of the bridge. Key issues in this work concerned the arrangements of the tolling and border crossing facilities, and the necessary navigational clearances to ensure that shipping lines were not disrupted.

In May 2008, following a worldwide **tender**, the Qatar-Bahrain Causeway Foundation representing the two governments of Qatar and Bahrain awarded a 'design and build' contract to a consortium led by Vinci Construction (of France) and involving Hochtief (of Germany), and CCC (of Greece) and Qatari Diar Vinci Construction (of Qatar), while dredging work and construction of embankments were awarded to Middle East Dredging Company (partially owned by Dredging International of Belgium).

A separate **project management contract** was awarded to KBR (USA) and Halcrow (UK), for design management, project management and construction management services. They will be overseeing the contracting consortium on behalf of the two governments. Once finished, it will be a truly international bridge!

Sources: Variety of news reports including *New Civil Engineer* (www.nce.co.uk), *Construction Week* (www.constructionweekonline.com), *Arabian Business* (www.arabianbusiness.com), COWI website (www.cowi.com); Halcrow website (www.halcrow.co.uk).

---

such work, are now on a global offensive to take on their Western rivals. Finally, firms that rely on outsiders to perform a lot of R&D may in the long run lose some of their core R&D capabilities.

Firms may know how to run a business, but they do not want to assume the financial risks of large real estate investments. A management contract would allow them to run the business, even though they don't own it. This is common for example in the hotel business or for infrastructure operators. Next time you stay at a Sheraton or Hilton hotel, remember that the bed you are sleeping in is unlikely to be owned by Sheraton or Hilton. More likely, it is owned by a local business and managed either by the international chain under a management contract, or by a local franchisee.[29] The business model has been pushed furthest by Intercontinental, a British hotel chain that also owns the Holiday Inn and Crown Plaza brands. They own a mere 16 of the 4186 hotels that bear their brand name.[30]

Tender
A competition for a major contract.

Project management contract
A contract to manage the whole of a project from inception to conclusion.

Management contract
A contract over the management of assets or a firm owned by someone else.

IN FOCUS 11.3

Scandinavia A/S: A small publisher for small people worldwide

Copenhagen-based Scandinavia A/S is publishing illustrated children's books, fairytales, Hans Christian Andersen fairy tales, inspirational and gift books all over the world. In an interview with Klaus Meyer (KM), Anthony Sten Höglind (AH), who spent ten years in managerial roles with Scandinavia A/S, explains the firm's business model:

KM: *Scandinavia A/S is selling European children's books all over the world – yet you only have a workforce of eight people. How do you do that?*

AH: Scandinavia A/S works with publishers, NGOs and distributors around the world in creating and developing quality illustrated books at affordable prices. Our Children's products appeal to children and parents around the world breaking barriers of language and culture. We combine the benefits of modern technology with traditional books.

Scandinavia A/S was founded in 1973 following an idea the founder had been dwelling on while working for an NGO in India. The company started as a monthly paper, then expanded into posters and eventually books with the introduction of the appropriately titled 'In The Beginning' in 1980. Scandinavia has continued to grow selling books around the world with their titles translated in over 80 different languages.

Scandinavia A/S has worked by maintaining its core competencies of product development, finance, production, quality control, marketing and sales in Copenhagen while all other functions involving the printing, finding authors, illustrators and shipping have been outsourced to firms specializing within those areas. This gives us the opportunity to find art that is not limited to the taste of Denmark but is more international and also allows us to shift production from one country or printer to another depending on a number of factors.

KM: *What are the main resources of Scandinavia A/S, and how do you exploit them?*

AH: The way it works is focusing the core competencies of product development, marketing, production and sales in Copenhagen. This is the knowledge base, with everything else sourced out. Product development is a combination of in-house ideas combined with ideas from illustrators and others who approach us with their concepts as well as collaborating with printers who are increasingly giving their input as well and suggestions for new products.

Scandinavia has a database of illustrators it has worked with over the years from diverse countries as Argentina, Denmark, France, Holland, Indonesia and Spain. The challenge is of course trying to find a style that will appeal to as many cultures and countries as possible. It doesn't always work but it did for quite a number of the products. Production is also sourced out to printers around the world where Scandinavia works with printers in China, Hong Kong, Singapore, Poland, Slovakia, Belarus, Japan and other countries. It is a combination of quality and price. There is also a learning curve involved in the communication process with the printers and trying to get them to understand what is needed. Since the founder has moved to Hong Kong, he often visits the printers and discusses with them what is needed.

KM: *Your business model seems very attractive as it allows you to focus on the high value added part of the value chain. Yet, how do you make sure the final product is of a quality that Scandinavia A/S would be proud off?*

AH: What Scandinavia actually sells is the concept with the design and the combination of the book. The publisher in the respective country does the translation to their language and sends their print files to Scandinavia who then combine the printing of the same title to the various publishers in a combined print run. This is called co-production in the industry. The publishers in the respective countries are free to change the text but cannot change the illustrations or the concept unless they produce it on their own under a special agreement.

Co-production is the process where a book is created and sold to publishers in different countries in a joint production. The firms adapt or translate the book into their local language sending the digital files for printing back to the originator who co-ordinates the overall production.

RESOURCES SUPPORTING INTERNATIONALIZATION

Internationalization process models

How do companies move from their first steps abroad to becoming major players on the global stage? How do they build the resources required to succeed in unfamiliar foreign markets? A single export transaction may capitalize on a specific opportunity. Yet to succeed continuously in other countries requires considerable networks and knowledge on how to do business in each host country. These capabilities are to a large extent based on experiential knowledge, that is they have to be learned by engaging in the particular activity and context. This focal role of experiential knowledge leads to a path-dependency in firms' growth: A firm may by chance start to export to Japan, then learn more about the country, and then set up a local sales subsidiary. This path-dependency is reflected in internationalization process models, (1) the Uppsala learning model of internationalization, (2) the network internationalization model and (3) stages models of internationalization.

Experiential knowledge Knowledge learned by engaging in the activity and context.

First, Uppsala model by Jan Johansen and Jan-Erik Vahlne was developed at the University of Uppsala in Sweden.[31] The essence of this model is that internationalization is a dynamic process of learning in which firms take decisions over their next step based on what they know at the time. Thus, a firm may make an initial commitment of resources to a market, which provides a basis for learning about the particular environment, and thus allows building context specific experiential knowledge and reduces the liability of outsidership. This knowledge then shapes the firm's ability to recognize business opportunities,[32] its perception of risk and the cost of deepening its involvement (Figure 11.2). Thus, internationalization tends to be a process of incremental decisions that one-by-one reduce market uncertainty. For example, Sweden's IKEA, took 20 years (1943–1963) before entering a neighbouring country, Norway. Then it focused on building Western European operations over the next decades. Only more recently has it accelerated its internationalization.[33]

Uppsala model A model of internationalization processes focusing on learning processes.

Second, the internationalization of a firm is often interdependent with the internationalization of its network. Smaller firms and entrepreneurs can draw on resources that they do not own, but that they can access through relationships with other businesses (and sometimes government agencies). In particular, networks provide access to assets, talent and technology, as well as knowledge of potential customers, suppliers and competitors. The Uppsala model thus has been extended to incorporate firms' networks.[34] Network relationships play an important role in facilitating access to information and organizational learning, and thus help to reduce resource deficiencies. Over time, firms in a network reinforce each others' internationalization processes, thus the expertise in a firm's network grows both with new members joining, and with existing members gaining more experience. For small businesses, these networks often overlap with the personal networks of individual entrepreneurs. For example, a study of small Danish businesses in the Baltic Sea region found that the Estonian-born wife of a CEO was pivotal in building business activity in Estonia, while a Polish-born manager helped another firm to outsource production to Poland.[35]

Some scholars have interpreted the internationalization process model as prescribing that firms need to go through distinct stages before they can successfully operate an FDI. These stages models suggest that firms go through this process in a slow, stage-by-stage process.[36] Thus, firms would go through a sequence of

Stage models Models depicting internationalization as a slow stage-by-stage process an SME must go through.

Figure 11.2 Internationalization processes

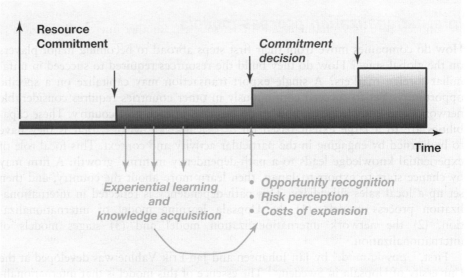

modes that reflect increasing degrees of commitments, for example, first licensing, then joint ventures, finally wholly owned subsidiaries. The specific modes vary, however, across industries and business models.[37] Moreover, there is considerable evidence that distance raises costs of doing business, yet experienced firms are better able to manage the obstacles of distance, and thus face fewer such costs.[38] Hence, firms would enter culturally and institutionally close markets first, spend enough time there to accumulate overseas experience, and then gradually move to distant markets, and from more simple modes such as exports to more sophisticated strategies such as FDI. Another interpretation of the internationalization process model suggests that the evolution of international expansion follows a discontinuous path. 'Epochs' of rapid change are followed by periods of incremental growth, or even retreat, before another boost of activity.[39]

Accelerating resource acquisition

The internationalization process model provides a good explanation of the patterns of internationalization in the 1950s to 1980s.[40] However, the Uppsala model has arguably become less powerful to explain recent expansion paths as many firms are internationalizing early in their life, and appear to jump over stages of the traditional model. These firms are known as born globals or international new ventures (INV), defined as businesses that, 'from inception, seeks to derive significant competitive advantages from the use of resources and the sale of outputs in multiple countries'.[41] How can they achieve that?

Consider Logitech, now a global leader in computer peripherals.[42] It was established by entrepreneurs from Switzerland and the USA, where the firm set up dual headquarters. R&D and manufacturing were initially split between these two countries and then quickly spread to Ireland and Taiwan through FDI. Its first commercial contract was with a Japanese company. As another example, consider Genmab, one of Europe's largest biotech firms. It was created in 1993 by two scientists, one

Born global (international new venture)
Start-up company that from inception, seek to derive significant competitive advantages from the use of resources and the sale of outputs in multiple countries.

American and one Dutch, with finance from a Danish investor. It was registered in Denmark and listed on the Copenhagen stock exchange in 2000. Yet, its main research laboratory was from the outset in the Netherlands, and its main customers are globally operating pharmaceutical companies.[43] Another interesting example is a medical equipment venture, Technomed, which was set up in France. From its inception, the founders did not see it as a French company; instead, it was viewed as a global company with English as its official language, very uncharacteristic of French firms. Only nine months after its founding, Technomed established a subsidiary through FDI in a key market, the USA.

There is little doubt that international business requires certain resources and capabilities that aspiring entrepreneurs need to build. INVs thus must have found other ways to build their resources and capabilities.[44] Their strategies include (1) building an entrepreneurial team with international competences, (2) cooperating with internationally active firms, (3) learning from others and (4) acquiring resources abroad (Table 11.2).

First, a key differentiator between rapidly and slowly (or not) internationalizing firms is the international experience of the entrepreneurial team, a fact well documented in management research.[45] Personal experience is an important resource, which is particularly important in young firms where the firm itself has not yet built embedded knowledge. Thus, entrepreneurs who have previously worked in an international role for a major company are better positioned to engage in international business: They know their industry and potential customers worldwide. Likewise, people who have lived abroad often have networks and local knowledge that help building export relationships.[46] Even studying abroad provides experiences, tacit knowledge and networks that help budding entrepreneurs to go international early. With solid previous experience abroad, doing business internationally is not so intimidating. For example, Logitech was established by a team comprising of a Swiss and an Italian, who met when studying at Stanford University in California, and a former manager of Olivetti and IBM.[47] For them bridging between Europe and America came naturally.

Second, firms may build competences for international business by working with foreign investors coming into their country. To save costs, most foreign investors are looking for local suppliers and distributors, and they may help upgrading

Table 11.2 Building resources for international business

Traditional Internationalization Processes	Accelerated Internationalization Processes
● Experiential learning and knowledge acquisition ● Network building and exploitation	● Building an entrepreneurial team with international experience ● Learning from importing and inward foreign investors ● Learning from others operating in the foreign country ● Acquiring resources in the foreign country, possibly entire firms

product quality and supply chain management practices. Such interaction with inward investors provides opportunities for learning, building international networks and establishing a reputation beyond the home ground. Some firms even find opportunities for piggybacking on the foreign partner by securing an international supply contract, or by selling through the partner's network. For example, one Northern Irish bakery for chilled part-bake bread secured supply contracts with an US firm, Subway, which entered Ireland in the mid-1990s. So successful was this relationship that the firm now supplies Subway franchisees throughout Europe, thus becoming an exporter.[48] Similarly, importing provides experiences in interacting with international partners, which helps building export markets abroad.[49] Thus, experiences in one sort of international activity facilitate acceleration of another international activity.

Third, firms may learn not only from their own experiences but from observing others. Notably, late entrants can learn by observing earlier entrants' successes and failures, and incorporate such knowledge into the design of their operations.[50] Moreover, they may imitate the behaviour of others as a means to reduce uncertainty:[51] if others (who presumably did their homework before entering) find it appropriate to use sales agents, then this appears to be an appropriate strategy. Such mimetic behaviour is a common way for firms to reduce the uncertainty associated with entering unfamiliar countries, and to speed up international growth.[52] However, it can also lead to everyone following the same fad until it eventually collapses: the fact that your rivals are rushing into China does not necessarily mean that now is the time for *you* to invest in China.

Fourth, ambitious firms may speed up their international growth by acquiring specific resources locally. At a basic level, they may rent offices, buy real estate, source local raw materials and hire people with specialist technical expertise or local knowledge. More challenging is the acquisition of brand names, distribution networks and legitimacy in the local context. These sorts of resources are rarely available to buy other than by taking over an entire firm. Foreign entrants thus may build relationships with local firms or take over local firms to access to the knowledge embedded in teams, organizational structures and routines.[53] The acquisition of local firms with sought-after capabilities thus helps overcoming the uncertainty that slows internationalization of firms following the traditional Uppsala model.[54]

INSTITUTIONS AND INTERNATIONALIZATION

The ability of internationally inexperienced firms to engage in international business is to a large extent shaped by (1) the institutional environment of the home country and (2) the institutional distance between the home country and the host countries.

First, the general institutional environment of the home country shapes firms' incentives, and thus the relative merits of pursuing international growth or domestic business opportunities. For instance, open economies with low trade barriers allow foreign entrants to challenge local firms, and thus indirectly encourage firms to pursue their opportunities abroad.[55] On the other hand, high tariffs encourage growth behind these protective barriers, for instance by expanding in related industries or by integrating suppliers. Thus, institutional environments have been shown empirically to have a major impact on firms' exports, and the profitability of such exports.[56]

Mimetic behaviour
Imitating the behaviour of others as a means to reduce uncertainty.

LEARNING OBJECTIVE

3 Explain how institutions influence exporting behaviour

In addition, some countries have designed specific institutions to help SME exporters overcome the uncertainty associated with international business. For example, export credit insurance schemes, such as the HERMES scheme in Germany, indemnify exporters against default of trade credits provided to customers abroad, thus reducing the risk of exporting to high risk countries, notably emerging economies.[57] A different type of scheme is operated by the Danish Foreign Ministry: its 'go global' initiative collects information on specific target markets to help smaller businesses in identifying suitable business partners.[58]

Second, cultural distance is the difference between two cultures along some identifiable dimensions (such as individualism).[59] Considering culture as part of institutional frameworks governing a particular country, institutional distance is 'the extent of similarity or dissimilarity between the regulatory, normative and cognitive institutions of two countries.'[60] The costs of doing business increase with such distance, both the costs of market transactions and the costs of coordinating with people in the same organization.[61]

Internationalization process models suggest that firms normally enter first where the cost of entry and the perceived risks are lowest, which is in culturally similar countries. Based on learning experiences in these countries, they may then venture further afield and enter culturally distant countries in later stages. This line of argument suggests that Belgian and Russian firms should first enter France and the Ukraine respectively, taking advantage of cultural and linguistic affinities, before venturing further afield. Business between countries that share a language on average is three times greater than between countries without a common language. Similarly, MNEs from emerging economies perform better in other developing countries, presumably because of their closer institutional distance and similar stages of economic development.[62]

However, keep in mind that these distance effects only moderate the basic rationale for doing business.[63] For instance, natural resource seeking firms have some compelling reasons to enter culturally and institutionally distant countries (such as Papua New Guinea for bauxite, Zambia for copper and Nigeria for oil). For example, Sakhalin Island is a remote part of Russia with a business environment that is quite hostile to foreign investors. Yet, Western oil majors have been flocking there because of rich oil reserves.[64] Under these conditions, cultural, institutional and geographic distance become secondary for businesses chasing profit opportunities. Moreover, some companies may have expertise in a particular distant country, or special network relationships that reduce their liability of outsidership.[65] Even personal networks matter, maybe the wife of the CEO hails from that country and opens the doors. Thus, for any specific firm it may be quite appropriate to stand out from the crowd and enter a distant market first because institutional considerations only represent one of several important sets of considerations.

Cultural distance
The difference between two cultures along some identifiable dimensions (such as individualism).

Institutional distance
The extent of similarity or dissimilarity between the regulatory, normative and cognitive institutions of two countries.

DEBATES AND EXTENSIONS

Designing and combining entry modes

Foreign entry is often presented first and foremost as a choice between a given set of entry modes. This may be true for firms establishing simple transactions across borders. Yet, as businesses mature, they usually develop more complex nets of relationships and contracts.[66] First, they may combine different types of transaction in one business relationship, for instance licensing technologies and exporting components to the same customer. Second, they may serve different segments of a market with different operation modes, for example exporting to a small market while

LEARNING OBJECTIVE

4 Participate in two leading debates on early stage internationalization

licensing to a mature market where a strong local partner has emerged. Thus, the alternative modes introduced in this section are like the building blocks for international business. New forms of contracts are designed to share resources, responsibilities, risk and returns in ways that best suit the partners in the deal.

Moreover, the decision on how to enter a foreign country is interdependent with other activities that a company may already have in the country, and with operations in other locations. An existing distributor may thus become sales agent for a new product line, or an intermediary to negotiate with local suppliers. Therefore, foreign entry decisions are highly interdependent, such that it may be more appropriate to talk about foreign operation modes configuration.[67]

Cyberspace versus conventional entry

The internet provides many avenues to support international business activity, or to create entirely new business models that by their nature transcend national boundaries. Exporters can use the internet to complement their traditional offerings: For example, they may strengthen their direct exports by using the internet as an advertising board and a catalogue, to facilitate communication with suppliers, and to process and track orders.[68] Others have developed entirely new types of business models where the entire value chain is created online, based on digital products such as software, or online services such as Google's search engine, eBay's auctions and Facebook's social networking sites. These trends require reassessment of established models of internationalization.[69]

From a resource-based perspective, the internet lowers the resource needs of entering international markets because it offers new opportunities for cost effective cross-national advertising, communication and coordination. However, firms need to develop new capabilities to utilize these new technologies effectively, and to integrate them with their business models.[70] This includes delivery of goods and services in locations where they do not have a physical presence. At the same time, competitors may spring up anywhere on the world, which keeps internet-based firms on their toes.

From an institution-based view, the key question is, whose rules of the game should e-commerce follow? Although pundits argue that the internet is undermining the power of national governments, there is little evidence that the modern nation-state system is retreating. At early stages of new technologies, investors and early commercial users push the boundaries of technology to build their markets – informality rules. As a technology matures, businesses become more concerned about protecting their property rights, while governments feel compelled to intervene to constrain businesses growing too powerful. Thus, like for earlier waves of technology, we can expect regulation to eventually catch up.[71] National governments, so far, often find it difficult to enforce such rules, as evidenced by the battle of the US authorities with gambling websites based in countries in the Caribbean. However, governments find ways to enforce rules even beyond their territories using inter-governmental negotiations, focusing on the firms' operations that are within their territory, and even by implementing screening software that blocs access to unwelcome websites. For example, British online gambling providers face legal obstacles to transactions with US banks (and thus US-based clients),[72] while Facebook negotiated with the Canadian government about its protection of the privacy of its individual members.[73] Google adapted its search engines in China to censorship demands of the Chinese government in 2006,[74] but threatened to withdraw when censorship requirements and privacy intrusions escalated in 2010.[75]

IMPLICATIONS FOR PRACTICE

As an entrepreneur or a small business who finds the home market 'too small for your shoes', how should you go about growing your business on an international stage? This chapter makes several suggestions (Table 11.3). First, a wide range of operation modes are available, even for a small firm (see Table 11.1 above). The strategic challenge is to analyze both your own resources and capabilities (Chapter 4), and the host context you are targeting (Chapters 2 and 3). On that basis, you can design an appropriate mode or combination of modes that link capabilities and contexts. Competitive advantage is often gained by finding innovative ways to combine resources to compete in a foreign market.

Second, continuous learning is essential in international business. A lot of this learning has to take place 'in action' rather than in a classroom. Therefore, plan ahead how you will be building your experiences when you design your firm's international operation. In particular, create interfaces with the local environment, and with customers in particular. A website or a licensing deal may give you quick market access. Yet, they provide you with limited customer feedback. Thus, competitors may overtake you by adapting better to the needs of consumers in that country.

Third, the dynamic view of internationalization implies that initial arrangements need to be built for flexibility. An initial entry mode may not last forever, thus contracts need to be designed to allow for change: switching from one agent to another, taking an equity stake in the agent or replacing an agent by a sales subsidiary.[76] For example, Danish packing materials manufacturer Scanbech appointed sales agents in Germany with explicit buyout options and dual distribution agreements for the time when Scanbech would increase its commitment and establish its own sales subsidiary.[77]

Fourth, entrepreneurial teams that think global *from the outset* can design their operations for global markets and supply chains, and avoid creating a domestic organization that later needs to be re-organized.[78] Reorganization is usually a very costly process that may be resisted by some people in the organization. Therefore, entrepreneurial firms without an established domestic orientation (such as Logitech, Genmab and Technomed) may outperform their rivals that wait longer to internationalize.[79] In other words, there may be inherent advantages of being young when venturing abroad, provided the entrepreneurial team can assemble the relevant competences.

LEARNING OBJECTIVE

5 Draw implications for practice

Table 11.3 Implications for action

- Design operations to link your capabilities with the local contexts you are targeting.
- Design operations to facilitate learning about IB in general and the host country in particular.
- Design operations for flexibility to enable later adjustment to changes in both your own capabilities and in the external environment.
- If your medium-term target markets are international, design your business models accordingly from the outset.

CHAPTER SUMMARY

1 Explain the different options for firms to start engaging in international business:

- Goods can be exported and imported with and without intermediaries such as agents and distributors.

- Services can be exported by attracting customers to your site, or by sending the outcome of the services across borders.

- A wide variety of contracts are available to combine different transfers of goods, services, and rights, including (1) licensing, (2) franchising, (3) turn-key projects, (4) subcontracting and (5) management contracts.

2 Explain how firms develop resources for international business:

- Traditional models of internationalization emphasize the gradual nature of knowledge accumulation and network building processes, which are reflected in stages models.

- Internationalization processes have accelerated as firms find new ways to build the capabilities needed in international business, including (1) building an experienced managerial team, (2) cooperating with experienced firms, (3) mimicking others and (4) acquiring local resources.

3 Explain how institutions influence exporting behaviour:

- Institutions of the home environment shape the relative costs and risks associated with international versus domestic growth.

- Cultural and institutional distance increase the costs of doing business, and thus lead many firms to start international business in locations in close proximity of their origins.

4 Participate in two leading debates on early stage internationalization:

- A new line of research suggests focusing on the combination of different entry modes

- The internet creates new challenges for resource exploitation and for interacting with institutions in many countries simultaneously.

5 Draw implications for practice:

- Operations abroad should be designed to (1) link with local contexts, (2) facilitate learning and (3) allow for flexibility.

- Start-up businesses aiming for global markets may benefit from creating global structures from the outset.

KEY TERMS

Born global (international new venture)
Build–operate–transfer (BOT)
Consortium
Cross-border services
Cultural distance
Design and build (DB) contract
Direct exports
Distributor
Entrepreneurial teams
Entrepreneurs
Experiential knowledge
Export intermediary

Exporter
Franchisee
Franchising
Franchisor
Importer
Indirect exports
Institutional distance
Letter of credit (L/C)
Licensee
Licensing
Licensor
Management contract
Mimetic behaviour

Project management contract
R&D contract
Sales agent
Servicing foreign visitors
Small- and medium-sized enterprises (SMEs)
Sporadic (or passive) exporting
Stage models
Subcontracting
Tender
Turnkey project
Uppsala model

CRITICAL DISCUSSION QUESTIONS

1 Some suggest that foreign markets are graveyards for entrepreneurial firms to over-extend themselves. Others argue that foreign markets represent the future for SMEs. If you were the owner of a small, reasonably profitable domestic firm, would you consider expanding overseas? Why?

2 Your Kazakh classmate offers you 15 per cent commission if you sell hand-made, fashionable clothing from Kazakhstan to local distributors in your home town. Would you consider this offer?

3 Your company receives an enquiry by e-mail from an unknown customer in Australia. The customer asks for detailed information about your latest high tech products, and envisages a very large order. How do you react?

4 Your former high school buddy invites you to join an entrepreneurial start-up that specializes in cracking the codes of protection software, which protect CDs and DVDs from being copied. He has developed the pioneering technology and lined up financing. The worldwide demand for this technology appears enormous. He offers you the job of CEO and 10 per cent of the equity of the firm. How would you respond to his proposition?

CLOSING CASE

Better Generation: the global generation of business

By Amber Guan, MBA Graduate, University of Bath and Klaus Meyer, University of Bath.

Green energy is a hot topic worldwide as government aim to limit greenhouse gas emissions in response to targets set by the Kyoto protocol, which came into force in 2005. One stream of innovations focuses distributed power generation, that is small scale generation of electricity with capacities from 1 KW to 100 KW close to the energy user. Individual owners of land or buildings (factories, farm-yards, private homes) thus install small windmills or solar panel to serve their own needs. In the words of British entrepreneur Toby Hammond:

> '... rather than building fewer large, expensive and polluting power stations, we should encourage generation from lots of renewable sources, such as wind and solar, closer to the point of consumption. This has an interesting context for global distribution, product standardization and manufacturing cost savings, as the industry and these technologies mature.'

However, these new technologies still face substantial obstacles: high costs of installation, lack of knowledge what technology works where and inconsistent (or absence) of governmental regulation. To overcome the technological barriers, Toby Hammond developed a tool called 'Power Predictor', a combined wind and solar power measuring device that collects local data from the site where it is mounted. These data enable an assessment of the specific site's wind and solar generation potential, forecasts the payback time for renewable energy investments and recommendations for the most cost-effective form of renewable energy equipment.

Toby Hammond holds degrees in Environmental Biology and in Sustainable Development, and has experience as an environmental consultant advising private and public sector clients on sustainability. In 2006, he founded Better Generation (BG) to manufacture and distribute his device. In 2008, he teamed up with Graham Brant, a venture capitalist with 28 years' experience in global business. From 1991 to 2001 Graham Brant held a number of senior positions with Microsoft, including the role of CEO of Microsoft Hong Kong, and he was one of the pioneers who established Microsoft's business in Mainland China. Since leaving Microsoft, he has been managing investments in hybrid Chinese/Western companies, before focusing on his role as CEO of BG. The partnership with

Reproduced with permission of Better Generation Group Ltd.

This device is called a 'Power Predictor', it is a combined wind and solar power measuring device that collects local data from the site where it is mounted.

Graham Brant enabled Toby Hammond to pursue his ideas on a global scale.

The essence of BG's business models is to focus on a key bottleneck for micro-generation industry: the difficulties of obtaining detailed data about the viability of individual sites for micro-generation, and of obtaining supplier-neutral advice about the most appropriate solution for the site. Their Power Predictor comes in two parts: a measuring device and a web-based software. The device collects the data, which are uploaded and analyzed using web-based software and BG's own databases to create reports for individual customers. The most strategic element of this business model is BG's ownership of the data uploaded by the Power Predictor's users. BG is thus building a global database of renewable energy micro generation resource data. This database of micro solar and wind conditions is expected to be of great value to both future customers and to developers of new technologies. BG uses this database to connect turbine manufacturers, distributors, retailers and installers

and to unlock the adaptation barriers to micro generation systems. This business model enables BG to explore distribution channels and to lock-in potential micro generation system buyers. It thus also provides a platform for the company to enter the market for micro wind turbines in the future. Graham Brant explains:

'Establishing a worldwide wind and solar resource database is an ambitious plan. It involves an enormous effort to research the worldwide wind and solar micro-generation technologies, complete the list of approved micro-generation system installers and distributors in each country and distribute Power Predictor worldwide. The way of doing it is to internationalize the business as early as possible. We are learning as we are doing, once the right model is established, we will just copy it to other countries.'

The success of this business model depends on the scale and scope of the operation. The value of the database depends on its volume and reach. Therefore, international growth and building market shares are essential goals for BG. In the words of Graham Brant:

'... with our unique product concepts and the value proposition in the market place, we could sell our product at a much higher price than we do now. However, by charging a relatively low price, we are aiming to drive sales volume and grab market share. Therefore, the success of our business is base on building volume. This is the case not just in the UK market, but also for the international market. What we really want to be is the Google of the micro-energy generation industry.'

Better Generation is organized as a group of three companies. BG Group is based in Hong Kong, and created as the parent company, while BG UK is responsible for European marketing and product design. BG China is a joint venture with a young technology firm in Chengdu manufacturing wind sensor products and large wind turbine control systems. BG Group controls 51 per cent of this joint venture. This structure is designed to support a tax efficient trading strategy, to operationally integrate the China-based manufacturing unit and to support a cost efficient global sales platform.

The micro-generation industry is in its infancy, but boosted by various government initiates around the world in the wake of the Kyoto protocol. However, many incentive schemes and subsidies focus on large scale energy generation. Micro-generation facilities still face high initial set-up costs and uncertainty regarding the efficacy of available technologies. Therefore, the market potential exists primarily where governments offer incentives to help consumers with the high up-front cost. Moreover, obtaining local planning permission to install wind turbines creates further obstacles that vary not only between countries, but across provinces and even municipalities.

The institutional environment for the renewable energy industry is therefore crucial for prioritizing which potential markets to enter. The market size and the generally supportive policies for micro-generation led BG to focus on the USA. For example, the federal government offers tax credits for energy generation from wind turbines, including a special scheme for small wind turbine for home, farm and business use. However, the specific regulation of the energy sector and of building policies falls mainly in the responsibility of individual states of the USA, which creates a very fragmented market. Other countries, such as continental Europe, focus their energy policies on larger scale power generation and thus offer less immediate market potential for BG. In its initial entry to the US market, BG used local distributors to reach markets fast, yet carefully designing distributor agreements to be sure to retain the rights to its database.

CASE DISCUSSION QUESTIONS

1 What motivates Better Generation to become international very fast?

2 What are the risks of a fast internationalization strategy for Better Generation?

3 How can Better Generation build the resources required for a fast internationalization strategy?

4 How should Better Generation develop its international strategy in terms of countries chosen and entry modes?

Sources: This case was prepared by Amber Guan (MBA Graduate, University of Bath) and Klaus Meyer. It is based on archival data and personal interviews. Copyright © Amber Guan and Klaus Meyer.

RECOMMENDED READINGS

O. Andersen, 1993, On the internationalization process of the firm, *JIBS*, 24: 209–231 – A critical review paper of the internationalization process literature.

M. Forsgren, 2002, The concept of learning in the Uppsala internationalization model: a critical review, *IBR*, 11: 257–277 – A review of alternative ways of learning how to do international business.

J. Johansen & J.E. Vahlne, 2009, The Uppsala internationalization process model revisited: From liability of foreignness to liability of outsidership, *JIBS*, 40, 1411–1431 – The fathers of the Uppsala model review and extend the literature that builds on their original work published in 1977.

L. Welch, G. Benito & B. Petersen, 2007, *Foreign Operation Methods*, Cheltenham: Elgar – A specialized textbook covering a wide range of modes with focus on non-equity modes.

S. Young, J. Hamill, C. Wheeler & J.R. Davies, 1989, *International Market Entry and Development: Strategies and Management*, Englewood Cliffs, NJ: Prentice Hall – An older book providing a very concise treatment of alternative modes of foreign entry.

NOTES

1 I.M. Kirzner, 1973, *Competition and Entrepreneurship*, Chicago: University of Chicago Press; M.C. Casson, 2010, *Enterpreneurship: Theory, Networks, History*, Cheltenham: Elgar;.

2 A. Zacharakis, 1998, Entrepreneurial entry into foreign markets, *ETP*, Spring: 23–39; K.E. Meyer, 1998, *Direct Investment in Economies in Transition*, Aldershot: Elgar (Chapter 4).

3 R. Chen & M. Martin, 2001, Foreign expansion of small firms, *JBV*, 16: 557–574.

4 F.H.R. Seringhaus & P.J. Rossen, 2001, Firm experience and international trade fairs, *JMM*, 17: 877–901; K.E. Meyer & A. Skak, 2002, Networks, serendipity and SME entry into Eastern Europe, *EMJ*, 20: 179–188.

5 L. Leonidou & C. Katsikeas, 1996, The export development process, *JIBS*, 27: 517–551; R. Salomon & J. M. Shaver, 2005, Export and domestic sales, *SMJ*, 26: 855–871; M.J. Matanda & S. Freeman, 2009, Effects of perceived environmental uncertainty on exporter-importer inter-organizational relationships and export performance improvement, *IBR*, 18: 89–107.

6 G. Balabanis, 2000, Factors affecting export intermediaries' service offerings, *JIBS*, 31: 83–99.

7 M.W. Peng & A.Y. Ilinitch, 1998, Export intermediary firms, *JIBS*, 29: 609–620; H. Trabold, 2002, Export intermediation: An empirical test of Peng and Ilinitch, *JIBS*, 33: 327–344; H. van Driel, 2003, The role of middlemen in the international coffee trade since 1870, *BH* 45(2): 77–101.

8 M.W. Peng & A. York, 2001, Behind intermediary performance in export trade, *JIBS*, 32: 327–346; P. Dimitratos & S. Lioukas, 2004, Greek perspectives on international entrepreneurship, in: P. Dana, ed., *Handbook of Research on International Entrepreneurship*, Cheltenham: Elgar; M.W. Peng, Y. Zhou & A. York, 2006, Behind make or buy decisions in export strategy, *JWB*, 41: 289–300; P.D. Ellis, 2010, Trade intermediaries and the transfer of marketing knowledge in transition economies, *IBR*, 19, 16–33.

9 M.W. Peng, Y. Zhou & A. York, 2006, Behind make or buy decisions in export strategy, *JWB*, 41: 289–300.

10 D. Skarmeas, C. Katsikeas & B. Schlegelmilch, 2002, Drivers of commitment and its impact on performance in cross-cultural buyer-seller relationships, *JIBS*, 33: 757–783; L. Li, 2003, Determinants of export channel intensity in emerging markets, *APJM*, 20: 501–516; C. Zhang, S. T. Cavusgil & A. Roath, 2003, Manufacturer governance of foreign distributor relationships, *JIBS*, 34: 550–566; H. Lau, 2008, Export channel structure in a newly industrialized economy, *APJM*, 25: 317–333.

11 C.A. Solberg & E.B. Nes, 2002, Exporter trust, commitment and marketing control in integrated and independent export channels, *IBR*, 11: 385–405; F. Wu, R. Sinkovics, S. T. Cavusgil & A. Roath, 2007, Overcoming export manufacturers' dilemma in international expansion, *JIBS*, 38: 283–302.

12 B. Petersen, D.E. Welch & L.S. Welch, 2000, Creating meaningful switching options in international operations, *LRP*, 33: 688–705.

13 J. Margretta, 1998, An interview with Victor Fung, *HBR*, September–October 102–118; V.K. Fung, W.K. Fung & Y. Wind, 2007, *Competing in a Flat World*, Upper Saddle River: Wharton School Publishing.

14 Office for National Statistics (UK), 2009, *Balance of Payment: The Pink Book*, Cardiff: ONS.

15 T.R. Lituchy & A. Rail, 2000, Bed and breakfast, small inns and the internet, *JIMktg*, 8: 86–97.

16 K. Larsen, J.P. Martin & R. Morris, 2002; Trade in educational services, *WE*, 25, 849–868; OECD, 2004, *Internationalization and Trade in Higher Education; Opportunities and Challenges*, Paris: OECD; M.R. Czinkota, 2006, Academic freedom for all in higher education, *JWB*, 41, 149–160.

17 P. Ghemawat, 2007, *Redefining Global Strategy*, Cambridge, MA: Harvard Business School Press (Chapter 6).

18 G. Anand, 2009, The Henry Ford of heart surgery, *Wall Street Journal*, November 26.

19 Klaus Meyer's interviews with a hospital director and a B&B host in Johannesburg, South Africa.

20 R. Luostarinen & L.S. Welch, 1990, *International Business Operations*, Helsinki: Export Consulting KY; B. Petersen & L.S. Welch, 2000, International retailing operations: downstream entry and expansion via franchising, *IBR* 9: 479–496; L.S. Welch, G.R.G. Benito & B. Petersen, 2007, *Foreign Operation Methods*, Cheltenham: Elgar (Chapters 3 & 4); J. Barthélemy, 2009, Le choix de la franchise ou de l'intégration verticale, *MI/IM/GI*, 13(4): 65–72.

21 J. Combs & D. Ketchen, 1999, Can capital scarcity help agency theory explain franchising? *AMJ*, 42: 196–207; A. Fosfuri, 2006, The licensing dilemma, *SMJ*, 27: 1141–1158.

22 Klaus Meyer's personal communication with the managing director of Bang & Olufsen UK.

23 A. Arora & A. Fosfuri, 2000, Wholly owned subsidiary versus technology licensing in the worldwide chemical industry, *JIBS*, 31: 555–572; P. Aulakh, S. T. Cavusgil & M. Sarkar, 1998, Compensation in international licensing agreements, *JIBS*, 29: 409–420.

24 W. Streitz, 2004, Karstadt und Starbucks: Das Ende der Frapuccino-Escapaden, *Der Spiegel*, September 29.

25 R. Tesker, 2002, Pepperoni power, *Far Eastern Economic Review*, November 14.

26 R. Aron & J.V. Singh, 2005, Getting offshoring Right, *HBR*, 83 (December): 135–143; R. Metters &

R. Verma, 2007, History of offshoring knowledge services, *JOM*, 26: 141–147; A. Stringfellow, M.B. Teagarden & W. Nie, 2007, Invisible costs in offshoring services work, *JOM*, 26: 164–179.

27 L.P. Hartman, D.G. Arnold & R.E. Wokutch, eds, 2003, *Beyond Sweatshops*, New York: Praeger.

28 B. Ambos, 2005, Foreign direct investment in industrial research and development, *RP,* 34: 395–410; L. Håkanson, 2007, Managing cooperative research and development, *RDM*, 23: 273–285; K. Asakawa & A. Som, 2008, Internationalization of R&D in China and India, *APJM*, 25: 375–394; A.Y. Lewin, S. Massini & C. Peeters, 2009, Why are companies offshoring innovation? The emerging global race for talent, *JIBS*, 40: 901–925.

29 F.J. Contractor & S.K. Kundu, 2003, Modal choice in a world of alliances: analyzing organizational forms in the international hotel sector, *JIBS*, 29, 325–357.

30 *The Economist*, 2009, Hotels: Outsourcing as you sleep, February 21.

31 R. Carlsson, 1966, *International Business Research*, Uppsala: Acta Universitatis Upsalienis; J. Johanson & J.E. Vahlne, 1977, The internationalization process of the firm, *JIBS*, 4: 20–29; G.R.G. Benito & L.S. Welch, 1994, Foreign market servicing, *JIMktg* 2: 7–27; J. Johanson & J.E. Vahlne, 2009, The Uppsala internationalization process model revisited, *JIBS*, 40, 1411–1431.

32 J. Johanson & J.E. Vahlne, 2006, Commitment and opportunity development in the internationalization process, *MIR*, 46: 165–178; M. Johanson & J. Johanson, 2006, Turbulence, discovery and foreign market entry, *MIR*, 46: 179–205.

33 K. Kling & I. Goteman, 2003, IKEA CEO Anders Dahlvig on international growth, *AME*, 17: 31–45.

34 J. Johansen & L.G. Mattson, 1988, Internationalization in industrial systems, in: N. Hood & J.E. Vahlne, eds, *Strategies in Global Competition,* New York: Croom Helm; N.E. Coviello & K.A. Martin, 1999, Internationalization of service SMEs, *JIMktg*, 7: 42–66; S. Chetty & D. Blankenburg Holm, 2000, Internationalization of small to medium-sized firms: A network approach, *IBR*, 9: 77–93; N.K. Malhotra, J. Agarwal & F.M. Ulgado, 2003, Internationalization and entry modes, *JIMktg*, 11: 1–31; K.E. Meyer & M. Gelbuda, 2006, Process perspectives in international business, *MIR*, 46: 143–164; S. Prashantham, 2009, *The Internationalization of Small Firms*, London, Routledge.

35 K.E. Meyer & A.T. Skak, 2002, *as above*.

36 A. Hadjikani, 1997, A note on the criticisms against the internationalization process model, *MIR* 37: 1–23; L. Li, D. Li & T. Dalgic, 2004, Internationalization process of small and medium-sized enterprises, *MIR*, 44: 93–116.

37 N.K. Malhotra & C.B. Hinings, 2010, An organizational model of understanding internationalization processes, *JIBS*, 41: 330–349.

38 G.Y. Gao, Y. Pan, J. Lu & Z. Tao, 2008, Performance of multinational firms' subsidiaries, *MIR*, 6: 749–768. P.Y. Li & K.E. Meyer, 2009, Contextualizing experience effects in international business, *JWB*, 44: 370–382.

39 M. Kutschker, I. Bäuerle & S. Schmidt, 1997, International evolution, international episodes, and international epochs, *MIR*, 37 (special issue 2): 101–124; M. Kutschker & S. Schmidt, 2008, *Internationales Management*, 6th ed., Munich: Oldenbourg.

40 Johanson & Vahlne, 2009, *as above*; R.P. Amdam, 2009, The internationalization process theory and the internationalization of Norwegian firms 1945–1980, *BH* 445–461.

41 B. Oviatt & P. McDougall, 1994, Toward a theory of international new ventures, *JIBS*, 25: 45–64.

42 P. McDougall, S. Shane & B. Oviatt, 1994, Explaining the formation of international new ventures, *JBV*, 9: 469–487.

43 *The Economist*, 2008, Face value: From across the divide, June 14.

44 T.K. Madsen & P. Servais, 1997, The internationalization of born globals, *IBR* 6: 561–583; G. Knight & S. T. Cavusgil, 2004, Innovation, organizational capabilities and the born-global firm, *JIBS*, 35: 124–141; M. Gabrielsson & V.H.M. Kirpalani, 2004, Born globals: how to reach new business space rapidly, *IBR,* 13: 555–572; M.V. Jones & N.E. Coviello, 2005, Internationalisation: conceptualizing an entrepreneurial process of behaviour in time, *JIBS*, 36: 284–303; S.A. Zahra, 2005, A theory of international new ventures, *JIBS*, 36: 20–28.

45 A.B. Reuber & E. Fischer, 1997, The influence of the management team's international experience on the internationalization behaviors of SMEs, *JIBS*, 28: 807–825; P. Westhead, M. Wright & D. Ucbasaran, 2001, The internationalization of new and small firms, *JBV*, 16: 333–358; S. Chetty, K. Eriksson & J. Lindbergh, 2006, The effect of specificity of experience on a firm's perceived importance of institutional knowledge in an ongoing business, *JIBS*, 37: 699–712; N.E. Coviello, 2006, The network dynamics of international new ventures, *JIBS*, 37: 713–731; Z. Fernandez & M. Nieto, 2006, Impact of ownership on the international involvement of SMEs, *JIBS*, 37: 340–351; H. Sapienza, E. Autio, G. George & S. Zahra, 2006,

A capabilities perspective on the effects of early internationalization on firm survival and growth, *AMR*, 31: 914–933.

46 K. Gillespie, L. Riddle, E. Sayre & D. Sturges, 1999, Diaspora interest in homeland investment, *JIBS*, 30: 623–634; I. Filatotchev, X. Liu, T. Buck & M. Wright, 2009, The export orientation and export performance of high technology SMEs in emerging markets: The effects of knowledge transfers by returnee entrepreneurs, *JIBS*, 40: 1005–1021.

47 V.K. Jolly, M. Alahuhta & J.P. Jeannet, 1992, Challenging incumbents, *SC*, 1: 71–82.

48 J. Bell, R. McNaughton & S. Young, 2001, Born-again global firms (p. 184), *JIM*, 7: 173–189.

49 L.S. Welch & R. Luostarinen, 1993, Inward-outward connections in internationalization, *JIMktg*, 1: 44–56; H. Korhonen, R. Luostarinen & L.S. Welch, 1996, Internationalization of SMEs: inward-outward patterns and government policy, *MIR*, 36-315-329; T. Buck, X. Liu, Y. Wei & X. Liu, 2009, The trade development path and export spillovers in China, *MIR* 47: 683–706.

50 M.B. Lieberman & D.B. Montgomerry, 1998, First mover (dis-)avantages, *SMJ*, 19: 1111–1125.

51 P.J. Di Maggio & W.W. Powell, 1983, The iron cage revisited: Institutional isomorphism and collective rationality in organizational fields, *ASQ*, 48: 147–160; J. Lu, 2002, Intra- and inter-organizational imitative behavior, *JIBS*, 33: 19–37.

52 M. Forsgren, 2002, The concept of learning in the Uppsala internationalization process model. *IBR*, 11: 257–277; C. Schwens & R. Kabst, 2009, How early opposed to late internationalizers learn, *IBR*, 18: 509–522.

53 J. Anand & A. Delios, 2002, Absolute and relative resources as determinants of international acquisitions, *SMJ* 23: 119–134. K.E. Meyer, M. Wright, S. Pruthi, 2009, Managing knowledge in foreign entry strategies: A resource-based analysis, *SMJ*, 31: 557–574; S. Freeman, K. Hutchings, M. Lazaris & S. Zynier, 2010, A model of rapid knowledge development, *IBR*, 19, 70–84.

54 Forsgren, 2002, *as above*.

55 T. Hutzschenreuther & F. Gröne, 2009, Product and geographic scope of multinational enterprises in response to international competition, *JIBS*, 40: 1149–1170.

56 G.A. Shinkle & A.P. Kriauciunas, 2010, Institutions, size and age in transition economies: Implications for export growth, *JIBS*, 41, 267–286; G.Y. Gao, J.Y. Murray, M. Kotabe & J. Lu, 2010, A 'strategy tripod' perspective on export behaviors, *JIBS*; 41: 377–396; M.R. Schneider, C. Schulze-Bentrop & M. Paunescu, Mapping the institutional capital of

high-tech firms: A fuzzy set analysis of capitalist variety and export performance, *JIBS*, 41: 246–266.

57 G. Dewitt, 2001, Intervention in risky export markets, *EJPE*, 17: 575–592.

58 www.goglobal.dk, accessed October 2009.

59 B. Kogut & H. Singh, 1988, The effect of national culture on the choice of entry mode, *JIBS*, 19: 411–432.

60 D. Xu & O. Shenkar, 2002, Institutional distance and the multinational enterprise (p. 608), *AMR*, 27: 608–618.

61 S. Shane & H. Singh, 1998, National cultural distance and cross-border acquisition performance, *JIBS*, 29: 137–158; J.F. Hennart & J. Larimo, 1998, The impact of culture on the strategy of MNEs, *JIBS*, 29: 515–538; S. Estrin, D. Baghdasaryan & K.E. Meyer, 2009, The impact of institutional and human resource distance on international entry strategies, *JMS*, 46: 1171–1196; N. Prime, C. Obadia & I. Vida, 2009, Psychic distance in exporter-importer relationships, *IBR*, 18: 184–199; D. Dow & S. Ferencikova, 2010, More than national cultural distance, *IBR*, 19, 46–58; B. Ambos & L. Hakanson, 2010, The antecedents of psychic distance, *JIM*, 16: 195–210.

62 E. Tsang & P. Yip, 2007, Economic distance and survival of foreign direct investments, *AMJ*, 50: 1156–1168.

63 J. Steen & P. Liesch, 2007, A note on Penrosian growth, resource bundles and the Uppsala model of internationalization, *MIR*, 47: 193–206.

64 *The Economist*, 2006, Don't mess with Russia, December 16: 11.

65 A. Ojala, 2009, Internationalization of knowledge-intensive SMEs: The role of network relationships in the entry to a psychically distant market, *IBR*, 18: 50–59.

66 J. Puck, D. Holtbrugge & A. Mohr, 2009, Beyond entry mode choice, *JIBS*, 40: 388–404; D. Tan, 2009, Foreign market entry strategies and post-entry growth, *JIBS*, 40: 1046–1063; G.R.G. Benito, B. Petersen & L.S. Welch, 2009, Towards more realistic conceptualisations of foreign operation modes, *JIBS*, 40, 1455–1470

67 C.G. Asmussen, G.R.G. Benito & B. Petersen, 2009, Organizing foreign market activities: From entry mode choice to configuration decisions, *IBR* 18: 145–155.

68 A. Morgan-Thomas & S. Bridgewater, 2004, The internet and exporting, *IMR*, 21: 393–406; Y. Luo, J.H. Zhao & J. Du, 2005, The internationalization speed of e-commerce companies, *IMR*, 22: 693–709; P. Servais, T.K. Madsen & E.S. Rasmussen, 2006, Small manufacturing firms' involvement in international e-business activities, *AIM*, 17: 297–317.

69 V. Mahnke & M. Venzin, 2003, The internationalization process of digital information good providers, *MIR*, 43: 115–142; M. Yamin & R.R. Sinkovics, 2006, Online internationalisation, psychic distance reduction and the virtuality trap, *IBR*, 15: 339–360.

70 B. Petersen & L.S. Welch, 2003, International business development and the internet, post-hype, *MIR* 43 (special issue) 7–29; S. Loane, R.B. McNaughton & J. Bell, 2004, The internationalization of internet-enabled entrepreneurial firms, *CJAS*, 21: 79–96.

71 D.L. Spar, 2001, *Ruling the Waves: Cycles of Discovery Chaos and Wealth from the Compass to the internet*, New York: Harcourt.

72 *The Economist*, 2006, Online gambling: Busted flush, October 5; R. Blitz, 2009, Brussels intensifies transatlantic fight over online gambling, *Financial Times*, March 27.

73 D. Gelles, 2009, Canada forces tighter Facebook privacy, *Financial Times*, August 28.

74 M. Dickie, 2006, Google to launch censored China service, *Financial Times*, January 25; *The Economist*, 2006, Here be dragons, January 26; *The Economist*, 2007, The internet: Who's afraid of Google?, August 30.

75 *The Economist*, 2010, Google and China: Flowers for a funeral, January 13.

76 B. Petersen, L.S. Welch & G.R.G. Benito, 2010, Managing the internationalisation process, *MIR*, 50: 137–154.

77 Petersen, Welch & Welch, 2000, *as above*.

78 E. Autio, H. Sapienza & J. Almeida, 2000, Effects of age at entry, knowledge intensity and imitability in international growth, *AMJ*, 43: 909–924.

79 P. Liesch & G. Knight, 1999, Information internationalization and hurdle rates in small and medium enterprise internationalization, *JIBS*, 30: 383–394; J. Mathews & I. Zander, 2007, The international entrepreneurial dynamics of accelerated internationalization, *JIBS*, 38: 387–403; S. Nadkarni & P.D. Perez, 2007, Prior conditions and early international commitment, *JIBS*, 38: 160–176.

© David Joyner/iStock

CHAPTER TWELVE

FOREIGN ENTRY STRATEGIES

LEARNING OBJECTIVES

After studying this chapter you should be able to:

1 Explain why MNEs establish subsidiaries abroad (*why* enter)

2 Identify relevant location-specific advantages that attract foreign investors (*where* to enter)

3 Compare and contrast first- and late-mover advantages (*when* to enter)

4 Compare and contrast alternative modes of entry (*how* to enter)

5 Explain the interdependence of operations and entry strategies

6 Apply the institution-based view to explain constraints on foreign entry strategies

7 Participate in leading debates on foreign entry strategies

8 Draw implications for action

OPENING CASE

Pearl River Piano enters foreign markets

A grand piano from a famous maker is the aspiration and passion of pianists around the world. Professionals swear for their favourite brands, like Bösendorffer (from Vienna, Austria) or Steinway (from New York, USA). Some with a lot of money to spend go for a hand-made piano from a traditional family business like Grotrian-Steinweg (from Braunschweig, Germany). The manufacture of a piano is a traditional craft that requires highly specialist skills, true to the Latin origins of the word (*manu* = hand). Most mortals with a passion for music make do with more mundane brand, such as Yamaha (from Yokohama, Japan). Yamaha brought together Japanese traditional passion for manufacturing excellence, and more, a recent

passion for classical music, to become the largest piano-maker of the world in the 1990s. In 2008, Yamaha acquired the leading European manufacturer, Bösendorffer, for a stronger positioning in the premium segment.

With such a strong field of incumbents, and strong loyalty to traditional brands, it may come as a surprise that a new kid on the bloc is rolling up the market: In 2002, Pearl River (of Guangzhou, China) overtook Yamaha to become the largest piano producer in the world producing about 100 000 pianos every year. How did it achieve that? Given the relatively low prestige associated with made-in-China goods, few would associate an aspirational product like a piano with 'made in China'. The Pearl River Piano was founded in 1956 in Guangzhou, where the Pearl river flows by.

© Peter Harmsen/AFP/Getty Images

How can an industry based on traditional craft-based skills expand internationally?

Pearl River in fact exported its very first piano to Hong Kong. Yet, its centre of gravity has remained in China, where pianos have become more affordable with rising income. The one-child policy induced families to invest heavily in their only child's education. As a result, the Chinese now buy half of the pianos produced in the world.

Pearl River succeeded in becoming the top selling brand in China. This may sound like an attractive market position. Yet, rising demand has attracted numerous new entrants, many of which compete at the low end in China. More than 140 competitors have pushed Pearl River's domestic market share from 70 per cent at its peak a decade ago to about 25 per cent now – although it is still the market leader.

Facing price competition at home, Pearl River sought new opportunities overseas. In North America, it started exporting in the late 1980s by relying on US-based importers. Making its first ever foreign direct investment (FDI), it set up a US-based sales subsidiary, Peal River Piano Group America, Ltd., in California in 1999. Acknowledging the importance of the US market and the limited international experiences of its management team, Pearl River hired an American with long experience in the piano industry, to head the subsidiary. In two years, the greenfield subsidiary succeeded in getting Pearl River pianos into about one-third of the specialized US retail dealers. In ten years, the Pearl River brand became the leader in the low end of the upright piano market in North America. Efforts to penetrate the high end market, however, were still frustrated.

Despite the enviable progress in the USA, the Pearl River brand suffers from all the usual trappings associated with Chinese brands. 'We are very cognizant that our pricing provides a strong incentive to buy', Rich noted in a media interview, 'but $6000 is still a lot of money'. In an audacious move to overcome buyers' reservation about purchasing a high-end Chinese product, Pearl River made a second strategic FDI move in 2000, by acquiring the brand Ritmüller. Founded in 1795, Ritmüller had manufactured pianos in Göttingen, Germany, for over one hundred years, yet the factory had closed during the recession of the late 1920s. The brand continued to be appreciated among connoisseurs of antique pianos, and thus helped Pearl River to position itself within the European piano-making tradition, and to move up-market. A new office, opened in Munich in 2004, focuses on design, research and development. A newly designed product line aims to signal commitment to a classic heritage and standard of excellence. Moreover, Pearl River commissioned international master piano designer Lothar Thomma to integrate German craftsmanship with the latest manufacturing technology. Pearl River executives as well as branding experts and media gurus debate whether the company should invest solely on building up the Pearl River brand or to inject major resources into reviving the Ritmüller brand.

While Pearl River is aggressively entering markets around the globe, using a combination of exports, greenfield investments and acquisitions, competitors are facing the pressure. Several smaller European piano makers had to close down; others were acquired by investors from Japan or Korea. The largest German manufacturer, Schimmel, went through insolvency procedures during the 2009 recession, and survived by a whisker. However, European brands remain popular, allowing craftsmanship driven businesses to occupy the premium segment worldwide. Even family business Grotrian-Steinweg pianos is setting up in China targeting the professional market: Their new agent invested €75 000 in English antiques to create an ambience of tradition and luxury for customers in Beijing who consider spending a small fortune for special sound and prestige of a piano handmade in Germany.

Sources: (1) W. Ding, 2009, The return of the king, *Beijing Review*, May 21; (2) Funding Universe, 2009, Guangzhou Pearl River Piano Group Ltd., www.fundinguniverse.com; (3) Y. Lu, 2009, Pearl River Piano Group's international strategy, in M.W. Peng, *Global Strategy*, 2nd ed. (pp. 437–440), Cincinnati: South-Western Cengage Learning; (4) Pearl River Piano Group, 2009, www.pearlriverpiano.com; (5) D. Behrendt, 2009, Tradition gibt den Ton an, *Hannoversche Allgemeine Zeitung*, March 4; (6) A. Reimann, 2009, Klavierhersteller Schimmel is insolvent, *Handelsblatt*, August 4; (7) Stadtarchiv Göttingen, no date, *Stationen der Stadtgeschichte*, www.stadtarchiv.goettingen.de.

How do numerous companies such as Pearl River enter foreign markets? Why did they start their ambitious international growth in Hong Kong and later the USA, before entering Europe? Why did Pearl River establish a greenfield operation in the USA, but acquired a business in Germany? What are the advantages of building your own brand, and when is a combination with an acquired brand appropriate?

Figure 12.1 The building blocks of an entry strategy

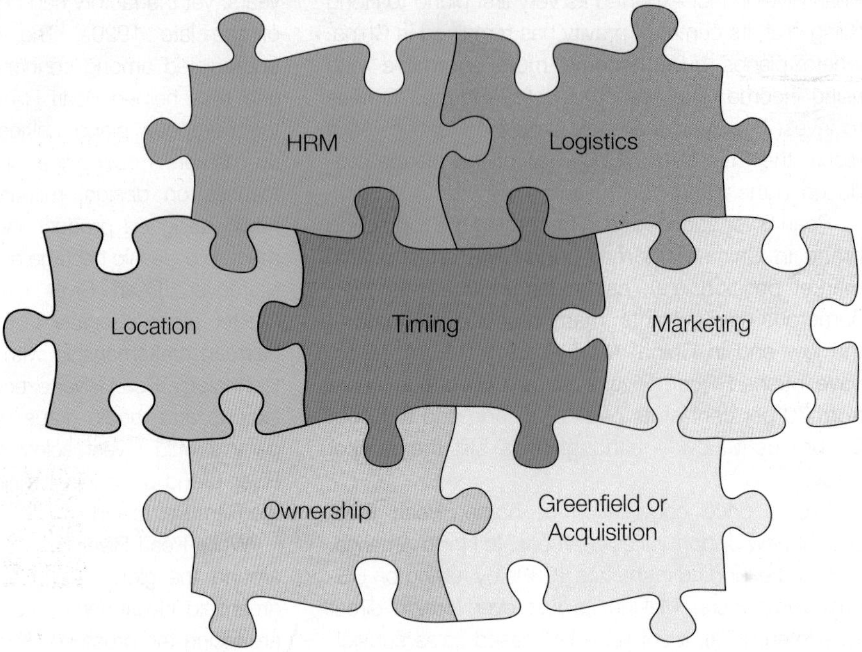

Foreign subsidiaries
Operations abroad set up by
foreign direct investment.

These are some of the key questions in this chapter. Recall from Chapter 6 that multinational enterprises (MNEs) engage in foreign direct investment (FDI) by establishing subsidiaries abroad. The establishment of foreign subsidiaries is a key strategic decision for MNEs expanding their global operations and entering foreign markets. Preparing such an investment, MNEs need to design an entry strategy that specifies their objectives and how they intend to achieve these objectives. In particular, the entry strategy has to match the needs and resources of the MNE with the opportunities and constraints in the specific local environment.

Entry strategy
A plan that specifies the
objectives of an entry and
how to achieve them.

This chapter provides you with an analytical framework to analyze how MNEs can best enter foreign countries. We approach foreign entry in this chapter from the perspective of mature firms with sufficient resources to establish their own subsidiaries. This complements Chapter 11, which focused on smaller firms and non-equity modes. We start with a review of the objectives that motivate firms to establish subsidiaries abroad. Foreign entry requires several strategic decisions, including location, timing, entry mode, marketing, human resources and logistics.[1] Most textbooks focus on the entry mode decision: exports, contracts, joint ventures or wholly owned subsidiaries? However, this choice of entry mode is interdependent with other aspects of the entry strategy. Our framework of foreign entry strategies integrates these various aspects. When designing an entry strategy, MNEs generally have to consider them together, ensuring a good fit between the different elements of the strategy – like the pieces of a jigsaw puzzle (Figure 12.1).

STRATEGIC OBJECTIVES
OF ESTABLISHING FOREIGN SUBSIDIARIES

LEARNING OBJECTIVE

1 Explain why MNEs
establish subsidiaries
abroad (*why* to enter)

If you want to advise a company on how to set-up an operation overseas (a very common topic for BA and MSc dissertations), then the first question you should ask the company is 'what *exactly* do you want to achieve?' MNEs establish foreign subsidiaries for a variety of reasons, and each operation contributes to the global MNE in a different way. Hence, every entry decision has to be considered in relation to the overall strategy of the MNE, and make best use of both the local context and the global resources of the MNE. There are four common objectives for establishing subsidiaries abroad and thus to engage in FDI:[2]

- Firms interested in natural resource seeking aim to access particular resources such as minerals, oil or renewable resources including timber or agricultural produce that they need in their production processes. Their main questions thus are, where do we find these resources, and how can we best secure access to them?

- Market seeking firms aim to sell their products or services to new customers. They would identify the relevant market and then seek a central location for sales, marketing and distribution operations. In some industries, also the actual production needs to be located close to the customer or the point of consumption, notably in service industries such as hotels and financial services, and for manufactured goods that face high transportations costs. Hence, market-seeking investors ask, where are our potential future customers, and what do we have to do to reach them better than our competitors do?

- Efficiency seeking firms aim to reduce their overall costs of production. They often single out the most efficient locations featuring a combination of low-cost inputs – especially labour force, economies of scale and good transportation linkages. There main questions is, how can we lower the costs of our production and the delivery of products and service to customers? For example, Indian IT company Tata Consultancy Services set up operations in Hungary because Hungary offered the best combination of labour costs and proximity to European clients.

- Innovation seeking firms aim to access new ideas and technologies that help them stay in touch with latest developments in their industry, and to accelerate their own innovations. Such entries aim to access innovation potential in the host country, and thus to generate knowledge that may help the entire MNE to advance its organizational learning and growth.[3] Innovation-seekers thus ask, where are the latest technologies and ideas, and how can we link them with our own innovation activities?

Natural resource seeking Firms' quest to pursue natural resources in certain locations.

Market seeking Firms' quest to go after countries that offer strong demand for their products and services.

Efficiency seeking Firms' quest to single out the most efficient locations featuring a combination of scale economies and low-cost factors.

Innovation seeking Firms target countries and regions renowned for generating world-class innovations.

These four strategic goals, while analytically distinct, are not mutually exclusive. Thus, investors may pursue several objectives when establishing a particular subsidiary. However, it is important to have a fairly clear idea of *what* you want to achieve, before you consider *how* to achieve it – in designing foreign entry strategies as well as in life in general. For example, a natural resource-seeker needs to specify the resources sought, and a market-seeker needs to identify the target customers. Having established the objectives of a foreign entry, we can proceed to discuss entry strategies, starting with location decisions.

WHERE TO ENTER?

Like real estate, the motto for international business is 'Location, location, location'. In fact, such a *spatial* perspective (that is, geography beyond one's home country) is a defining feature of international business.[4] Location decisions involve (at least) two levels, first the country and second the site. The considerations for

LEARNING OBJECTIVE

2 Identify relevant location-specific advantages that attract foreign investors (*where* to enter)

Location-specific advantages
Advantages that can be exploited by those present at a location.

these between-country and within-country location decisions tend to be similar. Favourable locations in certain countries may give firms operating there access to location-specific advantages, that is advantages that can be exploited by those present at a location. We may regard the continuous expansion of international business as a continuous search for locational advantages. As we discussed in Chapter 6, locational advantages relate in particular to markets, resource endowments, agglomeration, and institutions. Prospective foreign investors access the locational advantages of possible host countries and – critically – match them with their own needs. Thus, the weighting of different locational advantages varies for firms with different objectives (Table 12.1).

The quality and costs of local resources are a prime concern of natural resource and efficiency seeking investors. Their key decision parameters are the specific local resources that they require for their operations. For example, oil majors seek accessible oil deposits, software developers seek trained software engineers, and manufacturers seek reliable workers and suppliers of intermediate goods. Some of these resources are available only at a limited number of locations, which takes certain industries to far off locations, such as oil exploration in the Middle East, Russia, and Venezuela.

The costs and productivity of the local labour force is a prime consideration for efficiency seeking investors. Numerous MNEs have entered China with efficiency seeking motives. China now manufactures two-thirds of the world's photocopiers, shoes, toys, and microwave ovens; half of its DVD players, digital cameras, and textiles; and one-third of its desktop computers.[5] Shanghai alone reportedly hosts over 300 of the *Fortune* Global 500 firms. It is important to note that mainland China does not present the absolutely lowest labour costs in the world, and Shanghai is the *highest* cost city in China. However, its attractiveness lies in its ability to enhance foreign entrants' efficiency by lowering *total* costs. Total costs arise from the combination of costs of labour and the productivity of costs – plus costs of other inputs, and the costs of bring goods to market. Since the key efficiency concern is lowest total costs, it is also not surprising that some nominally 'high-cost' countries (such as the USA) continue to attract significant FDI. For instance, Grupo

Table 12.1 Matching strategic goals with locations

Strategic goals	Location-specific advantages	Illustrative locations mentioned in the text
Natural resource seeking	Quality and costs of natural resources	Oil exploration in the Middle East, Russia, and Venezuela
Market seeking	Strong market demand and customers willing to pay	Marketing and sales of consumer goods anywhere in the world
Efficiency seeking	Economies of scale, abundance of low-cost labour force and suppliers, transport and communication infrastructure	Manufacturing in Guandong, China; Logistics in Rotterdam, Vienna and Miami
Innovation seeking	Innovative individuals, firms and universities, industry agglomeration	Chinese acquisitions of technologies and brands in Germany; Bio-tech firms in Cambridge and Copenhagen; IT in Silicon Valley and Bangalore

organization. A greenfield option thus is preferred in particular by MNEs with competitive advantages grounded in the firm's organizational structure and culture. For example, Japanese car manufacturers have set up their UK plants as greenfield investments because this allows transfer of the work practices that are central for their competitive advantage.[19] In particular, they allow selecting and training suitable people rather than working with a workforce used to a different culture. Second, a greenfield WOS gives an MNE complete equity and management control. This, eliminates the headaches associated with JVs and providing better protection of proprietary technology, and allows for centrally coordinated global actions. Third, greenfield investments may be designed to be small initially, and to grow with the market development (especially for sales units), thus limiting the up-front capital commitment.

In terms of drawbacks, a greenfield WOS tends to add new capacity to an industry, which will make a competitive industry more crowded, and thus increases the intensity of competition (Chapter 13) – think of the Japanese automobile transplants built in the UK, like Nissan in Sunderland and Honda in Swindon. Finally, greenfield operations, relative to acquisitions, suffer from a slow entry speed because it normally takes two or more years to plan and build a new plant and new distribution channels. In terms of risk, greenfield investments reduce the risk of failure due to conflict between the JV partners or with employees in an acquired firm. However, it usually takes quite some time to build a greenfield plant, which means pay-back periods are likely to be long, and investment risks are high.

The second way to establish a WOS is through the acquisition of a local business.[20] An acquisition provides local organizationally embedded resources, such as human capital and networks with local authorities. Acquisitions are probably the most important mode in terms of the amount of capital involved, representing approximately 70 per cent of worldwide FDI flows. In addition to sharing many benefits of greenfield WOS, acquisitions enjoy two other advantages, namely, (1) adding no new capacity to the industry and (2) faster entry speed. Foreign entry by full acquisition is particularly feasible when another foreign investor is withdrawing from the market. For example, Cadbury acquired Wedel in Poland from PepsiCo when PepsiCo decided to focus on its core business in fizzy drinks and to divest confectionary businesses (see In Focus 12.3). As another example, Behr, a German manufacturer of automotive air conditioning and engine cooling systems, acquired its South African operation in 1993 from a US firm, Federal Mogul, who wanted to divest from this sub-segment of automotive supplier industry. This acquisition allowed Behr to strengthen its position as supplier to its key customers VW, Mercedes and BMW, who had recently upgraded their South African manufacturing plants.[21] Full ownership was desirable for Behr because it needed to integrate the new operations with its existing operations, and it was feasible because a facility of high technological standard was for sale at that time.

Acquisition
Take over of another business.

In terms of drawbacks, acquisitions are most likely to attract political resistance from both individuals working in the plant, and from nationalistic sentiments – especially if high profile companies are involved. In addition, acquisitions have to confront a different and potentially devastating disadvantage – the restructuring and integration of the acquired business (see Chapter 14). The restructuring challenges are particularly acute when acquiring firms that were previously run very inefficiently, such as state-owned enterprises in transition economies. Restructuring challenges are considerably easier when acquiring a business formerly owned by another foreign investor, such as the Cadbury and Behr examples above. In terms of risks, acquisitions present a high investment risks because of the high capital commitment required up front, and the chance of the integration process going wrong.

IN FOCUS 12.2

Joint venture ZF Kama in Russia

By Irina Jormanainen, Helsinki School of Economics

In 2005, ZF Friedrichshafen AG (ZF), a German automotive industry supplier, and Kamaz Corporation, a Russia commercial vehicle manufacturer, set up a joint venture 'ZF Kama' to produce commercial vehicle transmissions in Russia. The partners combined their resources to pursue complementary objectives, access to new markets and access to advanced technology.

ZF is one of the world's leading suppliers of driveline and chassis technology with an annual turnover of €12.5 billion, over 61 000 employees and 125 production sites worldwide (of which 31 are in Germany). The JV in Russia was an important step towards building a strong market position in the Russian market, where ZF was not yet present with a production operation. The cooperation with Kamaz was expected to help this objective by creating an association with a highly respected truck manufacturer and its extensive dealer network in Russia. In addition, the technological and managerial capabilities of Kamaz were significant criteria

for the choice of partner. The Russian JV generated an increase in demand for parts produced in ZF plants in Western Europe, and thus contributed to the growth and viability of these established business units.

Kamaz Corporation is one the largest automobile corporations in the Russian Federation with about 59 000 employees. It operates an integrated production complex that incorporates the whole technological cycle of truck production from development, production of components, assembly of vehicles, to the marketing of vehicles and after sales services. Kamaz produces a wide range of trucks, trailers, buses, tractors, engines, power units and a variety of machine tools, and operates the largest automotive distribution and service network in Russia and the former Soviet Union. The JV was an important element of the development strategy of Kamaz. The overall objective was to access advanced technologies of ZF, and to ensure the supply of high quality auto components. Hence, the primary criterion for the choice of JV partner was the possession of product technology. Moreover, a track record of sincere cooperation

© RIA Novosti/Alamy

What is the best way to build a manufacturing joint venture in Russia?

initiatives and a willingness to share risks were also important arguments for partnering with ZF.

ZF Kama was founded in 2005 to manufacture commercial vehicle transmissions. This was the first production facility established at Kamaz jointly with a foreign firm, and producing under its trade mark. The JV's production facilities are located within industrial site of Kamaz in the city of Naberezhnye Chelny in Tatarstan. ZF holds 51 per cent of the equity of the JV, while Kamaz holds the remaining 49 per cent. Both partners actively participate in the management of the JV, and they both have representatives in the management team. The Russian parent company, Kamaz, contributes a great deal of assistance in managing the various business relationships such as customers, suppliers and government authorities. Also, day to day

operations of the JV are mainly the responsibility of Kamaz. ZF contributes primarily through product technology and expertise. The main customer of the JV is Kamaz itself. A small numbers of products are also sold to other truck, bus and agricultural equipment manufacturers in Russia, Belarus and the Ukraine.

Both parent companies are quite satisfied with the JV's operations and aim to extend the scope and scale of its activity. Following the successful establishment of ZF Kama, Kamaz entered further JVs with automotive suppliers Cummins and Federal Mogul (both from the USA) and Knorr Bremse (Germany).

Source: This In Focus was prepared by Irina Jormanainen (Helsinki School of Economics) based on interviews with the companies. Copyright © Irina Jormanainen.

The control dimension

A joint venture (JV) is a 'corporate child' that is a new entity jointly owned by two or more parent companies.[22] It has three principal forms: minority JV (the focal firm holds less than 50 per cent equity), 50/50 JV, and majority JV (more than 50 per cent equity). A JV with a local partner has three advantages. First, an MNE shares costs, risks, and profits with a local partner thus limiting the financial risk of the investment. Second, the MNE gains access to knowledge about the host country, and the local firm, in turn, benefits from the MNE's technology, capital, and management. Third, JVs may be politically more acceptable.[23]

Joint venture (JV)
A new corporate entity given birth and jointly owned by two or more parent companies.

In terms of disadvantages, first, JVs often involve partners from different backgrounds and goals; conflicts are natural. Second, effective equity and operational control may be difficult to achieve because everything has to be negotiated (and in some cases, fought over). Finally, the nature of the JV does not give an MNE the tight control over a foreign subsidiary that it may need for global coordination (such as simultaneously launching new products around the world). In terms of risks, JVs reduce the investment risks because less capital is committed. However, JVs are highly exposed to internal risks such as conflicts between the parent firms, and they constrain the investors' ability to change its strategy. Hence, the risk of not reacting sufficiently flexible to changing internal or external circumstances is high.

JVs thus are appropriate in special situations, namely when three conditions are met: (a) the new business unit depends on resource contributions from two or more firms, (b) the transfer of these resources or the expected benefits for the investors is subject to high transaction costs, and (c) it is not feasible for the entire parent firms to be integrated into one firm, for instance because they are big relative to the envisaged project, or one of them is a state-owned enterprise.[24] In other words, JVs are common where two firms are trying to achieve something that neither could do on its own, and where the outcomes are highly uncertain. An area where JVs are common is entries into emerging economies: MNEs that lack local knowledge of their target markets may best obtain such knowledge access by collaborating with a local firm (In Focus 12.2). JVs thus provide an avenue to operate in unfamiliar contexts, especially in countries with weak market supporting institutions, such

IN FOCUS 12.3

Relocating and growing: Cadbury invests in Poland

In 1991, an equity stake of 40 per cent in Poland's leading chocolate manufacturer Wedel was auctioned off by the Polish privatization agency. Cadbury, Britain's leading manufacturer of confectionary, submitted a bid for this iconic Polish brand, yet American PepsiCo outbid their British competitors and took control of Wedel. With no attractive acquisition opportunities available, Cadbury entered Poland in 1993 by building a greenfield plant near Wrocław in the southwest of the country. It introduced its world-famous brands, which were hardly known in Poland at the time. Cadbury's market share grew, but from a very low basis.

In 1998, the opportunity arose to acquire Wedel. After the acquisition in 1991, PepsiCo had restructured Wedel, introduced new production technologies and turned it into a very profitable operation. Yet, PepsiCo is a drinks business and not a chocolatier, so a worldwide refocusing on its core lines of business created an opportunity for Cadbury to take over Wedel. However, Wedel's share price had risen more than

tenfold under PepsiCo's management, making the purchase price much more expensive. When PepsiCo sold Wedel to Cadbury in 1998, PepsiCo's shareholders made a good profit, and Cadbury could restart its entry strategy in Poland.

Cadbury developed its brand portfolio with a strong emphasis on the local brand, with its own Cadbury brand only positioned in a niche market. The joint company had sales of €55 million, employed about 110 people and commanded a market share of 28 per cent. Cadbury integrated the two operations with a strong focus on the Wedel brand. The Cadbury brand was positioned in the premium segment, but not as well recognized as competitors like Lindt, and too expensive for Polish consumers. Cadbury thus heavily invested in further strengthening the Wedel brand while partially withdrawing Cadbury-branded products. The merged company grew: by the end of 2003 about 1250 people were working for Cadbury in Poland. Production was expanded in Wrocław where Cadbury had its modern production facility, and labour costs were lower – some production employees from Warsaw were moved or had to be laid off. In Wedel's old headquarters in Warsaw, Cadbury concentrated in

© Caro/Alamy

How could Cadbury build a worldwide chocolate with production facilities in, for example, Poland?

administrative and marketing activities, thus the number of white-collar workers in Wrocław was reduced.

In 2007, Cadbury announced a major shift in its global strategy that involved spinning off its drinks business (Dr Pepper), strengthening the confectionary business with the aim for the top place worldwide, and stronger focus on shareholder value. This revised strategy included heavy investment and expansion of the Polish operations. The historical chocolate factory in Warsaw was modernized and expanded for €15 million; the plant near Wrocław was expanded to the tune of €200 million, while construction started for a new facility near Skarbimierz. The Polish Information and Foreign Investment Agency recognized Cadbury with the accolade of 'Most Significant Investor in Poland' in 2008. Cadbury is appreciated not only for creating employment, but for its friendly work environment fostering teamwork, and for its social initiatives. The Wedel brand continues to be one of the most

esteemed Polish brands, and it started to appear in supermarkets in Western Europe, eagerly awaited by the growing Polish Diaspora.

Meanwhile, Cadbury announced in 2007 that it would rationalize its four plants in the UK to lower costs. This would lead to a reduction of the workforce by 700, most of which in Keynesham, near Bath, where the local plant was to close entirely in 2010. Trade Unions launched a high profile campaign against 'moving jobs to Poland', but they could not convince the Cadbury board to change its mind. The decision remained unchanged when Kraft took over Cadbury after a hostile take-over battle in early 2010.

Sources: (1) P. Kulawczuk, 2007, Purchase of national brand no. 1 to rescue entry strategy, in: K.E. Meyer & S. Estrin, eds, Acquisition Strategies in European Emerging Markets, Basingstoke: Palgrave; (2) *BBC News*, 2007, Cadbury factories shed 700 jobs, October 3, (3) www.cadbury.pl, (4) www.paiz.pl.

as China or Russia. JVs are also used, for example, when two multinationals want to jointly conduct research and development, or merge a particular business unit (see Chapter 14).

In consequence of their operational disadvantages, many JVs operate only for a limited lifetime. Some JVs are designed for a specific purpose, and discontinued once this purpose has been achieved. Other JVs have no explicit termination agreement, but they are subject to conflicts between its parents and shifting interests and bargaining positions. Thus, ownership stakes may change, and most JVs are eventually dissolved.[25] Only a few JVs, such as Fuji-Xerox, defy the trend and successfully operate for several decades.

Shared control can also be established by an acquisition of an equity stake but not full ownership. Such partial acquisitions occur in particular (1) if a seller is unwilling to sell the business in full or if (2) the previous owners are still needed to run the operation. For example, privatization agencies in Central and Eastern Europe in the 1990s often sold only a small equity stake, and kept the remainder or gave it to domestic investors.[26] France Telecom acquired an equity stake of 35 per cent Polish Telecom in 2000, with local investors and the Polish Treasury holding the remainder. The company needed major improvements in efficiency as standards of telephone and internet communications were lagging. For example, Polish Telecom employed far more people per customer than other European telecom service providers. This restructuring led to tough negotiations with trade unions that resisted layoff and outsourcing of jobs until generous redundancy payments had been agreed.[27]

Partial acquisitions are also common for MNEs buying out entrepreneurial firms: If the entrepreneurs retain an ownership stake, they are probably more motivated to continue to pull their weight for the company. The advantage of partial acquisitions is to provide access to a firm that otherwise would be 'not for sale', while limiting the capital commitment. The main disadvantage of partial acquisition is that acquirers may have to implement organizational change without full equity control, and thus without the power to enforce changes in structures or processes.

Partial acquisition
Acquisition of an equity stake in another firm.

In terms of risks, partial acquisitions face less investment risks because the initial capital investment is limited, and it is often easier to sell again than a stake in a custom-designed JV. However, the risks arising from the integration process and potential conflict with co-owners are likely to be higher than in JVs.

JVs and partial acquisitions are special cases of strategic alliances, that is collaborations between independent firms using equity modes, non-equity contractual agreements, or both. However, the term strategic alliance is very broad. Understanding the relationship between two firms normally requires a more detailed specification of contributions, control, and risk sharing arrangements. Therefore, we prefer to use more specific terms to describe the nature of a relationship between two firms.

Strategic alliances Collaborations between independent firms using equity modes, non-equity contractual agreements, or both.

HOW TO ORGANIZE YOUR OPERATIONS?

LEARNING OBJECTIVE

5 Explain the interdependence of operations and entry strategies

It is tempting to make entry decisions one aspect at a time, and thus move step by step from one section in this chapter to the next. However, different the aspects are interdependent. Even specific operational questions can have an impact on firms' location, timing and entry mode. The resource-based view suggests three reasons why that may be so. First, the planned local operations require resources that the parent controls; second, the global operation requires resources controlled by the subsidiary (for example resources acquired from a local firm), and third the global competences of the MNE depend on a tight coordination and integration of its constituent parts, including foreign subsidiaries. These considerations imply that the management of resources and capabilities is central to entry strategies. They may reside in functional areas, notably (1) marketing, (2) human resources and (3) logistics may be central to entry strategy design.

First, a key issue in marketing is global standardization versus local adaptation of products, processes and brands (see Chapter 17).[28] Advantages of standardization across the operations of the MNE include economies of scale in the exploitation of capabilities of the global firm, including product development, production and marketing. In contrast, local adaptation strategies aim to accommodate local needs and preferences. They normally require the creation or acquisition of local resources such as mass market brands. This is common for instance in food and beverage industries. The Polish brewing industry is dominated by three global players: Heineken, SABMiller and Carlsberg. Yet, most Polish pub revellers probably don't know this. The leading brands in Poland are Tyskie, Zywiec and Okocim, all of which are local brands owned by one of the big three.[29] These brewing MNEs pursue multi-tier strategies that combine international premium brands with local brands aimed at the mass market – all acquired by taking over local breweries. The importance of local brands, however, implied that first mover advantages and the acquisition of local brands were important, which put constraints on other aspects of entry strategy.

Second, human resources are critical to foreign entry because each subsidiary needs qualified and motivated people, especially to facilitate knowledge sharing within an organization (see Chapter 16). This involves both the transfer of organizational practices to the new operation, and the tapping of headquarters into local knowledge. Foreign investors thus have to send expatriate managers, while recruiting, training and motivating local staff. Expatriates play a pivotal role in managing subsidiaries, as do locally recruited people who can liaise with other units of the MNE. Firms with a pool of experienced managers that can be posted overseas to lead a new operation without a local JV partner. On the other hand, firms without locally knowledgeable people are more likely to need contributions from a local JV partner.

Third, logistics is an important aspect of a foreign entry strategy because lower labour costs are only valuable for a business, if the products can be transported to the customer in good time at acceptable costs (see Chapter 17). Likewise, serving a local market is only feasible if you can get your products to the customer in good condition at acceptable costs. Effective supply chain management practices thus are crucial capabilities for companies aiming to exploit synergies between operations around the globe. For example, modern transportation and communication systems enable MNEs to optimize the integration of their internal operations as well as supplier relations. A foreign entry often triggers changes in these systems. In particular, the choice of location for production sites is interdependent with the choice of logistics systems.

INSTITUTIONS AND FOREIGN ENTRY STRATEGIES

Foreign entry strategies are often constrained by the institutional environment in the host economy. Institutions may (1) prohibit certain types of operations or transactions, (2) create a need for local knowledge, (3) change the relative (transaction) costs of alternative strategies, or (4) motivate tariff-jumping FDI. Table 12.4 illustrates the possible impact of such constraints on entry mode and location decisions.

First, some governments discourage or ban wholly-owned subsidiaries (WOSs), thereby leaving JVs with local firms as the only entry choice.[30] For example, the

> **LEARNING OBJECTIVE**
>
> **6** Apply the institution-based view to explain constraints on foreign entry strategies

Table 12.4 Institutional constraints on foreign entry

Types of Constraints	Impact of Entry Mode (examples)	Impact on Location (examples)
Certain operations of transactions are not permitted	• Establish JVs where WOSs are not permitted	• Locate where planning permissions are easier to obtain
Need for local knowledge	• Establish JVs to access local knowledge	• Locate in agglomerations of foreign investors that help attaining local knowledge
Higher transaction costs due to costly contract enforcement	• Avoid complex arm's-length contracts with unfamiliar partners	• Locate in areas where local uncertainty is lower
Higher transaction costs due to lack of financial intermediaries	• Avoid full or partial acquisitions of local firms	–
Higher tariffs or other trade barriers	–	• Locate production in the target market (see In Focus 12.1 'Ford Vietnam')

Indian government dictates the maximum ceiling of foreign firms' equity position in the retail sector to be 51 per cent, forcing foreign entrants to set up alliances such as JVs with local firms. The Indian retail market is an attractive target for multinational retailers as it is still highly fragmented. Yet, foreign investors have to accept the ownership constraint. Thus, in 2009 American Wal-Mart formed a 50/50 JV with Bharti Retail with the goal of setting up wholesale cash-and-carry stores throughout India. French Carrefour negotiated a similar deal with the Future Group of Indian magnate Kishore Biyani, combined with a wholly-owned wholesale operation as foreign ownership in wholesale trade is not restricted.[31] Legal restrictions such as the building code also affect where hypermarkets are opened. Supposedly, the inability to obtain planning for new stores has been a major reason for the withdrawal of Wal-Mart from Germany.[32]

Recently, there is a general trend towards less restrictive policies as many governments (such as those in Mexico and South Korea) that historically only approved JVs now allow WOSs. As a result, there has been a noticeable decline of JVs and a corresponding rise of acquisitions in emerging economies.[33] However, despite the general movement toward more liberal policies, many governments still impose considerable requirements, especially when foreign firms acquire domestic assets. For example, only shared ownership is permitted in industries considered strategic, such as automobile assembly in China and the oil industry in Russia. US regulations only permit up to 25 per cent of the equity of any US airline to be held by foreign carriers, and EU regulations limit non-EU ownership to 49 per cent of EU-based airlines.

Second, the institutional environment in many emerging economies is characterized by idiosyncratic rules and extensive use of networks. Such institutions, often characterized as 'weak institutions' by Western investors, create a need for local knowledge, local network relationships and other tacit resources held by local firms. For example, even after the legal restrictions have been removed, many foreign entrants use JVs to enter countries like China and Vietnam because they lack the necessary local knowledge and contacts. Hence, foreign entrants are likely to see a greater need to cooperate with local partners, for instance by establishing a JV. An alternative route to access local knowledge is to locate near other foreign investors, and to participate in the knowledge exchange within informal 'expatriate networks'.

Third, 'weak institutions' also increase transaction costs such as search costs arising from information asymmetries, and contract enforcement costs associated with inefficient legal systems. This implies that businesses are to a larger extent based on relationships rather than arm's-length transactions. Licensing or franchising contracts with a stranger thus would be costly. Moreover, acquisitions are costly where financial market institutions are underdeveloped, for instance due to the lack of reliable accounting and auditing information and non-existence of intermediaries such as financial advisors and consultants.[34] Foreign investors may thus avoid complex arm's-length relationships and may locate in advanced regions where legal uncertainties have been reduced.

Fourth, institutions inhibiting international trade may in some circumstances actually increase foreign entry with local production facilities. For example, local production allows entrants to overcome tariffs and non-tariffs barriers that inhibit serving a market through an export strategy. For example, Ford is operating a production facility in Vietnam at well below it efficient scale; yet it is important to gain access to the Vietnamese market (In Focus 12.1). Another institution that may attract foreign investors is local content requirements that may induce manufacturers to ask their suppliers to set up a local operation.

DEBATES AND EXTENSIONS

This chapter has already covered some crucial debates, such as first- versus late-mover advantages. Here we discuss two *recent* debates: (1) the scale of entry, and (2) dynamics of acquisitions.

Scale of entry: commitment and experience

Small firms facing resource constraints typically enter with a small operation that they gradually expand, as suggested by the internationalization process model (Chapter 11). However, resource-rich companies face a strategic choice between entering with a large up-font investment, or with a small foothold operation. In some highly competitive industries, heavy up-front investment is required to prevent retaliation from incumbents or to realize first-mover advantages, as for branded consumer goods. A number of European financial services firms, such as HSBC, and ING Group, have spent several billion dollars to enter the USA by making a series of acquisitions. The benefits of these large-scale entries demonstrate strategic commitment to certain markets. This both helps assure local customers and suppliers ('We are here for the long haul!') and deters potential entrants. The drawbacks of such hard-to-reverse strategic commitment are (1) limited strategic flexibility elsewhere and (2) huge losses if these large-scale 'bets' turn out wrong. Moreover, in some capital-intensive industries, for instance oil exploration, only large scale operations are economically viable.

On the other hand, small scale entry reduces the costs and risks of entry. They focus on organizational learning by getting firms' feet 'wet' – learning by doing – while limiting the downside risk.[35] Such platform investment provides investors with a small foothold from where to observe the local industry and to flexibly react to business opportunities if and when they emerge.[36] For example, to enter the market of Islamic finance in which no interest can be charged (per teaching of the Koran), Citibank set up a subsidiary Citibank Islamic Bank, HSBC established Amanah, and UBS launched Noriba. They were designed to experiment with different interpretations of the Koran on how to make money while not committing religious sins. This capability cannot be acquired outside the Islamic world; it needs to be developed locally. Such development of new capabilities internally takes time. The main drawback of small-scale entries is a lack of strong commitment, which may lead to difficulties in building market share and capturing first-mover advantages.

Acquisition dynamics

Recall from Chapter 11 that internationalizing firms can use a range of different strategies to build resources specific to contexts they want to enter (Table 11.2). The acquisition of a local firm can greatly accelerate this process. However, a single acquisition is often insufficient to create the operation that the foreign investor needs to achieve its objectives. Hence, acquisitions are often followed by extensive restructuring and additional investments or divestments.[37] This leads to complex strategies involving acquisitions (Table 12.5).

Sometimes the subsequent investment completely overlays the acquired organization, we then talk of a brownfield acquisition.[38] In these cases, the foreign investor may be interested only in a particular asset, such as an operating license, a distribution outlet, or a brand name. Yet, often this asset is not 'for sale' on its own, and can only be accessed by taking over the entire company. For example, cosmetics company Beiersdorf of Germany acquired Pollonia-Lechia in Poland, which owned

LEARNING OBJECTIVE

7 Participate in leading debates on foreign entry strategies

Scale of entry
The amount of resources committed to foreign market entry.

Brownfield acquisition
Acquisition where subsequent investment overlays the acquired organization.

Table 12.5 Types of acquisitions

Types	Purpose (example)	Risks
Conventional acquisition	• Take over a company that has complementary resources and capabilities	• Not overpaying • Post acquisition integration
Brownfield acquisition	• Obtain specific asset controlled by another firm, but upgrade it to fit the global operation	• Very high capital investment • Complex post-acquisition upgrading and integration
Multiple acquisitions	• Build a strong market share in a previously highly fragmented market	• Very high capital investment • Integration of multiple local units, as well as integrating them with the global operation
Staged acquisition	• Take over a firm whose sellers are unwilling to let go, or where their continued commitment is important	• Integration process with initially limited control • Uncertainty over long-term ownership structure

the rights to the Nivea brand in Poland yet had few other assets of interest. Beiersdorf added a new, parallel organizational structure to market the Nivea brand on Western standards, but operated largely independent of the old structures. This set up allowed the restructuring to run smoothly. Once the new operation was up and running, the old structure was closed down.[39]

In other cases, foreign investors may want to build an operation that incorporates several local businesses, especially when the local industry is highly fragmented. Thus, investors may pursue a strategy of multiple acquisitions, that is a strategy based on acquiring and integrating several businesses. A single acquisition may be insufficient to build the kind of operation that the foreign investor aspires, notably economies of scale and a leading market share. The acquisition of smaller firm in a new market may make only sense in the context of a broader strategy that involves further acquisitions. For example, Carlsberg in Poland acquired four different breweries – yet they still ended up in third place behind two competitors that were even more aggressive: Heineken and SABMiller.[40]

We have noted before that some acquisitions only involve the acquisition of an equity stake – partial acquisitions. However, this is rarely a stable arrangement. Often the foreign investor soon increases its equity stake, sometimes based on a preagreed schedule. In such staged acquisitions the ownership transfer takes place over stages: what looks like a shared ownership arrangement to outsiders is actually a way to implement an acquisition. For example, in the case of Skoda Auto, VW initially acquired a minority equity stake but attained management control over the company in 1993. Thus, VW led the restructuring of the company while it still formally was a JV with the Czech state. Only later did VW acquire full ownership and then fully integrated Skoda in its global operations. The advantages of staged acquisitions are, first, reduced political sensitivity, second, less up-front capital needs, and third, continued commitment of the previous owners. The disadvantages and risks are similar to partial acquisitions (Table 12.3).

Multiple acquisitions
A strategy based on acquiring and integrating multiple businesses.

Staged acquisition
Acquisition where ownership transfer takes places over stages.

IMPLICATIONS FOR PRACTICE

LEARNING OBJECTIVE

8 Draw implications for action

Foreign market entries represent a *foundation* for overseas actions. Without these crucial first steps, firms will remain domestic players. The challenges associated with internationalization are complex, and the stakes high. Returning to our fundamental question, we ask: What determines the success and failure in foreign market entries? The answers boil down to the two core perspectives: institution- and resource-based views. Consequently, three implications for action emerge (Table 12.6). First, from an institution-based view, managers need to understand the rules of the game, both formal and informal, governing competition in each of their foreign markets. Entry strategies need to 'fit' these institutions, notably by complying with local regulation and informal norms, as well as by building legitimacy with local interest groups.

Second, from a resource-based view, managers need to bring together the capabilities of their MNE with complementary local resources. Few investors would be able to compete in foreign markets solely based on their existing resources: their liability of outsidership works against them. Different entry strategies allow building or acquiring local capabilities in different ways: A gradual entry with a platform investment would emphasize learning along the lines of the internationalization process models (Chapter 11), a JV would facilitate leaning from the partner, while an acquisition would provided embedded capabilities of the acquired firm. With competition from both local firms and other foreign investors, managing your resources and capabilities is key to succeeding in foreign countries.

Finally, managers need to match the different elements of an entry strategy with their strategic goals. Decisions on one element influence other aspects. If timing and speed of entry are crucial for an investor – for example when pursuing a first-mover advantages – then an acquisition or a JV may offer quick market access. On the other hand, if global integration of marketing, logistics and human resource management, are important, then the existing structures and practices of an acquired firm may pose major obstacles, and a greenfield entry may be more appropriate. Thus, foreign entry decisions have to reflect the complex interdependence of multiple dimensions. Decision-makers may develop alternative scenarios and compare their respective merits, for example an acquisition of a specific firm in the Czech Republic versus a greenfield investment in a specific industrial zone in Poland.

Overall, appropriate foreign market entries, while important, are only a beginning. To succeed overseas, post entry strategies are equally or more important. These would entail managing competitive dynamics (Chapter 13), developing global strategies (Chapter 14), and creating dynamic and efficient operations (Chapter 15 to 17), all of which will be covered in later chapters.

Table 12.6 Implications for action

- Understand the rules of game – both formal and informal – and fit your strategies to the constraints and opportunities of these institutions.
- Bring together the MNEs global capabilities and complementary local resources.
- Match the different elements of an entry strategy with the firm's strategic goals.

CHAPTER SUMMARY

1 Explain why MNEs establish subsidiaries abroad (*why* to enter):

- Firms' strategic goals can be grouped in four categories (1) natural resources, (2) market, (3) efficiency, and (4) innovation.

2 Identify relevant locational advantages that may attract investors (*where* to enter):

- Foreign entrants seek locational advantages that match their strategic objectives.

3 Compare and contrast first- and late-mover advantages (*when* to enter):

- First-movers can attain advantages such as early brand building, yet there are countervailing benefits for fast followers.

4 Compare and contrast alternatives modes of foreign market entry (*how* to enter):

- Entry modes vary by the degree of control that entrants attain over the local operation.
- Entry modes provide access to local resources in different ways.

5 Explain the interdependence of operations and entry strategies:

- entry strategies need to take (1) marketing, (2) human resource, and (3) logistics operations into account.

6 Apply the institution-based view to explain constraints on foreign entry strategies:

- Formal and informal institutions may restrict the options for foreign entry, create needs for local knowledge, and increase transaction costs of certain forms of transaction.

7 Participate in two leading debates on foreign market entries:

- These leading debates are (1) the scale of a foreign entry, (2) and acquisition dynamics.

8 Draw implications for action:

- From an institution-based view, managers need to fit their strategies to the constraints and opportunities of local institutions.
- From a resource-based view, managers need to bring together the MNEs global capabilities and complementary local resources.
- Managers must match the different elements of an entry strategy with the firm's strategic goals.

KEY TERMS

Acquisition	Greenfield operation	Natural resource seeking
Agglomeration	Innovation seeking	Non-equity mode
Brownfield acquisition	Joint venture (JV)	Partial acquisition
Efficiency seeking	Late-mover advantages	Scale of entry
Entry strategy	Location-specific advantages	Staged acquisition
Equity mode	Market seeking	Strategic alliances
First-mover advantages	Modes of entry	Wholly owned subsidiaries (WOS)
Foreign subsidiaries	Multiple acquisition	

CRITICAL DISCUSSION QUESTIONS

1 Since joining the EU, countries like Poland and Hungary have seen an increase of foreign direct investment. Yet, some foreign investors move their operations from these countries to locations further East, complaining about rising labour costs. Use institution-based and resource-based views to explain these changes.

2 From institution- and resource-based views, identify the obstacles confronting MNEs from emerging economies interested in expanding overseas. How can such firms overcome them?

3 In what situations should companies consider sharing control over an operation with a local firm that is directly or indirectly owned by the host country's government?

4 In what situations should branded consumer goods manufacturers consider to forego potential first-mover advantages and delay their entry until after a competitor has entered?

CLOSING CASE

Danone and Wahaha: 'failed' joint ventures

By Sunny Li Sun, University of Texas, and Hao Chen, University of Texas.

In 1996, France's Groupe Danone SA established five joint ventures (JVs) with China's Wahaha Group. Danone owned 51 per cent of each of these JVs and Wahaha and its employees owned the remainder. Founded in 1987, Wahaha has one of the best-known beverage brands in China. By 2006, the total number of JVs between Danone and Wahaha had grown from 5 to 39. A huge financial success for both Danone and Wahaha, their JVs' revenues increased from $100 million in 1996 to $2.25 billion in 2006. These JVs, which cost Danone $170 million, paid Danone a total of $307 million in dividends over the past decade. By 2006, Danone's 39 JV subsidiaries in China, jointly owned and managed by Wahaha, contributed 6 per cent of Danone's total global profits.

In addition to the JVs with Wahaha, Danone also bought stakes in more than seven Chinese food and dairy firms, spending another $170 million (besides what was spent on Wahaha) over the past decade in China. In 2006, Danone became the biggest beverage maker by volume in China, ahead of rivals such as Coca-Cola and PepsiCo. At the same time, Wahaha also pursued aggressive growth in China, some of

which was beyond the scope of the JVs with Danone. By 2006, Wahaha Group managed 70 subsidiaries scattered throughout China. All these subsidiaries use the same brand 'Wahaha', but only 39 of them had JV relationships with Danone.

A major dispute erupted concerning Wahaha's other 31 subsidiaries that had no JV relationships with Danone. In 2006, after profits from the 39 JVs jumped 48 per cent to $386 million, Danone wanted to buy Wahaha's other subsidiaries. This would enable Danone to control the 'Wahaha' brand once and for all. This proposal was rejected by Wahaha's founder Zong Qinghou, who served as chairman of the 39 JVs with Danone. Zong viewed this offer as unreasonable because the book value of the non-JV subsidiaries' assets was $700 million with total profits of $130 million, while the price/earnings ratio of Danone's $500 million offer was lower than four. Zong also asserted that the buyout would jeopardize the existence of the 'Wahaha' brand, because Danone would phase it out and promote global brands such as Danone and Evian.

The heart of the dispute stemmed from the master JV agreement between Danone and Wahaha, which granted the subsidiary JVs exclusive rights to produce, distribute and sell food and beverage products under the 'Wahaha' brand. This meant that every product using the 'Wahaha' brand should be approved by the board of the master JV. Danone thus claimed that the non-JV subsidiaries set up by Zong and his managers were illegally selling products using the 'Wahaha' brand and were making unlawful use of the JVs' distributors and suppliers. However, Zong claimed that the original JV agreement to grant exclusive rights to use the 'Wahaha' brand was never approved by the Chinese trademark office and so was not in force or effect. He further stated that Danone had not made an issue when Wahaha embarked on its expansion and openly used the subsidiary JVs' assets – it seemed that Danone preferred Wahaha to shoulder the risk first. According to Zong, when Wahaha's expansion proved successful, Danone, driven by greed, wanted to reap the fruits. Finally, Zong argued that forcing Wahaha Group to grant the exclusive rights for the 'Wahaha' brand to the JVs with Danone was unfair to Wahaha Group, because Danone was actively investing in other beverage companies around the country and competing with Wahaha. Wahaha pointed out that in human marriage terms, these would be extra-marital affairs.

The board room dispute spilled into the public domain when Zong publicly criticized Danone in April 2007. In response, Danone issued statements and initiated arbitrations against Wahaha in Stockholm, Sweden. Danone also launched a lawsuit against a company owned by Zong's daughter in the United States, alleging that it was using the Wahaha brand illegally. Outraged, Zong resigned from his board

chairman position at all the JVs with Danone. Wahaha's trade union, representing about 10 000 workers of Wahaha Group, sued Danone in late 2007, demanding $1.36 million in damages. This made the dispute worse, and revenues of the JVs only increased 3 per cent in 2007, 17 per cent less than the industry's average growth.

Between 2007 and 2009, both sides spent most of their energy dealing with over 21 lawsuits and arbitrations in several countries, including British Virgin Islands, China, France, Italy, Sweden, and the United States. Even the French president and Chinese minister of commerce called for the two parties to stop lawsuits and to settle. Danone spent $83 million in litigation fees in three years but won no victory. Finally, Danone gave up its 51 per cent share in the JVs and sold it to Wahaha in September 2009. Yet, newspaper reports suggested that it was substantially less than the figure Danone cited in previously published financial accounts as the value of its Wahaha holdings, $555 million.

From an ethical standpoint, we can wonder whether the divorce was caused by opportunism from the start or by 'changed circumstances' as the relationship evolved. Even with the painful divorce, Danone still earned enviable financial returns. A Danone spokesman defended the JV strategy: 'If we now have 30 per cent of our sales in emerging markets and we built this in only ten years, it's thanks to this specific

How can global brand manufacturers like Danone manage their brands when entering a market through a joint venture?

[JV] strategy. We have problems with Wahaha. But we prefer to have problems with Wahaha now to not having had Wahaha at all for the last ten years.' Wanhaha's Zong said in the settlement announcement: 'Chinese companies are willing to cooperate and grow with the world's leading peers on the basis of equality and reciprocal benefit.'

DISCUSSION QUESTIONS

1 Was a series of joint venture the appropriate mode for Danone to enter China? What would have been the alternatives?

2 How would you design a joint-venture contract for an entry in China?

3 How would you suggest Danone should have managed its relationship with Wahaha?

Sources: This case was written by Sunny Li Sun and Hao Chen (both at the University of Texas at Dallas) under the supervision of Professor Mike W. Peng. It was based on (1) *China Daily*, 2007, Chinese drinks giant brands Danone 'despicable' over lawsuit, June 8; (2) finance.sina.com.cn/focus/2007wahaha; (3) M.W. Peng, S.L. Sun, & H. Chen, 2008, Managing divorce: How to disengage from joint ventures and strategic alliances, *Peking University Business Review*, April; (4) *Wall Street Journal*, 2009, Danone pulls out of disputed China venture, October 1.

RECOMMENDED READINGS

J.H. Dunning & S. Lundan, 2008, *Multinational Enterprises and the Global Economy*, 2nd ed., Cheltenham: Elgar – The most comprehensive book reviewing scholarly work on how companies are setting up foreign investment.

J.-F. Hennart, 2009, Down with MNE-centric theories! market entry and expansion as the bundling of MNE and local assets, *JIBS*, 40, 1432–1454 – A conceptual paper that integrates the perspective of a foreign investor with that of local partner firms.

K.E. Meyer & Y.T.T. Tran, 2006, market penetration and acquisition strategies for emerging Economies, *LRP*, 39, 177–197 – A study that illustrates many of the issues discussed in this chapter using the case of Carlsberg.

A. Verbeke, 2009, *International Business Strategy*, Cambridge: Cambridge University Press – A textbook that develops concepts of business strategy out of the economics-based theory of the MNE.

NOTES:

"FOR JOURNAL ABBREVIATION, PLEASE SEE PAGE XXVI-XXVII."

1 K.E. Meyer, 2009, Foreign market entry, in: R.S. Rajan & K.A. Reinert, eds., Princeton *Encyclopedia of the World Economy*, Princeton: Princeton University Press.

2 J.H. Dunning & S. Lundan, 2009, *Multinational enterprises and the global economy*, 2nd ed., Cheltenham: Elgar.

3 M.W. Peng & D.Y.L. Wang, 2000, Innovation capability and foreign direct investment, *MIR*, 40: 79–93. Some authors refer to this category as 'strategic asset seeking', see Dunning and Lundan, 2009, *as above*.

4 R. Belderbos & L. Sleuwaegen, 2005, Competitive drivers and international plant configuration strategies, *SMJ*, 26: 577–593; J.H. Dunning, 1998, Location and the multinational enterprise, *JIBS*, 29: 45–66.

5 Economist Intelligence Unit, 2006, *CEO Briefing* (p. 9), London: EIU.

6 G. Smith, 2003, Mexico: Was NAFTA worth it? (p. 72), *Business Week*, December 22.

7 K.E. Meyer & H.V. Nguyen, 2005, Foreign investment strategies and sub-national institutions in emerging markets: Evidence from Vietnam, *JMS*, 42: 63–93.

8 S. Sohm, B.M. Linke & A. Klossek, 2009, *Chinese Companies in Germany*, Bielefeld: Bertelsmann Foundation.

9 S. Mariotti & L. Piscitello, 1995, Information costs and locations of FDIs within the host country: Empirical evidence from Italy, *JIBS*, 26: 815–841; M.J. Shaver, & F. Flyer, 2000, Agglomeration economics, firm heterogeneity, and foreign direct investment in the

United States, SMJ, 21: 1175–1193; J. Alcacer &
W. Chung, 2007, Location Strategies and Knowledge
Spillovers, MSc, 53: 760–776.

10 M.B. Lieberman & D. Montgomery, 1988, First-mover
advantages, SMJ, 9: 41–58; Y. Luo & M.W. Peng,
1998, First mover advantages in investing in transition
economies, TIBR, 40: 141–163; G. Dowell &
A. Swaminathan, 2006, Entry timing, exploration, and
firm survival, SMJ, 27: 1159–1182; J.G. Frynas,
K. Mellahi & G. Pigman, 2006, First mover advantages
in international business and firm-specific political
resources, SMJ, 27: 321–345.

11 M.W. Peng, S. Lee, & J. Tan, 2001, The keiretsu in
Asia, JIM, 7: 253–276.

12 L. Fuentelsaz, J. Gomez, & Y. Polo, 2002, Followers'
entry timing, SMJ, 23: 245–264; J. Shamsie,
C. Phelps, & J. Kuperman, 2004, Being late than
never, SMJ, 25: 69–84.

13 B. Tan & I. Vertinsky, 1996, Foreign direct investment
by Japanese electronics firms in the United States and
Canada, JIBS, 27: 655–681; T. Isobe, S. Makino, &
D. Montgomery, 2000, Resource commitment, entry
timing, and market performance of foreign direct
investments in emerging economies, AMJ, 43:
468–484; V. Gaba, Y. Pan, & G. Ungson, 2002, Timing
of entry in international market, JIBS, 33: 39–55.

14 M.W. Peng, 2000, Controlling the foreign agent, MIR,
40: 141–165; F. Suarez & G. Lanzolla, 2007, The role
of environmental dynamics in building a first mover
advantage theory, AMR, 32: 377–392.

15 J.F. Hennart, 1982, The Multinational Enterprise, Ann
Arbor: University of Michigan Press. M.C. Casson,
1987, The Firm and the Market, Cambridge, MA: MIT
Press; P.J. Buckley &
M.C. Casson, 1998, Analyzing foreign market entry
strategies, JIBS, 29, 539–561.

16 D. Teece, 1977, Technology transfer by multinational
firms, EJ, 87: 242–261; B. Kogut & U. Zander
1993, Knowledge of the firm and the evolutionary
theory of the multinational enterprise, JIBS, 24:
625–645.

17 Y. Pan & D. Tse, 2000, The hierarchical model of
market entry modes, JIBS, 31: 535–554. See also
C.W.L. Hill, P. Hwang, & W.C. Kim, 1990, An eclectic
theory of the choice of international entry mode, SMJ,
11: 117–128; K.D. Brouthers, L.E. Brouthers &
S. Werner, 2003, Transaction cost-enhanced entry
mode choices and firm performance, SMJ, 24:
1239–1248; H. Zhao, Y. Luo & T. Suh, 2004,
Transaction cost determinants and ownership-based
entry mode choice, JIBS, 35: 524–544.

18 J.F. Hennart & Y.R. Park, 1993, Greenfield vs.
acquisition: The Strategy of Japanese investors in the.

United States, MS, 39, 1054–1070; J. Anand &
A. Delios, 1997, Location specificity and the transfer of
downstream assets to foreign subsidiaries, JIBS, 28,
579–604; H.G. Barkema & F. Vermeulen, 1998,
International expansion through start-up or
acquisition, AMJ, 41: 7–26; A.W.K. Harzing, 2002,
Acquisitions versus greenfield investments, SMJ, 23:
211–227.

19 B. Wilkinson, J. Morris & M. Munday, 1995, The iron
first and the velvet globe, JMS, 31: 819–830; J. Lowe,
J. Morris & B. Wilkinson, 2000, British factory,
Japanese factory and Mexican factory, JMS 37:
541–560.

20 H. Barkema & F. Vermeulen, 1998, International
expansion through start-up or acquisition, AMJ, 41:
7–27; K.D. Brouthers & L.E. Brouthers, 2000,
Acquisition or greenfield start-up? SMJ, 21: 89–98;
Harzing, 2002, as above K.E. Meyer &
S. Estrin, 2007, Acquisition Strategies in European
Emerging Economies, Basingstoke: Palgrave.

21 S. Gelb & A. Black, 2004, South African case studies,
in: S. Estrin & K.E. Meyer, eds., Investment Strategies
in Emerging Markets, Cheltenham: Elgar, 209–242.

22 K.R. Harrigan, 1988, Joint ventures and competitive
strategy, SMJ, 9, 141–158; B. Kogut, 1988, Joint
ventures, SMJ 9: 319–332.

23 S. Chen & J.F. Hennart, 2002, Japanese investors'
choice of joint ventures versus wholly-owned
subsidiaries in the U.S., JIBS, 33: 1–18; J.F. Hennart
& S. Reddy, 1997, The choice between mergers/
acquisitions and joint ventures, SMJ, 18: 1–12.

24 P.J. Buckley & M.C. Casson, 1998; Models of the
multinational enterprise, JIBS, 29: 21–44;
K.D Brouthers & J.F. Hennart, 2007, Boundaries
of the firm: Insights from international entry mode
research, JM, 33: 395–425; J.F. Hennart, 2009,
Down with MNE-centric theories, JIBS, 40:
1032–1054.

25 A.C. Inkpen & P.W. Beamish, 1997, Knowledge,
bargaining power, and the instability of international
joint ventures, AMR, 22, 177–200.

26 S. Estrin, 2002, Competition and corporate
governance in transition, JEP, 16, 101–124;
K.E. Meyer, 2002, Management challenges in
privatization acquisitions in transition economies,
JWB, 37, 266–276.

27 P. Kulawczuk, 2007, The purchase of a monopoly:
France Telecom acquires TPSA, in: K.E. Meyer &
S. Estrin, eds, Acquisition Strategies in European
Emerging Markets, Basingstoke: Palgrave Macmillan,
133–146.

28 C.A. Solberg, 2000, Standardization or adaptation of
the international marketing mix, JIMktg, 8: 78–98;

M. Theodosiou & L.C. Leonidou, 2003, Standardization versus adaptation of international marketing strategy, *IBR*, 12, 141–171.

29 K.E. Meyer & Y.T.T. Tran, 2006, Market Penetration and Acquisition Strategies for Emerging Economies, *LRP*, 39, 177–197; M. Bák, 2007, Growth through multiple acquisitions: Carlsberg Breweries in Poland, in: K.E. Meyer & S. Estrin, eds, *Acquisition Strategies in European Emerging Markets*, Basingstoke: Palgrave Macmillan.

30 D. Chen, Y. Paik & S. Park, 2010, Host-country policies and MNE management control in IJVs, *JIBS* (in press).

31 H. Hauschild, 2010, Carrefour pant Einstieg in India, *Handelsblatt*, March 7.

32 A. Verbeke, 2009, *International Business Strategy*, Cambridge: Cambridge University Press.

33 M. Desai, C.F. Foley & J. Hines, 2004, The costs of shared ownership, *JFE*, 73: 323–374; S. Rossi & P. Volpin, 2004, Cross-country determinants of M&As, *JFE*, 74: 277–304; H.K. Steensma, L. Tihanyi, M. Lyles & C. Dhanaraj, 2005, The evolving value of foreign partnerships in transitioning economies, *AMJ*, 48: 213–235; P. Kale & J. Anand, 2006, The decline of emerging economy JVs, *CMR*, 48: 62–76; M.W. Peng, 2006, Making M&As fly in China, *HBR*, March: 26–27.

34 K.E. Meyer, S. Estrin, S.K. Bhaumik & M.W. Peng, 2010, Institutions, Resources, and Entry strategies in emerging economies, SMJ, 31: 61–80.

35 Y. Luo & M.W. Peng, 1999, Learning to compete in a transition economy, *JIBS*, 30: 269–296; M.D. Lord & A.L. Ranft, 2000, Organizational learning about new international markets, *JIBS*, 31: 573–589.

36 B. Kogut & N. Kulatilaka, 1994, Options thinking and Platform investment, *CMR*, 36(2): 52–71; B. Kogut & S.J. Chang, 1996, Platform investments and volatile exchange rates, *RES*, 78: 221–232; D.J. McCarthy & S.M. Puffer, Strategic investment flexibility for MNE success in Russia, *JWB*, 32: 293–319.

37 L. Capron, P. Dussage & W. Mitchell, 1998, Resource deployment following horizontal acquisitions in Europe and North America, *SMJ*, 19, 631–661; L. Capron, W. Mitchell & A. Swaminathan, 2001, Asset divesture following horizontal acquisitions: A dynamic view, *SMJ,* 22: 817–844.

38 K.E. Meyer & S. Estrin, 2001, Brownfield Entry in Emerging Markets, *JIBS*, 32: 257–267; S. Estrin & K.E. Meyer, 2011, Brownfield acquisitions: A reconceptualization and extension, MIR, in press.

39 S. Blazejewski, W. Dorow, H.J. Stüting, 2003, The Case of Beiersdorf-Lechia S.A. Pozan, in: S. Blazejewski, W. Dorow, eds.: *Change Management in Transformation Economies,* Basingstoke: Palgrave.

40 K.E. Meyer & Y.T.T. Tran, 2006, *as above*.

© Neustockimages/iStock

CHAPTER THIRTEEN

COMPETITIVE DYNAMICS

LEARNING OBJECTIVES

After studying this chapter you should be able to:

1 Explain how attacks and counter-attacks are used in dynamic competition.

2 Explain how and why firms sometimes like to collude.

3 Outline how competition policy and anti-dumping laws affect international competition.

4 Articulate how resources and capabilities influence competitive dynamics.

5 Discuss how firms can compete during a major recession.

6 Participate in two leading debates concerning competition.

7 Draw implications for action.

OPENING CASE

Huawei challenges a world leader

By Sunny Li Sun, University of Texas, Dallas.

Founded in 1986, Cisco is a worldwide leader in networking for the internet. Numerous rivals challenged Cisco but none was really threatening – until the rise of Huawei. Founded in 1988, Huawei distinguished itself as an aggressive company that led the telecommunications equipment market in China. It is remarkable that Huawei, despite being a non-state-owned company, was able to not only beat all state-owned rivals but also a series of multinationals in China. In 1999, Huawei launched an overseas drive. Starting with $50 million sales (4 per cent of overall sales) in international markets in 1999, Huawei's sales outside of China reached $11 billion (65 per cent of overall sales) in 2006. What is Huawei's secret weapon? Relative to offerings from competitors such as Cisco, Lucent, Nokia and Siemens, Huawei's products offer comparable performance at a 30 per cent lower price. This is music to the ears of telecom operators. As a result, Huawei not only penetrated many emerging economies, but also achieved significant breakthroughs in developed markets such as Japan and Western Europe. As of 2007, Huawei served 31 of the world's top 50 telecom operators, including Vodafone, Telefonica, KPN, FT/Orange and Italia Telecom. Yet, North America remained the toughest nut to crack.

In 2002, Huawei turned to North America – Cisco's stronghold. In Supercomm 2002 (a trade show) in Atlanta, Huawei's debut in North America, two guests visited the Huawei booth and asked detailed questions for 20 minutes. Only after the two guests left did one of Huawei's executives recognize that

© vario images GmbH & Co.KG/Alamy

How has Huawei been challenging market leader Cisco?

one of the guests was John Chambers, Cisco's CEO. Chambers thus personally experienced the arrival of his aggressive new rival from China. Thanks to Huawei, Cisco's sales in China peaked in 2001 at $1 billion and then never reached anything above $600 million. Correspondingly Cisco's share in the Chinese router market went from 80 per cent to 50 per cent. In North America, facing suspicious buyers, Huawei offered 'blind' performance tests on Huawei and Cisco machines whose logos were removed. Buyers often found that the only difference was price.

Cisco's response was both audacious and unexpected. On January 22, 2003, Cisco filed a lawsuit in Texas, alleging that Huawei unlawfully copied and misappropriated Cisco's software and documentation. Cisco's actions totally caught Huawei off guard – the first time it was sued by a foreign rival. Even the day of the attack was deliberately chosen. It was on the eve of the Spring Festival, the main annual holiday in China. Thus, none of the Huawei top executives was able to spend a day with their family in the next few weeks. The media noted that this lawsuit squarely put Huawei 'on the map' as Cisco's acknowledged enemy number one.

Huawei's response was also interesting. Huawei noted that as a firm that consistently invested at least 10 per cent of its sales on R&D, it had always respected intellectual property rights (IPR). In addition to hiring top American lawyers, Huawei also announced a joint venture with Cisco's rival 3Com several days before the court hearing in March 2003. Consequently, 3Com's CEO, Bruce Claflin, provided testimonial supporting Huawei. By using an American CEO to fight off another American firm, Huawei thus skilfully eroded the 'us versus them' feeling permeating this case at a time when 'China bashing' was in the air.

While both Cisco and Huawei fought in court, negotiations between them, often involving American and Chinese officials, also intensified. In July 2004, Cisco dropped the case. While the details of the settlement were confidential, both Cisco and Huawei declared victory. Huawei agreed to change the software and documentation in question, thus partially meeting Cisco's goals. More importantly, Cisco delayed Huawai's North America offensive by one and a half years. Huawei not only refuted most of Cisco's accusations, but also showcased its technological muscle under intense media spotlight for which it did not have to spend a penny. In part thanks to this high-profile case, Huawei's international sales doubled – from approximately $1 billion in 2003 to $2 billion in 2004. Clearly, Huawei rapidly became a force to be reckoned with. In December 2005, Chambers visited Huawei and for the first time met its CEO Ren Zhengfei. The former plaintiff and defendant shook hands and had friendly discussions like pals, as if nothing had happened between them. However, Huawei continued its aggressive technology driven leadership, and by 2008 it filed the largest number of patent applications in the *world*.

Sources: We thank Sunny Li Sun (University of Texas at Dallas) for his assistance. Based on (1) www.cisco.com; (2) Cisco Systems *et al.* v. Huawei Technologies, Co. *et al.*, Civil Action No. 2:03-CV-027, Marshall, TX: US District Court for the Eastern District of Texas; (3) www. huawei.com; (4) J. Wu & Y. Ji, 2006, *Huawei's World*, Beijing: China CITIC Press.

In the rivalry between Cisco and Huawei, why did they take certain actions but not others? Once one side initiates an action, how does the other respond? How can they compete so fiercely, yet earn handsome profits for their owners? When there are only a few companies competing an industry, we call it an oligopoly. In an oligopoly, firms don't compete by driving down prices; they rather interact in strategic ways to beat their competitors, yet make handsome profits at the same time. This chapter focuses on such competitive dynamics – actions and responses undertaken by competing firms.[1] Since one firm's actions are rarely unnoticed by rivals, the initiating firm would naturally like to predict rivals' responses *before* making its own move. Anticipating rivals' actions, the initiating firm may want to both revise its plan and prepare to deal with rivals' responses in the next round. This process is called competitor analysis, advocated a long time ago by the ancient Chinese strategist Sun Tzu's teaching 'if you know the enemy and know yourself, your victory will not stand in doubt'. As military officers have long known, a good plan never lasts longer than the first contact with the enemy because the enemy does not act according to our plan(!). The key word is *interaction* – how firms interact with rivals.

Oligopoly
A market form in which a market or industry is dominated by a small number of sellers (oligopolists).

Competitive dynamics
The actions and responses undertaken by competing firms.

Competitor analysis
The process of anticipating a rivals' actions in order to both revise a firm's plan and prepare to deal with rivals' responses.

While militaries fight over territories, waters and airspaces, firms compete in markets. Note the military tone of terms such as *attacks* and *price wars*.[2] Obviously, military principles cannot be directly applied in business because the marketplace, after all, is not a battlefield where the motto is 'kill or be killed'. Fighting to the death would destroy the value firms create, and nothing would be left. In fact, if your competitor has to shut down and allows you to dominate the market, the media and the competition authorities will subject your actions to greater scrutiny, which is not necessarily a good position to be in. Thus, businesses compete to win, but not necessarily to kill the opposition. Moreover, businesses fight for market share because it helps their profitability, thus their aggressiveness will be tempered by the need to protect profits. Hence, business often is simultaneously rivalry and cooperation.[3]

This chapter first deals with the dynamics of competition, and with the ways firms cooperate to undermine competition by collusion and signalling. Then, we draw on institution- and resource-based views to shed light on competitive dynamics, before discussing a specific challenge for competition: how firms can compete in a global recession. Debates and extensions follows.

DYNAMICS OF COMPETITION

Businesses continuously vary the intensity of their competitive efforts, placing their resources where they expect the 'biggest bang for their bucks'. They can intensify competition by an attack, defined as an initial set of actions to gain competitive advantage, which may take the form of price cuts, advertising campaigns, market entries or new product introductions. An attack is worthwhile if it is expected to yield a stronger position and/or higher profitability, at least in the long run.

When companies enter a new market, or attack an existing rival in a new way, they tend to think of that rival as it is 'today'. However, when attacked, rivals may launch a counter-attack, defined as a set of actions in response to an attack. Firms considering an attack thus need to anticipate possible reactions. The awareness, motivation, capability (AMC) framework gives some indication of rivals' likely response:[4]

Attack
An initial set of actions to gain competitive advantage.

Counter-attack
A set of actions in response to an attack.

Awareness, motivation, capability (AMC) framework
A conceptual framework indicating when firms are likely to attack and counter-attack each other.

Blue ocean strategy
A strategy of attack that avoids direct confrontation.

- **Awareness** is a prerequisite for any counter-attack. If an attack is so subtle that rivals are not aware of it, then the attacker is likely to succeed. A new competitor is more likely to be noticed when making a high profile entry, for example by acquiring another firm, or by launching a major marketing campaign. Moreover, rivals with very similar operations and marketing practices are more aware of each other than of rivals operating in very different ways. Limited interaction and low similarity reduce managers' cognizance of the relationship with a competitor, and thus their awareness of the potential threat.[5] For example, importers may be perceived less threatening than competitors setting up a local subsidiary.[6] One interesting idea is the 'blue ocean strategy' that avoids attacking core markets defended by rivals.[7] A direct attack on rivals' core markets is very likely to result in a bloody price war – in other words, a 'red ocean'. Therefore, an entrant taking small steps to establish a foothold is less likely to get much attention from the incumbent.[8]

Consider Haier's entry into the US white goods market. Although Haier dominated its home country, China, with a broad range of products, it chose to enter the US market in a low profile segment: compact refrigerators for hotels and student residences. Does anyone remember the brand of the

IN FOCUS 13.1

Lev Leviev fights De Beers

In the diamond industry, De Beers of South Africa has been the undisputed 'king of the hill' for more than 100 years. It has skilfully organized a cartel known as the Diamond Syndicate whose purposes were to keep supply low and price high. Historically dominating the global diamond production (mostly in South Africa), De Beers sold rough diamonds only to a select group of merchants (called 'sightholders') from the world at take-it-or-leave-it prices. For independent producers, De Beers often urges them to sell rough diamonds only to De Beers. De Beers would purchase all of the output at prices it sets. In exchange, the producers reap the benefits of a cartel: stable prices, guaranteed purchases and little competition. At present, De Beers still controls approximately 60 per cent of the worldwide rough diamond sales.

As in all cartels, the incentives to cheat are substantial. De Beers's reactions are typically swift. In 1981, Zaire broke away from De Beers to directly market its diamonds. De Beers drew on its stockpiles to flood the market, forcing the Zairians to change their mind. In 1978, some Israeli sightholders began hoarding rough diamonds. De Beers ruthlessly purged one-third of sightholders, forcing many Israeli buyers out of business.

It is against such formidable forces that the Lev Leviev Group of Israel has risen. Lev Leviev is a Russian-speaking, Uzbeki-born, Israeli citizen. As one of Israel's largest diamond polishers, Leviev was invited to become a sightholder by De Beers in 1985. However, Leviev has proven to be De Beers's worst enemy. His actions are characterized by their subtlety, complexity and unpredictability. Leviev has subtly cultivated political connections in key countries. Dating back to the Soviet days, Russia had always sold its rough diamonds to De Beers. Leviev befriended Presidents Yeltsin and Putin and convinced the state-owned Russian producer, now called Alrosa, to set up a joint venture with him to cut $140 million worth of diamonds a year.

Leviev has cultivated a complex web of businesses scattered in numerous industries and countries. The Russian venture is only the tip of an iceberg of his deals in the former Soviet Union. In Angola, De Beers was engulfed in a public relations disaster associated with 'conflict diamonds'. In 1996, Leviev took advantage of the De Beers fiasco by putting together an Angola Selling Corporation, in which he gave the government a 51 per cent share in exchange for exclusive rights to purchase Angolan rough diamonds. In Namibia where locals also preferred to process their own diamonds instead of selling them to De Beers, Leviev first set up a joint diamond polishing factory with local players and then bought out their shares.

Finally, Leviev's actions are often unpredictable in the tradition-bound diamond business largely dictated by De Beers. Leviev has become the first diamond dealer with his finger on every facet of the value chain, from mining and cutting to polishing and retailing. Leviev is innovatively branding his best stones dubbed the Vivid Collection. Outraged, De Beers kicked Leviev out as a sightholder in 1995. De Beers has also set up a diamond polishing factory in Namibia and sought to launch its own brand. Today, as the world's largest cutter and polisher and a primary source of rough diamonds, Leviev has become De Beers's enemy number one.

Sources: Based on (1) P. Berman & L. Goldman, 2003, The billionaire who cracked De Beers, *Forbes*, September 15: 108–115; (2) M.W. Peng, 2006, Lev Leviev, in *Global Strategy* (pp. 327–328), Cincinnati, OH: Cengage.

compact refrigerator in the last hotel room you stayed in? Evidently, not only you failed to pay attention to that brand, but incumbents such as GE and Whirlpool also dismissed this segment as peripheral and low margin. In other words, they were not aware of the competitive threat until Haier had built a substantive operation in the USA. Meanwhile, Haier builds a 50 per cent US market share in compact refrigerators and has built a factory in South Carolina to go after more lucrative product lines.

- **Motivation** is also crucial. Rivals will launch a counter-attack if they expect long-term benefits from doing so. These benefits are likely to be large if the incumbent has a lot to lose, e.g. when market dominance is crucial for the incumbents profitability. On the other hand, if the attacked market segment is of marginal value, managers may decide *not* to counter-attack. Moreover, incumbents operating in a competitive environment and under private ownership have stronger incentives to react than firms in regulated industries that mainly depend on interaction with policy makers.

- **Capability** is the ability to engage in a battle for markets. Even if an attack is identified and a firm is motivated to respond, it requires strong capabilities to carry out counter-attacks. First, firms with strong financial resources are able to make critical investments, or to engage in a price war. For example, Microsoft has recently fought back Apple's near double-digit share of the PC market (with the Mac selling for US$ 2700) and a new generation of US$ 500 'netbook' computers that run on the free Linux operating system. Leveraging its deep pockets (a hard-to-imitate capability), Microsoft has charged PC makers only US$ 15 for Windows, which is normally priced at US$ 70. As a result, Mac sales are no longer increasing, and Linux has disappeared from most netbooks. In 2009, approximately 95 per cent of netbooks run Windows, up from 10 per cent in 2008.[9] Apple, however, did not sit idle and in turn launched a counter-attack on Microsoft by launching its iPad in 2010.

  Second, technological capabilities are crucial for firms to react to entrants using new technologies. To succeed against innovative competitors, firms have to connect new knowledge with existing knowledge, and to transform it for application in their own context. Firms with their strong human capital and innovation-facilitating organizational structures are better positioned to exploit such knowledge spillovers.[10]

Overall, minimizing the awareness, motivation and capabilities of the opponents is more likely to result in successful attacks. Carrying out frontal, simple and predictable attacks will find rivals ready to launch a counter-attack. Rivals, however, will also be subtle in their counter-attacks, launching attacks where they can catch the attacker unaware. Winning firms excel at making subtle, complex, but unpredictable moves. In Focus 13.1 illustrates how Lev Leviev manoeuvres to challenge the mighty De Beers.

COMPETITION AND COLLUSION

Competition is at the core of interaction between firms, and thus the main focus of economic analysis. However, the real world of competition is more ambiguous. 'People of the same trade seldom meet together, even for merriment and diversion', wrote Adam Smith in *The Wealth of Nations* (1776), '... but their conversation often ends in a conspiracy against the public'. In modern jargon, this means that competing firms in an industry may have an incentive to engage in collusion, defined as collective attempts to reduce competition.

Collude or not to collude?

Collusion can be tacit or explicit. Firms engage in tacit collusion when they indirectly coordinate actions by signalling their intention to reduce output and maintain

Collusion
Collective attempts between competing firms to reduce competition.

Tacit collusion
Firms indirectly coordinate actions by signalling their intention to reduce output and maintain pricing above competitive levels.

pricing above competitive levels. Explicit collusion exists when firms directly negotiate output, pricing or division of markets. Explicit collusion leads to a cartel – an
output- and price-fixing entity involving multiple competitors. Cartels are also
known as a trust, whose members have to trust each other for honouring agreements. As we will discuss in the next section, such collusion is usually illegal.

In addition to legal prohibition, collusion is often crushed by the weight of its
own incentive problems. Chief among these problems is the prisoners' dilemma.[11]
The term 'prisoners' dilemma' is used in game theory (a theory on how agents interact strategically to win) to describe a situation where two prisoners are suspected of
a major joint crime (such as burglary), but the police do not have strong evidence.
The two prisoners are separately interrogated and told that if either one confesses,
the confessor will get a one-year sentence while the other will go to jail for ten
years. If neither confesses, both will be convicted of a lesser charge (such as trespas-
sing) and go to jail for two years. If both confess, both will go to jail for ten years.
At first glance, the solution seems clear enough. The maximum *joint* payoff would
be for neither of them to confess. However, both prisoners have strong incentives to
confess – otherwise known as defect.

Translated to an airline setting, Figure 13.1 illustrates the payoff structure for
both airlines A and B in a given market, let's say, the connection between Paris
and Rome. Assuming a total of 200 passengers, cell 1 represents the ideal outcome
for both airlines to maintain the price at €500, and each gets 100 passengers and
makes €50 000; the 'industry' revenue reaches €100 000. However, both airlines
can increase their own revenues by lowering prices and attracting their competitors
customers. In cell 2, if B maintains its price at €500 while A aggressively drops it to
€300, B is likely to lose all customers. Assuming perfectly transparent pricing information on the internet, who would want to pay €500 when they can get a ticket for
€300? Thus, A may make €60 000 on 200 passengers and B gets nothing. In cell 3,
the situation is reversed. In both cells 2 and 3, although the industry *decreases* revenue by 40 per cent, the price drop *increases* the revenues of the firms charging the
lower price by 20 per cent. Thus, both A and B have strong incentives to reduce
price. Yet, if both do so simultaneously, they end in cell 4, whereby each still gets
100 passengers but with a 40 per cent reduction of revenue. A key insight from this

Explicit collusion
Firms directly negotiate
output, fix pricing and divide
markets.

Cartel
An entity that engages in
output- and price-fixing,
involving multiple
competitors.

Prisoners' dilemma
In game theory, a type of
game in which the outcome
depends on two parties
deciding whether to
cooperate or to defect.

Game theory
A theory on how agents
interact strategically to win.

Figure 13.1 A prisoners' dilemma for airlines

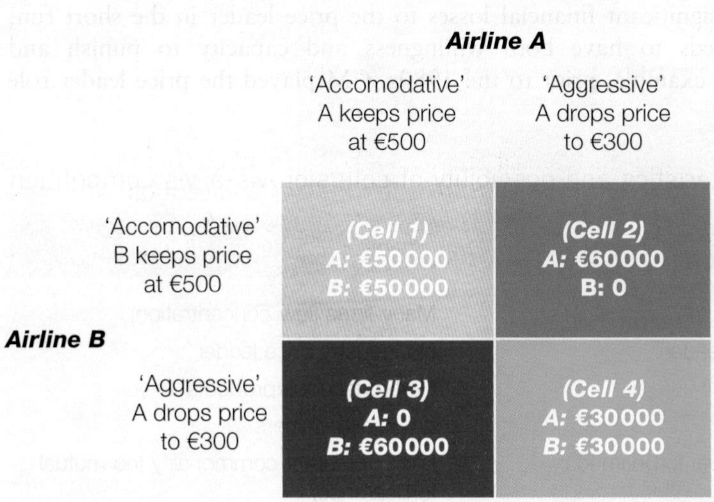

application of game theory is that even if A and B have a prior agreement to fix the price at €500, both still have strong incentives to cheat, thus pulling the industry to the competitive outcome in cell 4 where consumers benefit from lower prices, but both firms are worse off due to lower profits.

However, what happens if the situations remains the same over several periods of time? Of course, in a repeated game both players know the trade-offs in the next period, and that affects their behaviour in the first round. If someone plays 'aggressive' in a repeated game, they can expect to be punished in the next round of the game. This expected punishment, however, can prevent aggressiveness in the first place. Hence, if the two airlines in the theoretical example compete in a stable market for many years, they actually have some incentives to accommodate each other, and thus to remain in cell 1, knowing that any attempt to get to the more favourable outcome in cell 2 or 3 would invariably lead them into cell 4 in the next period.

Hence, companies can play a game of 'tit-for-tat', which means that they would react aggressively once their opponent plays 'aggressive', but act 'accommodative' when the other acts 'accommodative'.[12] If both firms understand the rules of tit-for-tat, they will play 'accommodate' and thus not deviate from a situation that suits them both. In fact, experiments have shown that in real life situations players do best when they play 'tit-for-tat' but occasionally play 'accommodate' when the other plays 'aggressive' because some actions perceived as aggressive are actually based on misunderstandings, which can unintentionally lead to a path of permanent aggressive play from both sides.

Market structure and collusion

Given the benefits of collusion and incentives to cheat, which industries are conducive to collusion? Five factors emerge (Table 13.1). The first is the number of firms or, more technically, concentration ratio, the percentage of total industry sales accounted for by the top 4, 8 or 20 firms. In general, the higher the concentration, the easier it is to organize collusion.

Second, the existence of a price leader – defined as a firm that has a dominant market share and sets 'acceptable' prices and margins in the industry – helps tacit collusion. The price leader needs to possess the capacity to punish defectors. The most frequently used punishment entails undercutting the defector by flooding the market, thus making the defection fruitless. Such punishment is costly because it brings significant financial losses to the price leader in the short run. The price leader needs to have both willingness and capacity to punish and bear the costs. For example, prior to the 1980s, GM played the price leader role in the US

Repeated game
A game plays over several periods of time.

Tit-for-tat
A strategy of matching the competitors move being either aggressive or accommodative.

Concentration ratio
The percentage of total industry sales accounted for by the top 4, 8 or 20 firms.

Price leader
A firm that has a dominant market share and sets 'acceptable' prices and margins in the industry.

Capacity to punish
Sufficient resources possessed by a price leader to deter and combat defection.

Table 13.1 Industry characteristics and possibility of collusion vis-à-vis competition

Collusion possible	Collusion difficult (competition likely)
• Few firms (high concentration)	• Many firms (low concentration)
• Existence of an industry price leader	• No industry price leader
• Homogeneous products	• Heterogeneous products
• High entry barriers	• Low entry barriers
• High market commonality (mutual forbearance)	• Lack of market commonality (no mutual forbearance)

automobile industry, announcing in advance the percentage of price increases. Ford and Chrysler would follow; otherwise, GM would punish them. More recently, with declining market share, GM is no longer able to play this role. Thus, the industry has become much more turbulent and competitive.

Third, in an industry with homogeneous products, in which rivals are forced to compete on price, it is easier to collude than if everyone offers slightly differentiated products. This is because it is easier to observe whether rivals stick to the agreement. Firms in commodity industries may have stronger incentives to collude because their price competition is often cut-throat, and it is easier to monitor members' compliance with the agreement (see In Focus 13.1). In other words, the more transparent the market, the easier it is to identify those that 'cheat' on a collusive agreement. This is a paradox, because normally, market transparency helps consumers. However, its also helps cartels to quickly identify cheaters, and to increase awareness of potential competitors. For example, price comparison websites set up to help consumers to find the cheapest price for their gas or electricity supplier have the side-effect of facilitating (tacit) collusion between the firms.

Fourth, an industry with high entry barriers for new entrants (such as shipbuilding) is more likely to facilitate collusion than an industry with low entry barriers (such as restaurants).[13] New entrants are likely to ignore the existing industry 'order' and to introduce less homogeneous products with newer technologies (in other words, 'disruptive technologies'). As 'mavericks', new entrants 'can be thought of as loose cannons in otherwise placid and calm industries'.[14] For example, in the 1990s Virgin Atlantic upset the cosy competition in transatlantic air travel between the UK and the USA after overcoming high barriers to entry to the industry.

Finally, multimarket competition occurs when firms engage the same rivals in multiple markets. Multimarket firms may respect their rivals' spheres of influence in certain markets, and their rivals may reciprocate, leading to tacit collusion.[15] For example, companies competing in several European countries have reasons not to upset each other too much. If firms have a high degree of market commonality, defined as the degree of overlap between two rivals' markets, this also affects the intensity of rivalry as it is likely to restrain firms from aggressively going after each other.[16]

Such mutual forbearance primarily stems from deterrence. A high degree of market commonality suggests that if a firm attacks in one market, its rivals have the ability to engage in cross-market retaliation, leading to a costly all-out war that the businesses do not really want – though consumers might love the lower prices.

Multimarket competition
Firms engage the same rivals in multiple markets.

Market commonality
The overlap between two rivals' markets.

Cross-market retaliation
The ability of a firm to expand in a competitor's market if the competitor attacks in its original market.

Cooperation and signalling

Some firms choose to compete and attack, and others choose to cooperate. How can a firm signal its intention to cooperate to *reduce* competitive intensity? Short of illegally talking directly to rivals, firms have to resort to signalling their actions through their actions:

- Firms may enter new markets not really to challenge incumbents but to seek mutual forbearance by establishing multimarket contact. Thus, MNEs often chase each other, entering one country after another.[17] For example, across Central and Eastern Europe, the Big Four global brewing MNEs (Heineken, SABMiller, AB-Inbev and Carlsberg) dominate the market in every country.[18] However, in each country, there are only two or three of the Big Four. They say that they aspire market leadership in each market where they compete, and exit those markets where they do not foresee becoming at least number two. This strategy reduces the intensity of competition compared to a hypothetical market where all four go head-to-head. Similarly, Airlines that meet on many routes are often less aggressive than airlines that meet on one or a few routes.[19]

- Firms can send an open signal for a truce. As GM faced grave financial difficulties in 2005, Toyota's chairman told the media *twice* that Toyota would 'help GM' by raising Toyota prices in the USA. As far as signalling goes, Toyota's signal could not have been more unambiguous, short of talking directly to GM, which would be illegal. Toyota, of course, was self-interested. Should GM indeed declare bankruptcy, Toyota would attract all the 'machine-gun fire' from protectionist backlash (as indeed it happened in 2010). Nevertheless, US anti-trust authorities reportedly took note of Toyota's remarks – they interpreted the message as an invitation to GM for price fixing.[20]

- Firms can also use certain pricing schemes that discourage competitors to aggressively underbidding them. In particular, it is in most countries perfectly legal to offer a price match guarantee: 'if you see the same product in the local area for a lower price, we pay you the difference'. Such a strong commitment send two signals: to consumers it says 'we have the lowest price', to competitors to says 'don't try to compete on price'. Hence, they won't. Hence, the firms try to gradually jack up prices to the levels of the competitors.

- Sometimes, firms can send a signal to rivals by enlisting the help of governments. Because direct negotiations with rivals on what consists of 'fair' pricing are often illegal, holding such discussions is legal under the auspices of government investigations. Thus, filing an anti-dumping petition or suing a rival does not necessarily indicate a totally hostile intent. Sometimes, it signals to the other side: 'We don't like what you are doing; it's time to talk'. Cisco, for instance, dropped its case against Huawei after both firms negotiated a solution (see Opening Case).

- Some alliances and joint-ventures can also help reduce the competition, for example when two competitors form a joint venture for their operations in the same industry.[21] Such alliances are, however, subject to competition policy review, and thus only feasible between non-leading firms in a market.

INSTITUTIONS GOVERNING COMPETITION

LEARNING OBJECTIVE

3 Outline how competition policy and anti-dumping laws affect international competition

In their aspiration for market share and profitability, it is important for firms to 'play by the rules'. In particular, collusion to enhance profits is usually against the rules. These rules are set by the legislators to protect consumers and smaller businesses. In the EU, the European Commission is responsible for monitoring and enforcing competition rules for business operating across countries, with national authorities retaining responsibility for purely domestic matters (Chapter 8). The institution-based view emphasizes that managers need to be well versed in these rules of the game governing competition.

Formal institutions: competition policy

Competition policy (anti-trust policy)

Policy governing the rules of the game in competition in a country.

The formal institutions governing competition are known as competition policy (or anti-trust policy). These institutions shape the mix of competition and cooperation within a market economy.[22] Without competition policy, firms are likely to sooner or later collude, for instance by forming cartels, or agreeing not to invade each others' market. This might be good for corporate profits, but it would be bad for consumers: prices rise.[23] Consumer prices vary considerably across countries (Table 13.2). European consumers often pay higher prices than Americans: for example British consumers pay the highest prices for agriculture and fishery products, cars and professional products, while Dutch consumers pay most for drugs and for petrol. Competition policy is probably a major cause of such differences (though probably not the only one), and the authorities have been getting tougher in enforcing the rules. Here we focus on (1) collusion to raise prices, (2) collusion to divide markets, (3) anti-competitive practices by dominating a market (Table 13.3).

First, classic cartels of the 19th and early 20th century included agreements between major companies to keep prices in a given market at a higher than competitive level. Such collusive price setting has been outlawed in many countries starting in the USA with the Sherman Act of 1890 and the Clayton Act of 1914, which were followed by similar antitrust laws in Europe early in the 20th century. By the end of the 20th century, trade liberalization had opened many formerly protected markets, which created new motivations for firms to collude across borders.[24] Competition watchdogs in Europe and North America reacted to this trend by increasing their collaboration to investigate international cartels, such as the international Vitamin

Collusive price setting
Price setting by monopolists or collusion parties at a higher than competitive level.

Anti-trust laws
Laws that attempt to curtail anticompetitive collusion by businesses.

Table 13.2 International price comparisons

(Ratio of Domestic Retail Prices to World Market Prices)							
	Australia	Canada	Germany	Japan	Netherlands	UK	US
Agriculture and fisheries	**1.067**	1.112	1.529	1.584	1.080	*1.648*	1.158
Processed food	**1.086**	1.192	1.447	*2.099*	1.299	1.202	1.090
Textiles	1.111	1.163	1.101	*1.478*	1.140	1.237	**1.051**
Printing and publishing	1.120	1.205	1.024	1.186	*1.342*	1.029	**1.005**
Drugs and medicines	**1.001**	2.680	2.643	1.217	*3.349*	1.845	3.105
Petroleum and coal	2.127	1.320	2.847	3.359	*4.335*	4.067	**1.007**
Motor vehicles	1.224	1.197	1.315	**1.000**	1.648	*1.680*	1.106
Professional goods	1.125	1.082	1.379	1.077	1.369	*1.586*	**1.074**
Weighted means	1.266	1.270	1.539	*1.567*	1.541	1.48	**1.118**

Source: Adapted from OECD, 2004, Product market competition and economic performance in the United States (p. 14), Economics Department working paper no. 398, Paris: OECD. **Bold** typeface indicates the lowest price in this category, *Italics* indicates the highest price in this category.

Table 13.3 EU Competition Policy

Fairness of Competition	Creation and Protection of Competition
● Price fixing cartels ● Market dividing agreements ● Anti-competitive practices by dominant firms	● Mergers and acquisitions (Chapter 14) ● Liberalization of regulated or state-controlled industries (Chapter 8) ● Limits on subsidies from states to firms (Chapter 8)

cartel (In Focus 13.2).[25] In the EU, the position of Competition Commissioner (held by Joaquin Almunia of Spain in 2010–14) has become one of the most powerful positions in Brussels. When regulators catch companies colluding at the costs of consumers, punishments tend to be severe. In countries such as the USA, the UK and Ireland, not only companies are fined but individuals involved in the price fixing can receive personal fines and jail sentences.

Regulators are getting smarter and more powerful when it comes investigating and punishing cartels. Both the EU and the USA have 'leniency programmes' that take advantage of the prisoners' dilemma discussed earlier: under certain circumstances, firms that are first to report a cartel (and thus 'defect' from the collusion) get a lesser punishment than others caught in the same cartel (In Focus 13.2). This increases the incentives for members of a cartel to cheat on each other, and hence makes it less likely that cartels are established in the first place. For example, in the lifts and escalators cartel in the Benelux countries, Kone of Finland was first to come forward and received immunity for Belgium and Luxemburg, whereas Otis of the USA received immunity with respect to the cartel in the Netherlands. Even so, the Commission imposed the largest cartel fines ever, a total of €992 million. The largest share, €480 million, was borne by ThyssenKrupp of Germany.[26] In addition to these fines, the companies faced indirect costs from legal and consulting fees, the pressure on management time and the negative publicity. Hence, if you are colluding and fear being caught, it actually pays to be the first 'to blow the whistle'. Moreover, once under investigation, it pays to collaborate early with the regulators!

In contrast, regulators in emerging economies often have neither the capabilities to investigate cartels, nor the legal means to punish wrong doing. For example, in Mexico the authorities have to give notice to targets of their investigations before conducting a search – guess how much evidence they find? Also, the maximum penalty is limited to about €5 million – compared to 10 per cent of the offender's sales in the EU. Thus, in Mexico, collusion may be profitable even if it is detected, an abnormality that the parliament tried to correct in spring 2010.[27]

Second, in market division collusion, companies may divide markets among each other. This is a major concern in Europe because many market leaders have traditionally dominated their home market, and the option of invading each others 'home market has emerged only when the single European market came into effect in 1993. Moreover, it is difficult to objectively assess for an outsider whether two companies stay in each others' home market because they lack the capability to compete in that market, or because of (tacit) collusion. Even so, the European Commission has in recent years prosecuted a number of cases. For example, Carlsberg and Heineken fiercely compete in many countries, but they stayed out of each others home markets, respectively Denmark and the Netherlands, until the

Leniency programmes
Programmes that give immunity to members of a cartel that first report the cartel to the authorities.

Market division collusion
A collusion to divide markets among competitors.

IN FOCUS 13.2

The Global Vitamin Cartel

The largest and most wide-reaching cartel ever convicted is the global vitamin cartel in operation during 1990–1999. It mainly involved four firms that controlled more than 75 per cent of worldwide production: (1) Hoffman-La Roche of Switzerland, (2) BASF of Germany, (3) Rhône-Poulenc of France (Now Aventis) and (4) Eisai of Japan. Four other Dutch, German and Japanese firms were also involved. The ringleader was the industry leader, Hoffman-La Roche. This cartel was truly extraordinary: By 1999, prices were meticulously set in at least *nine* currencies. Its discovery led to numerous convictions and fines during 1999–2001 by US, EU, Canadian, Australian and South Korean antitrust authorities. According to the US assistant attorney general:

> 'The criminal conduct of these companies hurt the pocketbook of virtually every American consumer – anyone who took a vitamin, drank a glass of milk or had a bowl of cereal ... These companies fixed the price; they allocated sales volumes; they allocated consumers; and in the United States they even rigged bids to make absolutely sure that their cartel would work. The conspirators actually held "annual meetings" to fix prices and to carve up world markets, as well as frequent follow-up meetings to ensure compliance with their illegal scheme'.

While this statement only referred to the damage to the US economy, it is plausible to argue that *every* vitamin consumer in the world was ripped off. Average buyers paid 30 per cent to 40 per cent more. The total illegal profits – known as 'global injuries' – were estimated to be $9 to $12 billion, of which 15 per cent accrued in the USA and 26 per cent in the EU. Firms and managers in this conspiracy paid a heavy price:

Worldwide, firms paid record fines of almost €4 billion, including penalties by the EU of €462 million for Hoffman-La Roche and €296 for BASF, plus penalties of equal magnitude from the US authorities. In addition, for the first time in US anti-trust history, Swiss and German executives working for Hoffman-La Roche and BASF served prison terms of three to four months and paid personal fines of US$ 75 000 to US$ 350 000.

This case has both triumphs and frustrations. A leading triumph stems from the corporate leniency programme. Tapping into the powerful incentive to defect in this *real* prisoners' dilemma, this programme offers the first company to voluntarily confess blanket amnesty from criminal prosecution while its fingered co-conspirators are hit with criminal fines and jail time. The amnesty prize goes only to the *first* company that comes forward. In this case, it was Rhône-Poulenc that provided anti-trust authorities overwhelming evidence that made other defendants decide not to contest the charges and to plead guilty. In terms of frustrations, despite the record fines and penalties, the criminal and civil justice systems of the world have failed to recover more than half of the cartel's illegal profits. In other words, given the low probability of detection, as experts noted, it may still be 'utterly rational for would-be cartelists to form or join an international price-fixing conspiracy'. Overall, the deterrence, as powerful as this case indicates, may still not be enough.

Sources: Based on (1) D. Bush et al., 2004, *How to Block Cartel Formation and Price-Fixing*, Washington, DC: AEI-Brookings Joint Center for Regulatory Studies; (2) *Guardian*, 2001, Vitamin cartel fined for price fixing, November 21; (3) C. Hobbs, 2004, The confession game, *Harvard Business Review*, September: 20–21; (4) US Department of Justice, 2000, Four foreign executives agree to plead guilty to participating in international vitamin cartel, April 6, Washington, DC: DOJ.

Commission intervened. In another case, in July 2009 the Commission fined gas suppliers Eon (Germany) and Gaz de France (France) €553 million *each* because they had agreed to divide markets, i.e. not to sell gas into the partner's home market.[28]

Third, dominant players in a particular market may use anti-competitive practices to inhibit competition, in particular by using their market power to dominate related markets, or raise barriers to entry for potential competitors. For example, it

Anti-competitive practices (by a dominant firm) Business practices by a dominating firm that make it more difficult for competitors to enter or survive.

Why is the gas distribution industry prone to anti-competitive behaviour?

sounds fairly reasonable that a food manufacturer offering a retailer a free display freezer stipulates that this freezer may be used exclusively for products of this manufacturer and not for competitors' products. However, if this manufacturer is the sole supplier of certain goods, then this tactic allows a dominant firm to keep out potential challengers. For example, Unilever used to provide display freezers to small shops in Ireland at low/no costs, provided that the freezers were used *exclusively* for Unilever-made ice creams. This exclusivity agreement inhibited the entry into the Irish ice cream market by Mars, a US confectionary producer. Mars complained to the competition authorities, and the European Commission eventually decided in its favour and declared the exclusivity agreement an anti-competitive practice of a dominant firm. This decision was upheld by the European Court of Justice (ECJ) in 2006, and Unilever eventually had to pay Mars compensation.[29]

Anti-competitive practices by dominant players are a major issue in industries where one firm controls a crucial element of the infrastructure, such as telecommunications, software and internet services. For example, the Commission argued that Deutsche Telecom was using its control of telecommunication *networks* in Germany to inhibit potential entrants competing with its telecommunication *operations* business. Specifically, the price that Deutsche Telecom charged other operators for the use of the network was too high, according to a ruling of the Commission backed by the European Court in 2008.[30] Another focus of Commission investigation has been various information technology sectors (In Focus 13.3). In several such cases, the EU has taken a tougher interpretation of what constitutes an anti-competitive practice by a dominant firm than US courts did in comparable cases.[31]

A related practice is predatory pricing, defined as (1) setting prices below cost *and* (2) intending to raise prices to cover losses in the long run after eliminating rivals ('an attempt to monopolize'). In a rare case in the 1990s, British bus company Stagecoach was found guilty of predatory pricing when it offered free rides on certain lines where it had a serious competitors, but not on others. However, it is difficult to prove predatory pricing. First, it is not clear what exactly is 'cost'. Second, even when firms are found to be selling below costs, courts would want to see

Predatory pricing
An attempt to monopolize a market by setting prices below cost and intending to raise prices to cover losses in the long run after eliminating rivals.

IN FOCUS 13.3

Brussels fight anti-competitive practices in the IT sector

The European Commission is not only fighting old incumbents of networks, but using the same principles of market dominance and anti-competitive practices to assess big players in the computer, software and internet industries. In particular, Microsoft has been the target of several investigations due to its dominance of the software industry with its Windows operating system. In one case, triggered in 1998 by Sun Microsystems, also a US firm, the Commission ruled that Microsoft had to make more information available about its proprietary software code to facilitate other software firms to develop software products that link into Windows. This highly controversial case has been going on for many years, with Microsoft being ordered to pay fines, which set the stage for new rounds of negotiations. Essentially the Commission considers Windows a basic infrastructure similar to the cables used by telecom companies, and thus infers that others have to access the system. In 2007, Microsoft was fined €899 million, but it continued to appeal.

In addition, the Commission investigated whether by bundling its Media Player into the Windows operating system, Microsoft was effectively freezing out competing products. In a similar conflict, when Microsoft tied its Explorer browser into Windows, this enabled Microsoft to pull customers away from the competitor Netscape, which eventually led to the demise of the Netscape browser. In 1995, Netscape had 90 per cent of the market, but 1999 Microsoft had become market leader with 70 per cent. In 2010, the Commission and Microsoft agreed that Microsoft offers a 'choice screen' from which users can themselves choose which browser they use. By then Netscape had disappeared from the market and Firefox was emerging as the main competitor.

In IT hardware sector, the Commission prosecuted Intel because it was using anti-competitive practices to exclude its competitor AMD from the market for micro-processors. More recently, the Commission started investigating whether Google was abusing its dominant position in the internet search engines to provide preferential links to its own businesses (or businesses it was associated with) by manipulating the sequence of search results.

Sources: P. Windrum, 2004, Leveraging technological externalities: Microsoft's exploitation of standards in the browser war, *RP*, 33: 385–394; S. McGuire & M. Smith, 2008, *The European Union and the United States*, Basingstoke: Palgrave. E.J. Morgan, 2009, Controlling cartels – Implications of the EU policy reforms, *EMJ*, 27: 1–12

evidence that the initially incurred loss will subsequently be recovered, which is hard to provide. These two legal tests have made it extremely difficult to win a predation case within the EU or in the USA – but the argument prevails in international trade.

In addition to collusion and anti-competitive practices, EU competition policy also covers issues discussed elsewhere in this book: the control of mergers and acquisitions (Chapter 14), state aid and liberalization of regulated industries (Chapter 8). Competition policy is (almost) always a subject to bitter disputes between businesses and the regulators, be they national or at the EU level. Businesses complain that the procedures are too bureaucratic, and that they cannot be challenged sufficiently in independent courts.[32] On the other hand, consumers feel that MNEs still have too much market power to dictate prices, especially in utilities such as telecommunications, gas supplies and transport.

Dumping
An exporter selling below cost abroad and planning to raise prices after eliminating local rivals.

Formal institutions: a focus on anti-dumping

The rules of international trade (Chapter 5) can also be used as weapons in competition. In the spirit of predatory pricing, dumping is defined as (1) an exporter selling below cost abroad and (2) planning to raise prices after eliminating local rivals. Although domestic predation is rarely investigated or prosecuted, cross-border dumping is often emotionally accused of being 'unfair'.

If a steel producer in *Indiana* enters a new market, Texas, under US antitrust laws, a predation case like this will have no chance of succeeding. However, if the 'invading' firm is not from Indiana but *India*, Texas steel producers 'would almost certainly obtain legal relief on the very same facts that would not support an anti-trust *claim*, let alone anti-trust relief'.[33] Note that imposing anti-dumping duties on Indian steel imports reduces the incentive for Texas firms to counter-attack by entering India, resulting in *higher* prices in both Texas and India, where consumers are hurt. These two scenarios are not merely hypothetical; they are highly realistic. An OECD study in Australia, Canada, the EU and the US reports that 90 per cent of the practices found to be unfairly dumping in these countries would never have been questioned under their own anti-trust laws if used by a domestic firm in making a domestic sale.[34] In a nutshell, foreign firms are discriminated against by the formal rules of the game.

Discrimination is also evident in the actual investigation of anti-dumping.[35] A case is usually filed by a domestic firm with the relevant government authorities, who then requests comprehensive, proprietary data on their cost and pricing, in English, using US generally accepted accounting principles (GAAP), within 45 days. Many foreign defendants fail to provide such data on time because they are not familiar with US GAAP. The investigation can have the four following outcomes:

- If no data are forthcoming from abroad, the data provided by the accusing firm become the evidence, and the accusing firm can easily win.

- If foreign firms do provide data, the accusing firm can still argue that these 'unfair' foreigners have lied – 'There is no way their costs can be so low!' In the case of Louisiana versus Chinese crawfish growers, the authenticity of the $9 *per week* salary of Chinese workers was a major point of contention.

How do you know whether the Chinese were dumping crayfish in the USA?

© anssi ruuska/iStock

- Even if the low-cost data are verified, US and EU anti-dumping laws allow the complainant to argue that these data are not 'fair'. In the case of China, the argument goes, its cost data reflect huge distortions due to government intervention because China is still a 'non-market' economy; the wage may be low, but workers may be provided with low-cost housing and benefits subsidized by the government. The crawfish case thus boiled down to how much it would cost to raise hypothetical crawfish in a market economy (in this particular case, Spain was mysteriously chosen). Because Spanish costs were about the same as Louisiana costs, the Chinese, despite their vehement objections, were found guilty of dumping in America by selling below *Spanish* costs. Thus, 110 per cent to 123 per cent import duties were levied on Chinese crawfish.

- The fourth possible outcome is that the defendant wins the case. But this happens to only 5 per cent of the anti-dumping cases in the USA.[36]

Simply filing an anti-dumping petition (regardless of the outcome), one study finds, may result in a 1 per cent increase of the stock price for US listed firms (an average of $46 million increase in market value).[37] Evidently, Wall Street expects 'Uncle Sam' to be on the side of US businesses. It is thus not surprising that anti-dumping cases have now proliferated throughout the world.[38]

RESOURCES INFLUENCING COMPETITION

A number of resource-based imperatives, informed by the VRIO framework were first outlined in Chapter 4, drive decisions and actions associated with competitive dynamics. The key question is whether the firms have sufficient resources to engage in a competitive battle.

LEARNING OBJECTIVE

4 Articulate how resources and capabilities influence competitive dynamics

Value-creation

Firm resources must create value when engaging rivals in dynamic competition. To stay ahead in the competition, moreover, a firm has to create more value for its customers than its competitors do. Otherwise, customers will defect to the rival – no matter how shrewd a competitive game is played. In addition, firms may need resources to persevere in a competitive battle. For example, the ability to attack in multiple markets – of the sort that enabled Gillette to launch its Sensor razors in 23 countries *simultaneously* – throws rivals off balance. Likewise, the ability to rapidly lower prices depends on the availability of resources.[39] Another example of a strong resource is a dominant position in key markets (such as flights in and out of London-Heathrow by British Airways). Similar, Saudi Arabia's vast oil reserves enable it to become the enforcer (price leader) of OPEC cartel agreements. Such a strong sphere of influence poses credible threats to rivals, which understand that the firm will defend its core markets vigorously.

Rarity

By definition, only rare resources help in a competitive battle. If a resource is not rare, then the competitor can easily get hold of it as well and eliminate any advantage gained.

Imitability

Most rivals watch each other and probably have a fairly comprehensive (although not necessarily accurate) picture of how their rivals compete. However, the next hurdle lies in how to imitate successful rivals. It is well known that fast-moving rivals tend to perform better.[40] Even when armed with this knowledge, competitively passive and slow-moving firms will find it difficult to imitate rivals' actions. Many major airlines have sought to imitate successful discount carriers such as Southwest, Ryanair, and Hainan (see Chapter 4 Opening Case) but failed.

Patent race

A competition of R&D units where the one first to patent a new technology gets to dominate a market.

Another barrier to imitation is patenting, which is a particularly effective means to prevent the imitation of the products created by rivals. Patents provide rights to technology that may be value-creating. Whoever is first to patent a new technology can prevent other from imitating it. Thus, firms are expanding their scale and scope of patenting, resulting in a 'patent race'.[41] Microsoft now holds approximately 3000 patents, up from a mere five in 1990. Intel sits on 10 000 patents. Only about 5 per cent of patents end up having any economic value.[42] So why do firms spend so much money on the patent race (on average, half a million dollars in R&D for one patent)? The answer is in part defensive and competitive. The proliferation of patents makes it very easy for one firm to unwittingly infringe on rivals' patents. When being challenged, a firm without a defensive portfolio of patents is at a severe disadvantage: It has to pay its rivals for using their patents. On the other hand, a firm with strong patents can challenge rivals for their infringements, thus making it easier to reach some understanding – or mutual forbearance. Patents thus become a valuable weapon in fighting off rivals. For this reason, China's Huawei (Opening Case) now files about 1800 patents a year (Table 13.4).

Table 13.4 Top ten patent applicant companies

	Company	Number of applications
1	Huawei (China)	1737
2	Panasonic (Japan)	1729
3	Philips (Netherlands)	1551
4	Toyota (Japan)	1364
5	Robert Bosch (Germany)	1273
6	Siemens (Germany)	1089
7	Nokia (Finland)	1005
8	LG Electronics (South Korea)	992
9	Ericsson (Sweden)	984
10	Fujitsu (Japan)	983

Source: *Data extracted from World Intellectual Property Organization, 2009, Top 50 PCT applicants in 2008, Geneva: WIPO (www.wipo.int). The number of applications refers to international patent filings under WIPO's Patent Cooperation Treaty (PCT) during 2008.*

Organization

Some firms are better organized for competitive actions, such as stealth attacks and willingness to answer challenges 'tit-for-tat'. The intense 'warrior-like' culture not only requires top management commitment but also employee involvement down to the 'soldiers in the trenches'. It is such a self-styled 'wolf' culture that has propelled Huawei to become Cisco's leading challenger (Opening Case). It is difficult for slow-moving firms to suddenly wake up and become more aggressive.[43]

On the other hand, more centrally coordinated firms may be better mutual forbearers than firms whose units are loosely controlled. For an MNE competing with rivals across many countries, a mutual forbearance strategy requires some units, out of respect for rivals' sphere of influence, to sacrifice their maximum market gains by withholding some efforts. Of course, such coordination helps other units with dominant market positions to maximize performance, thus helping the MNE as a whole. Successfully carrying out such mutual forbearance calls for organizational reward systems and structures (such as those concerning bonuses and promotions) that encourage cooperation between units. Conversely, if a firm has competitive reward systems and structures (for example, bonuses linked to unit performance), unit managers may be unwilling to give up market gains for the greater benefits of other units and the whole firm, thus undermining mutual forbearance.[44]

COMPETING IN A GLOBAL RECESSION

Competition is relatively easy when new markets are opening up, waiting to be conquered. However, markets do not always grow, sometimes they shrink. The global recession that followed the financial crisis in 2008 triggered broader awareness of the changing nature of competition over the business cycle. Competition is much harder in shrinking markets.[45] How can companies compete when adverse events such as a major recession hits their markets? They have to address to two challenges simultaneously (1) short-term survival and (2) preparation for the next upswing.

LEARNING OBJECTIVE

5 Discuss how firms can compete during a major recession

Short-term strategies and survival[46]

The dynamics of competition change in a recession: rather than seeking to outgrow their rivals, firms first and foremost are concerned about their own survival. Survival strategies focus on liquidity and the immediate preservation of resources. For example, during a credit crunch, companies find it more difficult to raise capital by borrowing from the banks or by raising equity. Hence, retention of cash flow becomes a priority. Similarly, a slump in demand requires firms to adjust their output to cut costs or to focus on markets that are likely to be resilient (Table 13.5).

What are people and businesses likely to do *more* during the recession? Reflecting over this question points to business opportunities during the recession, For example, in the 'value for money' segment of consumer goods retailers such as ASDA, Primark and the German newcomers Aldi and Lidl have been reporting substantive sales growth in 2008 recession in the UK. Likewise, manufacturers focus on 'value for money' products.[47] This may involve innovations that aim not at advancing new technologies, but at modifying products, production processes and business models to deliver almost the same level of benefit to customers at much lower costs.[48] In business-to-business markets, suppliers face customers tightening their budgets, with disproportionate effects on external suppliers. For example, if IT budgets are cut by 25 per cent, while 70 per cent of the budget is spend on maintenance, then only 5 per cent of the budget are available for new acquisitions of

Survival strategies
A strategy designed to ensure survival by ensuring liquidity and positive cash flow.

Table 13.5 Resilient strategies

Opportunity	Examples	Challenging Decisions
Low cost retail	Discount supermarkets for food and clothing.	Is it worthwhile going downmarket, thus taking the risk of downgrading the brand?
Basic need goods	Non-branded consumer goods, foods	How can we innovate to deliver essentials at lower costs?
Help customers save costs	IT system providers, energy saving technologies	How can we convince customers that recession is a good time to invest?
Help customers manage uncertainties	Risk sharing contracts	How will the risk assumed on behalf of customers affect our own risk profile?
Career breaks	Education, especially post-experience programmes, gap year travel, social work	How can we invest in new programmes when our customers' budgets are tight?
Entertainment	Domestic tourism, home entertainment, take-away food, sports	How can we develop 'budget' services during recession by prepare to go upmarket when the economy picks up?

hardware or software. Thus, opportunities for IT service providers like SAP or Microsoft are very limited unless they can help their customers to save IT maintenance costs, or costs elsewhere in the organization.

An additional obstacle to major purchases is often the risk of adverse events during the life time of the item that may affect the value of the item, or buyers' ability to pay for it. For example, people worried about loosing their job are likely to postpone buying a new car, especially if they need to finance it with a bank loan. If sellers can help managing this risk, this may ease the purchasing decisions. For example, Hyundai USA generated considerable attention – and sales – by offering to buy back cars if customers within a year of the purchase lost their job. Effectively, Hyundai offered an insurance policy along with the purchase of a car.[49] While this needs to be factored into the purchase price, this approach helps customers managing the investment risk.

Another industry that tends to be fairly resilient to economic downturns is entertainment. People may spend less on long distance travel and expensive days out, but they are substituting such activities by stay-at-home entertainment. This creates opportunities for businesses that provide for an enjoyable day at home, or nearby. Survival strategies thus include focus on consumer experiences such as sports (both spectator and participant), video games, children's' toys, take-away and ready-to-eat meals (substituting for days eating out), and beverages (invite your mates home rather than to the pub). Similarly, tourism may suffer from a decline of long-distance travel, but benefits from people spending their home at domestic tourism locations. In the recession of 2008/09, British hotels reported brisk trading: not only did the British seek nearby tourist spots for their holidays, but the depreciation of the British pound made Britain cheaper for foreign visitors.

What are the opportunities and risks for tourism businesses such as the London Eye during a recession?

Resilient strategies also target people who wish to use their involuntary career break (more commonly known as unemployment) in a useful way. In particular, they may invest in their own future and enrol for education programmes, especially mid career programmes (such as MBA), and career preparing programmes (such as MSc). Thus, applications for all sorts of university courses went up in 2009, creating growth opportunities for entrepreneurial higher education institutions.

Long-term strategies and strategic positioning

Survival strategies may achieve just that – survival – but not prosperity in the longer term. Like farmers using the winter to fix their tools for the next spring, businesses have to think ahead – even during a deep crisis – to use the time of the downturn to position themselves for the next upswing. For example, Renishaw, a British engineering company specializing on precision measurement systems continued to invest in R&D during the crisis of 2008, while laying of half of its 2000-strong workforce and cutting salaries by 20 per cent. Yet, by 2009, its turnover grew by 17 per cent on the basis of its R&D investment.[50]

Entrepreneurs may view a crisis as an opportunity to enter new markets. They ask, how are we going to benefit from the next economic upswing? How can we take advantage of rivals that drop out – headhunting their best people, invading their markets or acquire the bankrupt business? These questions resemble those you may have asked yourself when choosing your course at university: what skills will be in demand in a few years when *you* graduate? They questions concern the strategic positioning of the firm (or yourself) during the next economic cycle. Answering these questions, however, requires some idea of what the market will be like in the future. Strategic decision-makers frequently have to make such long-term decisions without 'knowing' what the future will look like.

Economic forecasting
A technique using econometric models to predict the likely future value of key economic variables.

Conventionally, businesses try to look into the future by economic forecasting. This approach employs complex econometric models that incorporate estimated relationships between key variables, and extrapolations of trends. These models generate point estimates of the most likely future state of the world, along with a range ('confidence interval') in which the actual outcome will be with, say, 90 per cent probability. In a stable environment, such forecasts provide reasonably good guidance for decision-makers. However, the forecast may be insufficient in highly volatile environments. Indeed, the precision of point estimates can be misleading. For example, a crisis may induce people to change their shopping habits, which changes key parameters in the econometric model. Therefore, forecasts are usually not very good at predicting when trends change, and they provide little insights into the range of possible developments.

Scenario planning
A technique generating multiple scenarios of possible future states of the industry.

An alternative is scenario planning.[51] Scenario approaches emphasize uncertainty and the range of *possible* outcomes rather than focusing on the *most likely* outcome. Scenario planning brings together a diverse set of experts to speculate about the future, generate ideas and then to condense these ideas into 'scenarios' capturing key variations. The experts would aim to identify the dimensions that are most crucial for shaping the future of the industry. Different combinations allow envisaging possible future states of the world. For example, at the onset of the financial crisis in 2008, consultants McKinsey developed possible scenarios for the world economy in 2009/10 along the dimensions of 'severe *versus* moderate global recession' and 'global credit and capital markets reopen and recover *versus* close down and remain volatile'.[52] The process of discussing the scenarios with internal and external experts may be as important as the written-up scenarios as it provides them with insights into the factors likely to be important in the future. Other scenarios look even further into the future, such as those developed by Wärtsilä for the global energy industry (see Chapter 9, Closing Case).

Scenarios serve several purposes. First, they create a mindset aware of the nature of uncertainty, framing the future as in terms of possibilities rather than probabilities. Decision-makers – as well as those who have to implement decisions – thus are mentally and practically prepared for having to change their course of action on short notice, yet having a clear sense of direction once a contingency plan is activated. Second, they provide a basis for assessing the robustness of alternative strategies.[53] Businesses would want their strategies to generate profitable operations under most of the likely scenarios. Hence, assessing the likely outcomes of proposed strategies under a set of alternative scenarios provides insights in their robustness.

Contingency plans
Plans devised for specific situations when things could go wrong.

Third, scenarios provide a basis for contingency plans that may be implemented when certain events happen or benchmarks are reached. Contingency plans allow preparation for both offensive as well as defensive actions, and may address questions such as: What acquisitions might be attractive on what terms? What new products might be launched under different scenarios? Which conditions would trigger a market exit, and how can an exit be managed while minimizing losses?

DEBATES AND EXTENSIONS

LEARNING OBJECTIVE

6 Participate in two leading debates concerning competition

Competition involves many sensitive issues of government policy, with businesses and governments as representatives of consumers disagreeing about the appropriate approaches. We here discuss (1) competition against overwhelming rivals, and (2) competition versus anti-dumping.

Local firms versus big MNEs

Some firms face competitors that are much bigger than themselves, yet sometimes they win. How is that possible?[54] They can adopt four strategic postures depending on (1) the industry conditions and (2) the nature of their firm's competitive assets. Shown in Figure 13.2, these factors suggest four strategic actions.[55]

In Cell 3, in some industry segments, the pressures to globalize are relatively low, and local firms' strengths lie in a deep understanding of local markets. Therefore, a defender strategy, by leveraging local assets in areas in which MNEs are weak, is often called for. For example, in Israel, facing an onslaught from MNE cosmetics firms, a number of local firms turned to focus on products suited to the Middle Eastern climate and managed to defend their turf. Ahava has been particularly successful, in part because of its unique components extracted from the Dead Sea that MNEs cannot find elsewhere.[56] In essence, a defender strategy is making the best of local resources to compete in domestic and regional markets where the local firms has unique advantages allows the local firm to stay ahead of its foreign competitors. Even in highly global industries such as brewing, local firms may find a niche market where they can avoid head-on competition with the global players. For example, Innis & Gunn, a Scottish speciality brewer established in 2004, has grown to sell 500 000 cases of bottled ale a year. Yet, it isn't even brewing the beer itself – the brewing is outsourced to one of the large brewers, Innis & Gunn solely focuses on building and selling the brand. It found a niche market where it can compete, and even export (also see Closing Case).[57]

In Cell 4, in some industries with less pressure for globalization, local firms may possess some skills and assets that are transferable overseas, thus leading to an extender strategy. This strategy centres on leveraging home-grown competencies abroad. For instance, Asian Paints controls 40 per cent of the house paint market in India. Asian Paints developed strong capabilities tailored to the unique environment in India, characterized by thousands of small retailers serving numerous poor consumers who only want small quantities of paint that can be diluted to save

Defender strategy
This strategy centres on leveraging local assets in areas in which MNEs are weak.

Extender strategy
This strategy centres on leveraging home-grown competencies abroad.

Figure 13.2 How local firms may respond to MNE actions

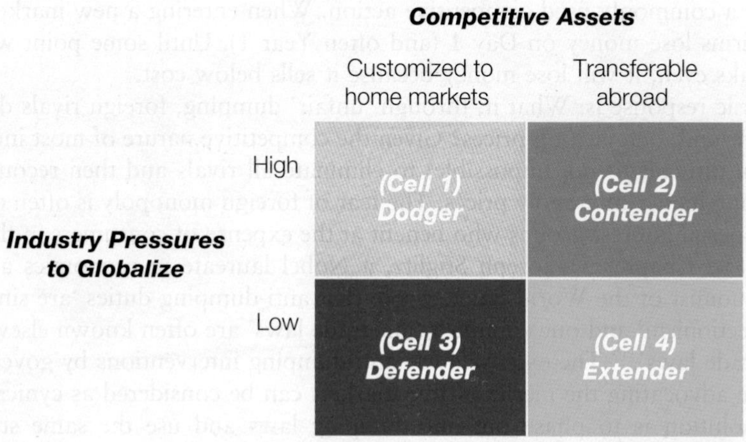

Source: Adapted from N. Dawar & T. Frost, 1999, Competing with giants: Survival strategies for local companies in emerging markets (p. 122), *HBR*, March–April: 119–129.

money. Such capabilities are not only a winning formula in India but also in much of the developing world.

Cell 1 depicts a most difficult situation for local firms that compete in industries with high pressures for globalization. Thus, a dodger strategy is necessary, which involves some form of collaboration. For example, local firms may cooperate through joint ventures (JVs) with MNEs and sell-offs to MNEs. In the Chinese automobile industry, *all* major local automakers have entered JVs with MNEs. The essence of this strategy is that to the extent that local firms are unable to successfully compete head on against MNEs, cooperation becomes necessary. In other words, if you can't beat them, join them!

Finally, in cell 2, some local firms, through a contender strategy, engage in rapid learning in their home environment and then expand overseas. A number of Chinese mobile phone makers such as TCL and Bird have rapidly caught up with global heavyweights such as Motorola and Nokia. By 2003, local firms, from a 5 per cent market share five years earlier, commanded more than 50 per cent market share in China. Engaging in a 'learning race', TCL and Bird moved to attack their rivals overseas once they had build the necessary competences. To do this successfully, however, requires a lot of resources.

How local firms respond is especially crucial in emerging economies opening up to international competition. In China, after an initial dominance, MNEs are not always 'kings of the hill'. In numerous industries (such as sportswear, cellular phone, personal computer and home appliance), many MNEs have been 'dethroned'. Although weak local players are washed out, some of the leading local players (such as Huawei in Opening Case), having won the game in the highly competitive domestic environment, now challenge MNEs overseas. In the process, they become a new breed of MNEs themselves.[58]

Competition versus anti-dumping

To most people, 'fair competition' also implies that governments play 'fair' and don't use legal tricks such as dumping investigations to prevent foreign entry. There are two arguments against the practice of imposing anti-dumping restrictions on foreign firms. First, because dumping centres on selling below cost, it is often difficult (if not impossible) to prove the case, given the ambiguity concerning cost. The second argument is that if foreign firms are indeed selling below cost, so what? This is simply a commonly used competitive action. When entering a new market, virtually all firms lose money on Day 1 (and often Year 1). Until some point when the firm breaks even, it will lose money because it sells below cost.

A classic response is: What if, through 'unfair' dumping, foreign rivals drive out local firms and then jack up prices? Given the competitive nature of most industries, it is often difficult (if not impossible) to eliminate all rivals and then recoup losses by charging higher monopoly prices. The fear of foreign monopoly is often exaggerated by special interest groups who benefit at the expense of consumers in the entire country (see Chapter 5). Joseph Stiglitz, a Nobel laureate in economics and then chief economist of the World Bank, wrote that anti-dumping duties 'are simply naked protectionism' and one country's 'fair trade laws' are often known elsewhere as 'unfair trade laws'.[59] The extensive use anti-dumping interventions by governments otherwise advocating the merits of free markets can be considered as cynical.

One solution is to phase out anti-dumping laws and use the same standards against domestic predatory pricing. Such a waiver of anti-dumping charges has been in place between Australia and New Zealand, between Canada and the USA, and within the EU. Thus, a Portuguese firm, essentially treated as a domestic firm, can be accused of predatory pricing but cannot be accused of dumping in France or

Dodger strategy
This strategy centres on cooperating through joint ventures (JVs) with MNEs and sell-offs to MNEs.

Contender strategy
This strategy centres on a firm engaging in rapid learning and then expanding overseas.

Germany. However, domestically, as noted earlier, a predation case is very difficult to make. In such a way, competition can be fostered, aggressiveness rewarded and 'dumping' legalized.

IMPLICATIONS FOR PRACTICE

LEARNING OBJECTIVE

7 Draw implications for action

Let us revisit our fundamental question: What determines the success and failure in managing competitive dynamics around the world? Drawing on the two core perspectives (institution- and resource-based views), we suggest that to successfully manage competitive dynamics, managers not only need to become masters of manoeuvres (both confrontation and cooperation) but also experts in government regulations if they aspire to successfully navigate the global landscape.

Consequently, three clear implications for action emerge for managers (Table 13.6). First, managers need to understand their competitors, and how they are likely to react to any competitive move. The reaction depends on the competitor's awareness, motivation and capability, but also on their ability to use the institutional context to their advantage.

Second, managers need to understand how the rules of the game governing competition vary around the world, and how they can use these rules to their advantages. For example, if you are drawn into collusion with a competitor, or you discover someone else in your company is, it is important to understand the nature of leniency programmes: Often it pays to get out quickly and report your collaborators to the authorities, else you may face very large fines indeed.[60] Likewise, in anti-dumping cases or patent protection, firms with capabilities in managing legal processes and interactions with the regulatory authorities are often one step ahead of their competitors.[61]

Third, managers need to strengthen their capabilities to effectively compete and/or cooperate. In attacks and counter-attacks, subtlety, frequency, complexity and unpredictability are often helpful to improve a firm's market position. In cooperation, market similarity and mutual forbearance may be better. As Sun Tzu advised 2500 years ago, you, as a manager, need to 'know yourself' – including your unit, your firm and your industry.

Table 13.6 Implications for action

- Analyze your competitor to be able to predict likely reactions and counter-attacks.
- Understand the rules of the game governing domestic and international competition around the world.
- Strengthen resources and capabilities that more effectively compete and/or cooperate.

CHAPTER SUMMARY

1 Explain how attacks and counter-attacks are used in dynamic competition:

- Attackers need to consider possible counter-attacks, which are driven by (1) awareness, (2) motivation and (3) capability.

2 Explain how and why firms sometimes like to collude:

- Collusion may enable firms to collectively earn higher return at the expense of their customers and/or suppliers.

- Industries primed for collusion tend to have (1) a smaller number of rivals, (2) a price leader, (3) homogeneous products, (4) high entry barriers and (5) high market commonality.

- Without talking directly to competitors, firms can signal to rivals by various means.

3 Outline how competition policy and anti-dumping laws affect international competition:

- Competition policies outlaw (1) price-raising cartels, (2) division of markets and (3) anti-competitive practices by dominant firms.

- Internationally, anti-dumping laws discriminate against foreign firms and protect domestic firms.

4 Articulate how resources and capabilities influence competitive dynamics:

- Resources meeting the VRIO criteria are necessary for long-term success in a competitive battle.

5 Discuss how firms can compete during a major recession:

- Survival strategies focus on liquidity and preservation of resources.

- Strategies for the next upswing focus on the strategic positioning in post-recession markets.

- Scenario analysis is a powerful tool to better understand the possibilities of the future.

6 Participate in two leading debates concerning the politics of competition:

- They are (1) small firms competing with Big MNEs and (2) anti-dumping versus competition.

7 Draw implications for action:

- Analyze your competitor to be able to predict likely reactions and counter-attacks.

- Understand the rules of the game governing competition around the world.

- Strengthen resources and capabilities that more effectively compete and/or cooperate.

KEY TERMS

Anti-competitive practices (by a dominant firm)
Anti-trust laws
Attack
Awareness, motivation, capability (AMC) framework
Blue ocean strategy
Capacity to punish
Cartel
Collusion
Collusive price setting
Competition policy (anti-trust policy)
Competitive dynamics

Competitor analysis
Concentration ratio
Contender strategy
Contingency plans
Counter-attack
Cross-market retaliation
Defender strategy
Dodger strategy
Dumping
Economic forecasting
Explicit collusion
Extender strategy
Game theory
Leniency programmes

Market commonality
Market division collusion
Multimarket competition
Oligopoly
Patent race
Predatory pricing
Price leader
Prisoners' dilemma
Repeated game
Scenario planning
Survival strategies
Tacit collusion
Tit-for-tat

CRITICAL DISCUSSION QUESTIONS

1 As CEO, you feel the price war in your industry is undermining profits for all firms. However, you have been warned by corporate lawyers not to openly discuss pricing with rivals, who you know personally (you went to school with them). How would you signal your intentions?

2 As a CEO of a French firm, you are concerned that your firm and your industry in the EU are being devastated by non-EU imports. Trade lawyers suggest filing an anti-dumping case against leading foreign rivals in China and assure you a win. Would you file an anti-dumping case or not? Why?

3 As part of an attack, your firm (firm A) announces that in the next year, it intends to enter country X, where

the competitor (firm B) is very strong. Your firm's real intention is to march into country Y, where B is very weak. There is actually *no* plan to enter X. However, in the process of trying to 'fool' B, customers, suppliers, investors and the media are also being intentionally misled. What are the ethical dilemmas here? Do the pros of this action outweigh its cons?

4 You are running a restaurant and wish to serve your country's leading brands of wine and beer to your customer. The distributor of these brands is happy to supply you on the condition that you exclusively sell these brands. How do you react?

CLOSING CASE

Wolters: a local brand competes with global giants

Globalization has transformed the brewing industry in the 1980s and 1990s. Once dominated by local brewers brewing for town and county, at the onset of the 21st century a handful of global players dominate most European markets: Heineken, AB-Inbev, SABMiller and Carlsberg. The industry concentration happened later in Germany, but once it started, it seemed inevitable.

Hofbrauhaus Wolters, established in 1627, was the focus of local brewing tradition in the city of Braunschweig, Germany. It had been honoured with the title 'Hofbrauhaus' ('purveyors to the court of the duke') in 1882, a title it kept even after the duke fell in a revolution in 1918. Wolters became the regional market leader in the city of Braunschweig and its vicinity, but in 1986 Glide brewery from neighbouring Hanover acquired a majority stake and took over strategic control. Gilde brewery in turn was in 2003 acquired by Belgian Interbrew, who operationally integrated their operations across Germany, centralized administration and distribution, and focused on marketing its best-selling

brand, Hasseröder, through the distribution channels of the acquired firms. In 2005, Interbrew merged with Ambev of Brazil to form Inbev, and the brewery in Braunschweig with close to 120 employees became a minor site in a global MNE employing thousands of people. When Inbev decided at the end of the year to close down this brewery because it was not sufficiently profitable, they expected a smooth streamlining of their operations.

Yet, they underestimated the rebelliousness and determination of the people of Braunschweig. Wolters was highly embedded in the local community, and held in high esteem because of its long-running sponsorship of local cultural and sports events. When the closure of Wolters was announced, many local clubs feared for their future, and events such as the annual cycle race and the annual ATP tennis tournament seemed to be in danger. Local people mobilized in pubs, clubs and the internet, and special Wolters parties added spice to the nightlife of the city. Meanwhile, local politicians led by an energetic lord mayor committed to do their best to save the brewery.

Negotiations were pursued behind closed doors, while the local media speculated about possible

How can a local brewery compete against the Big Four brewing multinationals?

acquirers. Eventually, a surprised public learned that Wolters would be reborn: Four former managers had agreed to take over the company, the local saving bank had arranged a large loan and the city bought the brewery's real estate in a lease-back deal that helped liquidity. However, the four 'musketeers' faced formidable organizational challenges: Due to the centralization of business functions in Inbev, the local brewery had no administration, marketing or distribution organization; the whole organizational structure had to be rebuild from scratch.

Braunschweigers celebrated this miraculous survival with a cold Wolters beer, and despite the operational challenges, sales jumped upwards quickly after the sale of the company. The newly independent Wolters build on its traditional strength in the on-trade (pubs and restaurants), regaining old customers and signing new ones – gradually expanding beyond its traditional 50km radius around Braunschweig, even invading neighbouring Hanover where locals were disgruntled about Gilde brewery being downsized by Inbev. With strong sales, Wolters was able to pay off its debt to Inbev in 2009 ahead of schedule, and thus gained full control over the rights to its brand name.

It also resumed its role as lead sponsor of local sport events, including the football team of Eintracht Braunschweig.

Meanwhile local rival Feldschlößchen faced a similar fate. It had become part of the Holsten Group, which was acquired by Carlsberg. In 2009, Carlsberg decided to sell the brewery, but – crucially – insisted on keeping the brand name. The physical assets were acquired by Öttinger a fast growing brewing company producing supermarket own brand beers, and other products for the mass market. Wolters used the opportunity to strike a deal with Carlsberg: The Feldschlößchen brand is now brewed under contract in Wolters' facilities – but each beer strictly by its own traditional recipe.

However, not all was clear sailing, the global giants fought back. In 2010, Wolters lost a court case against the association of brewers in Munich regarding the use of the name Oktoberbier (October beer), which Wolters had used for 13 years. The Munich breweries (some of which owned by Inbev) claimed it could be confused with their Octoberfest. In a different battle, Wolters was fighting against tighter rules on advertising of alcoholic beverages, which it believed would strengthen global players with bargaining power vis-à-vis supermarkets where they quite literally buy up shelf space. In contrast, local brewers operating in niche markets are relying on local marketing and brand recognition.

Meanwhile, Inbev merged in 2008 with Anheuser-Busch of the USA to form AB-Inbev, the world largest brewing company employing some 120 000 people, and operating literally in all time zones.

DISCUSSION QUESTIONS

1 What are the key competitive strategies used in the global brewing industry?

2 How can a small brewery such as Wolters survive and generate profits in a globally concentrated industry?

3 What are the advantages, disadvantages and ethical considerations of sports sponsoring as a marketing strategy?

Sources: (1) *Handelsblatt*, 2002, Mehrheit will Verkauf von Gilde an Interbrew, November 15; (2) P. Lehna, 2006, Wolters-Chef: Unser Bier schmeckt auch ohne Lemon (interview), *Braunschweiger Zeitung*, October 26; (3) J. Fiene, 2009, Wolters zahlt Restforderung von Inbev, *Braunschweiger Zeitung*, April 15, (4) E.J. Zauner, 2009, Münchner Gericht verbietet Wolters Oktoberbier, *Braunschweiger Zeitung*, May 7; (5) C. Böse-Fischer, 2010, Bier braucht doch Heimat, *Hannoversche Allgemeine*, January 15, and other news items in the same local newspapers.

RECOMMENDED READINGS

A. Dixit & B. Nalebuff, 1991, *Thinking Strategically*, New York: Norton – A very practical book that extracts ideas from game theory that help businesses (and individuals) make decisions in competitive situations.

A. Brandenburger & B. Nalebuff, 1996, *Co-opetition*, New York: Doubleday – A strategy book that uses ideas from game theory to explain how firms interact, often competing and cooperating at the same time.

M.J. Chen, 1996, Competitor analysis and inter-firm rivalry, *AMR*, 21: 100–134 – Theoretical paper that introducing the awareness, motivation, capability framework on dynamic competition.

E.J. Morgan, 2009, Controlling cartels – Implications of the EU policy reforms, *EMJ*, 27: 1–12 – A synthesis of the institutional framework regarding collusion and cartels in the EU.

D.F. Spulber, 2007, *Competitive Strategy*, Cambridge: Cambridge University Press – A strategy textbook that focuses on competition in the global economy.

NOTES:

"FOR JOURNAL ABBREVIATION, PLEASE SEE PAGE XXVI-XXVII."

1 K. Coyne & J. Horn, 2009, Predicting your competitors' reaction, *HBR*, April: 90–97; N. Kumar, 2006, Strategies to fight low-cost rivals, *HBR*, December: 104–112.

2 V. Rindova, M. Becerra & I. Contardo, 2004, Enacting competitive wars, *AMR*, 29: 670–686; G.D. Markman, P.T. Gianiodis & A.K. Buchholtz, 2009, Factor-market rivalry, *AMR*, 34: 423–441.

3 A. Brandenburger & B. Nalebuff, 1996, *Co-opetition* (p. 4), New York: Currency Doubleday.

4 M.J. Chen, 1996, Competitor analysis and interfirm rivalry, *AMR*, 21: 100–134; K.G. Smith, W. Ferrier & H. Ndofor, 2001, Competitive dynamics research, In: M.A. Hitt, R.E. Freeman & J.S. Harrison, eds: *Blackwell Handbook of Strategic Management*: 315–361. London: Blackwell.

5 M.J. Chen, K.H. Su & W. Tsai, 2007, Competitive tension: The awareness-motivation-capability perspective, *AMJ*, 50: 101–118; J.S. McMullen, D.A. Shephard & H. Patzelt, 2009, Managerial

(In)attention to competitive threats, *JMS*, 46: 157–181.

6 K.E. Meyer & E. Sinani, 2009, When and where does foreign direct investment generate positive spillovers? *JIBS,* 40: 1075–1094; T. Hutzschenreuter & F. Gröne, 2009, Product and geographic scope changes of multinational enterprises in response to international competition, *JIBS*, 40: 1149–1170.

7 W.C. Kim & R. Mauborgne, 2005, *Blue Ocean Strategy*, Boston: Harvard Business School Press.

8 T. Yu & A.A. Cannella, 2007, Rivalry between multinational enterprises, *AMJ,* 50: 665–686.

9 *Business Week*, 2009, How Microsoft is fighting back (finally), April 20.

10 M. Blomström & A. Kokko, 2003, The economics of foreign direct investment incentives, NBER Working Paper #9489; J.W. Spencer, 2008, The impact of multinational enterprise strategy on indigenous enterprises, *AMR*, 33: 341–361.

11 G. Tullock, 1985, Adam Smith and the prisonners' dilemma, *QJE*, 100, 1073–1081; J.B. Baker, 1999, Newdevelopments in antitrust economics, *JEP*, 13, 181–194.

12 R. Axelrod & W.D. Hamilton, 1983, The evolution of cooperation, *Science*, 211, 1390–1396; D.F. Midgey, R.E. Marks & L.G. Cooper, 1997, Breeding competitive strategies, *MS*, 43, 257–275.

13 A. Mainkar, M. Lubatkin & W. Schulze, 2006, Toward a product-proliferation theory of entry barriers, *AMR*, 31: 1062–1075.

14 J.B. Barney, 2002, *Gaining and Sustaining Competitive Advantage* (p. 359), Upper Saddle River, NJ: Prentice Hall.

15 F. Smith & R. Wilson, 1995, The predictive validity of the Karnani and Wernerfelt model of multipoint competition, *SMJ*, 16: 143–160; M. Semadeni, 2006, Minding your distance, *SMJ*, 27: 169–187.

16 Chen, 1996, *as above*.

17 F. Knickerbocker, 1973, *Oligopolistic Reaction and Multinational Enterprise*, Boston: Harvard Business School Press; J.F. Hennart & Y.R. Park, 1994, Location, governance, and strategic determinants of Japanese manufacturing investment in the United States, *SMJ*, 15: 419–436; J. Anand & B. Kogut, 1997, Technological capabilities of countries, firm rivalry, and foreign direct investment, *JIBS*, 28: 445–465; K. Ito & E. Rose, 2002, Foreign direct investment location strategies in the tire industry, *JIBS*, 33: 593–602.

18 K.E. Meyer & Y.T.T. Tran, 2006, Market penetration and acquisition strategies for emerging economies, *LRP*, 39: 177–197.

19 J.A.C. Baum & H. Korn, 1996, Competitive dynamics of interfirm rivalry, *AMJ*, 39: 255–291.

20 *USA Today*, 2005, Price remarks by Toyota chief could be illegal, June 10.

21 T.W. Tong & J.J. Reuer, 2010, Competitive consequences of interfirm collaboration, *JIBS*, 41: 1056–1073.

22 M. Motta, 2004, *Competition Policy: Theory and Practice*, Cambridge: Cambridge University Press; M. Furse, 2008, *Competition Law of the EC and UK*, Oxford: Oxford University Press.

23 J. Clougherty, 2005, Antitrust holdup source, cross-national institutional variation and corporate political strategy implications for domestic mergers in a global context, *SMJ*, 26: 769–790.

24 S. Evenett, M. Levenstein & V. Suslow, 2001, International cartel enforcement, *IE,* 24: 1221–1245.

25 C. Damro, 2006, The new trade politics and EU competition policy, *JEPP*, 13: 867–886; S. McGuire & M. Smith, 2008, *The European Union and the United States*, Basingstoke: Palgrave.

26 E.J. Morgan, 2009, Controlling cartels, *EMJ*, 27: 1–12.

27 *The Economist*, 2010, Mexico's competition policy: Busting the cartels, March 6.

28 *Frankfurter Allgemeine Zeitung*, 2009, Milliarden-Bußgeld für Eon und GdF, July 9.

29 P. Meller, 2003, European court tells Unilever it can't restrict store freezers, *New York Times*, October 24; European Court of Justice, 2006, *Unilever v Commission*, C-552/03 P.

30 European Court of First Instance, 2008, *Deutsche Telekom v Commission*, T-271/03.

31 J. Vickers, 2009, Competition policy and property rights, Department of Economics Discussion paper Series #436, University of Oxford.

32 *The Economist*, 2010, Antitrust in the European Union: Unchained watchdog, February 20.

33 R. Lipstein, 1997, Using antitrust principles to reform antidumping law (p. 408, original italics), in E. Graham & D. Richardson (eds.), *Global Competition Policy* (pp. 405–438), Washington, DC: Institute for International Economics.

34 OECD, 1996, *Trade and Competition: Frictions after the Uruguay Round* (p. 18), Paris: OECD.

35 J.P. Lindeque, 2007, A firm perspective of anti-dumping and countervailing duty cases in the United States, *JWT*, 41: 559–579.

36 T. Prusa, 2001, On the spread and impact of antidumping (p. 598), *CJE*, 34: 591–611.

37 S. Marsh, 1998, Creating barriers for foreign competitors, *SMJ*, 19: 25–37.

38 M. Finger, F. Ng, & S. Wangchuk, 2001, Antidumping as safeguard policy (p. 6), Working paper, World Bank.

39 J. R. Baum & S. Wally, 2003, Strategic decision speed and firm performance, *SMJ*, 24: 1107–1129; V. Terpstra & C. Yu, 1988, Determinants of foreign investment of US advertising agencies, *JIBS*, 19: 33–55.

40 W. Ferrier, K.G. Smith & C. Grimm, 1999, The role of competitive action in market share erosion and industry dethronement, *AMJ*, 42: 372–388.

41 D. Fudenberg, R. Gilbert, J. Stiglitz & J. Tirole, 1983, Preemption, leapfrogging and competition in patent races, *EER*, 22, 3–31.

42 *The Economist*, 2005, A market for ideas, October 22.

43 C. Pegels, Y. Song, & B. Yang, 2000, Management heterogeneity, competitive interaction groups and firm performance, *SMJ*, 21: 911–923.

44 B. Golden & H. Ma, 2003, Mutual forbearance, *AMR*, 28: 479–493; A. Kalnins, 2004, Divisional multimarket contact within and between multiunit organizations, *AMJ*, 47: 117–128.

45 J.A. Schumpeter, 1939, *Business Cycles: A Theoretical, Historical, and Statistical Analysis of the Capitalist Process*, vol. II, New York: McGraw Hill; K. Galbraith, 1957, *The Great Crash of 1929*, London: Penguin; P. Krugman, 2008, *The return of depression economics*: Penguin.

46 This section is based on K.E. Meyer, 2009, Thinking strategically during the global downturn, *AIB Insights* 9 (2): 2–7.

47 J.A. Quelch & K.E. Jocz, 2009, How to market in a recession, *HBR*, April: 52–62.

48 P.J. Williamson & M. Zeng, 2009, Value-for-money strategies for recessionary times, *HBR*, March: 66–74.

49 *The Economist*, 2009, Hyundai's surprising success: Sui genesis, March 7.

50 P.K. Yuk, 2010, Investing in new products and markets pays dividends, *Financial Times*, March 12.

51 P.J.H. Shoemaker, 1995, Scenario planning: A tool for strategic thinking, *SMR*, 36: 28–40; H. Courtney, 2001, *20/20 foresight: Crafting strategy in an uncertain world*, Cambridge, MA: Harvard Business School Press; I. Wilson, 2000, From scenarios thinking to strategic action, *TFSC*, 65: 23–29.

52 L. Bryan & D. Farrel, 2008, Leading through uncertainty, *MQ*, December, p. 1–13.

53 P. Goodwin & G. Wright, 2001, Enhancing strategy evaluation in scenario-planning, *JMS*, 38, 1–16.

54 Ferrier et al., 1999, as above K.G. Smith, W.J. Ferrier & C.M. Grimm, 2001, King of the hill, *AME*, 15: 59–70.

55 N. Dawar & T. Frost, 1999, Competing with giants, *HBR*, March–April: 119–129.

56 D. Lavie & A. Fiegenbaum, 2000, Strategic reaction of domestic firms to foreign MNC dominance, *LRP*, 33: 651–672.

57 A. Bolger, 2010, The accidental beer business, *Financial Times*, March 10.

58 J. Mathews, 2006, Dragon multinationals, *APJM*, 23: 5–27; A. Cuerco-Cazurra, 2008, The multinationalization of developing country MNEs, *JIM*, 14: 138–151; R. Ramamurti & J.V. Singh, eds, 2009, *Emerging Multinationals in Emerging Markets*, Cambridge: Cambridge University Press.

59 J. Stiglitz, 2002, *Globalization and Its Discontent* (pp. 172–173), New York: Norton.

60 Morgan, 2009, *as above*.

61 Lindeque, 2007, as above; C. Roquilly, 2009, La cas de l'iPhone en tant qu'illustration du rôle des resources juridiques et de la capacité juridique dans le management de l'innovation, *M@n@gement*, 12: 142–174.

CHAPTER FOURTEEN

© Mark Evans/iStock

BUILDING GLOBAL STRATEGIES

LEARNING OBJECTIVES

After studying this chapter you should be able to:

1   Articulate the strategic advantages of globally operating firms.

2   Explain different business modes to exploit the advantages of a globally operating firm.

3   Explain why global firms engage in mergers and acquisitions and alliances.

4   Apply the institution-based view to explain patterns of acquisitions.

5   Apply the resource-based view to explain when acquisitions are likely to succeed.

6   Participate in two leading debates on acquisitions.

7   Draw implications for action.

OPENING CASE

Danisco: the evolution of a global niche leader

When in March 2009, Danisco announced the completion of the sale of its Sugar division to its German competitor Nordzucker, many Danes were rubbing their eyes. For them, the name 'Danisco' was synonymous with Sugar. What was Danisco doing now? The answer is that Danisco has been undergoing a steady transformation over 20 years. Experts in the industry and financial analysts have been following the remarkable transformation of one of Denmark's leading companies. Yet, the wider public knew little about what they actually were doing. Why? Because most people know companies with famous consumer brand names. Danisco, however, had become a market leader in business-to-business markets – apart from its now sold Sugar division.

After the transformation, Danisco was positioned as a specialized supplier of food ingredients based on natural raw materials. Its customers included global food giants such as Unilever, Kraft, Danone and Nestlé, as well as regional and local players in all major economies. Danisco specialized on ingredients that alter the properties of processed foods such as yoghurts, ice cream, sauces and bread. Its business model included not only the development and manufacture of these ingredients, but the development of applications for the ingredients jointly with customers. For example, Danisco was involved in the creation of Magnum ice cream which is successfully marketed by major brand manufacturers around the world.

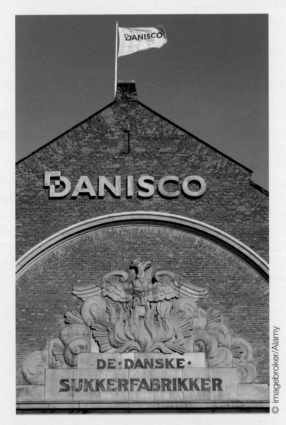

Danisco's historical headquarters in Copenhagen advertise "The Danish Sugar Factories"; how does this history shape the strategies for the future?

To emphasize the innovation-driven nature of their business, Danisco adopted the slogan 'First you add knowledge'.

When the global financial crisis hit in 2008, Danisco's first priority was to advance ingredients that would help its customers save costs. A major market research project investigated how people change their food purchasing behaviour during the recession. On this basis, Danisco determined which kinds of solutions were required in specific food industry sectors; and focused its marketing on product properties that help reduce costly ingredients (like fats) or extend shelf-life. For example, they advanced a functional stabilizer that enables efficient replacement of egg without any alteration to processing lines, while also being easier and cheaper to store than liquid egg yolk.

How did Danisco become a global market leader in this niche? Danisco had been created in 1989 by a merger of three companies aiming to create a strong Danish company that could compete in the EU common market after its completion in 1992. The merger was hoped to keep traditional businesses in Danish hands, and enhance their viability. The new company was a diversified conglomerate operating mainly in Denmark and other parts of Northern and Western Europe. From the outset the company aimed to focus its profile and to strengthen its core businesses. In the first annual report (1989/1990), the corporate strategy was stated as 'to be a first-class supplier to the international food industry on the global market and be a supplier of high quality foods and branded goods on selected European markets'. Over the next years, the foods, food ingredients and packaging businesses were grown, while businesses in the machine building segment were sold.

In the sugar sector, Danisco first consolidated its dominant position in Denmark, and then grew by acquisitions around the Baltic Sea in Sweden, (East) Germany, Poland and Lithuania. The sugar market was shaped by EU regulation that aimed to protect sugar beet farmers, but that also constrained the intensity of competition and limited the scope for aggressive growth. Liberalization of this market had long been anticipated, and it finally came into effect in 2009.

In 1999, Danisco announced a new strategy focusing solely on food ingredients, and acquired Finnish ingredients manufacturer Cultor OY to cement this strategic shift. At the same time, Dansico began to sell its businesses in branded foods and food packaging including Danish icon brands like Aalborg Snaps. Two divisions thus remained: Danisco Ingredients was developing, manufacturing and distributing emulsifiers, stabilizers, flavours and enzymes, while Danisco Sugar dominated northern European sugar markets. During this transformation, the internationalization of sales rapidly increased, with sales outside Denmark rising from 69 per cent 1995 to 88 per cent in 2004 and over 95 per cent after the sale of the sugar division. In 2009, Danisco generated €1.7 million turnover, of which 38 per cent came from Europe, 40 per cent from the Americas and 17 per cent from Asia-Pacific. Danisco employed 6800 people in 17 countries, in part to serve local markets, such as China, and in part to process natural ingredients only found in specific locations, such as Chile. Expansion in Europe, North America and Australia occurred mainly through acquisitions, while business in emerging markets grew to a larger extent by greenfield projects.

The sale of the sugar division in 2009 thus was the logical consequence of the two-decade long transformation process. The synergies between the sugar and ingredients sectors had diminished, while liberalization of the EU sugar regime led to the expectation of changing competitive dynamics in the sector. However, before completing the sale to Nordzucker AG of Germany, clearance needed to be obtained from competition authorities in those countries where both Nordzucker and Dansico held substantive market shares.

Sources: Based on Cortzen, J. 1997. *Merchants and Mergers: The Story of Danisco*, Copenhagen: Børsens Forlag; Meyer, K.E. and Møller, I.B. 1998. Managing Deep Restructuring: Danish Experiences in Eastern Germany, *EMJ*, 16: 411–421; Meyer, K.E. 2006. Globalfocusing: From domestic conglomerate to global specialist, *JMS*, 43(5): 1109–1144; Danisco (various years): Danisco annual reports; Danisco (2009): Latest News, www.danisco.com (accessed March 2010).

Why did Danisco change the focus of its business so drastically? Why did it make aggressive acquisitions around the world, while selling some of its former core businesses? How do companies like Danisco create value in such dispersed yet integrated operations around the world? The diversity of the global economy creates both challenges and opportunities for companies transcending borders and

Global strategies
Strategies that take advantage of operations spread across the world.

continents. This chapter focuses on the opportunities of global strategies, and how companies can make best use of the diversity of the world. Global strategies take advantage of operations spread across the world, they do *not* imply that the company is present everywhere, or that different parts of the world are equally important. In fact, most companies with global strategies have a major share of their operation close to their origins.

We first summarize different types of advantages that firms may be chasing when they develop global strategies. Then, we introduce the AAA typology of strategies that illustrates different ways in which firms can create value by integrating operations across countries: aggregation, adaptation and arbitrage.[1] Thereafter, we explore how firms use acquisitions to develop the kinds of global operations that allow them to deploy these strategies on the global stage, and discuss how institution- and resource-based views help explain the patterns and performance of acquisitions. Debates and extensions follow.

AAA typology
Aggregation, adaptation and arbitrage strategies.

COMPETITIVE ADVANTAGES OF THE GLOBAL FIRM

LEARNING OBJECTIVE

1 Articulate the strategic advantages of globally operating firms

International operations can help multinational enterprises entrepreneurships (MNEs) to develop competitive advantages in several ways, providing MNEs an edge over firms that operate only in a single country (Table 14.1).[2] Not every MNE exploits all of these potential advantages, but many benefit from several of them. Their relevance varies with the nature of the industry and the company's business models.

Global scale

Economies of scale
Reduction in unit costs achieved by increasing volume.

A basic advantage of MNEs over their typical domestic rivals is simply their size. Advantages of size are known as economies of scale, that is the reduction in unit cost that is achieved by increasing the volume of production. In manufacturing, economies of scale arise from higher capacity utilization, or from larger production facilities. Thus, the fixed costs of setting up a factory or a production line are distributed over a larger number of products. Large volume production thus reduces the costs of each unit. MNEs selling from a single manufacturing facility to many countries thus achieve economies of scale in their production.

In addition, scale advantages at other stages of the value chain are of increasing importance in the 21st century. In particular, MNEs may share their costs of

Table 14.1 Strategic advantages of global firms

- global scale advantages reduce costs in production, product development and marketing
- global sourcing provides access to a wider range of inputs
- global knowledge management enhances innovation
- global operation allows better servicing of global customers
- risk diversification reduces the corporate risk profile

designing and developing new products across products manufactured and sold at multiple locations. In sectors such as the car industry, these scale advantages of development can be enormous. Selling more cars by serving many countries thus makes a big difference to the price the manufacturer has to charge to recoup their R&D investment. Even if cars produced around the world vary in their design, they may share a common platform of technologies and components, which greatly reduces the development costs of new models.

Scale economies also arise in numerous other activities. For example, the volume of purchasing increases bargaining power vis-à-vis suppliers. Like in your weekly shopping, bulk buying reduces the unit prices paid by MNEs purchasing components or raw materials. Similarly, the scale of global brands reduces costs of development and marketing a brand.

Global sourcing

Businesses operating on the global stage can access resources in a variety of locations. Hence, they can source every input where it is available at the best quality or the lowest price. Exploiting even small cost differences, especially for raw materials, components and labour can make a substantial difference to a firm's cost structure – provided they are not eaten up by transport costs. Moreover, global sourcing enables firms to access specific qualities of raw materials available only at a limited number of locations. For example, Danisco (see Opening Case) set up a specialized plant to processes specific types of algae that were only available in the sea off the coast of Southern Chile.

Global sourcing
Buying inputs all over the world.

Bringing together operations at different locations in a single organization, MNEs thus can exploit comparative advantages (Chapter 5). Exporters and importers also exploit comparative advantages, yet MNEs do so internally, which enhances their operational flexibility by allowing smooth shifts of production from one site to another should circumstances change.[3] Especially activities that have low set-up costs can be moved in response to, for example, changes in exchange rates or labour costs.[4] MNEs can organize production geographically dispersed, yet integrated in a global supply chain.

Global innovation and knowledge management

Global companies can spread their research and development (R&D) units to tap into capabilities available at different sites. For example, a presence in Silicon Valley, California provides access to latest ideas in information technology, while biotechnology firms cluster around Cambridge, England or Copenhagen, Denmark. At the same time, innovation centres around the world provide exposure to different customer expectations when developing new products or services.

MNEs with dispersed yet inter-connected centres of excellence thus can reap several benefits. First, they can overcome the potential replication and inconsistency of standards that may evolve in case of disconnected R&D operations. Second, the interaction between research units at different locations enhances creativity and idea generation, and thus innovation. Third, centres of excellence allow exploitation of comparative advantages in for example specialized human resources, such as IT skills in India. A study by consultants Booz & Company demonstrates these benefits empirically. They show that international linkages between R&D units, rather than increased R&D spending per se, enhance innovation MNEs that deployed more than 60 per cent of their R&D outside their home countries were found to perform better on several indicators.[5]

Centres of excellence
Specialized centres for innovation that serve the entire MNE.

Moreover, global operations allow companies to share and exploit knowledge better than firms with only arm's-length relationships across borders.[6] MNEs connect people and businesses that operate in different environments, yet may face similar business challenges. Bringing these people together within one organization allows them to exchange knowledge, experiences and competences, which in turn facilitates the creation of new innovations and competencies. Global knowledge management thus allows firms to create a shared pool knowledge that supports each individual operation. Chapter 15 explores some of the operational challenges of global knowledge management.

Global customers

Global key accounts
Customers served at multiple sites around the world, but that negotiate centrally.

Global operations are especially valuable when it comes to serving customers that themselves are operating at multiple locations. Such global customers, also known as global key accounts, may source their inputs internationally. In other words, they negotiate contracts with suppliers who would provide the same product or service at multiple sites. The automotive industry has been at the forefront of developing supply networks on a global scale. Manufacturers work closely with suppliers when developing new models, and expect them to deliver modules or components at any of their assembly sites. Danisco (Opening Case) similarly is developing relationships with global key accounts such as food manufacturers Nestlé, Danone and Unilever. Also, many business services, such as consultancy, accounting or advertising work with global key accounts.[7] Firms with a global distribution network and production sites close to key locations of their customers have a distinct advantage in serving such global customers.

Diversification of risk

Operations in multiple countries also reduce the financial risk profile of the overall company. Like portfolio investment, sales revenues from a variety of sources reduce the overall risk profile as long as they are less than perfectly positively correlated. It is rare that a recession hits every country at the same time. Thus, companies with global sales may be able to shift the focus of their activities to locations that are doing relatively well. In consequence, their global sales are less volatile over time than sales generated in a single market. Similarly, locating production at multiple sites reduces exposure to adverse events affecting any particular site, including not only economic events (such as a recession) but also natural disasters, wars and terrorism or a flu pandemic. With increased frequency of unexpected events disrupting global trade, risk management practices that allow companies to react flexibly to the unexpected can be a vital competitive advantage.

GLOBAL BUSINESS MODELS

LEARNING OBJECTIVE

2 Explain different business modes to exploit the advantages of a globally operating firm

Global strategies provide competitive advantages to companies that think and act on the international stage, rather than in a single country. In view of these advantages, scholars have been arguing for MNEs to globalize their offerings. The origins of this movement can be traced to a 1983 article published by Theodore Levitt, with a self-explanatory title: 'The Globalization of Markets'.[8] Levitt argued that there is a worldwide convergence of consumer tastes. As evidence, Levitt pointed out Coke Classic, Levi Strauss jeans and Sony colour TVs, which were successful on a worldwide basis. Levitt predicted that such convergence would characterize most product markets in the future.

Figure 14.1 AAA Strategies

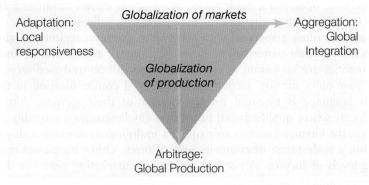

Source: Based on *'Redefining global strategy'* by P. Ghemawat, 2007, Harvard Business School Press, copyright © Harvard Business School Publishing, 2007. Reproduced with permission.

Levitt's article has often been used as the intellectual underpinning propelling many MNEs to globally integrate their products while minimizing local adaptation. Ford experimented with world car designs. MTV pushed ahead with the belief that viewers would flock to 'global' (essentially American) programming. Unfortunately, most of these experiments have not been successful. Ford finds that there are wide-ranging differences among consumer tastes around the globe. MTV has eventually realized that there is no global song. In a nutshell, one size does not fit all.[9] As we discussed in Chapter 1, globalization is about more intensive interfaces, not necessarily about convergence. Hence, global strategies are about making use of differences as well as communalities around the world. But how?

There is no single strategy that suits every firm – in fact coming up with a business idea that no one else has yet has thought of is a good basis for success. To classify business models, Harvard and IESE Professor Pankaj Ghemawat introduced three types: Arbitrage, Aggregation and Adaptation[10] (Figure 14.1). These strategies are not exclusive as many MNEs combine aspects of two or even all three strategies. However, trying to realize all three strategies at the same time may well overstretch organizational capabilities. Thus, choosing the right strategy is about finding a business model that best fits the specific firm, and its global competitive environment.

Aggregation strategy

An aggregation strategy focuses on the realization of synergies between operations in different locations by integrating them above the national level. It does not necessarily imply standardization, it may simply involve sharing of resources and integration of processes. For example, R&D laboratories serving a variety of activities may be pooled at a small number of strategic locations. Aggregation strategies are designed to exploit economies of scale, and to foster innovation and knowledge management. At the same time, activities that are best done differently may be located close to local resources and customers. For example, product development, sourcing and finance are often handled in regional or global business units, while sales, marketing and human resources are typically managed locally.

Aggregation may imply global centralization at headquarters (especially in smaller businesses), but not necessarily. Aggregation is often regional rather than global, thus reflecting the regional nature of much business. Global brand companies like Dell and Toyota in fact have supply chains that are region-based with separate hubs in Asia, Europe and North America.[11] Large organizations can vary their

Aggregation strategy
Strategy of realizing synergies between operations at different locations.

levels of aggregation, say global R&D, regional supply chains and local sales operations to fine-tune operations. Such varied aggregation allows optimizing synergies, yet it also increases complexity and thus cooperation challenges.

Aggregation is often associated with geography: country, region and global. But it can also follow other patterns. For example, cultural, administrative and linguistic communalities are important in consultancy and call-centre-based services. They may pool customers sharing a common language if communicating in the customers' own language is essential for the quality of their services. Alternatively, they may locate where qualified staff fluent in many languages are readily available. For instance, the Greater London area offers a multilingual workforce due to immigration from a wide range of countries and cultures. Other businesses may aggregate along levels of income as product design and marketing practices depend on how much consumers can afford.

Adaptation strategy

Adaptation strategy
Strategy of delivering locally adapted products in each market.

An adaptation strategy aims to deliver locally adapted products in each market. It thus allows serving consumers on their local terms despite differences in their needs, preferences and purchasing power. Adaptation is particularly important when entering distant countries, such as European businesses entering East Asia. In emerging economies, adaptation to local customers may take into consideration in particular (1) lower incomes, (2) higher variability of customer groups and (3) lower labour costs.[12] First, low incomes imply that marketing strategies imported from developed countries may not work: TV and internet advertising may not reach the target audiences cost-efficiently. Moreover, products designed in Europe may be too expensive or too complex, even if produced locally. Second, variations within the country may require even more fine-grained adaptations, for examples between rural and urban areas. Third, low labour costs create opportunities for business models that rely more on people, for instance by substituting capital-intensive sales and distribution processes by more labour intensive ones: sales assistants may hand out free samples to target customers, or promote drinks in restaurants and bars. Such an approach would be prohibitively expensive in Western Europe.

Yet adaptation does not mean that everything is done locally, or done differently in every country. MNEs can achieve variation without giving up the benefits of a global company. Ghemawat proposes four levers of adaptation (Table 14.2):[13] First, companies may focus on those activities and products where only a minimum of adaptation is required. For example, fast moving consumer goods MNEs may focus on young urban consumers whose consumption patterns vary less across countries than older or rural populations. Firms may also focus on stages of the value chain that require less adaptation, or sell the same product but position it in a different segment. A standard product from Western Europe may be positioned as a premium brand in an emerging economy, and thus be sold using different marketing and sales processes.[14] For example, Heineken and Carlsberg are considered mainstream beer brands in their home countries, yet in countries such as Vietnam they compete for leadership in the premium segment.[15]

Second, MNEs may externalize the costs of adaptation by working with local partners that contribute investment and local knowledge. For example, they may focus on business-to-business segments providing high-value added components that are incorporated variety of customized products by local firms. Other MNEs, such as McDonalds or KFC, have developed franchising models that empower local franchisees to vary products within the scope of the corporate brand and to carry the costs and risks associated with such adaptation.

Table 14.2 Levers of adaptation

Ideas	Examples
● Focus on activities and products that require less adaptation across markets	● Marketing to young urban consumers with cosmopolitan values ● Specialize in technologies or components used in a variety of final products
● Externalize the costs of adaptation by working with local partners	● Allow local franchisees and distributors to modify products and service delivery ● Enable users to modify the products to fit their needs
● Design the basic product in ways that increase flexibility of the final product to be produced for different markets	● Design products with shared platforms that economize on base technologies ● Design modular products that can be variously combined for different purposes
● Organize innovation processes with effectiveness of variation in mind	● Localize innovation to capitalize on local knowledge ● Recombine competences across the multiple locations

Source: Based on P. Ghemawat, 2007, *Redefining global strategy*, Boston: Harvard Business School Press.

Third, adaptability can be achieved through business models designed to share some communalities, but allow for adaptation to specific user groups or locations. For example, car manufacturers have developed their models around platforms and modules that allow production of a wide range of different cars with a small range of components and technologies. Fourth, local innovation allows creation of new products by locally knowledgeable people that can combine competences of the MNE with ideas available in the local context, and geared towards local needs. This increases variety of products without stretching central research and development units.

Arbitrage strategies

An arbitrage strategy exploits differences in prices in different markets. Prices for many goods vary across countries, which provides the basis for international trade (see Chapter 5) and provides many opportunities to earn money by moving products from one location to another. MNEs may be better positioned to exploit arbitrage as their subsidiaries can access local markets directly.[16]

Traditionally, arbitrage strategies opportunities were associated with labour, capital and natural resources. Strategies of labour arbitrage exchange the services of a labour force, and thus allow exploiting low cost labour or specialist human capital. Capital arbitrage is less common as financial markets are generally more efficient. Yet, some companies found ways to access capital at lower costs in foreign capital markets that are more internationalized and liquid. For example, many Chinese companies list on the Hong Kong stock market, while South African firms such as SABMiller list in London. Natural resource arbitrage exploits variation in geology and climate to trade energy resources (such as oil, gas and coal) minerals

Arbitrage strategy
Strategy of exploiting differences in prices in different markets.

How does the mining industry compete globally?

(such as copper, aluminium, zinc, gold, silver, diamonds) as well as agriculture, forestry and fishery products.

Location-bound humans capital also gives rise to arbitrage of knowledge-intensive services For example, educational institutions – from boarding schools and language classes to universities – sell their services to students, who come to their classrooms from all parts of the world. Similarly, entertainment experiences attract global audiences, such as musicals in London and New York, opera in Milan and Verona, or gambling in Monaco, Las Vegas and Macau. Similarly, medical services for patients worldwide are provided by hospitals in Singapore, Thailand, South Africa (beauty treatments!) and Eastern Europe who offer operations at much lower prices than for example in Western Europe.

Even used goods and waste can be an opportunity for arbitrage. Do you know how the world's richest self-made women, Cheung Yan, made her millions? From used paper![17] She is running the biggest paper mill business in the world by recycling paper from the USA in China. Now you may wonder how it can be worthwhile to ship paper all the way across the Pacific. Well, think of the US trade deficit. For years, the USA have been importing more products than they have been exporting. Full ships have crossing the Pacific eastbound, and returning comparatively empty westbound. Thus, freight rates from the USA to China have been rather low, making it economically viable to ship low value products. The diversity and communalities across the world thus provide a basis for a wide range of business models for firms with internationally dispersed operations.

LEARNING OBJECTIVE

3 Explain why global firms engage in mergers and acquisitions, and alliances

GROWTH BY ACQUISITIONS

Global operations provide competitive advantages, yet how do firms build global operations? One possibility would be organic growth with successive opening of new operations across the world. However, few firms choose this path – it simply

Figure 14.2 The variety of cross-border mergers and acquisitions

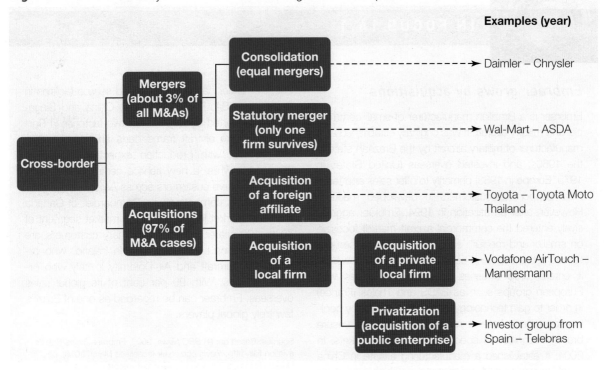

takes too much time. Companies with global ambitions thus typically grow through mergers and acquisitions (M&As).

An acquisition is a transfer of the control of operations and management from one firm (target) to another (acquirer), the former becoming a unit of the latter. For example, Danisco (Opening Case) acquired Cultor of Finland and integrated it in its own operations; Cultor ceased to exist as a firm. A merger is the combination of operations and management of two firms to establish a new legal entity. For instance, the merger in 2005 between Interbrew (Belgium) and Ambev (Brazil) created Inbev, which merged in 2009 with Anheuser Busch (USA) to form AB-Inbev. However, only 3 per cent of M&As are mergers (Figure 14.2). Even many so-called 'mergers of equals' turn out to be one firm taking over another. A recent *World Investment Report* opines that 'The number of "real" mergers is so low that, for practical purposes, "M&As" basically mean "acquisitions".'[18] Consequently, we will use 'M&As' and 'acquisitions' interchangeably.

Most large M&As are cross-border (international) M&As; they account for approximately 30 per cent of all M&As. In 2007 (a record year), M&A deals topped €2.9 trillion, of which €1.3 involved European companies. During the recession of 2009, the worldwide value of M&As dropped to €1.5 trillion, reflecting the lower asset prices, mirroring a similar drop after the 'internet bubble' of 2001 when M&A volume fell from €2.4 trillion to €0.9 trillion.[19] M&As represent the largest proportion of FDI flows, reaching approximately 70 per cent of worldwide FDI. Most of the largest MNEs of the world have grown by acquisitions, as have many MNEs from emerging economies that recently entered the global stage, such as Brazilian Embraer (In Focus 14.1) and Indian Bharti Airtel (Chapter 6, Closing Case).

Acquisition
The transfer of the control of operations and management from one firm (target) to another (acquirer), the former becoming a unit of the latter.

Merger
The combination of operations and management of two firms to establish a new legal entity.

IN FOCUS 14.1

Embraer grows by acquisitions

Embraer is a Brazilian manufacturer of small commercial and military aircraft. It was originally established as a manufacturer of military aircraft by the Brazilian state in the 1960s, and invested overseas (United States in 1979, Europe in 1988) primarily to offer sales and technical support to customers in developed markets. However, after privatization in 1994, Embraer aggressively entered the commercial aircraft market focusing on smaller and medium size jets. To build its competences in this segment, especially from 1999 onwards, it entered into a series of strategic alliances with European groups such as EADS and Thales (France) in order to gain technology (and to reduce risk by pooling resources). Later it made acquisitions to ensure brand recognition in specialist aerospace markets. In 2004, it established a manufacturing affiliate in China (in which it owns a 51 per cent stake), which assembles final aircraft for the Chinese and regional market. In

2009, Embraer had production and service facilities in Brazil, the USA, France, Portugal, China and Singapore, and started construction of two factories in Portugal to make aircraft frame parts and carbon fibre components, with production expected to start in 2012. Meanwhile, a new service centre in India was opened to serve customers across Asia.

Embaer is competing with Bombardier of Canada for world market leadership in the market segment of 70 to 100-seater aircraft. Its primary customers are regional airlines such as Jetbird in Ireland, who ordered 100 aircraft and Air Dolomity in Italy who ordered 30 jets. With 90 per cent of its global sales overseas, Embraer can be regarded as one of Brazil's few truly global players.

Sources: Based on: (1) *BBC News*, 2005, Embraer shows Brazil's aviation flair, http://news.bbc.co.uk (accessed March 2010); (2) United Nations, 2006, *World Investment Report 2006* (p. 159), Geneva: United Nations; (3) P. Blum, 2009, Brazilian jet maker expects to outlast crisis, *New York Times*, June 15.

Motives for acquisition

Synergies
Value created by combining two organization that together are more valuable than the two organizations separately.

What drives acquisitions? Table 14.3 shows three drivers: (1) synergies, (2) hubris, and (3) managerial motives.[20] First, synergies between two merging organizations mean that the new organization is more valuable than the two organizations separately, for example because only one central administration and one distribution channel is needed. Acquisitions may help firms to build the global operations they aspire, adding for example complementary market positions, production facilities or operational capabilities. The strategic complementarity of the resources of the two (or more) organizations thus forms the basis for synergies, and thus for the creation of value in the M&A.[21]

For example, when MOL, the Hungarian integrated oil refinery and distribution company, took over its Slovakian counterpart Slovnaft, it identified a wide range of synergies, including optimization of refinery production, linking of logistics networks, shared R&D, coordinated sales and marketing and integrated financial management. However, not all these synergies could be realized, for example in the area of logistics, while synergies in marketing and finance exceeded expectation.[22] The realization of synergies is a challenging managerial task that only some firms have mastered.

A related M&A driver is to establish a strong market position, or to enhance market power.[23] Mittal Steel's acquisition of European market leader Arcelor in 2007, propelled the Indian-owned MNE into a global leadership position with almost 10 per cent of world steel output. Arcelor's high-tech steel plants, particularly in France and Belgium, added new capabilities to Mittals's existing less sophisticated

Table 14.3 Motives for acquisitions

Synergistic motives	• Leverage superior organizational capabilities
	• Enhance market power
	• Reduce costs by eliminating duplicate units and exploiting scale economies
	• Access to complementary resources
Hubris motives	• Managers' overconfidence in their capabilities
Managerial motives	• Self-interested actions such as empire building and bonuses

Why do you think Lufthansa acquired Austrian Airlines in 2008?

facilities, and enabled it to raise the quality of its products, especially for technologically demanding buyers, such as the car industry. Moreover, the acquisition gave Mittal a bridgehead into new Latin American markets.[24]

While synergistic motives, in theory, add value, other motives can reduce shareholder value. Hubris refers to managers' overconfidence in their capabilities.[25] Managers of acquiring firms make two strong statements. The first is, 'We can manage *your* assets better than you [target firm managers] can!' The second statement is even bolder. Given that acquirers of publicly listed firms have to pay an acquisition premium, this is essentially saying: 'We can achieve something no one else can'. Capital markets are (relatively) efficient and the market price of target firms reflects their intrinsic value. Yet, an acquirer offering a premium suggests to create more value in the acquired firm than other owners, usually due to expected synergies. Empirical studies, however, show that very often the premium is too high, and

Hubris
A manager's overconfidence in his or her capabilities.

acquiring firms have overpaid.[26] For example, Kraft was widely believed to have overpaid for British chocolate maker Cadbury in 2010 as outside observers wondered how Kraft would be able to realize the synergies implied in its acquisition premium. One explanation of this frequent overpayment is that managers – often encouraged by their financial advisors – overestimate their own abilities.

While the hubris motives suggest that managers may *unknowingly* overpay for targets, managerial motives posit that for self-interested reasons, some managers may *knowingly* overpay for target firms in their personal quest for more power, prestige and money. This behaviour is caused by agency problems. Managers as 'agents' are supposed to act in shareholders best interest, yet they can use their inside knowledge to advance their own goals because shareholders lack effective mechanisms of control. While managerial self-interest is usually hard to prove, it is often suggested by opponents of a deal. For example, when German state railway company Die Bahn took over British bus and train operator Arriva, several politicians suggested that managers were pursuing their own interests rather than those of the owners, in this case the German state.[27]

Acquisitions versus alliances

Strategic alliances
Collaborations between independent firms using equity modes, non-equity contractual agreements, or both.

An alternative to a full take over of another firm is a collaboration with that firm, also known as a strategic alliance. We already discussed one form of strategic alliance, namely joint ventures (JVs) as a means to enter new markets (Chapter 12). Here we look at two further forms of strategic alliances: (1) business unit joint ventures (JVs), and (2) joint production, marketing or distribution arrangements.

First, some major MNEs pool their activities in specific industry segments with a competitor or another firm offering complementary resources. For example, Ericsson formed a JV with Sony to develop and market mobile phones, combining Ericsson's technological expertise and Sony's design competences. Similarly, Nokia has pooled is network operating systems with Siemens and Siemens pooled its white goods business with Bosch in Bosch-Siemens Hausgeräte, while competing with Bosch as an automotive supplier. Why do companies engage in such business unit JV under shared ownership?

Business unit JV
A JV in which existing business units from two firms are merged.

Like other JVs (Chapter 12), business unit JVs draw on competences of two (or more) parent firms. They are an attractive options if three conditions are met: First, two entities can together achieve something that neither could achieve on its own, for example market leadership in their industry or next-generation innovations. Second, the merged unit depends on inputs such as technologies from both parent firms that may be disrupted by legal separation (in other words, market transaction costs are high). Third, a full take-over is not feasible, perhaps because the competition authorities would object – see next section. Divisional JVs can develop a life of their own and become long-running success stories in their industry: Nokia Siemens Networks, Bosch Siemens Hausgeräte and Sony-Ericsson Mobile Phones have been key players in their industries for several years. Even longer, Fuji Xerox, a Japanese-American JV has been manufacturing printers since 1962. In other cases, JVs are discontinued when the original purpose has been achieved. For example, HP and Ericsson created a JV at a time when telecommunications and computer industries were merging. They set out to jointly develop new technologies to conquer the emerging telecommunications network market. After several years of a volatile relationship, these objectives were achieved and Ericsson took over the JV.[28]

Operation collaboration
A form of strategic alliance that includes collaboration in operations, marketing or distribution.

Second, a strategic alliance may consist of far-reaching operational collaboration, yet stopping short of full acquisition. Such alliances are common for example in the airline industry, where national flag carriers have formed alliances that allow them to connect to all major travel destinations. Their collaboration includes, for example, code sharing and shared frequent flyer programmes, which enables both (or more) partners to offer services that draw on resources of the partner. For example, when buying a Lufthansa ticket from Germany to the UK, you may actually be flying on a British Midlands aircraft.

Strategic alliances may also serve to prepare a full acquisition. Alliances cost less and allow for opportunities to learn by working with each other before a take-over.[29] Acquisitions are often one-off deals swallowing both the excellent capabilities and mediocre units of target firms, leading to 'digestion' problems.[30] Many acquisitions (such as DaimlerChrysler) probably would have been better off had firms pursued alliances first.

INSTITUTIONS GOVERNING ACQUISITIONS

Mergers and acquisitions are subject to formal and informal institutions such as restrictions on foreign ownership (Chapter 12), often simultaneously in several countries. Managers pursue M&As to enhance the profitability of their firms (or to further their personal interest), yet such mergers are not necessarily in the best interest of society. Therefore, legislators have created anti-trust laws that merging firms have to respect in every market in which they are operating. For example, when US firms GE and Honeywell wished to merge in 2001, the European Commission intervened fearing negative implications for European markets. However, authorities use different processes and criteria to approve or disallow proposed mergers, which implies that multiple approvals may be required. In the GE-Honeywell case, this led to conflicting decisions in Europe and the USA.[31] Eventually, the Commission lost its case in the courts, and GE and Honeywell were allowed to merge. Subsequently, the EU has refined its processes and guidelines and hired more economists specializing in competition analysis, which contributes to convergence of regulatory practice in the EU and the USA. Thus, merging firms now act within a somewhat clearer and more predictable institutional framework.[32] For businesses contemplating an M&A, the key concerns are (1) what are regulators looking for in horizontal M&As? (2) what are regulators looking for in vertical M&As? and (3) how can merging companies get approvals even when there are initial concerns?

LEARNING OBJECTIVE

4 Apply the institution-based view to explain patterns of acquisitions

Horizontal M&A

The key criterion for M&As within the same industry is whether the removal of competition will allow the merging companies to raise prices after the merger (Table 14.4). Traditionally, the main way to assess this criterion has been the joint market share. Yet, in recent years regulators have shifted to also consider potential positive effects of reduced costs and accelerated innovation for consumers. Moreover, the definition of the market focuses on substitutability of the products and services, as many competitors are not exactly in the same market, but sell close substitutes. These assessments based on new methods of economic analysis that had first been introduced in the USA, and are increasingly applied by the EU as well. For example, the European Commission prohibited the merger between Irish airlines Ryanair and Air Lingus, who both had their main hub in Dublin and together accounted for 80 per cent of passengers on many short-haul routes between Dublin and European destinations. Ryanair argued that it is operating in a different market segment, 'budget travel', and its customers choose between not travelling *versus* Ryanair rather than Ryanair *versus* Air Lingus. The Commission investigated this claim not only by economic analysis with by a questionnaire survey of passengers

Table 14.4 What regulators are looking for when assessing mergers and acquisitions

Horizontal M&A	Vertical and Conglomerate M&A
● Will the merged firm attain a dominant market share?	● Will the merged firm have the ability to use its control over multiple stages of the value chain to limit access to suppliers or customers for competitors operating in only in one stage?
● Will consumers benefit from cost savings or accelerated innovation in the merged firm?	● Will the merged entity have economic incentives to behave in such manner?
● Will the removal of competition enable the merged firm to raise prices?	● Will such behaviour give rise to significant impediment to effective competition?

using Dublin airport, and ruled that indeed the two companies were direct competitors, and thus the merger was not allowed to go ahead.[33]

Companies know these rules, and they design their acquisition strategies accordingly. For example, Heineken (Netherlands) had long wished to take over Scottish and Newcastle (S&N) to enter the attractive UK beer market. Yet in other countries such as France, they both held large market shares, and the competition authorities would not have approved the merger. Meanwhile, Carlsberg was keen to acquire S&N because of their co-owned business in Russia and other attractive operations in emerging economies. Yet, the British authorities would not have approved a merger of two of the four largest brewers in the UK. Thus, Heineken and Carlsberg launched a surprise *joint* attack: They acquired S&N, and then sliced it up in such a way that no national competition authority would have reasons to object. Thus, Heineken took over the operations in the UK, Finland, Belgium and Portugal, while Carlsberg took over S&N's share in the joint operation in Russia as well as businesses in France and Greece. The Kronenbourg brand thus is now being owned by Carlsberg in France, and by Heineken in the UK. Otherwise, the two archrivals continue to compete in many countries, softened by even stronger multipoint competition.

Vertical M&A

Vertical acquisitions tends to give less rise to competition concerns as efficiency gains between the partners are more likely due to the cost reductions that come with the internalization of markets. Usually, vertical mergers do not lead to a loss of direct competition. However, competition authorities may intervene if the merged entity is able to use its control over multiple stages of a value chain to make it harder for rivals competing only in one of the stages. For example, a vertically integrated company with dominance in the upstream stage may make it more difficult for rivals who compete in the downstream stage, because they would depend on the merged firm's inputs ('input foreclosure'). As a hypothetical example, if a dominant supplier of essential goods, such as milk, was to acquire a retail chain, the competition authorities may object because they fear that the merged firm might use its control over the milk market to the disadvantage of other retailers.

Likewise, a vertically integrated firm with dominance over the downstream stage may make it difficult for companies competing only in the upstream segment because they would have to sell to one their competitors ('customer foreclosure'). As a hypothetical example, an electricity grid operator that also operates power plants may grant competing power generators access to its network under less favourable conditions than its own plants. Thus, a vertical integration between a network operator and its suppliers would be a concern to competition authorities. When assessing vertical mergers, the European Commission would look for ability, incentives and detrimental effects of such behaviours (Table 14.4). In practice, these issues are important in the assessment of anti-competitive behaviour (Chapter 13), yet there have been few blocked vertical mergers, apart from the GE-Honeywell case.

Remedial actions

If a regulator is concerned that a merger negatively affects competition, it can (1) prohibit the merger, (2) ask for divestment of selected operations or (3) ask for commitment to specific actions that ensure competition.

First, an outright prohibition is the simplest solution, because it is easiest to implement and monitor, yet it does not allow the merging partners to achieve their goals. Second, the regulators may ask the merging firm to sell a business unit to ensure that competition is maintained in a particular market. This solution is however more tricky than might seem at first sight: it is essential that the sold unit is a viable business that will emerge as a substantive competitor in the hands of the new owners. As many businesses depend on knowledge transfer, licences or distribution channels shared with their parent firm, this condition is not easy to meet. If the regulator forces a sale, the merged firm has incentives to create a weak competitor that does not pose a substantial threat. For example, when Carlsberg merged with the brewing activities of Norwegian conglomerate Orkla, the Lithuanian authorities forced Carlsberg to sell one of its breweries in the country. Carlsberg complied by selling the brewery to a small Danish brewery with few international activities, making sure not to let any of its global rivals into this small but highly profitable market.

Third, the regulator may impose behavioural constraints, such as a commitment to give rivals access to critical infrastructure on a non-discriminatory basis, or to licence technologies. Such a commitment was used for example when Vivendi, the owner Canal+, merged with Seagram, which owned Universal, one of Hollywood's prime movie studios. Concerns were raised that preferred access of Canal+, a leading pay-TV operator, to Universal's movies would make life more difficult for competing pay-TV operators. Thus, the merging parties committed not to grant Canal+ 'first window rights' covering more than 50 per cent of Universal's new releases.[34] Such commitments are naturally difficult to assess and to monitor; thus regulators see them as a less preferred option.

A major concern of businesses about the competition policy is that the Commission has to deal with very complex matters, yet it has far fewer people working on these issues than comparable authorities in the USA. Thus, rulings are often less evidently supported by sophisticated economic analysis (a nice revenue earner for economics professors in the USA) and may take quite some time, especially if they are challenged in the European Court of Justice. In response to such criticism, the Commission has increased the resources it has allocated to its competition policy monitoring work.

RESOURCES INFLUENCING ACQUISTION PERFORMANCE

Value-destruction?

Do acquisitions create value? Obviously, managers believe they would add value, mainly by exploiting synergies. However, the overall performance of M&As is

LEARNING OBJECTIVE

5 Apply the resource-based view to explain when acquisitions are likely to succeed

Acquisition premium
The difference between the acquisition price and the market value of target firms.

sobering. As many as 70 per cent of acquisitions reportedly fail. On average, acquiring firms' performance does not improve after acquisitions.[35] Target firms, after being acquired and becoming internal units, often perform worse than when they were independent firms. The only identifiable group of winners is shareholders of target firms, who may experience increase in their stock value during the period of the transaction – thanks to the acquisition premium (the difference between the acquisition price and the market value of target firms).

Acquirers of EU firms on average pay an 18 per cent premium, and acquirers of US firms pay even more, 20 to 30 per cent premium.[36] Shareholders of acquiring firms experience a 4 per cent loss of their stock value during the same period. The combined wealth of shareholders of both acquiring and target firms is marginally positive, less than 2 per cent.[37] Thus, on average, M&As destroyed value.[38] Consider DaimlerChrysler. In 1998, Daimler paid $35 billion, to acquire Chrysler, a 40 per cent premium over market value. The high premium is an indication of (1) strong capabilities to derive synergy, (2) high levels of hubris, (3) significant managerial self-interests or (4) *all of the above*. In 2007, Chrysler was sold to Cerberus Capital, a private equity firm, for $7.4 billion – four-fifths of the value had been lost (either Daimler over-paid, or value was destroyed after the acquisition). For another example, in 2006, Google paid $1.6 billion to acquire YouTube, a 20-month-old video-sharing site with *zero* profits. Microsoft CEO Steven Ballmer commented that 'there's no business model for YouTube that would justify $1.6 billion'.[39]

Value-creation

In the presence of so much apparent value-destruction, how can acquirers actually create value in M&As? Successful M&As have to address numerous challenges in both pre- and post-acquisition phases (Table 14.5). Firms with capabilities to manage these processes are able to create value in acquisitions, even when others cannot.

Table 14.5 Causes of acquisition failures

Problems for all M&As	Particular problems for cross-border M&As	
Pre-acquisition: Overpayment for targets	• Managers overestimate their ability to create value • Inadequate pre-acquisition screening • Poor strategic fit	• Lack of familiarity with foreign cultures, institutions and business systems • Nationalistic concerns against foreign takeovers (political and media levels)
Post-acquisition: Failure in integration	• Poor organizational fit • Failure to address multiple stakeholder groups' concerns	• Clashes of organizational cultures compounded by clashes of national cultures • Nationalistic concerns against foreign takeovers (firm and employee levels)

A primary pre-acquisition challenge is due diligence, that is the assessment of the target firm's financial status, its resources and the fit between the target and the acquirer. Fundamentally, whether acquisitions add value boils down to how merged firms are organized. It concerns, first, strategic fit, which is about the effective matching of complementary strategic capabilities that allow to jointly achieve more, or achieve the same at lower costs.[40] In addition, but often not considered as carefully, it is crucial that the two firms have good organizational fit, which is the compatibility of cultures, systems and structures.[41] On paper, Daimler and Chrysler had great strategic fit in terms of complementary product lines and geographic scope, but there was very little organizational fit. American managers resented the dominance of German managers, and Germans disliked being paid two-thirds less than their Chrysler colleagues. These clashes led to an exodus of American managers from Chrysler – a common phenomenon in acquired firms.[42] The cultural clashes between the American and German units of DaimlerChrysler greatly contributed to the eventual failure.

During the post-acquisition phase, the merging organization faces numerous integration challenges. The key challenge is to realize the synergies that motivated the merger in the first place, which involves the often conflicting objectives between the creation of new capabilities and exploitation of existing resources in the larger organization.[43] At the same time, firms need to address genuine concern of many different stakeholders, who fear job losses and diminished power, and who may engage in self-serving action to undermine the efforts of the new owners. Inappropriate management of these human factors often results in low morale and high staff turnover.[44]

In cross-border M&As, integration difficulties may be worse because clashes of organizational cultures are compounded by clashes of national cultures.[45] When Four Seasons acquired a hotel in Paris, the 'American' request that employees smile at customers was resisted by French employees and laughed at by the French media as 'la culture Mickey Mouse', which the Americans found offensive.[46] Such problems of cross-cultural management in post-acquisition integration are even more profound when entering culturally distant countries, such as US firms entering China (In Focus 14.3). Hence, to create value in cross-cultural M&A, capabilities in managing post-acquisition processes are particular important.

Rarity, imitability and organization

Although many firms undertake acquisitions, a much smaller number have mastered the art of post-acquisition integration.[47] The high failure rate of acquisitions in combination with strong track records of some firms, such as General Electric, in managing acquisitions, suggests that capabilities to manage acquisition are indeed quite rare. For example, GE Capital, a finance firm associated with General Electric, developed acquisition competences by conducting one acquisition after the other. Their integrated the process over four stages pre-acquisition, foundation building, rapid integration and assimilation, which includes drawing lessons from the next acquisition.[48]

These acquisition process-related capabilities are grounded in tacit knowledge in various units of GE capital, and thus they are *hard-to-imitate*. As another example, at Northrop, integrating acquired businesses is down to a 'science'. Each must conform to a carefully orchestrated plan listing nearly 400 items, from how to issue press releases to which accounting software to use. Unlike its bigger defence rivals such as Boeing and Raytheon, Northrop thus far has not stumbled with any acquisitions.

Due diligence
The assessment of the target firm's financial status, resources and strategic fit.

Strategic fit
The effective matching of complementary strategic capabilities.

Organizational fit
The similarity in cultures, systems, and structures.

The capabilities to manage M&A processes are complex and specific to each organization. Hence they would be both hard to identify and imitate by outsiders, and they are embedded in the organization. They involve both manuals and 'to do lists', but also processes and assessments that draw on tacit knowledge of teams and individuals managing the post-acquisition integration.

DEBATES AND EXTENSIONS

LEARNING OBJECTIVE

6 Participate in two leading debates on acquisitions

This chapter has introduced a number of debates (such as the merits of acquisitions), and this section discusses two debates of concern to contemporary medium-sized European businesses (1) hidden champions and (2) globalfocusing.

Hidden champions

International business is often presented as primarily a matter of big MNEs competing for market share, especially in American textbooks. Smaller firm are often seen as fringe players in local or regional markets. With limited human and financial resources, a firm of, say, 1000 employees can hardly implement a global strategy – or can it?

In fact, across Europe, firms with 1000 or 5000 employees operate on the global stage in a specific, narrowly defined industry. Germany's infamous *Mittelstand* (medium size) firms have achieved market leadership in such global niche markets. They are often privately held, operate in business-to-business markets and are not widely known. Thus, they are often nicknamed hidden champions, a term coined by German professor turned consultant Herrman Simon.[49] They are leading in their selected niche markets world wide with competitive advantages grounded in highly specialized technological competences that are exploited worldwide.[50] The most famous examples of such firms have grown so fast that they are no longer able to hide: SAP, a developer of business software (see Chapter 4, Opening Case), Fresenius, a leader in dialysis care and Wuerth who sells fixing and assembly materials.

Hidden champions
Market leaders in niche markets keeping a low public profile.

Their (relative) smaller size typically leads them to conduct an aggregation strategy by focusing on elements of the value-chain that are shared around the world. Some combine this with arbitrage by offshoring production, while others, such as Kärcher (Closing Case) operate primarily out of their hub in Germany. Firms resembling the German hidden champions are also found in many other continental European countries with traditions in family businesses and commitment to manufacturing excellence. However, smaller size can be distinct disadvantage when competing head on with by big MNEs, as we discussed in Chapter 13.

Globalfocusing

Globalization has made global strategies more attractive. Yet, how can companies formerly diversified in a local or regional market develop a global strategy? The answer is, in part, that acquisitions and divestments, the sale of business units, are often closely related.[51] Many companies developed as an entrepreneurial company that initially experimented with a variety of different businesses ideas, before suceeding with a particular product or business model, and henceforth focusing all development on this line of business. Entrepreneurial teams often experiment with a variety of ideas and technologies before developing a core competence – which then becomes the focus on the company.

Divestment
The sale or closure of a business unit or asset.

IN FOCUS 14.2

The transformation of Nokia

Nokia is renown as a leading brand for mobile head-sets, yet as recently as two decades ago, the mobile phone business generated merely 10 per cent of the revenues of what was then an industrial conglomerate in Finland. Nokia quite literally 'hit gold' with its mobile handset design and marketing and then focused its resources on exploiting this goldmine, selling its other business units along the way. The main restructuring occurred in one major wave in the early 1990s, and since then Nokia has grown its competences in mobile telephony and is exploiting these competences increasingly by developing and marketing other communications devices. While focusing its product scope, Nokia has established its brand globally, backed up by global operations.

The transformation of the company can be traced in its annual reports. In 1990, Nokia presented itself as:

'a European technology company, ... 84 per cent of turnover comes from EFTA and EC countries. The group is divided into six divisions, ... Main products are colour TVs and monitors, micro computers and terminals, mobile phones, digital telephone exchanges and telecommunication networks, cables and cable machinery as well as tyres and chemicals for forest industry.'

In contrast, in 2009, the Nokia website introduced the company as:

'We make a wide range of mobile devices with services and software that enable people to experience music, navigation, video, television, imaging, games, business mobility and more. Developing and growing our offering of consumer Internet services, as well as our enterprise solutions and software, is a key area of focus. We also provide equipment, solutions and services for communications networks through Nokia Siemens Networks.'

The synergies between the mobile phone handset business and the network business gradually diminished. Mobile phones increasingly are about design, fashion and user software, which brought Nokia into new consumer appliances such as satellite navigation. The network industry went through a concentration process, and had to face new competitors such Huawei of China. In 2006 Nokia created a joint venture with Siemens in which both firms merged their network business. The German –Finnish joint venture is led by Rajev Suri, an Indian who spend most of his professional career with Nokia in Asia.

Source: Based on (1) K.E. Meyer, 2009, Globalfocusing: Corporate Strategies under Pressure, SC, 18: 195–207; (2) www.Nokia.com; (3) Nokiasiemensnetworks.com (accessed August 2009).

Other focused companies have their roots in diversified conglomerate of the 1950s and 1960s. They mainly focused on their home countries because barriers to trade and investment were substantial. Yet, with the reduction of trade barriers, they changed their strategies from competing in several industries in their home country to a global scope within a much sharper defined industry. Such a global-focusing strategy, that is the conversion of domestic conglomerate to a global niche player, has motivated many acquisitions and divestments.[52] This strategic change is driven by external pressures of institutional change and consequently shifts in the ways in which the firm's resources can add value. The change process itself involves a realignment of the firm's resources, and thus acquisition and sale of business units as we have seen in the evolution of Danisco (Opening Case). Similarly, Nokia (In Focus 14.2; Figure 14.3) has transformed itself in the 1990s from a Finnish conglomerate to the global mobile phone handset developer and marketer it is known for today.

Globalfocusing
A strategic shift from diversification to specialization which increasing the international profile.

The relative merits of alternative corporate growth paths, and hence the optimal scope in terms of product diversification and internationalization, are grounded in the transferability of the firm's resources across industries and countries. Some capabilities may be specific to a country, but may be profitably transferred to other industries within this country. For example, the in-depth knowledge of consumers and marketing practices may enable strategies of 'brand extension' to loosely related products. Other resources are more specific to an industry but may be exploited in this industry in other countries. For example, technological expertise for product development can be a foundation for international growth.

Figure 14.3 Nokia OY 1990–2008

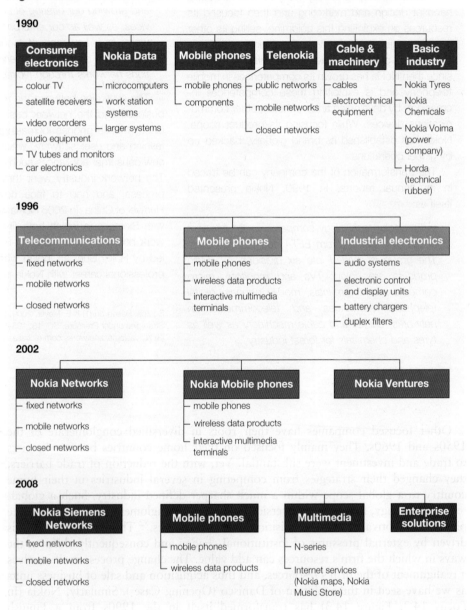

IN FOCUS 14.3

Making M&As fly in China

The first wave of foreign direct investment (FDI) in China, in the 1980s, mostly took the form of joint ventures (JVs). A second wave followed in the 1990s in the form of wholly foreign-owned enterprises (WFOEs). Now a third wave of FDI – cross-board mergers and acquisitions (M&As) – is gaining strength.

Consider the forces driving this third wave. China has a massive appetite for FDI; it is one of the world's largest FDI recipients. Yet, M&As account for only 10 per cent to 15 per cent of FDI flowing into China, compared with approximately 70 per cent of FDI outside China that takes the form of M&As. One reason for this disparity is that, until China joined the World Trade Organization in 2001, national regulations often encouraged (or required) foreign entrants to form JVs or set up WFOEs, while explicitly discouraging M&As. But China has since gradually loosened the regulations that govern foreign takeovers of Chinese assets, especially state-owned enterprises (SOEs), and has made explicit moves to attract foreign M&As. In many industries, including financial services and manufacturing, constraints on M&As are just now being lifted. At the same time, Chinese firms are increasingly engaging in cross-border M&As of their own, as evidenced by their recent bids for Unocal, Maytag, and IBM's personal computer division. To the extent that the Chinese government supports the outbound M&As, it must in most cases clear the path for inbound M&As, according to international norms of reciprocity.

Given the environment, how should foreign companies proceed? In many ways, strategies for M&As in China overlap those for M&As elsewhere. But my recent research has uncovered some idiosyncrasies that are specific to acquisitions in China.

First, Chinese SOEs are rife with organizational slack. Government agencies have restructured some SOEs to reduce underutilized resources and to make the SOEs more attractive M&A targets for foreign firms. Although slack usually indicates inefficiency, in certain firms, some slack – such as unabsorbed cash flow in the form of depreciation funds reserve funds, and retained earnings – may indicate the potential for increased performance, actually enhancing targets' attractiveness.

Second, it is well known that many Chinese SOEs maintain three sets of books: one set that exaggerates performance, to brag to administrative superiors; one that underreports performance, for tax purposes; and one that is fairly accurate, for managers themselves. Acquisition targets are likely to show foreign negotiators the bragging books initially. As a result, foreign firms need to be aggressive in conducting due diligence to uncover an accurate picture of targets' assets and resources. This is particularly relevant when investigating slack.

Finally, most Western firms launching JVs and WFOEs in China have believed that ethnic Chinese managers – those from overseas Chinese economies, such as Hong Kong and Taiwan, who are well versed in the local language – were the best choice for running their operations in China. Meanwhile, they have presumed that Western managers would be less effective because of language and cultural barriers. But evidence from Mike Peng's own research and others' suggests the *opposite*: Using surveys, interviews and other tools, researchers are finding that ethnic Chinese managers hired by Western companies to run these businesses are, on average, *less* effective than their non-Chinese counterparts, as measured by the length of their tenures and attainment of performance goals. How could this be?

One reason appears to be that ethnic Chinese managers often struggle with an ambiguous managerial identity: Western corporate headquarters views them as 'us', and local Chinese employees also expect them to be 'us'. When these managers favour headquarters on issues where headquarters and locals conflict – such as whether Western employees and locals should receive equal compensation or whether chopsticks or forks should be used at company banquets – local employees may regard them as traitors of sorts. That corrodes employees' trust, ultimately undermining ethnic Chinese managers' performance. On the other hand, employees give Western managers the benefit of the doubt. They expect these managers to behave differently, to commit cultural errors, and to show allegiance to the parent firm. This tolerance by local employees of Western managers' differences can enhance these managers' confidence and performance.

Of course, not every non-Chinese manager outperforms every ethnic Chinese manager. It is clear, however, that managerial effectiveness in China does not depend on one's ability to use chopsticks. This point is crucial as more M&As flow into China and more acquiring companies staff their target firms' management.

Source: Adapted from M.W. Peng, 2006, Making M&A fly in China, *Harvard Business Review*, March: 26–27.

IMPLICATIONS FOR PRACTICE

LEARNING OBJECTIVE

7 Draw implications for action

What determines the success and failure in global strategies? Our two core perspectives shed light on this 'big question'. The institution-based view argues that thorough understanding and skilful manipulation of the rules of the game governing acquisitions are often behind the fate of acquisitions. The resource-based view calls for the development of firm-specific capabilities to make a difference in enhancing acquisition performance.

Consequently, three implications for action emerge (Table 14.6). First, each firms needs a business model, a basic idea on how it is creating value from the resources at its disposal around the world. For many companies, this business model is the basis for achieving leadership in its chosen industry (or industries). For example, Danisco (Opening Case) is developing and producing food ingredients using natural ingredients from in a wide variety of locations, processing them, and delivering them into customers food processing factories worldwide. Kärcher (Closing Case) is manufacturing a great variety of customized cleaning machines exploiting its core technologies, and selling them around the world.

Second, when managing acquisitions, managers are advised not to overpay for targets and to focus on both strategic and organizational fit.[53] The strategic fit is about the contribution of the acquired firm – or a series of acquisitions and divestments – to the firms overall business model. Equally important is to manage the integration process after the deal is struck, by addressing the concerns of multiple stakeholders and try to keep the best talents. Be prepared to deal with roadblocks thrown out by people whose jobs and power may be jeopardized!

Third, managers need to understand and master the rules of the game – both formal and informal – governing acquisitions. Lenovo clearly understood and tapped into the Chinese government's support for home-grown multinationals. IBM likewise had a better understanding of the necessity for the new Lenovo to maintain

Table 14.6 Implications for action

- Appreciate and advance the global business model of the firm
- When managing acquisitions, do not overpay, focus on both strategic and organizational fit and thoroughly address integration concerns
- Understand and master the rules of the game governing alliances and acquisitions around the world

an American image by persuading Lenovo to set up its world headquarters in New York. This highly symbolic action made it easier to win approval from the US government in 2005. The upshot is that in addition to the economics of alliances and acquisitions, managers need to pay attention to the politics behind such high-stakes strategic moves.

Finally, when your boss or your business partner proudly announces the formation of a 'strategic alliance', your first question ought to be 'what exactly do you mean?' The term strategic alliances may be disguising a wide range of different transactions. It may be (1) a fancy term for a joint venture, (2) a partial acquisition that is the first step towards a full take-over (Chapter 13), (3) a divisional merger that secures the long-term viability of a struggling business unit, (4) an extensive operational collaboration that maintains both firms' independence or a range of other forms of working together. To assess the merits and risks of an alliance (including the impact on your own job), you need to know a bit more than the consultants' buzz words.

CHAPTER SUMMARY

1 Articulate the strategic advantages of globally operating firms:

- Advantages include global scale advantages, global sourcing, global knowledge management, servicing of global customers and risk diversification.

2 Explain different business modes to exploit the advantages of a globally operating firm:

- Aggregation strategies focus on the realization of synergies between operations in different locations.

- Adaptation strategies aim to deliver locally adapted products in each market.

- Arbitrage strategies exploit the differences in prices in different markets.

3 Explain why global firms engage in mergers and acquisitions, and alliances:

- Acquisitions may be driven by expected synergies, by managerial hubriad or by self-interest of the individuals involved.

- Alliances provide an alternative to a full acquisition, for example by merging business units, or collaborating on operations.

4 Apply the institution-based view to explain patterns of acquisitions:

- Horizontal acquisitions may not be permitted if they result in a reduction of competition that is judged to be harmful to consumers.

- Vertical acquisitions may not be permitted if they allow a dominant player to inhibit competition in an upstream or downstream industry.

- Remedial measures include prohibition of the merger, required divestments or behavioural constraints.

5 Apply the resource-based view to explain when acquisitions are likely to succeed:

- The impact of resources on acquisitions is illustrated by the VRIO framework.

6 Participate in two leading debates on global strategies:

- They concern (1) how hidden champions can succeed, and (2) how globalfocusing allows conglomerate to become global specialists.

7 Draw implications for action:

- Managers need to understand and master the rules of the game governing alliances and acquisitions around the world.

- When managing acquisitions, the savvy manager should focus on both strategic and organizational fit.

KEY TERMS

AAA typology	Divestment	Hubris
Acquisition	Due diligence	Merger
Acquisition premium	Economies of scale	Operation collaboration
Adaptation strategy	Global key accounts	Organizational fit
Aggregation strategy	Global sourcing	Strategic alliances
Arbitrage strategy	Global strategies	Strategic fit
Business unit JV	Globalfocusing	Synergies
Centres of excellence	Hidden champions	

CRITICAL DISCUSSION QUESTIONS

1 As an employee in a middle management role, you hear that your company has been acquired by a competitor based in a different country. What are your immediate and long-term concerns? What actions might you take?

2 As an investor, would you rather put your money in a domestic firm operating in multiple industries, or in a global company specialized in a single industry? What are the risks associated with either type of strategy?

3 As a CEO, you are trying to acquire a foreign firm. The size of your firm will double, and it will become the largest in your industry. On the one hand, you are excited about the opportunity to be a leading captain of industry and the associated power, prestige and income (you expect your salary, bonus and stock option to double next year). On the other hand, you have just read this chapter and are troubled by the fact that 70 per cent of M&As reportedly fail. How would you proceed?

4 During the courtship and negotiation stages of a merger, managers often emphasize equal partnerships and do not reveal (or try to hide) their true intentions. What are the ethical dilemmas here?

CLOSING CASE

Kärcher cleans up – worldwide

By Klaus Meyer and Bernd Venohr, Berlin School of Economics.

Cleanliness is often seen as a typical German trait. Alfred Kärcher GmbH & Co KG, a family-owned company based in Winnenden, a small town near Stuttgart, has built on this stereotype, and developed world market leadership for cleaning equipment and services. Kärcher became a global player in its industry segment selling more than 6.3 million cleaning machines annually in more than 190 countries, employing over 6800 people worldwide, and generating €1.3 billion in turnover in 2009.

Two ideas have guided Kärcher's strategy since the 1970s. First, the firm pursued a 'bottleneck-focused strategy' inspired by German management thinker Wolfgang Mewes. Essentially, this strategy suggests that the key to success is to concentrate on a specific 'burning challenge' (the bottleneck) for a well-defined customer group. Mewes advised companies to create maximum benefits for a target group by solving their most burning challenges. Based on its own resource profile the company should analyze which specific customer problem it can solve best, and find a customer segment that matches its resources. A supplier's attraction for its target group would raise sales, and correspondingly profits. Hence, Kärcher stopped product

© Pixonnet.com/Alamy

How can a German Mittelstand firm like Kärcher become a world leader?

diversification and focused all resources on what it considered as Kärcher's core competence: developing and selling high-pressure cleaning equipment.

Second, Kärcher's product diversification was inspired by evolutionary biology. Charles Darwin recorded 14 different but closely related species of finches on the Galápagos Islands. The birds were of similar size but differ in the size and shape of their beaks, which are highly adapted to food sources available on different islands. This discovery led Darwin to the idea that different species could have developed from a small number of 'ancestral finches'. Kärcher thus developed specialized cleaning equipment, treating its high-pressure steam cleaner as the 'ancestral finch'. This allowed the company to solve previously untapped cleaning challenges, and led to its slogan 'Kärcher: cleaning is our business'. The company transformed itself from a manufacturer of high-pressure water cleaners into a 'think tank' that specializes in solving the cleaning challenges of an increasing array of customer groups.

Kärcher sells about 2500 products addressing cleaning needs of finely defined customer groups, included both businesses and private households. It is an innovation driven company that has about 400 engineers and technicians in the central R&D unit continuously developing new solutions to solve cleaning challenges. Growth comes primarily from new

products because most products are quite durable, which limits replacement demand. Thus, 80 per cent of products sold are less than four years old. This rapid pace of innovation is supported by R&D investments of 4 per cent to 5 per cent of revenues.

A customer-driven innovation routine has become a core element of the organizational culture. Kärcher probably understands its customers' cleaning challenges better than the customers themselves. This know-how is based on intellectual property accumulated over 30 years, and continuously developed further. In 2007, the company held 342 patents and registered designs. Innovation is mostly incremental but may lead to major customer benefits: for instance a redesigned turbo/rotary nozzle increased the cleaning efficiency of building surfaces and roads by a factor of five.

Kärcher's international expansion initially focused on countries with a comparable standard of living, where cleaning needs were fairly similar. Thus, international market penetration targeted European countries from in 1974, then the USA in 1982 and Japan in 1987. By 2007, the company had 41 wholly-owned sales and service subsidiaries worldwide. Kärcher served most its key markets direct rather than via agents or other intermediaries, and by setting up greenfield sales operations. Only in the USA, Kärcher acquired several established companies to build its market position.

Many of Kärcher's products are under pressure from Asian low-cost producers, while the success has attracted larger competitors into this market. Kärcher therefore has to operate cost efficiently to remain price competitive, in addition to its innovative and customer-oriented differentiation. Kärcher still manufactures about half of its worldwide sales in Germany, while Germany accounts for only one fifth of its revenues. Four of its largest factories are in Germany, employing about 1250 people, with other plants located in Italy (3), USA (3), Mexico, Brazil and China.

How can Kärcher compete in view of German labour costs being among the highest in the world? Several factors contribute to the competitiveness of their German plants:

- The Kärcher product range is fairly complex, ranging from high volume consumer products to sophisticated small series of large professional cleaning equipment. All products are continuously improved, such that proximity between production and R&D, which is mostly in Germany, is crucial.

- In Kärcher's demand-led production system, all products are built to order. Factories are segmented into lines for different product types: within each line, employees can substitute for each other, which substantially enhances flexibility. Each factory specializes on one product group producing on a world scale to exploit economies of scale. This set-up enables Kärcher to deliver a complex product range with a high degree of flexibility and to adapt to seasonal variations in demand.

- Kärcher works with outside suppliers to develop new products and to share investments for new production equipment. Components are to a high degree outsourced, yet Kärcher decided against total outsourcing and is keeping most of the final assembly of its products in house. In particular, it retains some manufacturing capacity for its key technologies to strengthen its bargaining power vis-à-vis outside suppliers.

DISCUSSION QUESTIONS:

1 From an institution-based perspective, what influences may have influenced Kärcher's path of growth?

2 From a resource-based perspective, what motivated Kärcher's strategy of combining related diversification and internationalization?

3 How would you classify Kärcher in terms of the AAA-typology of global strategies? How did Kärcher manage to integrate these different aspects?

Sources: This case was prepared by Klaus Meyer and Bernd Venohr of Berlin School of Economics. Based on (1) H. Haas 1988. *Der Hai im Management*, Munich: Langen-Müller; (2) T. Rupp 2004. Ein Glücksfall für Kärcher, *Strategie Journal* 6: 11; (3) H. Witzel & R. Kamm 2006. *Unternehmenswachstum, die natürlichste Sache der Welt*, Hamburg: Books on Demand; (4) B. Venohr & K.E. Meyer, 2006, The German Miracle keeps Running: How Germany's Hidden Champions stay ahead in the Global Economy, working paper, Berlin School of Economics; (5) Kärcher website: www.karcher.com.

RECOMMENDED READINGS

P. Ghemawat, 2007, *Redefining Global Strategy*, Boston: Harvard Business School Press – A practitioner oriented book outlining ideas how companies can develop global strategies.

P.C. Haspeslagh & D.B. Jemison, 1989, *Managing Acquisition*, New York: Free Press – A classic book grounded in the resource-based view on how to manage acquisitions.

M. Kenney & R. Florida, eds, 1994, *Locating Global Advantage: Industry Dynamics in the International Economy,* Stanford: Stanford University Press – A study exploring the changing patterns of global strategies in a variety of different industries.

T. Levitt, 1984, The globalization of markets, *HBR*, May–June: 92–102 – Classic article arguing for the merits of a global strategy.

K.E. Meyer, 2006, Globalfocusing: From domestic conglomerates to global specialists, *JMS*, 43: 1109–1144 – A study following acquisitions and divestments of two companies over time, and interpreting the process from an resource-based view by introducing the concept of globalfocusing.

G.S. Yip, 2003, *Total Global Strategy II*, Prentice Hall – A textbook targeted at MBA students with the ambition to lead global firms.

NOTES:

"FOR JOURNAL ABBREVIATION, PLEASE SEE PAGE XXVI-XXVII."

1 P. Ghemawat, 2007a, *Redefining Global Strategy*, Boston: Harvard Business School Press.

2 S. Ghoshal, 1987, Global strategy, *SMJ*, 8: 425–440; G. Yip, 1989, Global Strategy … In a world of nations? *SMR*, 31, 29–41; K.E. Meyer, 2006, Globalfocusing: From domestic conglomerates to global specialists, *JMS*, 43, 1109–1144; J.H. Dunning & S. Lundan, 2008, *Multinational Enterprises and the Global Economy*, 2nd edition, Cheltenham: Elgar; P.J. Buckley, 2009, Internalisation thinking, *IBR*, 18: 224–235.

3 M. Kenney & R. Florida, eds, 2004, *Locating Global Advantage*, Stanford: Stanford University Press; T.J. Sturgeon 2002, Modular production networks, *ICC*, 11, 451–496; P.J. Buckley, 2009; The impact of the global factory on economic development, *JWB*, 44, 131–143.

4 B. Kogut, 1985, Designing global strategies: Profiting from operational flexibility, *SMR* 27: 27–38. B. Kogut & N. Kulatilaka 1994. Option thinking and platform investment, *CMR*, Winter, 52–71.

5 B. Jaruzelski & K. Dehoff 2008. Beyond Borders: The Global Innovation 1000, *Business + Strategy* 53: 53–68.

6 R. Mudambi, 2001, Knowledge management in multinational firms, *JIM*, 8, 1–9; N.J. Foss & T. Pedersen, 2001, Transferring knowledge in MNCs, *JIM*, 8: 49–67.

7 R. Greenwood, T. Morris, S. Fairclough & M. Boussebaa, 2010, The organizational design of transnational professional service firms, *OD*, in press.

8 T. Levitt, 1983, The globalization of markets, *HBR*, May–June: 92–102; also see K. Ohmae, 1989, Managing in a borderless world, *HBR*, May/June 1989; F. Fukuyama, 1992, *The end of history*, New York: Free Press.

9 C.W.F. Baden-Fuller & J.M. Stopford, 1991, Globalization frustrated, *SMJ*, 12: 493–507; A.M. Rugman, 2001, *The End of Globalization*, New York: AMACOM.

10 P. Ghemawat, P. 2007b. Managing Differences, *HBR*, (March): 58–68.

11 Ghemawat, 2007a, *as above* (pp. 144–156).

12 N. Dawar & A. Chattopadhay 2002. Rethinking marketing programs for emerging markets, *LRP*, 35: 457–474; T. London & S.L. Hart, 2004, Reinventing strategies for emerging markets, *JIBS*, 35: 350–370.

C.K. Prahalad. 2004, *The Fortune at the Bottom of the Pyramid*, Philadelphia: Wharton School Publishing.

13 Ghemawat, 2007a, *as above* (119–130).

14 Dawar & Chattopadhay, 2002, *as above*.

15 K.E. Meyer & Y.T.T. Tran, 2006, Market penetration and acquisition strategies for emerging economies, *LRP*, 39: 177–197.

16 B. Kogut, 1985, Designing global strategies: comparative and competitive value-added chain: SMR, 26(3): 15–28; S. Rangan, 1998, Do Multinationals operate flexibly? *JIBS*, 29: 217–237.

17 *The Economist,* 2007, Cheung Yan: Paper Queen, June 9.

18 United Nations, 2000, *World Investment Report 2000* (p. 99), New York: United Nations.

19 *Financial Times Online*, 2010, Mergers and acquisitions data 2000–2009, March 17.

20 K.D. Brouthers, P. van Hastenburg & J. van den Ven, 1998, If most mergers fail why are they so popular? *LRP*, 31: 347–353; A. Seth, K. Song & R. Pettit, 2000, Synergy, managerialism, or hubris? *JIBS*, 31: 387–405.

21 R. Larsson & S. Finkelstein, 1999, Integrating strategic, organizational and human resource perspectives on mergers and acquisitions, *OSc*, 10: 1–26; D. Loree, C. Chen, & S. Guisinger, 2000, International acquisitions, *JWB*, 35: 300–315; D.M. Schweiger & P. Very, 2001, International M&As special issue, *JWB*, 36: 1–2; J. Anand & A. Delios, 2002, Absolute and relative resources as determinants of international acquisitions, *SMJ*, 23: 119–134; T. Saxton & M. Dollinger, 2004, Target reputation and appropriability, *JM*, 30: 123–147.

22 Z. Antal-Mokos & K. Tóth, 2007, The emergence of the Central European MNE: MOL, in: K.E. Meyer & S. Estrin, eds, *Acquisition Strategies in European Emerging Economies*, Basingstoke: Palgrave, 190–202.

23 A.L. Ranft & M.D. Lord, 2002, Acquiring new technologies and capabilities, *OSc*, 13: 420–441.

24 P. March, 2009, Steel magnate steered Mittal to success with Arcelor, *Financial Times*, December 30.

25 R. Roll, 1986, The hubris hypothesis of corporate takeovers, *JB*, 59: 197–216.

26 P.R. Haunschild, A. Davis-Blake & M. Fichman, 1994, Managerial overcommitment in corporate acquisition processes, *OSc*, 5: 528–540; S.B. Moeller,

F.P. Schlingemann & R.M. Stulz, 2004, Firm size and the gains from acquisitions, *JFE*, 73: 201–228.

27 *Handelsblatt*, 2010, Deutsche Bahn tätigt teuersten Zukauf ihrer Geschichte, April 22.

28 B. Büchel, 2002, Joint venture development, *JWB*, 37, 199–207.

29 P. Porrini, 2004, Can a previous alliance between an acquirer and a target affect acquisition performance? *JM*, 30: 545–562.

30 J.F. Hennart & S. Reddy, 1997, The choice between M&As and JVs, *SMJ*, 18: 1–12.

31 E.J. Morgan & S. McGuire, 2004, Transatlantic divergence: GE-Honeywell and the EU's merger policy, *JEPP*, 11: 39–56; S.T. Anwar 2005. EU's competition policy and the GE-Honeywell merger fiasco, *TIBR* 47: 601–626; Y. Akbar & G. Suder, 2006, The new EU merger regulation, *TIBR*, 48, 667–686.

32 C. Damro, 2006, The new trade politics and EU competition policy, *JEPP*, 13: 867–886; S. McGuire & M. Smith, 2008, *The European Union and the United States*, Basingstoke: Palgrave.

33 A. Weitbrecht, 2008. Ryanair and more – EU Merger Control in 2007, *ECLR*, 341–348.

34 M. Motta, M. Polo & H. Vasconcelos, 2007, Merger remedies in the European Union: An overview, *Antitrust Bulletin*, 52: 603–632.

35 D. King, D. Dalton, C. Daily & J. Covin, 2004, Meta-analyses of post-acquisition performance, *SMJ*, 25: 187–200; K. Uhlenbruck, M.A. Hitt & M. Semadeni, 2006, Market value effects of acquisitions involving Internet firms, *SMJ*, 27: 899–913.

36 C. Moschieri & J.M. Campa, 2009, The European M&A industry (p. 82), *AMP*, November: 71–87.

37 G. Andrade, M. Mitchell & E. Stafford, 2001, New evidence and perspectives on mergers, *JEP*, 15, 103–120.

38 J. Doukas & O. Kan, 2006, Does global diversification destroy firm value? *JIBS*, 37, 352–371.

39 *Business Week*, 2006, Ballmer: They paid how much for that? October 23.

40 J.Y. Kim & S. Finkelstein, 2009, The effects of strategic and market complementarity on acquisition performance, *SMJ*, 30: 617–646.

41 S. Cartwright & C.L. Cooper, 1993, The role of culture compatibility in successful organization marriage, *AME*, 7, 57–70; P. Puranam, H. Singh & M. Zollo, 2006, Organizing for innovation, *AMJ*, 49: 263–280;

M.Y. Brannen & M. Peterson, 2009, Merging without alienating, *JIBS*, 40: 468–489; R. Chakrabarti, S. Gupta-Mukherjee & N. Jayaraman, 2009, Mars-Venus marriages, *JIBS*, 40: 216–236.

42 J.A. Krug & W.H. Hegarty, 2001, Predicting who stays and leaves after an acquisition, *SMJ*, 22: 185–196; A.K. Buchholtz, B.A. Ribbens & I.T. Houle, 2003, The role of human capital in post-acquisition CEO departure, *AMJ*, 46:506–514.

43 M. Iborra & C. Doiz, 2007, El papel de conflicto en la exploración y explotación de conocimiento en las adquisiciones, *M@n@gement*, 10, 1–21.

44 J.M. Birkinshaw, H. Bresman & L. Håkanson, 2000, Managing the post-acquisition integration process, *JMS*, 37: 395–425; A. Risberg, 2001, Employee experiences of acquisition processes, *JWB*, 36: 58–84; E. Vaara, 2003, Post-acquisition integration as sensemaking, *JMS*, 40: 859–894.

45 P. Morosini, S. Shane & H. Singh, 1998, National cultural distance and cross-border acquisition performance, *JIBS*, 29: 137–158; J. Child, D. Faulkner & R. Pitkethly, 2001, *The Management of International Acquisitions*, Oxford, UK: Oxford University Press; K.E. Meyer & E. Lieb-Dóczy, 2003, Post-acquisition restructuring as evolutionary process, *JMS*, 40: 459–482; A. Slangen, 2006, National cultural distance and initial foreign acquisition performance, *JWB*, 41: 161–170; R.M. Sarala & E. Vaara, 2010, Cultural differences, convergence, and crossvergence as explanations of knowledge transfer in international acquisitions, JIBS, 2010: 1365–1390.

46 R. Hallowell, D. Bowen & C. Knoop, 2002, Four Seasons goes to Paris (p. 19), *AME*, 16: 7–24.

47 J. Haleblian, J.Y. Kim & N. Rajagopalan, 2006, The influence of acquisition experience and performance on acquisition behavior, *AMJ*, 49: 357–370.

48 R.N. Ashkenas, L.J. Demonaco & S. Francis, 1998, Making the deal real: how GE Capital integrates acquisitions, *HBR*, (January-February): 5–15.

49 H. Simon, 1996, *Hidden Champions*, Boston, MA: Harvard Business School Press.

50 B. Venohr, 2006, *Wachsen wie Wuerth*, Frankfurt, Campus; B. Venohr, 2008, Die kommenden Weltmeister, *Handelsblatt*, October 24; H. Simon, 2009, *Hidden Champions of the 21st Century*, New York: Springer; B. Venohr & K.E. Meyer, 2009, Uncommon common sense, *BSR*, 20(1): 38–43.

51 L. Capron & W. Mitchell, 1998, Bilateral resource redeployment and capabilities improvement following horizontal acquisitions, *ICC*, 7: 453–484; L. Capron & M. Guillen, 2009, National corporate governance institutions and post-acquisition target reorganization, *SMJ*, 30: 803–833; L. Capron, W. Mitchell & A. Swaminathan, 2001, Asset divesture following horizontal acquisitions, *SMJ*, 22: 817–844.

52 K.E. Meyer, 2006, *as above*; K.E. Meyer, 2009, Globalfocusing *SC*, 18:195–207.

53 H. Bresman, J.M. Birkinshaw & R. Nobel, 1999, Knowledge transfer in international acquisitions, *JIBS*, 30: 439–469; L. Capron & N. Pistre, 2002, When do acquirers earn abnormal returns? *SMJ*, 23: 781–795; R. Larsson & S. Finkelstein, 1999, Integrating strategic, organizational and human resource perspectives on M&As, *OSc*, 10: 1–26; J.J. Reuer, O. Shenkar & R. Ragozzino, 2004, Mitigating risk in international M&As, *JIBS*, 35: 19–32; F. Vermeulen & H.G. Barkema, 2001, Learning through acquisitions, *AMJ*, 44: 457–477.

PART FIVE

OPERATIONS IN THE GLOBAL MNE

CHAPTER FIFTEEN

© Andresr/iStock

STRUCTURING AND ORGANIZING MNEs

LEARNING OBJECTIVES

After studying this chapter you should be able to:

1 Articulate the relationship between multinational strategy and structure

2 Outline the challenges associated with learning, innovation and knowledge management

3 Explain how institutions and resources affect strategy, structure and learning

4 Participate in two leading debates on multinational strategy, structure and learning

5 Draw implications for action

OPENING CASE

The global organizational design of the 'Big Four'

By Mehdi Boussebaa, University of Bath.

The global accountancy profession is dominated by four players that offer their services virtually all over the world: PricewaterhouseCoopers (PwC), Deloitte Touche Tohmastu, Ernst & Young and KPMG. These 'Big Four', like other professional service firms such as management consultancies and law firms, are very important for today's economy because they broker complex business transactions and offer managerial advice to the world's largest companies. They offer a diversified range of intangible, knowledge-based services that go beyond their traditional core offerings – audit and assurance – to include financial advice and management consulting. These services are targeted at Fortune 500 corporations as well as smaller, local clients and government agencies. The Big Four are also important because they are often held to be organizations of the future towards which other types of enterprises are converging. In the past, exemplary organizations were generally drawn from the manufacturing and re-

tailing sectors but in the present era professional service firms such as the Big Four are regarded as *the* source of managerial and organizational inspiration.

Over the last few decades, the Big Four have continued to expand internationally, becoming enormous multinational organizations as a result. For instance, PricewaterhouseCoopers (PwC), the largest of the Big Four, employs more than 160 000 people in 757 offices across 151 countries. In comparison, General Motors operates in 34 countries and Wal-Mart in 15. Such an international spread creates significant managerial and organizational challenges for the firms. In particular, the Big Four face the major challenge of serving large multinational clients who expect not only cutting edge and *customized* professional expertise but also *seamless* cross-national service. These clients also expect their advisors to not only provide different professional services but also to know about the countries and the industries in which they operate, creating a pressure on the Big Four to be structurally differentiated along three different axes: service line, geographic location and industry/market. Specific contracts with clients often require the integration of competences held by

How can professional service firms, such as Ernst & Young, bring together the expertise required by their global clients?

© Kevin Foy/Alamy

individuals and teams in different parts of the professional service firm, often in different places around the world.

How do the Big Four respond to these managerial and organizational challenges? Research conducted in these firms shows that they have been developing a 'multiplex' organizational form that consists of an unique mélange of both structural and cultural features. Specifically, the multiplex form has three core elements. First, it is characterized by several axes of *deep specialization*: professional expertise (produced through service lines), client expertise (developed through industry and market research) and geographical expertise (built through an international network of local offices). For example, Ernst & Young offers not only a range of services (e.g. Assurance, Advisory Services, Tax, etc.) but also claims expertise in 14 major industries (e.g. Energy, Financial Services, Health Care, Pharmaceuticals, etc.). The firm is also organized into several geographical regions through which

client service delivery is coordinated. Second, the multiplex form operates a sophisticated *client management system*, which connects teams of professionals drawn from the different expertise axes and focuses their efforts on the task of satisfying client needs. Third, the multiplex is supported by a *culture of reciprocity* that holds the firm together and ensures that the differentiation forces do not overpower the effectiveness of its client management system. This culture of reciprocity is achieved by building relationships across the different specialization axes and reinforcing these through the development of an array of organizational processes, including career, communication, recruitment and socialization practices.

Sources: This case was prepared by Mehdi Boussebaa, University of Bath, based on R. Greenwood, T. Morris, S. Fairclough & M. Boussebaa, 2010, The organizational design of transnational professional service firms. *Organizational Dynamics*, 39: 137–183. See also M. Boussebaa, 2009, struggling to organize across national

How can multinational enterprises (MNEs) such as PwC and KPMG organize their operations to be successful both locally and internationally? How can they make sure that people within the organization work together constructively? How can they foster the exchange of knowledge and improve the odds for better innovation? These are some of the key questions we address in this chapter.

MNEs operate in many different local contexts, and their ability to make connections between local contexts is crucial to achieve competitive advantage in global strategies (Chapter 14).[1] However, realizing such competitive advantages requires complex organizations that have to achieve many things simultaneously. Global MNEs are rarely hierarchical monoliths where the boss knows and decides everything, and thousands of people implement the decisions. Such central decision-making would kill creativity and initiative in the organization, and thus undermine many of the firm's capabilities. MNEs are typically knowledge-intensive firms, that is firms where the creation, dissemination and/or exploitation of knowledge are essential for their competitive advantage. Hence, how MNEs organize creative people and diverse subunits in distinct local contexts is at the core of this chapter.

We start by introducing a traditional view on organizing the MNEs based on the conflicting pressures for integration and local responsiveness, followed by a modern view focused on knowledge management. Next, the institution- and resource-based views shed additional light on these issues. Debates and extensions follow.

ORGANIZATIONAL STRUCTURES IN MNES

The integration-responsiveness framework

The trade-offs between arbitrage and adaptation strategies (Chapter 14) provides the foundation for a popular conceptual framework known as the integration-responsiveness framework. First, aggregation benefits such as economies of scale,

---

LEARNING OBJECTIVE

1 Articulate the relationship between multinational strategy and structure

Integration-responsiveness framework
A framework of MNE management on how to simultaneously deal with two sets of pressures for global integration and local responsiveness.

Local responsiveness
The necessity to be responsive to different customer preferences around the world.

Home replication strategy
A strategy that emphasizes international replication of home country-based competencies such as production scales, distribution efficiencies and brand power.

global innovation and global sourcing often call for global integration, while idiosyncratic local consumer demand and institutions call for local responsiveness.[2] Pressures for local responsiveness arise from different consumer preferences and host country institutions, formal and informal. Consumer preferences vary tremendously around the world. For example, McDonald's beef-based hamburgers obviously would find few (or no) costumers in India, a land where cows are sacred. Thus, McDonald's developed vegetarian products offerings specifically for India. Likewise, throughout Europe, Canadian firm Bombardier manufactures an Austrian version of railcars in Austria, a Belgian version in Belgium and so on. Bombardier believes that such local responsiveness is essential for making sales to railway operators in continental Europe, which tend to be state-owned.

Being locally responsive may please local customers and other stakeholders, but these adaptations may increase cost because they reduce the potential for economies of scale. Given the universal interest in lowering cost, some globally operating MNEs downplay (or ignore) the different needs and wants of various local markets and market a 'global' version of their products and services – ranging from the world car to the global iPod. Integration and responsiveness, however, may not be incompatible. Management gurus Chris Bartlett and Sumantra Ghoshal argue that MNEs may be able to pursue both objectives simultaneously.[3] Hence, integration-responsiveness is not a scale but can be depicted as a 2x2 matrix with four strategies: (1) home replication, (2) localization, (3) global standardization and (4) transnational strategy (Figure 15.1, Table 15.1). Each strategy has a set of pros and cons.[4]

Home replication strategy, often known as 'international' strategy, is based on replication of home country-based competencies such as production scales, distribution efficiencies and brand positioning. Essentially, the operation abroad is built to resemble the home operation in the belief that this is the best way to transfer

Figure 15.1 Multinational strategies and structures: The integration-responsiveness framework

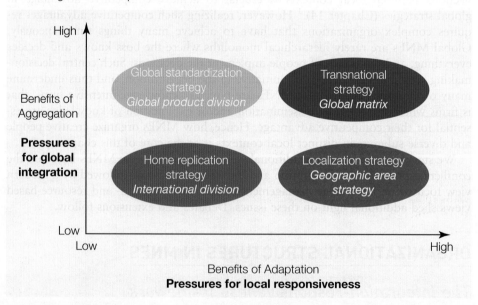

Note: In some other textbooks, 'home replication' may be referred to as 'international' strategy, 'localization' as 'multidomestic' strategy, and 'global standardization' as 'global' strategy. Some of these labels are confusing because one can argue that all four strategies here are 'international' or 'global'. The present set of labels is more descriptive and less (hopefully) confusing.

Table 15.1 Four strategic choices for multinational enterprises

	Advantages	Disadvantages
Home replication	• Leverages home country-based advantages • Relatively easy to implement	• Lack of local responsiveness • May result in foreign customer alienation
Localization	• Maximizes local responsiveness	• High costs due to duplication of efforts in multiple countries • Too much local autonomy
Global standardization	• Leverages low-cost advantages	• Lack of local responsiveness • Too much centralized control
Transnational	• Cost efficient while being locally responsive • Engages in global learning and diffusion of innovations	• Organizationally complex • Difficult to implement

competences of the firm. This strategy is relatively easy to implement and may be used by firms venturing abroad for the first time.

On the disadvantage side, this strategy suffers from a lack of local responsiveness. This makes sense when the majority of a firm's customers are back home. However, when the firm aspires to broaden its international scope to reach more foreign customers, failing to be mindful of foreign customers' needs and wants may result in their alienation. For instance, Wal-Mart, when entering Brazil, set up an exact copy of its stores in the USA, with a large number of *American* footballs. Obviously, in Brazil, the land of football, nobody (perhaps other than a few home-sick US expatriates) plays American football. Setting up an exact replica only makes sense as a starting point for experimentation and learning on how best to adapt while retaining the core features of the business model.[5]

Localization (multidomestic) strategy is an extension of the home replication strategy. It considers each country or region as a stand-alone 'local' market worthy of significant attention and adaptation. Although sacrificing global efficiencies, this strategy is effective when there are clear differences among national and regional markets and few pressures for global economies of scale. When first venturing overseas, MTV started with a home replication strategy (literally, broadcasting American programming). It then gradually moved to a localization strategy with eight channels, each in a different language, for Western Europe alone.

In terms of disadvantages, the localization strategy has to shoulder high costs due to duplication of efforts in multiple countries. The costs of producing such a variety of programming at MTV are obviously greater than the costs of producing one set of programming. As a result, this strategy is only appropriate in industries where economies of scale are not substantial. Another drawback is potentially too much local autonomy. Each subsidiary regards its country to be unique, and it is difficult to introduce corporate-wide changes. For example, Unilever had 17 country subsidiaries in Europe in the 1980s, and it took as long as four *years* to 'persuade' all 17 subsidiaries to introduce a single new detergent across Europe.

Localization (multidomestic) strategy
A strategy that focuses on a number of foreign countries/regions, each of which is regarded as a stand-alone 'local' (domestic) market worthy of significant attention and adaptation.

Global standardization strategy
A strategy that relies on the development and distribution of standardized products worldwide to reap the maximum benefits from low-cost advantages.

As the opposite of the localization strategy, the global standardization strategy is sometimes simply referred to as 'global strategy'. Its hallmark is the development and distribution of standardized products worldwide to reap the maximum benefits from economies of scale and shared product development. Global standardization does not imply that all core operations are based at home. In a number of countries, the MNE may designate a centre of excellence, defined as a subsidiary explicitly recognized as a source of important capabilities that are leveraged by and/or disseminated to other subsidiaries.[6]

Centre of excellence
An MNE subsidiary explicitly recognized as a source of important capabilities, with the intention that these capabilities be leveraged by and/or disseminated to other subsidiaries.

Global integration also helps serving global clients.[7] MNEs in business-to-business markets, such as the Big Four accountancy firms (Opening Case) serve global key accounts, that is customers who themselves operate at multiple sites and expect delivery of products or services across various countries. Most original equipment manufacturers (OEMs) – namely, contract manufacturers that produce goods *not* carrying their own brands (such as the makers of Nike shoes and Microsoft Xbox) – use this structure. Singapore's Flextronics, the world's largest electronics OEM, has dedicated global accounts for Dell, Palm and Sony Ericsson. Hence, all negotiations with these clients are channelled through the same person (or office), the global key account manager.

In terms of disadvantages, a global standardization strategy sacrifices local responsiveness. It makes sense in industries where pressures for cost reductions are paramount and pressures for local responsiveness are relatively minor. For example, Japanese consumer electronics firms conquered the world in the 1980s with fairly standardized radios, CD-players and other gadgets. However, as noted earlier, in numerous industries, ranging from automobiles to foods, a one-size-fits-all strategy may be inappropriate.

Transnational strategy
A strategy that endeavours to be cost efficient, locally responsive and learning driven simultaneously around the world.

A transnational strategy aims to capture the best of both worlds by endeavouring to be cost efficient and locally responsive.[8] A hallmark of this strategy is global learning and diffusion of innovations. Traditionally, the diffusion of innovations in MNEs was a one-way flow from the home country to various host countries. Underpinning such a one-way flow was the assumption that the home country is the best location for generating innovations, an assumption that is increasingly challenged, for two reasons. First, given that innovations are inherently risky and uncertain, there is no guarantee that the home country will generate the highest quality innovations.[9] Second, for many large MNEs, their subsidiaries have acquired a variety of innovation capabilities, some of which may have the potential for wider applications elsewhere.[10] GM has ownership stakes in Daewoo, Opel, Vauxhall, Subaru and Suzuki as well as the Shanghai GM joint venture with China's SAIC. Historically, GM employed a localization strategy, and each subsidiary could decide what cars to produce by themselves. Consequently, some of these subsidiaries developed locally formidable but globally underutilized innovation capabilities and patents. It makes sense for GM to tap into some of these local capabilities (such as Opel's prowess in what Americans call 'compact' cars) for wider applications. MNEs that engage in a transnational strategy promote global learning and diffusion of innovations. Hence, knowledge flows from the home country to host countries (which is the traditional flow) but also from host countries to the home country and among subsidiaries in multiple host countries.[11]

The IR-framework is well established but it is not without problems. First, a transnational strategy is organizationally complex and difficult to implement. The large amount of knowledge sharing and coordination may slow down decision speed. Simultaneously trying to achieve cost efficiencies, local responsiveness and global learning places contradictory demands on MNEs (discussed later in this chapter). Second, the IR-framework does not take account of other important dimensions of global strategy, such as the stage in the value chain of the subsidiary.[12]

Four organizational structures

Also shown in Figure 15.1, there are four organizational structures approximately matching the four strategic choices just outlined: (1) international division structure, (2) geographic area structure, (3) global product division structure and (4) global matrix structure.

An international division is typically set up when firms initially expand abroad, often engaging in a home replication strategy. For example, Figure 15.2 shows Starbucks' international division is complementing its four product divisions that primarily focus on the USA. Although this structure is intuitively appealing, it often leads to two problems. First, foreign subsidiary managers, whose input may be channelled through the international division, are not given sufficient voice relative to the heads of domestic divisions.[13] Second, by design, the international division serves as a 'silo' whose activities are not coordinated with the rest of the firm that focuses on domestic activities. Consequently, such an organizational structure is mainly used by firms where international sales contribute only a small share of their revenues. It is more commonly found in the USA than in Europe, though, for example, British retailer Marks & Spencer also has such kind of structure.

A geographic area structure organizes the MNE according to different geographic areas. It is the most appropriate structure for a localization strategy. Figure 15.3 illustrates such a structure for Mittal Steel, a Europe-based, Indian-owned steel company. A geographic area can be a country or a region, led by a country or regional manager. Each area is largely stand-alone. In contrast to the limited voice of subsidiary managers in the international division structure, country and regional managers carry a great deal of weight in a geographic area structure. Interestingly and paradoxically, *both* the strengths and weaknesses of this structure lie in its local responsiveness. Although being locally responsive can be a virtue, it also encourages the fragmentation of the MNE into autonomous, hard-to-control 'fiefdoms'.[14] Few global companies still use such a structure, unless they are focused on a single line of business. Indeed, after merging with Arcelor in 2007, Mittal-Arcelor implemented a mixed structure combining elements of product and regional structure.

A global product division structure, which is the opposite of the geographic area structure, supports the global standardization strategy. Figure 15.4 shows such an example from EADS, whose most famous unit is Airbus. This structure treats each product division as a stand-alone entity with full worldwide – as opposed to

International division
A structure that is typically set up when firms initially expand abroad, often engaging in a home replication strategy.

Geographic area structure
An organizational structure that organizes the MNE according to different countries and regions.

Country or regional manager
The business leader of a specific geographic area or region.

Global product division
An organizational structure that assigns global responsibilities to each product division.

Figure 15.2 International division structure at Starbucks

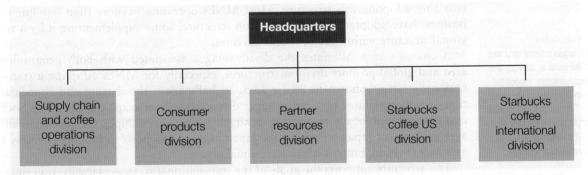

Source: Adapted from (1) www.cogmap.com; (2) www.starbucks.com. Headquartered in Seattle, USA, Starbucks operates coffeehouses around the world.

Figure 15.3 Geographic area structure at Mittal Steel

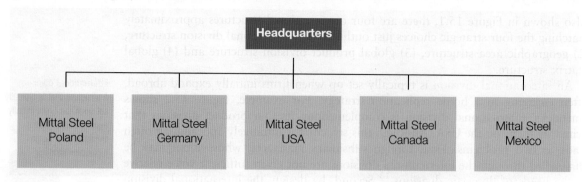

Source: Adapted from http://www.mittalsteel.com (accessed March 20, 2007). Headquartered in London, United Kingdom, Mittal Steel was the world's largest steelmaker. After its merger with Arcelor in 2007, it moved to a mixed geographic/product structure.

Figure 15.4 Global product division structure at European Aeronautic Defence and Space Company (EADS)

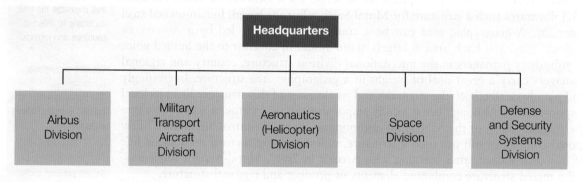

Source: Adapted from http://eads.com. Headquartered in Munich, Germany, and Paris, France, EADS is the largest commercial aircraft maker and the largest defence contractor in Europe.

domestic – responsibilities. This structure greatly facilitates attention to pressures for cost efficiencies because it allows for consolidation on a worldwide (or at least regional) basis and reduces inefficient duplication in multiple countries. For example, Unilever reduced the number of soap-producing factories in Europe from ten to two after adopting this structure. Most MNEs operating in more than one line of business have adopted a product division structure, some supplementing it by a regional structure within each product division.

A **global matrix** alleviates the disadvantages associated with both geographic area and global product division structures, especially for MNEs adopting a transnational strategy. Shown in Figure 15.5, its hallmark is the sharing and coordination of responsibilities between product divisions and geographic areas to be both cost efficient and locally responsive. In this hypothetical example, the country manager in charge of Japan – in short, the Japan manager – reports to Product Division 1 and Asia Division, both of which have equal power.

This structure supports the goals of the transnational strategy. However, in practice, it is often difficult to deliver. The reason is simple: Although managers (such as

Global matrix
An organizational structure often used to alleviate the disadvantages associated with both geographic area and global product division structures, especially for MNEs adopting a transnational strategy.

Figure 15.5 A hypothetical global matrix structure

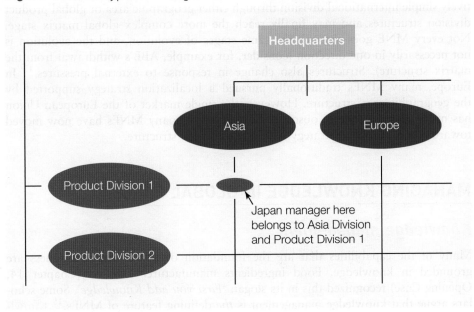

the Japan manager) usually find there is enough headache dealing with one boss, they do not appreciate having to deal with two bosses, who are often in conflict (!). For example, Product Division 1 may decide that Japan is too tough a nut to crack and that there are more promising markets elsewhere, thus ordering the Japan manager to *curtail* investment and channel resources elsewhere. This makes sense because Product Division 1 cares about its global market position and is not attached to any particular country. However, Asia Division, which is evaluated by how well it does in Asia, may beg to differ. It argues that to be a leading player in Asia, it cannot afford to be a laggard in Japan. Therefore, Asia Division demands that the Japan manager *increase* investment in the country. Facing these conflicting demands, the Japan manager has to satisfy two bosses, which can lead to complex and time-consuming negotiations between all the parties involved.

Taken together, the global matrix structure, despite its merits on paper, may add layers of management, slow down decision speed, and increase cost while not showing significant performance improvement. There is no conclusive evidence for the superiority of the matrix structure.[15] Having experimented with the matrix structure, a number of MNEs, such as the Swiss-Swedish engineering conglomerate ABB, have now moved back to the simpler and easier to manage global product structure. Even when the matrix structure is still in place, global product divisions are often given more power than geographic area divisions. The following quote from the then CEO of an early adopter of the matrix structure, Dow Chemical, is sobering:

> 'We were an organization that was matrixed and depended on teamwork, but there was no one in charge. When things went well, we didn't know whom to reward; and when things went poorly, we didn't know whom to blame. So we created a global product division structure, and cut out layers of management. There used to be 11 layers of management between me and the lowest level employees, now there are five.'[16]

Neither strategies nor structures are static. They evolve typically from the relatively simple international division through either geographic area or global product division structures and may finally reach the more complex global matrix stage. Not every MNE goes through the same stages of evolution, and the evolution is not necessarily in one direction (consider, for example, ABB's withdrawal from the matrix structure). Structures also change in response to external pressures.[17] In Europe, many MNEs traditionally pursued a localization strategy supported by the geographic area structure. However, the single market of the European Union has made such a structure obsolete. Consequently, many MNEs have now moved toward a pan-European strategy with a region-wide structure.

MANAGING KNOWLEDGE IN GLOBAL FIRMS

Knowledge management

Many of the capabilities that are the foundation of MNEs competitiveness are grounded in knowledge. Food ingredients manufacturer Danisco (Chapter 14, Opening Case) recognized this in its slogan *First you add Knowledge*. Some scholars argue that knowledge management is *the* defining feature of MNEs.[18] Knowledge management can be defined as the structures, processes and systems that actively develop, leverage and transfer knowledge.

Knowledge is a broad concept that includes not only factual information but the know-how and know-why held by individuals and by the firm as a whole. Hence, sophisticated information technology (IT) such as software provided by SAP (Chapter 4, Opening Case) is an important foundation, but knowledge management concerns also the informal social relationships within the MNE that facilitate the creation and sharing of knowledge. This is because there are two categories of knowledge:

Knowledge management
The structures, processes and systems that actively develop, leverage and transfer knowledge.

Explicit knowledge
Knowledge that is codifiable (that is, can be written down and transferred with little loss of its richness).

- Explicit knowledge is codifiable (that is, can be written down and transferred with little loss of its richness). Virtually all the knowledge captured, stored and transmitted by IT is explicit.
- Tacit knowledge is non-codifiable and its acquisition and transfer require hands-on practice.[19] For instance, mastering a driving manual (containing a ton of explicit knowledge) without any road practice does not make you a good driver. Tacit knowledge is evidently more important and harder to transfer and learn; it can only be acquired through learning by doing (driving, in this case).

Knowledge is often held by individuals – you know how to study and get a good mark in your exam, employees in companies individually 'know' how to do their specific job. However, there is also knowledge held by the team or organization. For example, a football team knows how to launch an attack, or defend, based on patterns of interaction between the members of a team. This organizational (or team-embedded) knowledge is more than the sum of the knowledge held by individuals; it is held by the organization either in shared repositories of documents and data, or embedded in the practices and routines of the members of the team. Based on the two distinctions explicit/tacit knowledge and individual/organizational knowledge, Japanese scholar Ikujiro Nonaka distinguished four types of knowledge that organizations have to manage (Figure 15.6).

Organizational (team embedded) knowledge
Knowledge held in an organization that goes beyond the knowledge of the individual members.

Knowledge management requires transformation of different forms of knowledge, such that knowledge held by individuals can be shared, and individuals utilize knowledge held in the organization in their own work. Thus, tacit knowledge of

Figure 15.6 Knowledge conversion

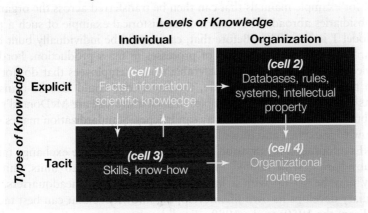

Source: 'Knowledge conversion' from 'A dynamic theory of organizational knowledge creation' by Ikujiro Nonaka in *Organization Science*, Vol 5(1) 1994, pp. 14–37. Published by Informs, Institute for Operations Research and Management of Science. Permission conveyed through Copyright Clearance Centre.

individuals (cell 3) has to be made explicit (cell 1), for example by writing manuals or by entering it into databases. At the same time, individuals have to adopt the explicit knowledge, and integrate it with their personal, tacit knowledge. The organization needs to combine the explicit knowledge of individuals to make it accessible to others, and to create new knowledge in the form of, for example, databases, rules or organizational systems (cell 2).

However, organizations 'know' more than the content of their databases. Think of a professional football team, such as Manchester United: they may have video recordings and analyses of their main competitors, such as Real Madrid, codified in databases. However, individual players may have played against them before, or they have experiences competing with Spanish teams playing in a similar style. They develop organizational routines (such as how to launch a counter-attack, how to score from a free kick or a corner) partly by studying the organizational explicit knowledge, and partly by sharing knowledge from player to player in a process known as socialization (cell 4). As a result, the team shares organizational knowledge that is more that the sum of the knowledge of individuals and that, due to its tacit nature, is hard to describe. Yet, everyone knows it is there. Football teams that have played together for a long time have more such team-embedded knowledge than those just recently assembled for a game. That is why teams with few star players sometimes can beat the teams assembled of many stars – think of 'minnows' such as Croatia, Denmark or Greece beating major football nations such as England or Germany in the European Championships.

Managing knowledge in a football teams is easy – compared to MNEs. There are only 11 players (plus their support staff) and they all work at the same location, the football pitch. However, many MNEs comprise thousands of people dispersed all over the world. How can they manage their knowledge? We start by looking at the four types of strategy.

Knowledge management in four types of MNEs

Knowledge flows from the centre to the periphery is the essence of a home replication strategy. Subsidiaries largely adapt and leverage parent company competencies. Thus, knowledge about new products and technologies is mostly developed at the centre and transferred to subsidiaries, representing the traditional one-way flow.

To be able to do that, the company has to make the tacit knowledge of its people explicit in for example manuals that can then be transferred across the organization – and to subsidiaries abroad. The most famous historical example of such a process is Ford's Model T in the 1920s. Before that, cars would be individually built by skilled craftsmen. With the standardization of processes in mass production, Ford codified the knowledge and thus made it transferable to new employees that do not need the craftsmen training.[20] In the same way, the knowledge could also be transferred to new plants abroad. More recent examples of such a strategy are McDonald's hamburgers, Starbuck's coffeehouses or Subway sandwiches. Standardization makes organizational knowledge explicit and thus allows its transfer abroad.

In MNEs adopting a localization strategy, most knowledge exchange takes place within subsidiaries, with limited knowledge transfer between units. Initially, the subsidiary may be set up with a knowledge transfer from headquarters, yet then the subsidiary develops its own life, developing knowledge that can best tackle local markets. From the 1950s to the 1980s, Ford developed cars in Europe for European customers with limited flows of knowledge from and to headquarters.

In MNEs pursuing a global integration strategy, the interdependence is increased. Knowledge is developed and retained at headquarters and a few centres of excellence at other locations. Consequently, there is an extensive flow of knowledge and people from these centres to other subsidiaries. Knowledge flows within the centre(s) thus involves the full cycle of knowledge creation and codification, while knowledge from the centre may be codified to facilitate the transfer. For example, Yokogawa Hewlett-Packard, HP's subsidiary in Japan, won a coveted Japanese Deming Award for quality. The subsidiary was then charged with transferring

Table 15.2 Knowledge management in four types of multinational enterprises

Strategy	Home replication	Localization	Global integration	Transnational
Interdependence	Moderate	Low	Moderate	High
Role of foreign subsidiaries	Adapting and leveraging parent company competencies	Sensing and exploiting local opportunities	Implementing parent company initiatives	Differentiated contributions by subsidiaries to integrate worldwide operations
Development and diffusion of knowledge	Knowledge developed at the centre and transferred to subsidiaries	Knowledge developed and retained within each subsidiary	Knowledge mostly developed and retained at the centre and key locations	Knowledge developed jointly and shared worldwide
Flow of knowledge	Extensive flow of knowledge and people from headquarters to subsidiaries	Limited flow of knowledge and people in both directions (to and from the centre)	Extensive flow of knowledge and people from centre and key locations to subsidiaries	Extensive flow of knowledge and people in multiple directions

Sources: Adapted from (1) C. Bartlett & S. Ghoshal, 1989, Managing across Borders: The Transnational Solution (p. 65), Boston: *Harvard Business School Press*; (2) T. Kostova & K. Roth, 2003, Social capital in multinational corporations and a micro-macro model of its formation (p. 299), *Academy of Management Review*, 28 (2): 297–317.

such knowledge to the rest of the HP family that resulted in a tenfold improvemen *corporate-wide* quality in ten years.[21]

Transnational MNEs are built on extensive and multi-directional flows (knowledge.[22] For example, extending a popular ice cream developed in Argentina based on a locally popular caramelized milk dessert, Häagen-Dazs introduced this flavour, Dulce de Leche, throughout the USA and Europe. Within one year, it became the second most popular Häagen-Dazs ice cream (next only to vanilla).[23] Particularly fundamental to transnational MNEs is knowledge flows among dispersed subsidiaries. Instead of a top-down hierarchy, the MNE thus can be conceptualized as an integrated network of subsidiaries (sometimes called the 'N-form'), each not only developing locally relevant knowledge but also aspiring to contribute globally beneficial knowledge that enhances corporate-wide competitiveness of the MNE as a whole.

The multiple-embedded MNE

In MNEs with a global or transnational strategy, codification is often not sufficient for effective knowledge exchange of varying degrees of complexity between many different parties. Knowledge is created at many places in the MNE. Each subsidiary is generating knowledge through the interactions of people within the subsidiary, and through the interaction of the subsidiary with (1) other units of the MNE and (2) with people and organizations in its local context, but outside the MNE (Figure 15.7). Some MNEs deliberate invest in innovation-seeking operations abroad, aiming to tap into such local knowledge.[24] As a result, MNEs themselves are embedded in multiple local contexts (countries) at home and in multiple host countries.[25] This multiple embeddedness creates complex patterns of knowledge creation and knowledge sharing.

Most knowledge creation takes place in groups of people doing similar or related tasks, known as communities of practice (CoP).[26] When people work, their

Communities of practice (CoP)
Groups of people doing similar or related work and sharing knowledge about their practices of work.

Figure 15.7 Multinational enterprises and local context

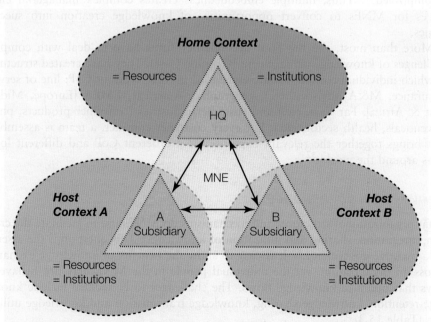

practices may not follow exactly the rules laid down in manuals, but they evolve with experimentation and innovation on the job. If people doing the same or similar types of work are closely connected by a social network, they can exchange such new knowledge before it gets codified. Knowledge exchange within CoP thus is more timely and relevant to the participants' practice than the traditional process of codifying knowledge, and then sharing it with relevant parties. CoP can be a powerful forum to share knowledge within a firm. Thus, firms may foster social interaction between people doing similar jobs. One simple way to do that is to offer free coffee in the office: the coffee machine becomes a point where people meet, gossip and exchange practical knowledge about their job.

Organizing CoP is more complex in MNEs operating across multiple locations, and where people speak different languages and originate from different cultures. Some MNEs take deliberate steps to facilitate the formation of CoP. For example, Shell recognizes the contribution of CoP to innovation, and systematically supports initiatives by staff to establish them.[27] CoP can operate through face to face interaction, for instance by bringing experts on specialist topics together in workshops and 'away days'. Other CoP operate as virtual communities of practice, sharing information on the intranet of the MNE. If members of a virtual CoP share common professional qualifications and other tacit knowledge, they can extent share tacit knowledge more effectively than corporate databases.[28] For example, Siemens introduced a system for knowledge sharing through codification and shared databases (see In Focus 15.1). Yet, beyond identifying the relevant experts, the more effective means to share knowledge often remains direct interaction within CoP.

On a local level, CoP can easily cross organizational boundaries: think of IT geeks in Silicon Valley hanging out at the same parties, exchanging tacit knowledge about the latest trends in the industry. A presence in different local contexts with varying institutions and resources is an important stimulus to innovation. Overseas R&D provides a vehicle to access a foreign country's local talents and expertise.[29] Collaborative research with external partners such as other firms or university research labs provide important sources of innovation.[30] However, connecting such local CoP with the MNE's internal (virtual) CoP is a challenge that few firms have accomplished.[31] Thus, multiple embeddedness creates complex managerial challenges for MNEs to convert opportunities of knowledge creation into success stories.

More than most, the Big Four accountancy firms have to deal with complex challenges of knowledge management (Opening Case). They have created structures in which individual consultants are embedded in three types of CoP: line of service (assurance, M&A advisory, etc), geographic (Americas, EMEA [Europe, Middle East & Africa], Far East, etc.) and customer industries (consumer products, pharmaceuticals, health sector, etc.). For every customer contract, a team is assembled that brings together the relevant expertise from different CoP and different locations around the world.[32]

Knowledge governance

What organizational structures and mechanisms do MNEs use to facilitate the creation, integration, sharing and utilization of knowledge? This question is the essence of knowledge governance.[33] It is easy to show the benefits of knowledge exchange across an organization, yet the individual people in the MNE may not behave in ways that optimize knowledge flows. The challenges to be tackled include knowledge retention, knowledge sharing, knowledge transmission and knowledge utilization (Table 15.3).[34]

Virtual communities of practice
Communities of practice interacting via the internet.

Knowledge governance
The structures and mechanisms MNEs use to facilitate the creation, integration, sharing and utilization of knowledge.

IN FOCUS 15.1

Siemens' ShareNet: A knowledge management system

Siemens, headquartered in Munich, is an engineering conglomerate that produces power generation equipment, transportation systems, medical devices and numerous other industrial products. In 1992, Siemens, in the words of its then CEO, was: 'an introverted, some would say arrogant, company, particularly in Germany, where 50 per cent of our business and more than 50 per cent of the people were still located at that time.' In 2009, Siemens had 85 per cent of sales, 77 per cent of assets and 73 per cent of its 405 000 work force outside Germany. As Siemens expands around the world, how to tap into and rejuvenate its employees' comprehensive knowledge and expertise that is geographically dispersed in 190 countries (!) remains a key challenge. Thus, since 1998, Siemens has developed a knowledge management (KM) system, ShareNet, that endeavours to put its employees' combined knowledge to work.

The ShareNet initiative went through four steps. The first step was concept definition. ShareNet was envisioned not only to handle explicit knowledge but also tacit knowledge. To overcome the drawbacks of traditional, repository-based KM systems, the new system had to integrate interactive components such as a forum for urgent requests and a platform for sharing rich knowledge. Pilot tests were carried out in Australia, China, Malaysia and Portugal to gain cross-cultural insights from users far from Munich.

The second step was the global rollout for 39 countries. Balancing global integration and local responsiveness, strategic direction for the project came from Munich, with ShareNet managers in each local subsidiary. They were people from the local subsidiaries assigned to become the nucleus in their regions. To jump-start the system, ShareNet managers held local workshops and encouraged participants to post an unsolved problem as an urgent request that would be sent to all users worldwide. Without exception, by the end of the day, the posting would get at least one reply, and inevitably, the person who had posted it would be 'stunned'. Not surprisingly, local workshops would

lead to an increase in urgent requests from that country.

Resistance was extensive. In Germany, attitude toward the English-only ShareNet was initially negative. Some employees thought that a Germany-based firm should use German. Although the English proficiency of German employees was relatively high, many employees still dared not post a question in a forum where thousands of people could see their grammatical or spelling errors. Over time, such resistance was gradually overcome as users personally experienced the benefits of the system.

The third step was generating momentum. Many people said: 'I don't have time for this'. Others put it more bluntly: 'Why do I have to share?' In 2000, Siemens provided incentives for local country managers and rewarded a country's overall participation. For a successful sale resulting from ShareNet collaboration, a bonus was given to both the country that had contributed the knowledge and the country that used it. Individual contributors were rewarded with various gifts and prizes, such as Siemens mobile phones, books and even trips to visit knowledge exchange partners. Interesting patterns emerged. Contrary to expectations, the average number of contributed knowledge pieces per contributor in China (16.67) was much higher than that in the USA (3.29). Indian employees were also enthusiastic. The ShareNet team suspected that this was in part because rewards were more attractive to Chinese and Indian employees (who were usually paid less) than to US employees. In India, some employees became overzealous, made low-quality contributions, and even neglected their 'day jobs'. The ShareNet team consequently adjusted rewards to less expensive goods such as books.

The fourth step was consolidating and sustaining performance. By 2002, ShareNet had 19000 users in more than 80 countries, supported by 53 ShareNet managers in different countries. After the initial establishment, the ShareNet team was trimmed to fewer than ten members worldwide. User behaviour also changed substantially. There was a noticeable decline in knowledge contributions, although the level of urgent requests was maintained. The rationale was simple: An urgent request could directly help solve an immediate problem in a tough time, whereas knowledge contributions did not yield an immediate payoff to the contributor. To demonstrate value added, the ShareNet team documented €5 million direct profits that had been generated by the KM system.

Sources: Based on (1) *Economist*, 2007, European business: Home and abroad, February 10; (2) www.siemens.com; (3) T. Stewart & L. O'Brien, 2005, Transforming an industrial giant, *Harvard Business Review*, February: 115–122; (4) S.C. Voelpel, M. Dous, & T. Davenport, 2005, Five steps to creating a global knowledge-sharing system: Siemens' ShareNet, *Academy of Management Executive*, 19: 9–23; (5) www.siemens.com.

Table 15.3 Selected challenges in knowledge governance

Elements of Knowledge governance	Challenges	Common obstacles
Knowledge retention	Can the firm keep the knowledge it has accumulated?	Employee turnover and knowledge leakage
Knowledge sharing	Are people willing to share knowledge with others inside the firm?	'How does it help me?' syndrome and 'knowledge is power' mentality
Knowledge transmission	Is knowledge communicated effectively between people and business units?	Inappropriate channels, language barriers
Knowledge utilization	Do potential recipients appreciate and utilize knowledge available elsewhere in the organization?	'Not invented here' syndrome, lack of absorptive capacity

Source: Based on A. Gupta & V. Govindarajan, 2004, *Global Strategy and Organization* (p. 109), New York: Wiley.

A basic problem is the retention of knowledge. Since knowledge, especially tacit knowledge, is often embedded in individuals, the departure of key individuals, such as star designers or R&D personnel can lead to the loss of knowledge-based capabilities. In the worst case, employees may take their knowledge to competitors.[35]

In knowledge sharing, the key question is whether those who have knowledge are willing to share this knowledge with those in the organization who need it. Specifically, managers of the source subsidiary may view outbound sharing of knowledge as a diversion of scarce time and resources, asking 'how does it help me/us?'. Further, some managers may believe that 'knowledge is power', and monopolizing certain knowledge may be viewed as the currency to acquire and retain power within the MNE.[36] Even when certain subsidiaries are willing to share knowledge, inappropriate transmission channels may still undermine the effectiveness knowledge sharing.[37] Virtual CoP help, but they are less effective than face-to-face interaction. Finally, recipient subsidiaries may present two problems that block successful knowledge inflows. First, the 'not invented here' syndrome causes some managers to resist accepting ideas from other units. Second, recipient subsidiaries may have limited absorptive capacity – 'ability to recognize the value of new information, assimilate it, and apply it'.[38]

As solutions to combat these problems, corporate headquarters can manipulate the formal rules of the game, such as (1) tying bonuses with measurable knowledge

Absorptive capacity
The ability to recognize the value of new information, assimilate it and apply it.

outflows and inflows, (2) using high-powered, corporate- or business-unit-based incentives (as opposed to individual- and single-subsidiary-based incentives) and (3) investing in codifying tacit knowledge. Siemens used some of these measures when promoting its ShareNet (In Focus 15.1). However, these formal policies fundamentally boil down to the very challenging (if not impossible) task of how to accurately measure inflows and outflows of tacit knowledge. The nature of tacit knowledge simply resists such formal bureaucratic practices. Moreover, high powered incentives may undermine a corporate culture of sharing knowledge, as individuals focus on initiatives that are measured and rewarded, while reducing informal means of sharing that can be more timely and effective. In other words, large bonuses can undermine a cooperative culture.[39]

Consequently, MNEs often rely on a great deal of informal integrating mechanisms, such as (1) facilitating management and R&D personnel networks among various subsidiaries through joint teamwork, training and conferences and (2) promoting strong organizational (that is, MNE-specific) cultures and shared values and norms for cooperation among subsidiaries.[40] The key idea is that instead of using traditional, formal command-and-control structures that are often ineffective, knowledge management is best facilitated by informal social capital, which refers to the informal benefits individuals and organizations derive from their social structures and networks.[41] Because of the existence of social capital, individuals are more likely to go out of their way to help friends and acquaintances. Consequently, managers of the China subsidiary are more likely to help managers of the Chile subsidiary if they know each other and have some social relationship. Otherwise, managers of the China subsidiary may not be as enthusiastic to provide such help if the call for help comes from managers of the Cameroon subsidiary, with whom there is no social relationship. Overall, informal interpersonal relationships among managers of different units may greatly facilitate inter-subsidiary cooperation among units.

Social capital
The informal benefits individuals and organizations derive from their social structures and networks.

Subsidiary mandates

If MNEs are no longer monolithic, hierarchical organizations, and if knowledge originates throughout the global network of the MNE, then subsidiaries have more important roles than implementing decisions by headquarters. This leads subsidiaries to attain, potentially, considerable autonomy within the MNE, and the possibility to become world wide leaders in certain specializations. Many MNEs have created centres of excellence with a worldwide (or global) mandate – namely, the charter to be responsible for one MNE function throughout the world. HP's Singapore subsidiary, for instance, has a worldwide mandate to develop, produce and market all HP handheld products.

Many MNEs provide subsidiaries the autonomy to design their own *subsidiary-level* strategies and agendas.[42] These activities are known as subsidiary initiatives, defined as the proactive and deliberate pursuit of new opportunities by a subsidiary to expand its scope of responsibility.[43] For example, Honeywell Canada requested that headquarters designate itself as a global centre for excellence for certain product lines (In Focus 15.2). Such initiatives may inject a much needed spirit of entrepreneurship throughout the larger, more bureaucratic corporation. Subsidiary autonomy is however generally constrained by internal decision-making rules and processes of the MNE. For example, the China subsidiary of AKZO Nobel has been authorized to take smaller strategic decisions itself, yet major decisions need to be proposed to divisional headquarters, where they are scrutinized and – possibly – approved (see Closing Case).

Worldwide (or global) mandate
The charter to be responsible for one MNE function throughout the world.

Subsidiary initiative
The proactive and deliberate pursuit of new opportunities by a subsidiary to expand its scope of responsibility.

IN FOCUS 15.2

A subsidiary initiative at Honeywell Canada

Honeywell Limited is a wholly owned Canadian subsidiary – hereafter Honeywell Canada – of the Minneapolis-based Honeywell, Inc. that produces a variety of consumer products and engineering systems. Until the mid-1980s, Honeywell Canada was a traditional branch plant that mainly produced for the Canadian market in volumes approximately one-tenth of those of the main manufacturing operations in Minneapolis. By the late 1980s, the winds of change unleashed by the US-Canadian Free Trade Agreement (later to become NAFTA in the 1990s) threatened the very survival of Honeywell Canada, whose inefficient (suboptimal scale) operations could face closure when the high tariffs came down and Made-in-USA products could enter Canada duty-free. Canadian managers in the subsidiary entrepreneurially proposed to the US headquarters that their plant be given the mandate in certain product lines to produce for the entire North America. In exchange, they agreed to

shut down some inefficient lines. Although some US managers were understandably negative, the head of the homes division was open-minded. Negotiations followed and the Canadian proposal was eventually adopted. Consequently, Honeywell Canada was designated as a Honeywell centre of excellence for valves and actuators. At present, Honeywell Canada is Canada's leading controls company.

Although this is a successful case of subsidiary initiative, a potential ethical problem is that from a corporate headquarters' standpoint, it is often difficult to ascertain whether the subsidiary is making good-faith efforts acting in the best interest of the MNE or the subsidiary managers are primarily promoting their self-interest such as power, prestige, and their own jobs. How corporate headquarters can differentiate good-faith efforts from more opportunistic manoeuvres remains a challenge.

Sources: Based on (1) J. Birkinshaw, 2000, *Entrepreneurship in the Global Firm* (p. 26), London: Sage; (2) http://www.honeywell.ca; (3) http://www.honeywell.com.

Subsidiary autonomy, however, makes it more difficult to realize the benefits of integration, in particular economies of scale and shared standards and practices. When headquarters want to introduce common practices throughout the organization (such as quality circles), some subsidiaries may be happy to comply, others may pay lip service, and still others may object, citing local differences.[44] In such situations, subsidiary employees often argue that headquarters, especially those staffed by parent country nationals only, take decisions in more or less ignorance about the local context of the subsidiary, and that practices imported from, say, the USA will do more harm than good.

From the perspective of corporate headquarters, it is often hard to distinguish between good-faith subsidiary initiatives and opportunistic 'empire building'. For instance, a lot is at stake when determining which subsidiaries become centres of excellence with worldwide mandates.[45] Subsidiaries that fail to attain this status may see their roles marginalized and, in the worst case, their facilities closed. Subsidiary managers often identify with the subsidiary and the host country (such as Canada at Honeywell Canada in In Focus 15.2), and naturally prefer to strengthen their subsidiary. The challenge thus is to create systems of international competition and performance assessment, that constrain self-seeking behaviours while encouraging entrepreneurial initiatives.

INSTITUTIONS AND THE CHOICE OF ORGANIZATIONAL STRUCTURE

MNEs face different sets of institutions that influence the ways in which they can organize their business, including institutions (1) in their home country, and (2) in their host countries. We discuss them in turn.

LEARNING OBJECTIVE

3 Explain how institutions and resources affect strategy, structure and learning

Home country institutions

MNEs are subject to the national institutional frameworks in each context in which they are operating. These institutional differences influence organizational forms in several ways, including the adaptation of the multi-divisional form. Historically, most firms were organized either as holding companies (if they operate in multiple businesses), or by functions along the value chain, separating purchasing, manufacturing and sales units (if they operate in a small number of industries). However, with increasing diversity of products and markets, such an organizational form was no longer appropriate. Starting in the USA in the 1950s, companies started introducing product division structures or geographic division structures discussed earlier.[46] These 'multi-divisional' forms were favoured in particular by outside financial investors who wanted clearer transparency and more efficient stock markets. The new forms were soon adopted by British MNEs that faced a similar institutional context as US firms, especially the financial market.[47] Yet, in France and Germany, individual owners, bankers and the state play a larger role in the context of a coordinated market economy (Chapter 2). This institutional context led to considerably slower adaptation of multi-divisional forms in French or German firms.[48] Similarly, institutional differences explain why US and British firms tend to be more focused on a single line of business, whereas German, French and Japanese businesses tend to have a higher degree of product diversification.[49]

The four modern organizational structures also vary across home countries. US companies traditionally were more likely to use home replication strategies, and due to the huge size of their home market many of them continue to use an international division structure, even if this division is allowed to localize its strategy. European MNES were operating traditionally in very distinct national markets, which encouraged localization strategies and geographic division structures. With the introduction of the EU single market in 1993, these differences diminished, and reduced the case for a geographic structure, leading firms to integrate operations more across countries and moving to product division or matrix structures.

Host country institutions

Host country governments, on the other hand, often attract or encourage MNEs into undertaking activities. For example, basic manufacturing generates low-paying jobs, but does not provide substantial technology spillovers to local businesses, and carries little prestige. Advanced manufacturing, R&D and regional headquarters, on the other hand, generate higher paying jobs and provide more technology spillovers.[50] Therefore, host country governments often use a combination of 'carrots' (such as tax incentives and free infrastructure upgrades) and 'sticks' (such as threats to block market access) to attract MNE investments in higher value added activities (see Chapter 6).

Many government incentive schemes specifically focus on attracting MNEs that contribute to the science and technology base of the country by establishing R&D units. Numerous subsidy schemes and tax breaks have been created to attract

How can MNEs interact with universities such as Oxford?

© Li Kim Goh

R&D operation. However, MNEs tend to look more broadly for the institutional framework influencing innovation activity, also known as national innovation systems.[51] Thus, MNEs locate their R&D units near quality universities and research laboratories, and where networks between business and academia facilitate knowledge flows.[52]

There are also numerous elements of informal institutions when dealing with *host* countries. For instance, Airbus spends 40 per cent of its procurement budget with US suppliers. While there is no formal requirement for Airbus to 'farm out' supply contracts, its sourcing decisions are guided by the informal norm of reciprocity: If one country's suppliers are involved with Airbus, airlines based in that country are more likely to buy Airbus aircraft. Such informal norms of producing or sourcing locally are particularly important when selling to government entities that are under political pressures to 'keep jobs at home'.

National innovation systems
The institutions and organizations that influence innovation activity in a country.

RESOURCE-BASED CONSIDERATIONS

The resource-based view – exemplified by the VRIO framework – adds a number of insights.[53] First, the question of value needs to be addressed. Hence, when making structural changes, whether the new structure (such as matrix) adds concrete value is crucial. Another example is the value of innovation.[54] A vast majority of innovations fail to reach the market, and most new products that do reach market end up being financial failures. R&D by definition contains a lot of experimentation: finding out what works and what does not. Hence, some innovations can be expected not to add value. The crucial questions for firms are whether their R&D programme as a whole creates value, and whether the organizational structure helps or hinders value-creating innovations.

A second question is rarity. Certain strategies or structures may be in vogue at one point in time. When rivals all move toward a global integration, this strategy cannot become a source of differentiation. To improve global coordination, many MNEs spend millions of dollars to equip themselves with enterprise resource planning (ERP) packages provided by SAP and Oracle. However, such packages are designed for broad appeal implementation, thus providing no firm-specific advantage for the adopting firm. Rarity comes not from adopting textbook structures or buying in systems and software; it comes from making it work by developing the tacit organizational knowledge that connects those systems with the needs of the firm.

Even when capabilities are valuable and rare, they have to pass a third hurdle, namely, imitability. Formal structures are easier to observe and imitate than informal structures. This is one of the reasons the informal, flexible matrix has been in vogue for many years. The informal, flexible matrix 'is less a structural classification than a broad organizational concept or philosophy, manifested in organizational capability and management mentality'.[55] It is obviously a lot harder, if not impossible, to imitate an intangible mentality than to imitate a tangible structure.

The last hurdle is organization – namely, are MNEs organized, both formally and informally, to exploit the values they are creating. A crucial difference exists between an innovator and a *profitable* innovator. The latter not only has plenty of good ideas but also lots of complementary assets (such as appropriate organizational structures and marketing muscles) to add value to innovation (see Chapter 4). Philips, for example, is a great innovator, having invented rotary shavers, videocassettes and compact discs (CDs). However, its abilities to profit from these innovations lag behind those of Sony and Matsushita, which have much stronger complementary assets.

DEBATES AND EXTENSIONS

The question of how to manage complex MNEs has led to numerous debates, some of which have been discussed earlier (such as the debate on the matrix structure). Here, we outline two of the leading debates not previously discussed: (1) top management teams and (2) relocating divisional headquarters.

LEARNING OBJECTIVE

4 Participate in two leading debates on multinational strategy, structure and learning

Top management teams

An important element in the structure of an MNE is the composition of the Top Management Team, and the leadership of subsidiaries. The nationality of the head of foreign subsidiaries is such an example.[56] MNEs essentially can have three choices when appointing a head of a subsidiary:

- A parent country national as the head of a subsidiary (such as a French person for a subsidiary of a French MNE in India).
- A host country national (such as an Indian for the same subsidiary).
- A third country national (such as a Briton for the same subsidiary).

MNEs from different countries follow different norms when making these appointments. Most Japanese MNEs seem to follow an informal rule: Heads of foreign subsidiaries, at least initially, need to be Japanese nationals.[57] In comparison, European MNEs are more likely to appoint host and third country nationals to lead subsidiaries. These staffing approaches reflect strategic differences.[58] Home country nationals, especially those long-time employees of the same MNE, are more likely to have developed a thorough understanding of the informal workings of the firm and to be better socialized into its dominant norms and values. Consequently, the Japanese propensity to appoint Japanese nationals is conducive to their preferred global integration strategy that values globally coordinated and controlled actions.[59] Conversely, the European comfort in appointing host and third country nationals is indicative of European MNEs' traditional preference for a localization strategy.

Beyond the nationality of subsidiary heads, the nationality of top executives at the highest level (such as board chair, CEO and board members) seems to follow another informal rule: They are (almost always) parent country nationals. To the extent that top executives are ambassadors of the firm and that the MNE headquarters' country of origin is a source of differentiation (for example, a German MNE is often perceived to be different from an Italian MNE),[60] parent country nationals would seem to be the most natural candidates for top positions.

However, in the eyes of stakeholders such as employees and governments around the world, a top echelon consisting of largely one nationality does not bode well for an MNE aspiring to globalize everything it does. Some critics even argue that this 'glass ceiling' reflects 'corporate imperialism'.[61] Consequently, such major MNEs as SAP (Chapter 4, Opening Case) have appointed foreign-born bosses to top posts, and this strategy is gathering pace worldwide (see In Focus 15.3). Such foreign-born bosses bring substantial diversity to the organization, which may be a plus. However, such diversity puts an enormous burden on these non-native top executives to clearly articulate the values and exhibit behaviours expected of senior managers of an MNE associated with a particular country.[62] Procter & Gamble (P&G), for example, appointed Durk Jager, a native of the Netherlands, to be its chairman and CEO in 1999. Unfortunately, his numerous change initiatives almost brought the venerable company to a grinding halt, and he was quickly forced to resign in 2000. Since then, the old rule is back: P&G has been led by an American executive.[63]

Moving (business unit) headquarters overseas

Some MNEs aggregate operations by locating *business unit* headquarters (HQ) away from home, while some are even moving their *corporate* HQ away from their country of origin. The question is: Why?

At the business unit level, the answer is straight-forward: the 'centre of gravity' of the activities of a business unit may pull its HQ toward a host country.[64] For example, the Danish 'East Asiatic Company' moved it operational HQ from Copenhagen to Singapore because most of its markets were in Asia or Latin America. Others move key functions overseas to be closer to their business partners. For example, IBM moved to global procurement office to Shenzhen, China in 2006.

At the corporate level, there are at least four strategic rationales. First, HQ location is a clear signal to various stakeholders that the firm is a global – rather than domestic or local – player. News Corporation's corporate HQ relocation from Melbourne, Australia to New York in 2004 is indicative of its global status, as opposed to being a remote firm from 'down under'. Lenovo's credibility among its US-based customers after the take-over of IBM's Laptop division has been greatly enhanced by the establishment of its worldwide HQ in the USA.

Second, it may facilitate access to capital markets. A corporate HQ in a major financial centre such as New York or London facilitates direct communication with institutional shareholders, financial analysts and investment banks. The MNE also increases its visibility in a financial market, resulting in a broader shareholder base and greater market capitalization. As a result, three leading (former) South African firms, Anglo American, Old Mutual and SABMiller moved their HQ to London, and later joined the FTSE 100 – the top 100 UK-listed firms by capitalization.

CLOSING CASE

Growing subsidiaries: AKZO Nobel Decorative Coating in China

By Jens Gammelgaard, Copenhagen Business School.

In the 1990s, AKZO Nobel Decorative Coatings (ANDC), a division of the Swedish-Dutch conglomerate AKZO Nobel, faced increasing competitive pressures in its core European markets for paints, varnishes and wood care products. It responded by rationalization, closing some European factories, and focusing more on Asian markets.

ANDC started in 1990 with a JV, a state-owned company in China, yet it failed due to problems with the distribution and the JV was terminated in 1992. A new JV was created in 1996 with another state-owned company and in 1998, ANDC established its first wholly-owned subsidiary with the mandate to market the company's products, mainly interior and exterior decorative paints manufactured outside China. The subsidiary was given a goal to sell five million litres, after which it was to receive a mandate for local production. This goal was reached in 2003.

The subsidiary, ANDC (China), negotiated a mandate to enter new market segments such as the construction industry, and to pursue acquisitions in China on the basis of AKZO Nobel's ambitious growth strategy. The mandate aimed to grow production capacity, to obtain local brands, and to reach geographically dispersed markets through subsidiaries spread across China. Thus, ANDC acquired a small local non-stick coating facility (10 million litres) in Dongguan (Guangzhou province), following negotiations over more than two and a half years. Further North, ANDC commissioned a coil coatings facility in Suzhou, and build two wood coatings factories on greenfield sites.

The construction industry is a major customer of ANDC, yet it also poses specific challenges such as the need to operate closely to the pertinent construction sites. Contracts are made with the architect or with the construction contractor. They typically place orders for the final product only late in the construction process,

Why and how do paints have to be locally adopted?

and then expect delivery on fairly short notice. This requires being close by. Moreover, paint formulations have to be adapted to specific requirements of the building, such as building materials, weather conditions and pollution, which often make standardized corporate formulations inappropriate. Thus, subsidiaries have to develop their own products, along with monitoring of the quality of raw materials and finished goods.

AKZO Nobel has traditionally been organized in a decentralized multi-divisional structure. However, a centralization process was initiated to better cope with the company's growing complexity in terms of both products and cultures. Thus, headquarters would take strategic decisions such as the geographical markets that subsidiaries should serve, and establish common practices and procedures for human resource management, corporate social responsibility and financial management. Subsidiaries could take strategic initiatives, and they frequently did, yet they had to present detailed project descriptions and budgets to a committee of the Swedish board of ANDC. Often, further clarifications and specifications were requested before the board would present the project to the corporate board of AKZO Nobel in the Netherlands. In the case of the acquisition of the coatings factory in Dongguan, ANDC (China) easily obtained the approval to search for acquisition targets, but it had to negotiate the screening criteria with the unit board in Sweden.

Compared to other subsidiaries, ANDC (China) had quiet a lot of influence over its mandate because of the strategic importance of the Chinese market and because it was managed by an expatriate. European headquarters were closely watching China due to the growth potential, and the board visited China at least once a year. The Chinese subsidiary thus was able to develop its role (e.g., gaining production mandates, building plants, making acquisitions) more autonomously than other subsidiaries.

However, every subsidiary depends on resources from headquarters. AKZO Nobel is organized as an 'internal market', where the subsidiaries compete for resources. Expatriate managers play a key role in this game, since they often have a competitive advantage – compared to local managers – in communicating and formulating the detailed reports required by headquarters. The Danish expatriate in charge of ANDC (China) at the time recalls:

'An expatriate manager is a key actor that can match and translate local business opportunities into project descriptions to be approved by headquarters – here I see myself as an intermediary between two worlds.'

The development of a subsidiary, therefore, depends on expatriate managers with ambitions and ideas to convert local opportunities into projects of interest for headquarters managers. Subsidiary power in AKZO Nobel, therefore, depends on the combination of local expertise and the position of the subsidiary in the corporate context. The former Danish expatriate recalls:

'You have negotiation power when you can formulate and sell your message to the board. You need to be embedded in the culture of writing of concrete executive summaries, to make budgets, etc., this is the way to convince. Secondly, performance counts. However, it is also important with the network – whom to make phone calls to. I can call informally the business unit CEO in Stockholm. I have known him for many years.'

Thus, personal networks are crucial. At the end of the day, the development of ANDC (China) depended on its ability to convince headquarters' management to allocate resources and mandates. It succeeded because of its strategic position in China, and the manager's ability to bridge the cultural distance between the Netherlands, Sweden and China.

CASE DISCUSSION QUESTIONS

1 From a resource-based view, why did ANDC pursue multiple acquisitions in China?

2 From an institutional perspective, what are the advantages and disadvantages of a fast growing subsidiary being led by an expatriate?

3 How does ANDC make strategic decisions regarding its decisions in China? Do you think this process is appropriate?

Sources: Jens Gammelgaard (Copenhagen Business School) prepared this case based on interviews with executives of the firm and archival sources. Also see Gammelgaard, J. (2008), Subsidiary Influence and its Impact on Role Development, in: V. Worm, ed., China: Business Opportunities in a Globalizing Economy. Copenhagen: Copenhagen Business School Press, p. 91–112.

RECOMMENDED READING

C. Bartlett & S. Ghoshal, 1989, *Managing Across Borders*, Boston: Harvard Business School Press – Classic book outlining the integration responsiveness framework and its implications.

J. Birkinshaw, 2001, *Entrepreneurship in the Global Firm*, London: Sage – A book discussing how managers in global MNEs, especially leaders of subsidiaries, can lead their unit entrepreneurially.

J. Birkinshaw, S. Ghoshal, C. Markides, J.M. Stopford, & G. Yip, eds, 2003, *The Future of the Multinational Company*, London: Wiley – Essays in memory of Sumantra Ghoshal, exploring various aspects of how best to manage a multinational company, and the integration-responsiveness framework in particular.

N.J. Foss & S. Michailova, 2009. *Knowledge Governance: Processes and Perspectives*, Oxford: Oxford University Press – Scholarly essays on knowledge processes with focus informal and informal governance mechanisms.

A. Gupta & V. Govindarajan, 2004, *Global Strategy and Organization* (p. 104), New York: Wiley – Discusses how companies can be organized to make best use of global opportunities, especially knowledge management.

NOTES:

"FOR JOURNAL ABBREVIATION, PLEASE SEE PAGE XXVI–XXVII."

1 U. Andersson, M. Forsgren & U. Holm, 2007. Balancing subsidiary influence in the federative MNC, *JIBS*, 38: 802–818; M. Forsgren, U. Holm & U. Andersson, 2007, *Managing the Embedded MNC: A Business Network View*. Cheltenham: Edward Elgar; K.E. Meyer, R. Mudambi & R. Narula, 2011, Multinational enterprises and local contexts: the opportunities and challenges of multiple-embeddedness, JMS, in press.

2 J.M. Stopford & L. Wells, 1972, *Managing the Multinational Enterprise*, New York: Basic Books ; C.K. Prahalad & Y. Doz, 1987, *The Multinational Mission*, New York: Free Press; J. Birkinshaw, S. Ghoshal, C. Markides, J. Stopford, & G. Yip (eds.), 2003, *The Future of the Multinational Company*, London: Wiley.

3 Bartlett, C.A. and Ghoshal, S. 1989. *Managing Across Borders: The Transnational Solution*, Boston, MA: Harvard Business School Press.

4 A.W.K. Harzing, 2000, An empirical analysis and extension of the Bartlett and Ghoshal typology of MNCs, *JIBS*, 31: 101–120; S. Venaik, D.F. Midgley & T.M. Devinney, 2005, Dual paths to performance: the impact of global pressures on MNC subsidiary conduct and performance, JIBS, 36: Pages: 655–675.

5 G. Szulanski & R. Jensen, 2006, Presumptive adaptation and the effectiveness of knowledge transfer, *SMJ*, 27: 937–957.

6 J. Birkinshaw, 2001, *Entrepreneurship in the Global Firm*, London: Sage; T. Frost, J. Birkinshaw, & P. Ensign, 2002, Centres of excellence in MNCs (p. 997), *SMJ*, 23: 997–1018; U. Andersson & M. Forsgren, 2000, In search of centres of excellence, *MIR*, 40: 329–350.

7 J. Birkinshaw & S. Terjesen, 2003, The customer-focused multinational, in Birkinshaw *et al.*, eds., *The Future of the Multinational Company* (pp. 115–127).

8 Bartlett & Ghoshal, 1989, *as above*.

9 J. Cantwell, J. Dunning & O. Janne, 2004, Towards a technology-seeking explanation of US direct investment in the United Kingdom, *JIM*, 10: 5–20; H. Berry, 2006, Leaders, laggards, and the pursuit of foreign knowledge, *SMJ*, 27: 151–168; N. Anand, H. Gardner, & T. Orris, 2007, Knowledge-based innovation, *AMJ*, 50: 406–428.

10 J. Birkinshaw & N. Hood, 1998, Multinational subsidiary evolution, *AMR*, 23: 773–796; J. Manea & R.D. Pearce, 2006, MNEs' strategies in Central and Eastern Europe, *MIR*, 46: 235–255; A.M. Rugman & A. Verbeke, 2001, Subsidiary-specific advantages in MNEs, *SMJ*, 22: 237–250.

11 J. Cantwell & R. Mudambi, 2005, MNE competence-creating subsidiary mandates, *SMJ*, 26: 1109–1128; K. Ruckman, 2005, Technology sourcing through acquisitions, *JIBS*, 36: 89–103.

12 S. Venaik et al., 2005, *as above*; A.M. Rugman, A. Verbeke & W. Yuan, 2011, Re-conceptualizing

Bartlett and Ghoshal's classification of national
subsidiary roles in the multinational Enterprise, JMS, in
press.

13 B. Lamont, V. Sambamurthy, K. Ellis & P. Simmonds,
2000, The influence of organizational structure on the
information received by corporate strategies of MNEs,
MIR, 40: 231–252; Y. Ling, S. Floyd & D. Baldrige,
2005, Toward a model of issue-selling by subsidiary
managers in MNCs, *JIBS*, 36: 637–654.

14 R. Edwards, A. Ahmad & S. Ross, 2002, Subsidiary
autonomy, *JIBS*, 33: 183–191; S. Miller & L. Eden,
2006, Local density and foreign subsidiary
performance, *AMJ*, 49: 341–355.

15 L. Burns & D. Wholey, 1993, Adoption and
abandonment of matrix management programs, *AMJ*,
36: 106–139; T.M. Devinney, D.F. Midgley &
S Venaik, 2000, The optimal performance of the global
firm, *OSc*, 11: 674–695; J. Johnson, 1995, An
empirical analysis of the integration-responsiveness
framework, *JIBS*, 26: 621–635.

16 R. Hodgetts, 1999, Dow Chemical CEO William
Stavropoulos on structure (p. 30), *AME*, 13: 29–35.

17 T. Murtha, S. Lenway & R. Bagozzi, 1998, Global
mind-sets and cognitive shift in a complex MNC, *SMJ*,
19: 97–114; G.R.G. Benito, B. Grøgaard & R. Narula,
2003, Environmental influences on MNE subsidiary
roles, *JIBS*, 34: 443–456; R. Whitley, G. Morgan,
W. Kelley & D. Sharpe, 2003, The changing Japanese
multinational, *JMS*, 40: 643–672.

18 B. Kogut & U. Zander, 1993, Knowledge of the firm
and the evolutionary theory of the multinational
corporation, *JIBS*, 24: 625–645; R. Grant, 1996,
Toward a knowledge-based theory of the firm, *SMJ*,
17: 109–122; H. Bresman, J. Birkinshaw &
R. Nobel, 1999, Knowledge transfer in international
acquisitions, *JIBS*, 30: 439–462; N.J. Foss &
T. Pedersen, 2005, Organizing knowledge processes
in the MNC, *JIBS*, 35: 340–349; N. Hashai,
2009, Knowledge transfer considerations and the
future of the internalization hypothesis, *IBR*, 18:
257–264.

19 X. Martin & R. Salomon, 2003, Knowledge transfer
capacity and its implications for the theory of the MNE,
JIBS, 34: 356–373; U. Schultze & C. Stabell, 2004,
Knowing what you don't know? *JMS*, 41: 549–573;
T. Felin & W. Hesterly, 2007, The knowledge-based
view, *AMR*, 32: 195–218.

20 R. Grant, 2008, *Contemporary Strategy Analysis*, 7th
ed., Chichester: Wiley.

21 M.E. Porter, H. Takeuchi, & M. Sakakibara, 2000, *Can
Japan Compete?* (p. 80), Cambridge, MA: Perseus.

22 Y. Luo & M.W. Peng, 1999, Learning to compete in a
transition economy, *JIBS*, 30: 269–296; T. Frost &

C. Zhou, 2005, R&D co-practice and 'reverse'
knowledge integration in MNCs, *JIBS*, 36: 676–687;
M. Kotabe, D. Dunlap-Hinkler, R. Parente & H. Mishra,
2007, Determinants of cross-national knowledge
transfer and its effect on firm innovation, *JIBS*, 38:
259–282; Q.A. Yang, R. Mudambi & K.E. Meyer,
2009, Conventional and reverse knowledge flows in
multinational Corporations, *JM*, 34: 882–902.

23 Y. Doz, J. Santos, & P.J. Williamson, 2001, *From
Global to Metanational*, Boston: Harvard Business
School Press.

24 P. Almeida, 1996, Knowledge sourcing by foreign
multinationals, *SMJ*, 17: 155–166; W. Kuemmerle,
1999, The drivers of FDI into R&D, *JIBS*, 30:
1–24; K. Asakawa & M. Lehrer, 2003, Managing
local knowledge assets globally, *JWB*, 38: 31–42;
R. Belderbos, 2003, Entry mode, organizational
learning, and R&D in foreign affiliates, *SMJ*,
24: 235–255; M. von Zedtwitz, O. Gassman & R.
Boutellier, 2004, Organizing global R&D, *JIM*, 10:
21–49.

25 U. Andersson, M. Forsgren & U. Holm, 2002, The
strategic impact of external networks, *SMJ*, 23:
979–996; R. Reagans & B. McEvily, 2003, Network
structure and knowledge transfer, *ASQ*, 48: 240–267.

26 J.S. Brown & P. Duguid, 1991, Organizational learning
and communities of practice, *OSc*, 2: 40–57;
E.C. Wenger & W.M. Snyder, 2000, Communities
of practice, *HBR*, (January/February): 139–145;
J. Roberts, 2006, Limits to communities of practice,
JMS, 43: 623–639.

27 J. McGee, H. Thomas & D. Wilson, *Strategy: Analysis
& Practice*, London: Wiley (p. 615).

28 M.K. Ahuja & K.M. Carley, 1999, Network structure in
virtual organizations, *OSc*, 10: 741–757; A. Ardichvili,
M. Mauer, W. Li, T. Wentling & R. Stuedemann, 2006,
Cultural influences on knowledge sharing through
online communities of practice, *JKM*, 10: 94–107;
J. Gammelgaard & T. Ritter, 2008, Virtual
communities of practice, *IJKM*, 4: 46–61.

29 M.W. Peng & D.Y.L. Wang, 2000, Innovation capability
and foreign direct investment, *MIR*, 40: 79–83;
J. Penner-Hahn & J.M. Shaver, 2005, Does international
R&D increase patent output? *SMJ*, 26: 121–140.

30 J. Hagedoorn & G. Duysters, 2002, External sources
of innovative capabilities, *JMS*, 39: 167–188; A. Lam,
2003, Organizational learning in multinationals, *JMS*,
40: 673–703; M. Mol, P. Pauwels, P. Matthyssens &
L. Quintens, 2004, A technological contingency
perspective on the depth and scope of international
outsourcing, *JIM*, 10: 287–305; R. Narula &
G. Duysters, 2004, Globalization and trends in
international R&D alliances, *JIM*, 10: 199–218.

31 S. Tallman & A. Chacar, 2010, Knowledge accumulation and dissemination in MNEs, JMS in press.

32 M. Bousssebaa, 2009, Struggling to Organise Across National Borders, HR, 62: 829–850; R. Greenwood, T. Morris, S. Fairclough & M. Boussebaa, 2010, The organizational design of transnational professional service firms, OD, in press.

33 A. Grandori, 2001, Neither hierarchy nor identity: knowledge governance mechanisms and the theory of the firm, JMS, 29: 459–483; N.J. Foss & S. Michailova, eds., Knowledge Governance: Perspectives, Process and Problems, Oxford: Oxford University Press; N.J. Foss, K. Husted & S. Michailova, 2010, Governing knowledge sharing in organizations, JMS, 47: 455–482.

34 A. Gupta & V. Govindarajan, 2004, Global Strategy and Organization (p. 104), New York: Wiley.

35 K. Asakawa & A. Som, 2008, Internationalizing R&D in China and India, APJM, 25: 375–394; Q.A. Yang & C. Jiang, 2007, Location advantages and subsidiaries' R&D activities, APJM, 24: 341–358.

36 S. Michailova & K. Husted, 2003, Knowledge sharing hostility in Russian firms, CMR, 45: 59–77; I. Björkman, W. Barner-Rasmussen & L. Li, 2004, Managing knowledge transfer in MNCs, JIBS, 35: 443–455; R. Mudambi & P. Navarra, 2004, Is knowledge power? JIBS, 35: 385–406.

37 R. Nobel & J. Birkinshaw, 1998, Innovation in MNCs, SMJ, 19: 479–496.

38 W. Cohen & D. Levinthal, 1990, Absorptive capacity, ASQ, 35: 128–152; J. Hong, R. Snell, & M. Easterby-Smith, 2006, Cross-cultural influences on organizational learning in MNCs, JIM, 12: 408–429; J. Jansen, F. van den Bosch & H. Volberda, 2005, Managing potential and realized absorptive capacity, AMJ, 48: 999–1015; D.B. Minbaeva, T. Pedersen, I. Björkman, C.F. Fey & H.J. Park, 2003, MNC knowledge transfer, subsidiary absorptive capacity, and HRM, JIBS, 34: 586–599.

39 M. Osterloh & B. Frey, 2000, Motivation, knowledge transfer and organizational form, OSc, 11: 538–550; M. Robertson & J. Swan, 2003, Control – what control? JMS, 40: 831–858.

40 H. Kim, J. Park & J. Prescott, 2003, The global integration of business functions, JIBS, 34: 327–344; S. O'Donnell, 2000, Managing foreign subsidiaries, SMJ, 21: 525–548; M. Subramaniam & N. Venkatraman, 2001, Determinants of transnational new product development capability, SMJ, 22: 359–378.

41 T. Kostova & K. Roth, 2003, Social capital in multinational corporations and a micro-macro model of its formation, AMR, 28: 297–317; A. Inkpen &

E. Tsang, 2005, Social capital, networks, and knowledge transfer, AMR, 30: 146–165; P. Gooderham, D.B. Minbaeva, & T. Pedersen, 2010, Governance mechanisms for the promotion of social capital for knowledge transfer in multinational corporations, JMS, 47: in press.

42 J. Taggart, 1998, Strategy shifts in MNC subsidiaries, SMJ, 19: 663–681; W. Newburry, 2001, MNC interdependence and local embeddedness influences on perception of career benefits from global integration, JIBS, 32: 497–507; M. Geppert, K. Williams & D. Matten, 2003, The social construction of contextual rationalities in MNCs, JMS, 40: 617–641; B. Ambos & B. Schlegelmilch, 2007, Innovation and control in the MNC, SMJ, 28: 473–486.

43 J. Birkinshaw, 2000, Entrepreneurship in the Global Firm, London: Sage; T.C. Ambos, U. Andersson & J. Birkinshaw, 2010, What are the consequences of initiative-taking in multinational subsidiaries? JIBS, 41: 1099–1118.

44 R. Edwards, A. Ahmad & S. Moss, 2002, Subsidiary autonomy, JIBS, 33: 183–192; T. Kostova & K. Roth, 2002, Adoption of an organizational practice by subsidiaries of multinational corporations, AMJ, 45: 215–233.

45 S.E. Feinberg, 2000, Do world product mandates really matter? JIBS, 31: 155–167.

46 A.D. Chandler, 1990, Scale and Scope, Cambridge, MA: Harvard University Press; A.D. Chandler, 1997, The United States, in: A.D. Chandler, F. Amatori & T. Hikino, eds, Big Business and the Wealth of Nations, New York: Cambridge University Press.

47 G. Jones, 1997, Great Britain, in A.D. Chandler et al., as above.

48 R. Whitley, 1994, Dominant forms of economic organization in market organizations, OSt, 15: 153–182; M. Mayer & R. Whittington, 2004, Economics, politics and nations: Resistance to the multidimensional form in France, Germany and the United Kingdom, 1983–1993, JMS, 41: 1057–1082.

49 B. Kogut, D. Walker & J. Anand, 2002, Agency and institutions: National divergence in diversification behavior, OSc, 13: 162–178; K.E. Meyer, 2007, Globalfocusing: From domestic conglomerate to global specialist, JMS, 43: 1109–1144.

50 S.E. Feinberg & S.K. Majumdar, 2001, Technology spillovers from foreign direct investment in the Indian pharmaceutical industry, JIBS, 32: 421–437; M. Wright, I. Filatotchev, T. Buck & K. Bishop, 2002, Foreign partners in the former Soviet Union, JWB, 37: 165–179; R. Narula & C. Bellak, 2009, EU Enlargement and consequences for FDI assisted industrial development, TNC, 18: 69–89.

51 B.Å. Lundvall, ed., 1992, National Systems of Innovation, London: Pinter; R. Nelson, 1993, ed., *National Innovation Systems: A Comparative Analysis*, New York: Oxford University Press.

52 J. Niosi, 1997, The globalization of Canada's R&D, *MIR*, 37: 387–404; R. Narula, 2003, *Globalization and Technology*, Cambridge: Polity; L.N. Davis & K.E. Meyer, 2004, Subsidiary research and development, and the local environment, *IBR*, 13: 359–382.

53 P. Cloninger, 2004, The effect of service intangibility on revenue from foreign markets, *JIM*, 10: 125–146; A. Delios & P.W. Beamish, 2001, Survival and profitability, *AMJ*, 44: 1028–1039; E. Danneels, 2002, The dynamics of product innovation and firm competences, *SMJ*, 23: 1095–1122; S. Tallman, 1991, Strategic management models and resource-based strategies among MNEs in a host country, *SMJ*, 12: 69–82.

54 G. Verona, 1999, A resource-based view of product development, *AMR*, 24: 132–142; K. Ojah & L. Monplaisir, 2003, Investors' valuation of global product R&D, *JIBS*, 34: 457–472.

55 Bartlett & Ghoshal, 1989, as above (p. 209).

56 N. Noorderhaven & A.W.K. Harzing, 2003, The 'country-of-origin effect' in MNCs, *MIR*, 43: 47–66.

57 P.W. Beamish & A. Inkpen, 1998, Japanese firms and the decline of the Japanese expatriate, *JWB*, 33: 35–50; R. Belderbos & M. Heijltjes, 2005, The determinants of expatriate staffing by Japanese multinationals in Asia, *JIBS*, 36: 341–354.

58 Y. Paik & J. Sohn, 2004, Expatriate managers and MNCs' ability to control international subsidiaries, *JWB*, 39: 61–71; R. Peterson, J. Sargent, N. Napier & W. Shim, 1996, Corporate expatriate HRM policies, internationalization, and performance in the world's largest MNCs, *MIR*, 36: 215–230.

59 J.K. Johansson & G. Yip, 1994, Exploiting globalization potential, *SMJ*, 15: 579–601; J. Sohn, 1994, Social knowledge as a control system, *JIBS*, 25: 295–325.

60 J. Birkinshaw, P. Braunerhjelm, U. Holm, & S. Terjesen, 2006, Why do some MNCs relocate their headquarters overseas? *SMJ*, 27: 681–700.

61 C.K. Prahalad & K. Lieberthal, 1998, The end of corporate imperialism, *HBR*, 76 (4): 68–79.

62 L. Palich & L. Gomez-Mejia, 1999, A theory of global strategy and firm efficiency, *JM*, 25: 587–606; O. Richard, T. Barnett, S. Dwyer, & K. Chadwick, 2004, Cultural diversity in management, firm performance, and the moderating role of entrepreneurial orientation, *AMJ*, 47: 227–240.

63 D. Leonhardt, 2000, Procter & Gamble shake-up follows poor profit outlook, *New York Times*, June 9; R. Berner, 2003, P&G: New and improved, *Business Week*, July 7.

64 Birkinshaw, et al., 2006, as above G.R.G. Benito, R. Lunnan & S. Thomassen, 2010, Moving abroad: Foreign located division headquarters in multinational Companies, JMS, in press.

65 *Wall Street Journal*, 2009, HSBC re-emphasizes its 'H', September 26.

CHAPTER SIXTEEN

INTERNATIONAL HUMAN RESOURCE MANAGEMENT

LEARNING OBJECTIVES

After studying this chapter you should be able to:

1 Distinguish ethnocentric, polycentric and geocentric management practices.

2 Explain how expatriates are managed in MNEs.

3 Explain how MNEs manage their employees in subsidiaries abroad.

4 Discuss how the institution-based view sheds additional light on HRM.

5 Discuss how the resource-based view sheds additional light on HRM.

6 Participate in two leading debates concerning HRM.

7 Draw implications for action.

EADS: managing human resources in a european context

By Professor Christoph Barmeyer, Passau University and Professor Ulrike Mayrhofer, Université Lyon 3.

In 2000, European Aeronautic Defence and Space Company (EADS) was created by a merger of the French Aerospatiale-Matra, the German DASA and the Spanish CASA. It aimed to join the strengths of three European nations with strong engineering traditions and to achieve market leadership and compete with world leaders such as Boeing and Lockheed Martin. However, merging firms from three different countries also meant bringing together three different organizational cultures that in turn were based on different national cultures. Human resource management teams faced important challenges, in particular due to cross-country mobility and cultural diversity.

Individuals from the three companies were selected to work on project teams outside their home country. These expatriates served important roles in facilitating the integration process. As cultural 'interface', they were to mediate between different systems of meaning and action in order to achieve mutual adaptation. English was adopted as an official language, which enables expatriates to better communicate with others in their team. However, expatriates also faced the challenge of integrating into another culture. Even though it was one company, the national culture where they worked was quite different. EADS considered this cultural diversity as an advantage, because it stimulates creativity and favours the dynamics of the group. In fact, expatriates had the opportunity to learn about different values that led to ideas and solutions that varied according to the problems they faced.

However, it creates personal challenges for the members of the teams as they were confronted with different ways of communicating and collaborating. Certain concepts of management such as cooperation or leadership have different meanings and interpretations in France and in Germany, which often leads to misunderstandings. For instance, for French engineers, the notion of cooperation implies that the goal should be achieved through work on an individual basis, whereas for German engineers, the

term cooperation means teamwork with the objective to obtain a common goal. Consequently, when working in German teams, the French sometimes felt frustrated by their lack of freedom and the necessity to reach a consensus. In the same way, when working in France, Germans attempted to find a consensus and had the impression that their French partners were individualists and difficult to predict. In the same way, expatriates learned about different conceptions of leadership. For example, German expatriates discovered that French authority was oriented towards paternalistic elements and personal power, favoured by centralized management structures. In contrast, French expatriates were surprised that German authority was mainly oriented towards function and professional competence and that German managers and engineers often graduated from public universities (in contrast to France where most managers and engineers graduate from highly selective and prestigious French 'Grandes Ecoles' like Ecole Polytechnique and Ecole Centrale).

Two metaphors highlight these different culturally embedded characteristics and conceptions of cooperation and leadership. The German organization has been described as a 'well-oiled machine': there is a clear technical structure to the regulation of functions in terms of tasks and responsibilities, and of processes in terms of sequential flow. The organization is understood as a *heterarchical* structure, the functions and goals of which are achieved – detached from personalized authority – according to its own agreed rules. In contrast, the French organization is like a 'pyramid of people': management holds a position of authority at the top of the pyramid, with subordinate participants below. The organization is understood as a *hierarchical* structure, in which interpersonal relations develop and personalized authority figures are needed to regulate power relations. As power is concentrated at the top of the pyramid, the persons below have to defend themselves by acting individually.

The human resource managers of EADS were aware that it was important to systematically explain such cultural characteristics and differences to expatriates in order to avoid conflicts which are likely to arise. The company, therefore, created its own corporate university for executive education, called *Corporate Business Academy (CBA)*, which offered intercultural

Nicolas Sarkozy and Angela Merkel visit the French Airbus plant

training seminars and helped to prepare expatriates for their work experience abroad. EADS also developed specific processes to build a new organizational culture based on teamwork. Several integration projects were conducted, and more than 80 employees worked on the harmonization and integration of human resources. The experiences of the expatriates and the initiatives taken to build a new corporate culture allowed EADS to successfully manage its human resources during the integration process, which is a crucial success factor in international mergers.

DISCUSSION QUESTIONS

1   What was the role of expatriates in the EADS merger?

2   Why is cultural knowledge of countries and organizations an important asset for managers to achieve efficiency?

3   How did EADS manage cultural diversity in order to facilitate the integration process?

4   How did human resource management contribute to the success of EADS?

Sources: This case was prepared by Professor Christoph Barmeyer (Passau University) and Professor Ulrike Mayrhofer (Université Lyon 3). Based on: (1) C. Barmeyer & U. Mayrhofer, 2002, Le management interculturel: facteur de réussite des fusions-acquisitions internationales?, *Gérer et Comprendre*, 70: 24–33; (2) C. Barmeyer & U. Mayrhofer (2007), Culture et relations de pouvoir: une analyse longitudinale du groupe EADS, *Gérer et Comprendre*, 88: 4–12; (3) C. Barmeyer & U. Mayrhofer, 2008, The contribution of intercultural management to the successes of international mergers and acquisitions: An analysis of the EADS Group, IBR, 17(1): 28–38.

How can multinational enterprises (MNEs) such as EADS manage a workforce of people originating from a variety of different cultures? How do they select, train and motivate people to take on postings to other countries? How do individuals in MNEs experience such postings abroad? These are some of the crucial questions we address in this chapter. This chapter explores international aspects of human resource management (HRM) – activities that attract, select and manage employees.[1] Specifically, we discuss HRM issues arising for different groups of people working in MNEs.

As a function, HRM used to be called 'personnel', and you can appreciate the rising importance of HRM just by looking at the evolution of the terminology. The term 'human resource management' clearly indicates that people are key resources of the firm to be actively managed and developed. No longer a pure administrative support function, HRM is increasingly recognized as a strategic function

Human resource management (HRM) Activities that attract, select and manage employees.

that, together with other crucial functions such as finance and marketing, helps accomplish organizational effectiveness and financial performance.[2]

HRM plays a particular crucial role in MNEs, where a great diversity of people work together at multiple locations, and where people frequently have to move between locations. This chapter first outlines three distinct approaches to international HRM. We then explore the management of (1) people sent abroad by the MNE, and (2) local employees in subsidiaries abroad. Then, we employ the institution- and resource-based views to shed further light on these issues. Debates and extensions follow.

APPROACHES TO MANAGING PEOPLE

There are three primary approaches to managing people in MNEs.[3] An ethnocentric approach emphasizes the norms and practices of the parent company (and the parent country of the MNE). Hence, subsidiaries are run largely in the same way as operations in the home country. To ensure the consistent implementation of management practices, subsidiaries are normally led by expatriates, who are non-native employees who work in the foreign country. In ethnocentric MNEs, these expatriates are typically parent country nationals (PCNs) that have been sent out specifically to work in this subsidiary. PCNs not only facilitate control and coordination by headquarters, but they may also be best qualified for the job because of special skills and experience (Table 16.1). An ethnocentric approach can be motivated by a *perceived* lack of talent and skills of host country nationals (HCNs), or by the need for headquarters to effectively communicate with the leader of the subsidiary, as illustrated by Akzo Nobel China (Chapter 15, Closing Case15.2).

The opposite of an ethnocentric approach, a polycentric approach focuses on the norms and practices of the host country. In short, 'when in Rome, do as the Romans do'. Who will be the best managers if we have an operation in Rome? Naturally, Roman (or Italian) managers – technically, HCNs. HCNs have no language and cultural barriers in the local environment. Unlike PCNs who often pack their bags and move after a few years, HCNs stay in their positions longer, thus providing more continuity of management. Further, placing HCNs in top subsidiary positions sends a morale-boosting signal to other HCNs who may feel that they, too, can reach the top (at least in that subsidiary). However, in some less experienced MNEs, HCNs in leadership positions may be an obstacle to effective communication between headquarters and subsidiaries.

Table 16.1 Multinational strategies and staffing approaches

Management practices	Typical top managers at local subsidiaries	Advantages
Ethnocentric	Parent country nationals	Strategies can be implemented most consistently, skills-base at home is fully utilized
Polycentric	Host country nationals	Local adaptation through local knowledge, career opportunity for local staff
Geocentric	A mix of parent, host and third country nationals	Utilization of the broadest worldwide talent pool, equal career opportunities for everyone

Disregarding nationality, a geocentric approach focuses on finding the most suitable managers, who can be PCNs, HCNs or third country nationals (TCNs) that come from neither the parent country nor the host country. In other words, a geocentric approach treats all employees the same. Geocentric firms develop a pool of managers recruited from a wide range of countries that serve in management roles across the MNE. For a geographically dispersed MNE, a geocentric approach can facilitate the emergence of a corporate-wide culture and identity. For example, the 400 top managers of Reckitt Benckiser, a leading household goods manufacturer, represent 55 different nationalities, with no country being recognized as 'home country' and many subsidiaries being run by a third-country national.[4] Likewise, EADS (Opening Case) is developing a geocentric approach, in part because it has tri-national roots (French, German, Spanish). Even so, the Opening Case illustrates the problems of implementing such a management approach. Moulding managers from a variety of nationalities is a lot more complex than integrating individuals from two (parent and host) countries. Each of the three management approaches has its advantages.

While the subsidiary leaders and specific experts may be PCNs or TCNs, the majority of an MNE's employees (that is, those in the lower and middle ranks) would be HCNs. For example, of HSBC's 28 400 employees worldwide, only a small cadre of 400 executives are expatriates, and another 1600 employees are on short-term assignments abroad.[5] A major concern is how to staff the *top* executive positions abroad, such as the subsidiary CEO, country manager and key functional heads (such as CFO and CIO).

Geocentric approach
A focus on finding the most suitable managers, who can be PCNs, HCNs or TCNs.

Third country national (TCN)
An employee who comes from neither the parent country nor the host country.

MANAGING EXPATRIATES

Expatriates play a critical role in managing subsidiaries of MNEs, and in facilitating communication between different units of the MNE.[6] Managing expatriates, however, is itself a challenging task for MNEs, including selecting, managing and motivating expatriates to work abroad. Shown in Figure 16.1, expatriates play four important roles:

LEARNING OBJECTIVE

2 Explain how expatriates are managed in MNEs

- Expatriates are *strategists* representing the interests of the MNE's headquarters, and ensuring control over the operations of the subsidiary.[7] Expatriates, especially PCNs who have a long tenure with a particular MNE, may have internalized the parent firm's values and norms. They not only enable headquarters to control subsidiaries, but also facilitate the socialization process to bring subsidiaries into an MNE's global 'orbit'.

Figure 16.1 The Roles of Expatriates

Source: P.J. Dowling, M. Festing & A.D. Engle, 2008, *International Human Resource Management*, 5th ed., London: Cengage.

- Expatriates are also *ambassadors*.[8] Representing headquarters' interests, they build relationships with host country stakeholders such as local managers, employees, suppliers, customers and government officials. At the same time, expatriates also act as ambassadors representing the interests of the subsidiaries when interacting with headquarters, as evident in the Akzo Novel China case (Chapter 15, Closing Case15.2).

- Expatriates act as *daily managers* to run operations and to build local capabilities. One of the reasons they are sent in the first place is often due to a lack of local management talent that fits the needs of the MNE.

- Finally, expatriates are *trainers* for local staff, including their own replacements, thus transferring knowledge from headquarters to subsidiaries.[9] Over time, MNEs usually aim to reduce the number of expensive (!) expatriates, calling for expatriates to train local employees.[10]

Selection of expatriates

Both in a managerial leadership role and in personal experience, an expatriate assignment is demanding. Selecting the right people for expat assignments thus is crucial for their success. Figure 16.2 outlines a model for expatriate selection, with six underlying factors grouped along situation and individual dimensions. In terms of situation dimensions, requirements of both headquarters and subsidiaries have to be considered. Headquarters may focus on loyalty to the company and leadership skills in implementing actions mandated from the top. Subsidiaries may be more concerned about sensitivity to local culture and in filling specific capability gaps.[11] In some Asian countries where seniority is highly respected,[12] younger expatriates may be ineffective. Also, it is preferable for expatriates to have some command (or better yet, mastery) of the local language.

Figure 16.2 Factors in expatriate selection

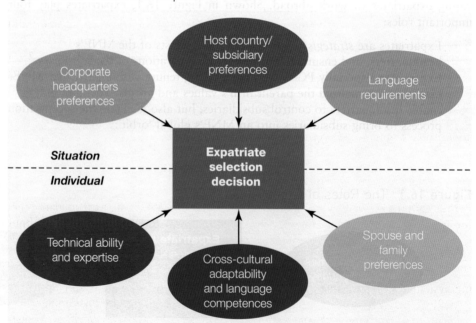

Source: P.J. Dowling, M. Festing & A.D. Engle, 2008, *International Human Resource Management*, 5th ed., London: Cengage. Reproduced with permission.

In terms of individual dimensions, a wide range of capabilities is required that goes beyond what is needed to succeed in the home environment.[13] One study suggests that in addition to the specific functional skills required for the job, successful expatriates combine three sets of capabilities:[14]

- Intellectual capabilities: knowledge of international business and the capacity to learn about new business contexts;
- Psychological capabilities: openness to different cultures and the capacity to change, along with receptiveness for new ideas and experiences;
- Social capabilities, including the ability to form connections, to bring people together and to influence stakeholders that have a different cultural background (for example colleagues, clients, suppliers and regulatory agencies).

That is quite a demanding personality profile! Last (but certainly not least), spouse and family preferences have to be considered.[15] The accompanying spouse may have to leave behind a career and a social network. He or she has to find meaningful endeavours abroad (to protect local jobs, many countries do not permit the spouse to work). Personal frustrations of family members are a frequent cause of expatriate failure.

In practice, MNEs often face the difficult choice between sending (1) a senior person with extensive industry experience and well-embedded in the company, and (2) an eager, young person who knows the local language and culture, but has limited understanding of the business. First, middle-aged expatriates (forty-somethings) often combine best experience, industry competence, ambition and adaptability. Yet, they are the most expensive because the employer often has to provide heavy allowances for children's education. High-quality schools are very expensive. In places such as Manila, Mexico City and Moscow, international schools cost €10 000 to €30 000 per year. Unfortunately, these expatriates also have the highest percentage of failure rates in part because of their family responsibilities. An alternative would be to send relatively older managers who no longer have school-age kids at home, but unless they have a track record of international assignments, they may find it more difficult to adapt to cultural differences.

Second, MNEs may promote younger managers with high career ambition and interest in the local culture – perhaps even fluency in the local language. Thus, expatriates in their late 20s and early 30s are often easier to motivate to take on a challenging assignment in an unfamiliar environment. Moreover, they are less costly to relocate because they may not yet have established a family (and have no school-age kids), and have not yet bought a house. The second preference has strong implications for students studying this book now: These overseas opportunities may come sooner than you expect – are *you* ready?

Pre-departure training for expatriates

Before sending key people on important assignments, MNEs ought to prepare them for the task by providing language and cross-cultural training.[16] However, about one-third of MNEs do not provide cross-cultural training for expatriates – other than wishing them 'good luck' – because many appointments are made on too short a notice to allow for in-depth preparation.[17] While the share of companies providing systematic preparation has been increasing in recent years, it is still up to the individual expatriate to ensure that they are well prepared for their assignment.

The extent of training should vary with the length of stay for expatriates. Longer and more rigorous training is imperative for stays of several years, especially for

Training
The specific preparation to do a particular job.

first-time expatriates. Three levels of training can be distinguished – the longer the stay, the higher the level of training that is appropriate.[18] At a basic level, training focuses on providing information on practicalities in so-called area briefings, cultural briefings and the use of interpreters. Language training may focus on survival phrases (such as 'good morning', 'thank you', and 'please take me to this address'). At an intermediate level, the training would include cultural assimilation training including for example role plays and discussion of cases and critical incidences.

At an advanced level, training may take an immersion approach that intensively exposes the expat-to-be to the foreign culture and language. For example, an expat may spend a few days at the new location in a situation resembling the future role. Yet, with a mentor at hand to explain and to teach the language. More enlightened firms involve the spouse and children in expatriate training as they will be sharing the expat experience, and can be an important source of personal support – or stress. Large MNEs usually also provide practical assistance, sometimes through specialist relocation service firms providing a comprehensive package for expatriates, including identifying a suitable place to live, organizing the removal of furniture, checking out suitable schools for the children and taking care of visa and work permit related matters.

Expatriates in action

Many of the practical challenges for expatriates are similar to experiences of students going abroad on exchange or to study for a degree course – except that few MNEs provide the sort of pastoral care that many universities offer their students. Arriving at the place of an expat assignment, the initial concerns are usually very practical matters such as finding your ways to the office, the home and local shops, and 'who does what' and 'who is who' at work (see In Focus 16.1). Once these essentials have been taken care off, you can settle down and get on with work – and life.

After a while abroad, essentially every expatriate experiences culture shock, defined as the expatriate's reaction to a new, unpredictable and therefore uncertain environment.[19] Students like yourself studying abroad also often experience culture shock; some of your classmates may indeed be going through this experience as you are taking your international business course. Essentially, when living in a different culture, your selective perception and interpretation systems don't function, you need to spend more effort on interpreting what local people do or say, and you find it more difficult to make yourself understood. Particularly troubling is that unconscious ways of communicating (such as body language) do not work, and hence the expat may not understand why he or she is less effective.[20] In other words, our cognitive system of interpreting what is happening is grounded in our culture, and when entering another culture, the home culture's perceptive system becomes ineffective. Another source of personal frustration of expatriates is to miss activities that used to be a normal part of daily life, notable 'oral pleasures' of speaking and enjoying entertainment in their own language, and of eating familiar foods.[21]

At the same time, when you work as an expat, you are normally under high expectations from both yourself and from your company. This imbalance between the effectiveness of your actions and your expectations cause expatriate stress (Figure 16.3). Even with a lot of financial and psychological support, few expatriates can simultaneously play the challenging multidimensional roles effectively.[22] Thus, it is common that expatriates fail to achieve what they set out to achieve, though this phenomenon appears to be more common for US expatriates[23] than for Australian or Nordic expatriates.[24]

Immersion approach
Placing a person in a situation where they will learn by practice

Culture shock
An expatriate's reaction to a new, unpredictable, and therefore uncertain environment.

Expatriate stress
Stress caused by an imbalance between expectations and abilities affected by culture shock.

IN FOCUS 16.1

Getting started in Asia

Your second author of this book, Klaus Meyer has spent two 'semesters abroad' teaching in Hong Kong and Taiwan. He offers some practical tips for getting started in Asia.

First, if you live in a foreign country, you need to take care of a few practicalities right at the start, and here the support of a local person is invaluable to communicate to other locals what your situation is, and what needs to be done. This includes getting your work permit, opening a bank account, and setting your account up with the employers' personnel office. If you are not being offered help, ask for someone to come along with you to make these crucial visits. In Taiwan, a basic need is to get a Chinese name: The university computer system reads only Chinese, and without being in that computer I would not have received my salary. I also urgently needed a name stamp because this is the normal means of identification for example when withdrawing money at the bank. Other important issues to do in the first week is to get a mobile phone (or a local SIM card), learn how to use the local buses and trains (taxies are expensive in the long run!).

Second, a major issue for many expatriates is food. In Asia, people are more likely to eat out at one of the small corner shops than to eat at home – the food is much cheaper and there really isn't much point in cooking yourself. If you don't read the local language, you may find it useful to memorize where your favourite dish is on the restaurant menu, or the supermarket shelf. However, if you are craving specific dishes from back home you will find that ingredients are hard to find and expensive, and home-cooking may often still be the best. In reverse, many Asian students learn how to cook after arriving England as going out is very expensive (compared to Asia), and English food doesn't please their taste buds.

Third, talk with expats and locals who have been to your country. They will be more able to help you with practicalities and with cross-cultural issues because they appreciate the differences in cultures. People who have never been abroad often find it difficult to explain their own country to outsiders because they lack understanding of your situation – or have their own prejudices (like, 'foreigners don't eat whole fish' just because earlier American visitors apparently have problems facing a whole fish-with-its-head on the table).

Figure 16.3 Sources of stress for expatriates

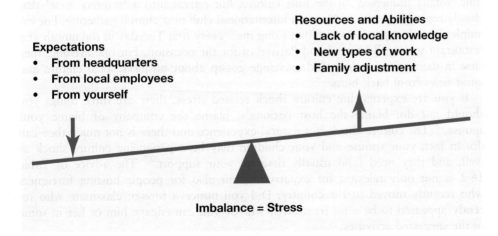

Expectations
- **From headquarters**
- **From local employees**
- **From yourself**

Resources and Abilities
- **Lack of local knowledge**
- **New types of work**
- **Family adjustment**

Imbalance = Stress

Figure 16.4 Culture shock: from honeymoon to normalization

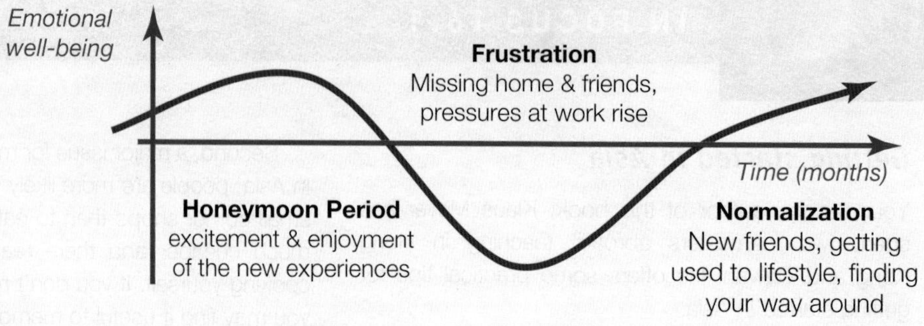

Culture shock tends to set in after a few weeks in the new culture. Initially, expatriate managers, like exchange students, are enthusiastic about all the new experiences (Figure 16.4). This initial enthusiasm – or honeymoon period – however wears off after a while. The pressures of work set in, and you may miss your friends back home. For students, unfortunately, this period often coincides with the time when the first assignments are due – to be written and assessed under rules that you are not familiar with. However, this period passes, you become more familiar with the local culture and – perhaps – the language, and you make new friends with other expats and/or locals. Thus, the mood recovers, and by the time the contract runs out, many would rather stay a bit longer.

When you are experiencing culture shock, the most important thing to know is that most other people also go through it. It is not a disease, but rather a *natural* response to living in an unfamiliar culture. In fact, culture shock is a *positive* sign of deep involvement with the host culture, rather than remaining isolated in an expatriate ghetto.[25] What can expatriates (or you as a student studying abroad) do to ease the impact of the culture shock? Past experiences suggest that different activities work for different individuals; Table 16.2 offers some suggestions. Some expatriates use extensive physical exercise, while others use meditation and relaxation techniques. For example, in many cities around the world, expat communities have organized social jogging events (hashes) that promote fitness and community. A particular powerful idea is 'stability zones', thus the expatriate would spend most of the time 'totally immersed' in the host culture, but retreat into a 'stability zone' that closely resembles home, such as an international club or a church gathering. For example, Danish expatriates in Hong Kong meet every first Tuesday in the month at a restaurant serving Biksemad and Pariserbøf for the occasion. For one evening, they chat in their native tongue and exchange gossip about business, local culture and latest news from back home.

If you are experiencing culture shock related stress, there are three things you should *not* do: blame the host nationals, blame the company or blame your spouse.[26] The culture shock is a natural experience and there is not much they can do. In fact, your spouse and your children may be experiencing culture shock as well, and they need (and usually deserve) your support.[27] The advice of Table 16.2 is not only relevant for expatriates, but also for people hosting foreigners who recently moved to the country: Did you notice a foreign classmate who recently appeared to be a bit frustrated? Maybe you can engage him or her in some of the suggested activities.

Table 16.2 Do's and don'ts for expatriates experiencing culture shock

Do's	Don't
● Physical exercise	● Blame the host nationals
● Meditation and relaxation techniques	● Blame the company
● 'Stability zones' such as groups in your own cultural community	● Blame your spouse
● Meet others in a similar situation such as fellow expats and internationally experienced locals	
● Modify expectation on the job	

Returning expatriates (returnees)

Coming home may be easier than leaving home, yet it presents challenges of its own. These challenges experienced by returnees (returning expatriates) often come unexpected, and concern both (1) professional re-entry and (2) private life (see Table 16.3).[28] Unfortunately, many MNEs are not doing a good job managing repatriation – the process of facilitating the return of expatriates.

Professionally, chief among the problems is career anxiety. A key concern is 'What kind of position will I have when I return?' Some major MNEs have systematic career development plans that include not only commitments by the employee to the company, but commitments by the company specifying what the employee will receive if certain performance objectives are met. It is, however, rare that companies commit to give the returnee a specific job several years in the future as, in a fast moving economy, such commitments are simply not feasible.

In large European MNEs, international experience thus is typically an asset, if not prerequisite for top management positions, and returnees are likely to find themselves working with colleagues that have gone through similar experiences. In many firms, however, commitments are informal and non-binding. Prior to departure, many expatriates are encouraged by their boss: 'You should take (or volunteer for) this overseas assignment. It's a smart move for your career'. Theoretically, this

Returnees
Returning expatriates.

Repatriation
The process of facilitating the return of expatriates.

Table 16.3 Challenges of repatriation

Professional Re-entry	● Career anxiety – what kind of position will I have when I return (if I do have a position)?
	● Work adjustment – from a big fish in a small pond (at the subsidiary) to a small fish in a big pond (at headquarters)
	● Loss of status and pay – expatriate premiums are gone; chauffeured cars and maids are probably unavailable
Private Life	● Friends and family have moved on, and cannot relate to the 'exotic' tales of the returnee
	● Difficult for the spouse and children to adjust to a more mundane life back home

Psychological contract
An informal understanding of expected delivery of benefits in the future for current services.

is known as a psychological contract – an informal understanding of expected delivery of benefits in the future for current services.[29] However, a psychological contract is easy to violate. Bosses may have now changed their mind. Or they may have been replaced by new bosses. Violated psychological contracts naturally lead to disappointments.

The international experience of a returning expat is less valued by smaller MNEs that are not using expats extensively, and that may have an ethnocentric view of their firm. Your boss may not appreciate how your rich experience may help the firm. Few (or nobody) at headquarters seem interested in learning from expatriates' overseas experience and knowledge. Having been a 'big fish in a small pond' in subsidiaries, returnees often feel like a 'small fish in a big pond' at headquarters. The initial job back home may be very similar to what you did before you left, and your performance will be similar to your pre-departure job (your boss' perspective) and less than what you did when abroad (your own perspective), which leads to stress. Returning expatriates may also experience a loss of status. Overseas, they are 'big shots', rubbing shoulders with local politicians and visiting dignitaries. They often command lavish expatriate premiums, with chauffeured cars and maids. However, most of these perks disappear back home. Encouragingly, however, the international experience tends to accelerate performance improvements and thus promotions in the longer run.[30]

Reverse culture shock
Culture shock experience by persons returning to their country of origin.

Privately, returnees experience a reverse culture shock, a common phenomenon, but less well understood than culture shock. When abroad, images of 'the green, green grass of home' often keeps expatriates going. Yet, coming home they realize that home is not what it used to be:

- The country has changed;
- The company has changed; and
- The expatriate him/herself has changed. In particular the personality and expectations have subtly changed under the experience of living abroad: some things that seemed to be important way back then (like the local sports club where your friends spend all their spare time) just aren't that important when seen from afar.

Many also realize that they held an idealistic view about the home country when abroad that was not true anyway – the streets aren't as clean and the food isn't always as good as you imagined. Re-establishing links with old friends can also be challenging because you may have quite literally developed away from each other. Some friends have moved, married, got children and their interests have shifted from, say, mountain climbing to playing with the kids. Moreover, many cannot relate to your experiences and may treat your constant temptation of telling stories from distant places as show off, partly being jealous and partly just being annoyed. Thus, a typical experience for an returnee is that: '*I came back with so many stories to share, but my friends and family couldn't understand them. It was as if my years overseas were unshareable.*'[31]

Finally, the spouse and the children may also find it difficult to adjust back home. The feeling of being a part of a relatively high-class, close-knit expatriate community is gone. Instead, life at home may now seem lonely, dull, unexciting, and in some cases, dreadful. In the USA, some wives of Honda executives enjoy being Avon Ladies (direct selling). When the long anticipated repatriation notice comes, they are excited about expanding their business back to Japan. However, prior to returning home, all husbands receive a letter from headquarters, demanding that their wives quit direct selling. This is because direct selling is viewed as a low-prestige occupation not worthy for the spouses of executives at a prestigious firm such as Honda – doesn't Honda pay executives enough? The letter ends with a warning that if their wives are found to continue selling Avon cosmetics in Japan, their husbands will be *fired*.[32] Likewise, children, being out of touch with current slang, sports and fashion, may struggle to regain acceptance into peer groups. Having been brought up overseas, (re)adjusting back to the home country educational system may be especially problematic.

Overall, repatriation, if not managed well, can be traumatic not only for expatriates and their families but also for the firm. Unhappy returning expatriates do not last very long.[33] Approximately one in four exits the firm within one year. Since MNEs make a heavy investment in each expatriate over the duration of a foreign assignment, losing that individual can wipe out any return on investment.[34] Worse yet, the returnee may end up working for a rival firm. The best way to prevent returnees from leaving is a career development plan that comes with a personal mentor (also known as a champion, sponsor or 'godfather').[35] The mentor helps alleviate the 'out-of-sight, out-of-mind' feeling by ensuring that the expatriate is not forgotten at headquarters and by helping secure a challenging position for the expatriate upon return.

MANAGING PEOPLE ABROAD

Although most international HRM practice and research focus on expatriates, it is important to note that HCNs deserve significant attention for their training and development needs (though there has been much less research on HCNs than on expatriates). In the ongoing quest for talent in China, whether employers can provide better training and development opportunities often becomes a key determining factor on whether top talent is retained or not. To stem the tide of staff turnover, many MNEs now have formal career development plans and processes for HCNs in China.

LEARNING OBJECTIVE

3 Explain how MNEs manage their employees in subsidiaries abroad

Building a committed workforce

How do you find people to work for you? Recruitment concerns the identification of suitable local employees, convincing them to apply for a job, and selecting the most suitable candidates for each job. In many countries, especially emerging economies, working for an MNE is a very popular career path. Hence, the main challenge is to sift through a large numbers of curriculum vitas (CVs) and to identify the most suitable candidates. Compared to HRM back home, foreign subsidiaries face two additional challenges. First, the candidates need to have not only the functional skills required for the job, but the ability to fit in with a multi-cultural work environment and to communicate with foreign employees, often in English. This creates difficult trade-offs and challenges in assessing the applicants' abilities. Some MNEs like to hire graduates with degrees in foreign languages and train them in functional skills, rather than hiring people with specialist degrees (say, engineers) whom they would have to train in English. Second, MNE subsidiaries, especially recently established ones, lack knowledge of how the local labour market works. For example, how do you make contact with the best university graduates? Which degrees from which schools or universities are best? Due to the need for such local

Recruitment
The identification, selection and hiring of staff.

IN FOCUS 16.2

Competing for talent in China

This may be hard to believe, but the most populous country in the world has a shortage of people – managers. Chinese and foreign firms need 75 000 globally competitive executives in China. At present, only approximately 3000 to 5000 Chinese executives fit the profile. Thus, MNEs of all stripes are going after the same pool of talent, and the pickings are especially slim at the top.

Although the average pay raise has been 10 per cent or more in recent years, for top talent, 'you see title inflation and raises of 50 per cent to 60 per cent a year', says an HR professional. Top talent is often snatched, quickly promoted and then, all too often, stolen away. One study finds that every year, 43 per cent of executives in China voluntarily quit, compared with 5 per cent in Singapore and 11 per cent in Australia. Another study puts the average turnover at 14 per cent. Although estimates vary, China probably now has the world's highest turnover rate for managers.

In a tight job market, money clearly matters. But beyond compensation, training and development are the new frontier for differentiation, with inpatriation in the MNE's parent country being one of the most highly sought-after prizes. At GE China, 60 per cent of the salaried employees are under 35. Young managers take on responsibilities that 20-something employees elsewhere can only dream about. A position that takes ten years to reach in Japan or five years to reach in the West often takes only three years to get in China; otherwise, the MNE risks losing such talent. GE finds that its executives are especially vulnerable after three years. This is a crucial point at which they have soaked up enough training and responsibility to make themselves attractive, but they are not yet really loyal to GE. In response, GE tries hard to make promising

managers stimulated, recognized and nurtured, and it manages to reduce its executive turnover to 'only' 7 per cent.

Both the shortage of talent and the rush of MNEs entering China for the first time with expats mean that the country now has more expats than ever with tremendous diversity. Kodak distinguishes among (1) full expats (from the US and the EU), (2) regional expats (from Hong Kong, Taiwan, and Singapore), (3) local foreigners (hired locally, who do not command expat packages) and (4) fully local hires (HCNs). Kodak tries to pay each group according to the going rate in its home region. Most MNEs aim to eventually replace expats with Chinese nationals. Such localization is often fuelled by a desire to reduce cost. However, trimming expats may not necessarily save money because compensation for HCNs has been skyrocketing recently.

Adding to the heat, Chinese firms have entered the fray. Alibaba, Gome, Haier, Huawei, Lenovo, Li Ning and TCL have successfully raided the managerial ranks of Microsoft, Nokia and other MNEs. This reflects a sea change. As recently as five years ago, no self-respecting executive would quit a *Fortune* 500 MNE to join a local outfit. Now such moves are considered very smart. Although Chinese firms do not necessarily outbid the MNEs in compensation, Chinese firms offer something that is hard to beat: no glass ceiling, no expats and the sky is the limit. There will be no shortage of Chinese rivals eager to snatch away managers trained by MNEs.

Sources: Based on: (1) Mike Peng's interviews in China; (2) *Business Week*, 2006, Management grab, August 21: 88–90; (3) *Business Week*, 2005, Stealing managers from the big boys, September 26; (4) V. Hulme, 2006, Short staffed, *China Business Review*, March–April: 18–23; (5) Y. Zhang, J. George, & T. Chan, 2006, The paradox of dueling identities: The case of local senior executives in MNC subsidiaries, *Journal of Management*, 32: 400–425.

knowledge, the HRM function is often among the most localized units in an MNE subsidiary.

At the top end of the organization, the challenges are quite different. Even in large countries like China, management talent for leadership roles is often quite scarce (In Focus 16.2). Especially people who can lead a major unit within a cross-cultural context are almost as scarce as expatriates. The main challenge thus is not to sort through a large numbers of applicants, but to find good people and convince them to apply. For this purpose, firms often employ headhunter (or 'executive search') companies that specialize in finding suitable people for senior positions, working through personal networks and trying to identify those who may seek promotions but didn't get promoted in their own firm. While using headhunters, MNEs naturally don't want their people to be headhunted. Thus, the ideal candidate shows a high degree of commitment to the MNE, which is hard to find in rapidly changing business environments.

Headhunter company
A company specializing on finding suitable people for senior positions.

Compensation, appraisal and retention

As an HRM area, compensation refers to the determination of salary and benefits.[36] At the bottom end of the compensation scale, low-level HCNs, especially those in developing countries, have relatively little bargaining power. The very reason that they have a job at the MNE subsidiaries is often because of their low labour costs – that is, they are willing to accept wage levels substantially lower than those in developed countries. To them, the benchmark groups are typically farmhands sweating in the fields making much less or unemployed taking home nothing to feed the family. Despite some social activist groups' accusations of 'exploitation' by MNEs, MNEs typically pay *higher* wages relative to similar positions in developing countries.

Compensation
The determination of salary and benefits.

On the other hand, HCNs in management and professional positions have increasing bargaining power. MNEs are rushing into Brazil, Russia, India and China (BRIC), where local supply of top talent is limited. Wage inflation in India's IT sector is 16 per cent a year, with a 40 per cent staff turnover.[37] It is not surprising that high-calibre HCNs, because of their scarcity, will fetch more pay (In Focus 16.2). The question is: How much more? Most MNEs aim to eventually replace even top-level expatriates with HCNs, in part to save cost. However, if HCNs occupying the same top-level positions are paid the same as expatriates, then there will be no cost savings. However, MNEs unwilling to pay top local talent top salaries may end up losing such high-calibre HCNs to competitors that are willing to do so. The quest for talent is essentially a bidding war for top HCNs.[38] Eventually, for qualified individuals in top positions, MNEs may have to pay international rates regardless of nationality.

Pay increases, however, depend on performance. Thus, firms conduct some form of performance appraisal defined as the evaluation of employee performance for promotion, retention or termination purposes. Although initial compensation is determined upon entering a firm, follow-up compensation usually depends on performance appraisal. It focuses on decision-making (to determine pay and promotion), development, documentation and subordinate expression. In our case, performance appraisal entails how expatriates provide performance appraisal to HCNs.

Performance appraisal
The evaluation of employee performance for promotion, retention or termination purposes.

When expatriates evaluate HCNs, cultural differences may create problems. Western MNEs emphasize feedback sessions with the opportunity for subordinates to express themselves. However, high power-distance countries in Asia and Latin America would not foster such an expression, which would potentially undermine the power and status of supervisors. Employees themselves do not place a lot of importance on such an expression.[39] Thus, Western expatriates pushing HCNs in these cultures to express themselves in performance appraisal meetings may be viewed as indecisive and lacking integrity.

Eventually, it is important for MNEs to retain the best of their local employees, which can be quite challenging in locations where staff frequently jump from one employer to another when better pay packages are offered. Even though Asian cultures traditionally emphasize loyalty and long-term employment, dynamic, competent and ambitious young people frequently depart from this traditional norm. Thus, MNEs have to create attractive career prospects, including possible training, travel and posting abroad to keep their best people on board.[40]

INSTITUTIONS AND HUMAN RESOURCE MANAGEMENT

LEARNING OBJECTIVE

4 Discuss how the institution-based views sheds additional light on HRM

HRM is significantly shaped by formal and informal rules of the game both at home and abroad, especially by employment law and practice.[41] Let us start with *formal* institutions. Every country has rules, laws and regulations governing employment relations, which set formal constraints for HRM. For example, the USA has very strict anti-discrimination laws that some foreign firms find difficult to accommodate. For instance, in Japan, firms routinely discriminate against women and minorities. When Japanese MNEs engage in such practices in the USA, they often face legal challenges. In the late 1980s, 60 per cent of Japanese MNEs doing business in the USA faced possible equal employment opportunity (EEO) litigation,[42] though they have since learned to implement such local laws.

On the other hand, US firms investing overseas are often amazed how difficult it is to lay off staff in countries such as France, Germany or India. For example, HP's subsidiary in France got a phone call from (then) President Jacques Chirac who complained after HP announced a plan to lay off 1200 employees.[43] Interestingly, France is a highly lucrative market for US-based Manpower. Manpower's expertise in providing part-time workers is highly valued by French firms reluctant to hire full-time employees. France is now Manpower's *largest* market, ahead of the USA (In Focus 16.3).

Other formal institutions relate to the education system. Many continental European countries have a vocational training system ('apprenticeships') that is organized jointly by firms, chambers of commerce and schools supported by the state. Access to skilled non-university educated staff de facto requires firms to participate

"Workers unite against shareholders". How can MNEs manage their multicultural workforce in line with local laws and local values?

in the system. Moreover, with certificates of their craftsmanship, staff would expect to be treated with a certain respect and status, and be entrusted with more complex tasks and responsibilities, than semi-skilled labourers in, for example, the UK.[44] Likewise, they would expect their bosses to have functional knowledge, and be able to do or explain critical tasks when the need arises. In reverse, German or Japanese managers are often frustrated about the low levels of basic skills, such as numeracy, in British workforces.[45] These differences in educational systems thus translate into differences in skill profiles, which make it difficult to transfer management practices between continental Europe, Japan and Anglo-American countries.[46]

Home country institutions also influence the HR practices employed in subsidiary. Often, there is no legal obligation that would force MNEs to transfer practices developed under the specific institutions conditions of their home environment, such as vocational training and employee participation processes. However, the internal consistency of the operations of an MNE is often enhanced by transferring HR practices.[47] Hence, some German MNEs would introduce apprenticeship style training in overseas affiliates as far away as Japan.

Informal rules of the game also assert a powerful influence (see Table 16.4). Although informal cultures, norms and values are important, HR managers need

Table 16.4 Some blunders in international HRM

- An American expatriate made a presentation to the prime minister of a small Caribbean country and his cabinet members by starting with 'Honourable Mr. Tollis and esteemed members of the cabinet'. The prime minister immediately interrupted him and asked him to start over. This went back and forth several times. Eventually, someone advised the bewildered and then embarrassed expatriate that Mr. Tollis was the *former* prime minister, who had been deposed by the current prime minister (the man sitting in front of the expatriate).

- A Spanish company sent to Saudi Arabia a team of expatriates, including a number of young, intelligent women dressed in the height of current style. Upon arrival, the Saudi immigration official took a look at their miniskirts and immediately sent the entire team on the next flight back to Spain. The expatriate team and the company belatedly learned that despite the heat, women in Saudi Arabia never show their bare legs in public.

- In Malaysia, an American expatriate was introduced to an important potential client he thought was named 'Roger'. He proceeded to call this person 'Rog'. Unfortunately, this person was a 'Rajah', which is an important title of nobility. In this case, the American tendency to liberally use another person's first name – and to proactively shorten it – appeared disrespectful and insensitive. The Rajah walked away from the deal.

- A Japanese subsidiary CEO in New York, at a staff meeting consisting entirely of Americans (except him), informed everybody of the firm's grave financial losses and passed the request from headquarters in Japan that everybody redouble their efforts. The staff immediately redoubled their efforts – by sending their résumés out to other employers.

- A female South Korean expatriate at a textile plant in Vietnam confronted a worker. She yelled in Korean 'Move!' The Vietnamese worker did not move because he did not understand Korean. The South Korean expatriate then kicked and slapped him. According to the media, in South Korea, it is common for employers to scold or even beat employees if they make a big mistake. But in this case, ten Vietnamese colleagues retaliated by beating up the expatriate, who was wounded, hospitalized and then deported. The workers went on to strike for four days and obtained 10 per cent to 15 per cent pay raises.

Sources: Based on text in (1) P. Dowling, M. Festing & A.D. Engle, 2008, *International Human Resource Management*, 5th ed. Cincinnati, OH: Cengage South-Western; (2) R. Linowes, 1993, The Japanese manager's traumatic entry into the United States, *Academy of Management Executive*, 7 (4): 21–38; (3) D. Ricks, 1999, *Blunders in International Business*, 3rd ed. (pp. 95–105), Oxford, UK: Blackwell.

to avoid stereotyping and consider changes. In the area of compensation, one study hypothesizes that the presumably collectivistic Chinese managers would prefer more equal compensation when compared with their individualistic US counterparts. The results turn out to be surprising: Chinese managers actually prefer more merit-based pay, whereas US managers behave exactly the opposite – in other words, the Chinese seem more 'American' than Americans (!).[48] Further digging reveals that these are not average Chinese; they are HCNs working for some of the most competitive Western MNEs in China. The upshot? Naïve adaptation to presumed local norms and values, often based on outdated stereotypes, may backfire.

RESOURCES AND HUMAN RESOURCE MANAGEMENT

LEARNING OBJECTIVE

5 Discuss how the resource-based view sheds additional light on HRM

Human resources are generally recognized as a critical foundation for firms' capabilities. Yet, how about the systems to manage these human resources? Applying the VRIO framework, managers' first question is: Does a particular HR activity add *value*?[49] Consider two examples. First, internal organization of labour-intensive chores, such as administering payroll, benefits and basic training, may not add value. They can often be outsourced (see In Focus 16.3). Second, training is expensive. Does it really add value?[50] Results pooled from 397 studies find that, on average, training adds value by leading to approximately 20 per cent performance improvement for that individual.[51] Thus, training is often justified.

Next, are particular HR practices *rare*? The relentless drive to learn, share and adopt 'best practices' may reduce their rarity and thus usefulness. If every MNE in China provides training to high-calibre HCNs, such training, which is valuable, will be taken for granted but not viewed as rare.

Further, how *imitable* are HR practices? It is relatively easy to imitate a single practice; however, it is much more difficult to imitate a complex HR *system* (or *architecture*) consisting of multiple, mutually reinforcing practices that work together.[52] Consider the Portman Ritz-Carlton hotel in Shanghai. Its expatriate general manager personally interviews *every* new hire. It selects HCNs genuinely interested in helping guests. It deeply cares about employee satisfaction, which has led to superb guest satisfaction. Each single practice here may be imitable, and the Portman Ritz-Carlton has been meticulously studied by its rivals (and numerous others) in China and around the world. Yet, none has been able to successfully imitate its system. On the surface, every firm says, 'We care about our people'. But the reality at many firms is under-investment by both employers and employees, which results in low loyalty and commitment.[53] Studies find that firms' performance is at its best with a mutual investment approach.[54] However, it is very difficult to imitate a mutual investment approach that comes together as a system (or architecture).

Finally, do HR practices support *organizational capabilities* to help the firm accomplish its performance goals? Consider teamwork and diversity, especially multinational teams consisting of members from different subsidiaries. Although most firms promote some sort of teamwork and diversity, it is challenging to organizationally leverage such teamwork and diversity to enhance performance.[55] Too little or too much diversity may hurt performance.[56] In teamwork, certain disagreements may be helpful to promote learning. But obviously too many disagreements may lead to conflicts and torpedo team effectiveness.[57] However, few managers (and few firms) master the art of drawing the line before disagreements within a team get out of control.

IN FOCUS 16.3

Manpower

Who is the largest private employer in the world now? Surprise – it's Manpower! Headquartered in Milwaukee, Wisconsin, USA, Manpower is a world leader in the employment services industry. The $18 billion company has a network of 4400 offices in 73 countries that 'employ' 400 000 part-time workers. Manpower has 27 000 full-time employees. Its core capabilities consist of its ability to provide 'flexible, ready-trained, on-demand and enterprise-ready talent'. In France, where the firing of full-time employees is difficult, Manpower has risen to the challenge by meeting the staffing needs of numerous firms that are afraid of being eventually stuck with unwanted full-time employees. As a result, France is now Manpower's largest market, contributing 33 per cent of its revenues. In comparison, the USA only contributes 13 per cent of its revenues.

Starting with the niche of providing part-time and temporary workers, Manpower is now a full-fledged employment services provider that also manages the recruitment of full-time staff for client organizations, conducts training for companies and governments and provides outsourcing and consulting services. In Australia, the military has outsourced all of its recruitment (9000 people every year) to Manpower, resulting in improved performance on recruiting goals and better retention rates. In Argentina, Manpower has partnered with the Ministry of Social Development to provide skill training to disadvantaged youth.

In a widely circulated white paper, 'Confronting the Talent Crunch', Manpower cites 41 per cent of employers worldwide that have difficulty filling positions. What is Manpower's advice for managers scratching their heads trying to confront the talent shortage? 'Making a strategic partnership with a specialist provider of employment services can be an extremely savvy move', obviously implying that Manpower is it.

Sources: Based on: (1) The Economist, 2007, The world of work, January 6; (2) Manpower, 2007, Confronting the talent crunch, White paper; (3) http://www.manpower.com.

DEBATES AND EXTENSIONS

This chapter has already alluded to a number of HR debates, such as the value of expatriates. Here, we focus on two previously untouched debates: (1) non-traditional forms of expatriation, and (2) expatriation versus inpatriation.

Non-traditional assignments

Traditionally, expat assignments consisted of a three to five year 'tour of duty' abroad, after which a big promotion was promised. In recent years, however, many MNEs have moved to shorter assignments and non-traditional forms of expatriation such as contract work, commuter assignments and global virtual teams.[58] First, firms use contract work when they need experts to implement specific tasks, for example in major construction projects such as power stations and bridges (see Chapter 3, Closing Case; Chapter 11, In Focus 11.2). These expatriates thus stay for shorter periods, and are often sent from one assignment to the next. Second, commuter assignments send people on a weekly or bi-weekly basis to work in another country, while keeping residency (and family) back home. Common within Europe, such commuter assignments enable firms to manage operations without an expatriate being 'on site' the year round. Both contract work and commuter assignments are more flexible and often less costly (no family relocation). However, individuals on frequent short-term assignment experience problems in maintaining

LEARNING OBJECTIVE

6 Participate in two leading debates concerning HRM

Contract work
A short assignment for a specific project or contract.

Commuter assignment
Assignments that involve regular stays abroad but with the main base remaining back home.

their social and family life, and they have to deal with a lot of complex regulatory regimes regarding for example work visas and income taxes.[59]

Third, globally operating firms often assemble project teams for a specific task or contract, drawing on the best people in the organization wherever in the world they are based. Such projects may relate to internal tasks (such as developing a new IT infrastructure) to external contracts (such as advising a specific global client, as is common for Big Four accounting and consulting firms) (Chapter 15, Opening Case). These teams may operate as global virtual teams, which do not meet face-to-face but rely heavily on communication technologies such as telephone, e-mail and video conferences. However, such teams often have to overcome substantial communication barriers and obstacles to building personal relationships.[60] For example, video conferences can hardly show body language, and provides little scope for informal chats. Hence, face-to-face meetings are still often necessary, which may take the form of short business trips. As virtual teams are an increasingly common feature of international business, managers have to be creative to make them work.[61]

Global virtual teams
Teams that are geographically dispersed and interact primarily through electronic communication.

Expatriation versus inpatriation

Addressing the expatriation problem, one solution is inpatriation – relocating employees of a foreign subsidiary to the MNE's headquarters for the purposes of (1) filling skill shortages at headquarters and (2) developing a global mindset for such inpatriates.[62] The term *inpatriation* of course is derived from *expatriation*, and most inpatriates are expected to eventually return to their home country to replace expatriates (see Closing Case). Examples would include IT inpatriates from India to work at IBM in the USA and telecom inpatriates from China to work at Alcatel in France. Technically, these inpatriates are expatriates from India and China, who will experience some of the problems associated with expatriation discussed earlier in this chapter.

Expatriation
Temporarily or permanently residing in a country and culture other than that of a person's upbringing or legal residence.

Inpatriation
Relocating employees of a foreign subsidiary to the MNE's headquarters for the purposes of (1) filling skill shortages at headquarters and (2) developing a global mindset for such inpatriates.

How can global virtual team members effectively communicate among themselves?

© leluconcepts/iStock

In addition, some inpatriates, being paid by the going rate of their home countries, are upset after finding out the compensation level of colleagues at headquarters doing equivalent work; the cost of an Indian IT professional is approximately 10 per cent to 12 per cent that of an American one. In Europe, however, inpatriates are subject to the labour law – and hence minimum wages – of the country where they work, which makes it unattractive for MNEs to import inpatriates except for specific skills in short supply. Different challenges arise when inpatriates brought to headquarters for training do not want to go back to take over the role they were destined for. Some may try to find work in their host countries with much higher pay, while others go back to their home countries but quit their sponsoring MNE and jump ship to rivals willing to pay more.

Even for inpatriates who return to assume leadership positions in subsidiaries in their home countries (as originally planned), unfortunately, many are ineffective. In China, inpatriated ethnic Chinese often struggle with an ambiguous identity: Western headquarters views them as 'us' whereas HCNs also expect them to be 'us'. When these managers favour headquarters on issues where HQ and locals conflict (such as refusing to pay HCNs more), HCNs view them as traitors of sorts. These problems erupt in spite of these inpatriates' Chinese roots – or perhaps, *because* of their Chinese roots. Overall, one lesson we can draw is that there will be no panacea in international staffing. Inpatriates, just like expatriates, have their fair share of problems and headaches.

IMPLICATIONS FOR PRACTICE

What determines the success and failure of HRM around the world? A simple answer is effectiveness of HR activities in areas such as staffing, training and development, compensation and labour relations. A more interesting question is: How much is the impact of effective HRM on firm performance?[63] Results from 3200 firms find that a change of one standard deviation in the HR system affects 10 per cent to 20 per cent of a firm's market value.[64] These recent findings validate a long-held belief among HRM practitioners and scholars: HRM is indeed *strategic*, as it has become a direct answer to the fundamental question of our field: What determines the success and failure of firms around the world?

LEARNING OBJECTIVE

7 Draw implications for action

Consequently, we identify four implications for action (Table 16.5). Centred on the four Cs developed by Susan Meisinger, president of the Society for Human Resource Management, the first three implications are for HR managers,[65] and the last one is for you as a student with the ambition to pursue an international career. First, HR managers need to be *curious*. They need to be well versed in the numerous formal and informal rules of the game governing HRM in worldwide operations. They must be curious about emerging trends of the world (such as the rise of outsourcing) and create people strategies to respond to these trends.

Second, HR managers must be *competent*. From its lowly roots as a lacklustre administrative support function, HRM is now acknowledged to be a more strategic function that directly contributes to the bottom line. As a result, HR managers need to develop organizational capabilities that drive business success. This starts with enhancing the basic business competencies of HR managers, who may have been trained more narrowly and with a more micro (non-strategic) focus. Now, HR managers not only must contribute to the strategy conversation but also need to take things off the CEO's desk as his or her full-fledged 'business partners'.

Third, HR managers must be *courageous* and *caring*. As guardians of talent, HR managers need to nurture and develop employees. This often means that as

Table 16.5 Implications for action

For HR managers: The four Cs

- Be *curious* – need to know formal and informal rules of the game governing HRM in all regions of operations
- Be *competent* – develop organizational capabilities that drive business success
- Be *courageous* and *caring* – as guardians of talent, HR managers need to nurture and develop people

For non-HR managers:

- Be proactive in managing your (international) career

employee advocates, HR managers sometimes need to be courageous enough to disagree with the CEO and other line managers if necessary. GE's recently retired head of HR, William Conaty, is such an example. 'If you just get closer to the CEO, you're dead', Conaty shared with a reporter. 'I need to be independent. I need to be credible'.[66] GE's CEO Jeff Immelt called Conaty 'the first friend, the guy that could walk in my office and kick my butt when it needed to be' – exactly how a full-fledged business partner should behave.

Finally, ambitious international managers need to have pro-active career management to develop a global mindset.[67] Given that international experience is now a prerequisite for reaching the top at many firms, managers need to prepare by investing in their own technical expertise, cross-cultural adaptability and language training. Some of these investments (such as language) are long term in nature, and just-in-time preparation will not cut it. This point thus has strategic implications for students who are studying this book *now*: Have you picked up a foreign language? Have you spent one semester or one year abroad? Have you made some friends from abroad who are studying in this class together with you now? Imagine a scenario for expatriate selection five to ten years down the road: Wouldn't you hate it when your colleague who speaks Chinese is tapped to go to China as a high-profile expat, but you are passed over because you have never studied Chinese (you and your colleague were classmates and studied this book together)? The difference may be that your colleague started investing in learning Chinese five to ten years ago, and you didn't. To make yourself 'China ready', you have to start now. The point of course is not just about China. You can pick any country likely to be an attractive place to do business in five years time. It is about arming yourself with the knowledge now, making proper investments and manoeuvring yourself to be picked eventually. In the global economy, it is *your* career that is in your hands.

CHAPTER SUMMARY

1 Distinguish ethnocentric, polycentric and geocentric management practices:

- International staffing may use ethnocentric, polycentric and geocentric approaches.

- Expatriates (primarily PCNs and to a lesser extent TCNs) play multiple challenging roles and often have high failure rates. They need to be carefully selected, taking into account a variety of factors.

2 Explain how expatriates are managed in MNEs:

- Expatriates play many crucial roles in MNE subsidiaries, and therefore need a variety of both financial and personal abilities.

- Pre-departure language tuition and cross-cultural training is essential but not always provided.

- Expatriates typically experience a period of culture shock cause by their limited understanding of the local context and pressures at work.

- Returnees face problems of re-integration both professionally and privately.

3 Explain how MNEs manage their employees in subsidiaries abroad:

- Training and development of HCNs are now an area of differentiation among many MNEs.

- Retention of top talent HCNs requires competitive pay, ongoing training, clear career prospects and culture-sensitive performance appraisal.

4 Discuss how the institution-based view sheds additional light on HRM:

- HRM is significantly shaped by formal and informal rules of the game both at home and abroad.

5 Discuss how the resource-based view sheds additional light on HRM:

- As HRM becomes more strategic, it should be assessed using the VRIO criteria.

6 Participate in two leading debates concerning HRM:

- These are (1) non-traditional forms of expatriation, and (2) expatriation versus inpatriation.

7 Draw implications for action:

- HR managers need to have the four Cs: being curious, competent, courageous and caring about people.

- Non-HR managers need to proactively develop an international career mindset.

KEY TERMS

Commuter assignment	Global virtual teams	Psychological contract
Compensation	Headhunter company	Recruitment
Contract work	Host country national (HCN)	Repatriation
Culture shock	Human resource management (HRM)	Returnees
Ethnocentric approach	Immersion approach	Reverse culture shock
Expatriate (expat)	Inpatriation	Third country national (TCN)
Expatriate stress	Parent (home) country national (PCN)	Training
Expatriation	Performance appraisal	
Geocentric approach	Polycentric approach	

CRITICAL DISCUSSION QUESTIONS

1 You have been offered a reasonably lucrative opportunity for an expatriate assignment for the next three years, and your boss will have a meeting with you next week. What would you discuss with your boss?

2 If you were an HCN, do you think pay should be equal between HCNs and expatriates in equivalent positions? If you were president of your subsidiary in a host country, as a PCN your pay is five times higher than the pay for the highest paid HCN (your vice president). What do you think?

3 As HR director for an oil company, you are responsible for selecting 15 expatriates to go to work in Iraq. However, you are personally concerned about their safety there. How do you proceed?

4 You have been assigned to an international team to develop a report on environmental pollution in the Mekong river delta in Southeast Asia. Experts joining the team are based in the Stockholm, Paris, Singapore and Sydney offices of your company. How are you going to make this team work effectively?

CLOSING CASE

Dallas versus Delhi

By Mike Peng, University of Texas, Dallas.

Prashant Sarkar is director for corporate development for the New Delhi, India, subsidiary of the US-based Dallas Instruments. Sarkar has an engineering degree from the Indian Institute of Technology and an MBA from the University of Texas at Dallas. After obtaining his MBA in 1990, he worked at a Dallas Instruments facility in Richardson, Texas (a suburb of Dallas), and picked up a green card (US permanent residence) while maintaining his Indian passport. In 2000, when Dallas Instruments opened its first Indian subsidiary in New Delhi, Sarkar was tapped to be one of the first managers sent from the USA. India of the early 21st century is certainly different from the India of the mid-1980s that Sarkar had left behind. Reform is now in the air, MNEs are coming left and right, and an exhilarating self-confidence permeates the country.

As a manager, Sarkar has shined in his native New Delhi. His wife and two children (born in 1995 and 1998 in the USA) are also happy. After all, curry in New Delhi is a lot more authentic and fresher than

that in Indian grocery stores in Dallas. Grandparents, relatives, and friends are all happy to see the family back. In Dallas, Prashant's wife, Neeli, a teacher by training, taught on a part-time basis but couldn't secure a full-time teaching position because she didn't have a US degree. Now she is principal of a great school. The two children are enrolled in the elite New Delhi American School, the cost of which is paid for by the company. New Delhi is not perfect, but the Sarkars feel good about coming back.

'Prashant, I have great news for you!' the American CEO of the subsidiary tells Sarkar at the end of 2011, 'Headquarters wants you to move back to Dallas. You'll be in charge of strategy development for *global* expansion, working directly under the group vice president. Isn't that exciting? They want someone with proven success. You are my best candidate. I don't know what design they have for you after this assignment, but I suspect it'll be highly promising. Don't quote me, but I'd say you may have a shot to eventually replace me or the next American CEO here. While I personally enjoy working here, my family sometimes still complains a bit about the curry smell. Or folks in

City skyline, Dallas, Texas, USA

© David Sucsy/iStock

Dallas may eventually want you to go somewhere else. Frankly, I don't know, but I'm just trying to help you speculate. I know it's a big decision. Talk to Neeli and the kids. But they lived in Dallas before, so they should be fine going back. Of course, I'll put you in touch with the folks in Dallas directly so that you can ask them all kinds of questions. Let me know what you think in a week.'

CASE DISCUSSION QUESTIONS

1 Going from Dallas to New Delhi, Sarkar, with his Indian passport, would be an HCN. With his green card, he could also be considered a US national

and thus an expatriate. Now if he goes from New Delhi to Dallas, would he be an expatriate or inpatriate? What difference does that make?

2 What questions should Sarkar ask the people at headquarters in Dallas?

3 Will Neeli and the children be happy about this move? Why?

4 Should Sarkar accept or decline this opportunity? Why?

Sources: Based on Mike Peng's interviews. All individual and corporate names are fictitious.

RECOMMENDED READINGS

N.J. Adler & A. Gundersen, 2008, *International Dimensions of Organizational Behaviour*, 5th ed., Cincinnati, OH: South-Western – A very practically oriented textbook focusing on expats, international teams, and careers.

N.A. Boyacigiller, R.A. Goodman, M.E. Phillips & J.L. Pearce, eds, 2004, *Crossing Cultures: Insights from Master Teachers*, London: Routledge – A book with practical tips and class room exercises for hands-on learning on cross-cultural management issues.

D.G. Collings & H. Scullion, eds, 2009, Special Issue on 'Global Staffing', *International Journal of Human*

***Resource Management*, 20(6), 1249–1450** – A special issue with research papers on various aspects of the management of expatriates.

P.J. Dowling, M. Festing & A.D. Engle, 2008, *International Human Resource Management*, 5th ed., London: Cengage – A textbook focused on international aspects of human resource management.

G.K. Stahl & I. Björkman, eds, 2006, *Handbook of Research in International HRM*, Cheltenham: Elgar – A collection of essays by leading scholars of the state of the art of research in the field.

NOTES:

"FOR JOURNAL ABBREVIATION, PLEASE SEE PAGE XXVI-XXVII."

1 G.K. Stahl & I. Björkman, eds, 2006, *Handbook of Research in International HRM*, Cheltenham: Elgar.

2 H. Scullion & K. Starkey, 2000, In search of the changing role of the corporate human resource function in the international firm, *IJHRM*, 11: 1061–1081; D. Bowen, C. Galang & R. Pillai, 2002, The role of HRM, *HRM*, 41: 103–122; W. Cascio, 2005, From business partner to driving business success, *HRM*, 44: 159–163; E. Lawler, 2005, From HRM to organizational effectiveness, *HRM*, 44: 165–169.

3 H. Perlmutter, 1969, The tortuous evolution of the multinational corporation, *CJWB*, 4: 9–18.

4 B. Becht, 2010, Building a company without borders, *HBR*, (April): 103–106.

5 *The Economist*, 2006, Traveling more lightly (p. 77), June 24.

6 J. Bonache, C. Brewster & H. Scullion, 2001, Expatriation: A developing research agenda, *TIBR*, 43: 3–20; H. Brewster & H. Scullion, 2001, The management of expatriates: Messages from Europe, *JWB*, 36: 346–365.

7 N. Boyaçigiller, 1990, The role of expatriates in the management of interdependence, complexity and risk in multinational corporations, *JIBS*, 21: 357–381;

A.W.K. Harzing, 2001, Of bears, bumble-bees and spiders, *JWB*, 36: 366–379; R. Marschan, D.E. Welch & L.S. Welch, 1996, Control in less hierarchical multinationals, *IBR*, 5: 137–150; D. Tan & J. Mahoney, 2006, Why a multinational firm chooses expatriates, *JMS*, 43: 457–484.

8 M. Janssens, T. Cappellen & P. Zanoni, 2006, Successful female expatriates as agents, *JWB*, 41: 133–148; A. Varma, S. Toh, & P. Budhwar, 2006, A new perspective on the female expatriate experience, *JWB*, 41: 112–120; D. Vora & T. Kostova, 2007, A model of dual organizational identification in the context of the multinational enterprise, *JOB*, 28: 327–350.

9 S. Pruthi, M. Wright & K.E. Meyer, 2009, Staffing venture capital firms' international operations, *IJHRM*, 20: 186–205.

10 K.S. Law, L.J. Song, C.S. Wong & D. Chen, 2009, The antecedents and consequences of successful localization, *JIBS*, 40: 1359–1373.

11 S.M. Toh & A.S. DeNisi, 2005, A local perspective to expatriate success, *AME*, 19: 132–146.

12 G. Graen, R. Dharwadkar, R. Grewal & M. Wakabayashi, 2006, Japanese career progress, *JIBS*, 37: 148–161; E. Pellegrini & T. Scandura, 2006. Leader-member exchange (LMX), paternalism, and delegation in the Turkish business culture, *JIBS*, 37: 264–279.

13 A. Vianen, I. Pater, A. Kristof-Brown & E. Johnson, 2004, Fitting in, *AMJ*, 47: 697–709; R. Takeuchi, P. Tesluk, S. Yun & D.P. Lepak, 2005, An integrative view of international experience, *AMJ*, 48: 85–100; P. Caligiuri, 2006, Developing global leaders, *HRMR*, 16: 219–228; A. Molinsky, 2007, Cross-cultural code-switching, *AMR*, 32: 622–640; S. Shin, F. Morgeson & M. Campion, 2007, What you do depends on where you are, *JIBS*, 38: 64–83; H.L. Cheng & C.Y.Y. Lin, 2009, Do as large enterprises do? *IBR*, 18, 60–75.

14 M. Javidan, M. Teagarden & D. Bowen, 2010, Managing yourself: Making it overseas, *HBR*, (April): 109–113.

15 M. Shaffer & D. Harrison, 2001, Forgotten partners of international assignments, *JAP*, 86: 238–254.

16 M.E. Mendenhall & G.K. Stahl, 2000, Expatriate training and development, *HRM* 39: 251–265; E. Drost, C. Frayne, K. Lowe & J.M. Geringer, 2002, Benchmarking training and development practices, *HRM*, 41: 67–86.

17 Brookfield Global Relocation Services, 2010, *Global Relocation Trends Survey* (accessed April 2010).

18 M.E. Mendenhall, E. Dunbar & G. Oddou, 1987, Expatriate selection, training and career-pathing, *HRM*, 26: 331–345.

19 J.S. Black, 1990, Locus of control, social support, stress and adjustment in international assignments, *APJM*, 7, 1–29; N.J. Adler & A. Gunderson, 2008, *International Dimensions of Organizational Behaviour*, 5th ed., Mason, OH: South-Western

20 J. Selmer, 1999, Culture shock in China? *IBR*, 8: 515–534.

21 J.C. Usunier, 1998, Oral Pleasures and expatriate satisfaction, *IBR*, 7: 89–110.

22 R.S. DeFrank, R. Konopaske & J.M. Ivancevich, 2000, Executive travel stress, *AME*, 14: 58–71; P. Bhaskar-Shrinivas, D. Harrison, M. Shaffer & D. Luk, 2005, Input-based and time-based models of international adjustment, *AMJ*, 48: 257–281; R. Takeuchi, D.P. Lepak, S.V. Marinova & S. Yun, 2007, Nonlinear influence of stressors on general adjustment, *JIBS*, 38: 928–943; I.C. Fischlmayr & I. Kollinger, 2010, Work-life balance, *IJHRM*, 21: 455–487.

23 J.S. Black, M. Mendenhall & G. Oddou, 1991, Toward a comprehensive model of international adjustment, *AMR*, 16: 291–317; R.L. Tung, 1982, Selection and training procedures for US, European, and Japanese multinationals, *CMR*, 25: 57–71.

24 P.J. Dowling & D.E. Welch, 1988, International human resource management: An Australian perspective, *APJM*, 6: 39–65; I. Björkman & M. Gertsen, 1993, Selecting and training Scandinavian expatriates, *SJM*, 9: 145–164.

25 Adler & Gunderson, 2008, *as above*.

26 Adler & Gunderson, 2008, *as above*.

27 H. de Cieri, P.J. Dowling & K.F. Taylor, 1991, The psychological impact of expatriate relocation on partners, *IJHMR*, 2: 377–414; B.J. Punnet, 1997, Towards effective management of expatriate spouses, *JWB*, 32: 243–257.

28 M.B. Lazarova & J.L. Cerdin, 2007, Revisiting repatriation concerns, *JIBS*, 38: 404–429.

29 A. Haslberger & C. Brewster, 2009, Capital gains: expatriate adjustment and the psychological contract in international careers, *HRM*, 48, 379–387.

30 G.K. Stahl, E.L. Miller & R.L. Tung, 2002, Toward the boundaryless career, *JWB*, 37: 216–237; V. Suutari & C. Brewster, Expatriation, *IJHRM*, 14: 1132–1151; J.M. Mezias & T.A. Scandura, 2005, A needs-driven approach to expatriate adjustment and career development, *JIBS*, 36: 519–538; S.M. Carraher, S.E. Sullivan & M.M. Crocitto, 2008, Mentoring across global boundaries, *JIBS*, 39, 1310–1326.

31 Adler & Gunderson, 2008, as above (p. 287).

32 Personal communication with Mike Peng from T. Amino, a retired Honda executive, May 2002.

33 S. Fineman, 2006, On being positive, *AMR*, 31: 270–291; Lazarova & Cerdin, 2007, as above

34 L. Bassi & D. McMurrer, 2007, Maximizing your return on people, *HBR*, March: 115–123; Y. McNulty, H. de Cieri, & K. Hutchings, 2009, Do global firms measure expatriate return on investment? *IJHRM*, 20: 1309–1326; D.E Welch, A. Steen & M. Tahvanainen, 2009, All pain, little gain? *IJHRM*, 20: 1327–1343.

35 J. Mezias & T. Scandura, 2005, A needs-driven approach to expatriate adjustment and career development, *JIBS*, 36: 519–538.

36 K. Lowe, J. Milliman, H. De Cieri, & P. Dowling, 2002, International compensation practices, *HRM*, 41: 45–66; E. Chang, 2006, Individual pay for performance and commitment: HR practices in South Korea, *JWB*, 41: 368–381; J. DeVaro, 2006, Strategic promotion tournaments and worker performance, *SMJ*, 27: 721–740; Y. Yanadori & J. Marler, 2006, Compensation strategy, *SMJ*, 27: 559–570.

37 *The Economist*, 2006, The world is our oyster, October 7.

38 T. Gardner, 2005, Interfirm competition for HR, *AMJ*, 48: 237–256; B.S. Reiche, 2009, To quit or not to quit, *IJHRM*, 20: 1362–1380.

39 J. Milliman, S. Nason, C. Zhu & H. De Cieri, 2002, An exploratory assessment of the purposes of performance appraisals in North and Central America and the Pacific Rim, *HRM*, 41: 87–102.

40 A.N. Vo, 2009, Career development for host country nationals, *IJHRM*, 20: 1402–1420.

41 I. Björkman, C.F. Fey & H.J. Park, 2007, Institutional theory and MNC subsidiary HRM practices, *JIBS*, 38: 430–446.

42 R. Schuler, P. Budhwar & G. Florkowski, 2002, International HRM (p. 56), *IJMR*, 4: 51–70.

43 *Business Week*, 2005, HP's French twist, October 10.

44 G. Delmestri & P. Walgenbach, 2005, Mastering techniques or brokering knowledge? Middle managers in Germany, Great Britain and Italy, *OSt*, 26: 197–220.

45 J. Lowe, J. Morris & B. Wilkinson, 2000, British factory, Japanese factory and Mexican factory, *JMS*, 37: 541–560.

46 G. Hofstede, 1993, Cultural constraints in management theories, *AME*, 7: 81–94; A. Klarsfield, 2004, Management development in Europe: Do national models persist? *EMJ*, 22: 649–658; C. Carr, 2005, Are German, Japanese and Anglo-Saxon decision styles still divergent in the context of globalization? *JMS*, 42: 1155–1188.

47 T. Kostova & K. Roth, Adoption of an organizational practice by subsidiaries of multinational corporations, *AMJ*, 45: 215–233; N. Beck, R. Kabst &

P. Walgenbach, 2009, The cultural dependence of vocational training, *JIBS*, 40: 1374–1395.

48 C. Chen, 1995, New trends in allocation preferences, *AMJ*, 38: 408–428.

49 K.S. Law, D.K. Tse & N. Zhou, 2003, Does HR matter in a transition economy? *JIBS*, 34: 255–265; S. Kang, S. Morris & S. Snell, 2007, Relational archetypes, organizational learning and value creation, *AMR*, 32: 236–256.

50 J. Selmer, 2002, To train or not to train? *IJCCM*, 2: 37–51.

51 W. Arthur, W. Bennett, P. Edens & S. Bell, 2003, Effectiveness of training in organizations, *JAP*, 88: 234–245.

52 D.P. Lepak & S. Snell, 1999, The HR architecture, *AMR*, 24: 31–48; B.A. Colbert, 2004, The complex resource-based view, *AMR*, 28: 341–358.

53 A.S. Tsui & J.B. Wu, 2005, The new employment relationship versus the mutual investment approach, *HRM*, 44: 115–121.

54 J. Shaw, M. Dufy, J. Johnson & D. Lockhart, 2005, Turnover, social capital losses, and performance, *AMJ*, 48: 594–606; A.S. Tsui, J.L. Pearce, L.W. Porter & A.M. Tripoli, 1997, Alternative approaches to the employee-organization relationship, *AMJ*, 40: 1089–1121; D. Wang, A. Tsui, Y. Zhang & L. Ma, 2003, Employment relationships and firm performance, *JOB*, 24: 511–535.

55 C. Boone, W. Olffen, A. van Witteloostuijn & B. Brabander, 2004, The genesis of top management team diversity, *AMJ*, 47: 633–656; Z. Simsek, J. Veiga, M. Lubatkin & R. Dino, 2005, Modeling the multilevel determinants of top management team behavioral integration, *AMJ*, 48: 69–84.

56 K. Dahlin, L. Weingart & P. Hinds, 2005, Team diversity and information use, *AMJ*, 48: 1107–1123.

57 J. Brett, K. Behfar & M. Kern, 2006, Managing multicultural teams, *HBR*, November: 84–91; P. Balkundi & D. Harrison, 2006, Ties, leaders, and time in teams, *AMJ*, 49: 49–68; C.J. Collins & K.G. Smith, 2006, Knowledge exchange and combination, *AMJ*, 49: 544–560; M. Zellmer-Bruhn & C. Gibson, 2006, Multinational organization context, *AMJ*, 49: 501–518.

58 H. Mayerhofer, L.C. Hartmann, G. Michelitsch-Riedl & I. Kollinger, 2004, Flexpatriate assignments, *IJHRM*, 15: 1371–1390; M. Meyskens, M.A. von Glinow, W.B. Werther, & L. Clarke, 2009, The paradox of international talent, *IJHRM*, 20: 1439–1450.

59 M. Tahvanainen, D.E. Welch & V. Worm, 2005, Implications of short-term international assignments, *EMJ*, 23: 663–673; D.E. Welch, L.S. Welch & V. Worm, 2007, The international business traveller,

IJHRM, 18: 173–183; T.L. Starr & G. Currie, 2009, Out of sight but still in the picture: short-term international assignments and the influential role of family, *IJHRM*, 20: 1421–1438.

60 J. Salk & M.Y. Brannen, 2000, National culture, networks, and individual performance in a multinational management team, *AMJ*, 43: 191–202; S. Chevrier, 2003, Cross-cultural management in multinational project groups, *JWB*, 38: 141–149; R. Lunnan & T. Barth, 2003, Managing the exploration vs. exploitation dilemma in transnational 'bridging teams', *JWB*, 38: 110–126.

61 PricewaterhouseCoopers, 2000, *Managing in a Virtual World*, London: PricewaterhouseCoopers; D.E. Welch, V. Worm & M. Fenwick, 2003, Are virtual assignments feasible? *MIR*, 43: 95–114.

62 M.G. Harvey, C. Speier & M.M. Novicevic, 2001, The role of inpatriation in global staffing, *IJHRM*, 10: 459–476; B.S. Reiche, 2006, The inpatriate experience in multinational corporations, *IJHRM*, 19: 1572–1590;

63 S. Colakoglu, D. Lepak, & Y. Hong, 2006, Measuring HRM effectiveness, *HRMR*, 16: 209–218; D. Datta, J. Guthrie, & P. Wright, 2005, HRM and labor productivity, *AMJ*, 48: 135–145.

64 B.E. Becker & M.A. Huselid, 2006, Strategic human resources management: Where do we go from here, *JM*, 32: 898–925. (p. 907).

65 S. Meisinger, 2005, The four Cs of the HR profession, *HRM*, 44: 189–194.

66 *Business Week*, 2007, Secrets of an HR superstar (p. 66), April 19: 66–67.

67 T. Cappellen & M. Janssens, 2005, Career paths for global managers, *JWB*, 40: 348–360; M. Dickman & H. Harris, 2005, Developing career capital for global careers, *JWB*, 40: 399–408; O. Levy, S. Beechler, S. Taylor, & N. Boyacigiller, 2007, What we talk about when we talk about 'global mindset', *JIBS*, 38: 231–258; D. Thomas, M. Lazarova, & K. Inkson, 2005, Global careers, *JWB*, 40: 340–347; C. Vance, 2005, The personal quest for building global competence, *JWB*, 40: 374–385.

©Dan Barnes/iStock

CHAPTER SEVENTEEN

INTERNATIONAL MARKETING AND SUPPLY CHAIN MANAGEMENT

LEARNING OBJECTIVES

After studying this chapter you should be able to:

1 Explain how companies may study consumer behaviour abroad.

2 Articulate four Ps in marketing (product, price, promotion and place) in a global context.

3 Outline the triple As in supply chain management (agility, adaptability and alignment).

4 Discuss how institutions affect marketing and supply chain management.

5 Discuss how resources affect marketing and supply chain management.

6 Participate in two leading debates concerning marketing and supply chain management.

7 Draw implications for action.

OPENING CASE

Zara: rewriting rules on marketing and supply chain management

Zara is one of the hottest fashion chains of the 21st century. Founded in 1975, Zara's parent, Inditex, has become one of the leading global apparel retailers. Since its initial public offering (IPO) in 2001, Inditex tripled its sales and profits and doubled the number of its stores of eight brands, of which Zara contributes two-thirds of total sales. Zara succeeds by breaking and then rewriting rules on marketing and supply chain management.

Rule number one: The country-of-origin of a fashion house usually carries some cachet. However, Zara does not hail from Italy or France – it is from Spain. Even within Spain, Zara is not based in a cosmopolitan city like Barcelona or Madrid. It is headquartered in Arteixo, a town of only 25 000 people in Galicia, a remote province of north-western Spain. Yet, Zara is active in Europe, the Americas, Asia and Africa. In 2006, Inditex launched 439 new stores – more than one per *day*. As of 2009, the total number of stores was over 4200 in 64 countries. Zara stores occupy some of the priciest top locations: Paris's Champs-Elysées, Tokyo's Ginza and New York's Fifth Avenue.

Rule number two: Avoid stock-outs (a store running out of items in demand). Zara's answer? Occasional shortages contribute to an urge to buy now. With new items arriving at stores *twice* a week, experienced Zara shoppers know that 'If you see something and don't buy it, you can forget about coming back for it because it will be gone'. The small batch of merchandize during a short window of opportunity for purchasing motivates shoppers to visit Zara stores more frequently. In London, shoppers visit the average store four times a year but frequent Zara 17 times annually. There is a good reason to do so: Zara makes about 20 000 items a year, about triple what Gap does. As a result, 'At Gap, everything is the same', according to a Zara fan, 'and buying from Zara, you'll never end up looking like someone else'.

Rule number three: Bombard shoppers with ads. Gap and H&M spend on average 3 per cent to 4 per cent of their sales on advertising. Zara devotes just 0.3 per cent of its sales to ads. The high traffic in the stores alleviates some needs for advertising in the media, most of which only serves as a reminder to visit the stores.

Rule number four: Outsource. Gap and H&M do not own any production facilities. However, outsourcing production (mostly to Asia) requires a long lead time, usually several months. Again, Zara deviates from the norm. By concentrating (most of) its production in-house and in Spain, Zara has developed a super-responsive supply chain. It designs, produces and delivers new garments to its stores worldwide in a mere 15 *days*, a pace that is unheard of in the industry. The best speed the rivals can achieve is two *months*. Outsourcing may not necessarily be 'low cost' because errors in prediction can easily lead to unsold inventory, forcing retailers to offer steep discounts. The industry average is to offer 40 per cent discounts across all merchandize. In contrast, Zara sells more at full price, and when it discounts, it averages only 15 per cent.

Rule number five: Strive for efficiency through large batches. In contrast, Zara intentionally deals with relatively small batches. Because of its flexibility, Zara does not worry about 'missing the boat' for a season. When new trends emerge, Zara can react quickly. More interestingly, Zara runs its supply chain like clockwork with a fast but predictable rhythm: Every store places orders on Tuesday/Wednesday and Friday/Saturday. Trucks and cargo flights run on established schedules – like a bus service. From Spain, shipments reach most European stores in 24 hours, US stores in 48 hours and Asian stores in 72 hours. Not only do store staff know exactly when shipments will arrive, regular customers also know that too, thus motivating them to check out the new merchandize more frequently on those days.

Overall, marketing and supply chain management have become an integrated system that mutually reinforces each other and propels Zara's formidable rise to new heights around the globe. In the fiscal year ended January 31, 2009, Gap was still bigger ($14.5 billion sales) than Inditex ($14.1 billion) – but barely. What is more striking is that in 2008 during worst global economic crisis since the 1930s, Inditex reported a 10 per cent sales gain. In contrast, Gap

Zara shop in Florence, Italy

suffered a 23 per cent sales decline in the same year. Out of desperation, Gap and other rivals had to resort to deep discounting, a practice Zara has been resisting thus far. In 2009, for the first time, *Business Week* ranked Zara's fashionable but affordable brand as one of the top 50 best global brands. While Gap also made the top 100, Gap's ranking (78) trailed behind Zara's (50).

Sources: Based on (1) K. Ferdows, M. Lewis, & J.A.D. Machuca, 2004, Rapid-fire fulfillment, *HBR*, November: 104–110; (2) *Business Week*, 2006, Fashion conquestador, September 4: 38–39; (3) http://www.zara.com.

How can firms such as Zara market themselves to attract customers? Having attracted customers, how can firms ensure a steady supply of products and services? This chapter deals with these and other important questions associated with marketing and supply chain management. Marketing refers to efforts to create, develop and defend markets that satisfy the needs and wants of individual and business customers. Developing marketing in international operations face additional challenges in creating appropriate variations in their marketing programmes across countries. Supply chain is the flow of products, services, finances and information that passes through a set of entities from a source to the customer.[1] Supply chain management refers to activities to plan, organize, lead and control the supply chain.[2] As the opening case illustrates, marketing and supply chain management are closely intertwined. Marketing will only succeed if the supply chain gets the right products to the right customers at the right time. Therefore, we discuss them together in this chapter.[3]

We start by briefly outlining the challenges of understanding diverse consumer behaviours around the world. Then we discuss how MNEs use marketing and supply chain management to deliver products that these diverse customers value. The institution- and resource-based views add further insights on the variations of marketing and supply chain management around the world. Finally, debates and extensions follow.

Marketing
Efforts to create, develop and defend markets that satisfy the needs and wants of individual and business customers.

Supply chain
Flow of products, services, finances and information that passes through a set of entities from a source to the customer.

Supply chain management
Activities to plan, organize, lead and control the supply chain.

UNDERSTANDING CONSUMERS

What consumers want varies across countries for lots of reasons discussed throughout this book. Probably, cultural differences (Chapter 3) are most important in explaining such differences, but differences in the regulatory environment (Chapter 2) and in resource endowments and incomes also matter. Marketers have a tool box (or marketing mix) of techniques to sell to different customers, but before deploying their tool box, they first need to understand their customers' needs. Often, this is more than asking customers what they want, but studying customer behaviours and coming up with new ideas to enhance their lives. For example, when Swedish truck maker Volvo started selling coaches in India, many wondered how they can succeed: Local buss are so much cheaper and few travellers would be able and willing to pay substantially extra simply for the luxury of travelling in a Volvo bus. However, Volvo's Indian marketers realized that their busses provided coach operators with a number of benefits. Most importantly, they were more reliable – and Volvo offered a service guarantee to repair busses breaking down en route. Stronger engines provided advantages in mountainous terrain, and more robust air-conditioned design made bus travel more comfortable. Last but not least, luggage could be stored inside the bus (rather than on the roof, as in traditional Indian buses) which reduced thefts and damages from adverse weather conditions – a major concerns during the monsoon season. Thus, by understanding the needs of bus operators (as customers) and travellers (as the customers' customers), Volvo was able to create an attractive product offering that led to rapid growth of its market share.[4]

More generally, when companies want to adapt their marketing consumers in different countries, they need to understand their (potential) consumers, media and distribution channels.[5] This can be quite a challenge if the consumers are far removed from the corporate boardrooms where marketing strategies are being designed. Three approaches can be considered: (1) experimental adaptation, (2) survey-based research and (3) anthropological studies. First, an experimental approach would transfer the firm's practices to the new location, and then use a trial-and-error approach to learning about consumers and identifying the optimal solution for each market through incremental changes. This approach reduces the initial costs of entry, but risks making major marketing blunders (huge mistakes). GM marketed its Chevrolet Nova in Latin America without realizing that *nova* means 'no go' in Spanish. Coors Beer translated its successful slogan 'Turn it loose' from English to Spanish as 'Drink Coors, get diarrhoea'.[6] Table 17.1 outlines some blunders that are hilarious to readers but *painful* to marketers, some of whom lost their jobs over these mistakes.

Second, consumer research thus has evolved as a major area of applied research, large numbers of consumers are surveyed by professional companies, and their responses are condensed in concise marketing reports.[7] You have probably been asked many times to complete little questionnaires by companies, often using the internet. Data from such surveys allow companies, for example, to test specific hypotheses about likely consumer responses to changes in prices or new product variations. However, indices developed from surveys are often difficult to compare across countries because cultural differences also affect how respondents interpret the questions that market researchers ask them.[8]

Third, an innovative approach is to directly observe potential consumers and to study their behaviours from an anthropological perspective. A British entrepreneur has built her business, Honest Films, by filming the life of ordinary people and preparing such visual insights for decision-makers in corporate boardrooms (see In Focus 17.1).

Table 17.1 Some blunders in international marketing

- One US toymaker received numerous complaints from American mothers because a talking doll told their children, 'Killing mommy!' Made in Hong Kong, the dolls were shipped around the world. They carried messages in the language of the country of destination. A packing error sent some Spanish-speaking dolls to the USA. The message in Spanish 'Quiero mommy!' means 'I love mommy!' (This is also a supply chain blunder.)

- AT&T submitted a proposal to sell phone equipment in Thailand. Despite its excellent technology, the proposal was rejected out of hand by telecom authorities because Thailand required a 10-year warranty but AT&T only offered a five-year warranty – thanks to standardization on warranty imposed by US headquarters.

- To better adapt its products to Egypt, one Chinese shoe manufacturer placed Arabic characters on the soles of the shoes. Unfortunately, the designers did not know Arabic and merely copied words from elsewhere. The words they chose meant 'God'. China's ambassador to Egypt had to apologize for this blunder.

- Japan's Olympia tried to market a photocopier to Latin America under the name Roto. Sales were minimal. Why? *Roto* means 'broken' in Spanish.

- In their eagerness to export to the English-speaking world, Chinese firms have marketed the following products: White Elephant brand batteries, Sea Cucumber brand shirts, and Maxipuke brand poker cards (the two Chinese characters, *pu ke*, mean poker, and they should have been translated as Maxi brand poker cards – but its package said 'Maxipuke').

Sources: Based on text in (1) T. Dalgic & R. Heijblom, 1996, International marketing blunders revisited – some lessons for managers, *JIMktg*, 4 (1): 81–91; (2) D.A. Ricks, 2006, *Blunders in International Business*, 4th ed., Oxford, UK: Blackwell.

THE MARKETING MIX

Figure 17.1 shows the four Ps that collectively consist of the marketing mix: (1) product, (2) price, (3) promotion and (4) place.[9] In this section, we explore how companies address these marketing challenges when operating across several national markets.

Product

Product refers to offerings that customers purchase. Although the word *product* originally referred to a physical product, its modern use includes services. To avoid confusion, we will use 'products and services' in this chapter. This makes sense because broadly speaking, when a customer purchases a product, this product also embodies service elements (such as maintenance and upgrades).

Even for a single category (such as women's clothing or sports cars), product attributes vary tremendously. For firms interested in doing business around the world, the leading concern is standardization versus localization.[10] Localization is natural. McDonald's, for example, sells wine in France, beer in Germany, mutton pot pies in Australia and Maharaja Mac and McCurry Pan in India. What is interesting is the rise of standardization, which is often attributed to Theodore Levitt's 1983 article, *'The Globalization of Markets'.*[11] This article advocated globally standardized products and services, as evidenced by Hollywood movies and Coke Classic. However, numerous subsequent experiments such as Ford's world car and MTV's global (essentially American) programming backfired. Thus, one size does not fit all, but most firms cannot afford to create products and services for just one group of customers. Thus, how much to localize remains a challenge,

Marketing mix
The four underlying components of marketing: product, price, promotion and place.

Product
The offerings that customers purchase.

IN FOCUS 17.1

Honest Films

Companies operating on the global stage often aim to sell to consumers in a wide variety of countries. Yet, these consumers live under different circumstances, and thus use globally standardized products in different ways, and perceive different benefits from the same product. As a marketing manager for a consumer goods sales operation in Asia, Sarah Thomas learned about these subtle differences of life styles and culture and their implications for the reception of marketing. However, she experienced major challenges in trying to communicate subtleties of local culture to senior managers and decision-makers, who often spend only a few days in Asia. The statistics and graphs generated in traditional marketing reports proved insufficient.

Have you ever been in a Chinese home? Imagine you are visiting a young middle class couple in Shanghai, the primary target group for consumer goods marketers. You walk up a narrow staircase, your are welcomed at the door and offered slippers to wear in the home, you are invited to sit down on the couch, and your eyes wonder around the small room … what do you notice? The furniture is space-saving and functional, combining traditional and modern designs, yet some decorative items are given special space – what is the significance of these objects? On the wall, you see pictures from the couple's holidays in Tokyo and Venice – how do these experiences influence their reception of Western consumer goods?

Out of the challenge of communicating these experiences to Westerners, Sarah Thomas developed her business idea for Honest Films. She joined forces with anthropologist filmmakers, documentary filmmakers and strategic planners to study life where it happens, as it happens. Their films about the lives of ordinary people uncover insights normally overlooked by traditional marketing research. They thus provide business decision-makers with a first-hand look at the issues, and engaging and inspiring them in a way no written report can. Such a real life perspective on how products might be used provides an alternative to statistics-filled consumer research reports, and facilitates innovations from customized advertising messages to new product developments.

Sources Based on: (1) Presentation by the entrepreneur at the University of Bath, February 2009; (2) www.honestfilms.net (accessed April 2010).

especially when entering markets that are very different than their home market, or that are internally very diverse (such as large emerging economies like BRIC).[12]

As noted in Chapter 15, localization is appealing (in the eyes of local consumers and governments) but expensive. A sensible solution is to have a product that *appears* locally adapted while deriving as much synergy (commonality) as possible in ways that customers cannot easily recognize. Consider the two global weekly business magazines, US-based *Business Week* and UK-based *Economist*.[13] In addition to its US edition, *Business Week* publishes two English (language) editions for Asia and Europe and a Chinese edition for China. Although these four editions share certain content, there is a lot of local edition-only material that is expensive to support and produce. In comparison, each issue of the *Economist* has the following regional sections: (1) the Americas (excluding the USA), (2) Asia, (3) Britain, (4) Europe (excluding Britain), (5) Middle East and Africa and (6) USA. Although the content for each issue is identical, the order of appearance of the regional sections varies. For US subscribers, their *Economist* starts with the USA section; for Asian subscribers, their magazine starts with the Asia section; and so forth. By doing that, the *Economist* appears to be responsive to readers with different regional interests without incurring the costs of running multiple editions for different regions, as *Business Week* does. Therefore, how many editions does one issue of the

Figure 17.1 The four PS of marketing mix

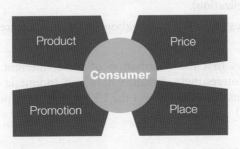

Economist have? We can say one – or six if we count the six different ways of stapling regional sections together and six different sets of advertisements.

One of the major concerns for multinational enterprises (MNEs) is to decide whether to market global brands (such as Nestlé) or local brands in their portfolio (see Table 17.2).[14] The key is market segmentation – identifying segments of consumers who differ from others in purchasing behaviour.[15] There are limitless ways of segmenting the market (males versus females, university versus high school educated, urban dwellers versus rural residents, French versus Italians). The million dollar question for marketers is: How does one generalize from such a wide variety of market segmentation in different countries to generate products that can cater to a few of these segments *around the world*?

One globally useful way of segmentation is to divide consumers into four categories:

- Global citizens (who are in favour of buying global brands that signal prestige and cachet).
- Global dreamers (who may not be able to afford, but nevertheless admire, global brands).

Market segmentation
A way to identify consumers who differ from others in purchasing behaviour.

Table 17.2 Top-20 global brands

1	Coca-Cola (USA)	11	Hewlett-Packard (USA)
2	IBM (USA)	12	**Mercedes-Benz (Germany)**
3	Microsoft (USA)	13	Gillette (USA)
4	GE (USA)	14	Cisco (USA)
5	**Nokia (Finland)**	15	**BMW (Germany)**
6	McDonald's (USA)	16	**Louis Vuitton (France)**
7	Google (USA)	17	Marlboro (USA)
8	Toyota (Japan)	18	Honda (Japan)
9	Intel (USA)	19	Samsung (South Korea)
10	Disney (USA)	20	Apple (USA)

Sources: Adapted from *Business Week*, 2009, The 100 top brands, September 28; European brands in bold.

- Anti-globals (who prefer local goods because of the perceived negative side effects of globalization).
- Global agnostics (who don't care about the global nature of the brands they buy).

Figure 17.2 shows that the distribution of these different groups within each country is uneven. Interestingly, Brazil, China and Indonesia have higher percentages of global citizens than the US and the UK, which correspondingly have higher percentages of global agnostics.[16]

Figure 17.2 Segmentation of consumers as they relate to global brands

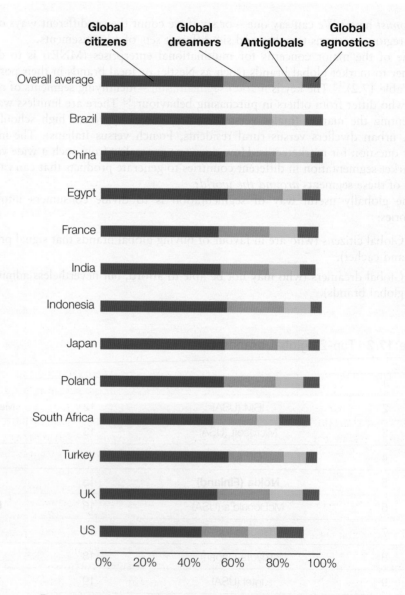

Percentage of respondents who fit into each consumer segment

Source: Based on D. Holt, J.A. Quelch, & E. Taylor, 2004, How global brands compete (p. 73), *HBR*, September: 68–75. Results are based on a survey of 1 500 urban consumers between 20 and 35 years old in 41 countries.

These data suggest that firms may reach the first two categories of global citizens and global dreamers (who total approximately 78 per cent of the consumers surveyed), by leveraging their global brands and their relatively more standardized products and services. 'Global brands make us feel like citizens of the world', an Argentinean consumer observed. However, MNEs do not necessarily have to write off the anti-globals because MNEs can market localized products and services under local brands. Moreover, many consumers may have positive attitudes to global brands, yet they still prefer local products – especially for culturally-bound products such as food and entertainment.[17] For such consumer goods, local brands often have the largest market share, with many consumers being unaware that the brands are actually owned by a major MNE.[18] For example, in Poland the leading brand of chocolate is Wedel, and the leading brands of beer are Tyskie, Zywiec and Okocim. Yet, Wedel has been owned by Cadbury of the UK since 1998, which in turn was acquired by Kraft of the USA in 2010. The three beer brands are owned respectively by Heineken, SABMiller and Carlsberg.

MNEs thus serve diverse consumer preferences with multi-tier branding, a portfolio of different brands targeted at different consumer segments: global brands for the premium segment, national brands for the mid-markets and/or for mass-markets, and further brands for specific niche markets.[19] Nestlé, for example, owns 8000 (!) brands around the world, most of which are local, country-specific (or region-specific) brands not marketed elsewhere.

Multi-tier branding
A portfolio of different brands targeted at different consumer segments.

Overall, Ted Levitt may have been *both* right and wrong. A large percentage of consumers around the world indeed have converging interests and preferences centred on global brands. However, a substantial percentage of them also resist globally standardized brands, products, and services. Armed with this knowledge, firms – both MNEs and locals – can better craft their products and services.

Price

Price refers to the expenditures that customers are willing to pay for a product. Most consumers are 'price sensitive'. The jargon is price elasticity – how demand changes when prices change. Basic economic theory of supply and demand suggests that when prices drop, consumers will buy more and generate stronger demand, which in turn will motivate firms to expand production to meet this demand. This theory, of course, underpins numerous firms' relentless drive around the world to cut costs and then prices. The question is *how* price sensitive consumers are. Holding the product (such as shampoo) constant, in general, the lower income of the consumers, the more price sensitive they are. American, European and Japanese consumers take it for granted that shampoo is sold by the bottle. But in India, shampoo is often sold in single-use packets, each costing about one to ten (euro-)cents, because many consumers there find the cost for a bottle of shampoo to be prohibitive. How to overcome such price elasticity thus is crucial as India develops its mass retailing.

Price
The expenditures that customers are willing to pay for a product.

Price elasticity
How demand changes when prices change.

However, not all consumers are highly price sensitive. Luxury products that are status symbols of upwardly mobile middle classes attain their status exactly because not everyone can afford these products. Thus, luxury goods usually compete on brand appeal and differentiation, not on price. For example, a Danish start-up company Pandora is designing and marketing jewellery that has become highly fashionable among women across Europe. The marketing strategy for their customizable combines fashion appeal with collector passion: A simple bracelet for €59 can be complemented with 'charms' that can be added and rearranged by the wearer – and they cost up to €1399. Pandora's model is highly successful with a profit margin of, reportedly, 45 per cent, but it is also a risky business model as fashion trends are highly volatile.[20]

असली निखार की नई पहचान।

© mark downey/Alamy

How do you sell consumer goods to poor people?

Total cost of ownership
Total cost needed to own a product, consisting of initial purchase cost and follow-up maintenance/service cost.

In addition to the price at the point of purchase, another dimension of price is the total cost of ownership. An example in consumer products is the HP laser printer. Owners typically spend two to three times more on HP print cartridges than on the printer itself. Although many individual consumers (such as buyers of HP printers) do not pay explicit attention to the total cost of ownership, it is obviously more important in business-to-business marketing and is often explicitly evaluated prior to purchase decisions. More important, after-sales (spare) products and services are less price sensitive and thus have a higher margin.[21] In fact, the lowest price that successful companies charge is zero. For example, anti-virus software by German start-up company Avira is available for free on the internet. Yet, the company is – according to its CEO – fairly profitable based on the sale of supplementary services, especially to business customers.[22] More generally, many firms compete on winning the initial sale with a low price, with the aim to capture more revenue through after-sales products and services.

Promotion

Promotion
Communications that marketers insert into the marketplace.

Promotion refers to all the communications that marketers insert into the marketplace. Promotion includes TV, radio, print and online advertising, as well as coupons, direct mail, billboards, direct marketing (personal selling) and public relations. Marketers face a strategic choice of whether to standardize or localize promotional efforts. Standardized promotion not only projects a globally consistent message (crucial for global brands) but can also save a lot of money. One large campaign may be more cost effective than 100 smaller campaigns.

However, there is a limit to the effectiveness of standardized promotion. The messages communicated in advertising are often culturally embedded, which implies that they would be received differently in different countries.[23] In the 1990s, Coca-Cola ran a worldwide campaign featuring a cute polar bear cartoon character. Research later showed that viewers in warmer weather countries had a hard time relating to this ice-bound animal with which they had no direct experience.

IN FOCUS 17.2

C&A: failed European standardization

C&A is a fashion retailer with German and Dutch roots operating across Europe. After more than hundred years of profitable growth, C&A fell on hard times in the late 1990s. It had failed to move with changing trends of fashion and shopping habits. Traditionally, C&A was positioned as affordable fashion for working class people, yet even these customers were no longer satisfied with C&A's sturdy but old-fashioned image. C&A offered low prices, but consumer surveys showed its image to be lagging behind competitors such as Marks & Spencer in the UK. Sales dropped to levels last seen in the early 1980s, and in 1998 C&A recorded a loss of about €130 million.

The management reacted by focusing on cost savings and synergies. Like in many European businesses, national subsidiaries were traditionally operating quite independently. Thus, there should be efficiency gains somewhere, shouldn't there? Centralization to headquarters in Amsterdam and Düsseldorf was seen as the answer: a Europe-wide fashion line communicated with a uniform marketing campaign featuring the same clothes and the same models, designed with the help of external designers. However, the strategy went spectacularly wrong. National differences were overlooked by designers and marketers in Düsseldorf. For example, Italian designers changed the suits to look great on the slim and sporty models featured in the ads. Yet, they failed to recognize that the typical male customer of C&A in Germany was middle aged with a tendency to overweight. After a number of faux pas like this, subsidiary managers revolted against the new centralization.

Especially the Spanish subsidiary was aggrieved. Children's clothes in violet colours wouldn't sell in Spain where that colour is associated with mourning. Ads showing children as clowns didn't fit how Spaniards like to see their kids. Lady's evening dresses designed in Germany were too short for Spanish culture. Men featuring swimming suits had body hair, another no-go in Spain. Many of these miscommunications might easily been rectified through effective internal communication, but feeling overruled from above, local staff aggravated small conflicts, and undermined the strategy. In 2000, C&A pulled back, returned more autonomy to the national subsidiaries, and focused on its traditional cheap but fashionable market appeal. The return to basic values turned C&A back to profitability, though it was too late for some – the UK operation was closed down.

Over the next decade, C&A adapted a more measured adaptation strategy for its 18 countries. This balanced localization is illustrated by C&A's internet presence: The front pages of national websites show a common lay-out, featuring the same fashion model. Yet beyond the front door, variations abound. The German site features online shopping services not available in other countries, while the Dutch site emphasizes the latest lines of fashion by two Dutch fashion designers. The same images are used in many national websites, suggesting a broad overlap of products. Yet, the Russian site features more low-cost sturdy clothing similar to the traditional clothes offered in Western Europe before the 1990s. Even during the economic crisis of 2008/09, this strategy helped C&A to grow its turnover across Europe.

Sources Based on: (1) P.J. McGoldrick, 1998, Spatial and temporal shifts in the development of international retail images, *JBR*, 42: 189–196; (2) B. Weiguny, 2005, *Die geheimnisvollen Herren von C&A*, Munich: Piper; (3) *Handelsblatt*, 2007, Billigheimer C&A gründet Tiefstpreiskette, November 11; (4) *Handelsblatt*, 2009, C&A widersetzt sich Kaufhaus-Krise, April 22; (5) websites of C&A in multiple countries: ru.c-and-a.com, www.c-et-a.ch, de-de.cunda.de, www.c-en-a.nl, tr.c-and-a.com, sk.c-and-a.com, www.cunda.at, www.c-e-a.pt, www.c-and-a.com.ro (all accessed April 2010).

In response, Coca-Cola switched to more costly but more effective country-specific advertisements. For instance, the Indian subsidiary launched a campaign that equated Coke with *thanda*, the Hindi word for 'cold'. The German subsidiary developed commercials that showed a 'hidden' kind of eroticism that would upset conservative consumers back in the USA.[24] As another example, consider fashion retailer C&A's ill-conceived attempts to save costs through a Europe-wide standardization strategy (In Focus 17.2). These examples suggest that even some of the most global brands (such as Coca-Cola) can benefit from localized promotion.

In addition to the traditional domestic versus international challenge, a new challenge lies in the pursuit of marketing via the internet.[25] Widely believed to be more effective in reaching specific target groups, online ads feature on a wide range of websites such as search engines, news sites, blogs and social networking sites. Growing up with the internet, today's teens and 20-somethings in many countries flock to social networks such as Second Life, MySpace and Facebook. These young people 'do not buy stuff because they see a magazine ad', according to one expert, 'they buy stuff because other kids tell them to online'.[26] What is challenging is how marketers can reach such 'generation Y' and 'generation Z' that have developed substantially different ways of social interaction and of accessing and processing information.[27] Firms such as Apple and Procter & Gamble (P&G) experiment with a variety of formats, including sponsorships and blogs, with some hits, some misses, and lots of uncertainty. The basic threat to such social networks is the whim of their users, whose interest in certain topics and networks themselves may change or even evaporate overnight.

Place

Place
The location where products and services are provided.

The 'place' in marketing refers to the location where a product is sold, which can be a physical location or a virtual location on the internet. In international business, a key decision is often when to enter which market – and in what sequence. Four sets of considerations come into play: (1) market potential, (2) costs, (3) strategic motives and (4) distribution channels. First, the potential of a market is usually estimated based on the size and growth of the market for the specific products, taking into consideration trends that may affect potential customers' buying behaviour. The initial analysis make use of industry level market statistics, but usually entrants employ additional customer surveys to assess the likely consumer behaviour. Second, expected revenues need to be converted to estimates of net revenues taking into account both cost of the initial entry and the unit cost that may be higher due to the adaptation of products and marketing programmes.

Third, strategic motives for the choice of market include test-markets, which are markets where trials are rolled out before a world-wide (or Europe-wide) introduction of new products. For example, Nordic countries are a popular test market because they resemble other European markets, but product introduction is much less expensive and errors can be rectified much easier. Moreover, bridge markets may offer avenues to enter broader markets, such as Latin American firms entering the Spanish market in view of eventually conquering Europe-wide markets. Fourth, the question of place is closely related to the question of distribution channel, how to bring the products to the customer. This brings us to the topic of supply chain management discussed next.

LEARNING OBJECTIVE

3 Outline the triple As in supply chain management (agility, adaptability and alignment)

SUPPLY CHAIN MANAGEMENT

Distribution channel
The set of business units and intermediaries that facilitates the movement of goods to consumers.

To be able to market their product, firms need a distribution channel – the set of business units and intermediaries that facilitates the movement of goods to consumers. Traditionally, firms used to have separate 'purchasing' and 'sales' units that would interact with respectively suppliers and customers, and intermediaries on either side. With changes in transportation, data-processing and communication technologies, these two aspects of business operations have converged. The new

Figure 17.3 Supply chain management

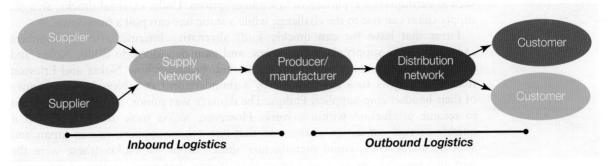

challenge thus is how to manage the longer channel from suppliers (and contract manufacturers) all the way to consumers[28] (see Figure 17.3). Consequently, a new term, supply chain, has been coined, and now almost replaced the old-fashioned 'distribution channel'. The sales and purchasing functions are increasingly interdependent as the entire process is managed 'on time', and the purchase of a component may be triggered by a customer ordering a final product, as in the case of Dell computers (Chapter 1, Opening Case). Strategy guru Michael Porter thus distinguishes 'inbound logistics' (purchasing) and 'outbound logistics' (sales) to indicate that the two functions complement each other like opposite sides of the same coin.[29] The new term supply chain thus covers all movements of goods at any stage of the value chain, encompassing both inbound and outbound logistics (see Chapter 4).

Traditionally, business logistics was a low prestige support function. However, if the supply chain covers the entire value chain, then supply chain management essentially handles the entire process of value creation. Consequently, supply chain management has now taken on new strategic importance and gained tremendous prestige. One indication of the more central role of supply chain management is the rapid growth of support industries, such as transportation service providers UPS and FedEx that have now become household names. On any given day, 2 per cent of the world's GDP can be found in UPS trucks and planes. 'FedEx' has become a verb, and even live *whales* have reportedly been 'FedExed'.[30] Next, we discuss the triple As underpinning supply chain management: (1) agility, (2) adaptability and (3) alignment.[31]

Inbound logistics
Purchasing and the coordination of intermediaries on the supply side.

Outbound logistics
Sales and the coordination of intermediaries on the customer side.

Agility

Agility refers to the ability to quickly react to unexpected shifts in supply and demand. Firms such as Zara thrive in large part because of the agility of their supply chain (see Opening Case). Zara's agility permeates throughout its entire operations, starting with design processes. As soon as designers spot certain trends, they create sketches and go ahead to order fabrics without finalizing designs. This speeds things up because fabric suppliers require a long lead time. Designs are finalized when reliable data from stores come. Production commences as soon as designs are complete. In addition, Zara's factories only run one shift, easily allowing for overtime production if demand calls for it. Its distribution centres are also highly efficient, allowing it to handle demand fluctuation without creating bottlenecks.

Agility may become more important in the 21st century because supply chains are more complex and therefore more sensitive to disruptions caused by a wide range of

Agility
The ability to quickly react to unexpected shifts in supply and demand.

different causes, including terrorist attacks, wars, flu epidemics and natural disasters such as earthquakes, typhoons or volcano eruptions. Under external shocks, an agile supply chain can rise to the challenge while a static one can pull a firm down.[32]

Firms that have (or can quickly find) alternative intermediaries or suppliers can continue to supply their customers, and gain new ones. In 2000, Nokia and Ericsson fought in the mobile handset market. Consider how Nokia and Ericsson reacted differently to a fire induced by a thunderstorm at a New Mexico factory of their handset chip supplier, Philips. The damage was minor, and Philips expected to resume production within a week. However, Nokia took no chances, and it quickly carried out design changes so that two other suppliers, one in Japan and another in the USA, could manufacture similar chips for Nokia (these were the only two suppliers in the world other than Philips that were capable of delivering similar chips). Nokia then quickly placed orders with these two suppliers. In contrast, Ericsson's supply chain had no such agility: It was set up to function exclusively with the damaged Philips plant in New Mexico – in other words, Ericsson had no plan B. Unfortunately, Philips later found out that the damage was larger than first reported, and production would be delayed for months. By that time, Ericsson scrambled to contact the other two suppliers, only to find out that Nokia had locked up all of their output for the next few months. The upshot? By 2001, Ericsson was driven out of the handset market as an independent player (it remain in the market with a joint venture with Sony called Sony Ericsson).[33]

Adaptability

Adaptability
The ability to change supply chain configurations in response to long-term changes in the environment and technology.

While agility focuses on flexibility that can overcome short-term fluctuation in the supply chain, adaptability refers to the ability to change supply chain configurations in response to long-term changes in the environment and technology. Enhancing adaptability often entails making a series of make-or-buy decisions. This requires firms to *continuously* monitor major geopolitical, social and technological trends in the world, make sense of them, and reconfigure the supply chain accordingly.[34] The damage for failing to do so may not be visible immediately or annually, but across a number of years, firms failing to do so may be selected out of the market.

Consider Lucent, the American telecommunications equipment giant. In the mid-1990s, in response to competitive pressures from its rivals Siemens and Alcatel that benefited from low-cost, Asia-based production in switching systems, Lucent successfully adapted its supply chain by phasing out more production in high-cost developed economies and setting up plants in China and Taiwan. However, Lucent then failed to adapt continuously. It concentrated its production in its own Asia-based plants, whereas rivals outsourced such manufacturing to Asian suppliers that became more capable of taking on more complex work. In other words, Lucent used foreign direct investment (FDI) to 'make' whereas rivals adopted outsourcing to 'buy'. Ultimately, Lucent was stuck with its own relatively higher cost (although Asia-based) plants and was overwhelmed by rivals. By 2002, Lucent was forced to shut down its Taiwan factory and to create an outsourced supply chain. But it was too late. By 2006, Lucent lost its independence and was acquired by its archrival Alcatel.

Alignment

Alignment
The alignment of interest of various players.

Alignment refers to the alignment of interests of various players involved in the supply chain. In a broad sense, each supply chain is a strategic alliance involving a variety of players, each of which is a profit-maximizing, stand-alone firm.[35] As a result, conflicts are natural. However, players associated with one supply chain must effectively coordinate to achieve mutually desirable outcomes.[36] Thus, supply chains are better at resolving conflicts of interest may be able to outperform other supply chains. For example, for Boeing's 787 Dreamliner, some 40 per cent of the $8 billion development cost is outsourced to suppliers: Mitsubishi makes the wings, Messier-Dowty provides the landing gear and so forth.[37] Many suppliers are responsible for end-to-end design of whole subsections. Headed by a vice president for global partnerships, Boeing treats its suppliers as partners, has 'partner councils' with regular meetings and fosters long-term collaboration.

Conceptually, there are two key elements to achieve alignment: power and trust.[38] Not all players in a supply chain are equal, and more powerful players such as Boeing naturally exercise greater bargaining power.[39] Having a recognized leader exercising power facilitates legitimacy and efficiency of the whole supply chain. Otherwise, excessive negotiation and bargaining will have to be conducted among supply chain members of more or less equal standing.

Trust stems from perceived fairness and justice from all supply chain members.[40] Although supply chains have become ever more complex and extended, modern practices, such as low (or zero) inventory, frequent just-in-time (JIT) deliveries and more geographic dispersion of production, have made all parties more vulnerable if the *weakest* link breaks down. Therefore, it is in the best interest of all parties to invest in trust-building mechanisms to foster more collaboration.

For instance, 7-Eleven Japan exercised a great deal of power by dictating that vendors re-supply its 9000 stores at three *specific* times a day. If a truck is late by more than 30 minutes, the vendor has to pay a penalty equal to the gross margin of the products carried to the store. This may seem harsh, but it is necessary. This is because Seven-Eleven Japan staff reconfigures store shelves three times a day to cater to different consumers at different *hours*, such as commuters in the morning and school kids in the afternoon. Time literally means money. However, Seven-Eleven Japan softens the blow by trusting its vendors. It does not verify the contents of deliveries. This allows vendors to save time and money because after deliveries, truck drivers do not have to wait for verification and can immediately move on to their next stop. The alignment of interest of such a supply chain is legendary. Hours after the Kobe earthquake in January 1995, when relief trucks moved at two miles an hour (if they moved at all) on the damaged roads, Seven-Eleven Japan's vendors went the extra mile by deploying seven helicopters and 125 motorcycles to deliver 64 000 rice balls to the starving city.

Sometimes, introducing a neutral intermediary (middleman) – more specifically, third-party logistics (3PL) providers – may more effectively align the interests in the supply chain. In the case of outsourcing in Asia, buyers (importers) include large Western retail businesses such as Gap, H&M and Toys 'Я' Us, while suppliers (exporters) are often smaller Asian manufacturers. Despite best intentions, both sides may still distrust each other. MNE buyers are not sure of the quality and timeliness of delivery. Further, MNE buyers are unable to control labour practices in supplier factories, some of which may be dubious (such as running 'sweatshops'). In the 1990s, Nike's reputation took a severe hit due to alleged questionable labour practices at its supplier factories. However, suppliers may also be suspicious. Since most contracts for shoes, clothing, toys and electronics are written several months ahead, suppliers are not confident about MNE buyers' ability to correctly forecast demand. Suppliers thus worry that in case of lower than anticipated demand, buyers may reject shipments to reduce excess inventory by citing excuses such as labour practices or quality issues.[41]

One solution lies in the involvement of 3PL intermediaries, such as the Hong Kong – based Li & Fung (Closing Case) that may add value by aligning the interests of all parties.[42] From humble roots of low-profile logistics, supply chain management has now come of age, supported by a huge transportation and logistics industry (In Focus 17.3).

Third-party logistics (3PL)
A neutral intermediary in the supply chain that provides logistics and other support services.

IN FOCUS 17.3

Ocean shipping: maxing out?

Everyday, container ships carry 90 per cent of the world's traded cargo by value. Taking off since the 1970s, container shipping has facilitated the emergence of global supply chains. This is because 'box trade' has reduced the cost of ocean shipping so significantly that brand owners in the West can afford to search the world for the lowest-cost suppliers. Thanks to the 'box trade', China's location in the Far East does not seem to be too far away from major markets in North America and Europe.

In 2007, with world merchandize trade growing by 15 per cent and China's exports at nearly double that rate, there were simply not enough ships. On top of the 4000 container ships, the industry ordered another 1300 and the average ship size became more gigantic. The mightiest is the *Emma Maersk*, which started to ferry toys from China to Europe by the end of 2006. This 150 000-ton ship can carry 11 000 20-foot containers (in the jargon, TEUs – 20-foot equivalent units). A train carrying that load would be 44 miles (71 kilometres) long (!). In comparison, until 1988, the biggest container ship had only carried 5000 TEUs, small enough to sail through the Panama Canal. Such ships are known as Panamax. The huge new container ships are labelled post-Panamax. They are far too big for the Canal.

However, fortunes turned abruptly. In 2008/09, the container shipping experienced its first decline in history; thanks to the global recession and the shrinking trade volume, 15 per cent of the industry capacity became idle. Approximately 750 ships were sheltering in Asian waters, with no containers to carry. Another 280 are laid up in European ports. In keeping with the tradition of the 'box trade' to cut shipping cost down, the price to move one container from China to Europe dropped from €1000 in summer 2008 to €300 in summer 2009. A cut-throat price competition over slices for a shrinking market had been unleashed.

To make the matters worse, pirates, especially those off the coast of East Africa, increased the cost of shipping. Kidnapping insurance usually covers legal fees and ransom (including the cost of the drop). Since 2009, a new type of insurance, simply known as pirate insurance, has emerged, costing €20 000 to €35 000 for a one-way transit through dangerous waters.

Sources Based on: (1) G. Stalk, 2006, The costly secret of China sourcing, *Harvard Business Review*, February: 64–66; (2) P.S. Benson, B. Lambek & S. Örskov, 2007, *Mærsk: Manden og Magten*, Copenhagen: Politikkens Forlag; (3) *Business Week*, 2009, Hedging bets on the high seas, April 27; (4) *The Economist*, 2007, Container ships, March 3; (5) *The Economist*, 2009, Sea of troubles, August 1.

INSTITUTIONS, MARKETING AND SUPPLY CHAIN MANAGEMENT

LEARNING OBJECTIVE

4 Discuss how institutions affect marketing and supply chain management

Standards in advertising
Formal rules designed by governments to protect consumers.

Formal and informal institutions in both target and home countries constrain the options for marketing and supply chain management. For example, standards in advertising, formal rules designed by governments to protect consumers, vary considerably across countries. Companies marketing controversial products such as tobacco or alcoholic beverages must be particularly adept at interpreting local rules and customs.[43] Other companies also occasionally fall foul of advertising standards. The British Advertising Standards Authority (ASA) frequently issues bans or public criticisms for a wide range of reasons, some of which are controversial. Cases in early 2010 included an ad with unproven emission reductions in cars, broadcasting of ads unsuitable for children in afternoon TV programmes and racial stereotyping in a bingo (gambling) ad. Even the government and politicians are not safe: criticism of the agency included a government sponsored ad with unproven statements on climate change, and election campaign ad with unproven claims on

IN FOCUS 17.4

India: forthcoming retail revolution

India has the world's highest density of retail outlets of any country. It has more than 15 million retail outlets, compared with 900 000 in the USA, whose market (by revenue) is 13 times bigger. At present, 97 per cent of retail sales in India are made in tiny mom-and-pop shops, mostly of less than 500 square feet (46 square meters). In Indian jargon, this is known, quite accurately, as the 'un-organized' retail sector. Even affluent urban Indians still do most of their daily shopping at traditional vendors such as corner shops and street vendors. The 'orga-nized' (more modern) retail sector commands only 3 per cent of total sales, of which 96 per cent is in the top-ten cities. This has substantial implications for those wishing to sell in India: Direct agreements with major supermarkets do not help much in building market share. Rather, it has to be attractive for those small ven-dors to carry the brand – which means consumer de-mand has to be created through brand awareness, and vendors need to be able to obtain the product through the wholesale trade.

However, the Indian retail sector is evolving fast. Major Indian business groups have diversified into retail and wholesale trade, not all of which are successful. Building a reliable supply chain that would deliver pro-ducts to the supermarket reliably is quite a challenge in the Indian context. Entrants experimented with different formats, business models, pricing and private labels to gather experiences on how to run a retail operation. For the time being, they could do so without foreign com-petitors, such as America's Wal-Mart, France's Carre-four, Germany's Metro and Britain's Tesco. These foreign retailers have been knocking at the door trying to expand the organized retail sector, yet the sector still remains closed to foreign direct investment (FDI). Millions of shopkeepers, supported by politicians and trade unionists, are worried about the onslaught of multinationals, citing the controversial 'Wal-Mart effect' being debated in the USA and elsewhere.

In response, the government delicately tries to bal-ance the interests of various stakeholders. FDI is still officially banned in *mass* retailing. However, a side door is now open. Foreign firms can take up to 51 per cent equity in *single-brand* shops that sell their own products, such as Nike, Nokia and Starbucks shops. Further, FDI in the supply chain is now permit-ted. Foreign firms can set up wholesale and sourcing subsidiaries that supply local mass retail partners. Moreover, the global players Tesco, Metro, Carrefour and Wal-Mart all have formed joint ventures with the retail arms of Indian business groups to establish a basis from where to grow in this promising market. Once this 'organized retail' sector takes off, other firms will have to adapt their sales strategy, possibly intro-ducing product placement on supermarket shelves similar to sales practices used in Western countries.

Sources Based on: (1) A. Mukherjee & N. Patel, 2005, *FDI in Retail Sector*, New Delhi: Department of Consumer Affairs; (2) *The Econo-mist*, 2006, Retailing in India: Coming to market, April 12; (3) *The Economist*, 2006, Retailing: Setting up shop in India, November 2; (4) A. Kazmin, 2010, Traditional vendors still dominate, *Financial Times*, April 21.

improvements in the quality of policing.[44] The challenge in international advertising is often to know what sort of proof may have to be provided when making claims about a product as this varies considerably across country. Moreover, some coun-tries such as Germany do not permit direct performance comparisons with compet-ing products.

Other constraints on marketing strategies arise from ownership restrictions. For example, In India, until 2006, FDI had not been allowed in the retail sector (see In Focus 17.4). Likewise, China forbids foreign retailers from operating wholly owned stores and only approves joint-venture stores. In China, France's Carrefour is the most aggressive foreign retailer with sales ahead of Wal-Mart. Yet, it was forced to sell a portion of its equity to Chinese partners and convert its wholly owned stores to joint-venture stores to be in compliance with ownership regulations.

Informal rules do not lead to official sanctions, but they can undermine the effectiveness of market strategies. In marketing, most of the blunders documented in Table 17.1 happen due to firms' failure to appreciate the deep underlying differences in cultures, religions, and norms – all part of the informal institutions.[45] Marketing managers thus need to be particularly sensitive to how informal norms affect consumers' perceptions of their products and promotions, as exemplified in In Focus 17.2 on C&A.

Supply chains not only create interdependencies between firms, they themselves can become a channel for the diffusion of practices and norms. If consumers expect their T-shirts to be produced by certain minimum labour standards, then retailers have to impose these standards (along with documentation) on the manufacturers and the entire supply chain (Chapter 10). Similarly, in the 1990s, many European firms adopted the ISO 9000 series of quality management systems. They then imposed the standard on their suppliers and partners throughout the world because every product is only as reliable as any of its components. Over time, these suppliers and partners spread ISO 9000 to other domestic firms. By 2005, more than 560 000 sites in more than 150 countries have been ISO 9000 certified. Similarly, the environmental standards known as ISO 14000 quickly spread through supply chains across the world.[46] In other words, suppliers and partners that export goods and services in a supply chain may be simultaneously *importing* their customers' norms and practices.[47]

RESOURCES, MARKETING AND SUPPLY CHAIN MANAGEMENT

LEARNING OBJECTIVE

5   Discuss how resources affect marketing and supply chain management

As before, we can evaluate marketing and supply chain management activities based on the VRIO criteria.[48] First, managers need to ask: Do these activities add *value?*[49] Marketing adds value to the firm if it helps increasing revenues by either increasing sales volumes or raising prices that can be charged to customers. It may also create value for consumers if it helps them identify products that best suit them. Supply chain management adds value for customers by providing products in a more timely manner, which increases value for customers, for instance by lowering inventory costs. However, marketers need to constantly reassess which techniques actually add value. Traditional media are losing viewers, readers and thus effectiveness. Yet, managers do not have a good handle of how advertising on the new online media adds value. This is especially unsettling in a cross-cultural context. Drivers for online value creation in a country with a very high internet adoption rate such as South Korea (which leads the world on this dimension) may be very different from drivers of such value creation elsewhere. Likewise, new practices in supply chain management may add value when transportation linkages run smoothly. Yet, dependence on certain suppliers and channels may destroy value at times of disruptions such as earthquakes, volcano eruptions or political upheavals.

Second, managers need to assess the *rarity* of marketing and supply chain activities. If all rival firms advertize on Google and use FedEx to manage logistics (all of which do add value), these activities, in themselves, are not rare. First movers into new techniques may attain rare advantages as first movers. For example, when radio frequency identification (RFID) tags were first introduced, they created extra benefits because they were rare.[50] However, as RFID has become more available, its rarity has diminished.

Third, having identified valuable and rare capabilities, managers need to assess how likely it is for rivals and partners to *imitate.*[51] Although there is no need to waste more ink on the necessity to watch out for rivals, firms also need to be careful about partners in the supply chain. As more Western MNEs outsource production to suppliers (or using a new jargon, contract manufacturers), it is always possible that some of the aggressive contract manufacturers may bite the hand that feeds them by directly imitating and competing with Western MNEs. This is not necessarily 'opportunism'. It is natural for ambitious contract manufacturers to flex their muscle. Such muscle is often directly strengthened by the Western MNEs themselves that willingly transfer technology and share know-how, which is often known as supplier (or vendor) development.[52] China's Haier (household appliances), TCL (televisions) and Galanz (microwaves) have become global leaders in just that way. While it is possible to imitate and acquire world-class manufacturing capabilities, marketing prowess and brand power are more intangible and thus harder to imitate. Hence, Western MNEs often cope by (1) being careful about what they outsource and (2) strengthening customer loyalty to their brands, such as Nike, to fend off contract manufacturers.[53]

Finally, managers need to ask: Is our firm *organizationally* ready to accrue the benefits of improved marketing and supply chain management? Oddly, in many firms, Marketing and Sales units do not get along well – to avoid confusion, here we spell the two terms with a capital letter to refer to these functional units. When revenues are disappointing, the blame game begins: Marketing blames Sales for failing to execute a brilliant plan, and Sales blames Marketing for setting the price too high and burning too much of the budget in high-flying but useless promotion. Marketing staff tend to be better educated, more analytical and disappointed when certain initiatives fail. In contrast, Sales people are often 'street smart', persuasive and used to rejections all the time. It is not surprising that Marketing and Sales have a hard time working together.[54] Yet, work together they must. Some leading firms have disbanded Marketing and Sales as separate functions and have created an integrated function – called Channel Enablement at IBM. An organization with warring functions cannot benefit from the values that any one unit may be creating.

DEBATES AND EXTENSIONS

There are some long-standing debates in this field, such as the standardization versus localization debate discussed earlier. Here, we focus on two important debates not previously discussed: (1) market orientation versus relationship orientation and (2) country of origin as liability or asset.

Market orientation versus relationship orientation

Market orientation refers to a philosophy or way of thinking that places the highest priority on the creation of superior customer value in the marketplace.[55] Although it originated as a marketing concept, its impact permeates throughout a firm and involves not only the marketing function but also strategy, supply chain, IT and numerous other functions.[56] A market-oriented firm genuinely listens to customer feedback and allocates resources accordingly to meet customer expectations. The debate centres on how firms benefit from market orientation *differently* around the world.

Another concept is relationship orientation, defined as a focus to establish, maintain and enhance relationships with customers.[57] Relationship orientation also originates from marketing (often known as 'relationship marketing'). Like market orientation, relationship orientation has more recently been expanded to touch many functions beyond marketing. Given the necessity for building trust and coordinating operations, business-to-business relationships within supply chains are

LEARNING OBJECTIVE

6 Participate in two leading debates concerning marketing and supply chain management

Market orientation
A philosophy or way of thinking that places the highest priority on the creation of superior customer value in the marketplace.

Relationship orientation
A focus to establish, maintain and enhance relationships with customers.

often based on long-term relationships. Instead of selling engines and then waiting for customers to order spare parts, Rolls-Royce (Integrative Case I.3) now builds deeper relationships with airlines by renting engines to them, providing 24/7 monitoring on every engine, carrying out full maintenance and getting paid for every hour the engine is in flight. Rolls-Royce can fix problems before they create damage, thus offering superior value for airlines.

Marketers have heavily debated how important relationship orientation is as complement to market orientation in global markets. Key to the debate is how firms benefit from market or relationship orientation differently around the world. Consider competition in China, where *guanxi* (relationship) reportedly is crucial. Firms have to allocate resources between building market-oriented capabilities (such as quality, pricing and delivery) and relationship-oriented assets (such as wining and dining). China thus offers a strong test for the debate between market and relationship orientation. Researchers find two interesting results. First, relationship-oriented assets do add value. Second, for truly outstanding performance, relationships are necessary but not sufficient. Market-oriented capabilities contribute *more* toward performance.[58] These results make sense in light of China's increasingly market-driven competition that gradually reduces (but does not eliminate) the importance of *guanxi*.

Viewed globally, the strongest effect of market orientation on performance has been found in US firms, which operate in arguably the most competitive market economy.[59] In weak market economies such as Russia and Ukraine, the returns from being market oriented are very limited.[60] In other words, firms there can 'get away' from a minimal amount of market orientation. Viewed collectively, these findings support the *institution-based* view: By definition, market orientation functions more effectively in a market economy.[61] In a comparative test between mainland Chinese and Hong Kong firms, market orientation has a greater effect on performance than does relationship orientation for Hong Kong firms. However, the pattern is reversed for mainland Chinese firms.[62]

Finally, it is important to note that all these studies take a snapshot, but economies constantly evolve. Although it is always the *combination* of market and relationship orientation that differentiates winning firms from losers, the debate boils down to the relative distribution between the two. There is reason to believe that as emerging economies develop further and follow more global rules of the game, market orientation may play an increasingly important role.[63]

Country-of-origin as liability or asset

Being an outsider, especially a foreigner, is often seen as a disadvantage. However, under certain circumstances, being foreign can be a competitive advantage. For example, in the 1880s, British industry lobbied their government to protect them by requiring importers to attach a 'made in ...' label to their products. To their great disappointment, 'made in Germany' quickly became a mark of quality and reliability, and ensured German manufacturing enduring success in the UK, interrupted only by two world wars. Similar positive country-of-origin effects emerged elsewhere in the world. American cigarettes are 'cool' among smokers in Central and Eastern Europe. Anything Korean – ranging from handsets and TV shows to *kimchi* (pickled cabbage) flavoured instant noodles – is considered hip in Southeast Asia. Conceptually, the country-of-origin effect refers to the positive or negative perception of firms and products from a certain country.[64]

Marketers have to decide whether to enhance or downplay such a country-of-origin effect.[65] This can be very tricky. Disneyland Tokyo became popular in Japan because it played up its American image. But Disneyland Paris received

Country-of-origin effect
The positive or negative perception of firms and products from a certain country.

In Paris Disneyland, is 'Americanness' an asset or a liability?

relentless negative press coverage in France because it insisted on its 'wholesome American look'.[66] Singapore Airlines projects a 'Singapore girl' image around the world. In contrast, Giordano downplays its Asian origin by adopting an Italian-sounding brand of a clothing line, made by a Hong Kong company that has no connection with Italy. Yet, Giordano figured that Italy has a positive country-of-origin image from which it can benefit.

Whether being a foreigner is indeed an advantage or a liability remains tricky. While some consumers may be attracted by the 'Americanness' of Disney entertainment, McDonalds hamburgers or Marlboro cigarettes, others are appalled by it. Normally, businesses only care about their (potential) consumers, but not about those who wouldn't buy their products or services anyway. Yet, broad social resentment against a brand can be harmful too.[67]

IMPLICATIONS FOR PRACTICE

What determines the success and failure in marketing and supply chain management around the globe? The institution-based view points out the impact of formal and informal rules of the game. In a nonmarket economy (think of North Korea), marketing would be irrelevant. In a world with high trade and investment barriers, globe-trotting FedEx jets would be unimaginable. The resource-based view argues that holding institutions constant, firms such as Zara that develop the best capabilities in marketing and supply chain management will emerge as winners (see Opening Case).

Consequently, three implications for action emerge (Table 17.3). First, marketers and supply chain managers need to know the rules of the game inside and out in order to craft their strategies. Regulations arising from specific legislation such as advertising standards or employment law force firms to adapt their strategies. In addition, informal norms exist in all societies, and they vary across countries. Violating informal norms may not trigger a lawsuit, but it can trigger negative media

LEARNING OBJECTIVE

7 Draw implications for action

Table 17.3 Implications for action

- Know the formal and informal rules of the game on marketing and supply chain management inside and out.
- In marketing, study local consumer behaviours, preferences and norms to avoid blunders.
- In supply chain management, focus on agility, adaptability and alignment (the triple As).

Table 17.4 Do's and don'ts to avoid blunders in international marketing

Do's	Don'ts
• Avoid ethnocentrism. Be sensitive to nationalistic feelings of local consumers, employees and governments.	• Don't be overconfident about the potential of your products or services – firms will be better off by continuously testing the 'water' and experimenting.
• Do your homework about the new market. Pay attention to details and nuances, especially those related to cultures, values and norms.	• Don't cut corners and save back-translation cost – always back-translate (after translating from English to Russian, get someone else to translate it from Russian to English to check accuracy).
• Avoid the pushy sales representative approach. The pace of business may seem too slow in some countries, but impatience does not bring sales.	• Don't use the same jokes across countries. Humour is often impossible to translate. What is viewed as funny by some may be offensive to others.
• Act like a diplomat – build relationships.	

Sources: Based on text in (1) T. Dalgic & R. Heijblom, 1996, International marketing blunders revisited – some lessons for managers, Journal of International Marketing, 4 (1): 81–91; (2) D.A. Ricks, 2006, Blunders in International Business, 4th ed., Oxford, UK: Blackwell.

exposure and consumer protests that severely harm a firm's reputation. Your local competitors will be ready to pounce on your errors to mobilize allies against the 'foreign invader undermining our culture'. This holds for essentially all countries – including your own!

Second, in marketing, focus on the four Ps. You know this from any marketing textbook. However, in international marketing, managers need to understand the behaviours of local consumers to avoid costly and embarrassing blunders (see Table 17.4). This includes mistakes made by your supply chain partners because if your name is on the product, you are likely to be held responsible, even if legally someone else is at fault. Remember: Despite their magnitude, blunders are *avoidable* mistakes. At the very least, international marketers should try very hard to avoid being written up as blunders in the next edition of this textbook.

Finally, in supply chain management, enhance your flexibility and responsiveness by focusing on the triple As. Underestimating the importance of a flexible response, many firms would only deliver container loads to minimize the number of deliveries and freight costs. When demand for a particular product suddenly rises, these firms often fail to react quickly; they have to wait until the container (or truck) is full. Such a practice may delay shipment, and thus cause stock-outs in stores that disappoint consumers. When firms eventually ship container loads, they often result in excess inventory because most buyers do not need a full container load. To get rid of such inventory, as much as a third of the merchandize carried by department stores is sold at a discount. Such discounts not only destroy profits for every firm in the supply chain but also undermine brand equity by upsetting consumers who recently bought the discounted items at full price. In contrast, the triple As urge savvy supply chain managers to focus on agility, adaptability and alignment of interests of the entire chain.

CHAPTER SUMMARY

1 Appreciate how international marketers can handle cross-cultural differences in consumer behaviour:

- Using marketing surveys and non-conventional methods, international marketers need to study consumer behaviours in the markets they wish to enter.

2 Articulate the four Ps in marketing (product, price, promotion and place) in a global context:

- In international marketing, the number-one concern on product is standardization versus localization.

- Marketers care about price elasticity – how responsive purchasing behaviour is when prices change.

- In promotion, marketers need to decide whether to enhance or downplay the country-of-origin effect.

- The place of sales is central to decisions where and in what sequence to enter foreign markets

3 Outline the triple As in supply chain management (agility, adaptability and alignment):

- The term *distribution channel* has been replaced by *supply chain management* in response to more outsourcing to suppliers, contract manufacturers and 3PL providers.

- Agility deals with the ability to quickly react to unexpected shifts in supply and demand.

- Adaptability refers to the ability to reconfigure supply chain in response to longer term external changes.

- Alignment focuses on the alignment of interests of various players in the supply chain.

4 Discuss how institutions affect marketing and supply chain management:

- Formal and informal rules such as advertising standards and employment law significantly impact these two areas.

5 Discuss how resources affect marketing and supply chain management:

- Managers need to assess marketing and supply chain management based on the VRIO criteria.

6 Participate in two leading debates concerning marketing and supply chain management:

- The debates are (1) market orientation versus relationship orientation, and (2) asset versus liability of countries-of-origin.

7 Draw implications for action:

- Knowing the formal and informal rules of the game will enable savvy managers to answer challenges in marketing and supply chain management.

- To avoid marketing blunders, managers should study consumer behaviour before deploying their marketing mix.

- Managers can enhance supply chain management by focusing on agility, adaptability and alignment (the triple As).

KEY TERMS

Adaptability
Agility
Alignment
Country-of-origin effect
Distribution channel
Inbound logistics
Market orientation
Market segmentation

Marketing
Marketing mix
Multi-tier branding
Outbound logistics
Place
Price
Price elasticity
Product

Promotion
Relationship orientation
Standards in advertising
Supply chain
Supply chain management
Third-party logistics (3PL)
Total cost of ownership

CRITICAL DISCUSSION QUESTIONS

1 Consider a novel product (such as a navigator or an iPad) and a country you know very little about (say China or Brazil). How are you going to find the information you need to design a marketing strategy?

2 Canada has an official animal: the beaver. Does your country have an official animal? If you were hired as a marketing expert by the government of Canada (or of whatever country), how would you best market the country using an animal?

3 In Hollywood movies, it is common to have product placement (have products, such as cars, from sponsored companies appear in movies without telling viewers that these are commercials). As a marketer, you are concerned about the ethical implications of

product placement via Hollywood, yet you know the effectiveness of traditional advertising is declining. How do you proceed?

4 You are a supply chain manager at a UK firm. In 2010, a volcano broke out in Iceland, disrupting air travel across Europe. On the one hand, you are considering switching to local suppliers in the UK. On the other hand, you feel bad about abandoning your Asian suppliers, with whom you have built a pleasant personal and business relationship, and who – in the long run – may be able to delivery products much cheaper. Yet, your tightly coordinated production cannot afford to miss one supply shipment. How do you proceed?

CLOSING CASE

Li & Fung: from trading company to supply chain manager

Founded in Guangzhou (then known as Canton), China, in 1906, the Li & Fung Group has been head-quartered in Hong Kong since the 1930s. Originating as a trading company, Li & Fung has emerged as the largest sourcing firm in the world. It manages the supply chain of high-volume, time-sensitive consumer

goods (especially clothes and toys) produced throughout Asia for some of the major retail brands, such as Limited Brands (with brands such as Victoria's Secret and Bath and Body Works), Liz Claiborne, Talbots, Timberland, Toys 'Я' Us and Sanrio, the Japanese merchandizer of Hello Kitty.

Although Li & Fung has over 70 offices in more than 40 countries, it does not own any factory. As

How did Victor Fung (right) and his company build a mega business managing the supply chain for retailers such as Toys 'Я' Us?

AFP/Getty Images

an intermediary, it adds value by linking smaller suppliers in Asia and larger retailers in the developed world. Li & Fung maintains a network of 8300 suppliers and factories throughout Asia. By bargaining on behalf of the 'small guys', Li & Fung enhances their bargaining power vis-à-vis multinational buyers. In exchange, Li & Fung enforces a code of conduct that prevents substandard quality and labour abuses. Suppliers found to violate this code are excluded from accessing Li & Fung's buyers. On the other hand, Li & Fung keeps multinational buyers honest. If they refuse shipments due to their own problems (such as faulty forecast or demand collapse), Li & Fung denies them future access to its supplier network. Of course, Li & Fung's buyers and suppliers pay a fee for its services, but the fee is lower than the transaction costs associated with the haggling, uncertainties and headaches when buyers and suppliers bargain directly.

Life as a trader and now a supply chain manager is not easy. In an effort for disintermediation, both buyers and suppliers relentlessly imitate Li & Fung's capabilities. Intermediaries such as Li & Fung thrive by working with small- and medium-sized client firms on both sides. When buyers such as IBM grow and expand their purchasing volume from Asia, they often set up their own procurement channels in Asia directly. Therefore, Li & Fung is bypassed. On the other hand, when suppliers such as Taiwan's BenQ become more successful overseas, their export volume justifies their investment to set up their own distribution channels in the West, again bypassing the likes of Li & Fung. Thus, Li & Fung lives in a precarious world, constantly under the threat of being bypassed from both sides by its clients. The solution is to make some its capabilities untouchable. For Li & Fung, this entails constantly developing and leveraging its intimate knowledge about both sides as a hard-to-imitate strategic weapon. Li & Fung often scouts for smaller and lower cost Asian manufacturers and for smaller Western buyers that would benefit from the wide selection and reliability that Li & Fung's network provides.

During the 2008/09 recession, the value from Li & Fung's services has shined more brightly. For example,

Liz Claiborne in early 2009 sold its sourcing operations to Li & Fung for $83 million. Liz Claiborne still designs and markets for brands such as Juicy Couture, Kate Spade, Liz Claiborne and Lucky Brand, but Li & Fung handles the rest. As US retailers cope with tough times, more are following Liz Claiborne's lead by turning to Li & Fung. As retailers slash costs, said Li & Fung managing director William Fung in an interview, 'they are asking themselves, "Is having our own buying office the way to go?"' The answer is increasingly no. For an order of 300 000 men's shorts, Li & Fung's abilities to tap into the best-in-breed suppliers in buttons, zippers, yarn, fabric and final production (sewing) scattered in various Asian countries and then to orchestrate the network to deliver high-quality products in a timely fashion are unrivalled. While Li & Fung doubled its revenue to $12 billion between 2004 and 2007, its revenue in 2009 is likely to reach a record $16 billion. As of May 2009, its Hong Kong-listed stock was up 63 per cent so far in 2009, compared with a mere 7 per cent increase for the Hang Seng Index. This does not mean all is rosy for Li & Fung. The devastation in the US retail sector has ex-posed Li & Fung's crucial vulnerability: 62 per cent of its revenues come from the Nevertheless, 'we expect to emerge stronger after this crisis', said Fung.

CASE DISCUSSION QUESTIONS

1 From a VRIO standpoint, what distinguishes Li & Fung from suppliers, buyers and other intermediaries?

2 Intermediaries such as Li & Fung need to be paid. Why, after paying Li & Fung a fee, buyers and suppliers still find it valuable to deal through an intermediary? In other words, why don't they trade directly?

3 Why is Li & Fung able to emerge stronger during the 2008–09 global economic crisis?

Sources: Based on (1) V. Narayanan & A. Raman, 2004, Aligning incentives in supply chains, *HBR*, November: 94–102; (2) V.K. Fung, W.K. Fung & Y. Wind, 2008, *Competing in a Flat World*, Philadelphia: Wharton School Publishing; (3) *Business Week*, 2009, How not to sweat the retail details, May 25: 52–54; (4) A. Chintakananda, A. York, H. O'Neill & M.W. Peng, 2009, Structuring dyadic relationships between export producers and intermediaries, *EJIM*, 3: 302–327.

RECOMMENDED READINGS

J. Mangan, C. Lalwani & T. Butcher, 2008, *Global Logistics and Supply Chain Management*, Chichester: Wiley – A textbook on the international supply chain part of this chapter.

M. de Mooij, 2005, *Consumer Behaviour and Culture*, London: Sage – Explores how variations across Europe affect consumer behaviour and its implications for marketing.

D.A. Ricks, 2006, *Blunders in International Business*, 4th ed., Oxford: Blackwell – Humorously tells the story of mistakes made by international business people, mostly in the area of marketing.

J.C. Usunier & J.A. Lee, 2009, *Marketing across Cultures*, 5th ed., London: Prentice Hall – A marketing textbook focusing on international and cross-cultural issues.

A.J. van Weele, 2005, *Purchasing and Supply Chain Management*, 4th ed, London: Cengage – A textbook on supply chain management analysis and practice.

NOTES:

"FOR JOURNAL ABBREVIATION, PLEASE SEE PAGE XXVI-XXVII."

1 M. Lejeune & N. Yakova, 2005, On characterizing the four C's in supply chain management *JOM*, 23: 81–100.

2 G.T. Hult, D. Ketchen, & S. Slater, 2004, Information processing, knowledge management, and strategic supply chain performance, *AMJ*, 47: 241–253; T. Choi & D. Krause, 2006, The supply base and its complexity, *JOM*, 24: 637–652.

3 D. Ketchen & G.T. Hult, 2007, Bridging organization theory and supply chain management, *JOM*, 25: 573–580.

4 J. Lehy, 2009, How Volvo took a lead in India, *Financial Times*, September 1.

5 C.S. Craig & S.P. Douglas, 2001, Conducting international marketing research in the 21st century,

IMR, 18: 80–90; M. De Mooij, 2005, *Consumer Behaviour and Culture*, London: Sage.

6 D.A. Ricks, 1999, *Blunders in International Business*, 3rd ed. (p. 88), Oxford: Blackwell.

7 M. Solomon, G. Bamossy, S. Askegaard & M.K. Hogg, *Consumer Behaviour: A European Perspective*, 3rd ed., Harlow: Prentice Hall.

8 C.B. Jarvis, S.B. Mackenzie, P.M. Podsakoff, D.G. Mick & W.O. Bearden, 2003, A critical review of construct indicators and measurement model misspecification in marketing and consumer research, *JCR*, 30, 199–218.

9 P. Kotler & K. Keller, 2005, *Marketing Management*, 12th ed., Upper Saddle River, NJ: Prentice Hall.

10 S. Jain, ed., 2003, *Handbook of Research in International Marketing*, Cheltenham, UK: Edward Elgar; M. Theodosiou & L.C. Leonidou, 2003, Standardization versus adaptation in international marketing strategy, *IBR*, 12: 141–171; D. Dow, 2006, Adaptation and performance in foreign markets, *JIBS*, 37: 212–226; C. Katsikeas, S. Samiee & M. Theodosiou, 2006, Strategy fit and performance consequences of international marketing standardization, *SMJ*, 27: 867–890; L. Lim, F. Acito & A. Rusetski, 2006, Development of archetypes of international marketing strategy, *JIBS*, 37: 499–524.

11 T. Levitt, 1983, The globalization of markets, *HBR*, May–June: 92–102.

12 M. Harvey & M.B. Myers, 2000, Marketing in emerging and transition economies, *JWB*, 35: 111–113; B. Money & D. Colton, 2000, The response of the new consumer to promotion in the transition economies, *JWB*, 35: 189–205; G. Cui & Q. Liu, 2000, Emerging market segments in an emerging economy, *JIMktg*, 9: 84–106; D. Rigby & V. Vishwanath, 2006, Localization, *HBR*, April: 82–92.

13 As the page numbers differ for different editions of these magazines, we do not report page numbers in our references, but suggest students searching for an article to type the title of the article in the magazine's website search function.

14 J. Townsend, S. Yeniyurt, & M. Talay, 2009, Getting to global, *JIBS*, 40: 539–558.

15 T.P. Beane & D.M. Ennis, 1987, Market segmentation, *EJM*, 21: 20–42; F.T. Hofstede, J.B. Steenkamp & M. Wedel, 1999, International market segmentation based on consumer-product relations, *JMR*, 36: 1–17; D. Yankelovich & D. Meer, 2006, Rediscovering market segmentation, *HBR*, February: 122–131.

16 D. Holt, J.A. Quelch & E. Taylor, 2004, How global brands compete, *HBR*, September: 68–75.

17 J. Klein, 2003, Us versus them, or us versus everyone, *JIBS*, 33: 345–363.

18 A. Schuh, 2000, Global standardization as a success formula for marketing in Central Eastern Europe? *JWB*, 35: 133–148.

19 K.E. Meyer & Y.T.T. Tran, 2006, Market penetration and acquisition strategies for emerging economies, *LRP*, 39: 177–197; A. Schuh, 2007, Brand strategies of Western MNCs as drivers of globalization in Central and Eastern Europe, *EMJ*, 41: 274–192.

20 C. Schlautmann, 2010, Pandora ist ein Glücksfall für Juweliere, *Handelsblatt*, March 13.

21 M. Cohen, N. Agrawal, & V. Agrawal, 2006, Winning in the aftermarket, *HBR*, May: 129–138.

22 J. Hofer, 2010, Interview: Die Idee kam uns beim Bier, *Handelsblatt*, March 7.

23 J.C. Usunier & J.A. Lee, 2009, *Marketing across Cultures*, 5th ed., London: Pearson.

24 K. Macharzina, 2001, The end of pure global strategies? (p. 106), *MIR*, 41: 105–108.

25 J.A. Schibrowsky, J.W. Peltier & A. Nill, 2007, The state of internet marketing research, *EJM*, 41: 722–733.

26 *Business Week*, 2005, The MySpace generation (p. 92), December 12: 86–96.

27 *Business Week*, 1999, Generation Y, February 15; S.M. Noble, D.L. Haylo & J. Phillips, 2009, What drives college-age generation Y consumers? *JBR*, 62: 617–628.

28 E. Rabinovich, A. M. Knemeyer, & C. Mayer, 2007, Why do Internet commerce firms incorporate logistics service providers in their distribution channels? *JOM*, 25: 661–681.

29 M.E. Porter, 1985, *Competitive Advantage*, New York: Free Press.

30 *The Economist*, 2006, The physical internet, June 17: 3–4.

31 The following discussion draws heavily on H. Lee, 2004, The triple-A supply chain, *HBR*, October: 102–112.

32 Y. Sheffi & J.B. Rice, 2005, A supply chain view of the resilient enterprise, *SMR*, 47: 41–48; E. Prater & S. Ghosh, 2006, A comparative model of firm size and the global operational dynamics of US firms in Europe, *JOM*, 24: 511–529; B. Avittathur & P. Swamidass, 2007, Matching plant flexibility and supplier flexibility, *JOM*, 25: 717–735.

33 *Economist*, 2006, When the chain breaks, June 17: 18–19.

34 R. Belderbos & L. Sleuwaegen, 2005, Competitive drivers and international plant configuration strategies, *SMJ*, 26: 577–593; F. Rothaermel, M.A. Hitt, & L. Jobe, 2006, Balancing vertical integration and strategic outsourcing, *SMJ*, 27: 1033–1056.

35 J.Y. Murray, M. Kotabe, & J. Zhou, 2005, Strategic alliance-based sourcing and market performance, *JIBS*, 36: 187–208.

36 D.A. Griffith & M.B. Myers, 2005, The performance implications of strategic fit of relational norm governance strategies in global supply chains, *JIBS*, 36: 254–269; M. McCarter & G. Northcraft, 2007, Happy together? *JOM*, 25: 498–511.

37 C. Niezen & W. Weller, 2006, Procurement as strategy, *HBR*, September: 22–23.

38 R.D. Ireland & J. Webb, 2007, A multi-theoretic perspective on trust and power in strategic supply chains, *JOM*, 25: 482–497.

39 W.C. Benton & M. Maloni, 2005, The influence of power driven buyer/supplier relationships on supply chain satisfaction, *JOM*, 23: 1–22; T.R. Crook & J. Combs, 2007, Sources and consequences of bargaining power in supply chains, *JOM*, 25: 546–555.

40 D. Krause, R. Handfield & B. Tyler, 2007, The relationships between supplier development, commitment, social capital accumulation and performance improvement, *JOM*, 25: 528–545; C. Rodriguez & D. Wilson, 2002, Relationship bonding and trust as a foundation for commitment in US-Mexican strategic alliances, *JIMktg*, 10: 53–76.

41 N. Morgan, A. Kaleka & R. Gooner, 2007, Focal supplier opportunism in supermarket retailer category management, *JOM*, 25: 512–527.

42 M.W. Peng, 1998, *Behind the Success and Failure of US Export Intermediaries*, Westport, CT: Quorum; V. Narayanan & A. Raman, 2004, Aligning incentives in supply chains, *HBR*, November: 94–102.

43 H. Saffer & F. Chaloupka, 2000, The effect of tobacco advertising bans on tobacco consumption, *JHE*, 19: 1117–1137; H. Saffer & D. Dave, 2002, Alcohol consumption and alcohol advertising bans, *AE*, 34: 1325–1334.

44 *The Guardian*, 2010, various news items on various dates: www.guardian.co.uk/media/asa; *Advertising Standards Authority*, 2010, various news items on various dates: www.asa.org.uk/Complaints-and-ASA-action/Adjudications.aspx.

45 K.S. Fam, D.S. Waller & B.Z. Erdogan, 2004, The influence of religion on attitudes towards the advertising of controversional products, *EJM*, 38: 537–555.

46 C.J. Corbett & D.A. Kirsch, 2000, International diffusion of ISO 14000 certification, *POM*, 9: 327–342;

47 S.W. Anderson, J.D. Daly & M.F. Johnson, 1999, Why firms seek ISO 9000 certification, *POM*, 8: 28–43; I. Guler, M.F. Guillén & J.M. Macpherson, 2001, Global competition, institutions and the diffusion of organizational practices, *ASQ*, 47: 207–232; O. Boiral, 2003, ISO 9000, *OSc OR OSt?*, 14: 720–737.

48 M.W. Peng & A. York, 2001, Behind intermediary performance in export trade, *JIBS*, 32: 327–346. See also N. Morgan, A. Kaleka, & C. Katsikeas, 2004, Antecedents of export venture performance, *JMktg*, 68: 90–108.

49 J.C. Anderson, J. Narus & W. van Rossum, 2006, Customer value propositions in business markets, *HBR*, March: 91–99; R. Priem, 2007, A consumer perspective on value creation, *AMR*, 32: 219–235.

50 C.C. Chao, J.M. Yang & W.Y. Jen, 2007, Determining technology trends and forecasts of RFID by a historical review and bibliometric analysis from 1991 to 2005, *Technovation*, 27: 268–279; E.W.T. Ngai, K.K.L. Moon, F.J. Riggins & C.Y. Yi, 2008, RFID research, *IJPE*, 112: 510–530.

51 F. Pil & S. Cohen, 2006, Modularity: Implications for imitation, *AMR*, 31: 995–1011.

52 S. Modi & V. Mabert, 2007, Supplier development, *JOM*, 25: 42–64; K. Rogers, L. Purdy, F. Safayeni & P.R. Dimering, 2007, A supplier development program, *JOM*, 25: 556–572.

53 S. Fournier & L. Lee, 2009, Getting brand communities right, *HBR*, April: 105–111.

54 P. Kotler, N. Rackham & S. Krishnaswamy, 2006, Ending the war between sales and marketing, *HBR*, July: 68–78.

55 A. Kohli & B. Jaworski, 1990, Market orientation, *JMktg*, 54: 1–18; J. Narver & S. Slater, 1990, The effect of a market orientation on business profitability, *JMktg*, 54: 20–35; C. Nobel, R. Sinha & A. Kumar, 2002, Market orientation and alternative strategic orientations, *JMktg*, 66: 25–39; K.Z. Zhou, C.K.B. Yim & D.K. Tse, 2005, The effects of strategic orientations on technology- and market-based breakthrough innovations, *JMktg*, 69: 42–60.

56 T. Dalgic, 1998, Dissemination of market orientation in Europe, *IMR*, 15: 45–60; G.T. Hult, D. Ketchen & S. Slater, 2005, Market orientation and performance, *SMJ*, 26: 1173–1181; S. Slater, E. Olsen & G.T. Hult, 2006, The moderating influence of strategic orientation on the strategy formation capability-performance relationship, *SMJ*, 27: 1221–1231.

57 L. Berry, 1995, Relationship marketing of services, *JAMS*, 23: 236–245; G. Hoetker, 2005, How much do you know versus how well I know you, *SMJ*, 26: 75–96.

58 M.W. Peng & Y. Luo, 2000, Managerial ties and firm performance in a transition economy, *AMJ*, 43: 486–501.

59 P.D. Ellis, 2006, Market orientation and performance, *JMS*, 43: 1089–1107.

60 P. Golden, P. Doney, D. Johnson & J. Smith, 1995, The dynamics of marketing orientation in transition economies, *JIMktg*, 3: 29–49; I. Akimova, 2000, Development of market orientation and competitiveness of Ukrainian firms, *EJM*, 34: 1128–1148.

61 J. Fahy, G. Hooley, T. Cox, J. Beracs, K. Fonfara & B. Snoj, 2000, The development and impact of marketing capabilities in Central Europe, *JIBS*, 31: 63–81; K.Z. Zhou, J.S. Brown, C.S. Dev & S. Agarwal, 2007, The effects of customer and competitor orientations on performance in global markets, *JIBS*, 38: 303–319.

62 L.Y.M. Sin, A.C.B. Tse, O.H.M. Yau, R.P.M. Chow & J.S.Y. Lee, 2005, Market orientation, relationship marketing orientation, and business performance, *JIMktg*, 13: 36–57.

63 M.W. Peng, 2003, Institutional transitions and strategic choices, *AMR*, 28: 275–296; K. Zhou & C. Li, 2007, How does strategic orientation matter in Chinese firms? *APJM*, 24: 447–466.

64 L.E. Brouthers, E. O'Connell, & J. Hadjimarcou, 2005, Generic product strategies for emerging market exports into Triad nation markets, *JMS*, 42: 225–245; J. Knight, D. Holdsworth, & D. Mather, 2007, Country-of-origin and choice of food imports, *JIBS*, 38: 107–125; S. Samiee, T. Shimps, & S. Sharma, 2005, Brand origin recognition accuracy, *JIBS*, 36: 379–397; P. Verlegh, 2007, Home country bias in product evaluation, *JIBS*, 38: 361–373.

65 J.C. Usunier, 2006, Relevance in business research: The case of country-of-origin research in marketing, *EMR*, 3: 60–73;

66 M.Y. Brannen, 2004, When Mickey loses face, *AMR*, 29: 593–616.

67 J.K. Johansson, 2005, *In Your Face: How American Marketing Excess is Fuelling Anti-Americanism*, Upper Saddle River: Prentice-Hall.

PART SIX

INTEGRATIVE CASES

A FEW TIPS ABOUT
CORRUPTION IN THE US

Andrew Delios
National University of Singapore

'Hey! Wait! Wait! Wait a minute, will you! You forgot something', the stylishly clad waiter yelled at Mr. Biswas, Mr. Lee and Mr. Lai as they exited the wharf-side restaurant in Monterey, California, in early September 2006.

'Thanks, what'd we forget?' inquired Mr. Biswas of the waiter.

'You left some junk on the table', replied the waiter as he tossed their $1.50 tip at the trio. 'Next time leave nothing, or leave a real tip, don't insult me by leaving a few quarters. Why don't you learn the local customs before you come here again!'

Andrew Delios wrote this case solely to provide material for class discussion. The author does not intend to illustrate either effective or ineffective handling of a managerial situation. The author may have disguised certain names and other identifying information to protect confidentiality.

Mr. Lee turned to Mr. Biswas and asked, 'What was that all about? I thought we were quite generous to the waiter. What we left could pay for a decent meal in any of our home countries'.

'Apparently we were not', piped in the pragmatic Mr. Lai. 'He's obviously angry with our tip. I never know how much to tip. I like the situation in China much better. We never have to tip, and never have to worry about the service. None of this silly calculation of some odd percentage and not knowing who to tip and when'.

'It's the same for me in India', said Mr. Biswas. 'I go to a restaurant and I don't have to worry about some extra charge to the base price. The waiters just do their jobs, the taxi drivers do their jobs, the bellboy does his job, and I don't have to pay them some bribe to have them do their job. In the US, I don't even know who I am supposed to tip: the waiter, the bellboy, the taxi driver, the hair stylist, the maid, the concierge; and the list just goes on and on'.

'Tipping is a crazy custom', Mr. Lee reinforced. 'The proprietors should just pay them for the work they do, and they should just do their work without trying to draw extra money from us. Instead, this doesn't happen and I always end up paying too little or too much and I don't even know if it improves the service at all'.

'The U.S. is an odd country', continued Mr. Biswas. 'It harps on us about corrupt practices in our parts of the world, yet it continues to not only allow, but support, this private sector corruption. Tipping, forget it, it's unnecessary and it's an archaic custom. The Americans should follow our lead and legislate it out of existence' (see Exhibit 1).

MR. BISWAS

Mr. Biswas was a 55-year-old home construction contractor from the large city of Mumbai, located on the central west coast of India. Mr. Biswas had worked in the housing industry from a young age, driven by a desire to build his own home. He had experienced several eras in the industry, most recently the opening-up of the construction industry following liberalization and other free-market reforms in India.

Although the market was opening up in India, Mr. Biswas still felt there was a high degree of bureaucracy in the market. State-level and local municipal officials wielded considerable power when it came to the sale of land necessary for Mr. Biswas's increasingly large developments.

Mr. Biswas did not let this feature of the business environment deter him. He was familiar with the procedures necessary to secure the cooperation of local officials in his land purchases. He understood the expectations of the local officials:

India is large country with a strong bureaucracy. From the days of the British Raj, through independence, to the days of liberalization, there has always been a great deal of power concentred in the civil service and government officials.

Even today, with the national government pushing for reforms and liberalization, there is still resistance at the state and local levels to the reforms. The local bureaucrats have entrenched power. They have a long legacy of power, and they aren't afraid to use their power to say yes, to say no, or to say nothing at all. The latter is the worst, where you put in an application or a form or a filing to do business in a particular area, and they just sit on the application.

Exhibit 1 Corruption perceptions index, 2005

2005 Rank	Country	2005 CPI	2005 Rank	Country	2005 CPI
1	Iceland	9.7	36	Bahrain	5.8
2	Finland	9.6	37	Cyprus	5.7
	New Zealand	9.6		Jordan	5.7
4	Denmark	9.5	39	Malaysia	5.1
5	Singapore	9.4	40	Hungary	5.0
6	Sweden	9.2		Italy	5.0
7	Switzerland	9.1		Korea, South	5.0
8	Norway	8.9	43	Tunisia	4.9
9	Australia	8.8	44	Lithuania	4.8
10	Austria	8.7	45	Kuwait	4.7
11	Netherlands	8.6	46	South Africa	4.5
	United Kingdom	8.6	47	Czech Republic	4.3
13	Luxembourg	8.5		Namibia	4.3
14	Canada	8.4		Slovakia	4.3
15	Hong Kong	8.3	51	Costa Rica	4.2
16	Germany	8.2		El Salvador	4.2
17	United States	7.6		Latvia	4.2
18	France	7.5		Mauritius	4.2
19	Belgium	7.4	55	Bulgaria	4.0
	Ireland	7.4		Colombia	4.0
21	Chile	7.3		Fiji	4.0
	Japan	7.3		Seychelles	4.0
23	Spain	7.0	59	Cuba	3.8
24	Barbados	6.9		Thailand	3.8
25	Malta	6.6		Trinidad and Tobago	3.8
26	Portugal	6.5	62	Belize	3.7
27	Estonia	6.4		Brazil	3.7
28	Israel	6.3	64	Jamaica	3.6
	Oman	6.3	65	Ghana	3.5
30	United Arab Emirates	6.2		Mexico	3.5
31	Slovenia	6.1		Panama	3.5
32	Botswana	5.9		Peru	3.5
	Qatar	5.9		Turkey	3.5
	Taiwan	5.9	70	Burkina Faso	3.4
	Uruguay	5.9		Croatia	3.4

2005 Rank	Country	2005 CPI	2005 Rank	Country	2005 CPI
	Egypt	3.4		Eritrea	2.6
	Lesotho	3.4		Honduras	2.6
	Poland	3.4		Kazakhstan	2.6
	Saudi Arabia	3.4		Nicaragua	2.6
	Syria	3.4		Palestine	2.6
77	Laos	3.3		Ukraine	2.6
78	China	3.2		Vietnam	2.6
	Morocco	3.2		Zambia	2.6
	Senegal	3.2		Zimbabwe	2.6
	Sri Lanka	3.2	117	Afghanistan	2.5
	Suriname	3.2		Bolivia	2.5
83	Lebanon	3.1		Ecuador	2.5
	Rwanda	3.1		Guatemala	2.5
85	Dominican Republic	3.0		Guyana	2.5
	Mongolia	3.0		Libya	2.5
	Romania	3.0		Nepal	2.5
88	Armenia	2.9		Philippines	2.5
	Benin	2.9		Uganda	2.5
	Bosnia and Herzegovina	2.9	126	Albania	2.4
	Gabon	2.9		Niger	2.4
	India	2.9		Russia	2.4
	Iran	2.9		Sierra Leone	2.4
	Mali	2.9	130	Burundi	2.3
	Moldova	2.9		Cambodia	2.3
	Tanzania	2.9		Congo, Republic of	2.3
97	Algeria	2.8		Georgia	2.3
	Argentina	2.8		Kyrgyzstan	2.3
	Madagascar	2.8		Papua New Guinea	2.3
	Malawi	2.8		Venezuela	2.3
	Mozambique	2.8	137	Azerbaijan	2.2
	Serbia / Montenegro	2.8		Cameroon	2.2
103	Gambia	2.7		Ethiopia	2.2
	Macedonia	2.7		Indonesia	2.2
	Swaziland	2.7		Iraq	2.2
	Yemen	2.7		Liberia	2.2
107	Belarus	2.6		Uzbekistan	2.2

2005 Rank	Country	2005 CPI	2005 Rank	Country	2005 CPI
144	Congo, Democratic Rep.	2.1	152	Côte d'Ivoire	1.9
	Kenya	2.1		Equatorial Guinea	1.9
	Pakistan	2.1		Nigeria	1.9
	Paraguay	2.1	155	Haiti	1.8
	Somalia	2.1		Myanmar	1.8
	Sudan	2.1		Turkmenistan	1.8
	Tajikistan	2.1	158	Bangladesh	1.7
151	Angola	2.0		Chad	1.7

Source: Transparency International, Corruption Perceptions Index 2005, available at www.transparency.org, accessed August 15, 2006.

As they say, sometimes you need to put grease in the wheels. Putting in the grease does not make the wheels turn in ways they are not supposed to turn, it just makes the wheels turn better. I don't want the bureaucrats to do something they are not supposed to do, like rig a contract or a bid for my company. I just want them to do what they are supposed to do and to do it fast.

I know what they would like, and I trust that what I give to them will help move the business process forward. Look, in the market today, you can't afford to sit and wait and let your competitors leapfrog you. If that requires me to secure the cooperation of bureaucrats to do the job they are supposed to do, then so be it. In any case, all these problems are caused by the politicians, who refuse to provide enough resources to upgrade the civil service and its staff. I should not have to pay the price for their incompetence, but a bit of money from me will help these poorly paid civil servants lead a better life.

MR. LEE

Mr. S.M. Lee was a fifth-generation Malaysian with distant Hokkien roots in China, who had founded and operated a large textile business. Although he originally began his business in the island-state of Penang in the 1970s, the commercial growth of this island through the 1980s soon made manufacturing in his local textile plants prohibitively costly.

Mr. Lee's response to the increasingly high-cost environment in Malaysia was rather dramatic. Recognizing the trend towards the development of electronic and high-technology industries in Malaysia, Mr. Lee made the decision to relocate his textile factory to Surabaya in Indonesia.

Mr. Lee relocated this plant in the mid-1980s. He subsequently expanded this plant in the early 1990s, since growth in Asia spurred growth in textile demand. As with many businesses in Asia, Mr. Lee's business grew rapidly through the mid-1990s, only to face a severe downturn following the Asian economic crisis in the late 1990s. With the return to growth in Asia in the early 2000s, Mr. Lee wanted to set up a new facility to replace his already aged textile factory.

Mr. Lee commented on the process of trying to establish another foreign-owned plant in Indonesia:

When I set up my first plant in Indonesia in 1986, it was quite a challenge. FDI [foreign direct investment] from Malaysia to Indonesia was not that common. There was a lot I had to learn about operating in Indonesia. I had to find local managers, I had to learn how to pay, train and motivate the textile workers. Should I use a piece-rate system or should I pay them a flat rate? Operational questions such as these arose nearly every day. I made my share of mistakes, but fortunately through hard work and some luck, I was able to succeed. Being able to understand Bahasa Indonesia [the national language of Indonesia], because I speak Malay, certainly helped.

If I can speak frankly, part of the reason I was able to succeed, is that I knew who to partner with. Setting up a plant in Indonesia at that time could not be done as a wholly owned subsidiary; I had to use a joint venture. I also had to obtain the agreement of the government for the plant. At that time, it was not a secret about what one had to do when establishing a foreign business in Indonesia. You had to go to Suharto [then President of Indonesia] and his family and somehow get them involved in the business. Either they were involved as a joint venture partner, most often in a silent role, or you involved them at the start-up stage, and after that they left you alone.

The good thing is that with the Suharto family's involvement, I knew which government official I had to work with, and I knew what the outcome would be. Remember the saying at that time, all would be good if you covered the standard 10 per cent requested by Suharto's wife Madam Tien, or as she came to be known, Madam Ten.

When making this payment, I had very little worry that I would be cheated or the official would not do what he said he would do. I could run the textile operation with my eyes closed. My friends questioned whether it was right for me to do this with the Suharto family, but I think they did much for Indonesia's development and helped reduce poverty greatly. So I was actually helping the country through my investments.

These days the situation is quite difficult. Now I know all the operational details. But the big problem for me is securing official approvals for the land and construction of the new plant. I don't know what my tax rates will be and I don't know who to contact in the government to help me with this. Also, the previous Indonesian President Megawati Soekarnoputri began the crackdown on corruption, collusion and nepotism that were prevalent during the Suharto regime. That said, corruption is still practiced collectively by those sitting in provincial legislative bodies, but now it is more risky to work with local government officials, and there is no guarantee that they will do what you have arranged with them to do. There was none of this uncertainty in the time of Suharto.

MR. LAI

Mr. X.C. Lai's family had a long and colorful history, as did many families in a country with as long a history as China. Originally from the inland province of Sichuan, Mr. Lai's family moved to the coastal city of Shanghai in the late 19th century. After three generations in Shanghai, in the late 1940s, the generation of Mr. Lai's grandparents went on a diaspora, with one brother moving to

Hong Kong, another to Taiwan and a third to the United States. Mr. Lai's grandfather remained in Shanghai, where Mr. Lai was raised.

Mr. Lai was raised in a tumultuous period in China's history. With the many changes that took place in China since the Communists achieved power in the late 1940s, the country where Mr. Lai grew up was quite different from the present-day China, as echoed in Mr. Lai's comments:

> When the open door policies began to gain traction in the late 1970s, I became acutely aware of the possibilities that existed should these reforms hold. I heard from my extended family in Hong Kong, Taiwan and the United States of the kinds of opportunities that could arise and I wanted to be in a position to capitalize on these.
>
> With a bit of effort in the early 1980s, I was able to travel to Shenzhen and I saw the opportunity for developing manufacturing operations. My cousin in Hong Kong ran a series of small manufacturing operations that produced toys for major companies in the US. My cousin saw that the rising wage costs in Hong Kong were at risk of pricing him out of his contracts.
>
> My cousin and I agreed that the proximity of Shenzhen to Hong Kong, coupled with the plentiful supply of low-cost labour in Shenzhen, as coupled with its status as a Special Economic Zone, could make for a very competitive manufacturing operation. My cousin had the contacts with the Western companies and he had the knowledge of how to develop the manufacturing plant. It was my task to secure the resources to actually build and operate the plant.
>
> At this time in China's opening there was no real market for me to gather everything I needed to run even a small, labour-intensive manufacturing plant. Many resource decisions such as the supply of electricity, the supply of building materials to build the facility, and even the supply of the plastics and other raw materials to make the toys, were still centrally allocated.
>
> Fortunately, I was not the only one who had wanted to develop manufacturing operations in Shenzhen. Through my associates from Shanghai, I was introduced to various officials in Shenzhen. Over time, I began to know these officials. Whenever I visited their offices, I was sure to bring along a gift, such as foreign wine or cigarettes or other items, often secured for me by my cousin in Hong Kong. This practice of gift-giving was nothing out of the ordinary in China at this time. Instead it would be more unusual if I hadn't brought gifts. I also hosted these officials to dinners at festive occasions. It was a nice way of thanking the officials for their service to the country, since they were paid so poorly by the government.
>
> Occasionally, there was pressure on me to deliver a bit more, especially once our operations started and we were known as being modestly successful, but I resisted this. I wanted to do what was necessary to maintain a good relationship, and to be fair and operate by normal practices, but I didn't want to engage in any overtly unusual practices.

BACK TO THE UNITED STATES

Mr. Biswas, Mr. Lee and Mr. Lai all agreed that what they were doing was not really different from tipping in the United States. They merely paid a small proportion of their full costs to ensure faster and better assistance from service staff in the government. Surely this could not be wrong?

Discussion questions

1 What is the definition of corruption? Is tipping in the private sector corruption? Why or why not?

2 Why do Mr. Lee, Mr. Biswas, and Mr. Lai have such difficulties understanding the practice of tipping? Should it not be second nature to know how to tip?

3 Is what Mr. Biswas does in India corruption? Why or why not?

4 Is what Mr. Lee does in Indonesia corruption? Why or why not?

5 Is what Mr. Lai does in China corruption? Why or why not?

6 Is corruption good or bad? Can it be both? Be prepared to defend your answer. Can this answer be used to develop a company policy for guiding its employees in their business decisions when operating domestically or abroad?

FROM INSOLVENCY TO WORLD LEADERSHIP: ROLLS ROYCE IS DEVELOPING AND EXPLOITING CAPABILITIES

Klaus E. Meyer
University of Bath

BRITAIN'S LONELY HIGH FLYER[1]

Rolls-Royce (RR) sticks out from the crowd: It is a rare case of a large British company leading in a high technology industry, aircraft engines. Although Britain was the cradle of the industrial revolution in the 19th century, it has, more than other European countries, shifted in the latter part of the 20th century to a service economy. The share of manufacturing in GDP fell to as little as 16 per cent in 2007, making RR look like the leftover of a bygone era. In fact, RR effectively went bankrupt in 1971, and was taken over by the government. Yet, since privatization in 1997 it went from strength to strength rising to second place behind General Electric (GE) in the market for civil aircraft engines, supplying the largest aircraft in the world, Boeing 787 and Airbus A350.

How did RR achieve its leadership position in such adverse conditions? This case traces the history of the company in search of the roots of its long-term success. Before we start, we need one clarification: In the 21st century, RR does not make cars – the famous Rolls-Royce motorcar brand is now owned by BMW of Germany.

This case was written by *Professor Klaus Meyer* of the University of Bath on the basis of archival sources. It is intended to be used as a basis for classroom discussion rather than to illustrate appropriate or inappropriate handling of managerial situations. © Klaus Meyer, 2010, Reprinted with permission.

ENTREPRENEURIAL ORIGINS[2]

Rolls-Royce was founded in 1904 by two entrepreneurs, Henry Royce, a perfectionist engineer, and Charles Rolls, a persuasive salesman. From the outset, RR integrated Royce's perfectionist approach and his attention to detail with Rolls' ability to relate customers' wishes and engineering feasibility shaped the credo of the company. Soon the media called their cars 'the best cars in the world'.

World War One (WWI) changed the priorities for RR. It started constructing aero engines, initially under a licence from Renault, but soon based on Royce's own engine designs. He drew on his extensive experience of building engines for motorcars, but needed major innovations because it takes far more energy to keep an aircraft in the air, than to keep a car rolling along the road. His success helped both the firm and nation: RR built the engines for half of all WWI aircraft of the Allies.

In the 1920s, the car sector boomed, and RR developed a highly sought after premium brand known for both the reliability of its engines and the originality of its designs. Its leading position was further strengthened by the acquisition of Bentley in 1931. However, technologies for aircraft and cars increasingly evolved along different trajectories, such that the synergies between the two lines of business declined. This case focuses on the aircraft engine business.

Competition increased during the 1920s, especially from US manufacturers. The main product at the time, an engine called *Merlin*, used a piston technology similar to that used in cars, but scaled up to produce much higher levels of power needed in aviation. The *Merlin* reached its peak during World War 2 (WWII, when 165 000 of RR's *Merlin* engines helped the Allied war efforts, of which 55 000 were build under license by Packard in the USA. Royce's philosophy of building ever better engines yielding constant improvements compelled the company forward. This philosophy of perfection established by the founder continued as the core of the company's corporate culture long after Royce's death in 1930.

In the early 1930s, an independent engineer, Frank Whittle, invented a completely new form of engine, the jet engine. In 1941, his first plane powered by a jet engine took to the air, and in 1943, RR took over Whittle's entrepreneurial operation. By the end of the war, the new jet-engine technology had largely replaced the traditional piston engines, and RR was leading in this technology.

COMPETITION AND INDUSTRY CONSOLIDATION[3]

After WWII, RR focused on the fast growing civilian airline sector. Its *Avon* engine became the first gas turbine to power fare-paying passenger services across the Atlantic. However, US-competitor Pratt & Whitney also invested in advanced gas-turbine technologies, notably with a new technology for turbine fan blades, and was able to leapfrog RR in the civilian airlines market. Losing its leadership in this market in the 1950s taught RR two lessons that, according to later CEO Ralph Robbins, shaped the strategic thinking over the next generation: First, 'engines must be sized for the world market and for a wide range of applications' and, second, 'once introduced, they must be developed continually'.[4] With long development cycles for new models, new technologies have often been researched several years, or even decades, before their introduction to the market.

The 1950s and 1960s saw a rapid consolidation of the UK aero engine industry from seven independent manufacturers to just one. The process was completed when RR acquired Bristol Siddeley in 1966 for £63.6 million, in part to prevent a link-up between Bristol Siddeley and their prime competitor, Pratt & Whitney.

This acquisition, however, tied up considerable financial resources because Bristol Siddeley owned shares in other businesses, and it took RR a while to sell them off to recover the costs of the acquisition. With that acquisition, RR had secured its position as number 1 manufacturer of aero engines in the UK – and in Europe. In the late 1950s, RR also became involved with nuclear energy, designing and manufacturing the reactors for the British nuclear submarine fleet.[5]

Yet, in this industry competition was already taking place on a global scale. The American competitors were flying ahead, in part because of government support. From the 1920s Pratt & Whittney had benefited from government-funded research and subsidies to aerospace industry. During WWII, the British handed their American allies jet-engine technology, which allowed GE to enter the aircraft engine industry in 1941. Dual licensing requirements by the US military let to this technology being shared with Pratt & Whittney from 1947 onwards. Both American firms took up these new ideas and advanced their own, even more advanced, jet engines. The technology received during WWII became the basis for GE's next generation turbo-fan engines, which it supplied to the US navy and air force, the biggest customer for military aircraft. In the 1960s, GE became the world's biggest aircraft engine manufacturer. Meanwhile, Pratt & Whittney became the prime supplier of engines to the rapidly growing American commercial airlines.

In the 1960s, RR was trying to catch up with its American competitors. It focused on bringing out the best of British engineering: A creed of engineering excellence guided the company, and it was reproduced generation after generation through recruitment and internal training. Employees tended to join the company young, and stayed with the company for most of their working life. The top management were mostly internally promoted engineers who took great pride in their history and their engineering skills. The pursuit of engineering excellence became the core of RR's organizational culture, and informed key decisions – excessively so, according to some commentators who felt that too little attention was paid to timing and cost considerations.

AN AMBITION TOO FAR[6]

In the early 1960s, RR started developing a new generation of turbofan engines. For larger aircraft, the two-shaft design of turbojet engines hit its technical limitations, and RR focused on a three-shaft configuration, which was expected to develop better aerodynamics, and thus be suitable for larger scale engines. In this development work, RR could draw on patents taken out in 1945 for a three-shaft engine design.

In 1967, RR started negotiations with Lockheed to supply their new L-1011 aircraft, which were widely expected to provide RR with the long sought break through into the American market. RR promised to develop a technological superior engine that was cheaper to run and easier to maintain, and fitted the demands of the next generation of aircraft. Eager to sign the deal, RR agreed to deliver the new engine at a price that undercut its American rivals: £200 000 compared to £250 000 (GE) and £280 000 (Pratt & Whitney). Lockheed announced the deal in March 1968 with an initial order of 450 engines, known as RB211 at the time. The news was well received by British financial markets and politicians.

However, the development of the new engine was a mammoth task, and entailed considerable economic risk. Not only was the new engine considerably bigger than RR's existing engine designs, it was in a different shape and thus required major investments in new machinery and new welding techniques. The development of the RB211 became RR's prime objective, and about half of its 84 000 strong workforce was allocated to the task. The British government supported the effort with initially £47 million of 'launch aid' (effectively an R&D subsidy).

At the time, the three shaft design of the RB211 was still an unproven technology, and it was difficult to raise capital for such a long-term and high risk project. The challenge increased with changes in Lockheed's design of the aircraft, which triggered needs for further adjustments to the engine. The aircraft became larger and heavier during the development process, which required even stronger engines. At the same time, RR encountered technological problems. The envisaged new carbon fibre fan blades failed the so-called 'bird-strike test', thus fan blades had to be redesigned, which increased both the weight and the costs of the engine. Various technical problems caused delays, and raised the prospect of having to pay severe late-delivery penalties.

In late 1969, the stress of the technological development started hitting financial numbers, and in 1970 RR reported £10 million in losses. At the same time, the costs of developing the RB211 surged: Initial estimates in September 1968 suggested £68 million, yet this number increased to £170.3 million in September 1970 and to 202.7 million in January 1971. The estimated production costs increased from originally £154 000 to £237 000 in 1970, which would translate in a loss of £37 000 for each engine sold.

When the crisis became apparent in September 1970, a rescue package was negotiated that included further £42 million of launch aid from the British government, and loans from the Bank of England and commercial banks. A turnaround plan was initiated, yet it was already too late. On February 4, 1971 RR went into receivership. Eventually, the attempt to develop the RB211 for the Lockheed drove RR into bankruptcy.

GOVERNMENT TO THE RESCUE[7]

Faced with the possible bankruptcy of one of the largest and prestigious British manufacturing enterprises, the Conservative government decided to nationalize RR. This move was motivated primarily by the importance of RR as a defence contractor, which made it a national interest. RR's car business was separated in 1973 and privatized again. Initially, cancellation of the RB211 was considered, which would have implied a massive downsizing of the company. However, the government soon thought better of it, and provided new launch aid to RR to continue its development plans, while renegotiating the terms of the contract with Lockheed. The government appointed new board members to join RR who were sympathetic to the RB211, but also had a sharp eye for the company's finances. As one insider later described it:

> 'the first thing we had to learn was that the company was not just a playground for engineers to amuse themselves'.[8]

After tough initial negotiations, the government gave the management of RR operational freedom to develop the company – and the RB211 programme – while retaining ultimate control over strategic decisions.

When the Labour government came to power in 1974, RR was placed under the National Enterprise Board, which interfered more directly in the management of what was now a state-owned enterprise. RR's management resisted the added bureaucracy, and the relationship with the Minister of Trade and Industry remained tense throughout the Labour government. Even so, RR was able to push the technological development of the RB211 engine, and repeatedly received financial support in the form of 'launch aid' from the government.

PRIVATIZATION[9]

When Margaret Thatcher was elected Prime Minister in 1979, the privatization of companies like RR was given a high policy priority. However, it took another eight years until the company could be turned over to private ownership. The RB211 had gone into production eventually, but the civil aviation industry was hit by a severe recession in the early 1980s. RR recorded losses of £58 million in 1979, which accelerated to a loss of £193 million in 1983. In 1983 and 1984 it sold only 126 new engines, much less than a 'worst case' prediction of 350 published in 1982. RR drastically cut its workforce from 62 000 to 41 000, while the government provided further launch aid of £437 million (of which £118 million was repaid from sales levies) in the 1980s.

At the height of the new crisis, RR considered exiting as an independent competitor from the large scale engine market. It entered a collaborative development with GE in 1984. RR took a 15 per cent stake in GEs latest high thrust development project, while GE took a 15 per cent stake in the development of a new medium-size engine aimed for the Boeing 757. However, in a recovering aircraft market, RR's leadership soon realized that they might not have to give up just yet. Engineers found new ways to increase the thrust of their engines without increasing the fan diameter. By 1986, RR was marketing its own high-thrust engine in direct competition to the joint project with GE. Understandably, the Americans were not amused, and the collaboration was soon terminated.

New engine developments during the 1980s were building on the designs and technologies of the 1970s and 1930s – and patents obtained back in the 1930s. The experience of the 1970s taught RR that the complexity of the technologies necessitated that new engine programmes be grounded in the R&D experience of the development team, and in previously demonstrated technologies. Thus, RR pursued a strategy of continuous development of technologies, well ahead of their market introduction.[10]

Eventually, RR started making profits again: In 1986, it recorded pre-tax profits of £120 million. In 1987, after 16 years under government ownership and massive financial injections, RR was privatized. The flotation raised £1.36 billion for the government, a handsome return on its investment (estimated to be £833 million since nationalization). The government, however, retained a golden share in the company (which it still holds) because of the national defence interests in the company. Foreign ownership was initially limited to 25 per cent, but under pressure of EU competition policy this was raised to 28.5 per cent in 1989 and to 49.5 per cent in 1998.

MORE RESTRUCTURING AND TAKE-OFF[11]

In the first years after privatization, RR experienced spectacular growth as its three-decade long investment in the three-shaft jet engine technology of the RB211 finally paid off. Its market share in the civil aircraft market grew from 5 per cent at the time of privatization to 20 per cent in 1990. Under new ownership, the strategy focused on core businesses, while more activities were outsourced. New management practices such as lean manufacturing, total quality management and business process reengineering aimed to cut costs and enhance productivity. Spending on R&D continued to rise in absolute values, staying at 6 per cent to 7 per cent throughout the 1990s.

Technologies for civil and military use increasingly diverged due to different demands to the aircraft. However, they would still draw on common underlying technologies. In earlier decades military advances often drove civilian innovation. By the 1990s, the reverse was often true, as civilian aircraft became more and more ambitious in their size and reach.

In 1989, RR acquired Newcastle-based Northern Engineering Industries, a power station equipment and heavy engineering group. This acquisition launched a diversification strategy that added gas turbines for use in energy and marine uses. New engines for the maritime sector, especially the navy, utilized technologies developed in aircraft related research, for example advances in fan blade technologies.

With continued emphasis on technology development, RR's stock market performance from 1987 to 2001 lagged the development of the stock market. The management was willing to accept lower short term financial performance, and value recognized by the stock market, by focusing on building its technologies and market positions.

During the 1990s, the industry went through another recession that exposed RR's low profitability. RR responded by further restructuring of its operations, including (from 1993 onwards) the layoff of 2900 people and the closure of 6 of the company's 12 manufacturing plants in the UK.

The privatized RR was a very focused company – limited to the largest segments of the aero engine market, and thus highly dependent on the fluctuations of this market. At the same time, RR was much smaller than its two American rivals and lacked the possibility to utilize its technologies across segments.[12] To diversify its activities and to utilize its technologies in a broader market, RR entered a JV with BMW of Germany in 1990. The JV was to develop new engines for two specific segments of the aircraft industry: medium-sized 100-seat aircraft and long-range business jets. The JV became a market leader in the business jet market. The regional jet market, on the other hand, declined when a major customer, Fokker, ceased business, while new entrants such as Embraer opted for a new technology supplied by GE. However, BMW-RR achieved a turnover well ahead of initial projections of US\$ 727 million in 1999. Eventually, BMW decided to refocus its strategy. RR bought the JV in 1999 and renamed it Rolls-Royce Deutschland.

ORGANIC AND ACQUISITIVE GROWTH

From the late 1990s, RR shifted its strategic priorities by applying it to engine technologies in the power industry and the marine sector. By now RR was a highly profitable business with a proven technology and a strong order pipeline, which made it much easier to raise capital on the stock market.

After regaining a profitable position in the industry, RR pursued growth both organically and by acquiring other businesses. In 1995, RR acquired Allison Engine Company in Indiana, USA for £328 million, following a cooperation that dated back to the 1960s. Allison strengthened RR's position in the USA, the world's largest aviation market, and provided access to the US military, the largest buyer of aircraft engines. However, the acquisition was subject to a special investigation into its national security implications, and Royce Rolls was required to manage Allison as a separate company and under a proxy board. Indiana henceforth became the hub of RR's North American operations employing over 9000 people.

RR expanded its business in two areas where its knowledge of building engines to highest standards was believed to be applicable, marine propulsion, power generation (especially nuclear power) and gas pumping. Navies around the globe shifted from piston engines to gas turbines to increase the power generated on limited space, while reducing maintenance costs. RR achieved leadership in this technology and supplied more than 50 navies around the globe.

In 1999, RR went on a shopping spree acquiring several complementary engineering businesses. The largest was Vickers, a company with a long-standing engineering tradition almost equal to that of RR. For £576 million in cash, RR obtained, in particular, capabilities for marine power systems, which enabled RR to pursue a leadership position for commercial ship engines. Further acquisitions in the same year were the rotating compression business of Cooper Cameron, and National Automotive, a service and repair facility on Oakland, California.

In the early 2000s, the marine sector has been the fastest growing division of RR, increasing turnover from £275 million in 1997 to £2.2 billion in 2007 (see Appendix). The shipbuilding industry has moved increasingly to Asia, with first Korean shipyards taking the lead, and more recently Chinese shipyards emerging as major players. Consequently, RR moved the headquarters of its marine division to Singapore to be closer to the main hubs of the shipbuilding industry in 2009. Competitor Wärtsilä made a similar move to Shanghai in 2008.

The energy division received a major boost in 2008 with the announcement that RR would enter the nuclear power industry. This coincided with a policy shift of the British government. Reversing its earlier policy, the Labour government announced that several new nuclear power stations be build in the UK. to cope with the diminishing capacity available in traditional coal and gas fired power stations. Politicians quickly added that such a major investment should be driven by British engineering. Yet, not having built any nuclear power stations for over two decades, such competences needed to be regained and upgraded to the state-of-the art.

COMPETITIVE DYNAMICS OF THE 21st CENTURY

The dynamics of competition in RR's core business, aero engines, shifted in two major ways around the beginning of the new millennium. First, the awareness and regulation on environmental matters has greatly increased. Thus, the airline industry is under pressure to reduce its emissions, and this pressure is passed onto aircraft manufacturers and their suppliers: Can you produce engines that produce less greenhouse gas emissions?

Second, the manufacture and servicing of engines is becoming more tightly integrated.[13] RR engineers are monitoring the performance of RR engines in real time: data collected from engines are directly transmitted from the aircraft to the RR service centre. In case of malfunctions, the service centre initiates corrections or sends instructions for work to be done once the aircraft has landed. Thus, maintenance (and if necessary repairs) can be completed more quickly, and the aircraft is much faster up in the air again. This new form of servicing blurs the boundaries between manufacturing and servicing, and opens new business opportunities to RR to exploit its competences. Independent maintenance businesses would not be able to draw on RR's extensive engineering competences and its databases. In 2008, the aero divisions earned more money through after sales services and spare parts than through the manufacture of engines, making the business less sensitive to the volatilities of the aircraft construction industry. More than half the engines manufactured by RR are sold with an after-sales service contract promising stable revenues for decades to come.

The importance of developing capabilities for the engineering sector was recognized by the British government, some would argue belatedly, in 2008. A new strategy was announced by Lord Mandelson, the Business Secretary providing funding of £151.5 million to manufacturing in technology-driven fields, of which 86 per cent is being channelled through RR. Recognizing the pivotal role of RR, Mandelson said: 'You have to recognize also that RR is making a strong commitment to the UK and is a global leader in what it does'.

In November 2010, RR was in the media for the wrong sorts of reasons. The engine of an Airbus A800 exploded in in flight after taking off from Singapore en route to Australia. The media quickly traced to fault to the Trent 900 engine made by RR, and RR's share price fell by 10 per cent that day.

Discussion questions

From the perspective of the institution-based view:

1   How did WWI and WWII influence the long term development of the company?

2   How did US defence policy influence the development of RR?

3   How did UK government policy influence the development of RR?

From the perspective of resource-based view:

1   Which resources are the sources of competitive advantage of RR in 2009?

2   What dynamic capabilities does RR have that have helped at different stages of its development?

3   If there was a new entrant in the market for aircraft engines, where would you expect it to come from?

APPENDIX

Figure 2.1a

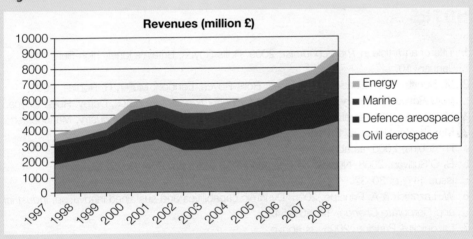

Source: Rolls-Royce Annual Reports, various years.

Figure 2.1b

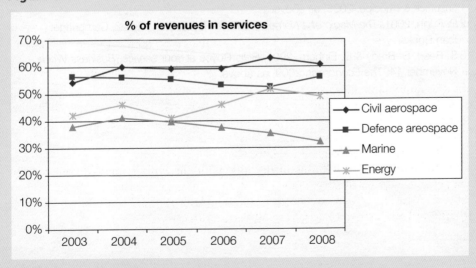

Source: Rolls-Royce Annual Reports, various years.

Figure 2.1c

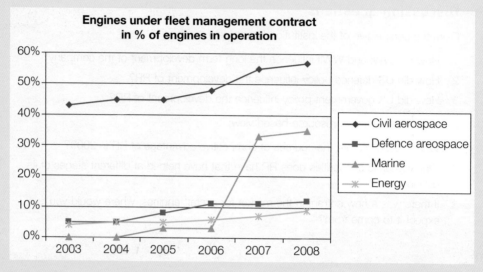

Engines under fleet management contract in % of engines in operation

Source: Rolls-Royce Annual Reports, various years.

NOTES

1 Title of an article in *The Economist*, 2009, Rolls-Royce: Britain's lonely high-flier, January 10.
2 M. Donne, 1981, Leader of the Skies: Rolls-Royce, London: Muller; R. Robins, 2005, *Rolls-Royce Centenary Lecture: Striving for perfection*, lecture notes, Derby: Rolls: Royce.
3 M. Donne, 1981, as above; K. Hayward, 1989, *The British Aircraft Industry*, Manchester: Manchester University Press.
4 R. Robins, 2005, as above.
5 B. O'Sullivan, 2008, Nuclear co-operation – 50 years no, *Rolls-Royce Magazine*, issue 117, p. 30–32.
6 W. Lazonick & A. Principe, 2005, Dynamic capabilities and sustained innovation, *Industrial and Corporate Change,* 14: 501–542.
7 Lazonick & Principe, 2005, *as above.*
8 K. Hayward, 1989, *as above* (p. 140).
9 Lazonick & Principe, 2005, as above.
10 R. Robins, 2005, as above (p. 24).
11 Lazonick & Principe, 2005, as above.
12 P. Pugh, 2001, *The Magic of a Name: The Rolls-Royce Story Part 2*, Cambridge: Icon Books.
13 S. Reed, D. Brady & B. Einhorn, 2005, Rolls-Royce at your service, *Business Week*, November 14; *The Economist*, 2009, as above.

VANGUARD SECURITY CORPORATION: INTERNATIONAL TRANSACTION DILEMMA

F. John Mathis
Director of the Global Financial Services Center
John G. Keat
Emeritus

A late spring day was dawning as Peter Levin, Vanguard Security Corporation's treasurer, arrived at the office to meet with his team to finalize a key decision. Vanguard Security was involved in a large sale to an American buyer, and Peter had to decide which of several foreign exchange hedging strategies was appropriate, if any. Sally Smith, Peter's bank relationship manager, and the bank's chief foreign exchange advisor had provided him with several possibilities. They were due to arrive in about an hour, giving Peter time to first meet with his team to consider which options would be best for the company. The urgency for the meeting was due to an unanticipated drop in currency exchange rates, which had already cost VSC a large sum of money.

COMPANY BACKGROUND AND THE TRANSACTION

Vanguard Security Corporation (VSC), a European corporation headquartered in Portugal, was founded in the early 1990s as a financial security provider for corporations with exposure to Internet fraud. Its main clients had been major commercial banks in Europe, but now it had an opportunity to enter the US market. VSC was primarily a computer software and hardware systems company with a strong reputation in the financial services industry as one of the leading providers as well as one of the most expensive providers.

VSC had experienced rapid expansion in revenues and profits during its early growth stages. However, increased competition from several companies in Asia had cut into its market and, as a result, revenues and profitability had deteriorated during the past several years. Many of VSC's top managers were still with the company, but when the company went public just prior to the bursting of the tech bubble in late 1999, several founding owners cashed out, and new management was recruited. Subsequently, on several occasions, VSC had been forced to cut its prices and historically high margins in order to retain customers. To remain competitive, the company had also begun to acquire long-term debt to fund research and build production capacity by purchasing new equipment. Because several private equity companies had been showing interest in VSC, senior management was increasingly concerned that they might be replaced. The US was viewed as a possible new market for VSC to deploy some of its existing technology and build revenue by developing a new customer base.

Barely a week ago, Peter had been scrambling to finalize VSC's year-end income statement and balance sheet (Table 3.1a). The American company, based in Boston, had insisted that Peter submit VSC's year-end financials before allowing it to bid for the project because they wanted to make sure that if VSC won the bid, they would have the financial resources to complete the project on time. This had delayed VSC's bid on the new project.

THE BID

VSC had bid on a rather large project in the United States which, if accepted, could help reverse a declining net income trend. The bid was for the design, construction, installation, testing and provision of a six-year service and warranty agreement. If the US company accepted VSC's bid, which included a 10 per cent down payment upon acceptance, the contract specified that the first part of the project must be completed within six months. The warranty would be paid for in equal annual installments over the life of the contract at the beginning of each year. Most of the components of the bid would have to be built specifically to meet American standards and be able to interface with the system currently in use by the US finance company. Also, under the terms of the agreement, VSC would have to secure a performance bond from a third-party vendor if awarded the bid. The performance bond would cost 0.35 per cent of the contract value according to Sally Smith, VSC's bank relationship manager. Under the terms of the performance bond, the US client would be paid the contract value if VSC failed to deliver.

The bid was tendered on April 1, and on May 15, VSC was notified that they had been awarded the contract (Table 3.1b). In accordance with the terms of the contract, the US company had e-mailed and faxed a letter of acceptance. The US company also had notified VSC that it would be wiring 10 per cent of the purchase price, also as stipulated in the contract, on the morning of May 16.

The remainder of the agreed price was due at the time the system was installed, tested and certified operational by the American company. The target date for VSC to fulfill the terms of the contract and be paid was November 17, six months from the day the down payment was received. The VSC chief operating officer had

Table 3.1a Sales and income statement

Year Ended Dec. 31	Sales Euros mil.	Net Income Euros mil.
2004	374.2	67.3
2005	401.8	88.4
2006	437.3	83.1
2007	379.9	46.3
2008	307.5	–8.7

Balance Sheet (2008) Assets	Euros mil.
Current assets:	
Cash and securities	2.1
Accounts receivable	122.7
Inventories	20.8
Total current assets	145.6
Property, plant and equipment	
Cost	526.8
Less: Accumulated depreciation	(106.0)
Goodwill and intangibles	209.8
TOTAL ASSETS	776.2
Liabilities	
Current liabilities	
Bank loans	122.0
Accounts payable	33.4
Notes payable	75.6
Long-term liabilities	
Debt	210.0
TOTAL LIABILITIES	441.0
Equity and retained earnings	335.2
TOTAL LIABILITIES AND EQUITY	776.2

verified with his suppliers that there would be no problems meeting this delivery schedule for hardware, although the product was not currently in inventory. Similarly, the software would have to be specially developed but, again, no problems were expected in terms of meeting the agreed-upon delivery schedule. On May 16, Peter Levin verified that VSC had received a funds transfer of US$16.103 million. The remaining, outstanding, balance of US$144.927 million was due on November 17, assuming all the terms and conditions of the contract were satisfied.

In preparing the bid, VSC had allowed for a modest markup of 12 per cent, which is less than what it would have charged normally. However, VSC was

Table 3.1b Bid preparation euro mil.

Design	3.7
Materials	68.9
Labour and installation	6.9
Shipping	1.2
Direct overhead	3.4
Allocation of indirect overhead	1.7
Service and warranty agreement (six years)	12.0
Subtotal	97.8
Markup (12%)	11.7
Total Bid in € mil.	€109.5
Conversion to US$ at April 1 spot rate of US$1.4706 = 1€	
Total Bid in US$ mil.	US$161.03

concerned about its declining net income and wanted to make sure it had a competitively priced bid, including the need to build new components. VSC knew that the quality of its product in the European market was recognized as outstanding. But because the company was not well known in the US, VSC realized that it would have to earn its outstanding brand recognition by proving it could successfully adapt its systems to American standards.

RELATIONSHIP BETWEEN THE US DOLLAR AND THE EURO

On May 16, when VSC's bank received the wire transfer deposit of US$16.103 million, it had to be converted into euros before VSC could begin to use the funds. Between April 1, when the bid was tendered, and May 16, when funds were received by VSC, the euro had appreciated by about 0.74 per cent relative to US currency. The exchange rate was now US$1.4815 = €1. Because of this exchange rate change between April 1 and May 15, VSC received just €10 869 389 million on May 16. This represented a loss of €80 611 due entirely to the drop in the exchange rate, something which VSC had not anticipated. VSC now realized that it had to focus on the value of the final payment of US$144.927 million expected on November 17. The change in the value of the US dollar relative to the euro had resulted because the US Federal Reserve Board of Governors had eased monetary policy and lowered interest rates by another 50 basis points. In contrast, the European Union had decided not to follow this US rate change and had kept its interest rates stable, thus making holding dollars less attractive. Furthermore, in the period ahead, interest rates in Europe were expected to rise, while the opposite was expected to happen in the United States.

Peter knew he had to act to protect the company from adverse exchange rate changes between mid-May and mid-November … but what? He had examined the movement of the US$/€ exchange rate over the previous several months before issuing the tender bid for the project, as reflected in the data in Table 3.1c.

Table 3.1c Exchange rates

Month	End of Period€/US$	End of Period US$/€
April 2007	0.73502	1.3605
May	0.74333	1.3453
June	0.74047	1.3505
July	0.72955	1.3707
August	0.72966	1.3705
September	0.70527	1.4179
October	0.69219	1.4447
November	0.71401	1.4005
December	0.70583	1.4168
January 2008	0.69154	1.4462
February	0.68593	1.4579
March	0.68254	1.4652

The data reflected a significant degree of volatility, with the US dollar both appreciating and depreciating relative to the euro. He saw no reason for this pattern to change. A particularly disconcerting characteristic of the data was that, at times, the US dollar would depreciate consistently against the euro over a period of several months. This meant that he could lose a significant share of the profit built in to his pricing of the project. He had to find a solution because he could not afford to take this risk as his profit margin was not that large. The decision would be made at that morning's meeting, after examining the various options and the economic outlook.

THE DECISION MENU: FOREIGN CURRENCY EXPOSURE MANAGEMENT ALTERNATIVES

The evaluation of expected macroeconomic developments in the United States and Europe confirmed Peter's concerns about a possible depreciation of the US dollar relative to the euro. Indeed, the dollar had depreciated from $1.4606 per euro to $1.4815 per euro during the time the bid was being evaluated by the US client. Further depreciation would reduce the profitability of the project for VSC. It was at this point that the bank's relationship manager for VSC arrived, accompanied by the bank's chief foreign exchange risk management executive. They explained that a foreign currency hedge would be an appropriate response to the expected foreign exchange risk faced by VSC. Since VSC had an outstanding dollar-denominated contract, or receivable, a hedge could be accomplished by any one of the following techniques:

1 **Forward currency contract**
   A forward foreign exchange contract would involve buying a contract
   from the bank committing VSC to deliver the exact amount of US dollars
   they would receive on November 17 from the American company if they
   performed on their agreement with them. The forward contract, if agreed to at

Table 3.1d Macroeconomic data

	2002	2003	2004	2005	2006	2007	2008
Real GDP Growth U.S. %	3.2	3.3	2.1	2.5	3.1	2.1	2.6
Real GDP Growth euro %	1.5	2.8	2.7	2.3	3.3	2.5	2.2
Inflation CPI U.S. %	3.4	3.2	2.6	2.6	1.9	3.4	2.3
Inflation CPI euro %	2.2	2.2	1.8	2	1.8	1.9	2
Unemployment U.S. % of labour force	5.1	4.6	4.6	4.8	4.5	4.7	4.9
Unemployment euro % of labour force	8.5	7.8	7.1	6.7	7.5	6.9	6.6
U.S. Gov't Deficit % GDP %	−3.8	−4.8	−4.6	−3.7	−2.3	−2.7	−2.6
Euro Gov't Deficit % GDP %	−2.5	−3.1	−2.8	−2.4	−1.6	−1	−0.7
U.S. Money Supply Growth % M2	5.6	5.3	4.1	5	6.5	6.5	6.2
Euro Money Supply Growth % M2	6.8	6.3	8.8	8.7	9.4	9	8.5
U.S. Short-term Interest Rates %	3.5	5.2	5.3	5	5.3	5.2	4.3
Euro Short-term Interest Rates %	2.2	3.1	4.1	4.3	3.6	4.3	4.3
U.S. Long-term Interest Rates %	4.3	4.8	4.7	4.8	4.6	4.8	4.3
Euro Long-term Interest Rates %	3.4	3.8	4.2	4.3	3.8	4.2	4.3
U.S. Current Account $ Bil.	−459.6	−522.1	−640.2	−754.9	−811.5	−784.3	−788.3
Euro Current Account $ Bil.	47.3	42.9	109.3	27.9	0.9	−21.2	−48.8
U.S. Financial Account $ Bil.	463.3	520.6	637.4	740.8	808.6	758.8	735
Euro Financial Account $ Bil.	50.3	−75.7	−124.9	−50.8	1.6	35	75
U.S. GDP $ Tril.	10.5	11	11.7	12.4	13.2	14	14.7
Euro GDP € Tril.	7.3	7.4	7.7	8	8.4	8.8	9.2
Euro Relative to U.S.$ Daily Avg.	1.061	0.885	0.805	0.805	0.797	0.745	0.670
US$ Real Effective Exchange Rate 2000 = 100	105.8	95.7	86.5	83.4	83.1	78.4	79.1
Euro Real Effective Exchange Rate 2000 = 100	104.66	115.35	119.93	120.45	121.72	127.87	125.2

Source: OECD and IMF.

the meeting, would guarantee that VSC could deliver US dollars to the bank and receive euros on November 17 at today's quoted six-month forward rate of US$1.4650 = 1€.

2 Foreign currency futures contract

A futures contact for euros is a standardized agreement to purchase or sell a specific amount of currency on a specific date. A euro futures contract, usually arranged through the Chicago Mercantile Exchange in the US – in this case, for €125 000 – could be purchased to buy or sell currency at the end of March, June, September, and/or December. The broker's fee for the purchase was US$50.00. The buyer or seller of the contract had to take or make delivery of the currency, and the position could only be eliminated if the futures contract was offset. The September futures price on that spring day was US$1.4635 = 1€, and the December contract price was US$1.4655 = 1€.

3 Foreign currency options

This currency hedging instrument would give VSC the right to either purchase (call) or sell (put) a currency at a specified price on a specific date in the future if it is a European-style option, or at anytime in the future if it is an American-style option. The purchaser of an option has the right, but not the obligation, to exercise the option. The purchaser can either receive the currency (call) or deliver the currency (put) if choosing to exercise the option, or allow the option to expire unexercised. The seller, or writer, of an option, on the other hand, must stand ready to fulfill an option obligation and surrender the currency on demand (call) or receive the currency on demand (put).

Since VSC had a contract to be paid in US dollars on November 17, it could hedge this foreign currency exposure by buying a US dollar put option or writing a US dollar call option. Buying a US dollar put option would protect VSC from any unfavourable downward movement in the US dollar exchange rate relative to the euro. Writing a US dollar call option would allow VSC to benefit if there was little or no change in the exchange rate of the US dollar against the euro. The purchase of a US dollar option would require an option premium to be paid at the time the contract was issued. Currently, the 180-day currency option premium on a strike price (or exercise price) of US\$1.4699 = 1€ was: for a call premium US\$0.03256 per unit, and for a put premium US\$0.0215 per unit. If VSC wrote a call option, it would receive the premium but might be called upon to exchange dollars for euros at a disadvantageous rate.

4 Tunnel forwards

One alternative for VSC which would not cost the company anything up front but would give it some exchange rate protection was a tunnel forward. This was a contractual agreement identifying a specific exchange rate band or defined range within which VSC would have to exchange currencies on a specific future date. The upper and lower limits of the range are like settlement rates if the actual exchange rate exceeds the limits of the range of the tunnel. Miller, VSC's banker, indicated that such a zero cost tunnel could be established with the strike on the euro put set at €0.7105 (US\$1.4075 = 1€) and the strike on the euro call set at €\$0.6429 (US\$1.5556 = 1€).

5 Foreign currency loan

This product would create a US\$ obligation 180 days in the future, which would be discharged by the final dollar contract payment to VSC in November. VSC could borrow today the present value of the dollars to be received in November. The dollars would be immediately exchanged for euros at the current spot rate, and either be used to fund working capital needs, pay down debt or invested in a euro financial instrument. Thus, VSC could borrow US\$ from the bank at today's meeting and convert the loan proceeds to euros to help finance the completion of the contract. The dollars received on November 17 from completing the contract would discharge the dollar loan, interest and principal. Any exchange rate gains or losses on the receivable due to a change in the value of the US\$ per euro exchange rate would be offset by matching losses or gains on the US\$ per euro value of the loan.

In his role as chief foreign exchange advisor, the banker believed that a 180-day loan in US dollars could be made today at a rate of 2.0 per cent above the US dollar prime rate of 6.00 per cent per annum plus an arrangement fee of 0.125 per cent. The comparable 'prime' euro interest rate was 5.50 per cent, with VSC receiving a spread of 1.85 per cent in the euro market for short-term investments.

6 Presale of foreign contract

Peter also knew that it was possible to presell the balance due on the foreign contract, or receivable, at a discount as an alternative method of hedging exchange rate risk and raising funds to help VSC finance the completion of the project. This alternative was different from a foreign currency loan in that it would not add to VSC's already large outstanding debt. The discount, or interest rate, for the presale was fixed for the 180-day period at US$ LIBOR (London Inter-Bank Offered Rate), currently at 4.15 per cent per annum plus a credit risk spread for VSC of 1.8 per cent. The arrangement fee for setting up this transaction was a flat upfront fee of 0.5 per cent. The current euro six-month LIBOR was 4.35 per cent plus a comparable credit spread.

Regarding the longer-term six-year service agreement, VSC's bankers recommended exploring the following options: check if VSC had any offsetting US dollar or parallel foreign currency payments (e.g., Canadian $) to match the US dollar receivable or determine if it made sense to use back-to-back or parallel loan arrangements, or cross-currency US dollar-euro swap to offset the expected US dollar receivable.

CURRENT ECONOMIC PERFORMANCE: EUROPE AND UNITED STATES

Economic activity was finally gaining momentum in Europe following a long period of sub par performance while, in contrast, the US economy, which had been growing at a healthy pace, was beginning to show signs of weakness. Neither region had had serious inflation problems for some time. Unemployment continued to be more of a problem in Europe than in the United States. However, in the period ahead, inflation and interest rates in Europe were expected to rise, while the opposite was happening in the United States. The US economic outlook had been revised downward from earlier forecasts to about 2.5 per cent, which was a slight improvement over the previous year's performance. The result would be a slight rise in unemployment and further easing in upward pressure on prices.

The US balance of payments was stabilizing following a brief period of improvement as export growth accelerated. Meanwhile, the US dollar, which had been volatile sporadically relative to the euro, was now showing signs of depreciating, reflecting weakening confidence triggered by the sub-prime banking crisis, uncertainties about US policy management and an upcoming election which would bring about a change in leadership. US monetary policy had been eased and is supportive towards restimulating growth. Earlier this year, interest rates began to decline as the Fed's policy shifted to ease credit conditions. In contrast, Europe has experienced relative stability in money supply growth and interest rates. Even so, Europe continues to face 'digestion problems' – politically and economically – absorbing all the newly entering countries into the euro zone.

Discussion questions

1   What type of international business transaction is VSC planning to undertake, and what expected international financial flows are involved in this transaction?

2   What risks are associated with these expected financial flows.

3   How can VSC protect itself against these risks using real or financial hedging?

AGRANA: FROM A LOCAL SUPPLIER TO A GLOBAL PLAYER

Erin Pleggenkuhle-Miles
University of Texas at Dallas

Headquartered and listed in Vienna, Austria, AGRANA is one of the leading suppliers to the multinational brands around the world. With revenues of US$2.6 billion and capitalization of $1.4 billion, AGRANA is the world's leader in fruit preparations and one of Central Europe's leading sugar and starch companies.

AGRANA was formed in 1988 as a holding company for three sugar factories and two starch factories in Austria. In the last two decades, it has become a global player with 52 production plants in 26 countries with three strategic pillars: sugar, starch and fruit. AGRANA supplies most of its fruit preparations and fruit juice concentrates to the dairy, baked products, ice-cream and soft-drink industries. In other words, you may not know AGRANA, but you have probably enjoyed many AGRANA products. How did AGRANA grow from a local supplier serving primarily the small Austrian market to a global player?

FROM CENTRAL AND EASTERN EUROPE TO THE WORLD

In many ways, the growth of AGRANA mirrors the challenges associated with regional integration in Europe and then with global integration of multinational

This case was written by Erin Pleggenkuhle-Miles (University of Texas at Dallas) under the supervision of Professor Mike Peng. © Erin Pleggenkuhle-Miles. Reprinted with permission.

production in the last two decades. There are two components of European integration. First, EU integration accelerated throughout Western Europe in the 1990s. This means that firms such as AGRANA, based in a relatively small country, Austria (with a population of 8.2 million), needed to grow its economies of scale to fend off the larger rivals from other European countries blessed with larger home country markets and hence larger scale economies. Second, since 1989, Central and Eastern European (CEE)[1] countries, formerly off limits to Western European firms, have opened their markets. For Austrian firms such as AGRANA, the timing of CEE's arrival as potential investment sites was fortunate. Facing powerful rivals from larger Western European countries but being constrained by its smaller home market, AGRANA has aggressively expanded its foreign direct investment (FDI) throughout CEE. Most CEE countries have become EU members since then. As a result, CEE provides a much larger playground for AGRANA, allowing it to enhance its scale, scope and thus competitiveness.

At the same time, multinational production by global giants such as Nestlé, Con-Agra, Coca-Cola, PepsiCo and Danone has been growing by leaps and bounds, thus reaching more parts of the world. Emerging as a strong player not only in Austria and CEE but also in the EU, AGRANA has further 'chased' its corporate buyers by investing in and locating supplier operations around the world. This strategy has allowed AGRANA to cater better to the expanding needs of its corporate buyers.

Until 1918, Vienna had been capital of the Austro-Hungarian Empire, whose territory not only included today's Austria and Hungary but also numerous CEE regions. Although formal ties were lost (and in fact cut during the Cold War), informal ties through cultural, linguistic and historical links had never disappeared. These ties have been reactivated since the end of the Cold War, thus fuelling a rising interest among Austrian firms to enter CEE.

Overall, from an institution-based view, it seems natural that Austrian firms would be pushed by pressures arising from the EU integration and pulled by the attractiveness of CEE. However, among hundreds of Austrian firms that have invested in CEE, not all are successful and some have failed miserably. Then, how can AGRANA emerge as a winner from its forays into CEE? The answer boils down to AGRANA's firm-specific resources and capabilities, a topic that we turn to next.

PRODUCT-RELATED DIVERSIFICATION

AGRANA has long been associated with sugar and starch production in CEE. Until 2003, AGRANA's focus on the sugar and starch industries worked well. However, the reorganization of the European sugar market by the European Union (EU) Commission in recent years motivated AGRANA to look in new directions for future growth opportunities.[2] This new direction – fruit – has since become the third and largest division at AGRANA (see Table 4.1a).

How to diversify? As a well-known processor in the sugar and starch industries, AGRANA wanted to capitalize on its core competence – the refining and processing of agricultural raw materials (sugar beets, cereals and potatoes). To capitalize on its accumulated knowledge of the refinement process, AGRANA decided to diversify into the fruit-processing sector (Table 4.1b gives a brief description of each of the three current divisions). First, entry into the fruit sector ensured additional growth and complemented AGRANA's position in the starch sector. Since the Starch Division was already a supplier to the food and beverage industry, this allowed AGRANA to benefit from those relationships previously developed when it entered

Table 4.1a AGRANA plant locations

Segment	1988–1989	2002–2003	2006–2007
Sugar	4	15	10
Starch	2	5	4
Fruit	0	0	39
Total	**6**	**20**	**53**

Source: AGRANA company presentation, June 2007, http://www.agrana.com and AGRANA International website, http://www.agrana.com.

Table 4.1b AGRANA divisions

Sugar: AGRANA Sugar maintains nine sugar factories in five EU countries (Austria, Czech Republic, Slovakia, Hungary and Romania) and is one of the leading sugar companies in Central Europe. The sugar AGRANA processes is sold to both consumers (via the food trade) and manufacturers in the food and beverage industries. Within this sector, AGRANA maintains customer loyalty by playing off its competitive strengths, which include high product quality, matching product to customer needs, customer service and just-in-time logistics.

Starch: AGRANA operates four starch factories in three countries (Austria, Hungary and Romania). The products are sold to the food and beverage, paper, textile, construction chemicals, pharmaceutical and cosmetic industries. To maintain long-term client relationships, AGRANA works in close collaboration with its customers and develops 'made-to-measure solutions' for its products. As a certified manufacturer of organic products, AGRANA is Europe's leading supplier of organic starch.

Fruit: This third segment was added to the core sugar and starch segments to ensure continued growth during a time when AGRANA reached the limits allowed by competition law in the sugar segment. The Fruit Division operates 39 production plants across every continent. Like the Starch Division, the Fruit Division does not make any consumer products, limiting itself to supplying manufacturers of brand-name food products. Its principal focus is on fruit preparations and the manufacturing of fruit juice concentrates. Fruit preparations are special customized products made from a combination of high-grade fruits and sold in liquid or lump form. Manufacturing is done in the immediate vicinity of AGRANA customers to ensure a fresh product. Fruit juice concentrates are used as the basis for fruit juice drinks and are supplied globally to fruit juice and beverage bottlers and fillers.

the fruit sector. Second, because the fruit sector is closely related to AGRANA's existing core sugar and starch businesses, AGRANA could employ the expertise and market knowledge it has accumulated over time, thus benefiting its new Fruit Division. AGRANA's core competence of the refinement process allowed it to diversify into this new segment smoothly.

AGRANA's CEO, Johann Marihart, believes that growth is an essential requirement for the manufacturing of high-grade products at competitive prices. Economies of scale have become a decisive factor for manufacturers in an increasingly competitive environment. In both the sugar and starch segments, AGRANA developed from a locally active company to one of Central Europe's major manufacturers in a very short timespan. Extensive restructuring in the Sugar and Starch divisions has allowed AGRANA to continue to operate efficiently and competitively in the European marketplace. Since its decision to diversify into the fruit-processing industry in 2003, Marihart has pursued a consistent acquisitions policy to exploit strategic opportunities in the fruit preparations and fruit juice concentrates sectors.

ACQUISITIONS

How does AGRANA implement its expansion strategy? In one word, acquisitions. Between 1990 and 2001, AGRANA focused on dynamic expansion into CEE sugar and starch markets by expanding from five plants to 13 and almost tripling its capacity. As the Sugar Division reached a ceiling to its growth potential due to EU sugar reforms, AGRANA began searching for a new opportunity for growth. Diversifying into the fruit industry aligned with AGRANA's goal to be a leader in the industrial refinement of agricultural raw materials. AGRANA began its diversification into the fruit segment in 2003 with the acquisitions of Denmark's Vallø Saft and Austria's Steirerobst. By July 2006, AGRANA's Fruit Division had acquired three additional holding firms and was reorganized so all subsidiaries were operating under the AGRANA brand.

AGRANA diversified into the fruit segment in 2003 through the acquisition of five firms. With the acquisition of Denmark's Vallø Saft Group (fruit juice concentrates) in April 2003, AGRANA gained a presence in Denmark and Poland. The acquisition of an interest (33 per cent) in Austria's Steirerobst (fruit preparations and fruit juice concentrates) in June 2003 gave AGRANA an increased presence in Austria, Hungary and Poland, while also establishing a presence in Romania, Ukraine and Russia. AGRANA fully acquired Steirerobst in February 2006. AGRANA first began acquiring France's Atys Group (fruit preparations) in July 2004 (25 per cent). The acquisition of Atys Group was complete in December 2005 (100 per cent) and was AGRANA's largest acquisition as Atys had 20 plants across every continent. In November 2004, AGRANA acquired Belgium's Dirafrost (fruit preparations) under the Atys Group and two months later (January 2005) acquired Germany's Wink Group (fruit juice concentrates) under the Vallø Saft Group. AGRANA's most recent expansion was a 50-50 joint venture under the Vallø Saft Group with Xianyang Andre Juice Co. Ltd. (fruit juice concentrates) in China. These acquisitions allowed AGRANA to quickly (within two years!) become a global player in the fruit segment. Table 4.1c provides an overview of AGRANA's present locations around the globe.

The strategy of AGRANA is clearly laid out in its 2006–2007 annual report:

'AGRANA *intends to continue to strengthen its market position and profitability in its core business segments ... and to achieve a sustainable increase in enterprise value. This will be done by concentrating on growth and efficiency, by means of investments and acquisitions that add value, with the help of systematic cost control and through sustainable enterprise management.*'

AGRANA's growth strategy, consistent improvement in productivity, and value added approach have enabled it to provide continual increases in its enterprise value and dividend distributions to shareholders. The key to AGRANA's global

Table 4.1c AGRANA plant locations as of 2007

	Sugar	Starch	Fruit	Ethanol
Argentina			1	
Australia			1	
Austria	2	2	3	1
Belgium			1	
Bosnia Herzegovina	1 (50%)*			
Brazil			1	
Bulgaria			1 (50%)	
China			2	
Czech Republic	2		1	
Denmark			1	
Fiji			1	
France			2	
Germany			1	
Hungary	2	1 (50%)	3	X**
Mexico			1	
Morocco			1	
Poland			5	
Romania	2	1	2	
Russia			1	
Serbia			1	
Slovakia	1			
South Africa			1	
South Korea			1	
Turkey			1	
Ukraine			2	
USA			4	
Total Plants	**10**	**4**	**39**	**1**

*AGRANA's holding is given in parentheses when not 100%.
**Hungrana, Hungary, plant also produces some ethanol.

Source: AGRANA 2006–2007 Annual Report.

presence in the fruit segment is not only its many acquisitions but its ability to quickly integrate those acquired into the group to realize synergistic effects.

In Table 4.1d, the annual revenue is given for each sector. Although the Sugar Division was the leader in 2005–2006 (contributing 50 per cent of the revenue), AGRANA's 2006–2007 annual report announced the Fruit Division as the new revenue leader (48 per cent), surpassing the projected expectations. AGRANA attributes its growth in the fruit sector to increases in dietary awareness and per capita income, two trends that are assumed to continue to rise in the future.

Table 4.1d AGRANA by division

	Sugar	Starch	Fruit	Total
Staff	2723	776	4724	8223
2005–2006 Revenue*	1040.04** (50%)	314.01 (15%)	730.62 (35%)	2084.67
2006–2007 Revenue	1059.34 (41%)	292.27 (11%)	1234.71 (48%)	2586.33

*Reported in USD, May 17, 2007, exchange rate used in calculation (US $1 = €0.74).
**Figures are reported in millions.

Source: AGRANA 2006–2007 Annual Report.

DIVERSIFYING INTO BIOFUEL

In light of further EU sugar reforms, AGRANA has continually looked for new growth opportunities. On May 12, 2005, the supervisory board of AGRANA gave the go-ahead for the construction of an ethanol facility in Pichelsdorf, Austria. Construction is estimated to be completed in October 2007. AGRANA first began making alcohol in 2005 in addition to starch and isoglucose at its Hungrana, Hungary, plant in a preemptive move to accommodate forthcoming EU biofuel guidelines. This move into ethanol was seen as a logical step by CEO Marihart. Similar to its move into the fruit sector, the production of ethanol allows AGRANA to combine its extensive know-how of processing agricultural raw materials with its technological expertise and opens the door for further growth.

Case discussion questions

1 From an institution-based view, what opportunities and challenges have been brought by the integration of EU markets in both Western Europe and CEE?

2 From a resource-based view, what is behind AGRANA's impressive growth?

3 From an international perspective, what challenges do you foresee AGRANA facing as it continues its expansion into other regions such as East Asia?

4 Compare the growth strategy of AGRANA to that of Danisco (Chapter 14, Opening Case), one of its competitors in the sugar market. Which strategy do you expect to be more sustainable in the long run?

NOTES

1 Central and Eastern Europe (CEE) typically refers to (1) Central Europe (former Soviet bloc countries such as the Czech Republic, Hungary, Poland, and Romania and three Baltic states of the former Soviet Union) and (2) Eastern Europe (the European portion of the 12 post-Soviet republics such as Belarus, Russia, and Ukraine).

2 One component of the Common Agricultural Policy (CAP) of the EU is the common organization of the markets in the sugar sector (CMO Sugar). CMO Sugar regulates both the total EU quantity of sugar production and the quantity of sugar production in each

sugar-producing country. It also controls the range of sugar prices, essentially limiting competition by assigning quotas to incumbent firms, such as AGRANA. In 2006, the EU passed sugar reforms reducing subsidies and price regulation, influencing the competition in the marketplace. These reforms included a reduction of sugar production by six million tons over a four-year transition period. Sugar reforms such as these have forced some of AGRANA's competitors to close a number of sugar facilities. However, AGRANA's executives are optimistic about AGRANA's future due to its investments in the fruit and starch markets.

SOURCES

Based on media publications and company documents. The following sources were particularly helpful: (1) AGRANA investor information provided by managing director, Christian Medved, to Professor Mike Peng at the Strategic Management Society Conference, Vienna, October 2006; (2) AGRANA Company Profile 2007; (3) AGRANA Annual Report 2005–2006 and 2006–2007, http://www.agrana.com (accessed August 1, 2007); (4) Sugar Traders Association, http://www.sugartraders.co.uk/ (accessed May 4, 2007); (5) N. Merret, 2007, Fruit segment drives Agrana growth, Food Navigator.com Europe, January 12; (6) N. Merret, 2006, Agrana looks east for competitive EU sugar markets, Confectionery News.com, November 29; (7) AGRANA Preliminary Results for Financial Year 2006–2007, press release, May 7, 2007; (8) C. Blume, N. Strang, & E. Farnstrand, *Sweet Fifteen: The Competition on the EU Sugar Markets*, Swedish Competition Authority Report, December 2002.

INTEGRATIVE CASE 5

ETHICS OF OFFSHORING: NOVO NORDISK AND CLINICAL TRIALS IN EMERGING ECONOMIES

Klaus Meyer
University of Bath

Richard Ivey School of Business
The University of Western Ontario

On a warm day in early spring 2008, the telephone is ringing in the office of Anders Dejgaard, chief medical officer of Novo Nordisk, a leading developer and manufacturer of insulin and related products. A business journalist of the Danish national newspaper *Berlingske Tidende* is on the line and asking for an interview. Dejgaard knows her from several conversations relating to business practices in the pharmaceutical industry.

The journalist is investigating the offshoring of clinical trials by Danish companies. A report recently published in the Netherlands alleges that multinational pharmaceutical companies routinely conduct trials in developing countries under allegedly unethical conditions. Also, the Danish National Committee on Biomedical Research Ethics has expressed concerns because Danish pharmaceutical companies are not obtaining ethical reviews in Denmark for such trials despite the offer from this committee. Thus, she wants to discuss Novo Nordisk's position on these issues.

Dejgaard reflects on how to react. Several articles on ethical aspects related to medical research in the Third World had appeared in the Danish press in recent months, creating an atmosphere of suspicion towards the industry.[1] Should he meet with the journalist and if so, what should he tell her? Or should he rather focus on his forthcoming business trip to new production facilities and send Novo Nordisk's press officer to meet the journalist? In his mind flashes the possibility of derogatory headlines in the tabloid press. As a company emphasizing corporate responsibility, the interaction with the media presents both opportunities and risks to Novo Nordisk.

NOVO NORDISK[2]

Novo Nordisk A/S had been created in 1989 through a merger between two Danish companies, Novo Industri A/S and Nordisk Gentofte A/S. Both had been established in the 1920s as manufacturers of insulin, a crucial medication for diabetes. Over decades of fierce competition, they had become leading providers of insulin and related pharmaceutical products. Novo Industri had been pursuing an internationally oriented strategy from the outset, and by 1936 was supplying insulin to 40 countries. A significant step in the internationalization of the company was a major push into the US market in 1979. At the time, Food and Drug Administration (FDA) regulations required Novo Industri to replicate its clinical studies in the United States to obtain the approval of the marketing of their new products. In 1989, the two companies merged and in 2000 the merged company spun off the enzyme business 'Novozymes'.

In 2008, Novo Nordisk presents itself as a focused company within the healthcare industry and a world leader in diabetes care. It claims the broadest and most innovative diabetes product portfolio in the industry, including the most advanced insulin delivery systems. In addition, Novo Nordisk holds leading positions in areas such as haemostasis management, growth hormone therapy and hormone replacement therapy. Sales reached DKr41.8 billion (about US$8 billion) in 2007, of which DKr30.5 billion were in diabetes care and DKr11.4 billion were in biopharmaceuticals.

Innovation is considered pivotal to the success of Novo Nordisk, as it was to its predecessor companies. Continuous innovations allow the development of more refined, and thus more effective, insulin preparations, and new delivery systems, such as Novopen(r), that facilitate the administration of the treatment, including self-administration by patients. In 2008, about 18 per cent of employees are working within research and development.

In 2008, Novo Nordisk holds market shares for insulin of about 56 per cent in Europe, 41 per cent in North America and 73 per cent in Japan and employs about 26 000 people, of whom 12 689 are located in Denmark, 3 411 in the rest of Europe, 3 940 in North America and the remainder in Asia Pacific and the rest of the world. Production facilities are located in six countries and products are marketed in 179 countries.

The shares of Novo Industri were first listed on the Copenhagen Stock Exchange in 1974 and on the London Stock Exchange in 1981 as the first Scandinavian company to be listed in London. In 2008, Novo Nordisk's B shares are listed on the stock exchanges in both Copenhagen and London, while its American depositary receipts (ADRs) are listed on the New York Stock Exchange.

Novo Nordisk emphasizes corporate social responsibility as part of its image, pursing a triple bottom line approach: environmental and social responsibility along with economic viability. This commitment is demonstrated through its values and its environmental and social responsibility policies that are reported on its website (see Appendix 1).

Critical milestones in Novo Nordisk's ambition to be recognized as a leader of corporate sustainability include the publication in 1994 of its Environmental Report. It was the first company in Denmark and one of the first in the world to do so. This was followed in 1999 by the first annual Social Report. In 2001, Novo Nordisk established the World Diabetes Foundation, a charity aiming to improve diabetes care in developing countries, where diabetes is becoming an epidemic as it had in Europe and North America a few decades earlier.

In recognition of its sustainability engagement, Novo Nordisk had been included in the Dow Jones Global Sustainability Indices, where it was ranked as "best in class" in the healthcare category in 2007. At home, Novo Nordisk is frequently ranked as having the most highly regarded corporate image by Danish magazines *Berlingske Nyhedmagasin*, *Børsen* and *Ingeniøren*.

NEW MEDICATIONS: DEVELOPMENT AND APPROVAL

Novo Nordisk, like other pharmaceutical and medical companies, heavily invests in the development of new medications offering more effective, safe and user-friendly treatments. New product development involves the creation of new drugs or modifications in their use, for instance their dosage and the form of administration.

To bring new drugs or medical devices to market, they must be approved by the relevant authorities – the FDA in the United States and European Medicines Agency (EMEA) in the European Union. The approval of drugs and medical devices requires proof of their efficacy and their safety. Efficacy refers to scientific evidence that the drug improves patients' conditions as claimed by the manufacturer. Safety refers to the absence of substantive negative side-effects. Thus, to obtain approval, pharmaceutical companies have to provide scientific evidence that the drug improves the conditions of patients and is free of disproportional side-effects.

This evidence has to be based on, among other data, clinical trials in which the drug has been tested on actual patients. The clinical trials are normally conducted in four stages. Phase 1 involves a small number of healthy volunteers and serves to assess the kinetic properties and tolerability of the drug. Phase 2 is performed on larger groups of patients to assess how well the drug works and to establish the doses that give the desired effect and to continue its safety assessment. Phase 3 trials often involve thousands of patients and aims to provide a definitive assessment of how effective and safe the drug is. All data generated in the three phases form an essential part of submissions to the regulatory authorities (FDA, EMEA and their counterparts in other countries) for drug approval. With this approval, the drug can then be marketed for the approved indications. Further trials, in phase 4, may be required to obtain permission to extend the labelling of a drug to new indications (e.g. a different disease) or specific groups, such as children or pregnant women.

Phase 3 and 4 trials require a large number of patients with the specific disease that the drug is to improve. A typical approval process conducted by Novo Nordisk might require six to eight different phase 3 trials with different patient groups or combinations of the drug component, each involving about 400 to 800 patients. Such trials are often conducted as multinational studies involving up to 15 countries. With increasing requirements for patient exposure for approval and increasing numbers of drugs being tested, the recruitment of patients is often a major challenge. Typically, trials are conducted at multiple hospitals that all must follow the same trial protocol to ensure the consistency of data and compliance with existing 'good clinical practice' (GCP) guidelines. Multi-site trials also facilitate the recruitment of patients with diverse backgrounds, for instance different ethnicities and diets, while helping to demonstrate their universal properties. Doctors and nurses but not patients are normally paid for this work and hospitals often find it attractive to participate in trials that allow access to new medications and front line research. Clinical trials, especially phase 3, are a major cost factor in the development of new medications and they often take many years to conduct (on average eight years).

In the early 2000s, major pharmaceutical industries increasingly moved parts of their trials, especially phases 3 and 4, to countries outside their traditional areas of operations, especially to Eastern Europe, South America, India and China. Hospitals in these areas provide access to qualified medical staff and larger numbers of patients with the specific conditions, while potentially being able to administer a trial at lower costs. Moreover, the efficacy of drugs may also vary across contexts, for instance due to genetic, dietary, climatic or other environmental conditions. In such cases, multi-site trials help to establish the efficacy of medications across contexts. Some countries, such as Japan, India and China, in fact require that trials are at least in part conducted locally to approve a new medication in the respective countries. However, the conduct of clinical trials in these areas also raises a range of ethical issues.

ETHICAL ISSUES IN MEDICAL RESEARCH[3]

Ethical issues in the pharmaceutical industry have received considerable media attention over several decades, as the industry has failed to live up to the expectations of some interest groups. In particular, clinical trials raise a number of widely recognized issues. Medical professionals, and with them many NGOs and media, focus on the medical ethics grounded in the Hippocratic oath that commits doctors to treat each patient to the best of their abilities, never to cause intentional harm and to maintain patient confidentiality. Scientists and approval authorities have been concerned about the scientific rigor of the tests to provide solid evidence of the effects of a new drug, and thus to protect potential future users of the drug. At the same time, pharmaceutical companies have to operate with limited financial resources and to satisfy shareholders and thus cannot spend more resources than expected future revenues would justify. Accordingly, the industry has been accused of performing trials in developing countries with lower attention to ethical principles – 'ethical bribing', with patients acting as guinea pigs that do not understand and/or care about the risk involved but just want to get free medication and with investigators not meeting the competence requirements, etc. Allegedly, all this just serves to generate documentation for compounds that are to be sold only in developed countries.

Medical (Hippocratic) ethics concern primarily the individual patients that are participating in any experiment. The relationship between the doctor and the subject participating in a trial is thus governed by the doctor's responsibility to care for his or her patient. Past incidences where this principle had been violated continue to affect popular perceptions of medical research. Most infamously, the Tuskegee syphilis study left 400 impoverished and unwitting African-American men in Macon County, Alabama, untreated to study how they developed the disease – an experiment initiated in 1932 and terminated only in the 1970s.

To prevent such scandals, professional medical organizations have developed guidelines and principles of ethics to guide their research, notably the Helsinki Declaration of the World Medical Association (see Appendix 2). These widely accepted ethical principles aim to protect subjects, e.g. patients, participating in such research. These include:

- Voluntary informed consent: Each patient has to agree voluntarily to participate in the research based on being fully informed about the purposes of the study and potential risks for the individual. Sponsors and local site investigators thus normally write an 'informed consent' document that informs potential subjects of the true risks and potential benefits, which is signed by each patient or their legal guardian before any trial procedure.

- Respect of patients: The privacy of the subject should be protected and they should be free to withdraw from the experiment at any time without reasoning. The doctor's professional responsibility to the patient should take precedence over any other considerations.

- Independent review: Any medical and pharmacological research has to be assessed on its scientific merits and ethicality by an independent review board (IRB) that is independent from those involved in or sponsoring the research.

Scientific ethics are concerned about the validity of the results of the scientific inquiry and thus the methodological rigour of the study. Thus, a study has to use valid measurements and statistical techniques and samples that are unbiased and sufficiently large that they can generate trustworthy and valid results.

Such scientific rigour is important to anyone who may in the future use an approved drug or medical device. Awareness of the need for rigorous tests prior to launching new medications had been triggered by various scandals of the 1960s, notably the Thalidomide scandal involving a pain killer used by women to ease sleep problems and pregnancy sickness. Due to side-effects of this medication, thousands of children worldwide were born with incomplete arms or legs, before the drug was withdrawn. In consequence to this and other scandals, the licensing and approval procedures for drugs have been tightened to ensure that only drugs with scientifically proven efficacy and safety are marketed.

Ethical businesses have to balance activities done in the interest of the wider society with their pursuit of profits. The late Nobel prize-winning economist Milton Friedman famously declared that the primary social responsibility of business is to make profits.[4] Under efficient markets, which he firmly believed in, this would generate the most mutually beneficial outcome. Thus, he argued, firms ought to give precedence to shareholders over any other interest groups.

Others argue that firms should engage in corporate social responsibility because it can be expected to benefit their bottom line in the long run, for instance through reputation effects. Yet others argue that firms have an intrinsic, normative responsibility to use their influence to do good for society and to aspire to the highest moral standards, independent of the profit motive. However, even so, their financial resources will be limited. Like organizations in the governmental or non-profit sector, businesses have to make critical decisions about how best to use their scarce resources.

ETHICS OF PLACEBO EXPERIMENTS[5]

Particular concerns have arisen for placebo trials, that is, trials where a control group of patients receives a treatment without any active ingredient for the disease. The purpose of placebo trials is, normally, to provide evidence of product efficacy by showing statistically significant improvements of the conditions of patients receiving the active treatment, compared to those receiving a placebo treatment.

Placebo trials are especially important for diseases that are affected by the so-called placebo effect, that is, patients' conditions improving because of the positive effect of receiving a form of treatment rather than the specific medication. This has been shown to be quite substantive, for instance, for schizophrenia and other psychiatric conditions. Both American and European authorities thus often require placebo trials as prerequisite for the approval of new medications.

Alternatives to placebo trials include the use of active controls, in which the control groups receive a previously marketed medication with known properties. Yet these types of trials are often not sufficient to provide the required rigorous evidence regarding the efficacy of the medication.[6] Placebo trials may create risks for patients in the placebo group, in particular when patients are denied a treatment that is known to improve their condition. The Helsinki Declaration therefore requires avoiding placebo experiments unless very special reasons require them or no alternative treatment of the illness is available (see Appendix 2, item 29). Ethics review boards have become very restrictive in permitting placebo trials. There have been arguments from some groups that one reason for the pharmaceutical industry to place studies in developing countries is the possibility of performing placebo trials that otherwise can be difficult to get approval for in developed countries.

Novo Nordisk generally avoids placebo trials. Usually, they are used only in phase 1 trials in healthy volunteers when new drug candidates are being developed. These trials are normally located near its main research centres in Europe and rarely in non-Western countries.

MEDIA SPOTLIGHTS

In February 2008, a report from the Dutch NGO SOMO raised public awareness of placebo trials conducted by major pharmaceutical companies in developing countries.[7] The report was critical of trials that had been submitted to the FDA and the EMEA for drug approval. Its primary concern was that key information about ethical aspects of these clinical trials was not available to it as an external observer and it found incidences where patients suffered serious harm after receiving a placebo in a trial.

The report focused on three case studies of clinical trials for recently approved drugs conducted in Eastern Europe and Asia, based on publicly available information. It concluded that:

> 'trial subjects in these countries are more vulnerable and their rights are less secured than in high income countries. Conditions such as poverty, illiteracy, poor health systems and inadequate research ethics committees result in international ethical standards not being met. Current EU legislation requires that results from unethical clinical trials … not be accepted for marketing authorization. With three case studies on recently approved drugs in the EU (Abilify, Olmetec and Seroquel), SOMO demonstrates that this principle is being violated. European authorities devote little to no attention to the ethical aspects of the clinical trials submitted, and they accept unethical trials as well as trials of poor quality'.[8]

In its conclusions, the report alleges that local regulation and the enforcement of ethical principles are less strict, partly because local independent review boards are less qualified and partly because they are less keen on restricting what is potentially a revenue earner. The authors thus advocate global harmonization of ethical criteria along the principles currently used by ethics committees in Europe: ' ... there must be no discrepancy between the ethical criteria used to approve research protocols in Western Europe and in low and middle income economies to avoid the creation of "easy countries"'.[9]

The media picked up, in particular, the case of a schizophrenic patient committing suicide while participating in a trial of the anti-schizophrenia medicine Seroquel by Astra-Zeneca. Moreover, media reported that 10 per cent of recipients in the placebo group had to be hospitalized because of worsening conditions. Careful reading of the original report suggests that 8.3 per cent (p. 64) of a group of 87 patients (p. 62) were affected, which adds to seven persons. No assessment of the likelihood of such incidents under alternative medication available at the time had been included in the report.

Concerns have also been raised by the Danish National Committee on Biomedical Research Ethics.[10] In particular, the committee criticizes the industry for not accepting the committee's offer to provide independent ethical reviews before submitting to local ethics committees as a service to the industry. The chairperson for the committee, Johannes Gaub, chief medical officer at Odense Hospital, told the media:

> 'Like production companies locate their factories in low wage areas, the medical industry is outsourcing its scientific experiments in the same way. The costs of conducting medical trials in developing countries are only a fraction of what they are in the West because of the low wages ... In the USA it costs about DKr 150 000 to move one patient through a trial. In Denmark, it costs DKr 80 000. I don't really know the price in developing countries, but it is a fraction of that'.

Gaub also rejects the concern of the industry that hospitals in Denmark would not be able to conduct trials of the necessary scale, given the growing requirements worldwide to provide clinical trial data for approvals around the world:

> 'We have considerable spare capacity in Denmark. Despite the high costs we have a well-functioning health system. We have data about patients because of our national identity number system, and there are many clinical researchers in the hospitals who would be happy to participate in the trials of new medications ... It is actually worrying that we do not receive more applications in Denmark. We need clinical research to maintain the high level of health science that we so far have had in the country'.[11]

Danish politicians also joined the debate. In a statement to the health committee of the national parliament, the minister for health emphasized that EU regulation for the approval of new medicines requires that trials conducted outside the European Union have been implemented in accordance with the European Union's own rules as well as with ethical principles such as the Helsinki Declaration. The minister thus concluded:

> 'I find no reason to take initiatives to constrain research projects by the Danish medical industry outside the EU. In this context, I consider it important to emphasize that all clinical trials that shall be used as a basis for applications for approval of marketing of a medication in the EU must comply with the EU's laws on good clinical practice and the ethical principles regarding medical research with human subjects'.[12]

Also, other politicians joined the debate. For example, Member of Parliament Birgitte Josefsen (V)[13] urged Danish pharmaceutical companies to hold the ethical flag high: 'The medical industry ought to be very careful about whom they use as test persons. That should be people who have resources to say "no". A poor Indian mother with three children is not the right one to become a test person'.[14]

NOVO NORDISK'S POSITION ON CLINICAL TRIALS

Anders Dejgaard is pondering the complexity of the ethical issues. As corporate sustainability features highly on Novo Nordisk's agenda, the ethically appropriate handling of clinical trials is important to the company. It conducts clinical trials globally to test the safety and efficacy of new drug candidates in order to obtain global marketing authorization. These trials always follow a common protocol and thus the same standards at all trials sites. Trials sites are selected based on a variety of criteria, including the quality of regulatory authorities, ethical review processes and medical practices. Moreover, drugs have to be tested on the types of patients who will later become users of the drug and trial subjects should have access to the drugs after the process has been completed. In addition, Novo Nordisk will only conduct trials in countries where it has affiliates with the necessary competence to arrange and monitor the trials. In 2008, these criteria were met in about 65 countries worldwide.

Novo Nordisk has adapted the global guidelines and recommendations by all the professional bodies and publishes its policies on clinical trials on its website (see Appendix 3). This includes enhanced global exposure of investigated products through its own website as well as websites sponsored by the FDA (see Appendix 3). Novo Nordisk conducts research in therapies that require global trials and the inclusion of different ethnic populations. The company also anticipates a need to increase the number of clinical trials due to an expanding pipeline and more extensive global and local regulatory requirements. Its ethical principles and standard operating procedures, which apply globally, are designed to ensure due respect for the safety, rights, integrity, dignity, confidentiality and well-being of all human beings participating in Novo Nordisk-sponsored trials. Novo Nordisk is auditing 10 per cent of all trials, while at the same time the American and European authorities, FDA and EMEA, are making random checks of about one per cent of Novo Nordisk's clinical trials. These random checks have never identified ethical problems in clinical trials in developing countries. Since trials are normally conducted in multiple countries, the same standards are applied everywhere, for both ethical and scientific reasons (consistency of results).

At the same time, Dejgaard is irritated about the request for an additional ethics approval by the Danish National Committee on Biomedical Research Ethics. He estimates that it would add three months to the preparation of each new trial. In his own experience, the ethical reviews in those locations he worked in are as rigorous as in Western countries and he does not recognize an added benefit, as the Danish committee would be no better in assessing a trial than a local ethics committee. On the contrary, he finds the suggestion more appropriate for a colonial empire. Moreover, specific local issues, such as ethnic or religious minorities, would be better understood by local committees.

Yet various issues come to mind. Is Novo Nordisk doing its research and development in an appropriate manner or are there issues that could be done better in view of Novo Nordisk's triple bottom line commitments? Are Novo Nordisk's standard operating procedures being properly implemented in all developing countries that participate in the programs and how is such compliance to be monitored? How should Novo Nordisk manage its simultaneous relationships with various regulatory authorities, independent review boards at various sites and with the Danish National Committee on Biomedical Research Ethics?

Most pressing is the decision on how to handle the journalist. Should he meet her in person, send a public relations person or not meet at all and reply in writing, citing the corporate website? If he is to meet her, what should be the key messages that he should get across and how should he prepare himself for any questions she might raise during the meeting?

Discussion Questions

1 Considering both economics and ethics, what are the principles that should guide decisions on where and how to administer clinical trials?

2 What interest groups are affected by the clinical trials, how are they becoming involved, and how should Novo Nordisk handle them?

3 If trials are conducted in emerging economies, what principles should guide them? How should Novo Nordisk manage such trials?

4 As Anders Deijgaard, how would you handle the journalist? How can you communicate effectively with her, and the media in general?

NOTES

1 See in particular B. Alfter, "De fattige er verdens nye forsøgskaniner. Krav om kontrol med medicinalindustrien," Information, Feb. 26, 2008, pp. 4-5, and B. Lambeck and S.G. Jensen, "Halvdelen af al medicin afprøves i den tredje verden," Politiken, Oct. 6, 2007.

2 This section draws on the company website, www.novonordisk.com, and an undated (circa 2002) document, "Novo Nordisk History," available via this website.

3 This section draws in particular on E.J. Emanuel, D. Wendler & C. Grady, "What makes clinical research ethical?" Journal of the American Medical Association, 283:20, 2000, pp. 2701-2711, and M.A. Santoro and T.M. Gorrie, Ethics and the Pharmaceutical Industry, Cambridge University Press, 2005.

4 M. Friedman, "The social responsibility of business is to increase profits," The New York Times Magazine, September 13, 1970; reprinted in K.E. Meyer, Multinational Enterprises and Host Economies, Elgar, Cheltenham, 2009.

5 This section draws on contemporary discussions in the medical literature, in particular E.J. Emanuel & F.G. Miller, "The ethics of placebo-controlled trials e- A middle ground," New England Journal of Medicine, 345:12, 2001, pp. 915-919, and R. Temple & S.S. Ellenberg, "Placebo-controlled trials and active-controlled trials in the evaluation of new treatments," Annals of Internal Medicine, 133:6, 2000, pp. 455-463.

6 An active-control trial infers efficacy from non-significant differences of performance compared to the active-control drug. Such non-significance, however, can be caused by a number of other influences. Moreover, this test is problematic if the active-control drug is subject to large placebo effects varying with study designs. On the merits and concerns of active-control trials, see e.g., Temple & Ellenberg, 2000, as above, and B.T. Walsh, S.N. Seidman, R. Sysko & M. Gould, "Placebo response in studies of major depression: Variable, substantial and growing," Journal of the American Medical Association, 287:14, 2002, pp. 1840-1847.

7 I. Schipper & F. Weyzing, "Ethics for Drug Testing in Low and Middle Income Countries: Considerations for European Market Authorisation," Stichting Onderzoek Multinationale Ondernemingen (SOMO), 2008, http://somo.nl/publications-en/Publication_2472, accessed October 2008.

8 Ibid, abstract on the cover page.

9 I. Schipper & F. Weyzing, 2008, as above.

10 For further information on the Danish National Committee on Biomedical Research Ethics, see www.cvk.im.dk/cvk/site.aspx?p=119.

11 Both citations are from B. Erhardtsen, "Medicinalindustrien dropper frivillig etisk blåstempling," Berlingske Tidende, April 5, 2008, Inland section, pp. 6-7 (case author's translation).

12 J.K. Nielsen, *Besvarlse af spørgsmal nr. 20 (alm. del) som Folketingets Sundhedsudvalg har stillet til indenrigs – og sundhedsministeren* (Written reply to a question in the health committee of the Danish parliament), January 9, 2008. (Archives of the Danish government: Indenrigs or Sundhedministeriet, Lægemiddlekontoret, J.nr. 2007-13009-599, Sagsbeh: nhj) (case author's translation).

13 (V) refers to Venstre, one of the parties of the minority government at the time.

14 *Berlingske Tidende* website, www.berlingske.dk/article/20080403/danmark/704030057, April 3, 2008, accessed October 2008 (case author's translation).

Appendix 1
CORPORATE SUSTAINABILITY AT NOVO NORDISK (EXTRACTS)

At Novo Nordisk, we refer to corporate sustainability as companies' ability to sustain and develop their business in the long-term perspective, in harmony with society. This implies a more inclusive view of business and its role; one in which engagements with stakeholders are not just used to legitimise corporate decisions, but rather the foundation for how it conducts and grows its business. It is about innovation, opportunity and planning for the long term.

The Triple Bottom is the principle behind our way of doing business. The company's Articles of Association state that it 'strives to conduct its activities in a financially, environmentally and socially responsible way.' This is a commitment to sustainable development and balanced growth, and it has been built into corporate governance structures, management tools and methods of assessing and rewarding individuals' performance …

The stakeholder dimension: Novo Nordisk needs to stay attuned to emerging trends and 'hot issues' on the global agenda in order to respond and to contribute to the debate. Stakeholder engagement is an integrated part of our business philosophy. We have long-standing engagements with stakeholders that are vital for building trust and understanding of a variety of issues. By involving stakeholders in the decision-making processes, decisions are better founded and solutions more likely to succeed. Stakeholders are defined as any individual or group that may affect or be affected by a company's activities.

Translating commitment to action: Corporate sustainability has made a meaningful difference to our business, and we believe it is a driver of our business success. This is best illustrated in three examples:

Business ethics: Surveys indicate that ethical behaviour in business is today the number one driver of reputation for pharmaceutical companies. Any company that is not perceived by the public as behaving in an ethical manner is likely to lose business, and it takes a long time to regain trust. While the Novo Nordisk Way of Management is a strong guide to our behaviour, we decided we needed more detailed guidance in the area of business ethics. In 2005 we therefore framed a new business ethics policy, in line with universally accepted high standards, backed by a set of procedures. Since then we have trained managers and employees, held workshops and offered e-learning on the new policy.

Climate change: We need to act to put a brake to human-induced climate change. While the implications of climate change pose major business risks, there are also opportunities. We have partnered with the WWF [World Wildlife Fund] in the Climate Savers programme and set an ambitious target to achieve a 10% reduction in our company's CO_2 emissions by 2014, compared with 2004 emission levels. This will occur through optimized production, energy savings and greater use of renewable energy supplies.

The diabetes pandemic: Today, diabetes is recognized as a pandemic. Novo Nordisk responds to this major societal challenge by working in partnerships with many others to rally the attention of policy-makers and influencers to change diabetes. We have made a promise of **Changing Diabetes**® and have framed **a strategy for inclusive access to diabetes care.** We established the **World Diabetes Foundation,** and have made several initiatives to advocate for change and build evidence of diabetes developments. **The National Changing Diabetes**® **programme** and **DAWN** are examples of education and awareness programmes implemented by Novo Nordisk affiliates in their respective countries. Our **Changing Diabetes**® **Bus** that promotes Novo Nordisk's global Changing Diabetes® activities had reached 86,000 people by the end of 2007 during its world tour. Its primary goal is to support the **UN Resolution on diabetes,** which was passed in December 2006.

Source: www.novonordisk.com, accessed November 2008.

Appendix 2
HELSINKI DECLARATION OF THE WORLD MEDICAL ASSOCIATION (EXCERPTS)

10. It is the duty of the physician in medical research to protect the life, health, privacy and dignity of the human subject.

13. The design and performance of each experimental procedure involving human subjects should be clearly formulated in an experimental protocol. This protocol should be submitted for consideration, comment, guidance, and where appropriate, approval to a specially appointed ethical review committee, which must be independent of the investigator, the sponsor or any other kind of undue influence. This independent committee should be in conformity with the laws and regulations of the country in which the research experiment is performed. The committee has the right to monitor ongoing trials. The researcher has the obligation to provide monitoring information to the committee, especially any serious adverse events. The researcher should also submit to the committee, for review, information regarding funding, sponsors, institutional affiliations, other potential conflicts of interest and incentives for subjects.

14. The research protocol should always contain a statement of the ethical considerations involved and should indicate that there is compliance with the principles enunciated in this Declaration.

15. Medical research involving human subjects should be conducted only by scientifically qualified persons and under the supervision of a clinically competent medical person. The responsibility for the human subject must always rest with a medically qualified person and never rest on the subject of the research, even though the subject has given consent.

16. Every medical research project involving human subjects should be preceded by careful assessment of predictable risks and burdens in comparison with foreseeable benefits to the subject or to others. This does not preclude the participation of healthy volunteers in medical research. The design of all studies should be publicly available.

17. Physicians should abstain from engaging in research projects involving human subjects unless they are confident that the risks involved have been adequately assessed and can be satisfactorily managed. Physicians should cease any investigation if the risks are found to outweigh the potential benefits or if there is conclusive proof of positive and beneficial results.

18. Medical research involving human subjects should only be conducted if the importance of the objective outweighs the inherent risks and burdens to the subject. This is especially important when the human subjects are healthy volunteers.

19. Medical research is only justified if there is a reasonable likelihood that the populations in which the research is carried out stand to benefit from the results of the research.

20. The subjects must be volunteers and informed participants in the research project.

21. The right of research subjects to safeguard their integrity must always be respected. Every precaution should be taken to respect the privacy of the subject, the confidentiality of the patient's information and to minimize the impact of the study on the subject's physical and mental integrity and on the personality of the subject.

22. In any research on human beings, each potential subject must be adequately informed of the aims, methods, sources of funding, any possible conflicts of interest, institutional affiliations of the researcher, the anticipated benefits and potential risks of the study and the discomfort it may entail. The subject should be informed of the right to abstain from participation in the study or to withdraw consent to participate at any time without reprisal. After ensuring that the subject has understood the information, the physician should then obtain the subject's freely-given informed consent, preferably in writing. If the consent cannot be obtained in writing, the non-written consent must be formally documented and witnessed.

23. When obtaining informed consent for the research project the physician should be particularly cautious if the subject is in a dependent relationship with the physician or may consent under duress. In that case the informed consent should be obtained by a well-informed physician who is not engaged in the investigation and who is completely independent of this relationship.

29. The benefits, risks, burdens and effectiveness of a new method should be tested against those of the best current prophylactic, diagnostic, and therapeutic methods. This does not exclude the use of placebo, or no treatment, in studies where no proven prophylactic, diagnostic or therapeutic method exists.

Note of clarification on paragraph 29 of the WMA Declaration of Helsinki

The WMA hereby reaffirms its position that extreme care must be taken in making use of a placebo-controlled trial and that in general this methodology should only be used in the absence of existing proven therapy. However, a placebo-controlled trial may be ethically acceptable, even if proven therapy is available, under the following circumstances:

- Where for compelling and scientifically sound methodological reasons its use is necessary to determine the efficacy or safety of a prophylactic, diagnostic or therapeutic method; or
- Where a prophylactic, diagnostic or therapeutic method is being investigated for a minor condition and the patients who receive placebo will not be subject to any additional risk of serious or irreversible harm.

All other provisions of the Declaration of Helsinki must be adhered to, especially the need for appropriate ethical and scientific review.

30. At the conclusion of the study, every patient entered into the study should be assured of access to the best proven prophylactic, diagnostic and therapeutic methods identified by the study.

Note of clarification on paragraph 30 of the WMA Declaration of Helsinki

The WMA hereby reaffirms its position that it is necessary during the study planning process to identify post-trial access by study participants to prophylactic, diagnostic and therapeutic procedures identified as beneficial in the study or access to other appropriate care. Post-trial access arrangements or other care must be described in the study protocol so the ethical review committee may consider such arrangements during its review.

Source: www.wma.net/e/policy/b3.htm, accessed October 2008.

Appendix 3
CLINICAL TRIALS: NOVO NORDISK'S POSITION

- Clinical trials sponsored by Novo Nordisk will always be conducted according to the Helsinki Declaration, which describes human rights for patients participating in clinical trials, and similar international ethical guidelines such as the Nuremberg code, the Belmont report and CIOMMS, and the International Conference of Harmonisation (ICH) guidelines for current good clinical practice (cGCP).

- The above guidelines and regulations are the foundation for our clinical Standard Operating Procedures (SOPs) including the SOP on the 'principles of clinical trials'. These standards are laid out to ensure the safety, rights, integrity, confidentiality and well-being of persons involved in Novo Nordisk trials globally.

- Novo Nordisk will apply the same procedures wherever we sponsor clinical trials. This means that all subjects enrolled in Novo Nordisk trials are protected by the same rights, high ethical standards and regulations irrespective of location of the study.

- The interest and well-being of the trial subject should always prevail over the interest of science, society and commerce.

- Novo Nordisk will not conduct clinical trials for drug development in countries where we do not intend to market the investigational drug. In any country where we do undertake clinical trials we will ensure that a proper internal organisation and a proper regulated external environment exist.

- Clinical trials should only be done if they can be scientifically and medically justified, and all Novo Nordisk-sponsored trials should be based on sound scientific methodology described in a clear and detailed protocol. Placebo will only be used as comparator when scientifically and ethically justified.

- No trial activity in Novo Nordisk-sponsored trials will start before approval is obtained from external local ethics committees and health authorities.

- We will always ensure that investigators involved in Novo Nordisk clinical trials are skilled in the therapeutic area and are trained in GCP. No procedure involving a person undergoing clinical trial activities will take place before the appropriate freely given informed consent is obtained based on proper information on potential risk of participation in the trial. A patient can at any time withdraw from a clinical trial without giving any reason. In cases where trial subjects are incompetent, physically or mentally incapable of giving consent, or if the person is a minor, Novo Nordisk will follow local regulations for obtaining consent.

- Products used in Novo Nordisk-sponsored clinical trials will be manufactured and controlled according to international and local regulations and laws. Novo Nordisk will conduct frequent site monitoring to ensure that the study is executed according to the study protocol, and that data used in statistical analysis and reporting reflects the data obtained from the involved patients during the trial. Safety information from any Novo Nordisk trial will be monitored on a continuous basis and appropriate actions will be taken if risks of the investigational product outweigh the potential benefits.

- Patients participating in Novo Nordisk-sponsored clinical trials will always be offered best available and proven treatment after study termination. The treatment will be offered at the discretion of the responsible physician. If study medication is not marketed the responsible physician can apply for medication on a named patient basis. Post-study medication will be described in the protocol and informed consent.

- Novo Nordisk will ensure proper indemnification of trial subjects in case a trial product or procedures in a Novo Nordisk-sponsored trial cause bodily harm to a trial subject.

- Novo Nordisk strives to have all clinical trial results published according to accepted international guidelines, and we will always ensure transparency of our studies by publishing protocol synopses on the external website: **www. clinicaltrials.gov**. Study results from trials involving marketed drugs can be accessed via **www.clinicalstudyresults.org**. Furthermore, Novo Nordisk has its own online repository for clinical trials activities: novonordisk-trials.com. Novo Nordisk is collating all information about bioethics in the R&D area on **www.novonordisk.com/R&D/bioethics**.

Source: www.novonordisk.com, accessed November 2008.

DENTEK'S UK DECISION

Anne D. Smith and Amber Galbraith Quinn
University of Tennessee

On a lovely spring day in 2003, John Jansheski, CEO of DenTek (http://www.
dentekoralcare.com), hung up the phone after a conversation with the distributor of his dental products in the United Kingdom. The distributor had given Jansheski (known as 'J. J.') a choice: a formal joint venture (JV) or potential termination of their annual distribution agreement. J. J. leaned back in his chair and thought about the past 21 years with the company he had created. J. J. realized that his domestic strategy was in place, growing at a 30 per cent annual rate (1986–2003) and yielding over $50 million in retail sales. DenTek and J. J. had faced large consumer products firms and lawsuits to build significant shelf space in major US discount and drugstore retailers. DenTek had continued to create a steady stream of new dental product innovations for consumers. However, J. J. was at a crossroads in his global strategy; specifically, should he enter into a JV with his UK distributor or not?

BACKGROUND

Dr. Jansheski, J. J.'s father, was a successful dentist in northern California. He had developed an innovative design for a metal tartar removal device, called the

This case was written by Professor Anne D. Smith and graduate student Amber Galbraith Quinn (University of Tennessee). The purpose of the case is to serve as a basis for classroom discussion rather than to illustrate the effective or ineffective management of issues related to a medium-sized entrepreneurial firm and its international expansion. © Anne D. Smith and Amber Galbraith Quinn.

Dental Pik. His patients had been asking for scalers to clean their teeth at home. Dr. Jansheski thought this product could be sold through dental offices and drugstores. J. J.'s older brother developed a business plan for manufacturing and marketing this product. Soon after, J. J.'s brother had the Dental Pik manufactured in the United States. With costs of about $2 per pick and a sales price to retailers of $4, consumers paid around $8 for the metal pick product. The largest retail contract was with Long's Drug Store for 13 of its Arizona stores. Yet, the business was floundering with limited end-user sales and significant business overhead. J. J.'s brother only generated $13 000 in sales, with no reorders from the drug chain. He eventually walked away from the business.

J. J. had undertaken a variety of endeavours while attending College of Marin, such as being a disc jockey, cleaning boats and distributing HerbaLife. When his father asked him to take over the family business, J. J. requested 50 per cent equity holdings and was given a 25 per cent interest. 'In 1985, I decided to give it a go ... but I did not know much about running a business.'[1] J. J. took over management of DenTek with $150 000 of debt and a product design (with no patent) that he believed needed a change. At this time, J. J.'s office consisted of two 6-foot-by-9-foot storage units, which he referred to as a 'doublewide'. He still recalls entering the 'office' for the first time, full of fear.

With no sales during J. J.'s first six months, he quickly realized that the metal instrument 'was a scary-looking product'. Facing sceptical distributors, J. J. set out to design a plastic version of the Dental Pik. He moved the manufacturing to China before the launch of a national ad campaign. However, he was working with only a $30 000 line of credit, which funded developing a mould for the Dental Pik plastic handle, buying out a DenTek partner,[2] building inventory, launching an advertising campaign and travelling to Asia to set up manufacturing. Back in the States, Jansheski developed low-cost advertising with product ads featuring his girlfriend in the *National Enquirer* magazine. Over time, his marketing and new product efforts led to the allocation of more drugstore shelf space to DenTek's products. By the late 1980s, retail sales approached $2 million.

Throughout the late 1980s and the 1990s, J. J. continued to develop new products (Table 6.1a) and expand into new US retail outlets. His most popular product was the plastic disposable flosser. Yet, his successes were somewhat tempered by lawsuits from larger consumer products firms. Around 1995, DenTek faced a lawsuit from Butler, a leading firm that marketed a 'G-U-M' product related to DenTek's Gingibrush electric toothbrush. J. J. described this experience:

'We were about $3 million in sales ... If we had lost, it would have bankrupted us ... We settled, after a $75 000 legal bill, and agreed not to trademark or contest the suit ... after all, Butler was part of a multibillion dollar global consumer products firm.'

After the Butler lawsuit, Jansheski faced a lawsuit from Johnson & Johnson in 1999, which alleged trademark infringement by a new DenTek product called Temparol. Temparol was a dental repair product that a consumer placed into a missing filling until a dentist could be seen. J. J. recounted to a business class in 2006, 'After $150 000 in legal fees, we settled ... we were spanked'. DenTek renamed the product Temparin.[3]

In 1999, J. J. decided to relocate his company from Petaluma, California, to Maryville, Tennessee. The decision to move to the East Coast 'was a no-brainer', according to J. J. 'With 80 per cent of our shipments heading east of the Mississippi, we needed to be closer to this base to reduce our distribution costs ... We

Table 6.1a Time Line of DenTek Product Development

Year Introduced	Product Name	Product Description
1984	Dental Pik	Consumers clean tartar between teeth
1990–1996	Temparin, Tempanol and Gingibrush	Temporary filling material; electric toothbrush
1997	Floss Picks	Plastic flossers for consumers; in bags of 30 or 60
1999	Breath Remedy	Line of products to address the source of bad breath; includes mouth rinse, tongue sprays, tongue drops and tongue cleaners
1999	Dental First Aid	Complete tooth pain and repair products for emergencies and the medicine cabinet
2000	Thin Set	First temporary cap and crown cement for consumers
2001	Explorer	Interdental pick for removing food between teeth
2002	Silk Floss Picks	For consumers with tight teeth, a hassle-free flossing experience
2002	Maximum Hold Temparin	Ten times stronger hold than Temparin product
Products under development in 2003		
	Silk Easy Angle Floss Picks	For hard-to-reach back teeth
	Individually wrapped Silk Floss Picks	Easy on-the-go flossing
	Fun Flossers	With fluoride, for children
	Evo Flossers	Longer reach flossers
	Narrow Brush Picks	Flossing made easier
	Wide Brush Picks	Cleaning around braces and bridges easier

have saved at least $1 million in distribution by relocating to Tennessee'. DenTek's facility includes a warehouse, a small assembly area and offices for design staff, training and executives. Its location in Maryville, Tennessee, puts DenTek in close proximity to major Interstate freeways and customers on the East Coast. 'It was the most important financial decision we've ever made', even though J. J. had to replace most of his 40 employees from California.[4] With cheaper rent, taxes and shipping costs, 'we are putting all that money back into the company, and as a result, sales are now twice what they were ... It's helped us double the size of the company'.[5] Construction had just been completed on a $1.7 million, 22 000 square foot addition that doubled the size of DenTek's Maryville facility, and plans were on the table for another 26 000 square foot addition.[6]

One consequence of the relocation was that J. J. lost or replaced all but one of his California executive team members, who had been primarily comprised of friends. As J. J. recounted, 'Around 2001, I began to build a more professional management team, which was needed at this point.'

Also in 1999, a serendipitous encounter at the National Association of Chain Drug Store trade show led to DenTek's early international expansion.

There, J. J. met Dr. D.,[7] the owner of a British distributor of consumer products. Dr. D. was a successful plastic surgeon who also distributed his own line of facial products. After a year of conversations, visits and negotiations, J. J. signed an agreement for Dr. D. to distribute DenTek products in the United Kingdom. By 2003, the distributor had built market presence for DenTek products at Boots, one of the largest drugstore chains in the UK. Dr. D. was a colourful character who J. J. stated 'had a different perception of money ... with many high-end sports cars to choose from in Beverly Hills'. J. J. told a story about when Dr. D. chartered a jet to take Boots salespersons to see the Rockettes in Nashville. 'This relationship over the past few years had gone swimmingly well ... then he decided to push us to JV with him'.

In 2001, J. J. hired an 'aggressive' vice president (VP) of international sales. J. J. explained what happened during this part of DenTek's international push:

'The VP proceeded to open offices in Brazil, Mexico and Germany in order to build a retail presence. We got greedy to go direct and boost our margins. We decided to bypass distribution to build retail. This was one of the dumbest decisions I've made. We lost over $1 million in three markets in two years. We had no sales in Mexico or Brazil, and I felt like every government official had their hand out to be greased. Germany was not a total loss; we still do some business there ... but it is difficult.'

By 2003, the VP and J. J. were both unhappy and decided to part ways.

NATURE OF COMPETITION

DenTek faced formidable competitors both at home and abroad. As J. J. explained, 'The US is the most difficult and competitive market for consumer packaged goods'. This $4 billion market is the battleground of large multinational firms such as Johnson & Johnson, Butler, Listerine and Procter & Gamble with Oral B.[8] These companies had deep pockets and were fierce competitors. J. J. was keenly watching the lawsuit between Johnson & Johnson and Listerine; Johnson & Johnson questioned Listerine's claim that its mouthwash was as effective in fighting gum disease as flossing. Jansheski was certainly aware that these consumer products firms were capable of targeting his products with versions of their own. The large companies' ability to quickly replicate products and to support them with large marketing budgets was one reason J. J. continued to innovate.

Despite the threat from large companies, J. J. stated that he was most worried about 'the smaller scrappy passionate companies ... The large multinationals, however ... are not going to get down and fight'. He continued, 'I can predict the price that Johnson & Johnson is going to offer on their dental products, they own certain segments ... The smaller scrappy ones are more unpredictable ... [yet] even though we are aware of others, we focus on our show.'

DenTek had a leading market share in many dental accessories and sold its products through Wal-Mart, Target, Walgreens, Rite Aid, Kmart, CVS and other retail chains. DenTek was the category leader in disposable flossers, with over 500 million units packaged and sold and an estimated 32 per cent US market share (see Table 6.1b). Because many of these major retailers prefer not to deal with multiple suppliers, DenTek helps manage the category of dental accessories for several large retail chains.

Table 6.1b MASS market sales (excluding Wal-mart): Dental accessories category

Top Brands	2003 Dollar Sales (in millions)	2003 Unit Volume (in millions)
DenTek (flossers only)	13.1	4.8
Water Pik	8.6	0.3
Oral-B	7.7	2.8
Doctor's Nightguard	6.1	0.3
Glide	5.8	1.2
Butler G-U-M	5.3	1.9
Stim-U-Dent	4.7	2.0
Oral B super floss	4.6	1.4
Butler Proxabush	3.9	1.3
Butler G-U-M Proxabrush	3.6	1.4

Source: *Chain Drug Review*, 2003, 25 (10), June 6: 223.

One benefit to competing in the dental accessories industry is the positive growth trends due to Baby Boomer demographics. Sales of commodity dental products were flat, but 'specialty segments' – particularly high-end products that offer increased cosmetic and therapeutic benefits – are driving category growth overall. 'As Baby Boomers come into mid-life, they are at the prime age for periodontal disease, expanding the market for products that address this condition.'[9]

CURRENT DILEMMA

In 2003, Jansheski was faced with a difficult decision related to his UK distributor. 'Right now I make, let's say, 25 cents on each product that I sell to my distributor. He in turn buys the product from me for 50 cents and sells for $1 to Boots, who then retails for $2'. This arrangement had worked well for many years. Yet, Dr. D. was adamant that their short-term yearly distribution arrangement was to end in a few months unless they could work out a JV. Additionally, Dr. D. wanted the rights to distribute to the entire EU. J. J. pulled a legal pad out of his desk and began to consider aspects of this important decision that he would discuss with his president at tomorrow's meeting.

Case discussion questions

1 Should DenTek abandon global expansion efforts right now to more fully concentrate on new product innovations against marketing powerhouses in the United States? Is now the right time in DenTek's growth to build market share outside the United States?

2 What caused DenTek's independent international expansion (2001–2003) into Brazil, Mexico and Germany to fail? If J. J. decides to pursue overseas opportunities again, what type of structure or safeguards should he put in place to ensure that it is not a repeat of its previous failed effort?

3 What are the pros and cons of entering into a JV with Dr. D.'s company? What are the risks associated with a 50/50 JV, a majority JV (in which DenTek has majority equity interest) or a minority JV (in which DenTek has minority equity interest)? What aspects are critical to include in JV legal documentation? What are the risks associated with passing on this JV proposal?

4 Which of the abovementioned options related to international expansion would enhance DenTek's attractiveness to a potential buyer (acquirer)? Why?

NOTES

1 Quotes without a linked publication are from interviews with or lectures by John Jansheski during 2006 and 2007.

2 During the 1980s, J. J. bought out all previous partners in the DenTek business, including his father. He has not had outside investors since that time.

3 DenTek currently markets a temporary filling product, launched in 1996. See Table 6.1a for DenTek's product innovation time line.

4 From http://www.entrepreneur.com/magazine/entrepreneur/2005/september/79358.html.

5 From http://www.entrepreneur.com/magazine/entrepreneur/2005/september/79358.html.

6 J. Stiles, 2003, New product helps DenTek expand plant, add jobs, Knoxville News Sentinel, June 5: C1.

7 Name disguised.

8 In January 2005, Gillette (and its Oral B brand) was purchased by Procter & Gamble.

9 Drug Store News, October 8, 2001.

THE LG-NORTEL JOINT VENTURE

Bill Turner

Joe Bentz

Steve Caudill

Christine Pepermintwalla

Ken Williamson

University of Texas at Dallas

Peter MacKinnon, chairman of the recently formed LG-Nortel joint venture (JV), is back in his Dallas office after two hard weeks in South Korea (hereafter Korea). Next week, he is off to Europe for a well-deserved vacation with his family. In his office, MacKinnon surrounds himself with family photos, awards and souvenirs from around the world. He is highly dedicated to the LG-Nortel JV and currently spends two weeks each month in Korea. When in Dallas, he leaves the headquarters in Korea in the capable hands of LG-Nortel JV CEO Jae Ryung Lee.

MacKinnon tackles his work and personal challenges with 100 per cent dedication, as shown in his drive to make the LG-Nortel JV a success. He has a passion

This case was written by Bill Turner, Joe Bentz, Steve Caudill, Christine Pepermintwalla, and Ken Williamson (University of Texas at Dallas, EMBA 2007) under the supervision of Professor Mike Peng. The purpose of the case is to serve as a basis for classroom discussion rather than to illustrate the effective or ineffective handling of an administrative situation. The authors thank Mr. Peter MacKinnon for his time and for sharing his expertise and experiences. The views expressed are those of the authors (in their private capacity as EMBA students) and do not necessarily reflect those of the individuals and organizations mentioned. © Bill Turner. Reprinted with permission.

for life and is one of those executives who 'works hard and plays hard'. This is evident by the ice hockey stick sitting an arm's-length from his desk chair and the fact that he plays in three hockey leagues when visiting Korea. Finding a balance between work and personal life remains a challenge with the current heavy workload and extended travel to Korea each month.

Having travelled around the globe and having been an expatriate in Europe previously, MacKinnon is no stranger to international travel. He describes some interesting cultural aspects of doing business in Korea and highlights 'respect' and 'knowledge for the cultural differences' as important. He is keenly aware of the dynamics of the corporate culture in Korea and its implications on the success of the JV, given the mixed management of Koreans and a few North Americans living in Korea.

With MacKinnon's new boss, Nortel CEO Mike Zafirovski (Mike Z.), driving for management excellence, there is little room for missteps. MacKinnon is currently a very hands-on full-time chairman as demanded by Mike Z. The LG-Nortel JV must satisfy the needs of both the corporate parents (Nortel and LG) as the conduit for their telecom products and also be Nortel's gateway to the Korean telecom market. In addition, MacKinnon must lead and leverage a highly capable and innovative group of Korean engineers to develop new products for the advanced Korean and worldwide telecom markets.

This is MacKinnon's first time chairing a board of directors (see his bio in Figure 7.1a). Managing this new JV, with a multicultural management, is presenting a number of challenges. For the first six months since the JV was established, MacKinnon has been spending 16-hour days tackling a number of 'start-up' problems. He has been driving this mixed cultural team to resolve the recent tactical and

Figure 7.1a Peter MacKinnon bio

Peter MacKinnon is chairman, LG-Nortel JV and president, LG-Nortel Business Unit – a joint venture between Nortel and LG Electronics. In these roles, MacKinnon is responsible for magnifying the success of the joint venture by scaling its products into Nortel's global channels as well as coordinating the LG-Nortel and Nortel portfolios across Nortel's various business units. The portfolio includes Enterprise products, with a renewed focus on SMB, UMTS evolution to LTE, WiBro/WiMAX and Wireline/IPTV.

Prior to this position MacKinnon was president, GSM/UMTS Networks for Nortel. With a global customer base in more than 100 countries, he was responsible for R&D, product management, sales, marketing and customer support.

MacKinnon's previous roles at Nortel include: senior vice president, Wireless Networks Americas; vice-president and general manager of the Asia-Pacific wireless business unit and global responsibility for the product management and marketing efforts of Nortel's GSM networks business. He has also held positions in the North American SONET Transport Group – in product management, marketing, operations and design.

MacKinnon is a director on the board of Guangdong Nortel Telecommunications Equipment Ltd (GDNT) in China.

MacKinnon earned an MBA as well as a BS degree in electrical engineering from McGill University in Montreal, Canada. He is fluent in English and French and enjoys experiencing different cultures. He also plays golf, ice hockey and tennis. Mr. MacKinnon is married and has two daughters and a son.

Source: http://www.nortel.com/corporate/exec/mackinnon.html (accessed July 5, 2006).

operational issues and is working to resolve cross-cultural and management tension. Lately, he has been contemplating how and when to shift to become more strategic and start to be a part-time chairman. His main challenge is how to establish the JV for success in the future and be the strategic part-time chairman that he wants and needs to be.

LG ELECTRONICS BACKGROUND

LG (Korea Stock Exchange: 6657.KS) was established in Korea as a private company in 1958 as GoldStar. As a global leader in home appliances, digital media devices, and display and information and communications products, LG has more than 64 000 employees globally and its 2005 revenues reached over $16.9 billion (unconsolidated). It is comprised of 30 companies with about 130 overseas subsidiaries. As part of the LG corporate conglomerate, LG Electronics's goal is to enable the intelligent networking of digital products that will make consumers' lives better than ever.[1]

NORTEL BACKGROUND

Nortel (NYSE: NT; Toronto TSX: NT) is a 110-year-old Canadian company doing business in more than 150 countries with 2005 revenues of $10.52 billion. Nortel's portfolio of solutions for telecommunications network providers, government and enterprises includes end-to-end broadband (packet and optical), Voice over IP, multimedia services/applications, wireless networks and wireless broadband networks.[2]

NORTEL'S EXPERIENCE IN NEW MARKETS

Expanding into new global markets, Nortel has had its share of successes and failures. Some expansions were accomplished through acquisition of wholly owned subsidiaries such as the acquisition of Matra in France and others through JVs. MacKinnon discussed one particular learning experience where Nortel entered into a 50-50 JV. Unfortunately, voting was deadlocked; the JV became ineffective and had to be shut down.

In 1998, with a presence in North America and Europe, Nortel entered into the rapidly expanding South Korean telecom market. This soon turned into a valuable lesson on how *not* to do business in Asia (through an understanding of the local culture but not of the 'business culture'). Nortel assumed that to do business in Korea, all you needed was a few local Korean employees in a local office. This was a vital misunderstanding. MacKinnon summed up the challenge by saying, 'You can't just hire a few Koreans and call yourself a Korean company; it's all about relationships'. This first attempt was not successful, and Nortel backed out of South Korea.

TELECOM IN SOUTH KOREA: AN INDUSTRY OVERVIEW

South Korea has the 10th largest economy in the world and has one of the leading telecommunications infrastructures in the world. This was not true just a mere

30 years ago. In the late 1970s, with a population of 40 million, there was barely one phone line to every 160 persons. Today, there is nearly one phone line to every two persons. However, the demand for phone line service is in decline as more advanced services eliminate the need for basic phone lines. Mobile technology has advanced rapidly, and the subscriber base has grown to nearly 40 million with an increasing number of these subscribers using their service for wireless digital transfer.

WIRELESS TODAY IN SOUTH KOREA: AN ACCELERATING INDUSTRY

South Korea's CDMA Network is the largest EVDO wireless network deployment in the world and has the most advanced early adopters with 75 per cent user penetration. As of 2004, Korea already had 11 million subscribers using EVDO. Korea also boasts the most advanced data applications in the world, estimated to be two years ahead of North America. The government originally mandated CDMA wireless technology to be used in South Korea. However, recent mandates to the more widely adopted UMTS technology represent a major technology shift for the country and local equipment providers like LG.

THE LG-NORTEL JOINT VENTURE

With the policy shift toward UMTS, LG was not prepared and did not have products for UMTS to meet these new government requirements. LG now found itself in need of a partner for UMTS products. Nortel had no footprint in the heavily competitive South Korean market since the 1998 retreat, and it needed a way to re-enter South Korea. LGE was the leader of the Korean consumer electronics market. It also was a major global force in electronics, information and communications products. Due to LGE's demonstrated innovative technology leadership position in Korea and Nortel's proven UMTS portfolio and worldwide reach, the mutual attraction was inevitable.

On August 17, 2005, LG and Nortel signed a definitive JV agreement with a contract closure target date of November 1, 2005. Nortel entered into the JV with a $145 million investment. For this investment, Nortel would receive ownership of 50 per cent plus one share of the company and control a majority of positions on the board. Gaining 50 per cent plus one share was a 'deal breaker' for Nortel given the past experiences on 50-50 partnerships. MacKinnon was named chairman and Jae Ryung Lee would become CEO. Other key positions were filled accordingly with Nortel and LG executives. The JV had over $500 million in sales in the first six months, but not without organizational and cultural issues to deal with.

ISSUES WITHIN THE FIRST SIX MONTHS

Of the 1400 LG-Nortel JV employees, 1350 are South Korean and 50 are American and Canadian. While building the JV organization, cultural differences surfaced immediately. A higher than normal attrition rate was seen in part as the result of placement of younger former Nortel employees over older former LG employees. This is not acceptable in Korean corporate culture, and thus, many Korean employees left. Mac-Kinnon had also seen the cultural divide when a Korean male employee started holding his hand and confiding in him about some issues the

Korean male employee was having. MacKinnon never pulled his hand away, heard the employee's message, and knew immediately that this kind of cultural exchange might happen to Americans and Canadians unaware or less tolerant of these differences in the future.

The burdens of implementing both US GAAP and Korean GAAP have taken their toll and created additional process and stress on the organization. In one instance, contract template issues caused revenue recognition problems, which in turn created a (financially) reported order backlog. The contract template issues were identified, and a plan to correct them was developed. Two contract templates accounted for 60 per cent of the revenue with another 15 more accounting for the other 40 per cent to be corrected. The implementation was now critical to finally recognizing the revenue needed to prove the JV was already a success to both parents, LG and Nortel.

Pre-JV, LGE had been mainly focused on Korea, concentrating on the requirements of the demanding high-growth and innovative local market. Now these highly qualified engineers needed to take a broader worldwide view of product development so products could be funnelled back through Nortel's non-Korean markets.

Nortel cancelled a major project within the JV as the project was just ramping up its development. This decision was made after the most recent planning and forecasting exercises used by Nortel had shown that the business case and market outlook would not provide the returns required by Nortel. Regardless of sunk costs for development by the JV, the project was cancelled. The shock and awe felt by the Korean members of the JV were hard. They did not agree with this decision and could not understand why this first major project would be killed so soon into development. This caused major tension in the relationships with the LG and Nortel counterparts and with the Nortel corporate parent. CEO Lee started asking direct questions, such as 'How could you do this?' and 'Now why are we working together?'

With tensions mounting, small internal conflicts were happening in private. Then one day, in a public meeting, CEO Lee had a very emotional reaction and vented upon MacKinnon many of Lee's frustrations of working with a North American company. Understanding this was not the norm for a Korean executive, MacKinnon listened intently to everything Lee had to say. Once Lee finished, MacKinnon recognized that he must respond and struck back with a ten-minute speech directed at Lee. Afterward, the Korean managers at the meeting asked MacKinnon to go for drinks, but he declined. Seeing that MacKinnon had his hockey equipment with him when leaving, they realized that he had other plans that evening. In fact, MacKinnon had not taken up their offer to go drinking on a number of other occasions and was always sure to have other plans.

THE FUTURE CHALLENGE OF THE LG-NORTEL JV

MacKinnon is currently a full-time chairman as directed by Nortel CEO Mike Z. However, Mike Z. is also concerned about the possibility that MacKinnon might be burned out. MacKinnon himself fully recognizes that eventually he needs to gracefully retreat, become more strategic and become a part-time chairman. To do this, he ponders how to set up the organization, processes and people to be most effective. In addition, he must ensure success before trade talks among Korea, the United States and Canada conclude, which would lower trade barriers and allow greater competition.[3] The big challenge for MacKinnon is: How can LG-Nortel be self-sustaining, and how can he pull away from the day-to-day operations of the JV?

Case discussion questions

1 Did Nortel make the right decision by (re)entering South Korea through a JV? What other market entry alternatives did Nortel have?

2 Discuss the advantages and disadvantages of having a strategic alliance such as the LG-Nortel JV. What are the unique advantages of controlling 50 per cent equity plus one share?

3 What are the skills and attributes that successful JV managers would ideally possess? Does MacKinnon possess these skills and attributes?

4 What can MacKinnon do to reduce cross-cultural conflicts within the JV?

5 What can Nortel and LG do to improve the odds for the success of this JV?

NOTES

1 LGE website: http://us.lge.com/about/company/c_profile.jsp.
2 Nortel website: http://www.nortel.com/corporate/index.html.
3 E. Ramstad, 2006, In US-Korea free-trade talks, tense mood highlights the stakes, *Wall Street Journal*, July 11: A6.

MANAGING A DUTCH – CHINESE JOINT VENTURE: WHERE TO START?

Christoph Nedopil
Prof. Ulrich Steger
International Institute for Management Development

W hen Jan van der Werde, director of Marketing for the Asia-Pacific region of Global Beverage, boarded the plane in Shanghai to fly to Qingdao in the Chinese Shandong Province he felt a bit uneasy.

It was the first meeting of the board of Dhangtu Beer, a regionally dominant brewery, in which Global Beverage had bought a 45.8% stake as part of its expansion strategy in China. Dhangtu Beer – Global Beverage's biggest investment in China so far – had formerly been a state-owned company; the majority was still in Chinese hands, mostly through the existing management and employees, and the local government, which still had a 10% stake.

Jan could not help thinking that Global Beverage had paid too much for its stake in Dhangtu Beer. However, what was preoccupying him more than reaping the economic benefits of the joint venture was to make an essential pre-condition work: To manage the complex corporate governance issues. During the due diligence of

Research Associate Christoph Nedopil prepared this disguised case under the supervision of Professor Ulrich Steger as a basis for class discussion rather than to illustrate either effective or ineffective handling of a business situation. Names of companies and individuals have been changed to secure anonymity.

Dhangtu Beer, when Jan had had a first glimpse of the company and its board members, he had told his boss:

'As one would expect in that remote area, Dhangtu Beer has serious transparency problems due to its very arcane accounting structures'.

What made the collaboration even more difficult was that all the board meetings had to be translated, as did the dinner conversations. Furthermore, Jan was worried by the holding structure of the group, since it would probably not provide fast decision making. Rather there were possible conflicts of interest on the horizon, since the former state bureaucracy had no tradition of behaving like a company in a competitive environment – neither on the board level nor further down in the organization. This became especially clear to Jan during the due diligence: Despite Dhangtu Beer's dominant position in the region being threatened by its competitors, Jan did not feel any sense of urgency in the company to react, especially not on the board.

COMPANY BACKGROUND

Dhangtu Beer had a long tradition of brewing beer. Established by Germans in the city of Qingdao in Shandong Province in 1899, the brewery became famous across the province borders. It was one of the oldest breweries in China and had a production volume of around ten million hectoliters in 2006 (the total beer volume in China was almost 212 million hectoliters in 2006 and the biggest beer producer, Tsingtao, had a market share of approximately 12 per cent).

Dhangtu Beer had been state owned for almost 60 years and was only officially privatized in 2005 when the government sold 10 per cent of the shares as an experiment to the Hong Kong-based One National Bank. Only after this trade was successful the government went on to find more shareholders.

At this point, 10 per cent of its stocks were still owned by the local government through the Jiao'ao Group Co. Ltd (Jiao'ao Group). The Jiao'ao Group itself was also a former state-owned holding company and was now partly privatized with different shareholder groups such as the local government (80 per cent) and various employee groups (20 per cent).

The remaining shares of Dhangtu Beer were held by several institutions: 20 per cent of the shares were held by the existing management and the employees through a private holding company – the Pilsnyu Group – and 14.2 per cent of the shares were floated on the Shenzhen Stock Exchange. The relative majority owner with 45.8 per cent though was Global Beverage, a Dutch-based brewing company with holdings in breweries around the world (refer to **Exhibit 1** for the ownership structure of Dhangtu Beer).

Global Beverage knew that this was a unique opportunity to acquire a share in one of the oldest and best-known breweries in China. But of course other investors were also aware of this, and with all of them vying to get their tenders accepted, the bidding went through the roof.

Finally, on June 21, 2005 Global Beverage signed an Equity Sales and Purchase Agreement with the Jiao'ao Group to acquire a 45.8 per cent stake in Dhangtu Beer. However, this acquisition did not come without demanding conditions. For example, Global Beverage had to agree to a five-year lockup period, as the shares were classified as 'Legal Person Shares'. By contrast, despite being the relative majority shareholder, Global Beverage was granted only few concessions by the Chinese, many of which had not yet been established, either formally or informally.

Exhibit 1 Ownership structure of Dhangtu beer

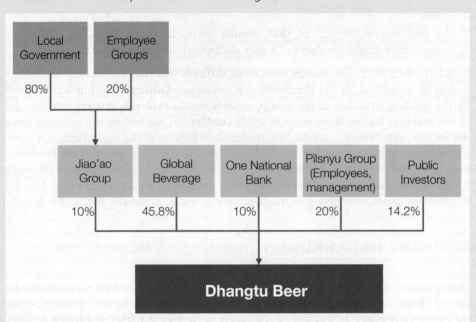

JAN VAN DER WERDE

Jan van der Werde, 43, was of Dutch origin and had worked for Global Beverage for over 15 years. He had quickly made a career for himself thanks to a dynamic and focused management style and, of course, his flexibility: In the last few years, he had not only held top management positions in Europe, South America and the Middle East but also had served on several boards of the companies Global Beverage had invested in. During the last 18 months he had been working in Asia as marketing director for the Asia-Pacific region for Global Beverage.

Jan van der Werde had already got to know Dhangtu Beer through his work in the due diligence team, which had been analyzing the company before Global Beverage took its final decision to buy the stake. Jan had also played a major role in the negotiations between the Chinese and Global Beverage.

Sitting in the plane and thinking about his past experience with Dhangtu Beer, Jan remembered the performance and governance issues that the due diligence team had revealed – and he knew that they had only scratched the surface.

GLOBAL BEVERAGE'S BIG PLANS FOR DHANGTU BEER

Dhangtu Beer had been a fairly successful company, considering its state ownership. However, since other breweries had been privatized earlier they had had a head start in streamlining their operations and had become much more competitive than Dhangtu Beer. When, during the due diligence, Jan asked a senior manager why Dhangtu was losing ground to its competitors, he replied:

'Jan, sorry to tell you that, but we currently have a rather weak position considering our production efficiency and our marketing capabilities compared to our competition'.

In fact, when the due diligence team compared Dhangtu Beer with one of Global Beverage's other investments – a smaller brewery in Shanghai – it found out that Dhangtu Beer's sales force productivity was only 40% of the other investment's productivity. This came as a big shock to Global Beverage, since they were not only looking for a great brand, but also they were urgently looking for a strategic distribution platform for other Global Beverage products in China.

Jan's boss was outraged when he received the information. Jan remembered the call he received shortly after he had sent the due diligence report:

'How the hell are we supposed to sell our products? How have things been working there for all this time? Jan, you've got to get things done over there! Dhangtu Beer is a real jewel and we really must make this work!'

But things were unfortunately not that easy and further investigations revealed that Dhangtu Beer was in fact operating below its RWA cost of capital.

THE GOVERNANCE STRUCTURE OF DHANGTU BEER

Directors

The board of directors of Dhangtu Beer had recently been extended from five to nine board members. According to the Shenzen Stock Market regulations, at least one-third of the board members of publicly listed companies had to be independent, non-executive directors.

Jan van der Werde himself was considered to be an outside director, but due to his engagement with Global Beverage, not independent. For that reason, Jan was afraid that he might be cemented in an *outsider* position without any influence.

Investors from the Shenzen Stock Exchange, the Jiao'ao Group and the Pilsnyu Group nominated the three independent, non-executive directors of Dhangtu Beer:

- Mr Jiang Flyu – Dean of the Business School of the local University, also consultant to the local government
- Mr Wang Zingzo – Director of a local accounting firm
- Mr Jungo Zhou – Director of the Chinese Beer Association

Whether these three directors would be considered as truly independent according to international standards remained unclear. For their work at Dhangtu they were compensated with RMB 30 000 (around €3000) per year without any stock options, which was in line with similar listed enterprises.

The remaining five members of the board were: one director from the Jiao'ao Group (government official), one director from One National Bank, two directors from the management through the Pilsnyu Group and Mr Liao Dxingdhu, the chief of operations for Global Beverage, China (*refer to* **Exhibit 2** *for the composition of the board*).

Mr Dxingdhu and Jan had worked together before, but things had not always been easy between them. Mr Dxingdhu was a Chinese local and it was only ten months since he had taken over the job as chief of operations from another Dutch expatriate. In fact, this had happened more as a sign of goodwill on the part of Global Beverage to accommodate Chinese employee groups than because of his qualifications.

Board Committees

The board had an audit committee as well as a recently established remuneration committee. The audit committee was composed of three members, none of whom

Exhibit 2 Board composition of Dhangtu beer

Name	Designation	Nominated by
Mr Lu Hongjing	Executive Director	Jiao'ao Group
Mr Bin Qu	Executive Director	Pilsnyu Gropu
Mr Qiang Sun	Executive Director	Pilsnyu Group
Mr Jan van der Werde	Non-Executive Director	Global Beverage (Marketing Director, Global Beverage Asia Pacific)
Mr Liao Dxingdhu	Non-Executive Director	Global Beverage (Chief of Operations, Global Beverage China)
Mr Ted Minko	Non-Executive Director	One National Bank
Mr Jiang Flyu	Independent, non-executive Director	Free-Flow Investors
Mr Wang Zingzo	Independent, non-executive Director	Pilsnyu Group
Mr Jungo Zhou	Independent, non-executive Director	Jiao'ao Group

were board members: two members from the internal audit were appointed by two shareholders and one member was appointed as a representative of the employees – certainly not a configuration that reflected international standards, which required the composition of the audit committee of non-management directors chaired by an independent non-executive director.

As yet, no members had been appointed to the remuneration committee since mostly the inside directors wanted to be on this committee. However, due to the nature of the work of this committee, it was necessary to select only non-executive directors.

THE STRUGGLE FOR PERFORMANCE

Jan lay back in his seat, trying to collect his thoughts, but his boss's words kept coming back into his head:

'Jan, you've got to get things done over there!'

He knew that his boss was mostly concerned about the economic performance of this joint venture. But as he looked out of the plane window onto the runway he pondered how he should push for economic performance with so many governance issues to resolve.

One of these issues was the remuneration of senior management – an important performance incentive in Western companies. Dhangtu Beer had recently engaged an HR consultant to revamp the compensation structure for senior management after Jan had pointed out that the structure and level of compensation were totally obscure.

Senior management remuneration was in fact a difficult topic in China, since the general level of compensation for senior managers was not yet high enough to provide sufficient incentive for managers to really care about the company performance. The HR consultant had explained to Jan:

'You've got to understand, Jan: China is traditionally a consensus-driven culture. Individual accountability is consequently difficult to institutionalize'.

Nevertheless, managers at Dhangtu Beer had the feeling that they were being compensated above average compared to other listed companies. The exact level and details of the compensation though were yet to be disclosed and then to be fairly determined by the remuneration committee.

Another issue Jan was musing about was the relationship with the Jiao'ao Group. Jan figured – also from past experience – that since the Jiao'ao Group was mostly a state owned holding group with employee interests, its goals for Dhangtu Beer might be very different from those pursued by Global Beverage. Some difficulties had already surfaced during the negotiations, when one of the government officials said:

'Even if you find one or two divisions which don't fulfil your expectations considering efficiency during your due diligence, please consider: There is no way that you will close any of them in the next 24 months. Remember, employment is our major concern and we expect shareholders to respect that obligation'.

The fact that the Jiao'ao Group only had one executive director on the board of Dhangtu Beer did little to appease Jan either, since he was afraid that the government might be able to influence decisions through the independent non-executive director they appointed as well as through party members on all management levels. As Jan was aware, through his work in the negotiations, the directors from the Jiao'ao Group had also established close ties with the three directors from the Pilsnyu Group, leaving him even less leverage in board negotiations.

Jan's best hope of getting more leverage on the board was through the director from One National Bank, although he had not yet met him. But since he was working for a bank in Hong Kong, Jan dared to hope that this director might pursue more economic interests than the others did.

HOW TO TACKLE THE DILEMMA

Jan van der Werde knew what it took to make a joint venture successful: shared and aligned goals, a trusting attitude, shared knowledge and, certainly in China, the involvement of people who had the right amount of influence to change things (*refer to* **Exhibit 3** *for a more comprehensive list of success factors of joint ventures). But would the current structure really allow this joint venture between Dhangtu and Global Beverage to flourish? How could it be changed in order to influence the performance? What would be needed to initiate the change and more importantly, what could Jan do?*

Yet Jan saw another dilemma for himself: Where should he start his battle – push for rationalization to make Dhangtu Beer more competitive again or make the board and the governance work? What were his leverages? Who could he trust?

Exhibit 3 Success factors in a joint venture

Success factors	Failure factors
1 Trusting attitude/behaviour	1 Absence of shared and aligned goals, objectives
2 Shared and aligned goals, objectives	2 Absence of clear/consistent goals, objectives
3 Open behaviour	3 Absence of trusting attitude/behaviour
4 Shared knowledge/information	4 Absence of open and unhindered communication
5 Clear roles	5 Presence of culture differences
6 Commitment	6 Absence of strong/proactive leadership
7 Co-operative/supportive behaviour	7 Presence of adversarial behaviour, non-co-operation and/or conflict
8 Openness, honesty, integrity, etc.	8 Absence of fair allocation of risks, rewards and profits
9 Integrated team, without inter-company boundaries	9 Absence of open behaviour and willingness to change
10 Involvement of people who can influence outcome	10 Absence of commitment of members to relationship

Sources: Hacque *et al.* (2004). Survey conducted 1999 – representative sample of 99 managers from UK oil and gas industry.

As the plane took off, he brushed aside his negative thoughts and remembered what his boss in headquarters had told him:

'In China the signing of the contract is the beginning of the negotiations!'

When he started reading the board book, his mind was focused on the questions: Where should he start with the negotiations? What priorities did he really need to set in this 'must-win battle?'

Discussion questions

1 From a resource-based view, what resources are the partners contributing, and what resources are they seeking from the partner? Would these contributions suggest that a JV is an appropriate organizational form?

2 From an institution-based view, how does the setting of the JV in China affect the costs and benefits of alternative organizational forms and contractual arrangements?

3 Consider the case of Danisco-Wahaha (Chapter 12, Closing Case): What lessons from that case are relevant to the negotiations between Global Beverage and Dhangtu Beer?

4 What are the next steps for Jan van der Werde in his forthcoming negotiations?

BAOSTEEL EUROPE

Bernd Michael Linke
Friedrich Schiller University of Jena, Germany
Andreas Klossek
Technical University of Freiberg, Germany

The name 'Baosteel' combines Baoshan, a district in Shanghai, China, and the English word 'steel.' 'Baosteel' stands for a Chinese company with global outreach. However, experts on Asia think that there is an additional twist at play, as is often the case with company names in this region. In Chinese 'bao' also signifies 'valuable' or 'precious', and a literal translation of Baosteel may be 'premium steel' – certainly something to which the company aspires.

This case was written by Bernd Michael Linke (Friedrich Schiller University of Jena, Germany) and Andreas Klossek (Technical University of Freiberg, Germany). It was first published in the authors' study *Chinese Companies in Germany: Chances and Challenges*, which was sponsored by Bertelsmann Foundation and Deloitte (the full study can be accessed at http://www.bertelsmann-stiftung.de/cps/rde/ xbcr/SID-12ED87F3-5090242B/bst_engl/xcms_bst_dms_27517_27534_2.pdf). The authors would like to thank both for granting the permission to reprint this case. © Bertelsmann Foundation. Reprinted with permission. Case discussion questions were added by Mike Peng.

Baosteel's home market is staggering. On the demand side, the market reflects the sheer and insatiable needs of the largest and most successful emerging economy in the world. However, on the supply side, it is fragmented unlike any other market in the world. Currently, the Chinese steel market is divided by 260 steelmakers of various sizes, and some sources say this number could be greater than 1000. While some of these firms are profitable, most are not. Thus, it is not surprising that the Chinese government is urging them to turn themselves into large steelmaking corporations following the lead of Baosteel.

Baosteel Group was founded in Shanghai in December 1978 under the name of Baoshan Iron and Steel Complex. Skipping some of the historical details, it is suffice to say that the current-day corporation is the result of a large merger between Shanghai Metallurgical Holding Group Corporation and Shanghai Meishan Group Co., Ltd. carried out in 1998 on the basis of a government decree. With continued growth, the most recent acquisition took place in April 2008, when Baosteel acquired the Bayi Steel Group in the province of Xinjiang.

Baosteel Group is a holding company consisting of five divisions: (1) financial, (2) steel trading, (3) equipment and spare parts engineering, (4) steel products and (5) Shanghai headquarters office (administrative and service). The company produces and sells steel primarily to carmakers, shipbuilders, electronics and household appliances makers, oil drilling and pipeline companies and construction companies. Baosteel has further diversified into areas such as financial services, trading and logistics services. In sum, the company's operational philosophy is to continue to 'diversify trading functions and operation products' while 'gradually expanding non-Baosteel trading business'.[1]

In comparison to international rivals, Baosteel displays a high degree of diversification. However, this is typical for many large Asian firm. Baosteel is a wholly owned state-owned enterprise (SOE). The largest business unit, Baoshan Iron and Steel Co., Ltd. (Baosteel Co., Ltd.), has been listed on the Shanghai Stock Exchange since 2000. Currently 78 per cent of the shares are held by Baosteel Group, and thus ultimately by the Chinese government.

In recent years, the turnover of Baosteel has risen annually by 10 per cent, from $19.5 billion in 2004 to $26.3 billion in 2007. During the same period, steel production has risen from 21.4 million to 28.6 million tons. Baosteel, which currently employs 122 780 workers, is China's largest producer of steel. It has worked on prestigious and complex building projects such as the principal venue of the 2008 Summer Olympic Games (the national stadium nicknamed 'Bird's Nest' in Beijing), the headquarters of CCTV state television in Beijing and the terminals of international airports in Beijing and Shanghai. In international terms the company is also one of the largest corporations of its kind. Since 2006, Baosteel has been in fifth place in the global steelmaker category. In 2004, Baosteel was the first Chinese manufacturing company to be included in the *Fortune* 500 list at 372 – by 2008 it had climbed to 259. Baosteel aims to become one of the three largest steel producers in the world as soon as possible, and is well on its way to achieving this goal.

STRATEGIC POSITIONING AND GLOBAL ACTIVITIES

Many experts believe that Baosteel's goal is attainable. Its accomplishments, which the Western media traditionally would not have thought possible in the case of a Chinese SOE, speak for themselves. Over the course of the most recent merger, the workforce was cut 43 per cent from 176 000 to 122 780. Baosteel believes that its future success is no longer going to be based on cheap labour, but instead on automated production. The main plant in Shanghai is considered to be one of the most modern and most efficient manufacturing sites for steel products in the *world*. At Baosteel, the new management focus is visible in many areas. For example, the 'Six Sigma' quality management system was successfully introduced in 2005. Further, Baosteel engages in strategic planning and has an integrated management system designed to regulate and assign responsibilities, executive order powers and communication channels between business entities.

Corporate social responsibility (CSR) has also become increasingly important in recent years. Baosteel is ahead of this social trend, embracing CSR and bankrolling numerous social projects as early as 1990. For example, the establishment of Baosteel Education Fund is one of the most visible education awards nationwide. Its foundation has set up 38 Hope elementary schools[2] and provides support for sustainability and environmental projects. To further substantiate its dedication to CSR, Baosteel is the first Chinese company to publish annual sustainability reports, which have appeared since 2005. Moreover, in 2006 the management announced a new slogan and goal centred around CSR. The slogan, 'Green Baosteel, our common home', is aligned with its goal of turning Baosteel into the cleanest and most sustainable steelmaker in the world.

The preconditions for turning the company into a global player are in place. First, Baosteel, since its founding, has never been a typical Chinese SOE. Second, it dates back only to December 1978, which coincides with the exact point at which the Chinese economic reforms got off the ground. Thus, unlike many SOEs, it was not burdened with the legacy of the Chinese communist past. Finally, it has been shaped by the cosmopolitan tradition of Shanghai, which is reflected in the long-lasting relationships and numerous joint ventures that the Baosteel Group holds with other global players.

Baosteel is prepared to confront the future and recognizes the enormous challenges it will bring. Special market segments in China have, for some time, seen higher growth rates and much higher demand levels than in other emerging markets such as India and Russia. To some extent, they have even caught up with those of industrialized countries such as the United States. The latest OECD research suggests that this trend is visible in every segment of the Chinese steel market and is projected to become more pronounced. At the same time, exports continue to grow despite the gigantic demand in China. In 2004, Chinese steel exports exceeded imports for the first time in history.

Endeavouring to meet the high demand at home, more than 90 per cent of Baosteel's turnover is in China. Additionally, to enhance its negotiating position in the competition for scarcer natural resources, it is planning further mergers and acquisitions at home and abroad, both horizontally and vertically (upstream and downstream) across the value chain. The current consolidation of the Chinese steel market and open access to international markets are making this strategy of acquiring new plants and integrating important mining sites possible. For example, currently, Baosteel imports 80 per cent of the iron ore it needs. However, as early as in 2001 the company took a 50 per cent share in the Brazilian iron ore mine Água Limpa, and in 2003 it acquired shares in Hamersley Iron, an Australian subsidiary of Rio Tinto. These equity positions are examples of Baosteel's vertical movement on the value chain. Moreover, loose partnerships and numerous meetings with other steel giants in Asia, such as Nippon Steel in Japan and Posco in Korea, nurture rumours that a merger may emerge.

Of decisive importance for the Baosteel Group's strategic planning are not only the economic goals, but also the acquisition of international management experience. As such, internationalization efforts, such as those detailed in the remainder of the case with a focus on Baosteel Europe, are crucial.

SETTING UP A SUBSIDIARY IN HAMBURG, GERMANY

Baosteel has been conducting business in Germany for a long time, though its activities have changed significantly over the years. In the beginning, it was impossible to think about selling steel products; rather its main task was to supply Chinese companies with vital replacement parts sourced in Germany for domestic production. This changed in 1993, when senior management decided to expand and founded Baosteel Europe GmbH with $6.64 million. Baosteel selected Germany for a very specific reason: the local courts provide European customers and suppliers with more legal protection than if business were to be conducted in Hong Kong or China. In other words, Baosteel considered the 'rules of the game' regarding the legal infrastructure and enforcement across countries and made its location decision using the institution-based view.

After deciding to locate in Germany, Baosteel also evaluated a number of German cities. Its decision to locate the business in the Hamburg metropolis was based on both economical motives (such as direct access to shipping routes) and cultural aspects. For example, Ye Meng, the current President of Baosteel Europe, states:

> 'Hamburg and China can look back on a long history of partnership. There really are quite a lot of Chinese companies and trading entities here. The parent of Baosteel Europe GmbH comes from Hamburg's sister city, Shanghai, which is also a port city. Both from a cultural perspective and for geographical reasons Hamburg in our opinion provides us with favourable conditions for the development of our company.'

Additionally, the workforce, technology and infrastructure in Germany are known to be world class. Further, Meng believes that earning the trust of German clients and selling 'Made in Germany' steel parts in China have benefited the company greatly.[3]

Indeed, Baosteel Europe's business has been booming. In the last three years, turnover increased to $732 million. This means that Baosteel Europe is among the largest Chinese companies in Germany. While making a profit, Baosteel Europe is certainly not resting on its laurels. Not only is Baosteel Europe strategizing to increase its share of the global market, it is also seeking to expand in Germany and Europe with new products and innovations. As such, the Hamburg subsidiary is due for expansion with new specialists recruited. Under Meng, the structure of Baosteel Europe GmbH has changed considerably in the last four years. For example, in 2004, there were 30 Baosteel employees in Germany, and today there are 55 – with additional employees in other offices throughout Europe, the Middle East, and Shanghai. The finance department and the Shanghai office are responsible for the internal organization of what happens in Hamburg. Looking after customers and suppliers is the task of each business areas (i.e., steel trading, spare parts and equipment and metal products). Recently, the new business department has been given the mandate of expanding into new business areas. In order to manage a variety of tasks, the company employs individuals from a number of countries. In Hamburg, Chinese expatriates work side by side with Germans. In other subsidiaries in Europe, employees from the various host countries are in the majority. Taken together, it is apparent that Baosteel is a transnational company with a global outlook.

BUSINESS AREAS OF THE
BAOSTEEL SUBSIDIARY IN GERMANY

Procurement, which was of considerable importance at the start of Baosteel's activities in Germany, continues to play an important role today. The transactions involved are complicated and inter-culturally demanding, requiring good coordination. The procurement process is set in motion by a firm in given location – for example a Chinese steelmaker in a province, which needs spare parts obtainable only from Europe. This requirement is relayed to the Baosteel head office in Shanghai, which subsequently transmits an inquiry to Baosteel Europe. The inquiry is received by a Chinese or German employee in Hamburg, who then places an order with a local (German) supplier. After the spare parts arrive, another Chinese or German Baosteel employee arranges for them to be sent to China. Inquiry, order processing and transport are dealt with in Chinese, German and English, meaning that employees of both nations transact on many tasks together and must engage in an ongoing dialogue. Thus, at the Hamburg location business success absolutely depends on Sino-German cooperation, which is based on years of experience and mutual understanding. A Chinese department head supervises four tandems, each consisting of a Chinese and a German employee, who know each other and work together in a coordinated manner.

Steel trading, however, has a fundamentally different procurement process, wherein ten Chinese co-workers – most of whom are engineers – work under the direction of the internationally-experienced deputy managing director, Guo Zheng. The working language is Chinese and in keeping with international business practices, English is used when communicating with the 'outside' world. In steel trading, the German market plays a subordinate role. Sales orders are sent via Hamburg, where the contracts are concluded, to the whole of Europe and the rest of the world. The majority of customers value Baosteel's quality, reliability, punctual delivery and service. Although price is important in certain countries, Baosteel does not position itself in the lower price segment, preferring to have a price level akin to that of ThyssenKrupp and ArcelorMittal. In order to increase its market share in Europe, Baosteel is pinning its hopes on premium quality and customer orientation. The turnover volume, currently about 500 000 to 600 000 tons annually, is still a very small percentage of the total output.

The new business department is also managed by a Chinese expatriate with international experience. 'New' refers both to new regions (such as the Middle East, Eastern Europe and Africa) and to new activities (such as investments in sectors other than the steel industry). The current planning phase involves conducting feasibility studies (with the help of external expertise) and studying market entry methods.

CORPORATE CULTURE AND WORK ATMOSPHERE

In recent years, Baosteel's senior management has come to realize the importance of a common corporate culture – for both Chinese and foreign employees. In 2004, Baosteel implemented a programme that stresses 'good faith' and 'synergy' as basic values and emphasizes the significance of culture as the basis of all economic action. It has been said that: 'Baosteel's culture is the soul of management, while Baosteel's management is the vehicle of culture'. The executives at Baosteel Europe emphasize words such as 'integrity', 'teamwork' and 'loyalty', and are thus transferring to all employees the essence and level of their cooperation with the head office in Shanghai. To stress the high opinion and importance of the local workforce, all German employees of Baosteel Europe were invited to stay in Shanghai for a week. There they were shown the organization of the head office, met their counterparts with whom they often telephoned or exchanged emails, and experienced Chinese hospitality – along with gratitude for their achievement and loyalty to the company. The German employees have also been included in the Chinese bonus system in order to encourage their participation in the success of the company.

At the bi-annual meeting involving all Baosteel Europe employees, management reports at length about the success and goals of the parent company and the Hamburg subsidiary, hoping to foster a community spirit. The German employees were also pleasantly surprised that the Chinese executives clearly try to respect German habits and customs by not expecting German employees to stay in the office until late in the evening, as is often the case with Chinese expatriates. Baosteel has come to understand and acknowledge that despite different work habits, in the end, the efficiency is the same.

The German employees are also particularly appreciative of the respect with which Chinese superiors treat their subordinates. The experience of working together on a daily basis means that German employees at Baosteel certainly do not share the typically negative picture of China that is often painted by the media. Instead, most have developed a far more positive picture of China.

Apart from the good atmosphere in the workplace, employees have additional motivations. Specifically, a large and expanding company is synonymous with safe jobs. This is especially true for Chinese companies, where protection against dismissal is based on the Chinese and Confucian belief that one has a duty to look after the well being of others. The high one-off bonuses for special accomplishments confirm the appreciative attitude of the senior management. Therefore, employee turnover is quite small in comparison to other companies within this industry.

To advance within Baosteel, it is necessary to occupy a position of responsibility at the head office. As such, it is necessary for individuals to possess not only professional qualifications, but also have the ability to speak fluent Chinese. Thus, many German employees who do not speak Chinese find it extremely difficult to reach the senior management level at Baosteel Europe. Overall, while challenge remain, Baosteel has overcome many of the cultural differences by taking time to understand those differences and finding ways to embed both the German and Chinese cultures within its organizational culture.

HUMAN RESOURCE MANAGEMENT (HRM)

In China, Baosteel enjoys a good reputation for its excellent compensation and career opportunities. To maintain its reputation and recruit top talent, Baosteel implements a very thorough recruiting process. Candidates for its comprehensive examination procedure are selected from a large number of applicants – of which all are university graduates. Unlike most companies in East Asia, Baosteel rarely recruits candidates jumping ship from other employers or at job fairs. However, once candidates are selected, the successful applicants are introduced to and trained in Baosteel's corporate culture, which is a customary practice in Chinese firms. If the candidate does well over the course of the year, the company may cover the cost of further education – for example, a one-year higher education programme at home or abroad. After this, the individual is likely to be promoted within the company and employed as a senior executive, alternating between China and other countries.

Interestingly, until recently it had been considered a welcome opportunity for Chinese employees to be offered the opportunity to work abroad for a number of years, since it coincided with good pay and enhanced qualifications. However, because income and career opportunities have developed enormously within China in recent years, many consider this same 'opportunity' or assignment to be a burden, especially since the quality of life in Shanghai is now higher than that in many Western cities.

In other words, Chinese expatriates now experience the same types of burdens as expatriates from developed countries, such as separation from their family or problems with their children's schools overseas. Although Baosteel takes into account these reservations and offers its Chinese expatriates numerous incentives such as increased compensation and job guarantees for spouses, the willingness to work in other countries is declining. However, for individuals trying to climb the career ladder, successful stints abroad considerably facilitate access to the senior management level and to executive posts in the subsidiaries and at the head office.

More recently, Baosteel has expanded the scope of its HRM, becoming more strategic in nature. In addition to regular assessments, the skills of its employees are continually being enhanced by means of systematic training. Further, preparatory country-specific or culture-specific instruction for foreign assignments is now available, as are returnees' programmes. Finally, the mentoring system is well organized and highly valued. Talented young executives are watched over and given advice by mentors appointed to look after and guide them. As mentors rise in the company hierarchy, it will eventually lead to advancement for their 'mentees', who may also receive recommendations for employment elsewhere. This network system not only leads to good professional work, but is indispensable if one wishes to advance to a decision-making position.

BAOSTEEL EUROPE PAVES THE WAY FOR INTEGRATION AND EXPANSION

For Baosteel, numerous economic and cultural aspects were of decisive importance when it chose Hamburg as its European location. Endeavouring for a win-win outcome, Baosteel Europe has developed a great relationship with the Hamburg city government, especially with its departments involved in economic development. Baosteel continuously manages this relationship by staying in touch with the media and having company representatives participate in and sponsor public events. Interestingly, Baosteel has also incorporated its German-oriented practices of external representation back in China, demonstrating its dedication to learning from global best practices. Baosteel has also begun to develop ideas regarding networking strategies with other Chinese organizations in Germany geared toward the joint promotion of their interests, and maintained loose partnerships with two other large Chinese corporations also located in Hamburg – COSCO and Bank of China.

Baosteel Europe is said to exemplify the 'large Chinese corporation abroad' and it occupies a frontrunner role in two senses – being both a 'test case' and a 'model'.[4] Many Chinese companies still find it difficult to be internationally competitive, and there is often a discrepancy between an impressive success story told at home and the hesitant progress overseas that may be marred by setbacks. This could change quickly if 'pilot projects', such as the internationalization of Baosteel, are a success and the senior management of other companies draws the right conclusions. However, it is not only the views within an industry that are of importance. Chinese companies, especially those with international ambitions, must assume that they are being watched intently by the public both at home and abroad, and must behave in a responsible manner.

After a rough start, Baosteel has made significant progress in recent years. Admittedly, the situation has been rather auspicious for the steel industry. An essential basis for further expansion in the international sector is a systematic development of HR beginning with recruiting, and leading to career planning and further education. Baosteel aims to use the talents of both German and third-country specialists and to form international leadership teams that will be in a position to meet the challenges of international management. Further, in the case of international customer-supplier relationships, it is important to pre-empt cross-cultural conflicts by increasing the level of intercultural competence and strengthening an overarching corporate culture.

Baosteel is well on its way to mastering these challenges, having already united a variety of very different companies in Shanghai and developing a distinct corporate culture among its employees. When discussing Baosteel's 'hard skills', the former chairwoman Qihua Xie once coined the slogan 'quality, not quantity'. The same can just as well be applied to Baosteel's 'soft skills'. Overall, the Baosteel Group is an exemplary company for which other Chinese companies can learn from.

Case discussion questions

1   What location-specific advantages did Hamburg, Germany, provide Baosteel? Evaluate other European locations that might offer similar advantages.

2   How did Baosteel manage its entry into Europe? What factors have enhanced its success?

3   What are the lessons on how to manage human resources in a subsidiary that we can draw based on Baosteel Europe's experience in Germany?

4   Why does Baosteel devote considerable resources to corporate social responsibility?

5   As the director of human resources for Baosteel, outline a strategic plan that will be implemented over the next three years that focuses on organizational culture and learning.

NOTES

1   Baosteel, 2009, Address by the President, Accessed November 11, 2009, www.baosteel. eu.
2   In Chinese jargon, Hope schools refer to schools set up in poor rural areas, where children would not have been educated had these schools not been set up. These schools are known to offer 'hope'.
3   Hamburg provides Chinese company with link to Germany, Europe, and the World, accessed November 12, 2009, http://www.gtai.com/homepage/info-service/publications/our-publications/germany-investment-magazine/vol-2008/vol-032008/foreign-direct-investment1/.
4   Handelsblatt no. 43, March 1, 2007

RIBE MASKINFABRIK A/S – DEVELOPING NEW BUSINESS AREAS

Bo Bernhard Nielsen

Torben Pedersen

Jacob Pyndt

Soren Frolunde

Copenhagen Business School

Richard Ivey School of Business
The University of Western Ontario

CEO Ole Juul Jørgensen evaluated the RM Group (RM) 2004 results and was highly satisfied. The company had recorded a net income of DKK9.2 million, which was the best result in the company's history (see Exhibit 1). Jørgensen looked at his great-grandfather, the company's founder, who was portrayed on the wall in

Professor Bo Bernhard Nielsen, Professor Torben Pedersen and Management Consultant Jacob Pyndt with assistance from Research Assistant Søren Frølunde wrote this case solely to provide material for class discussion. The authors do not intend to illustrate either effective or ineffective handling of a managerial situation. The authors may have disguised certain names and other identifying information to protect confidentiality.

Exhibit 1 RM holding financial performance 2001-2004

Key figures (DKK thousands)	2001/02	2002/03	2003/04
Gross profit	41 016	52 191	69 058
Profit before financial items	9 157	11 247	16 375
Profit for the year	4 188	4 429	9 257
Inventories	13 236	24 687	38 879
Trade receivables	16 515	36 638	22 346
Equity	10 256	14 685	23 857
Balance sheet	61 172	107 071	131 678
Key ratios (percentage)			
Return on equity	51	35	48
Equity ratio	17	14	18

Source: RM Holding annual report 2004.

his office. The painting served to emphasize the strong family values permeating the company. His grandfather would undoubtedly be proud of the company's achievements since he founded it in 1897, although he could not have anticipated the major strategic shifts and global orientation that took place starting in 1993.

Jørgensen represented the fourth generation of family members to serve as major shareholders in RM – a company comprised of Ribe Maskinfabrik, Rimadan A/S and RM-Group China (see Exhibit 2). An engineer by training, he had been responsible for the development of the company since 1994. RM's transformation and achievements did not pass unnoticed by the business media. As a supplier of processed (manufactured) steel, RM was often described in the Danish media as a prime example of how a supplier can capture opportunities arising from globalization. Instead of viewing globalization as a threat, RM used the apparent labour cost advantage by selling tailor-made outsourcing projects through which industrial clients bought access to RM's web of sub-suppliers, primarily those in Central and Eastern Europe (CEE).

In light of tough market conditions characterized by increasing steel prices, the 2004 results were gratifying. Group Director Peter Lønborg Nielsen commented on the state of the industry:

'Our industry has been under pressure as a consequence of production relocations and mounting steel prices, and it has been rather tough to pass on high raw material prices to the customer. I believe that steel prices are beginning to stagnate and that will give the company a better order prospect'.[1]

RM clearly demonstrated how to tackle global opportunities proactively. The question was how these positive developments could be sustained and new business opportunities could be realized. Globalization affected companies at a rapid pace and Jørgensen felt that the company had to be on the lookout for attractive production sites and supplier webs that could help generate new business. RM saw itself as a 'conductor', matching supplier capacity, quality and know-how with clients' needs. In that role, RM opted to find the best-suited supplier at the best possible

GLOSSARY OF KEY TERMS

AAA typology Aggregation, adaptation and arbitrage strategies.

Absolute advantage The economic advantage one nation enjoys that is absolutely superior to other nations.

Absorptive capacity The ability to recognize the value of new information, assimilate it and apply it.

Accommodative strategy A strategy that is characterized by some support from top managers, who may increasingly view CSR as a worthwhile endeavour.

Acquisition The transfer of the control of operations and management from one firm (target) to another (acquirer), the former becoming a unit of the latter.

Acquisition premium The difference between the acquisition price and the market value of target firms.

Adaptability The ability to change supply chain configurations in response to long-term changes in the environment and technology.

Adaptation strategy Strategy of delivering locally adapted products in each market.

Administrative practices Bureaucratic rules that make it harder to import foreign goods.

Agglomeration The location advantages that arise from the clustering of economic activities in certain locations.

Aggregation strategy Strategy of realizing synergies between operations at different locations.

Agility The ability to quickly react to unexpected shifts in supply and demand.

Alignment The alignment of interest of various players.

Andean Community A customs union in South America that was launched in 1969.

Anti-competitive practices (by a dominant firm) Business practices by a dominating firm that make it more difficult for competitors to enter or survive.

Antidumping duty Costs levied on imports that have been 'dumped' (selling below costs to 'unfairly' drive domestic firms out of business).

Anti-trust laws Laws that attempt to curtail anticompetitive collusion by businesses.

Appreciation (of a currency) An increase in the value of a currency.

Appropriability The ability of the firm to appropriate the values for itself.

Arbitrage strategy Strategy of exploiting differences in prices in different markets.

Artefacts of culture The visible surface of culture.

ASEAN-China Free Trade Agreement (ACFTA) An agreement to establish a free trade area encompassing ASEAN and China.

Asset specificity An investment that is specific to a business relationship.

Association of South-east Asian Nations (ASEAN) The organization underpinning regional economic integration in Southeast Asia.

Attack An initial set of actions to gain competitive advantage.

Australia-New Zealand Closer Economic Relations Trade Agreement (ANZCERTA or CER) A bilateral trade agreement between Australia and New Zealand.

Awareness, motivation, capability (AMC) framework A conceptual framework indicating when firms are likely to attack and counter-attack each other.

Balance of payments (BoP) A country's international transaction statement, including merchandize trade, service trade and capital movement.

Balance of trade The aggregation of importing and exporting that leads to the country-level trade surplus or deficit.

Bandwagon effect The result of investors moving as a herd in the same direction at the same time.

Bargaining power The ability to extract a favourable outcome from negotiations due to one party's strengths.

Base of the pyramid The vast majority of humanity, about four billion people, who make less than €1500 a year.

Basel Committee A group of central bankers establishing standards for banking supervision.

Basel II The name of a set of rules for banking regulation.

Benchmarking An examination of resources to perform a particular activity compared against competitors.

Bid rate The price offered to buy a currency.

Blue ocean strategy A strategy of attack that avoids direct confrontation.

Bologna Process A political process aimed at harmonizing European higher education.

Born global (international new venture) Start-up company that from inception, seeks to derive significant competitive advantages from the use of resources and the sale of outputs in multiple countries.

Bretton Woods system A system in which all currencies were pegged at a fixed rate to the US dollar.

Brownfield acquisition Acquisition where subsequent investment overlays the acquired organization.

Build–operate–transfer (BOT) A contract combining the construction and temporary operation of a project eventually to be transferred to a new owner.

Business unit JV A JV in which existing business units from two firms are merged.

Capability Firm-specific abilities to use resources to achieve organizational objectives.

Capacity to punish Sufficient resources possessed by a price leader to deter and combat defection.

Capital and financial account (of the BoP) Sales and purchases of financial assets.

Capital flight A phenomenon in which a large number of individuals and companies exchange domestic currencies for a foreign currency.

Captive (in-house) offshoring Setting up subsidiaries abroad – the work done is in-house but the location is foreign.

Cartel An entity that engages in output- and price-fixing, involving multiple competitors.

Case law Rules of law that have been created by precedents of cases in court.

Causal ambiguity The difficulty of identifying the causal determinants of successful firm performance.

Central and Eastern Europe The common name used for the countries east of the former Iron Curtain.

Centres of excellence An MNE subsidiary explicitly recognized as a source of important capabilities, with the intention that these capabilities be leveraged by and/or disseminated to other subsidiaries.

Child labour Working persons under the age of 16.

Civil law A legal tradition that uses comprehensive statutes and codes as a primary means to form legal judgments.

Civilization The highest cultural grouping of people and the broadest level of cultural identity people have.

Classical trade theories The major theories of international trade that were advanced before the 20th century, which consist of mercantilism, absolute advantage and comparative advantage.

Cluster Countries that share similar cultures together.

Code of conduct A set of guidelines for making ethical decisions.

Cognitive pillar The internalized, taken-for-granted values and beliefs that guide individual and firm behaviour.

Collectivism The idea that the identity of an individual is primarily based on the identity of his or her collective group.

Collusion Collective attempts between competing firms to reduce competition.

Collusive price setting Price setting by monopolists or collusion parties at a higher than competitive level.

Comecon The pre-1990 trading bloc of the socialist countries.

Command economy An economy in which all factors of production are government- or state-owned and controlled, and all supply, demand and pricing are planned by the government.

Common agricultural policy (CAP) The EU's policy for the agricultural sector.

Common currency Currency shared by a number of countries

Common law A legal tradition that is shaped by precedents and traditions from previous judicial decisions.

Common market Combining everything that a customs union has, a common market permits free movement of goods and people.

Communities of practice (CoP) Groups of people doing similar or related work and sharing knowledge about their practices of work.

Commuter assignment Assignments that involve regular stays abroad but with the main base remaining back home.

Comparative advantage Relative (not absolute) advantage in one economic activity that one nation enjoys in comparison with other nations.

Compensation The determination of salary and benefits.

Competition policy (anti-trust policy) Policy governing the rules of the game in competition in a country.

Competitive dynamics The actions and responses undertaken by competing firms.

Competitor analysis The process of anticipating a rivals' actions in order to both revise a firm's plan and prepare to deal with rivals' responses.

Concentration ratio The percentage of total industry sales accounted for by the top 4, 8 or 20 firms.

Consortium A project based temporary business owned and managed jointly by several firms.

Contender strategy This strategy centres on a firm engaging in rapid learning and then expanding overseas.

Context The underlying background upon which interaction takes place.

Contingency plans Plans devised for specific situations when things could go wrong.

Contract work A short assignment for a specific project or contract.

Coordinated market economy (CME) A system of coordinating through a variety of other means in addition to market signals.

Copenhagen Accord A declaration by developed and developing countries to combat climate change.

Copenhagen Criteria Criteria the new members have to fulfil to be admitted as members of the EU.

Copyrights Exclusive legal rights of authors and publishers to publish and disseminate their work.

Corporate governance Rules by which shareholders and other interested parties control corporate decision-makers.

Corporate language The language used for communications between entities of the same MNE in different countries.

Corporate social responsibility (CSR) The consideration of, and response to, issues beyond the narrow economic, technical and legal requirements of the firm to accomplish social benefits along with the traditional economic gains which the firm seeks.

Corruption The abuse of public power for private benefits, usually in the form of bribery.

Cosmopolitans The people embracing cultural diversity and the opportunities of globalization.

Council of Europe A loose association in which essentially all European countries are members.

Council of the European Union The top decision-making body of the EU, consisting of ministers from the national governments; it decides by qualified majority voting.

Counter party risk The risk of a business partner not being able to fulfil a contract.

Counter-attack A set of actions in response to an attack.

Country or regional manager The business leader of a specific geographic area or region.

Country-of-origin effect The positive or negative perception of firms and products from a certain country.

Crawling bands A policy of keeping the exchange rate within a specified range, which may be changing over time.

Cross-border services Supplying services across national borders.

Cross-market retaliation The ability of a firm to expand in a competitor's market if the competitor attacks in its original market.

Cultural distance The difference between two cultures along some identifiable dimensions (such as individualism).

Cultural intelligence An individual's ability to understand and adjust to new cultures.

Culture The collective programming of the mind that distinguishes the members of one group or category of people from another.

Culture shock An expatriate's reaction to a new, unpredictable, and therefore uncertain environment.

Currency board A monetary authority that issues notes and coins convertible into a key foreign currency at a fixed exchange rate.

Currency exchange market A market where individuals, firms, governments and banks buy and sell foreign currencies.

Currency hedging A transaction that protects traders and investors from exposure to the fluctuations of the spot rate.

Currency risk diversification Reducing overall risk exposure by working with a number of different currencies.

Currency swap A currency exchange transaction between two firms in which one currency is converted into another in Time 1, with an agreement to revert it back to the original currency at a specific Time 2 in the future.

Current account (of the BoP) Exports and imports of goods and services.

Customs union One step beyond a free trade area, a customs union imposes common external policies on non-participating countries.

Deadweight loss Net losses that occur in an economy as the result of tariffs.

Defender strategy This strategy centres on leveraging local assets in areas in which MNEs are weak.

Defensive strategy A strategy that focuses on regulatory compliance with little top management commitment to CSR causes.

Democracy A political system in which citizens elect representatives to govern the country on their behalf.

Depreciation (of a currency) A decrease in the value of a currency.

Design and build (DB) contract A contract combining the architectural or design work with the actual construction.

Development aid A gift from generous donors wishing to help developing countries.

Direct exports The sale of products made by firms in their home country to customers in other countries.

Directorate General (DG) A department of the EU commission, similar to a ministry of a national government.

Dispute settlement mechanism A procedure of the WTO to resolve conflicts between governments over trade-related matters.

Dissemination risks The risks associated with unauthorized diffusion of firm-specific know-how.

Distribution channel The set of business units and intermediaries that facilitates the movement of goods to consumers.

Distributor An intermediary trading on their own account.

Divestment The sale or closure of a business unit or asset.

Dodger strategy This strategy centres on cooperating through joint ventures (JVs) with MNEs and sell-offs to MNEs.

Doha Round A round of WTO negotiations started in Doha, Qatar, in 2001 – Officially known as the 'Doha Development Agenda'.

Domestic outsourcing Outsourcing to a firm in the same country.

Downstream vertical FDI A type of vertical FDI in which a firm engages in a downstream stage of the value chain in two different countries.

Due diligence The assessment of the target firm's financial status, resources and strategic fit.

Dumping An exporter selling below cost abroad and planning to raise prices after eliminating local rivals.

Dynamic capabilities Higher level capabilities that enable an organization to continuously adapt to new technologies and changes in the external environment.

Economic forecasting A technique using econometric models to predict the likely future value of key economic variables.

Economic system Rules of the game on how a country is governed economically.

Economic transition The process of changing from central plan to a market economy.

Economic union In addition to all features of a common market, members of an economic union coordinate and harmonize economic policies.

Economies of scale Reduction in unit costs achieved by increasing volume.

Efficiency seeking Firms' quest to single out the most efficient locations featuring a combination of scale economies and low-cost factors.

Emerging economies (emerging markets) Economies that only recently established institutional frameworks that facilitate international trade and investment, typically with low or middle level income and above average economic growth.

Entrepreneurial teams A group of people jointly acting as entrepreneurs.

Entrepreneurs Leaders identifying opportunities and taking decisions to exploit them.

Entry strategy A plan that specifies the objectives of an entry and how to achieve them.

Equity mode A mode of entry (JVs and wholly owned subsidiaries) that is indicative of relatively larger, harder to reverse commitments.

Erasmus Programme An EU programme encouraging student mobility in Europe.

Ethical imperialism The absolute belief that 'there is only one set of Ethics (with the capital E), and we have it'.

Ethical relativism A perspective that suggests that all ethical standards are relative.

Ethics The principles, standards and norms of conduct governing individual and firm behaviour.

Ethnocentric approach An emphasis on the norms and practices of the parent company (and the parent country of the MNE) by relying on PCNs.

Ethnocentrism A self-cantered mentality by a group of people who perceive their own culture, ethics and norms as natural, rational, and morally right.

Euro The currency of the European Monetary Union.

European Bank for Reconstruction and Development (EBRD) A multilateral bank designed to help transition economies.

European Central Bank (ECB) The central bank for the eurozone.

European Coal and Steel Community (ECSC) A predecessor organization of the EU.

European Commission The executive arm of the EU, similar to a national government.

European Constitution An ambitious project to create a new legal foundation for the EU, which failed.

European Convention on Human Rights A charter defining human rights in Europe.

European Council The assembly of heads of governments setting overall policy directions for the EU.

European Court of Human Rights An international court assessing human rights cases in Europe.

European Court of Justice (ECJ) The court system of the EU.

European Parliament The directly elected representation of European citizens.

European Union The political and economic organization of 27 countries in Europe.

Eurozone The countries that have adopted the euro as their currency.

Exchange rate The price of one currency in another currency.

Exchange rate risk (or currency risk) The risk of financial losses because of unexpected changes in exchange rates.

Expatriate (expat) A non-native employee who works in a foreign country.

Expatriate assignments A temporary job abroad with a multinational company.

Expatriate stress Stress caused by an imbalance between expectations and abilities affected by culture shock.

Expatriation Temporarily or permanently residing in a country and culture other than that of a person's upbringing or legal residence.

Experiential knowledge Knowledge learned by engaging in the activity and context.

Explicit collusion Firms directly negotiate output, fix pricing and divide markets.

Explicit CSR Voluntarily assuming responsibilities of societal concerns.

Explicit knowledge Knowledge that is codifiable (that is, can be written down and transferred with little loss of its richness).

Export intermediary A firm that performs an important 'middleman' function by linking sellers and buyers overseas.

Exporter Seller of products or services to another country.

Exporting Selling abroad.

Expropriation Governments' confiscation of private assets.

Extender strategy This strategy centres on leveraging home-grown competencies abroad.

Factor endowment theory (or Heckscher-Ohlin theory) A theory that suggests that nations will develop comparative advantage based on their locally abundant factors.

FDI flow The amount of FDI moving in a given period (usually a year) in a certain direction.

FDI stock The total accumulation of inbound FDI in a country or outbound FDI from a country across a given period of time (usually several years).

Femininity Values traditionally associated with female role, such as compassion, case and quality of life.

First-mover advantage Advantage that first entrants enjoy and do not share with late entrants.

Fixed exchange rate An exchange rate of a currency relative to other currencies.

Floating or (flexible) exchange rate policy The willingness of a government to let the demand and supply conditions determine exchange rates.

Footloose plant Plants that can easily be relocated.

Foreign direct investment (FDI) Investments in, controlling and managing value-added activities in other countries.

Foreign portfolio investment (FPI) Investment in a portfolio of foreign securities such as stocks and bonds.

Foreign subsidiaries Operations abroad set up by foreign direct investment.

Formal institutions Institutions represented by laws, regulations and rules.

Forward discount A condition under which the forward rate of one currency relative to another currency is higher than the spot rate.

Forward exchange rate The exchange rate for forward transactions.

Forward premium A condition under which the forward rate of one currency relative to another currency is lower than the spot rate.

Forward transaction A currency exchange transaction in which participants buy and sell currencies now for future delivery, typically in 30, 90 or 180 days, after the date of the transaction.

Four freedoms of the EU single market Freedom of movement of people, goods, services and capital.

Franchisee The company receiving a franchise.

Franchising Firm A's agreement to give Firm B the rights to use a package of A's proprietary assets for a royalty fee paid to A by B.

Franchisor The company granting a franchise.

Free float A pure market solution to determine exchange rates.

Free trade Trade uninhibited by trade barriers.

Free trade area (FTA) A group of countries that remove trade barriers among themselves.

Free Trade Area of the Americas (FTAA) A proposed free trade area for the entire Western Hemisphere.

Game theory A theory on how agents interact strategically to win.

General Agreement on Tariffs and Trade (GATT) A multilateral agreement governing the international trade of goods (merchandize).

General Agreement on Trade in Services (GATS) A WTO agreement governing the international trade of services.

Geocentric approach A focus on finding the most suitable managers, who can be PCNs, HCNs or TCNs.

Geographic area structure An organizational structure that organizes the MNE according to different countries and regions.

Global economic integration Efforts to reduce trade and investment barriers around the globe.

Global key accounts Customers served at multiple sites around the world, but that negotiate centrally.

Global matrix An organizational structure often used to alleviate the disadvantages associated with both geographic area and global product division structures, especially for MNEs adopting a transnational strategy.

Global product division An organizational structure that assigns global responsibilities to each product division.

Global sourcing Buying inputs all over the world.

Global standardization strategy A strategy that relies on the development and distribution of standardized products worldwide to reap the maximum benefits from low-cost advantages.

Global strategies Strategies that take advantage of operations spread across the world.

Global virtual teams Teams that are geographically dispersed and interact primarily through electronic communication.

Globalfocusing A strategic shift from diversification to specialization which increasing the international profile.

Globalization A process leading to greater interdependence and mutual awareness among economic, political and social units in the world, and among actors in general.

Gold standard A system in which the value of most major currencies was maintained by fixing their prices in terms of gold, which served as the common denominator.

Greenfield operation Building factories and offices from scratch (on a proverbial piece of 'green field' formerly used for agricultural purposes).

Gross domestic product (GDP) The sum of value added by resident firms, households, and governments operating in an economy.

Gross national income (GNI) GDP plus income from non-resident sources abroad. GNI is the term used by the World Bank and other international organizations to supersede the term GNP.

Gross national product (GNP) Gross domestic product plus income from non-resident sources abroad.

Harmonized sector Sectors of industry for which the EU has created common rules.

Headhunter company A company specializing on finding suitable people for senior positions.

Hidden champions Market leaders in niche markets keeping a low public profile.

High-context culture A culture in which communication relies a lot on the underlying unspoken context, which is as important as the words used.

Holy An item or activity that is treated with particular respect by a religion.

Home replication strategy A strategy that emphasizes international replication of home country-based competencies such as production scales, distribution efficiencies and brand power.

Horizontal FDI A type of FDI in which a firm duplicates its home country-based activities at the same value chain stage in a host country.

Host country national (HCN) An individual from the host country who works for an MNE.

Hubris A manager's overconfidence in his or her capabilities.

Human resource management (HRM) Activities that attract, select and manage employees.

Human resources Resources embedded in individuals working in an organization.

Hypernorms Norms considered valid anywhere in the world.

IMF conditionality Conditions that the IMF attaches to loans to bail out countries in financial distress.

Immersion approach Placing a person in a situation where they will learn by practice

Implicit CSR Participating in the wider formal and informal institutions for the society's interests and concerns.

Import quota Restrictions on the quantity of imports.

Import tariff A tax imposed on imports.

Importer Buyer of goods or services from another country.

Importing Buying from abroad.

Inbound logistics Purchasing and the coordination of intermediaries on the supply side.

Indirect exports A way for SMEs to reach overseas customers by exporting through domestic-based export intermediaries.

Individualism The perspective that the identity of an individual is fundamentally his or her own.

Infant industry argument The argument that temporary protection of young industries may help them to attain international competitiveness in the long run.

Inflation The (average) change of prices over time.

Informal institutions Rules that are not formalized but exist in for example norms and values.

In-group Individuals and firms regarded as part of 'us'.

Innovation seeking Firms target countries and regions renowned for generating world-class innovations.

Inpatriation Relocating employees of a foreign subsidiary to the MNE's headquarters for the purposes of (1) filling skill shortages at headquarters and (2) developing a global mindset for such inpatriates.

Institutional distance The extent of similarity or dissimilarity between the regulatory, normative and cognitive institutions of two countries.

Institutional framework Formal and informal institutions governing individual and firm behaviour.

Institutional transition Fundamental and comprehensive changes introduced to the formal and informal rules of the game that affect organizations as players.

Institution-based view A leading perspective in international business that suggests that firm performance is, at least in part, determined by the institutional frameworks governing firm.

Institutions Formal and informal rules of the game.

Instrumental view A view that treating stakeholders well may indirectly help financial performance.

Intangible assets Assets that are hard to observe and difficult (or sometimes impossible) to quantify.

Integration-responsiveness framework A framework of MNE management on how to simultaneously deal with two sets of pressures for global integration and local responsiveness.

Intellectual property rights Rights associated with the ownership of intellectual property.

Interest rate parity Hypothesis suggesting that the interest rate in two currencies should be the same after accounting for spot and forward in exchange rates.

Internalization The replacement of cross-border markets (such as exporting and importing) with one firm (the MNE).

Internalization advantages Advantages of organizing activities within a multinational firm rather than using a market transaction.

International business (IB) (1) A business (firm) that engages in international (cross-border) economic activities and/or (2) the action of doing business abroad.

International division A structure that is typically set up when firms initially expand abroad, often engaging in a home replication strategy.

International Monetary Fund (IMF) A multilateral organization promoting international monetary cooperation and providing temporary financial assistance to countries with balance of payments problems, in order to help secure macroeconomic stability.

Intra-firm trade International trade between two subsidiaries in two countries controlled by the same MNE.

Joint-venture An operation with shared ownership by several domestic or foreign companies.

Knowledge governance The structures and mechanisms MNEs use to facilitate the creation, integration, sharing and utilization of knowledge.

Knowledge management The structures, processes and systems that actively develop, leverage and transfer knowledge.

Knowledge spillover Knowledge diffused from one firm to others among closely located firms.

Kyoto Agreement An agreement committing developed countries to limit their greenhouse gas emissions.

Late-mover advantages Advantages that late movers obtain and that first movers do not enjoy.

Legal certainty Clarity over the relevant rules applying to a particular situation.

Legal system The rules of the game on how a country's laws are enacted and enforced.

Leniency programmes Programmes that give immunity to members of a cartel that first report the cartel to the authorities.

Letter of credit (L/C) A financial contract that states that the importer's bank will pay a specific sum of money to the exporter upon delivery of the merchandize.

Liability of outsidership The *inherent* disadvantage that outsiders experience in a new environment because of their lack of familiarity.

Liberal market economy (LME) A system of coordination primarily through market signals.

Liberalization The removal of regulatory restrictions on business.

Licensee The company receiving a license.

Licensing Firm A's agreement to give Firm B the rights to use A's proprietary technology or trademark for a royalty fee paid to A by B.

Licensor The company granting a license.

Lingua franca The dominance of one language as a global business language.

Lisbon Treaty A major treaty integrating earlier treaties of the EU, and changing the institutional structures of the EU.

Lobbying Making your voice heard and known to decision-makers with the aim of influencing political processes.

Local content requirement A requirement that a certain proportion of the value of the goods made in one country originate from that country.

Local responsiveness The necessity to be responsive to different customer preferences around the world.

Localization (multidomestic) strategy A strategy that focuses on a number of foreign countries/regions, each of which is regarded as a stand-alone 'local' (domestic) market worthy of significant attention and adaptation.

Location advantages Advantages enjoyed by firms operating in certain locations.

Location-bound resources Resources that cannot be transferred abroad.

Location-specific advantages Advantages that can be exploited by those present at a location.

Long-term orientation A perspective that emphasizes perseverance and savings for future betterment.

Low-context culture A culture in which communication is usually taken at face value without much reliance on unspoken context.

Maastricht Criteria Criteria that countries have to fulfil to join the eurozone.

Maastricht Treaty A major treaty deepening integration in Europe.

Managed float The practice of influencing exchange rates through selective government intervention.

Management contract A contract over the management of assets or a firm owned by someone else.

Market commonality The overlap between two rivals' markets.

Market division collusion A collusion to divide markets among competitors.

Market economy An economy that is characterized by the 'invisible hand' of market forces.

Market failure Imperfections of the market mechanism that make some transactions prohibitively costly.

Market orientation A philosophy or way of thinking that places the highest priority on the creation of superior customer value in the marketplace.

Market seeking Firms' quest to go after countries that offer strong demand for their products and services.

Market segmentation A way to identify consumers who differ from others in purchasing behaviour.

Marketing Efforts to create, develop and defend markets that satisfy the needs and wants of individual and business customers.

Marketing mix The four underlying components of marketing: product, price, promotion and place.

Masculinity Values traditionally associated with male role, such as assertive, decisive and aggressive.

Members of the European Parliament (MEPs) Parliamentarians directly elected by the citizens of the EU.

Mercosur A customs union in South America that was launched in 1991.

Merger The combination of operations and management of two firms to establish a new legal entity.

Mimetic behaviour Imitating the behaviour of others as a means to reduce uncertainty.

Mixed economy An economy that has elements of both a market economy and command economy.

Modern trade theories The major theories of international trade that were advanced in the 20th century, which consist of product life cycle, strategic trade and national competitive advantage.

Modes of entry The format of foreign market entry.

Moral hazard Recklessness when people and organizations (including firms and governments) do not have to face the full consequences of their actions.

Multilateral organizations Organizations set up by several collaborating countries.

Multimarket competition Firms engage the same rivals in multiple markets.

Multinational enterprise (MNE) A firm that engages in foreign direct investments and operates in multiple countries.

Multiple acquisition A strategy based on acquiring and integrating multiple businesses.

Multi-tier branding A portfolio of different brands targeted at different consumer segments.

Mutual recognition The principle that products recognized as legal in one country may be sold throughout the EU.

National innovation systems The institutions and organizations that influence innovation activity in a country.

Natural resource seeking Firms' quest to pursue natural resources in certain locations.

Nearshoring Offshoring to a nearby location, i.e. within Europe.

Non-equity mode A mode of entry (exports and contractual agreements) that tends to reflect relatively smaller commitments to overseas markets.

Non-governmental organizations (NGOs) Organizations, such as environmentalists, human rights activists and consumer groups that are not affiliated with governments.

Nontariff barrier (NTB) Trade barriers that rely on nontariff means to discourage imports.

Normative pillar The mechanism through which norms influence individual and firm behaviour.

Normative view A view that firms ought to be self-motivated to 'do it right' because they have societal obligations.

North American Free Trade Agreement (NAFTA) A free trade agreement among Canada, Mexico and the USA.

Obsolescing bargain Refers to the deal struck by MNEs and host governments, which change their requirements after the initial FDI entry.

Offer rate The price offered to sell a currency.

Offshore outsourcing Outsourcing to another firm doing the activity abroad.

Offshoring Moving an activity to a location abroad.

OLI paradigm A theoretical framework positing that ownership (O), locational (L) and internationalization (I) advantages combine to induce firms to engage in FDI.

Oligopoly A market form in which a market or industry is dominated by a small number of sellers (oligopolists).

Operation collaboration A form of strategic alliance that includes collaboration in operations, marketing or distribution.

Oportunistic behaviour Seeking self-interest with guile.

Opportunity cost Given the alternatives (opportunities), the cost of pursuing one activity at the expense of another activity.

Optimal currency area A theory establishing criteria for the optimal size of an area sharing a common currency.

Organizational (team embedded) knowledge Knowledge held in an organization that goes beyond the knowledge of theindividual members.

Organizational culture Employees' shared values, traditions and social norms within an organization.

Organizational fit The similarity in cultures, systems and structures.

Original brand manufacturer (OBM) A firm that designs, manufactures and markets branded products.

Original design manufacturer (ODM) A firm that both designs and manufactures products.

Original equipment manufacturer (OEM) A firm that executes the design blueprints provided by other firms and manufactures such products.

Outbound logistics Sales and the coordination of intermediaries on the customer side.

Out-group Individuals and firms not regarded as part of 'us'.

Outsourcing Turning over an organizational activity to an outside supplier that will perform it on behalf of the firm.

Ownership advantages Resources of the firm that are transferable across borders, and enable the firm to attain competitive advantages abroad.

Parent (home) country national (PCN) An employee who comes from the parent country of the MNE and works at its local subsidiary.

Partial acquisition Acquisition of an equity stake in another firm.

Patent race A competition of R&D units where the first one to patent a new technology gets to dominate a market.

Patents Legal rights awarded by government authorities to inventors of new technological ideas, who are given exclusive (monopoly) rights to derive income from such inventions.

Path dependency The present choices of countries, firms and individuals are constrained by the choices made previously.

Pegged exchange rate An exchange rate of a currency attached to that of another currency.

Performance appraisal The evaluation of employee performance for promotion, retention or termination purposes.

Philanthropy Donations for purposes that benefit the wider society.

Place The location where products and services are provided.

Political risk Risk associated with political changes that may negatively impact on domestic and foreign firms.

Political system A system of the rules of the game on how a country is governed politically.

Political union The integration of political and economic affairs of a region.

Pollution haven Countries with lower environmental standards.

Polycentric approach An emphasis on the norms and practices of the host country.

Post–Bretton Woods system A system of flexible exchange rate regimes with no official common denominator.

Power distance The extent to which less powerful members within a country expect and accept that power is distributed unequally.

Predatory pricing An attempt to monopolize a market by setting prices below cost and intending to raise prices to cover losses in the long run after eliminating rivals.

President of the Commission The head of the EU's executive, similar to a national prime minister.

President of the European Council The person chairing the meetings of the European Council.

Price The expenditures that customers are willing to pay for a product.

Price elasticity How demand changes when prices change.

Price leader A firm that has a dominant market share and sets 'acceptable' prices and margins in the industry.

Primary resources The tangible and intangible assets as well as human resources that a firm uses to choose and implement its strategies.

Primary stakeholder groups The constituents on which the firm relies for its continuous survival and prosperity.

Principle of non-discrimination A principle that a country cannot discriminate among its trading partners (a concession given to one country needs to be made available to all other GATT/WTO members).

Prisoners' dilemma In game theory, a type of game in which the outcome depends on two parties deciding whether to cooperate or to defect.

Privatization The change of ownership from state to the private owners.

Proactive strategy A strategy that endeavours to do more than is required in CSR.

Product The offerings that customers purchase.

Product life cycle theory A theory that accounts for changes in the patterns of trade over time by focusing on product life cycles.

Project management contract A contract to manage the whole of a project from inception to conclusion.

Promotion Communications that marketers insert into the marketplace.

Property rights The legal rights to use an economic property (resource) and to derive income and benefits from it.

Protectionism The idea that governments should actively protect domestic industries from imports and vigorously promote exports.

Psychological contract An informal understanding of expected delivery of benefits in the future for current services.

Purchasing power parity (PPP) A conversion that determines the equivalent amount of goods and services different currencies can purchase. This conversion is usually used to capture the differences in cost of living in different countries.

Purchasing power parity (PPP) hypothesis Hypothesis suggesting that, in the long run, baskets of goods would cost the same in all currencies ('law of one price').

R&D contract A subcontracting of R&D between firms.

Race to the bottom Countries competing for foreign direct investment by lowering environmental standards.

Reactive strategy A strategy that would only respond to CSR causes when disasters and outcries break out.

Recruitment The identification, selection and hiring of staff.

Reduce mobility Assumption that a resource used in producing a product for one industry can be shifted and put to use in another industry.

Regional economic integration Efforts to reduce trade and investment barriers within one region.

Regulatory pillar The coercive power of governments.

Relationship orientation A focus to establish, maintain and enhance relationships with customers.

Relative PPP hypothesis Hypothesis suggesting that changes in exchange rates will be proportional to differences in inflation rates.

Repatriation The process of facilitating the return of expatriates.

Repeated game A game played over several periods of time.

Resource (factor) endowments The extent to which different countries possess various resources (factors), such as labour, land and technology.

Resource mobility The ability to move resources from one part of a business to another.

Resource-based view A leading perspective in global business that posits that firm performance is fundamentally driven by firm-specific resources.

Resources The tangible and intangible assets a firm uses to choose and implement its strategies.

Returnees Returning expatriates.

Reverse culture shock Culture shock experience by persons returning to their country of origin.

Risk management The identification, assessment and management of risks.

Sales agent An intermediary receiving commission for sales.

Scale of entry The amount of resources committed to foreign market entry.

Scenario planning A technique generating multiple scenarios of possible future states of the industry.

Schengen Agreement The agreement that laid the basis for passport-free travel.

Schengen Area The area covered by the Schengen Agreement.

Schengen Visa Visa giving non-citizens access to the Schengen Area.

Schuman plan A plan in the 1950s that outlined the path for European Integration.

Secondary stakeholder groups Those who influence or affect, or are influenced or affected by, the corporation, but they are not engaged in transactions with the corporation and are not essential for its survival.

Secular society A society where religion does not dominate public life.

Servicing foreign visitors Supplying services to customers coming from abroad.

Single European Act (SEA) The agreement that established the basis for the single European market.

Single market The EU's term of its common market.

Small- and medium-sized enterprises (SMEs) Firms with fewer than 500 employees.

Social capital The informal benefits individuals and organizations derive from their social structures and networks.

Social complexity The socially complex ways of organizing typical of many firms.

Sovereign wealth fund A state-owned investment fund composed of financial assets such as stocks, bonds, real estate or other financial instruments.

Sporadic (or passive) exporting The sale of products prompted by unsolicited inquiries from abroad.

Spot market rate The exchange rate for immediate payment.

Spread The difference between the offered price and the bid price.

Stabilization Policies to combat macroeconomic imbalances.

Staged acquisition Acquisition where ownership transfer takes places over stages.

Stage models Models depicting internationalization as a slow stage-by-stage process an SME must go through.

Stakeholder Any group or individual who can affect or is affected by the achievement of the organization's objectives.

Standards in advertising Formal rules designed by governments to protect consumers.

Standards of engagement (code of conduct, code of ethics) Written policies and standards for corporate conduct and ethics.

Strategic alliances Collaborations between independent firms using equity modes, non-equity contractual agreements, or both.

Strategic fit The effective matching of complementary strategic capabilities.

Strategic hedging Organizing activities in such a way that currencies of revenues and expenditures match.

Strategic trade policy A trade policy that conditions or alters a strategic relationship between firms.

Strategic trade theory A theory that suggests that strategic intervention by governments in certain industries can enhance their odds for international success.

Subcontracting A contract that involves outsourcing of an intermediate stage of a value chain.

Subsidiarity The EU takes action only if it is more effective than actions taken at lower levels.

Subsidiary initiative The proactive and deliberate pursuit of new opportunities by a subsidiary to expand its scope of responsibility.

Subsidy Government payments to (domestic) firms.

Sunk cost Up-front investments that are non-recoverable if the project is abandoned.

Supply chain Flow of products, services, finances and information that passes through a set of entities from a source to the customer.

Supply chain management Activities to plan, organize, lead and control the supply chain.

Sustainability The ability to meet the needs of the present without compromising the ability of future generations to meet their needs.

Survival strategies A strategy designed to ensure survival by ensuring liquidity and positive cash flow.

SWOT analysis An analytical tool for determining a firm's strengths (S), weaknesses (W), opportunities (O) and threats (T).

Synergies Value created by combining two organization that together are more valuable than the two organizations separately.

Taboo An item or activity considered unclean by a religion.

Tacit collusion Firms indirectly coordinate actions by signalling their intention to reduce output and maintain pricing above competitive levels.

Tacit knowledge Knowledge that is non-codifiable, and whose acquisition and transfer require hands-on practice.

Tangible assets Assets that are observable and easily quantified.

Tariff barrier Trade barriers that rely on tariffs to discourage imports.

Tender A competition for a major contract.

Theory of absolute advantage A theory suggesting that under free trade, each nation gains by specializing in economic activities in which it has absolute advantage.

Theory of comparative advantage A theory that focuses on the relative (not absolute) advantage in one economic activity that one nation enjoys in comparison with other nations.

Theory of mercantilism A theory that holds the wealth of the world (measured in gold and silver) is fixed and that a nation that exports more and imports less would enjoy the net inflows of gold and silver and thus become richer.

Theory of national competitive advantage of industries (or 'diamond' model) A theory that suggests that the competitive advantage of certain industries in different nations depends on four aspects that form a 'diamond'.

Third country national (TCN) An employee who comes from neither the parent country nor the host country.

Third-party logistics (3PL) A neutral intermediary in the supply chain that provides logistics and other support services.

Tit-for-Tat A strategy of matching the competitors move being either aggressive or accommodative.

Total cost of ownership Total cost needed to own a product, consisting of initial purchase cost and follow-up maintenance/service cost.

Totalitarianism (dictatorship) A political system in which one person or party exercises absolute political control over the population.

Trade deficit An economic condition in which a nation imports more than it exports.

Trade diversion A change in trade pattern away from comparative advantages due to trade barriers.

Trade embargo Politically motivated trade sanctions against foreign countries to signal displeasure.

Trade surplus An economic condition in which a nation exports more than it imports.

Trademarks Exclusive legal rights of firms to use specific names, brands, and designs to differentiate their products from others.

Trade-Related Aspects of Intellectual Property Rights (TRIPS) A WTO agreement governing intellectual property rights.

Training The specific preparation to do a particular job.

Transaction costs The costs associated with economic transactions.

Transnational strategy A strategy that endeavours to be cost efficient, locally responsive and learning driven simultaneously around the world.

Treaties of Rome The first treaties establishing European integration, which eventually led to the EU.

Triad Three regions of developed economies (North America, Western Europe and Japan).

Triple bottom line Firms' economic, social and environmental performance.

Turnkey project A project in which clients pay contractors to design and construct new facilities and train personnel.

Uncertainty avoidance The extent to which members in different cultures accept ambiguous situations and tolerate uncertainty.

Union of South American Nations (UNASUR) An initiative to further economic and political integration in South America.

Uppsala model A model of internationalization processes focusing on learning processes.

Upstream vertical FDI A type of vertical FDI in which a firm engages in an upstream stage of the value.

USA-Dominican Republic-Central America Free Trade Agreement (CAFTA) A free trade agreement between the USA and five Central American countries and the Dominican Republic.

Value chain A chain of activities vertically related in the production of goods and services.

Varieties of capitalisms view A scholarly view suggesting that economies have different inherent logics on how markets and other mechanisms coordinate economic activity.

Vertical FDI A type of FDI in which a firm moves upstream or downstream in different value chain stages in a host country.

Virtual communities of practice Communities of practice interacting via the internet.

Voluntary export restraint (VER) An international agreement in which exporting countries voluntarily agree to restrict their exports.

VRIO framework The resource-based framework that focuses on the value creation (V), rarity (R), imitability (I) and organizational (O) aspects of resources.

Waves of globalization The pattern of globalization arising from a combination of long-terms trends and pendulum swings.

Wholly owned subsidiaries (WOS) A subsidiary located in a foreign country that is entirely owned by the parent multinational.

World Bank International organization that provides loans for specific projects in developing countries to support their economic development.

World Trade Organization (WTO) The organization underpinning the multilateral trading system.

Worldwide (or global) mandate The charter to be responsible for one MNE function throughout the world.

INDEX